The *Sams Teach Yourself in 24 Hours* Series

Sams Teach Yourself in 24 Hours books p
answers in a proven step-by-step approa
In just 24 sessions of one hour or less, yo
you need to get the results you want. Let our experienced
authors present the most accurate information to get you reliable
answers—fast!

MW01103613

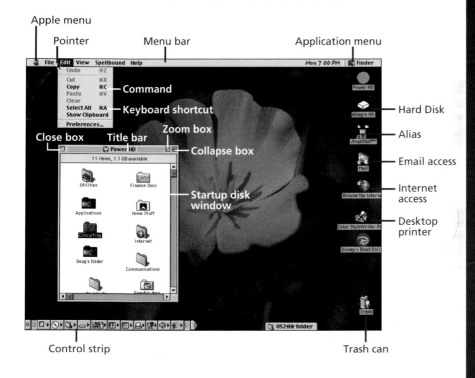

Apple menu

Pointer

Menu bar

Application menu

Command

Keyboard shortcut

Hard Disk

Alias

Email access

Close box

Title bar

Zoom box

Collapse box

Internet access

Startup disk window

Desktop printer

Control strip

Trash can

SAMS

Teach
Self

MAC OS 8.5

in 24 Hours

Apple Menu
(cropped from Desktop)

Application Menu
(cropped from Desktop)

Edit Menu
(cropped from Desktop)

File Menu
(cropped from Desktop)

Help Menu
(cropped from Desktop)

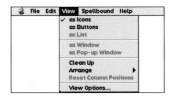

Special Menu
(cropped from Desktop)

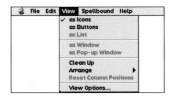

View Menu
(cropped from Desktop)

SAMS

How to Use This Book

This book is designed to teach you the essentials of the latest release of the Macintosh operating system (Mac OS 8.5, also known as "Allegro") in 24 one-hour sessions. The book focuses on the improvements in the OS 8.5 operating system and describes in appropriate level detail many of the improvements that are making this one of the most anticipated Mac OS releases to date.

Beyond improved speed and reliability, Allegro features significant improvements in the following features: Find, Help, System Folder, Folder Manager, and AppleScript. If you're not familiar with these terms, don't fear! This book provides useful tips and hands-on examples for readers who have not used the software before as well as for readers who have had some experience but want to learn more.

This book is the perfect resource if you want to get up and running with 8.5 quickly, efficiently, and effectively.

Rita Lewis
Lisa Lee

SAMS
Teach Yourself

Mac OS 8.5

in **24** Hours

SAMS

A Division of Macmillan Computer Publishing
201 West 103rd St., Indianapolis, Indiana, 46290 USA

Sams Teach Yourself Mac OS 8.5 in 24 Hours

Copyright © 1999 by Sams Publishing.

International Standard Book Number: 0-672-31335-9

Library of Congress Catalog Card Number: 98-84849

Printed in the United States of America

First Printing: October 1998

00   99   4   3   2

Trademarks

Warning and Disclaimer

EXECUTIVE EDITOR
Chris Will

DEVELOPMENT EDITOR
Kezia Endsley

PROJECT EDITOR
Kevin Laseau

COPY EDITOR
Bart Reed

INDEXERS
Greg Pearson
Christine Nelsen

TECHNICAL EDITOR
Lisa Lee

LAYOUT TECHNICIANS
Marcia Deboy
Susan Geiselman

PROOFREADER
Jennifer Earhart

Overview

Introduction   1

PART I MORNING HOURS: WELCOME TO MAC OS 8.5!   **5**

Hour 1   Introducing Mac OS 8.5   7

2   Installing Mac OS 8.5   23

3   Getting Oriented   41

4   The Finder   61

5   Customizing Your Mac   85

6   Applications and Mac OS 8.5   105

7   Optimizing Mac OS 8.5 Performance   127

8   Mobile Computing   151

9   Fonts   169

PART II AFTERNOON HOURS: PRINTING AND MULTIMEDIA   **197**

Hour 10   Printing   199

11   Color   225

12   QuickTime   243

13   Sound and Audio   263

14   Video   281

15   Web Publishing   293

16   File Sharing   325

PART III EVENING HOURS: NETWORKS AND INTERNET   **349**

Hour 17   Personal Web Serving   351

18   Entering the Internet   373

19   Using the Internet   399

20   Talking to the Other Guys   419

PART IV NIGHT HOURS: ADVANCED MAC OS 8.5   **439**

Hour 21   Working with Java   441

22   Automating Your Mac with AppleScript   457

23 The File System Extended 481

24 Troubleshooting Your System 495

APPENDIXES

Appendix A Internet Sources for Mac OS 8.5 519

B Quiz Answers 521

Index 547

Contents

INTRODUCTION   **1**

Who Should Read This Book? 1

How to Use This Book 1

Main Section 2

Term Review 2

Workshop 3

PART I MORNING HOURS: WELCOME TO MAX OS 8.5!   **5**

HOUR 1 INTRODUCING MAC OS 8.5   **7**

What's New in Mac OS 8.5 8

Using the Updated Installer 9

Using Those Helpful Assistants 10

Working with the Improved Finder 10

    Working with the Mac OS 8.5 GUI 10

    Introducing Burrowing Cursors, Contextual Menus, and Other

       Slick Finder Tools 11

What's New Under the Hood? 12

    Location Manager 12

    Open Transport Software 13

    Calibrating Your Mac with ColorSync 2.5 13

    Mac OS Runtime for Java (MRJ) 13

Exploring Mac OS 8.5 Multimedia Tools 14

    Introducing QuickTime 3.0 14

    QuickTime VR 15

    QuickDraw 3D 15

Browsing the Internet 16

    Personal Web Server 17

Introducing the New Extended File System 18

Third-Party Software 18

Summary 19

Term Review 20

Q&A 21

Workshop 21

    Quiz 21

HOUR 2 INSTALLING MAC OS 8.5   **23**

Preparing for Mac OS 8.5 Installation 23

    Checking Your Memory and Drive Capacity 24

    Making Sure Your Hard Disk Is Virus Free 26

Making Sure Your Hard Disk Is Error Free 26
Updating Your Hard Disk Driver..27
Backing Up Your Mac 29
One Last Preparation: Turning Off Security and Virus Protection 29
Installing Mac OS 8.5 29
Why Do a Clean Install? 30
How to Do a Clean Install 30
Customizing Your Mac OS 8.5 Installation 32
Performing a Custom Install of Mac OS 8.5 32
Determining What To Install 34
Things to Watch During and After Installation 34
Adding, Reinstalling, and Removing Components............................35
Cleaning Up After Installation 35
Restoring Your System Folder..36
Troubleshooting Extension Conflicts 37
Summary...37
Term Review 38
Q&A 38
Workshop 39
Quiz 39

HOUR 3 GETTING ORIENTED   41

Understanding the Desktop..41
The Menu Bar 43
Drives and Volumes 43
The Trash Can 44
Using the Windows and Menus 44
Spring-Loaded Windows 44
Pop-Up Windows...46
Collapsible Windows...46
Using Contextual Menus 46
Using the Control Strip 47
Using the Launcher 49
Manipulating Files and Folders 50
Creating Files and Folders...51
Creating Aliases of Folders 52
Moving and Protecting Folders 53
Starting Up and Shutting Down 53
Other Options for Shutting Down...54
Other Options for Starting Up...54
Ejecting and Throwing Things Away 55
Ejecting Disks and Volumes 55
Throwing Away Items 55

Using Copy, Cut, Paste, and Drag Operations 56
Summary 56
Term Review 57
Q&A 58
Workshop 59
    Quiz 59

HOUR 4 THE FINDER   **61**

What Is the Finder?...62
Organizing the Desktop 62
    Using Aliases 62
    Sweeping Clutter Under the Rug 64
    Some Additional Desktop Behaviors 65
    Using the Launcher 65
Viewing and Navigating Your Files 66
    Burrowing with the Mouse 67
    Navigating with the Apple Menu and Desktop...68
    Under the Finder's Hood..69
    Viewing Disks, Volumes, and Drives 70
Finding Files 71
    Find a File 71
    Search By Content..72
    Search the Internet..73
Opening and Grouping Documents 74
    Dragging Versus Double-Clicking Files 74
    Grouping and Opening Applications...75
CD-ROMs and the Finder..76
Using the Trash Can 77
    Emptying the Trash 77
    The Move to Trash Command..78
The Menu Bar...78
    Organizing the Apple Menu 79
Using the General Information Window..80
Customizing the Finder..81
    Changing Custom Icons 81
    Changing Files and Folders...82
Summary 82
Term Review 82
Q&A 83
Workshop 84
    Quiz 84

HOUR 5 CUSTOMIZING YOUR MAC   **85**

Changing the Desktop Format 85
   Setting Desktop Themes 87
   Setting Desktop Appearance 87
   Setting Desktop Fonts 88
   Setting Desktop Pictures and Backgrounds 88
   Setting Desktop Sounds..90
   Setting Other Desktop Options 91
Modifying the Extensions Manager 91
   How to Use Extensions Manager 92
   Creating Extension Manager Sets 93
Changing the Monitors & Sound Control Panel 94
   Sizing up Your Monitor 95
   Color Depth 96
   Resolution and Gamma 96
   Changing the Alerts 96
   Changing Multiple Displays 97
Changing the Keyboard Control Panel..98
Modifying the Numbers Control Panel 99
Modifying the Text Control Panel 99
More Customization Options..100
Summary 100
Term Review 100
Q&A 101
Workshop 102
   Quiz 102

HOUR 6 APPLICATIONS AND MAC OS 8.5   **105**

Introduction to Applications 106
   Different Kinds of Applications 107
   The Look and Feel of Applications...108
Installing and Removing Applications 108
   Installing Applications...108
   Removing Applications 109
   Application Protection...109
Opening, Closing, and Saving Applications..................................109
   Opening Applications 110
   Using Navigation Services 111
   Closing Applications 111
   Saving Documents 112
Understanding Multitasking 114
   The Finder's Role 115
   Doing More Than One Task with Mac OS 8.5 116
   Working with the Application Menu..117

Understanding Memory Management 119
   Determining How Much Memory You Have 119
   Managing Mac OS 8 Memory...120
   Managing Application Memory 121
Summary 123
Term Review 123
Q&A 124
Workshop 125
   Quiz 125

HOUR 7 OPTIMIZING MAC OS 8.5 PERFORMANCE   **127**

Understanding Performance 128
   Determinants of System Performance...128
   Performance of the Software...133
Maximizing the Default OS Settings 136
   Finder Settings..136
   Memory Control Panel 136
   File Sharing Control Panel 140
   AppleTalk Control Panel 140
   PowerBook Performance Issues 141
Tricks for Improving Performance 141
   General Performance Improvements...142
   Improving Performance Using Connectix Products 142
   Improving Performance of Extensions 143
   Improving Graphics and Video Performance 145
   Tools for Optimizing Hard Drives..146
Customizing Mac OS 8.5 for Performance 147
Summary 148
Term Review 148
Q&A 149
Workshop 150
   Quiz 150

HOUR 8 MOBILE COMPUTING   **151**

Independence Day...152
   The First PowerBooks 152
   PowerBooks Today 153
Using PowerBook Hardware 154
   Batteries..155
   Swappable Drives 156
   PC Cards 157
Using PowerBook Software 158
   Mac OS 8.5 PowerBook Features 158
   Applications..161

As Good as It Gets 163
    Using PowerBook Software 163
    Optimizing Software for Mobility..164
A Short Look at What's Coming Soon...165
Summary 165
Term Review 166
Q&A 166
Workshop 167
    Quiz 167

HOUR 9 FONTS   169

History of Fonts 169
What Are Fonts and Type?...170
    Basic Typography 171
    The Computer Vocabulary 175
    Working with Screen and Printer Fonts 179
Types of Type 180
    Apple's Original Bitmapped Fonts 181
    Adobe PostScript Fonts 181
    Type 3 PostScript Fonts 182
    TrueType Fonts 182
    Multiple Master Fonts 182
    OpenType and Open Font Architectures 183
Fonts and the Printing Process 184
Installing Fonts 185
Viewing Fonts 187
Adding Professional Polish..187
    Kerning 188
    Leading 189
    Typography 189
Layout Tips 191
Em, En, and Other Punctuation 192
Summary 192
Term Review 193
Q&A 194
Workshop 196
    Quiz 196

PART 2 AFTERNOON HOURS: PRINTING AND MULTIMEDIA   197

HOUR 10 PRINTING   199

Printing on the Mac 199
    Printing with Dot Matrix Printers 201
    Printing with Inkjet Printers 203
    Printing with Laser Printers...204

Using PostScript to Print 205
    PostScript Level 2 207
    PostScript 3 208
Preparing Your Mac for Printing 209
    Setting Up Your Printer Driver 209
    Setting Up Page-Description Documents 211
    Creating a Desktop Printer 212
    Stopping and Changing Print Jobs 212
Printing a Document..213
    Using Page Setup...213
    Using the Print Command 215
Printing with Color 218
    Color Halftoning and Dithering 218
    Inkjet Technology 219
    Color Laser Technology 219
    Thermal Wax Technology 220
    Dye Sublimation Technology 220
    PostScript Options for Color Printers 221
Summary..221
Term Review 221
Q&A 222
Workshop 223
    Quiz 223

HOUR 11 COLOR   **225**

What Is Color Management? 226
    Why Don't Colors Match? 226
    Working with RGB and CMYK Colors 227
    Setting Up Color Profiles 228
    Developing Color Management Systems 228
Using QuickDraw 229
Color Calibrating Your Mac 231
    Monitor Calibration Assistant 231
    Calibrating Other Devices 234
Using Color Picker 235
Other Uses of ColorSync 237
Summary..238
Term Review 239
Q&A 240
Workshop 240
    Quiz 240

HOUR 12 QUICKTIME   **243**

What Is QuickTime?..243
Using QuickTime 245
  Playing a Movie..245
  Controlling the Video 246
  Playing Back a Movie in a QuickTime-Savvy Program...............................247
  Saving a Video in the Scrapbook 248
Setting QuickTime Preferences 249
  Setting Up AutoPlay Preferences 249
  Setting Your Connection Speed..250
  Setting Up Music Preferences...250
  Setting Media Keys 251
  Setting Up QuickTime Exchange 252
Editing Videos with Movie Player Pro..252
  Editing Videos with Movie Player 2.5 252
  Drawing Vector Graphics in QuickTime..253
Using Picture Viewer 254
QuickTime and the Internet 254
  Working with the QuickTime Plug-In..254
  Saving Movies from the Web 255
  Creating QuickTime Movies for Fast Web Playback 256
  Embedding QuickTime in Your Web Page 257
Understanding QuickTime 3.0's Architecture 258
Introducing the QuickTime Media Abstraction Layer 258
Summary...259
Term Review 260
Q&A 260
Workshop 260
  Quiz 261

HOUR 13 SOUND AND AUDIO   **263**

History of Sound on the Macintosh 264
A Sound Primer 265
  Digital Audio 266
  Musical Instrument Digital Interface (MIDI) 267
  Customizing Your Mac with Sounds..268
  Audio File Formats 269
How to Use Sound 270
  Playing Audio CDs on Your Mac 270
  Using the Monitors & Sound Control Panel 271
  Using the Sound Control Strip Module...272
  Using the Sound Control Panel 273
  Recording Sound with Mac OS 8.5 274

MIDI Hardware...275
    MIDI-to-Mac Interface 275
    MIDI Connections 276
Sound and Music Software..277
    Software Options 278
    Applications for Editing and Creating Sound Files 278
Summary 279
Term Review 279
Q&A 279
Workshop 280
    Quiz 280

HOUR 14 VIDEO   281

You, Too, Can Be in Pictures 282
What Is Apple Video Player? 283
Using Apple Video Player..284
    Capturing Video Pictures...284
    Helpful Hints for Quality Pictures 285
    Playing Back Your Video...286
    Video Playback and CDs or Servers 286
Hardware Considerations 287
    AV Macs 287
    Cabling Considerations 288
Video Applications 288
Summary 289
Term Review 289
Q&A 290
Workshop 290
    Quiz 291

HOUR 15 WEB PUBLISHING   293

Planning for Electronic Publishing on the Web 294
    Content Design: Determining What to Say..294
    Appearance Design: Organizing Your Information.......................................297
    Physically Prototyping the Site 298
Constructing Your Site 302
    The Home Page 303
    Support Pages 304
    Designing Your Graphics for Navigation 304
    Setting Up Your Resources 305
    Tips for Speeding Up Download Times 305
    Testing Your Site 306

A Quick Primer on HTML 307

How HTML Works 308

The Logic Behind HTML 313

Web Publishing Software 316

Gaining Access to the Web 317

Uploading Your Page 318

Summary 319

Term Review 320

Q&A 323

Workshop 324

Quiz 324

HOUR 16 FILE SHARING   **325**

What Is File Sharing? 325

What's Under the Networking Hood in Mac OS 8.5? 326

Setting Up File Sharing 329

Sharing a Volume..332

Opening a Shared Volume at Startup 334

Ending a File Sharing Session..335

Understanding Network Permissions 335

The Owner 336

Guests 336

Registered Users 336

Groups of Users..337

Access Privileges..338

Shared Folders versus Shared Volumes..339

Using Networked Programs from Your Mac..................................340

Connectivity Options 341

Cabling Mediums 341

Cabling Topologies 342

Bus Designs..342

Cabling in a Nutshell..345

Summary..346

Term Review..346

Q&A 347

Workshop 348

Quiz 348

PART 3 EVENING HOURS: NETWORKS AND INTERNET   **349**

HOUR 17 PERSONAL WEB SERVING   **351**

Personal Web Sharing..352

Setting Up Web Sharing 353

Turning On Web Sharing..353

    Accessing the Server 354

    Working with CGIs in Personal Web Serving...............................356

Running a Dedicated Server 358

    Making Hardware Decisions 358

    Web Server Software 361

CGI Script Examples 363

    Forms and Guest Books 363

    Counters...364

    Active Images 365

    Animation 366

    Online Stores 367

    Database Processing 368

For More Information 370

 Summary 371

Term Review 371

Q&A 371

Workshop 372

    Quiz 372

HOUR 18 ENTERING THE INTERNET   373

The Mac's Role on the Web 374

The Underlying Architecture 375

    How TCP/IP Works 375

    Internet Service Providers 376

    Corporate Servers 378

    Open Transport Technologies 378

Using Internet Setup Assistant 382

Using the Internet Control Panel 386

    Working with Configuration Sets 386

    Working with the Personal Tab 387

    Working with the Email Tab 387

    Working with the Web Tab 388

    Using Other Internet Configuration Tabs 389

Getting Ready for the Web 389

    Dialing the Internet 389

    Now That You're In 391

Welcome to the Browser Wars 392

Summary 394

Term Review 394

Q&A 395

Workshop 396

    Quiz 396

HOUR 19 USING THE INTERNET 399

What Is the Internet?..399
    Enter the World Wide Web 401
    Browsers and the Web 401
Using Commercial Online Services 403
    Using AOL...404
    Growing Beyond AOL..406
Other Internet Services 407
    Electronic Mail 407
    Usenet Newsgroups 409
    Chat Rooms 411
Using Apple Data Detectors 412
Uploading and Downloading Documents..414
Using Fetch to Upload Files 415
Summary..415
Term Review 415
Q&A 417
Workshop 418
    Quiz 418

HOUR 20 TALKING TO THE OTHER GUYS 419

Sharing Data versus Sharing Documents 420
    Understanding File Types 420
    What Are File Formats? 422
Sharing Data Between Files 424
    Publish and Subscribe 425
    Object Linking and Embedding (OLE)..427
Sharing Files Between Programs 428
    Using File Exchange for Translation...428
    Using the PC Exchange Screen...429
Sharing Files over a Network and the Internet...431
Sharing Documents Online..433
    Portable Document Format (PDF) 433
    Common Ground, Envoy, and Replica 434
Summary..435
Term Review..435
Q&A 437
Workshop 438
    Quiz 438

PART 4 NIGHT HOURS: ADVANCED MAC OS 8.5   439

HOUR 21 WORKING WITH JAVA   441

What Is Java? 442
    Java Capabilities 442
    Understanding the Java VM 443
    Java and the Internet 445
Using Macintosh Runtime Java (MRJ)..445
    More About Applets 447
    Running an Applet...449
Using Component Software 451
Running Java Applications 453
Summary 454
Term Review 454
Q&A 455
Workshop 456
    Quiz 456

HOUR 22 AUTOMATING YOUR MAC WITH APPLESCRIPT   457

What Is AppleScript? 458
    Things You Can Do with AppleScript....................................458
    The Downside of Using AppleScript 3.0 459
    What's Under the Hood?...459
Scripting Fundamentals 461
Using Apple's Script Editor 463
    Generating a Script 464
    Saving Your Script 468
    Debugging and Compiling 469
    Extending the AppleScript Language 469
AppleScript Language Basics..471
    Data Types 471
    Variables 472
    Operators 473
    Commands..474
Advanced Tools and Scripting Resources 476
Summary 478
Term Review 478
Q&A 479
Workshop 480
    Quiz 480

HOUR 23 THE FILE SYSTEM EXTENDED   **481**

What Is a Hard Drive? 481
Initializing Disks..483
    Interleaving 483
    Tracks and Sectors..483
    Hard Formatting 484
    Logical Formatting 485
Understanding Mac OS Extended Format (HFS+) 485
    Drawbacks of HFS+ 486
    Initializing HFS+ Disks..487
    Using Alsoft PlusMaker 489
Summary..490
Term Review 490
Q&A 492
Workshop 493
    Quiz 493

HOUR 24 TROUBLESHOOTING YOUR SYSTEM   **495**

What to Do If There's a Problem 496
Problems You May Encounter 497
Collecting a Software Toolkit..497
Identifying the Problem 499
    Continuing Your Research..500
    Working with Problems..501
    Software Problem Symptoms 501
    Hardware Problem Symptoms..502
Finding Solutions 503
    Software Problem Resolutions 503
    Battling Software Conflicts..505
    Detecting Buggy, Poorly Designed, and Conflicting Applications...............508
    Detecting Viruses..508
    Hardware Problem Resolutions..509
Summary..513
Term Review 513
Q&A 515
Workshop 516
    Quiz 516

APPENDIXES

APPENDIX A: **INTERNET SOURCES FOR MAC OS 8.5**   **519**

APPENDIX B **QUIZ ANSWERS**   **521**

Hour 1 521
Hour 2 522
Hour 3 524
Hour 4 525
Hour 5 526
Hour 6 526
Hour 7 528
Hour 8 529
Hour 9 530
Hour 10 531
Hour 11 532
Hour 12 533
Hour 13 534
Hour 14 534
Hour 15 536
Hour 16 537
Hour 17 539
Hour 18 539
Hour 19 540
Hour 20 541
Hour 21 542
Hour 22 543
Hour 23 544
Hour 24 544

INDEX   **547**

About the Authors

Rita Lewis is a freelance writer with nine years of formal training in fine arts and design. She applied her MA in cultural anthropology to the participant observation of computer companies during her 10 years working as a proposal manager for various networking and mainframe organizations.

During that time she cut her teeth on the original 512K Mac and System 4.5 and grew up with the Mac until today's Power Computing Power Center Pro 180 running Mac OS 8.5.

Rita is the author of nine books on various Macintosh topics, including *PageMill 2.0 Handbook* and *Show Me the Mac*, both from Macmillan Publishing. She's also a collaborative author of the hardware sections of Hayden's *Maclopedia*.

Lisa Lee works as a software quality assurance engineer in Mountain View, California. She has been using Macintosh computers for over 12 years. She has worked at Apple and with many Macintosh hardware and software developers to create Macintosh products, including Mac OS.

Dedication

To my mother, Brigitte Freidin. You always said that I could do anything.
—Rita Lewis

To Mom and Dad
—Lisa Lee

Acknowledgments

I would like to thank the following people without whom this book could not have been written.

To Lisa Lee, co-author and technical editor, who brought patience and knowledge about Apple products that helped keep this book afloat. Lisa's always there when you need her.

To Brad Miser and Steve Trinkos, silent co-authors, whose chapters on troubleshooting and AppleScript were cogent and complete. Thanks for your support.

To Chris Will, executive editor, who had the fortitude to stand by me when I pushed for this book to be published and who has the kindness and patience to nurture my best writing. I'm glad you moved to Indianapolis when you did.

To Kezia Endsley, development editor, whose constant comments and reviews made this book ever so much better.

To Bart Reed, copyeditor, who did a seamless, professional job of making sure my English was up to snuff.

To Kevin Laseau, project editor, whose perfectionism makes sure that all the little details of book publishing happen. What would I do without you, Kevin?

To all of the folks in production who labor to take cryptic production instructions and numbered screen shots and create beautiful copy. Thanks.

As always, to my husband Doug, who is my coach, my sounding board, and best friend, as well as consummate babysitter. Thank you for your open-hearted ways.

To my two daughters, Lisa and Hannah, who were weaned on Macs and know more than I do. Thanks for your patience with your silly mother.

Finally, to Steve Jobs, who resuscitated Apple and gave us new Macs and Mac OS 8.5. This book is dedicated to you and all the people at Apple who think differently.
—Rita Lewis

Thanks to all my friends at Apple and the Macintosh development community for making Mac OS as great as it is today.
—Lisa Lee

Tell Us What You Think!

As the reader of this book, *you* are our most important critic and commentator. We value your opinion and want to know what we're doing right, what we could do better, what areas you'd like to see us publish in, and any other words of wisdom you're willing to pass our way.

As the Executive Editor for the operating systems team at Macmillan Computer Publishing, I welcome your comments. You can fax, email, or write me directly to let me know what you did or didn't like about this book—as well as what we can do to make our books stronger.

Please note that I cannot help you with technical problems related to the topic of this book, and that due to the high volume of mail I receive, I might not be able to reply to every message.

When you write, please be sure to include this book's title and author as well as your name and phone or fax number. I will carefully review your comments and share them with the author and editors who worked on the book.

Fax: 317-817-7070

Email: opsys@mcp.com

Mail: Executive Editor
        Operating Systems
        Macmillan Computer Publishing
        201 West 103rd Street
        Indianapolis, IN 46290 USA

Introduction

Apple introduced Mac OS 8 in 1997 to great fanfare. Since that time there has been a major revision, called Mac OS 8.1, and the latest revision, called Mac OS 8.5. The book also covers all of Mac OS 8.5's features extensively, including bugs, tricks and tips for performance, and how to optimize your Mac experience. We also include the "latest" facts on adjunct software, such as Internet Explorer 4.5, QuickTime 3.5, and other enhancments.

You must realize in reading and learning from this book that the Mac OS is a fluid construct whose features are enhanced on an almost daily basis. We include many URLs allowing you to update the information provided herein as it happens.

As with all Mac software, experimentation is the key to learning. This book provides you with a good grounding in how the parts of the operating system work. It's up to you to try out the pieces yourself. In other words, you should customize your Mac to fit your working style.

Who Should Read This Book?

This book covers all the essential elements of Mac OS 8.5 and is designed for readers who have not used a Mac before as well as readers who have some experience but want to learn more. I've also designed the book to be useful for those working in either an office environment or at home; both groups of readers will learn all the useful components of Mac OS 8.5.

How to Use This Book

This book is designed to teach you topics in one-hour sessions. All the books in the Sams *Teach Yourself* series enable the reader to start working and become productive with the product as quickly as possible. This book will do that for you! In fact, the first several lessons are concerned with showing you how to use the basic as well as power elements of Mac OS 8.5: It takes you through managing the desktop, file management, the Finder, installing the operating system and applications, getting help, and optimizing Mac OS 8.5. It's designed to teach you all the navigational skills you need to be an effective user of your Mac.

Although most computer books use jargon that's not easily understood, this book tries not to. I have consciously avoided terms that would be unfamiliar to most readers. Only where necessary do I use technical language, and at these points I make sure you can follow my discussion. A Term Review section is included at the end of each lesson, providing definitions for technical terms introduced during the session.

Each hour (or session) starts with an overview of the topic, informing you of what to expect during the lesson. The overviews help you determine the nature of the lesson and whether the lesson is relevant to your needs.

Main Section

Each lesson has a main section that discusses the lesson topic in clear, concise language, breaking the topic down into logical components and explaining each component thoroughly before going on to the next. Sometimes step-by-step directions are provided, and other times explanatory paragraphs are provided to guide you through a task.

Embedded into each lesson are Tips, Cautions, and Notes enclosed in boxes.

A *Tip* informs you of a trick or element that is easily missed by most computer users. Feel free to skip these hints and additions; however, if you skip reading them, you might miss a shorter way to accomplish a task than that provided in the main text.

A *Caution* deserves at least as much attention as the body of the lesson, because these sidebars point out a problematic element of the operating system or a "gotcha" you want to avoid while using the operating system. Ignoring the information contained in a caution could have adverse effects on the stability of your computer! Cautions are the most important information bars in this book.

A *Note* is designed to clarify the concept being discussed. Notes also contain additional information that may be slightly off-topic but interesting nonetheless. Notes elaborate on the subject, and if you're comfortable with your understanding of the subject, you can read these for more edification or bypass them with no danger.

Term Review

This portion of each lesson provides a mini dictionary of the concepts learned in the lesson. All words are defined as they are used so you have a way to review the technical terms used in the lesson.

Workshop

This section of each lesson provides exercises that reinforce the concepts you learned in the lesson and help you apply them in new situations. Although you can skip this section, you might find it helpful to go through the exercises to see how the concepts covered in the session can be applied to other common tasks.

PART I

Morning Hours: Welcome to Max OS 8.5!

Hour

1 Introducing Mac OS 8.5

2 Installing Mac OS 8.5

3 Getting Oriented

4 The Finder

5 Customizing Your Mac

6 Applications and Mac OS 8.5

7 Optimizing Mac OS 8.5 Performance

8 Mobile Computing

9 Fonts

HOUR 1

Introducing Mac OS 8.5

Before I get into the nitty-gritty of how every part of the Mac operating system works, I'll introduce you to some of the changes that have taken place between Mac OS 8.5 and System 7.6 (even the name of the operating system has changed).

Although Mac OS 8.5, the current manifestation of Mac OS 8, supports the same Finder, QuickDraw, desktop, and other graphical user interface (GUI) features you know and love, it's also revolutionary (right down to its machine-coded bones) in that it represents a total rewrite of the operating system, providing a more stable, faster, and more efficient computing experience. The changes are both subtle (such as the PowerPC-native Finder, QuickDraw, and AppleScript) and self-evident (such as the new Finder dialog boxes that provide enhanced file management and browsing, the Internet and Remote Access control panels, and the Appearance themes). This hour provides an overview of what's new in Mac OS 8.5. Topics covered include the following:

- The updated installer
- The Mac OS Information Assistant and Internet Assistant, as well as other information resources

- The new-and-improved multitasking Finder, which includes an enhanced Application menu that lets you select multiple documents at the same time
- New system components such as the Appearance Manager, Location Manager, and Internet Manager
- New Mac OS applications such as: Open Transport 1.3, ColorSync 2.5, QuickTime 3.5, and HTML-based AppleGuide.
- V-Twin-based Sherlock, which lets you search both your local hard disk and the Internet to find the documents you need.

What's New in Mac OS 8.5

Mac OS 8.5 represents the platform on which the Macintosh operating system will be built in the twenty-first century. Apple's operating system strategy builds on the features you will see in Mac OS 8.5, but will grow to include modern operating system functions such as pre-emptive multitasking, protected memory, hardware independence, and more integration with the Internet. The Mac is growing up and OS 8.5 is in adolescence.

Here's a short description of the surprises you'll find in Mac OS 8.5:

- **Appearance Manager**. The new Appearance Manager lets you customize the desktop exactly how you want it. For example, pictures can jazz up the desktop beyond those boring patterns (although you can still use them). In addition, the Appearance Manager lets you group fonts, pictures, highlight colors, and sounds together into "themes." It also supports third-party add-on schemes via such shareware programs as Kaleidoscope 2.1.
- **Multitasking capabilities**. The redesigned Finder lets you perform multiple background processes such as printing, copying, and moving documents simultaneously, with little processing degradation. In addition, you'll immediately notice the new Finder dialog boxes, which replicate the list view that's so useful for finding the exact document you need.
- **Internet management components**. Enhanced Internet setup and browsing is available via the Internet Setup Assistant and Remote Access and Internet control panels. Macintosh Runtime for Java (MRJ) lets you run programs you download directly onto your Mac, no matter what their origin, and enhanced printing and color controls provide better support for your Web and desktop publishing efforts.

- **New and improved system components**. Mac OS 8.5 provides extensive application updates. For example, Open Transport 1.3, the Mac OS extended file system, the ColorSync 2.5 color calibration management system, and the consolidated File Sharing tools all make the Macintosh computing experience fast and easy, as well as compatible with existing Macintosh software.

Let's look at the new features of the Mac OS 8.5 operating system one by one.

VOCABULARY LESSONS

Because Mac OS 8.5 contains so many new innovations, Apple has generated a lot of new terminology. You shouldn't be afraid of all this new jargon, though. Just look at the end of each chapter for the "Term Review" section, and you'll amaze your friends with your erudition (that is, how well you can speak "Mac").

Using the Updated Installer

Because Mac OS 8.5 consists of so many more components than older Mac system software, and because the new operating system provides more flexibility for setting up your system, Apple has built a new installer: Install Mac OS. Install Mac OS still walks you through four steps for setting up Mac OS; however, its interface has changed since its introduction in Mac OS 7.6 (see Figure 1.1). Each step contains a more detailed explanation of what's involved in preparing for Mac OS 8.5 installation and enables you to navigate back and forth between all the pages of information. Installer options have also changed. For example, the Clean Install option is on the second page of this application, and you can use it to update all the Apple hard disk drivers on your Mac prior to installation. For more information on Install Mac OS, see Hour 2, "Installing Mac OS 8.5."

FIGURE 1.1.

The new installer gives you more control over the installation of selected components as well as provides a safer installation.

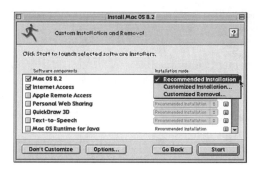

Using Those Helpful Assistants

Apple has thought of everything. If you're a novice user, for example, you won't be over-whelmed by all of the various settings and customization tools built into the operating system, because when you first start your new Mac OS 8.5–based Macintosh, various assistants are available to help you set up your location, network, printer, modem, and Internet connection, as well as some customization features. Here are some highlights:

- You can use the Mac OS Setup Assistant to configure your ideal Mac.
- You can use the Internet Setup Assistant to set up your Internet connection, includ-ing establishing a new Internet Service Provider account.
- You can use the control panel utility to designate your default browser and ISP settings.

On the other hand, if you're a Mac power user, you can exit the assistant and skip all its configuration features in lieu of manually setting up Mac OS 8.5. What's more, if you're not sure of all the settings you want to use with Mac OS 8.5, you can complete as much information as you feel comfortable with and wait until all your data is exactly the way you want it; then you can use the last page of the assistant to update all your Mac OS 8.5 settings.

Working with the Improved Finder

Finder 8 has native PowerPC code as well as 68K code, which means it will run faster on Power Macs. In addition to several new features, such as spring-loaded folders and pop-up windows, Finder now sports multiple Copy dialog boxes, context-sensitive menus, sticky menus, window view preferences (located in the Views menu), Finder preferences, tighter or wider grid spacing for icon views, and a method for displaying fewer Finder features (see Figure 1.2). Hour 3, "Getting Oriented," explores these new features of the Finder.

FIGURE 1.2.

Finder 8 provides easi-er navigating features as well as an updated desktop appearance.

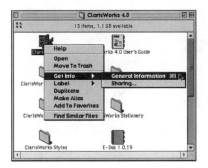

Working with the Mac OS 8.5 GUI

The first obvious change to Finder 8 is the appearance of the Mac OS 8.5 icons, folders, and Finder menus (see Figure 1.3). The three-dimensional platinum windows, sliders, and buttons make it easier to understand what each window tool does, whether you're snapping open a window, closing a window, resizing a window, or scrolling through a window. You can set up how you view your windows and folders: You can view them as icons or set them up as easy-to-read lists. In addition, you can create your own filing system by dragging selected folders onto the bottom of your desktop. When you drag any open folder window to the bottom of your desktop, it turns into a little tab that you can click to spring the contents of that folder open or shut. These neat tabs are also "drag sensitive." You can drag an item over the tab to see the window pop open to receive that item.

FIGURE 1.3.

Mac OS 8.5 desktop.

Folder in icon view

New scroll bars

Tabbed folder

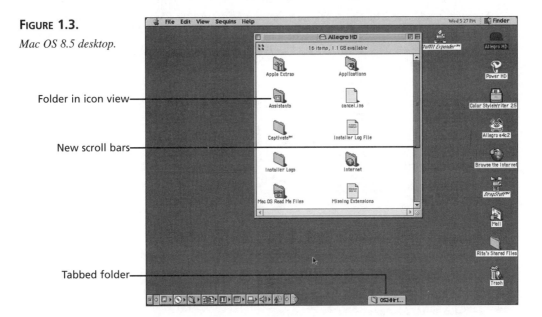

Introducing Burrowing Cursors, Contextual Menus, and Other Finder Tools

Try this: Press the Control key while clicking the mouse on your desktop. Something new popped up, didn't it? This new pop-up menu is called a *contextual menu*, and it can be filled with all sorts of commands, depending on where on the Mac you invoke it (and whether applications support it). Already, Apple has supplied what it calls *data detectors*, which let you use contextual menus within applications to call up the Internet for selected information to download into your document.

Another new feature of the Finder is the *click-and-a-half*, a new burrowing cursor that lets you pop open folders by passing this magic wand over their icons. In fact, several new cursors provide additional navigation information for your convenience. Hour 3 covers these features in more detail.

What's New Under the Hood?

In addition to its new look and feel, Mac OS 8.5 also has updated and new applications, including Location Manager, ColorSync 2.5, Open Transport technologies, and Macintosh Runtime Java.

Location Manager

Location Manager (see Figure 1.4) lets your PowerBook change configurations to reflect where your physical location is in the world. For example, it works with the Extensions Manager to change which extensions load with each Location Manager setup. It also changes settings in Date & Time, as well as your printer, file sharing, sound, and application settings.

FIGURE **1.4.**

The Location Manager control strip module.

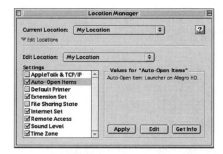

Location Manager uses the following files to provide the capability to localize your PowerBook:

- **Auto-Open.** Automatically opens documents or applications configured with a Location Manager set
- **Network (Open Transport's AppleTalk and TCP/IP control panels).** Lets you configure different network configurations with different Location Manager sets
- **Default Printer.** Selects the default printer for a particular Location Manager set
- **Extensions Manager.** Selects an Extensions Manager set within a particular Location Manager set
- **Sound volume.** Sets the sound volume as part of a Location Manager set

You can further customize how your PowerBook works by installing other localization software. Look for third-party modules for Location Manager on Apple's Web site at http://www.apple.com.

Open Transport Software

Open Transport is the Macintosh Internet Protocol (IP) software used to let a Mac easily network with other computers. Open Transport 1.3 contains quite a few more components that work hand-in-hand with Open Transport, such as Open Transport PPP (Point-to-Point Protocol), Apple Remote Access, File Sharing, AppleShare servers, Web servers, and all the Internet software available for Macs. The following list highlights some of Open Transport's features:

- You can use more than one networking system at once (for example, you can use AppleTalk to communicate with network printers and TCP/IP to connect to the Internet).
- You can save and modify different networking configurations.
- You can switch among networking configurations quickly and easily.

Open Transport consists of several shared libraries and control panels that are explained in more detail in Hours 16, "File Sharing," and 20, "Talking to the Other Guys."

Calibrating Your Mac with ColorSync 2.5

One of the most successful uses of Macs has been in the publishing business, both on the creative and prepress sides of the operation. With the advent of cheaper color printing, Apple recognized that a new revolution in the same vein as desktop publishing was brewing and stepped up with a solution to a vexing problem—how to make sure that the colors printed on your output device match those created on your computer. Color management is supported on the Mac both covertly (via ColorSync 2.5) and overtly (via the Color Picker tool and the ColorSync control panel). Now, using these tools, you can calibrate your monitor, printer, scanner, plotter, and software to match exactly the color system you want to use. Hour 11, "Color," discusses the wonders of ColorSync in more detail.

Mac OS Runtime for Java (MRJ)

Mac OS Runtime for Java (MRJ) is Apple's implementation of the Java runtime environment based on software from Sun Microsystems (see Figure 1.5). With MRJ, Mac OS applications can run Java applets and applications.

FIGURE 1.5.

A Mac OS Runtime for
Java applet.

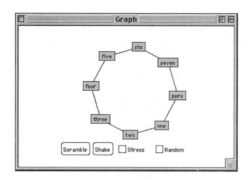

Exploring Mac OS 8.5 Multimedia Tools

Apple's multimedia software consists of several technologies, including QuickTime, QuickTime VR, and QuickDraw 3D. No doubt you'll want to install as many of these software technologies as your memory and hard drive can handle. These technologies hide behind the scenes until you need them for the seamless display and manipulation of three-dimensional spaces and objects, as well as for the painless display of audio and video documents. For more information about Apple's multimedia software, see Part II (Hours 9 through 15).

Introducing QuickTime 3.5

QuickTime 3.5 is Apple's technology that enables your computer to play audio and video files. You can play them directly on your Mac via the new MoviePlayer and PictureViewer components or over the Internet via the updated QuickTime browser plug-in. Although this technology looks deceptively simple, it represents over 175 different software features. These software components can be combined into about 20 categories of services that relate to multimedia, and Apple developers add these services to their products. What all this means is that QuickTime 3.0 brings a wealth of multimedia features to Mac OS 8.5 as well as to Macintosh multimedia hardware and software products.

You'll immediately notice several advertisements for QuickTime Pro that pop up whenever you open MoviePlayer or when QuickTime is invoked. QuickTime Pro is a fully functional professional-level audio and video editor you can use to create and edit QuickTime-based documents for use on the Internet or directly on the Mac. Note that QuickTime Pro is for sale and does not come free with Mac OS 8.5.

QuickTime 3.0 has many new features you can use to view many diverse audio and video formats. QuickTime's vast array of support tools include the MPEG1 extension, which was introduced with QuickTime 2.5. It lets you play back MPEG1-formatted files with applications such as MoviePlayer 2.5, which is included with QuickTime 3 on your Mac OS 8.5 CD-ROM (see Figure 1.6). Hour 14, "Video," discusses QuickTime in more detail.

FIGURE 1.6.

QuickTime MoviePlayer.

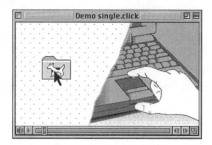

QuickTime VR

QuickTime VR is Apple's virtual reality technology. It turns a series of photos into a virtual world (see Figure 1.7). For example, you use a QuickTime VR file to navigate inside a room, including the ability to turn full circle as well as zoom toward or away from any visual element contained in the room. QuickTime VR files can be created with special virtual reality cameras, or they can be created purely with software-based images such as 3D worlds. Mac OS 8.5 installs QuickTime VR 2.0 along with the QuickTime software.

FIGURE 1.7.

QuickTime VR.

QuickDraw 3D

As its name implies, QuickDraw 3D is Apple's 3D technology (see Figure 1.8). Its API libraries support interactive rendering, 3D interface features, and the industry-standard 3DMF file format. A bug fix update exists for QuickDraw 3D in Mac OS 8.5.

QuickDraw 3D supports any application that uses this technology, as well as many 3D hardware cards, including Apple's QuickDraw 3D accelerator card. Bug fixes address critical feature-related problems and performance.

> Most 3D applications have adopted the QuickDraw 3D technology—they use the 3DMF file format as well as QuickDraw 3D's rendering capability and user interface. Some applications that use QuickDraw 3D include games (such as Descent) and 3D design applications (such as StrataVision 3D 4.0, Poser 2.0, and Bryce 2). The QuickDraw 3D technology is also used on the World Wide Web, enabling you to view and manipulate 3D objects on the Internet.

FIGURE 1.8.

QuickDraw 3D and SimpleText.

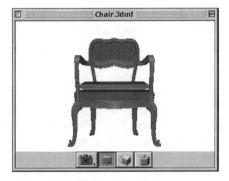

Browsing the Internet

One of the first things you'll notice about Mac OS 8.5 is the new Internet control panel, which provides the same configuration support once provided by the Internet Config shareware product. Here, in one handy place, is a way to manage all the numerous pieces of software required to connect you successfully to the Internet, including your browser, your PPP connection, your TCP/IP software, and your modem hardware and software.

The Mac OS 8.5 desktop lets you reach the Internet in several ways: via a browser button, a data detector contextual menu, an email button, an Apple menu item, and various AppleScript items. All these enhancements build on the Open Transport technologies that lie under the hood of Mac OS 8.5.

In addition, Apple has added two more Internet tools to Mac OS 8.5: Macintosh Runtime Java and Personal Web Server. You can also choose between Microsoft's Internet Explorer browser (the default) and Netscape's Navigator browser, because they're both included with Mac OS 8.5. For additional information on Mac OS 8.5 Internet software, see Hours 18, "Entering the Internet," and 19, "Using the Internet."

Mac OS 8.5 provides the following Internet and Internet-related software:

1

- **Microsoft Internet Explorer 4.5.** Microsoft's popular Web browser application is installed as your default browser in the Internet folder at the root level of the hard disk. You can substitute Microsoft Internet Explorer with Netscape's Navigator browser by installing it from the Mac OS 8.5 CD-ROM to your Internet folder and using the Internet control panel to designate it as your default browser.

- **The Internet control panel.** A useful utility that generates a universal Internet configuration across all your various Internet software so that you can easily switch between email programs and browsers without having to change your email address, news address, or home page designation.

- **Apple Remote Access (ARA).** (Formerly called PPP.) This is Point-of-Presence software that's used for dialing into the Internet or some other network. ARA provides a dialer, a status dialog box, a control strip component, and a control panel for managing the connection to your ISP.

- **StuffIt Expander.** Lets you expand compressed files downloaded from the Internet.

- **DropStuff Expander.** Lets you expand a compressed file by dropping it over this application's icon. StuffIt Expander and DropStuff Expander are standard Mac file decompression applications published by Aladdin.

- **Internet Setup Assistant.** Lets you configure all your Mac's network settings, including registering with an Internet Service Provider, without having to open any control panels. The Internet Assistants are four AppleScripts located in the Client Access folder within the Internet folder.

- **Acrobat Reader 3.0.** An application for reading PDF files. A set of fonts plus the Acrobat application and PDF file creator for Chooser are part of this software installation.

Personal Web Server

Licensed from Maxum, Web Sharing works with Apple's File Sharing technology to turn your Mac into a personal, miniaturized Web server (see Figure 1.9). Web Sharing lets you publish documents and HTML-based pages on the Internet from your Mac (albeit to a small group of connected Macs). You can also manage uploading and downloading tasks on its FTP server. This software adds a Web Sharing control panel to Mac OS 8.5, sets your Mac's Web Identity (for example, the location of your HTML files), and lets you turn Web Sharing "on" or "off" with some general access privileges.

The Web Sharing control panel.

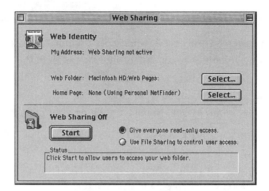

Introducing the New Extended File System

Every version of the Macintosh operating system up until now has been based on a filing system (called the Standard Format) that allocates 64K of disk space for each file, no matter how large a file actually is. In addition, your Mac had a limit to the number of files that could be stored on its hard drive. However, Mac OS 8.1 introduced the Extended Format file system (also called *Hierarchical Filing System Plus*, or *HFS+*). Now you can format your hard disks (as well as your removable disks) as Extended Format disks, thus optimizing the storage capacity of today's large multigigabyte hard disks by allocating the actual disk space required to store a file. An added benefit is that you can now save more than 65,000 files on your hard disk. The Extended Format is intended for hard disks of 1GB or greater.

One caveat to HFS+: When you reformat your disk drives to take advantage of HFS+, you need to use Mac OS 8.1 or later; otherwise, you can no longer read the contents of the reformatted disks. You must consider the operating system levels of all your Macs on your network before taking advantage of HFS+. Macs acting as servers can be formatted as Extended Format systems without having to upgrade client Macs to Mac OS 8.1.

Summary

In this hour, I introduced you to some of the new features you'll encounter in Mac OS 8.5. As you can see, Mac OS 8.5 is an evolutionary step forward from the older Mac operating systems. You'll find your computing experience is more reliable, faster, and more efficient because Mac OS 8.5 contains numerous built-in tools for performing daily work. The next hours cover each of these new features in detail so that you can learn how to get the most from each one. Hour 2 begins with a tour of the desktop, files, and folders of Mac OS 8.5.

Term Review

Appearance Manager   The system tool that controls how windows, icons, dialog boxes, buttons, radio buttons, text boxes, and so forth are displayed. The Appearance control panel lets you customize your desktop.

Desktop   The main interface of the Mac OS, where you see all the drives, the Trash, and so forth. The desktop is controlled by the Finder.

File Sharing   Peer-to-peer networking via the AppleTalk protocol that lets Macs and specially equipped PCs share documents and printers.

Finder   The system tool that controls how the Mac works with documents (opening, closing, saving, displaying, and managing files).

Hierarchical File System Plus (HFS+)   The new Extended Format file system introduced in Mac OS 8.1, which optimizes the storage of files on large disk drives by decreasing the minimum size of a single file. This is recommended for drives 1GB or larger.

installer   A program that lets you control how software is installed on your Mac. The Mac OS 8.5 installer provides additional services, such as checking the quality and size of your hard drive, updating Apple hard drives, and letting you customize which applications are placed on your computer.

Internet Setup Assistant   The application that automatically sets up an Internet Service Provider account and all the related pieces of information required on your Mac to enable you to quickly get on the Internet.

Macintosh Runtime for Java   A Java virtual environment on the Mac that lets you run Java-based programs directly on your Mac without conversion requirements.

Open Transport   A collection of system tools that provides TCP/IP and networking functions for your Mac.

Standard and Extended Formats   Mac OS file formats. The Standard Format was called the *Hierarchical File System (HFS)* and was the way that storage media was set up to store Mac files. The Extended Format is a new file format (also called *HFS+*) that increases the number of files that can be placed on storage media.

Q&A

Q How do I know the version of the operating system my Mac is currently running?

A Click the Apple icon and select About This Computer. The resulting dialog box lists the operating system currently running on your Mac.

Q How do I run my Mac from the Mac OS 8.5 CD-ROM so that I can install the new system?

A Insert the Mac OS 8.5 CD-ROM in your CD-ROM drive. Hold down the C key on your keyboard when restarting your Mac.

Q Where can I learn more about Mac OS 8.5's features to determine whether it's right for me?

A Go to the Mac OS Web page at http://www.macos.com for more information.

Q Where's the best place for me to begin to quickly acquaint myself with the new features of Mac OS 8.5?

A Open the About the Mac OS folder that comes on the CD-ROM. Mac OS 8.5 comes with an extensive online training guide you can access from the desktop by double-clicking the Mac Info Center icon.

Q Where can I learn more about the Macintosh hardware?

A Read the *Teach Yourself Macintosh in 24 Hours* companion to this book.

Workshop

The Workshop contains quiz questions to help you solidify your understanding of the material covered. You can find the answers to the quiz questions in Appendix B, "Quiz Answers."

Quiz

1. What does it mean that Finder 8 is now "native PowerPC code"? What new Finder features provide more control over how your Mac displays information?

2. Which control panels are no longer supported in Mac OS 8.5. Where's the best place to look for these features if you aren't sure where they are in Mac OS 8.5?

3. What's the name of the new file system used in Mac OS 8.1? What are some of the advantages to using it over the old system?

4. What benefits are provided with QuickTime 3.0?

5. What benefits are provided by ColorSync 2.5?

6. What is Open Transport and what does it do?

7. What piece of shareware has Apple emulated with the Internet control panel?

8. What navigation mechanisms have been added to the Finder in Mac OS 8.5?

9. What is Web Sharing?

10. What benefits are provided by the new Appearance Manager?

1

HOUR 2

Installing Mac OS 8.5

Now is the moment you've been waiting for. You're ready to install Mac OS 8.5! Installation is as easy as following the four steps outlined in the Install Mac OS application. You can also customize your installation to pick and choose those components of the Mac OS that fit your needs. This hour walks you through an installation and smoothes out the rough spots. The following issues are covered:

- Preparing for Mac OS 8.5 installation
- Installing Mac OS 8.5
- Adding, reinstalling, and removing components
- Cleaning up after installation

Preparing for Mac OS 8.5 Installation

Although the Mac is known for its ease of use, you should follow a few pre-installation steps to ensure a smooth transition when you're installing new system software:

1. Check to see how much memory and hard disk space you have available for the installation

2. Ensure that your hard disk is error and virus free

3. Update your hard disk driver

4. Back up your hard disk's contents

5. Reconfigure your extensions

Each of these issues is discussed in more detail in the following sections.

Checking Your Memory and Drive Capacity

Before you install Mac OS 8, check your hard drive to make sure you have enough free space to install the software packages you want to use. Gone are the days when you could fit your operating system on a single 400K floppy disk. This version of the operating system takes a whopping 154 MB if you want to install all of its components. Even a minimal installation requires at least 90 MB. In addition, you'll need at least 12 MB of RAM to run the operating system. If you don't know how much hard disk capacity and RAM you have installed on your Mac, you need to find out whether you have enough to support both Mac OS and other software you plan to use.

To see how much hard drive space is available on your Mac hard drive, use the following steps:

1. Select the hard drive icon on your desktop.

2. Double-click the icon or select Open from the File menu.

3. After the hard drive's window is open, select View as Icons from the View menu.

4. The amount of available space is displayed in the center of the hard drive window's title bar (see Figure 2.1). In fact, any folder opened from that hard drive will display this same information.

FIGURE 2.1.

A folder window showing the available space on disk.

HOW TO ADD HARD DRIVE SPACE

If you don't have enough hard drive space available to install Mac OS 8.5, there are several ways you can add more disk space to your computer:

- If you have an older Mac, replacing your internal hard drive is difficult because of the design of the computer. In this case, you can purchase an external hard drive and connect it to your Mac's external SCSI port. Install Mac OS 8.5 onto this drive. An added bonus is that you can immediately format this new external drive with HFS+ to gain additional storage space before installing the new software.

  In addition, if you have a second SCSI bus, you can install a second hard drive internally. Read the literature that comes with your Mac to see if it is equipped with a second SCSI bus. You can then swap files between your two volumes.

- If you have a more modern Mac whose drive is readily accessible, you can replace your internal hard drive with a larger drive. You'll have to remove the contents of the old drive prior to installation and then move your current files to the new drive. Again, you can format the new drive as HFS+ before reloading your files.

- You can purchase a removable drive, such as SyQuest SyJet or Iomega Jaz, that supports 1GB removable media. You can move files off your hard drive, freeing up space for installing Mac OS 8.5. This is a very expensive proposition, because Iomega Jaz drives start at $299 for a gigabyte. Use this method only if you have the cash flow. You should also realize that you'll probably have to go to a hard disk eventually, because Mac OS 8.5 really does not like to be run from a removable disk.

Table 2.1 presents an overview of the function of each Mac OS 8.5 component and its hard disk space requirements. Use these figures to estimate the amount of space you'll need for your new system.

TABLE 2.1. MAC OS 8.5 COMPONENT MEMORY AND SPACE REQUIREMENTS.

Software	Space Required	Function
Apple Remote Access 3.0	1.7 MB	Enables you to dial up the Internet and establish a connection with your ISP
ColorSync 2.5	1.2 MB	Color Management System for the Mac
Internet Access 1.2	12 MB	Includes all the software required to manage Web browsing and electronic mail services on the Internet
QuickDraw 3D	2.2 MB	Graphic image enhancement software

continues

TABLE 2.1. CONTINUED

Software	Space Required	Function
Mac OS Runtime for Java	3 MB	Macintosh Java virtual engine
Personal Web Sharing (requires browser and AppleShare)	1.1 MB	Turns your Mac into a Web page server Apple component software engine
QuickDraw 3D (requires supported software)	2.1 MB	3D graphics performance enhancement
Mac OS 8.5	140 MB or more	The Macintosh operating system software

Making Sure Your Hard Disk Is Virus Free

If you don't already check your Mac for viruses on a regular basis, you should definitely check for viruses before you install Mac OS 8.5. Both shareware and commercial software packages are available that search for viruses on your Mac. The good news is that the Mac has relatively few viruses compared to other computer platforms. Dr Solomon's Virex 5.8 and Symantec's Norton Anti-Virus 5.0 are two examples of virus-protection programs available for the Mac.

The most common way to get a virus onto your Mac is over a network or by downloading an infected file from a server. If you frequently use a Mac at a service bureau or are carrying floppy disks from one work location to another, it's possible you may have transferred a virus from one Mac to another.

Antivirus software works similarly to other Mac software applications. Most have a feature to scan specific files or folders, or even one or all hard drives, for all known viruses to that particular version of the antivirus software. Another feature lets you remove any viruses found on your computer. For example, in Disinfectant, this feature is the Disinfect menu item or button. Be sure to scan all your hard drives with Disinfectant or some other antivirus software before installing Mac OS 8.5.

Making Sure Your Hard Disk Is Error Free

Another task you need to perform before updating your operating system is to run a program that checks your disk for possible software and hardware errors. Several commercial products are available for checking HFS-formatted disks (for example, Symantec Norton Utilities 3.5, Apple Disk First Aid 8.1, and Micromat's TechTool Pro 2.0).

However, only three products are available that will check disks formatted with HFS+:
MicroMat's TechTool Pro, Symantec's Norton Utilities 4.0, and Disk First Aid. All these
products check your hard drive's file system for errors and repair most of them (see
Figure 2.2). For more information about troubleshooting your hard drive, see Hour 24,
"Troubleshooting Your System."

> The *file system* is part of the Mac's toolbox, and it's the piece of system soft-
> ware that tracks how and where all your files are mapped on any of your
> Mac's hard drives. It's also commonly referred to as the computer's *directory*.

2

FIGURE 2.2.

TechTool Pro is the
best system checker for
HFS and HFS+ disks.

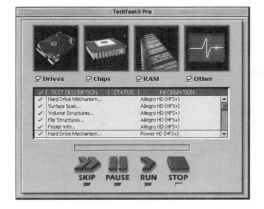

> Start up your Mac using the Mac OS 8.5 CD-ROM. (Press C while restarting
> your Mac to force the Mac to start up using the CD-ROM rather than its
> startup disk). You must isolate your startup disk so that the hard disk repair
> kit can repair as well as verify the status of your file system.

Updating Your Hard Disk Driver

The new installer automatically updates Apple internal SCSI and IDE hard drives using
the Drive Setup 1.4 utility included on the CD-ROM. You can also manually update your
Apple hard drive using the Drive Setup 1.4 software should you later choose to install
only portions of the operating system. Note that you can only use this version of Drive
Setup if you have upgraded your drive to the Mac Extended file system.

Drive Setup has a straightforward interface. However, if you don't use Install Mac OS to
update your hard disk's drivers, it might be a little difficult locating this feature in Drive
Setup. Follow these steps to update the driver of any Apple hard drives connected to your
Mac:

1. Launch Drive Setup.

2. Choose the drive you want to update in the Drive Setup window.

3. Select Update Driver from Drive Setup's Functions menu (see Figure 2.3).

If the driver updates successfully, a message will appear saying that you need to restart your Mac in order to use the new driver.

FIGURE 2.3.

The Drive Setup application.

You only need to update your Apple hard drive's driver once. You should update the drive that will run Mac OS 8.5 as well as any other hard drives or removable media that will be used with Mac OS 8.5. After a hard disk driver is updated, you can run previous versions of Mac OS, as well as Mac OS 8, from the drive.

Here are two things to be aware of when updating your drives:

- Drive Setup (or any other disk formatter) will erase and reformat your hard drive if you select the wrong command! Be sure to back up your hard drive before running this program.

- Don't use an older version of Drive Setup to update the driver with Mac OS 8.5. It will install an older driver and can cause incompatibilities between the operating system and the hard disk.

UPDATING MAC CLONE DRIVERS

Here's a "heads up" for you: The Mac OS installer will not update clone hard drives. You must update these drivers yourself prior to running the installer.

If you have a Power Mac clone, you need to use an updated hard drive formatter for the internal drive of the computer. Most clone machines use FWB's HardDisk Toolkit to manage the formatting and driving of Mac clone disks. Be sure to upgrade your copy of HardDisk Toolkit to version 2.5.2, because only this current version supports HFS+ and Mac OS 8.5. You can also use HardDisk Toolkit to update the driver for any external hard drive you may be using.

Backing Up Your Mac

As a last precaution, back up your existing System Folder before installing Mac OS 8.5. If you have enough time and media, you should back up your entire hard drive as a precursor to installing new system software. Don't forget to back up items on your desktop, and back up your RAM disk, too, if you're using one.

The basis of performing a backup is making a copy of the software on your hard drive. You can keep this copy on the same drive as the original. However, it's recommended that you copy or move any software being backed up to another hard drive, such as an external drive, removable media, or even a server. Besides using the Finder to create a copy, you can also use commercial backup software, such as Retrospect Remote, to back up the files on your hard drive to an external tape drive or second hard drive, such as a server.

One Last Preparation: Turning Off Security and Virus Protection

If you're running a virus protection program, screen saver, or security-related software, you should turn it off before installing Mac OS 8.5. These types of products will probably appear extensions residing in your System Folder. The easiest way to turn them off is to use the Extensions Manager (or a third-party manager) during startup.

To invoke Extensions Manager or Conflict Catcher 8 at startup, press the spacebar when you see the Mac OS splash screen and keep holding it until the extension's window appears. Select another set, such as 8.5 Base in the Extensions Manager, to turn off all extraneous extensions.

Note that you're going to have to reset these sets after installing Mac OS 8.5, because the system extensions and control panels have changed drastically from earlier systems.

Installing Mac OS 8.5

Installing Mac operating system software doesn't have to be a confusing exercise, but it can be persnickety. The thing to remember is that Mac OS 8.5 is considerably different than earlier Mac operating systems. You should start fresh and not install files over older files with the same name. In order to start with a "fresh" system, you perform a *clean install*. This is not an update of an existing System Folder, but a replacement of the current System Folder with a "brand new" one.

Don't be afraid of loosing all those third-party system extensions and desk accessories—the Mac installer is very smart and renames your System Folder as "Old System" before creating its new System Folder. Just compare the contents of the two folders when you're done and drag any files you need from the old to the new System Folder. It's a tedious and painstaking job, but it works.

Why Do a Clean Install?

A normal system software install modifies and updates the existing System Folder. A clean install disables the existing System Folder, leaving all files in place, and it forces the installer to create a new System Folder.

A clean system installation brings the system software back to the standard configuration. This is necessary when system software has been damaged or modified, preventing a normal installation. It's also useful for troubleshooting.

How to Do a Clean Install

You can follow these steps to create a clean install of Mac OS 8.5 on your hard disk. Begin by restarting your Mac with the Mac OS 8 Disk Tools or CD-ROM.

If you have a Disk Tools disk:

1. Shut down your Macintosh computer.
2. Insert Disk Tools in the floppy drive and turn on the computer.
3. At the desktop, the Disk Tools floppy disk's icon should be in the upper-right corner of your screen with your hard drive's icon below it.

If the computer ejects the Disk Tools disk, make sure that you have an Apple SuperDrive (formerly FDHD) that reads high-density disks and that you're using the Disk Tools that came with Mac OS 8.5.

If you have an Apple Macintosh CD-ROM that came with your computer:

1. Insert the Apple Macintosh CD-ROM in the CD-ROM drive.
2. Restart your Macintosh.
3. Hold down the C key on the keyboard immediately after you power on your Mac.

If Step 3 doesn't work with your computer, turn on the computer and immediately hold down the Command, Option, Shift, and the large Delete keys simultaneously. Keep these keys held down until you see the "Welcome to Mac OS" message.

At the desktop, the Mac OS 8.5 CD-ROM's icon should appear in the upper-right corner of your screen with your hard drive's icon below it. If any other hard drives appear above the Apple Macintosh CD-ROM, shut down the computer and all attached devices, remove the large SCSI cable from the rear of the Macintosh, and try again.

If the internal hard drive still appears above the Apple Macintosh CD-ROM, go to Control Panels under the Apple menu, open the Startup Disk item, select the Mac OS 8.5 CD-ROM, close all open windows, and then restart. The Mac OS 8.5 CD-ROM should then appear in the upper-right corner of the screen.

2

Performing a clean installation of Mac OS 8.5 from the Mac OS 8.5 CD-ROM is the most convenient way of doing a clean install if you have a Power Mac Desktop system or a PowerBook with a CD-ROM drive. Follow these steps to use the Mac OS 8.5 CD-ROM to do a clean install:

1. Double-click Mac OS Install on the Mac OS 8.5 CD-ROM.
2. Click the Welcome screen's Continue button.
3. On the next screen, select the hard disk you want to use as your startup disk (the place where you want to install the operating system).
4. Click Options.
5. In the resulting screen, make sure the Perform Clean Installation check box is selected. Click OK.
6. The installer returns you to the disk selection screen. Click Continue.
7. The installer walks you through the license agreement. Click Agree to continue the process.
8. A Mac OS 8.5 installation screen is displayed. Click Start.
9. Once the process is completed, click Restart to restart your Mac.

DOWNLOADING A MAC OS 8.5 UPDATE

Installing a downloaded update is very similar to installing from a CD-ROM, except you must remember to reboot the hard drive you're planning to use to house the System Folder (your new startup disk) so that it's not the active startup disk. You reboot by inserting your original Mac OS CD-ROM or Disk Tools disk and pressing C during restart so that your Mac is forced to use the CD-ROM or floppy drive.

It's smart to download the disk images for the update to a removable disk or another hard disk so that you can maintain a copy of the update offline for possible later use. Note that this is way too big to download to a floppy. Also, the update will not be bootable because it consists of disk images.

You must also make sure you have a little program called Disk Copy available to convert the downloaded disk images to volumes before the installation can occur.

Then, simply follow the instructions for performing a clean install, making sure to select your new startup disk as the installation target on the first screen of the installer.

Customizing Your Mac OS 8.5 Installation

Customizing a Mac OS 8.5 installation allows you to configure each software package that will be installed.

Perhaps the best benefit to custom installing your software is that you select exactly what's installed onto your hard disk. This could be an overwhelming amount of information if all the software installers were selected in one sitting; however, custom installation lets you upgrade system software at your own pace. It's also a convenient way to replace missing or corrupted software pieces.

Performing a Custom Install of Mac OS 8.5

The installer is very smart and knows whether you're installing Mac OS 8.5 for the first time. If you are, the program takes you to a splash screen that asks you to click Customize or Install. Click Customize to select the software you want to install. If you're returning to the installer to reinstall something or add a component, it knows this, too, and displays a dialog box asking whether you want to perform a complete install or a reinstall. Click the Add/Remove button. On the resulting Startup Disk selection screen, click Continue; then follow these steps:

1. In the resulting dialog box, deselect all the check boxes next to the software you do not want to install at this time. (See Figure 2.4.)

FIGURE 2.4.

The Custom Install dialog box.

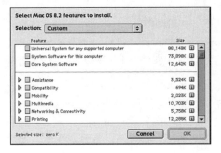

2. If you want to install only portions of Mac OS 8.5, select Customized Installation from the pop-up menu next to the software you want to install. You can selectively remove portions of software by selecting Custom Removal, or you can install all the software by leaving the pop-up menu on its default selection of Recommended Installation. Only those programs that offer customization will provide active pop-up menus. All other software will present "grayed out" pop-up menus.

3. If you don't want to update the Apple driver at this time, click Options at the bottom of the dialog box. In the resulting dialog box, deselect the appropriate check box. Click OK.

4. When the original dialog box with your list of selected software reappears, click Start.

5. The installer displays a list of components. Choose those components you want to install. Click OK.

6. The installer proceeds to perform the installation.

2

SUGGESTED CUSTOM INSTALLATION OPTIONS

If you have a huge amount of hard disk space (say 154 MB), select all the software packages available for installation in the Mac OS 8.5 disk and delete the ones you don't want to keep at a later time.

Not everyone has this option. If you have limited space (or are like me and hate clutter), you can install only those packages you want to use. Two levels of selection are available: extraneous packages outside of Mac OS 8.5 and selective installation of Mac OS 8.5 itself.

Here are some ideas for package combinations if you want to install all of Mac OS and selectively install additional software:

- If you're using your Mac as a word processor and a spreadsheet machine (basic business applications), there's no need to install Personal Web Sharing, Mac OS Runtime for Java, QuickDraw 3D, or Text-To-Speech. In fact, just install Internet Access, Apple Remote Access, and Mac OS 8.5.

- If you're using your Mac as an Internet-access device (say, the iMac), you really only need to install MRJ, Internet Access, ARA, and the operating system.

- If you're a graphic designer or Web designer, you'll need everything except Text-To-Speech and maybe Personal Web Sharing.

If you want to perform a customized installation of the operating system, think again about what you use your Mac for; then delete those components that do not apply (such as Token Ring, if you are running on a LocalTalk-based network, and so forth).

Determining What To Install

If you're familiar with all the software installers included with Mac OS 8.5, you'll most likely use the Customized Installation option in Install Mac OS. If you just want to install the system software, only select Mac OS 8.5—you can always add the other software packages at a later time. If you're unfamiliar with Mac OS 8 and its software installers, select the default Recommended Installation option. This gives you Apple's universal installation of Mac OS 8.5.

Although installing all the Mac OS 8 software has its benefits (for example, it gives you a complete dose of what's included with Mac OS 8.5), installing software installers one or two at a time can help you become more familiar with the features of each software package. For example, try installing the suggested Mac OS 8.5 package as a starting point. Then install one or two technologies or software packages at a time to see whether they contain something you can use. If you decide the hard drive space is better used for other software, you can always uninstall.

Things to Watch During and After Installation

As Install Mac OS progresses from one software installer to the next, each software package is updated with the status of the installation. If it's successful, the status will show that the software was installed. If there's a problem with the installation, the status will show that the package was selected but not installed.

If a software installer has a problem installing software onto the destination disk, an error message will appear in the Install Mac OS application. This happens while the software installer for a particular package is running. Therefore, if the software installation comes to halt, go to the Install Mac OS application and make sure the installation has not stopped due to an error. For example, QuickDraw 3D only installs on Power Macs. If you select this installation on a 68K Mac, the software installation will not move forward until you go to the Install Mac OS application and choose to stop or skip the installation in progress.

Once all the software installers have run, Install Mac OS displays a dialog box asking you whether you want to Continue or Restart if you installed software in the active System Folder. If you installed software onto a separate hard drive, Install Mac OS displays a dialog box asking whether you want to Continue or Quit.

Adding, Reinstalling, and Removing Components

After installing Mac OS 8.5, the software installers can be used again to reinstall, add, and remove software. You might choose to remove some software to free up disk space or, perhaps, because the particular software is not being used. Removing software can also help reduce System Folder file clutter as well as lessen the RAM requirements of the system. However, keep in mind that removing software often requires that the original installation path be retained, including the name of the file and the folder the software was installed in. Removing system software works best with Custom Remove. Otherwise, it's more efficient to just move software files to the Trash manually.

Adding software packages using the installer can be more efficient when evaluating a specific technology. In other words, you can add the software package, and if you don't like it, you can use the installer to remove it.

Reinstalling system software can be helpful for when the System Folder (or perhaps just one of its software files) needs to be reinstalled. For example, individual control panels or extensions might mistakenly be deleted (one of the CD-ROM software files, for example). Reinstalling the CD-ROM software from the Mac OS 8.5 installer conveniently puts these pieces back into your System Folder without you having to wade through your backup or wait for an entire system install.

While it's reinstalling, the Mac OS 8.5 installation software is aware of both enabled and disabled control panels and extensions. Therefore, if you reinstall a system software package and do not see the installed item in the expected folder, don't forget to also check the disabled folders.

Cleaning Up After Installation

Restart your Mac after completing a clean install of Mac OS 8.5. If everything starts up smoothly and gets to the desktop, you've probably had a successful installation.

Note that if you performed a "clean install," you'll have two System Folders—one called System Folder and the other labeled "Previous System Folder." You'll recognize the active System Folder because it will be the one with the system icon stamped on its folder. You'll also have used twice as much disk space because you now have duplicates of all of the contents of your System Folder. Don't worry, because when you're done transferring what you want out of the Previous System Folder, you can throw it away to recapture a substantial amount of hard disk space.

Restoring Your System Folder

You can now reinstall those system extensions, desk accessories, fonts, and preferences from the old System Folder (now named "Previous System Folder"). If possible, you should reinstall these items from their original disks.

> Mac OS 8.5 has done something cool to your System Folder: It has added folders for application drivers and other components, thus lessening slightly the clutter of your System Folder under System 7. Make sure you replace all your applications' driver folders (especially Adobe, Macromedia, Microsoft, and Claris), because these applications will not function without them. Luckily, this is easy to do, because each application's drivers resides in a folder labeled with the name of the software maker. Drag the folders into the Applications folder in your System Folder.
>
> Make sure you pay close attention to your old Preferences folder. This is where Netscape, Microsoft, and other vendors place files that personalize their software (such as Netscape's user profiles, mailboxes, bookmarks, and so on). Be sure to replace all third-party files, as well as any Apple settings, such as Users and Groups, that you want to keep.

If the original disks are not available, you may move the files from the old System Folder to the new System Folder. Be careful not to replace anything that's already in the new System Folder. In other words, you should only move items that are not already in the new System Folder. The following steps provide suggestions for moving items from the Previous System Folder to the new, clean System Folder:

1. Open each corresponding folder within the System Folder and the Previous System Folder and then compare the contents.

2. Move anything that's not already in the new System Folder and its subfolders from the Previous System Folder and its subfolders.

3. Restart your Macintosh.

> Casady & Greene's Conflict Catcher 8, the only version that's compatible with Mac OS 8.5, provides a very useful service: It synchronizes your old and new System Folders, accurately placing third-party software in your new folder from the Previous System Folder, thus saving you much anxiety.

Troubleshooting Extension Conflicts

Any system extensions or control panels installed appear as icons across the bottom of the screen when you restart your computer. They load into memory at startup time and modify the standard behavior of the operating system.

If the Macintosh fails to restart or behaves erratically, you probably have an incompatible or conflicting startup file (also known as a *system extension* or *control panel*). To verify this problem, follow these steps:

1. Restart, and after you see the picture of a computer with a smile, hold down the Shift key.
2. Release the Shift key when the "Welcome to Mac OS, Extensions Off" message appears.
3. When the Macintosh is ready, try to re-create the erratic behavior.
4. If the problem no longer occurs, you have a conflicting extension or control panel.

When the Macintosh behaves as expected and you're sure that all needed items in the Previous System Folder are transferred, move the Previous System Folder to the Trash and choose Empty Trash from the Special menu.

HELP WITH CONTROLLING SYSTEM EXTENSIONS

It's strongly recommended that you purchase a system extension manager, such as Casady & Greene's Conflict Catcher 8. Conflict Catcher will perform the tedious scan of your system extensions and regroup them should a conflict occur. An added bonus of running this program is that you can hook directly to your third-party software's Web site should you need to upgrade an extension. It's a great program.

Summary

Using Install Mac OS is recommended if you're installing Mac OS 8.5 on one Mac and you don't need to customize any of the software packages. It's also a timesaver for custom installs of one or all of the Mac OS 8.5 software packages. However, if you only need Mac OS 8.5 and do not want to bother with any other software with your initial Mac OS 8.5 install, you can run Disk First Aid, Drive Setup, and the Mac OS 8.5 installers manually.

Term Review

clean install   An installation that installs an entirely new version of your System Folder rather than copying over existing files.

directory   A location on your hard disk where data is stored.

file system   The collection of directories that make up your hard drive.

hard disk driver   The software that locates and manages directories on your hard drive.

installer   The application program that correctly places new or updated software on your Mac.

Random Access Memory (RAM)   The memory that stores information only while your Mac is turned on. This is also called *volatile memory*, because what's stored in such memory can be accessed very quickly but is lost if you turn off your Mac.

virus   An application that invades your Mac and does damage to your files through various nefarious means.

Q&A

Q How can I tell what version of the operating system my Mac is currently running?

A If your Mac is turned on, select About this Computer from the Apple menu. The resulting dialog box displays the current version of the operating system.

Q What if I need to install only one program, such as a new LaserWriter driver, out of the entire operating system?

A Use the individual installer for that piece of software. The installer resides with the software on your installation floppies or CD-ROM.

Q I have a lot of compatibility questions; where do I go to find out if my games and programs will operate with Mac OS 8.5?

A Check out www.versiontracker.com for a list of all current updates to Mac software.

Workshop

The Workshop contains quiz questions to help you solidify your understanding of the material covered. You can find the answers to the quiz questions in Appendix B, "Quiz Answers."

Quiz

1. What are the steps you should follow to perform an installation?

2. What is the benefit of performing a "clean install"? What are the drawbacks?

3. How much disk space does a full install require? How much RAM?

4. How can you tell how much disk space you have available?

5. What are some popular virus-protection applications?

6. How do you update your Apple hard drive's driver?

7. How do you update a Mac clone's hard disk driver?

8. How do you boot from a CD-ROM? From a disk?

9. How do you select which components within a given application you want to install if you choose to perform a custom installation?

10. What do you do to return your Mac to its original state once you've finished the installation?

2

HOUR 3

Getting Oriented

The magic of Mac OS is that it's easy to learn *and* easy to use. The technology behind the magic resides in the System Folder—in its icons, sounds, and extensions. Whether you're surfing the Net, working with a deadline, or troubleshooting a problem, when you understand more about the Mac OS, you'll gain insight into solving problems faster and optimizing your productivity. The following issues are covered in this hour:

- Understanding the desktop
- Using the menus and windows
- Creating files and folders
- Starting up and shutting down
- Ejecting disks
- Using cut, copy, paste, and drag operations

Understanding the Desktop

The Mac desktop is the heart and soul of the Mac. Here, you'll find icons representing hard disks, networked volumes, browsing tools, aliases to regularly used applications, the default printer, the Trash Can, and the menu bar, which lets you access the contents of your Mac. You'll quickly learn how to interpret the behavior of windows, icons, dialog boxes, menus, and aliases so that you can read the status of your Mac at a glance. The secret is that it's all done with pictures.

The desktop is similar to other windows in the Finder; however, it cannot be closed (except if the Mac is accessed over the network). You can only view items in "icon" mode in the desktop window. The desktop window is the most convenient place to store files, as well as aliases to folders or files, you use frequently.

The desktop, shown in Figure 3.1, consists of four main areas generated by the Finder. These areas are the Finder's menu bar, the hard drive icon (also called a *volume*), the Trash Can icon, and the desktop window (a.k.a. the *desktop*). From these areas, you can access everything from software applications to the world of the Internet.

FIGURE 3.1.

The Mac OS 8.5 desk-top.

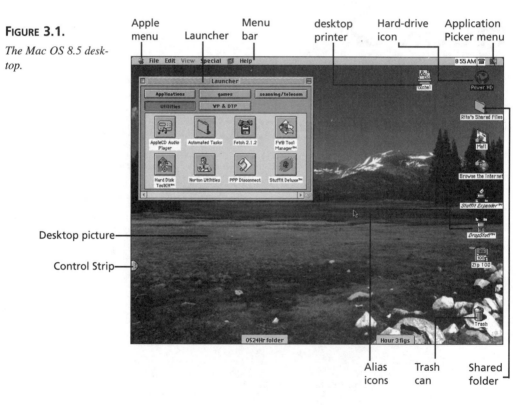

The Mac is a very versatile machine. You always have many different ways to perform your work, and all these methods work because the Mac's icons always operate the same way, no matter where you're working—on the desktop, in a window, or in an application. For example, you're given at least four ways to open documents:

- You can select an icon, click and hold down the mouse on a menu bar, and then drag the cursor down to select a command (such as Open in the File menu).

- You can press a keyboard equivalent (such as Command-O for Open).
- You can double-click one of those little pictures (called *icons*) to open a file (either an application or its related document).
- You can select a document's icon and drag it on top of an application icon or its alias.

Let's look more closely at the desktop's main components.

The Menu Bar

The menu bar, shown in Figure 3.2, provides access to many Mac OS software components, and it also monitors which applications are working with Mac OS. On the left end of the menu bar is the Apple menu. It consists of desk accessories, such as the Chooser and Key Caps, and applications, such as the Note Pad and Stickies. On the right end of the menu bar is the Application Picker menu. This menu contains a list of all currently open applications running on Mac OS. The Finder appears in this menu, as will any other open applications. The other menus (File, Edit, View, Special, and Help) provide commands that let you customize your Mac experience as well as open, print, save, copy, cut, paste, and view your Mac's contents in many different ways.

FIGURE 3.2.

The menu bar.

Drives and Volumes

The hard drive icon represents the internal hard drive in your Mac. Typically, this icon also represents your "startup" disk (the hard drive containing your active System folder). The startup disk's icon always appears at the very top of the stack of icons on your desktop.

From now on, when I omit the word "icon" from these discussions and just refer to "startup disk" or "window," for example, you can assume I mean their icon representations.

Double-clicking the hard drive icon opens a window that represents the root (or *base level*) of items on the hard drive. If you have other drives, such as a Zip drive or other external drives, they'll also appear as icons on the desktop. In addition, if you're connected to a network, you may see an icon representing the network volume. You work with network volumes in the same way you do the local hard disk.

The Trash Can

You can delete as many files and folders as you like by using the Trash Can icon located at the lower-right corner of your Mac's desktop. When the Trash Can has one or more items in it, its icon changes to a "full" Trash Can. Trash can be emptied by selecting Empty Trash from the Special menu.

Using the Windows and Menus

The first thing you see on your Mac OS 8.5 system is that everything is three dimensional. (Apple calls this the *platinum appearance*.) Windows stand out, the Trash Can has a shadow, and folders stand up. However, there's a method to this elegance. The 3D appearance provides visual cues as to where you are. For example, an "active" window (meaning the window you currently selected) appears three dimensional (see Figure 3.3). Click an inactive window and it bounces to the front and changes its appearance. New controls on this window let you manipulate it with fewer mouse clicks.

FIGURE 3.3.

Mac OS 8.5 windows provide elegant controls.

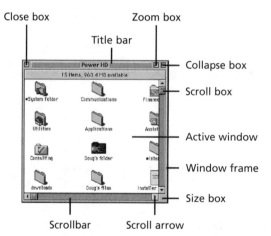

Mac OS 8.5 introduces some innovative window behaviors that prove very helpful when you want to move files and folders around without using extra mouse clicks. Mac OS 8.5's windows spring, pop, and scroll by themselves.

Spring-Loaded Windows

Drag a file or folder into another folder and watch the folder "spring open" to accept the item. Drag a file or folder onto a tabbed folder and the folder springs open to accept the item. These "spring-loaded" windows make it easy for you to move around your files and folders, and you can adjust the "springiness" (how fast a folder opens when you pass an item over it) using the Preferences command on the desktop's Edit menu. (See Figure 3.4.)

FIGURE 3.4.

The Preferences dialog box lets you set up your spring-loaded folders.

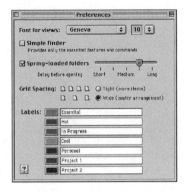

Another neat aspect of spring-loaded windows is that you're given the ability to burrow down through nested folders with a click of your mouse. If you want to find a file or folder that's hidden deep within nested folders, just double-click, but on the second click, hold down the mouse button on the folder. This "click-and-a-half" causes the cursor to change into a magnifying glass (see Figure 3.5). Pass the magnifier over a folder to cause its contents to spring open for viewing. Keep the mouse button pressed to continue digging. When you move the magnifier out of a window, the window collapses back to a folder.

FIGURE 3.5.

The cursor turns into a magnifying glass to signify jumps down into subfolders in a folder stack.

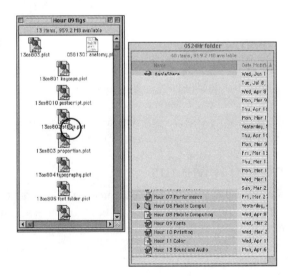

3

Pop-Up Windows

If you find yourself using a folder often, you can open the folder and then drag it to the bottom of your desktop. This turns the folder window into a tab. Now you can click the tab to open the window. This is called a *pop-up window*. This feature is great because it removes the clutter of multiple opened windows from your desktop and gives you direct access to your current folders.

You can place items in the pop-up window by dragging them onto the window's tab. The window pops up to receive the item and then collapses. Just drag the tab onto the desktop to convert the pop-up window back to a standard window. Figure 3.1 shows you a pop-up window on the desktop. If you want a way to quickly compare the contents of two or more folders, you can change the folders to "list" view by selecting As List from the View menu. Next, make them long and narrow and then drag them to the bottom of your screen to turn them into tabs. You can line up multiple windows along the bottom and click them open one by one to view their contents. As one window pops up, the previous one closes down.

> You can change the view in a pop-up window from "icon" to "list" or "button" by clicking the window's tab while holding down the Control key.

Collapsible Windows

You can close each window down to its title bar by using the collapse button. Clicking the collapse box while holding down the Option key collapses every window on your screen. You can also double-click a title bar while holding down the Option key to collapse all windows at once, or you can just double-click to collapse only one window at a time. Try these actions a few times on a basic window and you'll be a pro in no time.

Using Contextual Menus

If you've ever wanted to perform a command immediately without having to search through the menu bar or press a combination of keys, you'll love contextual menus. Mac OS 8.5 introduces the ability to Control-click an icon, window, or desktop to access frequently used commands. Figure 3.6 illustrates the contextual menu that pops up when you Control-click the desktop.

FIGURE 3.6.

Control-click an item to reveal a contextual pop-up menu.

You can use contextual menus to access control panels, such as Appearance (select Change Desktop Background), change the view, set up File Sharing privileges, and to turn on or off the desktop printer's print queue. In addition, third-party vendors are working furiously to build contextual menus into their applications. It's a whole new world out there. Experiment with Control-clicking to see what pops up.

The contextual menu is very handy and easy to use: Just release the mouse button and Control key, and the menu remains open until you click the mouse again.

Using the Control Strip

Control Strip is the narrow strip of software (most commonly seen on PowerBooks) that provides easy access to many system software features, such as AppleTalk, File Sharing, CD-ROM playback, sound volume, desktop printing, as well as various PowerBooks settings, such as battery level and hard disk sleep. Mac OS 8.5 installs Control Strip on all PowerBooks and Power Macs with PCI expansion slots (see Figure 3.7).

Each Control Strip module can be relocated within the Control Strip via dragging and dropping. The location of Control Strip can be changed by holding down the Option key and dragging the Control Strip to either side of your screen. The font and font size can also be configured in the Control Strip control panel.

FIGURE 3.7.

*Control Strip control
panel and modules.*

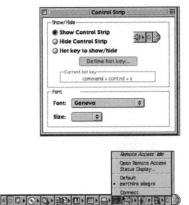

The following types of control strips are automatically installed with Mac OS 8.5:

- **AppleTalk Switch.** Changes AppleTalk from active to inactive (and vice versa)
- **CD Strip.** A mini version of an Audio CD player with track selection, volume, pause, stop, and play controls
- **File Sharing Strip.** Turns personal File Sharing on and off from this module
- **Location Manager.** Provides access to all the Location Manager modules installed in your System Folder
- **Monitor Bit Depth.** Provides access to all available bit depths for the monitor connected to your Mac
- **Monitor Resolution.** Provides access to all support monitor resolutions
- **Printer Selector.** Contains a list of desktop printers created by using Desktop Printing
- **Remote Access.** Lets you dial onto the Internet or an intranet from your desktop
- **Sound Volume.** Displays the sound volume and lets you change the setting

The following types of control strips can be found in the PowerBook folder in the Apple Extras folder. They're used on PowerBooks to manage battery life and other portable computing requirements:

- **Video Mirroring.** Turns video mirroring on and off.
- **PC Setup Switch.** Lets you switch from your Mac to your PC and back.
- **Battery Monitor.** Reflects the power source for your PowerBook. For example, it can tell you if your battery is running out of juice or whether you're using a socket-based power source.

- **Sleep Now.** Puts PowerBooks and supported Macs to sleep.
- **Power Settings.** Contains power-related settings for PowerBooks.
- **HD Spin Down.** Spins down the PowerBook's hard disk.

Control strips are available on such sites as MacAddict (www.macaddict.com) and Cnet's Download.com (www.download.com) as well as other shareware repositories. To add a new control strip, drag it onto the System Folder or manually place it in the Control Strip Modules folder in the System Folder.

Using the Launcher

The Launcher (see Figure 3.8) control panel is a floating window that contains buttons, representing applications, documents, servers, or folders, which enable you to open whatever is represented by the button with a single click. The button size can be changed by holding down the Command key and clicking in the Launcher window. A pop-up menu appears that enables you to select from a small, medium, or large button size.

FIGURE 3.8.

The Launcher control panel.

Items can be added to the Launcher window simply by dropping an icon into it. To remove an item from the Launcher window, hold down the Option key and move the button to the Trash Can icon. Launcher works with a folder that contains aliases in the System Folder, and its buttons look similar to those used in Apple's At Ease software.

You can organize your Launcher items by creating new folders within the Launcher Items folder. Open the Launcher Items folder in the Systems folder. Press Command-N to create a new folder. Give the folder a name beginning with a bullet •. The folder name will appear as a tab on the Launcher. Drag items into the folder or onto its tabbed name to organize your desktop.

Manipulating Files and Folders

Everything on a Mac is either a file or a folder. Folders open to reveal windows containing other files and folders (you can nest them inside each other *ad infinitum*). Figure 3.9 illustrates how files and folders can be nested.

FIGURE 3.9.

You can nest folders within folders, thus creating a "pyramid" filing system.

Files and folders are easily created, but can become difficult to locate and organize. The Mac provides several ways to manage the deluge of folders that can swamp your desktop. The View menu's View Options command, the Edit menu's Preferences command, and the General Controls control panel all let you set how files and folders are displayed: whether as icons, buttons on a bar, or lists; whether icons are displayed in a staggered or straight alignment; how the importance of files and folders can be labeled; how icons are displayed, and much more. (See Hour 5, "Customizing Your Mac" for more information.)

Apple sets up the hard disk window initially with a series of subject folders called: Applications, Apple Extras, Internet, System Folder, and Assistants. I like this system, but I add to it. I organize my files and folders two ways: I place all of my applications in the folder labeled Applications. I then make folders for each of my work functions: Graphics, Home, Finances, Consulting, and so forth. I create subfolders in these folders for each project (for example, I have a folder within my Consulting folder called "24Hours" for the contents of this book). Documents are stored by project, and I create aliases of a file or folder and place the alias in another folder if I want to reference it elsewhere. You can create a method for organizing your Mac using folders that best suits your working style.

The folder window is the second most basic feature of the Mac operating system. It contains devices to open, close, "window shade," enlarge, and move the window in order to get to where you want to be. Figure 3.10 presents a generic folder window and identifies its components.

FIGURE 3.10.

The folder window.

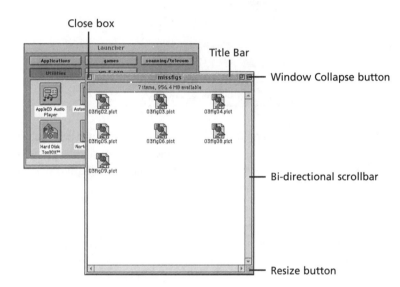

Close box

Title Bar

Window Collapse button

Bi-directional scrollbar

Resize button

3

You can select items in a folder window in many different ways after it's open. The easiest way is to click the item to be opened. However, if the item is not immediately visible, you can use the scrollbars to navigate around the window. The tab and arrow keys can also be used to scroll through the contents of a window. If the name of the item to be found is known, you can type its name and the Finder will reposition the window to show you that particular file or folder.

Creating Files and Folders

You can create a folder in any Finder window by selecting New in the Finder's File menu (or by pressing the keyboard combination Command-N). You can name a file or folder by selecting an item and pressing the Return key. This highlights the name of the file or folder, enabling you to rename it with a name containing up to 32 characters. You can get information on any file or folder by selecting General Information or Sharing Information from the Get Info submenu of the File menu (or by pressing Command-I). (See Figure 3.11.)

FIGURE 3.11.

Files, folders, and the Get Info window.

Files are created by applications. You can create a new file by selecting New from the application's File menu. First, input some text; then select Save (Command-S) from the File menu, and the file will be created on your Mac's hard drive. To open the file, select Open from the File menu or press Command-O.

Creating Aliases of Folders

You can create aliases to files or folders that you place in convenient locations so that you never have to dig into your nasty pile of folders. *Aliases* are icons that point to the location of an actual file. Creating aliases is easy. Select the icon and choose Make Alias from the File menu (or Command-M). You can also drag and drop icons onto the Launcher window or its title bar as well as the Apple menu to place aliases within these systems.

Aliases can be used for many purposes—from organizing your documents without moving their actual stored location to organizing your desktop to make it more manageable without moving actual files. For example, my husband likes to have two folder aliases on his desktop: one to create backups that points to his removable disk drive and another for active documents (so that he doesn't have to burrow through folders whenever he wants a Quicken template, for example).

The Mac uses aliases in its Recent Applications and Recent Documents Apple menu items. Because aliases are very small (about 33K, depending on the size of your hard disk), they're a great way to have access to large documents without actually moving them from their storage position (say, on a file server or backup disk).

Try to think of other uses for aliases.

One use of an alias to organize your desktop is to create a folder called "Documents." Use this folder to store all your most timely documents—the ones you don't want to loose. Make an alias (Command-M) of the folder and place the alias directly on your desktop.

Moving and Protecting Folders

To protect your system and application files and folders from losing their content, you can prevent them from being moved around unnecessarily. Go to the General Controls control panel and activate the protection check boxes for the System Folder and Applications Folder. If someone attempts to move a file or folder out of these folders (located at the root level of the hard drive), the Finder will show an alert and not allow anything to be moved or deleted from these folders.

You can move files and folders by selecting and dragging them to any other window or folder or to the desktop. You drag an item by clicking it while holding down the mouse button and then moving that item around a window or onto the desktop. If you drag a file onto a window from another hard drive, or a window or folder from a server, the Finder will copy those items to that drive (provided there's enough room or you have the adequate privileges on the server). When files and folders are copied, the originals remain on the source hard drive.

SPECIAL FILES AND FOLDERS

The System Folder stores a folder of files that contains settings for most software that runs on your Mac—the Preferences folder. The Preferences folder stores dozens of system preferences, as well as preferences for all types of software on your Mac.

Starting Up and Shutting Down

Turning on and off your Mac is as easy as pressing a button. In fact, that is all you do: press the Power key on your keyboard. When you press the Power key to start up the Mac, you get that old smiley face on your screen as the Mac commences its startup checks.

Shutting down is slightly more complicated. There are two types of shutdown:

- **Shut Down.** Turning off your computer hardware. You should always shut down before you completely turn off the machine.
- **Restart.** Turning off the Mac operating system.

Whenever you press the Power key, you're given the option of completely powering off the computer (such as when you're done for the day) or restarting the Mac OS (such as when you've installed a new application, updated a system extension, or ran Norton Utilities to fix your hard disk).

Figure 3.12 shows the alert box that appears when you press the Power key. Note that you can also put your Mac to sleep (meaning that it turns itself off without losing anything that may be in volatile memory).

FIGURE 3.12.

The Shut Down alert box.

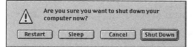

> **THE 11TH COMMANDMENT!**
>
> **Thou shalt not turn off thy Mac without shutting down first.**
>
> In other words, always shut down if you can.
>
> If your Mac happens to freeze, you can sometimes shut down the application you're working in so that you can properly shut down the Mac. Press the keyboard combination Command-Option-Esc to "force quit." If it works (depending on the nature of the bug or freeze), this causes the Finder to override the application and quit. You lose everything you haven't saved whenever you perform this function, so be careful and save often.

Other Options for Shutting Down

Of course, there are a couple other ways to shut down your Mac:

- Choose the Special menu and select Shut Down or Restart.
- In an emergency (a bomb or a freeze up), press the keyboard combination Command-Control-Power key. Your Mac will restart, destroying any information that you have not saved and possibly messing up your hard drive. Do this only if you cannot shut down any other way (because this violates the 11th commandment).

Other Options for Starting Up

Of course, because this is a Mac, you're given options for which programs will start up when you first turn on your Mac, as well as which programs shut down first or last when you turn off your Mac. The System Folder contains a folder for startup items and shut-down items. Any type of file, alias, document, sound, or application can be placed in either of these folders and will be launched by the system at startup or shutdown. If you use an application, such as a calendar or word processor, you might want to place it, or an alias to it, in your Startup Items folder. Placing an item in the Startup Items folder will automatically open that item when you start up your Mac. Similarly, if you place an alias, file, or application on the Shut Down Items folder, the system will attempt to quit out of that software when Shut Down is selected from the Special menu, or when your Mac is set up to shut down at a particular time.

Ejecting and Throwing Things Away

The Trash Can not only serves as a place to put items that you want to delete, it also works as a quick way to "throw away" a disk or volume you no longer want on your desktop. Keep the two uses of the Trash Can separate and you should have no problem.

Ejecting Disks and Volumes

Removing CD-ROMs, removable disks, and floppies from their drives is simply a matter of throwing the icon for the drive into the Trash Can. This seems scary, but the Mac knows the difference between a drive or volume and a file or folder. As with all things Macintosh, there are other ways to remove items from your desktop:

- Select Eject from the Special menu
- Press the keyboard combination Command-E
- Select the Put Away command in the File menu (Command-Y)
- Select the Move to the Trash command from the File menu (Command-Delete)

Throwing Away Items

The Trash Can also works to delete items from your Desktop directory. Placing an item in the Trash Can does not automatically erase it from your hard drive. You must select Empty Trash from the Special menu to formally erase the item. If you throw something away that you didn't mean to, simply double-click the Trash Can icon and you'll find it there (provided you haven't emptied the trash yet). Simply drag it out of the Trash Can to restore it. Hour 4, "The Finder," describes the Trash Can in more detail.

Macs are very forgiving computers. If you deleted something you really did-n't mean to and then emptied the Trash Can, don't despair. You have a trou-bleshooting toolkit that I discuss in Hour 24, "Troubleshooting Your System." TechTools 2.0 or Norton Utilities both have unerase features that help you retrieve deleted files most of the time (that is, if the computer hasn't already written over the file with a file of the same name).

Using Copy, Cut, Paste, and Drag Operations

Text, images, and other data can be transferred between applications and documents by using the Finder's Copy and Paste features (found in the Edit menu). The keyboard shortcuts for Copy and Paste are Command-C and Command-V, respectively. When you use the Copy function, it places any selected text, image, or other data into the Mac's Clipboard. From there, the data can be pasted into any other application or document.

Some applications also support drag-and-drop functionality. This is even simpler than using Copy and Paste, because it enables you to drag an object (text, image, and so on) directly to another document or application.

If you want to select several items in a window or document, you can Shift-click or Command-click to select any specific items (either in the Finder or in a document). To select all items in a document or window, press Command-A or choose Select All from the Edit menu.

Full and partial screen captures are both supported in Mac OS 8. The following information is a list of screen capture options available in Mac OS 8, courtesy of Apple Computer:

- Command-Shift-Control-3 copies a picture of the entire desktop to the Clipboard.
- Command-Shift-4 creates a picture file of a rectangular selection of the desktop. After pressing and releasing the key combination, position the cursor at the upper-left corner of the area you want to capture and then drag to the lower-right corner. If you continue to press the Shift key while dragging the cursor, the capture area will be constrained to a square.
- Command-Shift-4-Caps Lock creates a picture file of a window. After pressing this key combination, click the window you want to capture.
- To save the rectangle or window on the Clipboard instead of as a file, press the Control key as you click. To cancel a Command-Shift-4 screen selection, press the spacebar.

The Mac places all screen shots at the root level of your hard disk and labels them Picture 1, Picture 2, and so on. You need a graphic image viewer such as SimpleText or Lempke's GraphicConverter to view your screen shots.

Summary

During this hour, you learned your way around the desktop. You learned how to use a click-and-a-half to burrow through folders, how spring-loaded folders, pop-up windows, and collapsible windows operate, and how to recognize the status of windows and to change the view of files and folders within windows. The next hour presents information on customizing Mac OS 8.5.

Term Review

alias   An icon pointing to the location of an actual file. You use aliases to place files in more accessible locations, such as the Apple menu or desktop, without moving the actual file.

Apple menu   A special menu on the left side of your screen that contains small utilities such as Chooser and Scrapbook. AppleScript scripts are also launched from the Apple menu. You can also place aliases of commonly used applications in the Apple menu for easy launching.

Application menu   A special menu on the right side of your screen that is used to switch between open applications and the Finder.

contextual menu   A special pop-up menu accessed by Control-clicking any file or folder, including the desktop. Contextual menus change depending on where on the Mac you click, and they contain frequently used commands.

Control Strip   A pop-up bar residing at the bottom of your screen that contains commonly used utilities, such as Sound Level, Monitor Bit Depth, Color Depth, and Network Information.

desk accessory   A small utility program that performs a single function. Jigsaw Puzzle, Scrapbook, Stickies, and Calculator are all desk accessories.

Desktop   The root level directory on the Macintosh where the Finder operates.

Finder   A system application that manages files and folders on the Macintosh. The Finder controls the opening, saving, closing, and viewing of files and folders.

icons   Graphical representations of files available to your Macintosh. Icons can represent applications, documents, folders, hard drives, networked volumes, and so on. In fact, the entire Macintosh operating system consists of icons and rules for their manipulation.

Launcher   A special window that contains buttons used to launch applications.

menu bar   The row of pull-down menus along the top of your screen that contains most of the Finder commands. Every application also has a menu bar that contains a portion of the desktop menu bar (at least File, Edit, and Help).

platinum appearance   The new silver 3D appearance of windows and icons in Mac OS 8.5.

3

startup disk   The hard disk that contains your active System Folder.

Trash Can   The icon that represents the folder used to delete items. Use the Empty the Trash command to empty the Trash folder.

volume—A networked hard drive loaded on your desktop.

Q&A

Q What shareware is available to enhance contextual menus? Where can I find these programs?

A Check out the Control-Click! Web site (`www.control-click.com`) for the most up-to-date information about contextual menu add-ons. The best enhancement to contextual menus is provided by Turlough O'Connor's FinderPop control panel. FinderPop tacks on a special submenu with a user-determined list of applications, folders, and disks (akin to the Apple menu). Another cool shareware program lets you open contextual menus without Control-clicking. Look Mom No Hands! is available from the Tools & Toys Web site (`www.ToolsAndToys.com:81/Home/`) or from `www.download.com`.

Q What shareware is available to enhance the performance of aliases?

A The following shareware programs enable you to use aliases to their full potential:

- **Alias Crony.** Scans all your online volumes, creating lists of attached and unattached aliases. It retrieves aliases and their original files, links, and updates, and deletes these aliases. By Rocco Moliterno ($5).

- **AliasZoo.** Searches your hard drive or a specified folder and displays a report listing all the aliases it finds. Lets you delete orphaned aliases. By Blue Globe Software ($15).

- **a.k.a.** A drag-and-drop program that creates aliases. Freeware from Fred Monroe.

Q Where can I find out about Mac OS 8.5 utilities?

A Check out MacAddict's Web site (`www.macaddict.com/macos8/`) for a continuously updated list of utilities available to enhance Mac OS 8.5.

Q How can I tame my desktop aliases?

A If you find that you've dropped too many aliases on your desktop, place them in a folder and drag the folder to the bottom of your screen. Give the folder a descriptive name, such as "Printers" or "My Graphics" so that you know what the folder contains. When you drag the folder down, it becomes a pop-up menu accessed via a tabbed title bar. Click the title bar tab to pop open the alias folder.

Q How can I find something quickly on a CD-ROM?

A Make an alias of the contents of the CD-ROM (you have to create this on your hard disk because CDs are locked). Then, when you double-click the item with the CD-ROM loaded, you'll be automatically taken to that item on the CD-ROM. If you don't have the CD-ROM loaded, the Mac asks politely for it. (Note that you can do this with any type of removable disk.)

Workshop

The workshop contains quiz questions to help you solidify your understanding of the material covered. You can find the answers to the quiz questions in Appendix B, "Quiz Answers."

3

Quiz

1. How do you recover items from the Trash Can?

2. What are the various selection tools available in a dialog box?

3. How do you close a folder and still let it remain active or available on the desktop?

4. What is the difference between a local disk and a volume?

5. How do you move things around on the Control Strip?

6. How do you create a new container in the Launcher?

7. How do you add items to the Launcher?

8. How do you change the speed with which a folder springs open?

9. How do you access a contextual menu?

10. How do you change the sorting options in the Finder list view?

HOUR 4

The Finder

The Finder supplies Mac OS 8.5 with all the visible and interactive features for which the Mac operating system is famous. It's the application that implements the Macintosh computer's system software. Everything you see on a Macintosh—the desktop, and all windows, menus, and files—is ultimately connected to Finder. The following issues are covered in this hour:

- Understanding and customizing the Finder
- Organizing the desktop
- Viewing and navigating through the Mac
- Using drag-and-drop
- Accessing CD-ROMs, disks, and PC cards
- Understanding the menu bar

To be certain you're in the Finder, choose Finder in the Application menu.

What Is the Finder?

The Finder is the file manager for the Macintosh operating system. Without Finder, you wouldn't be able to open, close, save, print, or find files on your Mac. The most current version of Finder is Finder 8.0.

Finder 8.0 includes new features for long-time Macintosh users, while retaining its magical "ease of use" for those new to Mac OS 8.5. Many basic tasks work the same as with System 7, such as organizing files and folders, adjusting system settings and options, and using Mac OS to complete day-to-day tasks. Finder 8.0 includes new ways of doing these tasks, and it adds a new look to everything you'll work with in Mac OS 8.5. Finder 8.0 also enables you to return to the look and feel of System 7, thus offering the best of both worlds.

Organizing the Desktop

You could consider the desktop in Mac OS 8.5 to be the "home page" of the Macintosh. Internet metaphors aside, the desktop is the starting point for Mac OS. It consists of the Finder's menu bar, the Trash Can icon, an icon representing each hard drive and other disk volumes, and the preinstalled Mac OS 8.5 alias files. You can rearrange these items to create a working environment that's most suited to your tastes and needs.

The basic tasks for organizing files and folders in Mac OS 8.5 are simple. They involve setting up all the files and folders so that all the software is easy to find and efficient to use, yet personal enough to reflect how you use your Macintosh. Organizing the desktop also involves organizing any hard drives, other types of drives, and any network servers attached to your Macintosh.

Using Aliases

The key to organizing your desktop is the use of *aliases*, which are icons that look like the real thing (only with italicized names) but really only point to a file that's stored elsewhere on your Mac (sort of like a hypertext link on the Web). The alias of a file contains a pointer to its originating file (called subtly enough, its *original item*).

The beauty of aliases is that they're very small files that can be put almost anywhere on your desktop or in your folders. In addition, if you move or rename the original item, the alias is able to resolve the change and locate its originator. This makes it easy to move around files to create customized organizational motifs without touching actual storage locations.

Creating an Alias

Creating an alias is easy: Select the file or folder you want to make an alias for and press the keyboard combination Command-M. You can also choose Make Alias from the File menu. Then, drag the alias to the desktop or to wherever you want it to reside.

> You can also Control-click an item and select Make Alias from the resulting pop-up contextual menu. If you want to create an alias of an item at a location separate from its originator, drag the item while pressing the Command-Option keys. When you release the mouse button, an alias is created where you dragged the file. The mouse pointer changes shape (adding a tiny right-pointing arrow) to let you know you're successfully creating an alias.

Remember that after creating an alias, you can move it, rename it, copy it, or drag and drop it as you would any other file on your Mac. Just a word of caution: If you decide to name the alias with exactly the same name as its original item, the two cannot reside in the same folder. If you do want to store an alias in the same location as its original item, create a subtle difference in the name, such as adding a space after the name. The alias will always appear in italics, so you'll be able to tell which is which.

You can find the original item for an alias by selecting the alias and choosing Show Original (Command-R) from the File menu or the Contextual menu.

4

Manipulating Aliases

Here are some tricks you can use with aliases:

- Save on confusion between your Trash Can and the way you eject disks by creating an alias of your Trash Can, renaming it Remove Disk, and giving it a different icon (see the section "Customizing the Finder," for how to do this).

- Place an alias of your favorite folder on the desktop. Then, whenever you want to open a favorite file, you go to the desktop level of the Open dialog box and there's your folder in plain view. A good example of this is how Apple places an alias of a sharable folder on your desktop for your use during File Sharing to restrict access to your hard disk.

- Keep track of items on removable disks by creating an alias for these files on your hard disk. Then, whenever you double-click the alias, the Finder asks you for the appropriate removable disk and then opens the item.

- Make an alias of your Recent Servers folder (from the Apple Menu Items folder) and put it on your desktop. Then, whenever you want to save items to an unloaded volume, select its name in your Save dialog box as the target folder.

- Avoid using the Chooser to gain access to shared items by making an alias of the networked item after you've loaded it using the Chooser (see Hour 16, "File Sharing"). Then, select the shared item's alias whenever you want to link to that item over the network.

Sweeping Clutter Under the Rug

The Finder has three handy features you'll find yourself using over and over to clear up your desktop without closing windows: the Application Switcher, the Hide command, and the collapse box. Use these three features to keep your working area organized. There are also three ways to jump quickly between applications and three ways to hide windows on the Mac. (Didn't I say that the Mac always provides you with choices?) Use a combination of these tricks to move rapidly around your desktop and windows. The Application menu and Application Switcher are discussed in more detail in Hour 6, "Applications and Mac OS 8.5."

To jump quickly between applications, you can use any of the following approaches:

- **Using the Application Switcher**. Mac OS 8.5 has a handy little feature for those of you who like using buttons and the Launcher to open applications. After you open your applications and documents (and they're listed on the Application menu), just open the Application menu and slide the mouse down it and off the end. Notice that the menu seems to "peal off." The resulting little window filled with buttons is called the Application Switcher. Click an application button on the Switcher to open, close, or hide any windows.

- **Use the Application menu**. You can select another application from the Application menu.

- **Click another window with your mouse**. If the window you want is visible under the active window, click anywhere to bring that window to the front (thereby activating it). Click the desktop to return to the Finder.

To hide open windows, you can use any of the following approaches:

- **Use the Application menu's Hide command.** When you want to jump quickly from the Finder to an open document, choose Hide *<application name>* on the Application menu to remove an application and its document from your screen and to display the desktop. You can also use Hide Finder to jump back to your application while hiding any other open folders that may cause a distraction to your work.

- **Set up the General Controls control panel.** You can set up the General Controls control panel to hide all windows except the active one whenever you switch between applications.

• **Use the collapse button on the window.** The Window Shade option from System 7 is now part of every window in Mac OS 8.5; its functionality is implemented in the collapse box found in the upper-right corner of each window. You can use the collapse option to have several windows open on the desktop, with each window "collapsed" down to the title bar. If a window is collapsed, you can still use it to navigate through at least part of your hard drive. Command-click in the window's name in the title bar, and a menu appears showing the path in which the window resides.

 You can collapse all Finder windows by holding down the Option key while clicking the collapse box.

Some Additional Desktop Behaviors

You can change the view of icons on the desktop between two different types: button view and icon view. The Finder offers these additional standard behaviors:

• Finder will not let you open a device by dragging on top of it. Therefore, you cannot move the Trash Can icon or any device icons onto each other or off the screen.

• If you're running Mac OS 8.5 on an externally bootable drive that's been moved from a computer with a larger screen to one with a smaller screen, Finder automatically moves items into the smaller screen's desktop.

• If you have full access privileges, you can see the Desktop folder and Trash Can icon when accessing these folders from another Macintosh using File Sharing.

• If you're using File Sharing to access desktop items, you need to look for a Desktop folder at the root level of the hard drive to find those items.

Using the Launcher

A controversial method for accessing applications and folders without having to open windows is to use the Launcher control panel. I say *controversial* only because so-called power users don't use the Launcher, because it limits their ability to open and close items. The Launcher is a venerable part of the Mac Performa line that has been brought to Mac OS 8.5. I love the Launcher because I have children and do not want them clicking away at windows. I place applications, such as games, in the Launcher Items folder in my System Folder (dragging an item onto the Launcher does the same thing) and then they appear as buttons on the Launcher window. (See Figure 4.1.)

FIGURE 4.1.

*The Launcher provides
a safe way to start
applications.*

You can set up your Launcher, as shown in Figure 4.1, using various folders, thus organizing your documents and files for quick startup.

To add a folder to the Launcher, create a new folder with the File|New Folder command
(Command-N). Next, rename the folder, placing a bullet (Option-8) in front of its name,
and then Command-Option-drag the new folder onto the Launcher's tab bar. You remove
an item from the Launcher by pressing Option while dragging it to the Trash Can.

Viewing and Navigating Your Files

One of the nice features of the Finder is its flexible viewing options. You can change how
you view your documents and folders with the click of the mouse. Use the Views command to set up the view preference for each of your folders. Each window can be viewed
differently—whether as icons or via a list view—based on your working style and needs.

If you want to use the drag-and-drop technique to open documents, you should keep your
folders where applications are stored in icon view. If you want to view a history of a project, you should keep your folders in list view to present a hierarchical display. A third
option, usually for beginning users or as a safeguard for your files, is the button view,
where no one can move any items on your desktop. Figure 4.2 shows you the three different views.

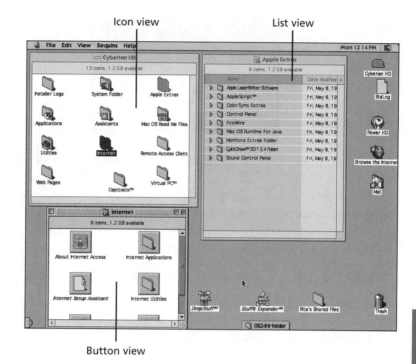

FIGURE 4.2.

The list, button, and icon views.

Button view

Burrowing with the Mouse

A new way to navigate through hard disks and folders, starting from your desktop, is to use your mouse. No, I don't mean doubling-click a folder as in System 7. Instead, hold down the mouse button at the second click; then, when you move the mouse over a folder and keep it there for a couple seconds, the cursor turns into a magnifying glass and the folder automatically opens (see Figure 4.3). Apple calls this action a *click-and-a-half*.

NEW CURSORS IN MAC OS 8.5

Mac OS 8.5 has several new cursors. In addition to the magnifying glass, there's also a submenu cursor for context menus, as well as a plus cursor for navigating while Option-copying a file in Finder 8.0.

4

FIGURE 4.3.

*The magnifying glass
cursor provides a new
navigation feature in
Mac OS 8.5.*

You can open as many folders in a row as you want. If you want to go through a different set of folders, you can move the mouse away from the current set of folders and windows, wait until they close, and then begin another navigation adventure by holding down the second click until your navigation is complete. This new way of navigating, indicated by the magnifying glass cursor, enables you to quickly navigate through multiple drives, CD-ROMs, disks, and servers.

Navigating with the Apple Menu and Desktop

The desktop is a great place to put frequently accessed folders, files, and aliases. Another way to access folders or files quickly is to place them on the Apple menu. Here are some key points:

- To place a folder, file, or alias on the desktop, select the file or folder icon and drag it to the desktop. Keep in mind that the file still exists on the hard drive on which it was created. Placing folders or files on the desktop is similar to placing them in another folder: that is, the Desktop folder. The Desktop folder (or the *desktop*) is unique from other folders because it's not device dependent. You can place files from different hard drives on the desktop, for example, without having to copy them from one drive to another.

- To place an item on the Apple menu, open the Apple Menu Items folder in the System Folder and drag an alias of the file or folder into this folder. Make it easier on yourself by creating an alias of the Apple Menu Items folder and placing it inside the Apple Menu Items folder. This way, you have a way to open Apple menu items quickly via the Apple menu. (Are you confused yet?)

- A new Mac OS 8.5 feature is the Favorites folder. Programs that support the new navigation services, such as the Finder, let you add your popular files and folders to the Favorites folder by clicking the Favorites button on the Finder's new Open dialog box. You can also add favorites to the Favorites folder by selecting the item (say, your hard disk) and choosing Add to Favorites from the File menu on the desktop. The Favorites folder can be accessed from the Apple menu as well as from the Finder's Open dialog box (see Figure 4.4). Select the item from the

Favorites submenu to open that item. You can remove items from Favorites in two ways: use the Remove Favorites command on the Open dialog box or drag unwanted favorites to the Trash Can from the Favorites folder in the System Folder.

FIGURE 4.4.

Use the Favorites menu to quickly access favorite applications or folders.

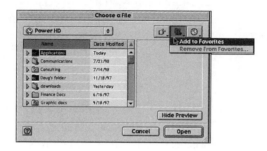

Under the Finder's Hood

A key element of Finder is its invisible desktop database, which is where all icon and some file information is stored on each hard drive or storage device. The desktop database also links files to applications by creating a cache of icons, bundles, and file information for the applications.

> The desktop database supports a limited number of icons for files and folders on a drive. This should not affect the day-to-day use of your Macintosh. If you notice documents or applications with a generic icon instead of a custom icon, however, this is a good indication that the limits of the desktop database have been reached and that it should be rebuilt. To rebuild the desktop database, hold down the Command and Option keys at startup.

Once in a while, you should rebuild the desktop database, either as part of regular maintenance, such as once a month if you use your computer daily, or to help with software troubleshooting.

To rebuild the desktop database, hold down the Command and Option keys at startup. Before the desktop is drawn, a dialog box appears asking whether you want to rebuild the desktop. Select OK. A progress bar appears that first saves comments in the Information window and then continues until the desktop has been rebuilt. (See Figure 4.5.)

FIGURE 4.5.

*Rebuilding the desk-
top.*

When the desktop is rebuilt, all Information window comments are saved in Mac OS 8.5. To view file comments, select any file or folder and then press Command-I (or select General Information from the Get Info pull-down menu on the File menu or contextual menu). Comments can be typed into the lower part of the General Information window.

Viewing Disks, Volumes, and Drives

The hard drive icon is the most frequently accessed device icon on the Macintosh, especially if you have only one drive with one partition configured on your Macintosh. Other devices that can be used with Mac OS include removable drives, such as Zip and Jaz 2 drives, and CD-ROM drives. In addition to using the magnifying glass, a menu, and the mouse to open and close folders and files, you can select devices and their contents a number of different ways. The following list explains different ways you can select and work with files and folders stored on hard drives, CD-ROMs, and removable media:

- You can use the Tab key to select an item in a window in list, icon, or button view.
- You can use the arrow keys to select an item in a window in list, icon, or button view.
- For faster access to an item in a window, type the filename, and Finder will select the filename that most closely matches what you entered.
- To rename an item, press the Return key.
- You can remove a hard drive or storage device from the desktop by placing its icon in the Trash Can, or you can choose Put Away from the File menu (Command-Y). Remember not to throw away your startup disk (the one at the top-right corner of your desktop).

WHAT IS A PARTITION?

In order to use a hard disk to store files and folders, it must have at least one partition formatted to work with Mac OS 8.5. Each partition is a volume created on the hard disk by using a software application such as Drive Setup. A hard drive can have one or more partitions created all at once, or erased and re-created over time. Each partition on the drive appears as a separate volume on the desktop.

Sherlock

Mac OS 8.5 has substantially updated the Find command to include the ability to save
search criteria for future searches as well as the ability to index your disk drives for rapid
searching. You can search across networks and save the results via the contextual menu
to the Clipboard. The Find application has been renamed Sherlock to reflect its enhanced
searching capabilities.

You can now perform three types of searches in the Sherlock application: Find a File,
Find by Content, and Search the Internet.

Find a File

Say you want to find a file with "Mac" in the name. Choose Find from the File menu or
select Sherlock from the Apple menu or Contextual menu (or press Command-F). In the
resulting Find dialog box, type the word "Mac" in the text box and then press Find.
Figure 4.6 shows you the results. In this case, 199 files were found containing the word
"Mac." Select a file to see exactly where on your local volumes it's located. Double-click
the filename in the lower list box to open that folder.

FIGURE 4.6.

*The Find File screen
locates files based on
criteria you enter.*

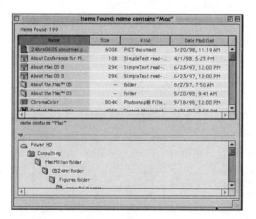

4

As shown in Figure 4.7, you can select where Find should seek your text by using the
Name pop-up menu to change your searching criteria. Use the next pop-up menu to
change how precise the search should be. Click More Choices to add more search criteria and precision levels to your search.

FIGURE 4.7.

Select your search criteria and precision from the pop-up menus.

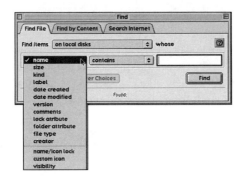

Search By Content

Here's where the neat stuff added in Mac OS 8.5 comes into play. Say you want to find a document containing the word "Mac" inside the document, not just the filename or Finder headings. You can perform a search of your local and networked disks using the V-Twin-based content search engine.

Open Sherlock again (Command-F) and click the Search Content tab. Figure 4.8 shows you the resulting Sherlock window. Select a volume to search and type the text you want to find in the Text box. In this case, I chose "Mac OS 8.5." The search may take some time, based on how large your disk drives are and how many you chose to search. In order to Find by Content, you must first index your volumes.

FIGURE 4.8.

Files containing your search phrase are listed in the dialog box.

Indexing creates a mini database of all the major words in all your documents on the selected drive. (Note that little words, such as "the," "and," "a," and so forth are deleted to shorten the list.) Sherlock uses this index to speed up its search. Click Index to index your drive. In the resulting dialog box, select a disk drive and click Index (see Figure

4.9). You can schedule updates to the index at regular intervals to ensure that the index is up-to-date.

FIGURE 4.9.

Indexing your volumes speeds up the search time.

Search the Internet

Here's a really cool new feature of Sherlock. Now you can search the Internet for any phrase you type into the Sherlock dialog box. You can also select where on the Internet you want to search. Narrow or broaden your search by selecting different search engines and Web sites, such as Excite or MacInSearch. You can add new search site plug-ins by downloading them from `http://www2.apple.com/sherlock/plugins.html` or `www.maccentral.com` and dropping them into the Internet Search Sties folder in the System folder. Search CNN for news articles, Internet Movie Site, Amazon Books, Barnes and Noble Books, and other internal sites using their proprietary engines. More plug-ins are being added daily.

Figure 4.10 shows a search for the phrase "QuickTime 4.0." When you click Find, Remote Access dials your ISP and initiates the search.

FIGURE 4.10.

Search the Internet for any topic by typing a phrase in the Search Internet window.

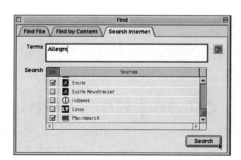

The results are displayed in Figure 4.11. Clicking a link automatically opens your browser to that page.

FIGURE 4.11.

Click a link to open the page in your browser.

Find lets you save all the search criteria you created in each of the three types of searches. Select Save Search Criteria from the File menu in the Find application (Command-S). If you want to use this criteria, select Open Search Criteria from the File menu of the Find application.

ADDING SHERLOCK PLUG-INS

One nice thing about the Macintosh developer community is that they do not sleep on the job. The minute Sherlock was introduced, developers increased the efficacy of the technology by creating plug-ins that let you search many more online databases such as Amazon.com, Barnes and Noble.com, MacCentral, and many more sites. To add a plug-in to Sherlock, download the plug-in from such repositories as Apple's Sherlock Plug-In Site at http//www2.apple.com/sherlock/plugins.html and then drag and drop the resulting file on to your System folder. The Mac will place the Sherlock plug-in into the Internet Searches folder in your System folder.

Opening and Grouping Documents

Another regular regimen on your computer is opening and saving documents. To make it easier to find files to open, try grouping related files in the same folder. You can group files and folders in several different ways. The most common method is to use a unique filename so that you can tell what the document is about or who it's from or for. You can also customize file and folder groupings by adding a space at the beginning of the name of a file and folder or by assigning a common label across selected items. To assign a label to any file or folder, select the item and then choose a label color from the Label pull-down menu located in the File menu or contextual menu. The selected file or folder will display the chosen label color.

> You should make at least one backup of whatever files and applications are
> created or frequently used.

Dragging Versus Double-Clicking Files

Double-clicking a file is probably the most intuitive way to open a file and its application. You can also choose Open from the File or contextual menu or press Command-O
to open files. Another way to open a file is to drag its icon over the icon of the
application with which you want to open the file. Some applications also support
dragging the file into an already opened window to open the file.

Dragging a file over the application you want to use can save more time than double-
clicking the file. For example, if you have more than one application on your hard disk
that can read text files, double-clicking a file may not open the application you want to
use. Also, if Mac OS Easy Open is "on," it will show a list of applications that may be
able to open the file.

Grouping and Opening Applications

Finder enables you to run multiple applications—memory permitting—at the same time.
Although only one application can be the front-most at any given time, most applications
can still process some data when they're in the background. Running multiple applications simultaneously reduces the amount of time you must wait for an application or file
to open.

Finder works with applications to use similar dialog boxes for opening and saving files
via a new toolbox called Navigation Services (see Figure 4.12). Technically, these dialog
boxes are referred to as standard Finder dialog boxes. The dialog boxes enable you to
navigate throughout both the desktop and storage devices either to find a file to open or a
location in which to save a file. Navigation Services lets you select and open more than
one document simultaneously, as well as preview the contents of the document directly
in the Finder dialog box window. Foreign files are automatically translated using the services of File Exchange. With Navigation Services, the contents of your networked volumes can be searched exactly as if they were resident locally.

Generally, Open and Save Finder dialog boxes appear in any application that lets you
open or save documents. You can use the General Controls control panel to change the
default location for where a file is saved.

4

The General Controls control panel has a Documents section located in the lower-right corner of its window. There are three options for opening or saving a document—in the folder that's set by the application, in the last folder used in the application, and in the Documents folder. Selecting the Documents folder option generates a Documents folder on the desktop after the control panel is closed.

FIGURE 4.12.

The standard Finder dialog box for opening a file in Microsoft Word 98.

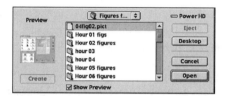

Usually when you're opening a file, you can see only supported filenames in the standard file dialog box. The file types include text, PICT, and 3D file formats for customizing application document formats for word processing, spreadsheets, and multimedia data storage. Most file types can be translated to some degree across applications. The best way to open a specific file format, however, is to have an application that can create or view the file being viewed or edited.

CD-ROMs and the Finder

All current Macintosh computers contain CD-ROM drives. The CD-ROM drive was the first multimedia component for the Macintosh, allowing you to store up to 600 MB of data. You can now purchase CD recorders for under $1,000 to use your own, personally created CDs with the CD-ROM drive. Additionally, CD-ROM drives are available that let you create more than one recorded session on the CD-recordable disk.

To use a software or audio CD with Mac OS 8.5, put the disc in the CD tray. After you close the drawer, Finder mounts the disc on the desktop. If Finder cannot read the disc, it asks you if you want to eject it. Keep in mind that CD media is read-only, so you can't add any items to CD media. For general file and folder navigation, CD media works the same as a hard drive.

After the CD-ROM is mounted on the desktop, double-click the CD-ROM icon to view its root level. If an audio CD is inserted, the QuickTime Settings control panel will automatically play the audio CD by default. For more information on QuickTime, see Hour 12, "QuickTime." Some CD-ROM software requires you to copy an application or folder to your Macintosh computer's hard drive to provide optimal performance. You can remove a CD-ROM from the desktop as follows:

- By dragging the CD-ROM icon to the Trash Can
- By pressing Command-Y
- By choosing Put Away from the File menu
- By choosing Eject from the Special menu
- By pressing Command-E

Using the Trash Can

The Trash Can is, as its name denotes, a place to remove files and folders from Mac OS (see Figure 4.13). It has a unique Trash icon when it's empty, and a full Trash icon when files or folders are put into it. The Trash icon is similar to the hard drive device icon; you cannot place it in another window or remove it from the desktop. The Trash Can is also similar to the desktop in the sense that when you share files, the Trash Can is a folder.

FIGURE 4.13.

You can view items in the Trash Can in list mode.

4

Emptying the Trash

There are no serious penalties for waiting to take out the trash. You can place items in the Trash Can until you're sure you want to delete them. Double-clicking the Trash icon opens a window in which you can view items in list, button, or icon mode. To remove items from the Trash Can, choose Empty Trash from the Special menu. A warning message asks you to confirm if you want to remove the items permanently. If you put a file or folder from a server into the Trash Can, it will be emptied when the server is dismounted from the desktop. Select Cancel if you want to keep an item in the trash. To bypass the warning message, hold down the Option key while selecting Empty Trash from the Special menu.

The warning for emptying the Trash Can can be turned off from the Get Info pull-down menu. The General Information window for the Trash icon contains a "Warn Before Emptying" check box at the bottom of its window. Uncheck this check box to turn the warning off.

Most files and folders are deleted when you empty the Trash Can. Some files, however, can be locked or busy, resulting in a dialog box telling you those types of files could not be deleted. For locked files, hold down the Option key while selecting Empty Trash. If a file is busy, try restarting the computer to make the file "unbusy" and then select Empty Trash.

After files or folders are deleted, they're removed from Finder's access. They are still on the hard drive, however. As new files or folders are created, they'll most likely be created over the hard disk where the previous deleted file was physically located on the disk. If you accidentally delete a file, you can use software such as Norton Utilities to recover it. Remember not to create or copy any additional files or folders onto the drive until after the file or folder you need has been recovered.

Occasionally, when Mac OS crashes or freezes, a folder titled "Rescued items from <hard drive name>" appears in the Trash Can. Mac OS uses the folder and its items to help restart system software. After you successfully restart the computer, you can delete the folder and its items without harming the Mac operation system.

The Move to Trash Command

A new feature in Mac OS 8.5 is the Move to Trash command, which appears in any file's or folder's context menu. Selecting Move to Trash for any item places that item directly in the Trash Can. You can also select an item and then press Command-Delete to move the file or folder to the Trash Can.

The Menu Bar

Finder's menu bar has changed a little in Mac OS 8.5. All the features in System 7 are still there, along with a few new ones. The menu items in Finder provide a wide range of services: creating new folders, copying files, formatting floppy disks, emptying trash, and selecting a view for any Finder window.

With sticky menus, one of the helpful new features in Mac OS 8.5, a menu remains onscreen after you click any item in the menu bar. After a menu appears, you can move the cursor to any other menu and view each list of menu options without having to hold down the mouse button.

The menu bar consists of the Apple, File, Edit, View, Special, Help, and Application menus. Most menu items are the same as in System 7. Along with windows, dialog boxes, and buttons, Finder 8.0 has added a new grayscale background and 3D Apple and Application menu icons to the menu bar. Note that the name of the active application is now listed in the menu bar beside its icon. The Edit and View menus have also been rearranged, and the Label menu item has been moved to the File menu. (See Figure 4.14.)

FIGURE 4.14.

The Label menu item now appears in the File menu.

The Edit menu contains a Finder Preferences menu item with which you can choose label names and colors. The View menu contains a wide range of Finder views as well as a View Options menu item. Depending on the view of the front-most window, View Options displays several icon- or list-oriented options. Any changes you make apply only to the front-most Finder window. Although the Help menu has been moved next to the Special menu, its menu items are the same as in System 7. In Mac OS 8.5, the Help menu has been changed from an icon to text.

Organizing the Apple Menu

You can save navigation time spent opening and closing folders by having an alias to them in the Apple menu. The Apple Menu Items folder is located in the System Folder. You can place an alias, or any other file or folder, in the System Folder by copying, dragging, or creating an alias to the item in the Apple Menu Items folder.

4

The Automated Tasks folder contains an AppleScript that can create an alias for any item and put it in the Apple menu.

When Apple Menu Options is "on," placing a hard drive icon in the Apple menu enables you to navigate through your drive using Finder menus instead of windows. You can browse menus a little faster than opening and closing Finder windows.

When adding items to the Apple menu, you should watch for duplicate items. Also, over time, access might not be as easy if broken aliases or items removed from the hard drive are not removed from the Apple menu.

Using the General Information Window

General Information contains many different types of information about an application, such as when it was created, where it's located on the disk, and how much memory it needs to run (see Figure 4.15). To see the General Information window, select an application icon, such as SimpleText, and then select General Information from the Get Info pull-down menu on the File menu. The following list identifies each item in the General Information window of an application:

- At the top of the window is the icon and name of the application.

- In the lower-right corner are the memory requirements for that application.

- Suggested Size is the amount of memory recommended to run the application.

- Minimum Size is the amount of memory the application must have to launch. For example, SimpleText has a Preferred Size setting of 512K and a Minimum Size setting of 192K. If 512K is not available in Finder, for example, SimpleText can open if there's more than 192K of available memory. This number can be adjusted to be higher or lower than Suggested Size. It's recommended, however, that the Minimum Size setting not be less than the Preferred Size setting.

FIGURE 4.15.

The General Information window for an application.

- Preferred Size is the amount of memory the application will use when opened. For many applications, you can increase this number, especially if you're working with large files. The recommended size varies from 20 percent up to a ratio based on the size of the file you want to open with the application.

In Mac OS 8.1 and higher, the default configuration has added 1 MB of virtual memory to decrease the amount of RAM an application uses.

The General Information window is the key to setting how much memory an application uses when open. If the preferred amount of memory is not available, the application will run in any amount of memory available between the Minimum Size and Preferred Size settings. For Power Macintosh computers, the note at the bottom of the window informs you of how much memory you can save if virtual memory is enabled.

Customizing the Finder

After you've become familiar with using Finder, you can start exploring new ways to extend Finder to make your Macintosh easier to use. Many shareware control panels and extensions are available that can change the way Finder appears. You can alter many facets of Finder—from menu bars to windows, dialog boxes to buttons.

Changing Custom Icons

A fun feature of Mac OS 8.5 is the ability to customize file and folder icons. The method for doing this involves the following steps:

1. Select a file or folder.
2. Select General Information from the Get Info pull-down menu (Command-I). The icon for that file or folder appears in the upper-left corner of the General Information window.
3. Open another file or folder whose icon you want to put on the first.
4. Select the icon located in the upper-left corner of the second item's General Information window.
5. Select Copy from the Edit menu.
6. Select the icon in the first item's General Information window.
7. Select Paste from the Edit menu. The first item's icon changes to the new icon.

When you start feeling comfortable adding custom icons to files and folders, you might want to try creating your own icons. For more information about creating custom icons, see Hour 5, "Customizing Your Mac."

4

A wealth of icons is available for Macs, both as shareware and commercial products. Most icons can be found in Macintosh software libraries in forum areas and FTP sites.

Changing Files and Folders

You can customize files and folders by using Finder features such as custom icons, labels, and descriptive filenames. Every file has two icons for the monitor's color depth: a regular icon and a small icon. If you put a window in View as Icons mode, regular-sized folder and file icons appear in the selected window. If you put a window in View by List mode, the medium-size icon appears (unless you change the default icon size to small or large).

Each filename can have a maximum of 32 characters. You can edit the name of any folder or file (except for files that are locked or on a server that has read-only file access). Undo, from the Edit menu, also reverts any edits made with filenames in Finder.

 You can change the sorting order for any column in list view by clicking the column's title in a window. Finder 8.1 also adds a sort button on every Finder window.

Summary

Apple has done a great job of improving Mac OS by keeping the best of System 7 and adding some great new features to Finder 8.0. This chapter reviewed some basic ways to use Mac OS as well as how to exploit Finder to do the same old tasks in new and different ways. This hour covered how to view documents in the Finder as well as how to find documents using the updated Find application. You also learned how to customize the Finder as well as how to optimize its behavior to meet your working style.

Term Review

alias   A small file that points to the location of its original. You use aliases to place multiple copies of a file in different locations on your desktop without actually having to move the original.

button view   A Finder view that presents files as clickable buttons.

Desktop database   A hidden file that contains information about file locations, aliases, and icons used by the Finder to maintain the desktop's integrity.

drag and drop A method of opening or saving a file by selecting it and dragging it on top of another file's icon.

Finder 8.0 Mac OS 8.5's file management application.

icon view A Finder view that presents files as small pictures that can be moved, copied, renamed, and opened.

Launcher A desk accessory that provides a way to open applications, documents, and folders via buttons that represent aliases of these items.

list view A Finder view that presents files and folders in their nested hierarchy.

original item The actual item represented by an alias.

Q&A

Q How can I change the label colors used to prioritize my documents?

A Select Preferences from the Edit menu. In the resulting dialog box, click the Labels tab. Click a color to bring up the Color Picker; then select another color from the Picker. See Hour 5 for a full discussion of how to customize your Mac.

Q What else can I do with aliases?

A Make an alias of your Apple Menu Items folder and place it on the Apple menu for quick access to that folder.

Make an alias of a removable disk's volume and use it as a drop box for backup copies of critical files.

Q How do I find a document using Boolean logic?

A Boolean logic uses "and," "or," as well as "contains" to create a more precise search. For example, set up your Find criteria to search for all files containing the word "Mac" that were modified yesterday. This would find only those files modified yesterday containing the word "Mac." Select these logical operators from the second pop-up menu on the Find dialog box. You can use more than one search parameter at a time by clicking the More Choices button.

Q What is a quick way to get to the desktop from an application?

A Click the Desktop window and then click the application's window to return to that application. See Hour 6 for a further discussion of the Application menu.

Q Why do I sometimes see a Finder-like list of folders and files in the Finder dialog box and sometimes the older Finder dialog box list when I select Open or Save As?

4

A The new Navigation Services feature in Mac OS 8.5 must be supported within applications to invoke its use. If the application is not Navigation Services savvy, it must use the older File Picker toolbox to display the Finder list. Not many programs are savvy as of yet.

Workshop

The Workshop contains quiz questions to help you solidify your understanding of the material covered. You can find the answers to the quiz questions in Appendix B, "Quiz Answers."

Quiz

1. What is the "root" directory?
2. How do you locate an original item for an alias?
3. Name three ways to create an alias of an item.
4. How do you hide an active window from view?
5. What icons on the desktop *cannot* be dragged into the Trash Can?
6. How do you add a document or application to the Launcher?
7. How do you create a new folder within the Launcher?
8. How do you index a local volume? Why would you want to?
9. How do you change the viewing preferences for a folder?
10. What is a "click-and-a-half" and how is it used?

HOUR 5

Customizing Your Mac

The power of the Mac operating system has always been the ease with which you can adapt it to the way you work instead of you having to adapt to the way it works. After you have Mac OS 8.5 installed, you may want to run it in the out-of-the-box configuration for awhile. Eventually though, you'll certainly want to mold the system to fit the way you work as well as your personality. Using a Macintosh, you can easily express yourself in many ways. The following issues are covered in this hour:

- Changing the desktop's format using the various screens of the Appearance control panel
- Using the Extensions Manager to change how your Mac behaves
- Changing the behavior of your display and system sounds using the Monitors & Sound control panel
- Creating custom icons

Changing the Desktop Format

Let's begin by exploring how to change the way Mac OS 8.5 looks. You have complete control over how your desktop appears, including menu bars, fonts, window formats, scrollbars, coloring, and highlights. You can add "wallpaper," such as tiled designs, to the desktop background or photographs that brighten your working atmosphere.

If you're familiar with older Mac system software, you know that you can change the appearance of your desktop, including its background, how windows are drawn, and how windows behave. To do this in Mac OS 8.5, you use the new Appearance control panel. With this control panel, you can set up desktop themes consisting of a desktop picture, background color, highlight colors, sounds, and fonts. You can also set up how you want the overall window to behave. The Appearance control panel consists of six tabs: Themes, Appearance, Fonts, Desktop, Sounds, and Options. (See Figure 5.1.)

FIGURE 5.1.

The Appearance control panel.

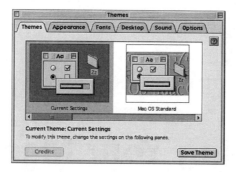

Setting Desktop Themes

The quickest way to change the appearance of your desktop is to select a desktop theme from those included with the Appearance control panel. (I'm assuming that hackers and shareware gurus will add to this list in the future.)

ADDING THEMES

Apple has included only one theme, called Platinum, with Appearance. If you wish to enhance your desktop with additional themes, download and pay for Kaleidoscope 2.1 (www.kaleidoscope.net). Kaleidoscope 2 schemes are fully compatible with the Appearance Manager. The K2 schemes archive at www.kaleidoscope.net/archive/ is full of shareware and freeware schemes such as Janet Parris' Wood Nymph Scheme ($10) shown in Figure 5.2.

Open the Appearance control panel and click the Themes tab to display the themes. Scroll through the themes and click the one you want to use. Your desktop changes to accommodate your choice.

If you use the other five tabs, you're given the option of saving your customized desktop as a new theme. Always return to the Themes tab to save your new desktop.

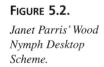

FIGURE 5.2.

Janet Parris' Wood Nymph Desktop Scheme.

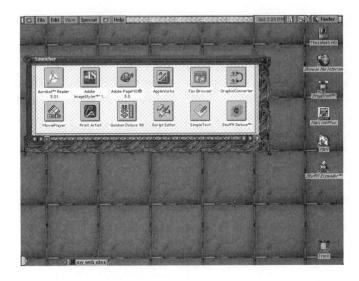

Setting Desktop Appearance

Using the Appearance tab, you can change the highlighting color used by applications to indicate selected items as well as the highlighting color used by the system to indicate the status of processes (see Figure 5.3). The Appearance tab lets you use the Color Picker to select a custom highlight color for both text and status markers. You're also given the option of changing the theme used to draw menu bars and windows.

FIGURE 5.3.

The Appearance tab lets you choose highlight colors.

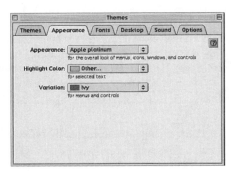

5

WHAT EVER HAPPENED TO?

If you're familiar with System 7.6, you're probably wondering why I haven't mentioned the old Color and Desktop Pictures control panels. They are gone, eaten by the Appearance control panel. Gone, too, is the old Mac OS 8.1 Appearance control panel that included color and desktop patterns. This centralizing of functions continues throughout Mac OS 8.5, as you'll see in later hours.

Setting Desktop Fonts

In Mac OS 8.5, you could change how system text was displayed by using the View|Options command. This always seemed counterintuitive to me. Well, Apple must have thought so, too, because now you can change the way menu bars, title bars, system text, and dialog box text are displayed using the handy Font tab on the Appearance control panel. (See Figure 5.4.)

FIGURE 5.4.

The Fonts tab lets you choose three types of system fonts.

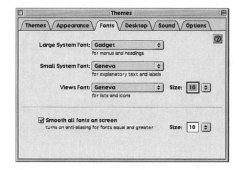

Use the pop-up menus to select a system font from the WYSIWYG menu. You can also select two other text fonts using any font resident on your Mac.

> **WHAT EVER HAPPENED TO?**
>
> Apple has added several jazzy new fonts, including Charcoal, Gadget, Techno, Capitals, and Sand, to the old standby Chicago font. Also note that Monaco and Geneva are no longer options for your large-size system text (that is, for menus, button names, and so forth). However, you can use these older bitmapped fonts for other system text. Geneva and Helvetica (the sans serif fonts) are the most legible for use as smaller-sized fonts. However, don't go crazy with your selections. You'll kill your eyes.

When you make a font change, the change is automatically reflected on the desktop so that you can see the results and adjust your selections accordingly.

Setting Desktop Pictures and Backgrounds

Desktop patterns have been on Macintosh computers since System 1.0; however, back then it was a simple gray background. System 7.5 added the Desktop Patterns control panel to make it easier to create and share patterns with other Macintosh computers. Originally, desktop patterns consisted of an 8.×8.-pixel square repeated across the desktop. With System 7.5, the size of desktop patterns were extended to range from 8×8 pixels to 128×128 pixels. The Desktop Pictures control panel, under Mac OS 8.5, supports these same features and also adds the capability to name patterns. Mac OS 8.5 updated Desktop Pictures by placing the functions of this control panel into the Appearance control panel. Click the Desktop tab to select either patterns or pictures (see Figure 5.5). In Mac OS 8.5, both the Desktop Patterns and Desktop Pictures control panels are obsolete.

FIGURE 5.5.

The Desktop tab lets you choose a pattern or picture for your desktop background.

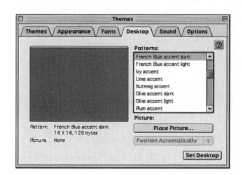

The patterns range from solid colors to pictures. Each pattern has a certain pixel and footprint size, and the pattern is repeated across the desktop (this is called *tiling*). The pattern size as well as the amount of memory required are displayed below the pattern in the control panel. All patterns work in any color depth mode; however, 256 or more colors is recommended.

Select a pattern name from the Patterns list box. An example is shown in the box to the left of the list. If you like the pattern, click Set Desktop to make it appear.

Choosing a Desktop Picture

Desktop pictures are larger than desktop patterns; you only use one to fill the desktop. Any PICT file or picture clipping can be used as a desktop picture. These images do not need to be any particular size to be a desktop picture. If you have a 17- or 20-inch monitor, an 832×624 pixel image is a good size to use at high-resolutions. If the desktop picture selected is smaller than the actual size of the desktop, the desktop pattern will fill up the rest of the desktop. One caveat: Although desktop pictures are aesthetically pleasing, they do take up more memory to display. Therefore, if your memory is limited, don't use pictures.

Click the Place Picture button on the Desktop tab to select a desktop picture. A standard file dialog box shows the available PICT files, with a preview snapshot to the left of the selected file. Choose Open for any of the files in this folder. The chosen file appears in the main window. Next, press the Set Desktop button to put the selected picture on to the desktop. After an image is selected, its dimensions and memory requirements appear below it in the control panel window.

5

Positioning the Desktop Picture

After a picture is selected, you can display it in five different ways on the desktop. Although the default is Position Automatically, you can also set the picture to Fill Screen, Scale to Screen, Center on Screen, or Tile on Screen.

The following list shows each type of position option as well as what each pop-up menu item does:

- **Position Automatically.** Allows the software to take a best guess at positioning the picture on the desktop. The image either fills, scales to, or centers onscreen.
- **Fill Screen.** Enlarges a smaller image to fill the selected screen size. If a screen is smaller than the selected image, this position does not change on the selected screen.
- **Scale to Screen.** Shrinks or enlarges the image to fit on the selected screen.
- **Center on Screen.** Places an image in the center of the screen without scaling or resizing it. This position does not apply to images that are too large to be displayed on the selected screen.
- **Tile on Screen.** Converts smaller images into a repeating tile for the desktop picture. This position does not apply to images that are too large to be displayed on the selected screen.

The context menu for positioning desktop pictures appears if you press the Control key and then click on the desktop image picture.

All the previously explained image positions are available in this context menu as well as two more: Find Picture File and Remove Picture. Find Picture File opens the folder of the image file. Remove Picture clears the selected image from the control panel window.

Removing the Desktop Picture

After a desktop picture has been set to the desktop, the Select Picture button changes to Remove Picture. You can select any number of different pictures in the control panel, but the desktop picture does not change until you click the Set Desktop button.

Setting Desktop Sounds

The Appearance control panel also lets you set individual sounds for different system functions, such as opening files, closing windows, throwing things away, as well as other activities. Click the Sound tab to display the sound options (see Figure 5.6). Select the system features to which you want to apply sounds and then select the sound theme you want to apply (again, for now, only Platinum is available).

Third-party developers offer sound sets on shareware sites such as `http://www.apple-donuts.com/sounds/index.html` that you can drop into the sound sets folder in the Appearance folder.

FIGURE 5.6.

The Sound tab lets you choose sounds for system functions.

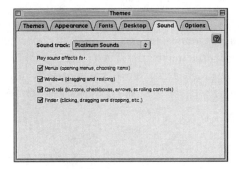

I personally find these sounds obnoxious over time and turn them off, but they are cute if you're used to Windows 95's cacophony. You turn off the sounds using the same Sound tab.

Setting Other Desktop Options

The final tab, shown in Figure 5.7, provides you the opportunity to change how your windows scroll. You can set the scroll arrows placed on the top, bottom, or both ends. The Options tab also lets you set how your scrollbars work (either they change shape when you resize a window or they function like they always have in earlier operating system versions). The Options tab also lets you turn on and off the Window Shade feature (which give you the ability to close windows down to their title bar).

FIGURE 5.7.

The Options tab lets you choose how your windows scroll as well as the appearance of the arrows and bars.

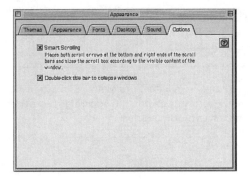

5

Modifying the Extensions Manager

Mac OS adds capabilities to the basic system by inserting system extensions into the operating system at startup. These startup extensions are controlled via the system extensions saved in the Extensions folder in System Folder, and they're managed by a very powerful application called Extensions Manager.

Although Mac OS 7.6 introduced the Extensions Manager, it fits in nicely with the look and feel of Mac OS 8.5. Extensions Manager can drastically affect how Mac OS looks, depending on which control panels, extensions, and other system files are turned on or off at system startup. Extensions Manager, or any of the third-party managers, manages what loads at startup in order to change the look and feel of your system. (See Figure 5.8.)

FIGURE 5.8.

The Extensions Manager sets in Mac OS 8.5.

How to Use Extensions Manager

You can launch Extensions Manager during startup or in Finder. To launch it at startup, hold down the spacebar when the Macintosh first starts up. The Extensions Manager window appears before any extensions load, enabling you to select which set or specific file to use to start up your Macintosh.

> You can sort any list in Extensions Manager in ascending or descending order. Use the arrow located in the upper-right corner of the list window to reverse the current sorting order.

Extensions Manager has a list view, similar to the list view in Finder windows. The selected column sorts all items in the window and has a slightly darker gray hue than the other window columns. In the Preferences window from the Edit menu, you can choose additional columns for viewing type and creator information.

You can view all Extensions Manager items in one of three modes:

- **View by Folder.** Viewing items by folder reflects the file location in the System Folder.

- **View as Package.** View as Package organizes all System Folder items by the version 2 resource of each file. The version 2 resource appears at the top of every Get Info window. This file descriptor is called "version 2" because its information is presented on the second row below the name of the file in the Get Info window. However, not all files contain information in this location.

- **View as Items.** View as Items displays all System Folder files without any folder or package affiliation.

Each folder and file also has an on/off check box to its left to indicate whether the file is going to load at startup. In lieu of remembering which files you need to use for different system software configurations, you can create sets in Extensions Manager. If you decide to add any third-party user interface, networking, video or game software, or if you want to leave out desktop printing or other software features, you can create an Extensions Manager set for each custom configuration of its System Folder files.

Creating Extension Manager Sets

Extensions Manager sets are saved to the Extensions Manager Preferences folder in the Preferences folder. The original Mac OS 8.5 sets are locked, so you need to duplicate them (using the Duplicate Set button) if you want to use them as a template to modify the new set. Sets are saved automatically, and Extensions Manager automatically updates its window if you move files or folders out of the System Folder while it's open. You can also use Extensions Manager sets with any other computer running Mac OS 8.5.

You can create custom sets with Extensions Manager. A set stores the "on" and "off" settings of all items displayed in the Extensions Manager window. Settings can represent a minimal set of extensions or extensions specific to using games, video, Internet, or application sets. If a computer is used by several people, you can create a set for each person, enabling you to start the computer without having to reinstall software or reconfigure the System Folder.

5

The steps that follow explain how to create a set of game settings using Extensions Manager:

1. Open Extensions Manager from the Apple Menu|Control Panels folder.

2. Selected Set, at the top of the Extensions Manager window, should be set to My Settings.

3. Duplicate this set by selecting File|DuplicateSet; then name it Game Settings.

4. If an item is "on," an × appears in the check box to its left. If the item is "off," its check box is empty. For this set, turn off the desktop printing extensions (Desktop PrintMonitor and Desktop Printer Spooler), any printer drivers, and any non-Apple control panels and extensions.

5. Once the set is created, you must restart your Mac to use the set. You can make a copy of the set and save it as a backup, or you can send it to a friend. A set can be selected at startup by holding down the spacebar. Once Extensions Manager appears, you can select a set and then press the Continue button to complete the startup.

SHOW ITEM INFORMATION

If you're not sure what to turn on or off in Extensions Manager, select Show Item Information and use the additional information (if available) in the text field to decide whether you need a particular extension or control panel in a set.

Changing the Monitors & Sound Control Panel

The Monitors & Sound control panel was introduced with the first PCI Power Macintosh computers in 1995. It has since been updated with some new features and works with all Mac OS 8.5 computers. Figure 5.9 shows the Monitors portion of the Monitors & Sound control panel.

Monitors & Sound is actually an application, not a traditional control panel. Because it's installed in the Control Panel folder, however, I'll refer to it as a control panel.

FIGURE 5.9.

The Monitors portion of the Monitors & Sound control panel.

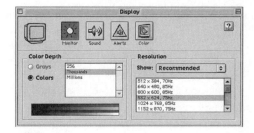

Sizing up Your Monitor

Monitor color depth and screen size depend on the size of the physical display, the type and capabilities of the graphics chips used by the computer or graphics card, and the amount of VRAM or RAM available to the display. Most displays are connected to the built-in video port on a Macintosh. Graphics cards, however, may offer more color depth and resolution options for the same monitor. Monitors & Sound shows only the color depths and resolutions available for any particular screen. The standard resolution size for most Macintosh computers is 640×480, although larger monitors will use larger resolution sizes.

FIGURING OUT WHAT YOUR MONITOR CAN DO

If you're not sure which resolutions or color depths your monitor supports, the Monitors & Sound control panel can tell you.

If Monitors & Sound shows more than one resolution, these resolutions are shown on the right side of the Monitor portion of the control panel window. If you have a 15" multi-sync monitor, multiple resolutions will appear on this window, reflecting both the capabilities of the monitor and the amount of VRAM installed on the computer. If only one resolution appears, you either only have enough VRAM to support one resolution or you have an RGB monitor. RGB monitors are designed to support only one resolution. A 14" or 15" RGB monitor displays a 640×480 desktop. A 21" RGB monitor displays a 1280×1024 desktop. The higher the selected resolution, the larger the desktop and the lower the available color depth. For example, if you have a monitor set to 1280×1024, you may only be able to use a color depth of thousands of colors instead of millions of colors.

The most common resolutions available for Mac monitors are 640×480, 800×600, 832×624, 1024×768, 1152×870, and 1280×1024. Each resolution also has a refresh rate. Higher refresh rates result in better quality images displayed on the monitor. A higher refresh rate, such as 75Hz, has less flicker than lower refresh rates, such as 67Hz.

The Monitors section of the control panel consists of two areas: Color Depth and Resolution. (Note that a new area called Color lets you calibrate your monitor to fit your output requirements using the new ColorSync 2.5 technology. ColorSync is covered in its own hour—Hour 11, "Color.") Earlier Macintosh computers, such as the Quadras and

PowerBook Duos, support color depths ranging from black and white through millions of colors with built-in video.

More recent Macintosh computers, such as the PCI Macs, only support 256 colors, thousands of colors, and millions of colors. Resolution affects multisync monitors connected to a Macintosh. These can support a range of screen sizes, such as 640×480 through 832×624, 1024×768, and even larger. After you select a resolution, the screen size automatically resizes.

Color Depth

Color Depth consists of three interrelated settings: a list of color depths, radio buttons for grays and colors, and a color table. Depending on the color depth selected in the list, the color table changes to reflect the current system color palette. The Grays radio button only applies to black and white, 4, 16, and 256 color depth settings.

Only the Color radio button is selectable in thousands and millions color depth modes. As mentioned previously, for most Macs, the number of colors depends on how much VRAM is installed in the computer or card. For lower bit depths, the number of color depths displayed reflect those supported in ROM for built-in video, or in the ROM of the NuBus or PCI video card.

Resolution and Gamma

The resolution of the monitor is related to the size of the desktop. This area of the control panel consists of two settings: a pop-up-menu with recommended settings and a list of supported monitor resolutions. Selecting any resolution updates the screen automatically. The number and size of available resolutions depends on the type of monitor connected to your computer and how much VRAM is installed.

Changing the Alerts

Simple Beep is the default alert sound for Mac OS 8.5. The Monitors & Sound control panel contains a short list of sounds you can use as the alert sound: Droplet, Indigo, Quack, Simple Beep, Sosumi, Wild Eep. These sound files are stored in the system file. Any sound recorded in this control panel is also stored in the system file. (See Figure 5.10.)

iMacs use a modified Monitors & Sound control panel that lets you adjust the vertical and horizontal screen as well as the contrast controls. Click Monitor to access these buttons.

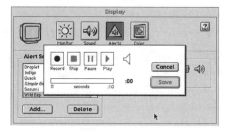

Figure 5.10.

The Alert screen of the Monitors & Sound control panel and the recording window.

The Alert window of Monitors & Sound consists of three distinct functions: System Alert Volume, the Alert Sound list, and the Alert Recording button (the Add button). You can set System Alert Volume at any setting between 0 and 7. This volume level also affects the computer system volume level.

The Add and Delete buttons at the bottom of the window enable you to create or remove any sounds from the Alert Sound list. Add brings up a simple recording window with the following controls: record, stop, pause, and play. The recording level of a connected microphone or audio CD is reflected in animation from the speaker icon. Selecting the Save button in the recording window adds the recorded sound to the Alert Sound list.

To record alert sounds for Mac OS 8.5, you can also use Simple Sound in the Apple menu as well as the Sound control panel in the Apple Extras folder.

Changing Multiple Displays

5

If you have more than one monitor connected to your computer, opening Monitors & Sound displays the control panel window on each separate screen. Each display reflects the features of that hardware model (such as AV-specific settings).

How to Use Multiple Monitors with Macs

Most Macs support only one display via a built-in video port. All PowerBooks and many Performas have a built-in monitor. PowerBooks have a video port that enables them to support an external monitor with a desktop of 800×600 at a setting of thousands of colors. Most Performas have only one slot for expansion. Granted, many Macintosh computers cannot support more than two displays; adding more than one monitor to a Mac requires an additional graphics card to support each additional monitor you want to connect to the computer.

The graphics card must fit into an expansion slot available on your computer. Desktop systems have either NuBus or PCI slots for expansion slots. Most Performas have a processor direct slot (or *PDS*). PowerBook Duos can be docked to connect with NuBus slots, and other PowerBooks have one expansion video connector. Once a graphics card is installed in the PDS, NuBus, or PCI slot, you can open the Monitors & Sound control panel to configure how you want each monitor's desktop to appear. Each monitor has its own resolution, desktop size, and color depth.

Changing the Keyboard Control Panel

The Keyboard control panel affects all Mac OS systems despite the fact that the top half of the control panel is specific to international keyboard layouts (see Figure 5.11). Mac OS 8.5 installs the following keyboard scripts into the system folder: Australian, Brasil, British, Canadian–CSA, Canadian–ISO, Canadian-French, Danish, Dutch, Espanol ISO, Finnish, Flemish, French, French–numerical, German, Italian, Norwegian, Spanish, Swedish, Swiss French, Swiss German, and U.S. You can select any number of keyboard layouts to support the appropriate keyboard for a specific country or language.

FIGURE 5.11.

The Keyboard control panel.

Changing the keyboard layout in the Keyboard menu changes the keyboard layout used by Mac OS 8.5. Check the French or German keyboard layout in the Keyboard control panel, for example. A flag icon appears in the Keyboard menu bar after you close the Keyboard control panel. Select French or German from this menu and then open the Key Caps desk accessory from the Apple menu to see how the keyboard layout has changed. You can rotate between keyboard layouts by choosing the Command-Option-spacebar check box in this control panel. If only one keyboard layout is selected in the Keyboard control panel, the Keyboard menu does not appear in the menu bar.

Key Repeat settings are located at the bottom of the Keyboard control panel. These settings affect almost all keys on the keyboard, except for the Command, Option, Control, Caps Lock, and Escape keys. Pressing any key on the keyboard causes a Macintosh computer to type that key repeatedly as long as the key is held down.

This can affect you if you use any alphabet keys for playing games or for inputting repetitive characters with your computer. Key Repeat options include slow to fast for the Key Repeat Rate setting and short to long (or off) for the Delay Until Repeat setting.

Modifying the Numbers Control Panel

The Numbers control panel can work with keyboard layouts scripts in the Keyboard control panel, or it can have its own settings, independent of other language settings in Mac OS 8.5. The Numbers control panel enables you to select how numbers are displayed in Finder and other applications (see Figure 5.12). The number formats available in the Numbers control panel are resources installed in the system file. Choosing the Number Format, Decimal, and Thousands options is easier in Mac OS 8.5 with sticky menus and the pop-up menu in the Numbers control panel.

FIGURE 5.12.

The Numbers control panel.

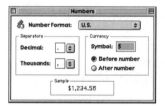

Use the Number Format field to select from Australian, Brasil, British, Danish, Dutch, Finnish, Flemish, French, French Canadian, German, Italian, Norwegian, Spanish, Swedish, Swiss French, Swiss German, Swiss Italian, and U.S. The Number format can be the same or completely different from the keyboard layout selected in the Keyboard control panel. Also, you can change the Number Format setting to match the settings in the Keyboard control panel, and you can check the Text control panel to make certain that the text behavior for the keyboard layout also matches the Number Format setting.

Modifying the Text Control Panel

The Text control panel can work with the Keyboard and Numbers control panels or independent of them (see Figure 5.13). It displays text behaviors for script resources installed in the system file. All keyboard layouts installed with Mac OS 8.5 use Roman script resources installed in the system file. Language kits for two-byte languages, however, such as Chinese, Japanese, and Korean, or complex one-byte languages add more items to the pop-up menu in the Text control panel.

5

Figure 5.13.

The Text control panel.

Both pop-up menus have the new grayscale pop-up menu look for Mac OS 8.5. Sticky menus enable you to click the Behavior menu to display all items. The default settings for Mac OS 8.5 in the United States are Roman Script with English behavior. To change the text behavior, select from Brasil, Danish, Dutch, English, Finnish, French, French Canadian, German, Italian, Norwegian, Spanish, and Swedish. Changes made to this control panel are independent of sort order, case conversion, and word definitions in Finder and any other applications.

More Customization Options

Of course, you have other ways to change the look, feel, and function of Mac OS 8.5. The Appearance, Extensions Manager, File Sharing, Keyboard, Numbers, Text, Monitors & Sound, and Desktop Pictures control panels are provided with Mac OS 8.5 to customize a wide range of Finder features. Numerous shareware and commercial software products provide additional ways of modifying Finder features.

> Mac OS can become unstable as a result of combining extensions and control panels in the System Folder. Some software products that modify the way Finder looks or works may have software conflicts with existing system software or other software installed with your computer.

Summary

Changing the look, feel, and function of Mac OS 8.5 starts with the Appearance control panel. You can use numerous other control panels, however, to modify your Macintosh. This hour covered several control panels that are part of Mac OS 8.5, including Monitors & Sound, Desktop Pictures, and Extensions Manager.

Term Review

accent color   The subtle color added to scrollbars, windows, and other Finder icons. You select an accent color by using the Appearance control panel.

Appearance control panel   A very important control panel that governs how icons and dialog boxes appear on your Mac. Use this control panel to set up accent and highlight colors, change the overall appearance of windows (platinum or grayscale), as well as change the system font used throughout the Mac's various dialog boxes.

color depth   The amount of colors (number of bits used to represent color) displayed by your monitor. You can set your monitor to display anything from 1 bit (black and white) to 24 bits (millions of colors).

Color Picker   A system extension that provides the capability to set how colors are displayed on your Mac's screen. Set the method of picking colors to match how your output will be processed—either Pantone spot colors, RGB (the standard Mac method), CMK (color output matching), or a new picker called Crayon (for simple color selection).

desktop patterns   Repeating patterns that can be displayed as a background on your desktop.

desktop pictures   PICT files that can be displayed over the entire screen or centered over a desktop pattern.

Extensions Manager   The desk accessory that manages your system extensions.

gamma   The hue or lighting that can be set for your monitor. Set the gamma in the Monitors & Sound control panel to match your output needs.

highlight color   The color used to indicate that you have selected something onscreen.

Monitors & Sound control panel   The control panel that manages how monitor colors and system sounds are used on the Mac.

resolution   The number of pixels that can be displayed on your screen. Set the monitor's resolution to enlarge or reduce how items are displayed by making a selection in the Monitors & Sound control panel.

Q&A

Q   How do I add my own desktop patterns to the Appearance control panel's Desktop tab?

A   Open the Desktop tab on the Appearance control panel and select Desktop Patterns. Drag a PICT or GIF image onto the Patterns box. The new tiled version of the pattern is displayed. You can create clips in an image-editing program such as Adobe Photoshop, get freeware from the Internet, or select and drag an image onto your desktop.

5

Q How do I add a clock to my menu bar?

A Open the Date & Time control panel. Click the "on" radio button under the menu bar's Clock section.

Q How do I change the appearance of my menu bar clock?

A Once you've turned on the menu bar clock, click the Clock Options button to display a dialog box that lets you change the color and font used to display the clock.

Q How do I add sounds to the Alerts tab of the Monitors & Sound control panel?

A Record the sound using the Add Sounds tab in the Monitors & Sound control panel. Click the Alert button on the control panel to display that screen. Click the Add button to get to the recording screen. You can also add sounds you download from repositories on America Online or the Internet. After creating the sound, drag the SND file into the system file (or onto the System Folder). Read Hour 12, "QuickTime," for more information about using sounds on the Mac.

Q What do I do with the Text and Numbers control panels?

A You can delete them if you're working in English and in the United States. These two panels assist you in setting up WorldScript options for displaying non-Western text on your Mac. You can also set up European methods of displaying numbers (using decimal points rather than commas for placeholders, for example).

Workshop

The Workshop contains quiz questions to help you solidify your understanding of the material covered. You can find the answers to the quiz questions in Appendix B, "Quiz Answers."

Quiz

1. What control panel and tab is used to change the background picture or pattern on your desktop?

2. What control panel and tab is used to set up a theme for your desktop?

3. What control panel and tab is used to assign sounds to system functions?

4. What control panel and tab is used to assign highlighting colors? How do you add custom colors?

5. How do you change the fonts assigned to desktop features?

6. How do you adjust the resolution of your monitor?

7. How do you remove a picture from your desktop?

8. How do you change the alert sounds used by the system?

9. How do you localize your keyboard?

10. Which application is used to set up the system extensions? How do you invoke this panel during startup procedures?

5

HOUR 6

Applications and Mac OS 8.5

Applications work with Mac OS to enable you to perform all kinds of tasks, from working with databases and spreadsheets, to word processing and page layout, to playing games and maintaining your computer. There isn't a whole lot you can do with your computer without applications. The following issues are covered in this hour:

- Understanding what applications are and how they work
- Installing and removing applications
- Opening, closing, and saving applications
- Multitasking applications
- Managing application memory
- Using applications

Introduction to Applications

The term *application* refers to any file you double-click to run on a Mac. It also refers to the user interface, functions, and all the software that might be required to make it work, such as data files, shared libraries, preferences, as well as image, database, or networking software. The Mac lets you work with more than one application at a time (although you cannot run two applications simultaneously). Background processing enables you to copy files, throw away trash, or print while you're working in an application. In fact, one of the biggest advantages of Finder 8.0 is its new ability to multitask in this manner.

One of the innovations of Mac OS 8.5 is the conversion of many operating system components such as control panels and System extensions into applications. Applications are more efficient and effective because they can take advantage of Mac OS toolbox managers without affecting the performance of crucial system resources. Mac OS 8.5 applications include:

- Control panels such as Internet, Remote Access, Appearance, Adobe Type Manager, and so forth
- Mac OS add-ons such as ColorSync, QuickTime, and Sherlock
- Specialized Mac OS software such as Disk Copy, Disk Drive Setup, and Drive Repair

---

WHAT IS COMPATIBILITY ANYWAY?

When users speak of *compatibility*, they mean two things: Can an application actually run on an operating system version, and do all the features of the operating system work in the application? All applications should be compatible with Mac OS 8.5 if they were compatible with Mac OS 7.6 or System 7.5. Note that I said *should be*. If the software is already installed, use it with caution until you're convinced it doesn't cause any instabilities with Mac OS.

Some of the earlier applications for System 7 may not have completely followed the *Macintosh Human Interface Guidelines*, or they may not be Mac OS 8.5 compatible. Use them with caution on your computer. They might not be as stable on Mac OS 8.5 as they were on System 7.0 and 7.1.

Some applications created for System 6 may still work with Mac OS 8.5. However, it's best to try to find an updated version of the software before installing or running older applications with Mac OS 8.5.

On the other hand, most older software will run but will not take advantage of Mac OS 8.5's newer features, such as Navigation Services, drag and drop, the platinum graphical user interface, and so forth. Such programs are termed "not savvy." You'll need to upgrade these older programs, if possible, to their most current versions to take advantage of newer OS features.

Different Kinds of Applications

One characteristic of applications is that some can work without any additional files, whereas others require dozens or hundreds of files to run. SimpleText, for example, does not require any other files to support its feature set; its guide file is only required for support and for navigating all the application's features (see Figure 6.1).

HOW THE MAC WORKS

What is spoken of as the Mac operating system is in reality a three-part construct. The uniqueness of the Mac software's deep relationship with Apple hardware lies in how much of the software that makes the Macs run actually resides on Read-Only Memory (ROM). What we call the System is in actuality patches to the basic Application Program Interfaces (APIs) residing in ROM. System extensions add or change the behavior of these APIs. The resulting collection of software modules is called the Toolbox. The Toolbox is accessed by calls from applications to Toolbox managers such as Navigation Services, Application manager, File manager, and so forth. It is this ability to call on Toolbox managers to perform functions typically performed by the applications themselves on other platforms that makes the Mac easy to use.

FIGURE 6.1.

SimpleText application with an open document.

6

The Look and Feel of Applications

One of the beauties of the Mac graphical user interface is that applications look and feel alike. The reason for this is that most applications use the Mac's built-in toolboxes to display dialog boxes, menus, palettes, and windows. Therefore, the Finder governs the entire Mac interface, not just the desktop.

This makes learning applications on the Mac much easier because once you learn where commands reside and how they work on one program, you can basically figure out how they work in all Mac programs. (Don't get me wrong, as graphic and layout programs become more sophisticated, their hidden palettes and nonstandard features become more pronounced. Also, the more cross-platform a software product becomes, the less Mac-like its interface will be.)

Installing and Removing Applications

Installers are designed to simplify application installation and to compact installed files to reduce the floppy disk or media footprint for the product. Some installers also support removing the software.

Installing Applications

Installing an application is similar to installing system software; however, most applications do not use Apple's software installer.

There are roughly six ways to install software. In general, most software installers put all installed pieces into one folder on the hard drive. Some installers also put preferences settings and support files in the System Folder. Some also have control panels or extensions placed in the System Folder; these can be identified by using Extensions Manager control panel. The following list describes the most commonly used installer applications for Mac OS:

- MindVision's installer is used to install most Mac software. It looks very similar to Apple's installer but has a few extra features, such as letting you select a particular folder in which to install the software.

- Some software products are compressed using StuffIt, Aladdin's compression utility. They also can use Aladdin's software installer, which usually places all installed files into one folder at the root level of the hard drive.

- Microsoft Office uses Microsoft's Setup application to install or remove any major or minor pieces of its software products that are included with Microsoft's Office suite.

- Adobe's PageMaker and Persuasion, as well as some of its other desktop publishing applications, use Adobe's custom software installer for placing files in the System Folder, as well as into a number of folders created on the hard drive.
- Software on CD-ROM may include directions to drag-copy some software on the CD-ROM to your local hard drive.
- Other installers are also available for installing Mac software. They work similarly to either Apple's installer or the other installers listed in this section.

In any case, you can begin installing the software in question by inserting the media (disk or CD-ROM, for example) into your drive and following the instructions that appear as part of the installation program.

Removing Applications

The easiest way to remove applications is to first check the original installer to see whether there's an uninstall option. If not, move the main software folder for that application to the Trash Can; then use Find File to look for related files and trash those as well. Be sure that any support files you find aren't used by other applications before you trash them (for example, many Microsoft applications share support files).

Application Protection

Performas were equipped with an Application folder that was installed at the root level of the hard drive. Mac OS 8.5 creates an Application folder at the root level of the hard drive if one does not already exist. To protect the software in that folder, a Protect an Application setting is located in the General Controls control panel. If this setting is active, the system will not let you move any files or folders out of the Application folder. If you need to remove or reorganize software in this folder, turn off this setting, uncheck the Protect Applications Folder check box in the General Controls control panel, and then make your changes.

Opening, Closing, and Saving Applications

6

One of the most important functions of the Finder is to make the process of opening, closing, and saving files transparent across all Mac applications. The Finder provides the dialog boxes and command menus for these tasks. The dialog boxes can be modified by different applications.

One of the most exciting changes in Mac OS 8.5 is the total rewrite of the Finder's Open and Save As system. In Mac OS 8.5, a new Toolbox manager called Navigation Services has been created that lets you use the new filing system to rapidly find files on your local volume or across networks. In addition, you can select from previously opened documents using a new pull-down menu. You'll only see these new Finder dialog boxes in the Finder until software vendors upgrade their programs to take advantage of the enhanced searching capabilities of Navigation Services.

In most applications, you'll continue to see the older Finder dialog boxes displayed in Figure 6.2. This Open dialog box from Word 98 has been enhanced by Microsoft to enable you to find a file using Microsoft's Find File function from within the dialog box. (See Hour 4, "The Finder," for a discussion of the new V-Twin-based Find command.)

FIGURE 6.2.

Word 98 still uses Finder's old Open dialog box.

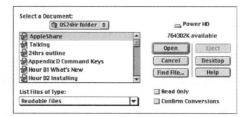

Navigation Services provides a similar but more powerful function via its Find command. Figure 6.3 (shown in the next section) displays the new Open command provided by Navigation Services.

Opening Applications

As with all things Macintosh, you have various ways to open an application and its documents:

- Select the application or document icon you want to open. Choose Open from the File menu.
- Select the application or document you want to open and press the keyboard combination Command-O.
- Double-click the document you want to open. If you aren't currently working on a document, double-click the application's icon.
- Place an alias of the application or document in the Launcher and then simply click its icon when you want to open it.
- Drag the document you want to open on top of the icon of its application. If you have MacLink Plus installed (it comes with Mac OS 8.5), you can drag a document onto any application and MacLink will find the appropriate one to open it.

The Mac OS 8.5 Open dialog box is extremely useful. As shown in Figure 6.3, you can rapidly scroll through folders in the Finder list box using the same arrows you use in the Finder. In addition, contextual menus work in the dialog box.

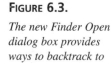

FIGURE 6.3.

The new Finder Open dialog box provides ways to backtrack to previously opened items.

Finder's new list box   Finder button   Favorites button

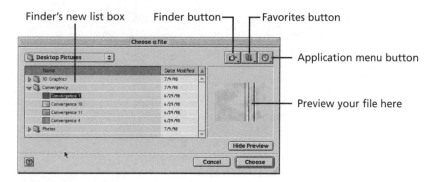

Application menu button

Preview your file here

Using Navigation Services

Navigation Services has some neat features. Using the three new buttons located in the top-right section of the dialog box, you can open documents both locally or on the Internet or network, collect files you use regularly and place them in a Favorites folder, and go to a recently accessed document with the click of your mouse.

The "pointing finger" button, which I call the *Finder button*, lets you access files both locally and remotely. This button replaces the arduous routine of clicking the desktop button, selecting a new volume, scrolling through the volume to a select folder, and so forth. Use the pop-up menu to open a new volume from those listed.

The "book shelf" button, which I call the *Favorites button*, opens your Favorites pop-up menu. You can add files to Favorites by selecting a file in the Finder list box and choosing Add to Favorites. You can choose a previously selected favorite by simply selecting it from the menu. You can also add folders or files to the Favorites pop-up menu from the File menu on the desktop.

The "clock" button, which I call the *Application Menu button*, lists documents you have recently selected. Here's where Navigation Services shines, because you can get to your regularly used documents without drilling through folders by selecting from this pop-up menu. It doesn't matter whether the document is stored locally or remotely.

Closing Applications

Closing an application can also be performed in several ways, depending on whether you want to end your working session (Quit) or just close a document to begin a new one (Close).

If you want to totally end a working session, use the Quit command from the File menu or press the keyboard combination Command-Q. Using the Quit command gives the application the chance to save any unsaved materials prior to quitting. You get a Save dialog box after using the Quit command if you haven't saved since the last change.

6

Use the Close command on the File menu (Command-W) to close a window, such as a document. Another way to close a window but remain in an application is to click the close box in the top-left corner of the window.

> You can close all open windows by pressing the Option key while clicking a close box or while pressing Command-W.

Saving Documents

Remember to save early and save often. There are several ways to save your data. If you've already given your document a name, choosing Save from the File menu will save information to this previously named file. You can also press the keyboard combination Command-S. Many applications have added a toolbar button for saving, which makes the task even easier.

If you've not previously named your document, using the Save command opens a special Finder dialog box called Save As. Use the Save As dialog box to assign a name to your document as well as a place where you want to save it. In the Save As dialog box displayed in Figure 6.4, you can see the Finder's standard list box and navigation buttons. Use these tools to select a folder where you want to save your document. You type a name for your document in the text box.

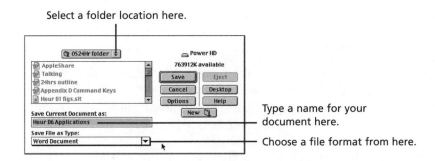

FIGURE 6.4.

The Save As dialog box.

You can then select a file format, such as Word 98, RTF, or Word 2 (Word for Windows 95), for your document. Select the format from the Format pop-up menu.

USING PROPER NAMING CONVENTIONS FOR EASY FILE TRADING

If you're sharing files with Windows 95 or 3.1 users, it's a good idea to follow standard DOS naming conventions. Identify the format of your document by using a three-letter suffix, such as .DOC for Word for Windows or Word 98 documents or .RTF for RTF-formatted documents. This enables the much dumber Windows program to be able to link your file to the appropriate application. Try to limit the actual name of your document to eight characters so that the name does not run into the three-digit suffix. Avoid using blank spaces by using an underscore to represent a space.

If you're dealing only with fellow Mac users, feel free to name your files whatever you like, because the Mac uses its hidden data fork to identify the application that owns the file.

The Save As command has two other very powerful uses—renaming and relocating files. Renaming and relocating files is an excellent way to produce fast backup copies of your critical documents. You can rename files to separate your Windows versions from your Mac versions (by adding that DOS suffix to the Windows version) or you can separate different versions of a document by numbering the revisions in the filenames. Alphabetize your documents by shifting their names (for example, I name my files by their chapters numbers so that they line up in the list view). This chapter is called MACOS06.DOC. The next document is called MACOS07.DOC, and so forth.

You can access the Save As command at any time by choosing the File menu and selecting Save As.

While in the Save As dialog box, you can speed up navigating among files and folders by typing the first letter of the folder in which you want to save your document. Use the Tab key to move from the Finder box to the Name text box. Click the Desktop button to move between volumes (such as removable disks and networked disks).

6

Understanding Multitasking

In 1984, when Apple introduced the Macintosh 128K microcomputer, multitasking was the providence of minicomputers and mainframes running operating systems such as UNIX and VM-CMS. Microcomputers performed one task at a time. You had to quit one program before proceeding to the next, and no way existed to easily share data between programs.

Multitasking is the capability to run several programs simultaneously. The first small programs that could be operated along side applications on the Macintosh were called *desk accessories* (or *CDEVs*).

CDEVs were tiny utilities such as a calculator, calendar, alarm clock, notepad, and puzzle. CDEVs were restricted in size to a couple of kilobytes so that they could fit into memory along side the applications.

As the Macintosh evolved, Apple took the idea of the CDEV and built from it the ability to work with more than one application at one time. Apple introduced the MultiFinder in System 6 as an optional way of running the Macintosh.

System 7 revolutionized multitasking, eliminating the memory limitation of CDEVs. All programs, regardless of their use or size, share memory and processing time. In fact, as stated earlier, most CDEVs have evolved into actual applications.

Like all multitasking systems, Mac OS 8.5 really runs only one program at a time. The illusion of several programs working at once is created by switching among applications so rapidly that it appears that everything is happening at once. The actual goal of multitasking is the capability of applications to share systems resources. The difference among types of multitasking is in how applications pass control from one to another. Three types of multitasking exist:

- **Context-switching multitasking.** This is also called *time sharing*. The resources are moved among programs on a fixed schedule. Even if an active program doesn't currently need resources, it's provided them. This method can be very wasteful of processing resources.

- **Cooperative multitasking.** Each program can request the use of the processing resources, but other applications are not forced to respond to these requests. This method assumes that the applications are well behaved in this type of environment.

- **Preemptive multitasking.** Each program is assigned a priority and can compete for resources. Preemptive multitasking is currently available only with sophisticated operating systems and generally on mainframe computers.

The Macintosh uses a combination of context-switching and cooperative multitasking methods. If an application requests resources, it's guaranteed a minimum share. Cooperative multitasking is used to perform background operations with programs that are designed to work in this environment.

Cooperative multitasking works by giving control to a program to perform one task or event and relying on that program to turn control over to the next application when the task is accomplished (or when a maximum time limit has passed). If an application is not designed to cooperate within this environment, context-switching—putting one application on hold to run a second one—is used to allow you to run even poorly behaved programs. Without this feature, most older DAs would operate only when placed in the foreground and would stop when moved to the background.

Although purists often do not accept the Macintosh operating system's multitasking capability because it's not preemptive (that is, the operating system does not interrupt an application's event to perform another application's event), Mac OS 8.5 provides extensive performance enhancements for those programs capable of cooperative multitasking (those that follow the Macintosh System Interface Standards).

Even without the added benefit of running other multitasking applications, the Mac OS 8.5 Finder's capabilities for printing, copying, and moving data in the background provide significant advantages without the overhead required for a preemptive multitasking system.

The Finder's Role

As you learned in Hour 4, the Finder is the Macintosh's file- and disk-management software. The Finder always runs in the background to assist you in managing disks, applications, and documents. The Finder performs several important functions that are related to multitasking. Many of these tasks are related to the Finder's primary task of file management, but some are specific to enabling Mac OS 8.5 to provide multitasking capabilities.

6

Running several applications at the same time is one way to maximize your use of Finder. This software "luxury," however, requires RAM. The suggested amount of memory for multitasking applications can range from 24 MB to well over 100 MB. A little information on memory management can help you utilize multiple applications more efficiently.

Doing More Than One Task with Mac OS 8.5

Multitasking with Mac OS 8.5 can involve having two, three, or more applications open at the same time (see Figure 6.5). While these are running, you can also copy several files and folders across several windows, as well as delete files and folders to the Trash Can. Multitasking lets you perform a number of different Finder tasks, such as copying, deleting, or formatting media, while also accessing applications that run in the foreground or in the background.

FIGURE 6.5.

Mac OS 8.5 with more than one application open.

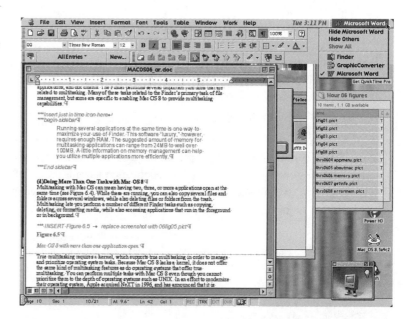

True multitasking requires a kernel, which manages and prioritizes operating system tasks. Because Mac OS 8.5 lacks a kernel, it doesn't offer the same kind of multitasking features that true multitasking operating systems do. You can perform multiple tasks with Mac OS 8.5 even though you cannot prioritize them to the extent of operating systems such as UNIX. In an effort to modernize its operating system, Apple acquired NeXT in 1996 and has announced that it's moving toward a newer architecture with future releases of its operating system.

ABOUT KERNELS

This *kernel* is not related to military ranking or fast-food chains. It's one of the core technologies of modern operating systems that manages everything the OS does, such as networking, printing, and running applications. The kernel is essentially responsible for creating and tracking processes that run in the OS. In UNIX-based operating systems, you can view all processes currently running and kill, or *quit*, any process you choose.

One of the best advantages to having a modern kernel built into the operating system is the improved stability for multitasking. This means that if several applications are running and one crashes, it will only affect that application process and won't bring down the entire system. Mac OS 8.5 works this way in many cases. This, of course, doesn't mean that operating systems that use kernels do not crash as often as Mac OS 8.5.

Working with the Application Menu

As mentioned earlier, the Application menu is the visible manifestation of the Mac's multitasking functions at work. You use the Application menu to switch between active windows, show or hide active windows, and return to the Finder. Figure 6.6 shows the open Application menu displaying several open programs as well as an indication of the currently active application.

Click here to hide all of your windows except the active window.

Click here to hide the active window.

Slider

Active Application

FIGURE 6.6.

The Application menu lets you switch between open applications.

Active window

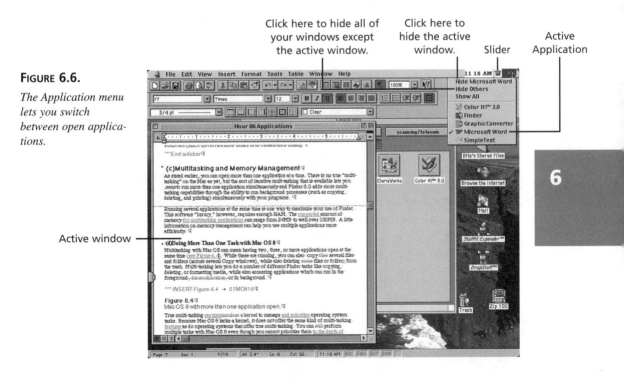

I keep throwing around the word *active*. Here's the easiest way to define an active window: It's the one on top. You can perform work in an active window's document. Active windows are indicated by a fully drawn title bar. Inactive windows are grayed out and lie behind the active window. There can be only one application active at one time, and the active application is running in the active window. (I'm not counting background processes such as copying, printing, or moving in my definition of *active applications* for simplicity's sake.)

You can switch between active and inactive windows by clicking any window lying beneath your active window to bring it to the front, thereby making it the active window.

Mac OS 8.5 provides several new features for the Application menu. For example, you can switch between applications without using the Application menu by pressing the keyboard combination Command-Tab. This switches you between applications in the order they appear on the Application menu.

Another new feature is the ability to display the active application's name in your menu bar along with its icon. If you don't like to use precious menu bar space with long application names, you can use the slide to move the name off the bar.

Select the Application menu and slide the mouse down the menu and past the end. Notice that a shadow menu follows your cursor on to the desktop. This tear-off palette is called the *Application Switcher* (see Figure 6.7). Use the Application Switcher's buttons to switch between or close applications.

FIGURE 6.7.

The new Application Switcher uses buttons to manage your applications.

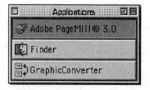

Understanding Memory Management

The down side of multitasking is how much Random Access Memory, or RAM (also called just *memory*), it requires. Every program you open is allocated a slice of memory. The more programs you open and close, the more memory you use. You must stay aware of your memory use so that you don't run out at critical junctures. Luckily, the Mac OS provides several ways to monitor and manage memory.

Managing memory on your Macintosh depends largely on how much memory you have installed, as well as which software runs in conjunction with your system software. Low memory error messages can sometimes be handled by simply increasing the amount of memory available to an application, quitting an application, or purchasing more RAM.

Determining How Much Memory You Have

Memory is stored in RAM located on your motherboard. When the Macintosh starts, it loads the instructions located on the PowerPC's ROM on the motherboard first, and then Mac OS; the memory occupied by Mac OS is referred to as the *system heap*. The system heap consists of the core system and Finder files as well as control panels, extensions, and fonts residing in the System Folder. The remaining memory is available for applications to run. This is known as the *application heap*.

To find out how much memory your system is using, select Apple|About This Computer. After an Easy Install of system software, Mac OS 8.5 generally occupies approximately 6 to 10 MB of memory (depending on the hardware it's running on). RAM requirements of applications currently running also appear in the About This Computer window (see Figure 6.8).

FIGURE 6.8.

The About This Computer window.

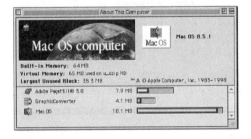

When you select Apple|About This Computer, you should see the following items:

- **Built-in Memory.** This is the amount of physical memory installed in your Macintosh (on the motherboard).
- **Virtual Memory.** This is activated automatically after a clean, Easy Install of Mac OS 8.5. You can turn virtual memory on or off in the Memory control panel.
- **Largest Unused Block**. This is the amount of memory currently available for applications to use.

6

The version number of Mac OS 8.5 is located in the upper-right corner of the About This Computer window. The Mac OS and any applications currently running are listed in the bottom half of the About This Computer window. For the system or any application, the amount of memory in use is reflected by the "fullness" of the progress bar. The more empty space in the progress bar, the more memory available to the application.

> You can also use the Balloon Help system in the About This Computer window to see more detailed information about how much memory each application is allocated and using. Select Show Balloons from the Help menu and then pass your cursor over an application's memory bar graph on the About This Computer window. The balloon displays more information about memory for that application. (See Figure 6.9.)

FIGURE 6.9.

You can learn how much memory out of a total memory partition an application is using by invoking the Balloon Help system.

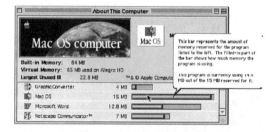

The About This Computer window displays some critical memory statistics about your Macintosh. It shows you how much memory is installed and available, as well as how much is in use by each application. You can use this information to make your System Folder more memory efficient, change the memory configurations of your applications, or quit an application you no longer need.

Managing Mac OS 8.5 Memory

The amount of memory used by Mac OS 8.5 should stay fairly constant while running applications. Some system features, such as the disk cache and RAM disk, can use a portion of memory that can be adjusted in the Memory control panel. Disk cache and RAM disk are "off," by default. When enabled, file sharing also increases the amount of your system memory by approximately 300K.

If you're running low on memory or are trying to minimize the amount of memory used by Mac OS, turn off file sharing and RAM disk and leave your disk cache around 96 to 256K.

You can dramatically increase the amount of memory used by Mac OS if you have a lot of extensions, control panels, and fonts in your System Folder. Extensions consist of printer drivers, shared libraries, startup extensions, and so on. If you don't print to a color StyleWriter or other Apple printer, for example, move these printer drivers out of your Extensions folder as well as the System Folder. If you plan on using several extension configurations, you might want to have one set with a minimal number of extensions and control panels, and another set with your preferred, full System Folder.

If you use a lot of fonts, you might want to reduce your System Folder memory usage by removing and archiving any fonts you no longer use.

Keep in mind that anything that adds functionality to your Macintosh or changes the appearance of the desktop requires memory to run. You always must make the determination whether a particular add-on is worth the additional memory required to run it.

Managing Application Memory

Applications are allocated a preselected amount of memory when they're opened. Any application can use any portion of the Largest Unused Block displayed in the About This Computer window. If an application in the About This Computer window displays more than a third of an empty bar, you should consider allocating a smaller amount of memory to it if possible. You can use the Application menu to identify which applications are currently open and running.

You can configure the amount of memory available to an application by using the new Memory screen in the General Information window. Open the General Information window and perform the following steps:

1. Make sure the application that you want to get information about is not running.

2. Select the application icon and then select Memory from the Get Info pop-up menu in the File menu (see Figure 6.10).

3. Press the Control key and click the application icon. A contextual menu appears over the application icon. Select Memory from this pop-up menu.

6

FIGURE 6.10.

The Memory Information window is used to designate preferred and minimum memory partitions for your application.

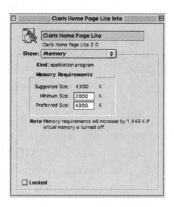

An application can't be running if you want to access information about it. Always quit an application before invoking Get Info.

Managing System or Application Memory-Related Error Messages

If your system or application runs low on memory, an error message appears notifying you that the software does not have enough memory available, and that you should save the document. If the system reports this type of error message, you might want to upgrade your Macintosh with more memory. If you already have upgraded, you might need to quit an application or two to free enough memory for the system to run in conjunction with other applications.

If not enough memory is available to open an application, Finder displays an error message. You should increase the amount of memory allocated to the application via the Memory Information window (accessed from the Get Info submenu on the File menu). You might want to start by increasing the memory by a few hundred kilobytes to see whether the error message goes away. When increasing the amount of memory available to the application, be sure to check About This Computer to make sure the amount of memory is free before reopening your application.

Some common error messages are Error Type 11 and Error Type 28. Although these error messages may not always be generated due to low memory, you might want to consider upgrading memory or increasing the amount of memory for an application if these error messages appear consistently when you're using large files with an application.

Memory Fragmentation

The About This Computer window will sometimes show that you have, say, 10 MB free but will give you an error message indicating there isn't enough memory to open an 8 MB application. This scenario can occur if you open three applications that take up 4 MB, 3 MB, and 6 MB—for a total of 13 MB—and then quit the 4 MB and 6 MB applications. Attempting to open the 8 MB application generates a `Not Enough Memory` message because Mac OS requires a contiguous block of memory in which to run an application. To open the 8 MB application, you must first quit the 3 MB application.

Summary

The rule of thumb when dealing with memory issues is *more is never enough*. The more memory you have, the more applications you can open simultaneously. Working with applications is totally about keeping watch on your memory use. This hour explained what makes an application an application on a Mac. The hour also reviewed how to optimize application memory as well as how to manage overall system memory via the Extensions Manager and the Memory control panel.

Term Review

application A program that performs a function. Applications can be as small as the calculator desk accessory or as large as Adobe Photoshop. Applications also may have many associated files, such as the OLE libraries associated with Microsoft Word. You can also think of applications as *programs* (versus files that contain information, which are called *documents*).

background processing Actions that occur behind the scenes while you're working in an application window. Activities such as copying, moving, and printing can work in the background.

built-in memory The actual amount of Random Access Memory (RAM) installed on your Mac.

cross-platform software Application software that's available to run on more than one type of operating system (be it Mac OS, Windows, or another OS).

foreground processing Actions that occur in an application that stop you from working until they're completed.

installers Specialized programs written to place pieces of software in their correct locations to ensure they will operate properly.

6

kernel   The part of a modern operating system that manages the creation and tracking of processes running in the operating system. Processes can be printing, copying, and running applications, as well as performing some specialized action within an application.

memory   Also called Random Access Memory (RAM). Contains a set of special addresses used by the computer to store data while it's being used. RAM is called *volatile* because its contents are lost whenever you turn off your Mac.

memory partition   The special location in RAM allocated to each application when it's opened. Applications use this specified area to store their data. The partition is given back to the system when you quit the application.

multitasking   The capability to perform more than one process simultaneously. There are three types of multitasking: cooperative, context-switching, and preemptive multitasking.

SimpleText   A rudimentary text editor provided with Mac OS 8.5. Use SimpleText to access ReadMe files and to write scripts.

virtual memory   Artificial memory created by borrowing space on your hard disk and swapping "pages" of data in and out as they are needed. Virtual memory is slower than real memory because the computer uses its input/output buses to transfer information rather than its memory addresses.

Q&A

Q How do I turn off background printing? Why would I want to?

A Select the Chooser from the Apple menu. In the Chooser dialog box, deselect the Background radio button. You would want to turn off background printing to release memory. You should print in the foreground if you're printing a large, complicated document with many graphics and fonts.

Q How can I improve the performance of applications on a Power Mac?

A In Mac OS 8.5, you'll find that the default setting for memory is set to have 1 MB of virtual memory turned on. You can turn off virtual memory to run hard disk repair software.

If you're running an earlier version of Mac OS 8.5, you can increase performance when you turn on virtual memory in the Memory control panel and set it to increase your memory by 1 MB. Be sure to restart your Mac.

See the next hour for more performance tricks.

Q How can I minimize the Application menu in the menu bar?

A Slide the small scrollbar to the right to hide the active application's name on the Application menu's menu bar. You can also press the Control key while clicking the Application menu to minimize the menu bar.

Q Why can't I use Navigation Services in all my Mac applications?

A Apple builds new technologies into its operating systems via Application Program Interfaces (APIs). It's up to the individual software vendors to update their programs to call on these APIs to take advantage of new features such as Navigation Services. Over time, you'll begin to see your applications using the new Open dialog box as well as other services.

Workshop

The Workshop contains quiz questions to help you solidify your understanding of the material covered. You can find the answers to the quiz questions in Appendix B, "Quiz Answers."

Quiz

1. What's the difference between applications, control panels, plug-ins, and system extensions?
2. Give at least three ways to open an application.
3. Give at least three ways to open a document.
4. How do you save a document to a different location on your hard disk?
5. How do you open a document located on a remote volume using the old-style Finder dialog box? How would you do the same task using the Navigation Services dialog box?
6. How do you hide an active window?
7. Give two ways to change the currently active application.
8. Give two ways to close a document.
9. How do you ensure that your document can be read by an Intel-based computer running Windows 95? What naming conventions should you use?
10. What's the safest way to remove an application from your Mac?

6

HOUR 7

Optimizing Mac OS 8.5 Performance

The goal of this hour is to cover three main Mac OS performance topics:

- How to make your Mac faster
- An explanation of the hardware roots of Mac OS performance
- How to use performance benchmark software to analyze your Mac's performance

Although you don't need to optimize Mac OS 8.5 to use it successfully, after using Mac OS 8.5 for some period of time, you may notice performance slow downs, or you may want to see if you can improve software performance. Just remember that no real performance tweak exists for slow hardware. Software performance, in the end, is driven by the design and speed of the hardware it runs on.

Understanding Performance

You have four general categories to consider when analyzing your system for performance:

- Hardware configuration
- Mac OS 8.5 settings
- Application configuration
- Performance monitoring or benchmarking

The hardware configuration running its original shipping version of Mac OS is a good baseline for measuring Mac OS 8.5 and general system performance. Mac OS 8.5's performance should be the same or faster than benchmarks created for the same hardware configuration running Mac OS 7.x.

Generally, benchmarks are created using the default settings for system software. However, it's possible for some benchmarks to be created using customized system settings, such as a custom disk cache or RAM disk, to make one Mac seem slower or faster than another, even though both have the same hardware and system software. The best baseline to use is one created on the same computer as the new performance numbers. Therefore, if you haven't already installed Mac OS 8.5, you should run benchmark software before doing so. Run it with Mac OS 7.6.1, or your favorite version of Mac OS, before installing Mac OS 8.5.

Determinants of System Performance

Although your Mac's performance is largely a result of the hardware itself, a faster processor does not necessarily mean faster system software or application performance. The system bus speed, as well as its subcomponents (such as memory, I/O, and video chip components), affect the overall hardware performance of a computer.

Overall, system performance on Macs is affected greatly by the addition of extensions and control panels in the System Folder. Virtual Memory (VM), file sharing, background printing, and background software calculations (such as finding items or counting folder contents) can slow your Macintosh to a crawl.

This is the dilemma most users face: You either customize the Mac to death and take a huge performance hit, or you turn everything off and enjoy a fast, Zen-like Macintosh.

However, you can have the best of both worlds by using an extension manager such as Now Software's Startup Manager, Casady & Greene's Conflict Catcher, or Extension Manager 4 in Mac OS 8.5, along with custom extension sets. If you're planning on doing a lot of processor-dependent work, you can use a minimal extension setup to avoid software incompatibilities or conflicts. If entertainment and adventure are your objectives, you can turn all the extensions on and spend time customizing and exploring software.

Hardware Performance Limitations

Although Mac OS 8.5 is a pure software product, its performance is determined by the hardware it's running on. Understanding how hardware plays a role with Mac OS 8.5 features can help explain three software-centric scenarios that you'll most likely encounter as you use Mac OS 8.5:

- No matter how well you fine-tune your system software for performance, it will never be able to go faster than the hardware's limitations.

- You need to understand Mac OS 8.5 hardware requirements so that you can upgrade software or hardware on your computer.

- If Mac OS 8.5 performance is extremely disappointing for you, it's unlikely software tweaking will be able to improve performance dramatically enough to make a difference.

The processor is the engine of your computer. Both the type of processor and its speed play a large role in the performance of any computer. In addition to the processor, the core hardware design also consists of memory (the speed of RAM, such as the SDRAM in G3s), the video chip (ATI on the G3), the I/O chipset, and related subsystem hardware controllers. These factors, combined with a data path on the motherboard to support the processor, comprise the core hardware design of a computer.

Also, any Internet software and networking hardware, such as the modem or network connection, plays a large role in network performance.

The New PowerMac G3 Processor

The faster and more efficient the processor, the better your Mac programs will operate. PowerPCs gone through three generations: 601, 603/604e, and 750 (nicknamed *G3*). Figure 7.1 displays a chart showing the evolution of these processors.

7

FIGURE 7.1.

The PowerPC micro-processor roadmap. (Photo courtesy of Apple Computer)

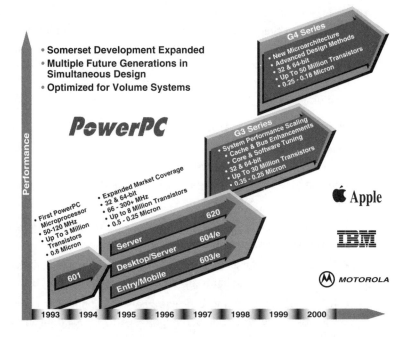

The new G3 processor performs up to twice as fast as its predecessors. This chip provides computer performances of up to 300MHz based on MacBench 4 benchmarks. Performance is provided by four enhancements:

- The G3 is optimized (meaning *it runs best*) for the Mac OS to ensure minimal branching and use of the shortest data transfer routes.
- Level 2 cache has been moved from the logic board to the processor card so that the CPU can access the cache directly using a dedicated bus specially designed for this purpose.
- A large Level 1 cache has been included. This cache has doubled from 32 bits to 64 bits to allow for 32-bit addresses for instructions and 32-bit addressing dedicated to data.
- The G3 uses a new 0.25-micron process in its manufacture that results in a cooler-running chip with very low power requirements.

Although the G3 was recently introduced, the G4 is already waiting in the wings. The G4 processor features the new IBM/Motorola copper process technology for an even more efficient high-performance chip.

I/O Performance Issues

The access time and interface of a hard drive plays a big role in determining its performance, especially if you're using your hard drive to record audio or video. Apple ships two types of hard drives with its Power Macs: IDE and SCSI. Most PowerBooks and midrange desktop computers have internal IDE drives, but they can have external SCSI (small computer serial interface) drives connected to them.

The new G3 desktop and tower Power Macs have an internal IDE bus and cables, but they perform extremely well because of the new Gossamer motherboard's design. Earlier high-end desktops, such as the 9500, 8500, 7500 and 7200 series Power Macs all have dual SCSI buses, one for the internal SCSI chain and one for the external SCSI chain of devices.

CD-ROM drives are also available with either a SCSI or IDE interface. Generally, SCSI drives have faster access times than IDE drives. However, IDE drives usually cost less than an equivalently configured SCSI drive. Slower hard drives are less expensive than drives with faster access times or larger caches, but the slower drive may not provide the performance for all computing tasks once you start using it.

Additionally, SCSI drives support faster interfaces, such as a RAID configuration or a PCI card providing an interface for Ultra-Wide SCSI. Attaching a PCI card to a SCSI drive increases the throughput of data moving between the Mac and the SCSI drive. The PCI card connects directly to the SCSI device, bypassing the traditional SCSI port connection.

A RAID configuration boosts performance even further by using a second SCSI drive to mirror data on the first drive.

Hard Drive Performance Issues

Overall, Mac OS 8.5 works with the factory-packaged internal hard drive that comes with the computer. It also works with any properly formatted SCSI hard drive. However, depending on what software you plan to use with your Mac, you may want to consider more than one hard drive option to optimize system performance. For example, one way to increase Mac OS 8.5 performance is to add an internal hard disk that has a fast RPM (7200 or higher) and a fast access time (10ms or faster).

The size of the hard drive also plays an important role with Mac OS 8.5. Although its RAM requirements have not changed considerably, the hard disk space needs have increased. Remember, you not only need disk space for Mac OS 8.5, but also for applications and other software. Mac OS 8.5 has cured one of the performance-slowing side effects of using an extremely large hard disk on a Mac. With Mac OS 8.5, you can

7

upgrade your hard disk driver to the Extended Format (called HFS+) to overcome the problem of inefficient file block sizes. HFS, or the Standard File Format, causes the minimum block size for a file to increase as the overall drive size increases. For example, a 2K file on a 200 MB hard disk can occupy 20K on a 9GB hard disk. HFS+ sets the minimum number of blocks to 4.26 billion, giving the file system much more latitude in allocating space. The downside of HFS+ is that you must reformat your hard drive in order to install the new file system. See Hour 23, "The File System Extended," for a discussion of how to implement HFS+ without destroying your data.

A hard drive of at least 500 MB is recommended but not required in order to use Mac OS 8.5. Some of the benefits of having more hard disk space available include the following:

- Mac OS 8.5 has a default setting of turning the Virtual Memory setting "on" following a clean installation. This creates a swapfile on the hard disk, which can occupy anywhere from 16 MB or more of hard disk space.

- A larger hard drive allows you to store more files over a longer period of time. What does this mean? If you copy and delete files frequently on a smaller drive, this can create fragmentation, and thus decrease the overall performance of the hard disk. Over time, as files are copied, moved, or deleted from the drive, newer files will be spread across a broader range of the hard disk, requiring the drive to work harder to find all the pieces of a file on the hard disk. A large drive lets you leave more files on it, thus decreasing the potential for defragmentation and performance degradation.

- Although using a file compression utility is not recommended for regular software application and document use, this becomes an option if you're running low on available hard disk space. Having a larger hard drive reduces the overhead of having to use software compression to store more information on a hard disk.

Regardless of what kind of hard disk is being used with Mac OS 8.5, the bottom line is that you need to make sure it's properly configured and maintained in order to ensure optimal performance.

Video Performance Issues

Video and graphics performance varies across computers supported by Mac OS 8.5. Video actually references two modes of technology. One is the video from the computer monitor to the CPU; the other is support for capturing, editing, and outputting moving picture video using the computer. Video performance in this section specifically refers to the former: performance of the computer screen to the components attached to the computer's motherboard.

Earlier Mac models with built-in video ports that relied on installed RAM for video have slower performance than those with an add-in video card or video chipset on the motherboard. However, the latest Macs with built-in video use dedicated VRAM and have comparable video and graphics performance to many add-in PCI cards. Third-party cards provide the best graphics acceleration, because they rely on additional hardware chips to boost performance beyond what the built-in video hardware can provide for specific graphics, video, or 3D functions. Current G3 Power Macs use ATI graphics chips on the motherboard. The ATI chips supports 2D and 3D acceleration as well as video playback support (via television input to the Mac screen).

Network Performance Issues

Network performance follows a similar paradigm to the rules for efficient performance. The baseline for network software performance is the network hardware and its supported protocol. For example, if a Mac is connected to a LocalTalk network, network software performance will never exceed the bandwidth of LocalTalk. To boost performance, the network hardware needs to be upgraded to support Ethernet protocols, such as 10-Base T or coaxial cabling.

Computers manage many types of tasks over the network. These include Internet and general network server access, email, printing, file sharing access, and so on.

The main bottleneck for networks can be the size and limits of the network itself. Network performance on your local computer can be optimized by understanding what's happening when performance slows down while your computer tries to complete a task via a network.

Background events—such as printing and file sharing—can take a heavy toll on Mac OS performance. For example, if you're sending email while a document is printing in the background or while someone is copying files from your Mac, the computer must manage both the foreground task of sending the email to the network as well as the background task of printing or copying a document.

There's no hard-and-fast number for this type of performance hit. However, performance will decrease dramatically if your Mac tries to do several tasks at once, especially if some of those tasks are on a network.

Performance of the Software

Hardware performance can be adversely affected if Mac OS 8.5 system software is not adjusted properly. These performance penalties can impact overall system performance or specific component performance, such as while printing or accessing the CD-ROM. Additional performance components to consider are discussed in the following sections.

7

What Is Native Software?

Native software is software created specifically to run on the PowerPC processor. This processor, used in all Power Macintosh computers and their clones, replaced the 680x0 Macintosh processor. Power Macs can also run traditional 68K Macintosh application software through a *software emulator* built into Mac OS 8.5. The 68K emulator is software that intercepts 68K code and acts as the 680x0 processor chip, although a PowerPC processor chip is actually processing the data.

One feature the 68K emulator does not support is 68K floating-point unit (FPU) instructions. Third-party software is available that provides 68K FPU emulation, but this software solution for the FPU will never match its hardware equivalent. If the software is still supported by a publisher, it might be worth upgrading to a Power PC version of that software.

In the past, system software contained both 68K and Power PC native code. That has not changed with Mac OS 8.5, because it's not entirely native. The software component that helps Power PC code work with 68K code in system software is called *Mixed Mode Manager*.

For faster performance, the goal of native software is to use the mixed mode as little as possible. Each time Power PC code must work with 68K code to complete a software task, system software must pass Power PC code to mixed mode and then to the 68K emulator. It must then pass those results back to the Power PC code to complete the startup extension-based task. As you might expect, these extra steps slow down the performance of the software running on the computer. One example of software that can be a catalyst for this type of performance slowdown is a system extension.

Software applications that contain Power Macintosh and traditional 680x0 code are known as *fat applications*. A fat application will run Power Macintosh native software if launched on a Power Mac and 68K software if launched on a traditional 68K Macintosh. Fat applications generally take up more hard drive space than 68K-only or PowerPC-only code. With Mac OS 8.5, Finder is now a fat application.

CD-ROM Settings

Although the raw speed of a CD-ROM drive depends on the access time and speed of the drive itself, system software settings can help either avoid or create a performance hit. CD-ROM performance can be affected by system software settings pertaining to virtual memory, file sharing, and the color depth of your computer monitor.

CD-ROM media ranges from audio CDs to interactive multimedia to 3D animation-packed software applications. To maximize CD-ROM playback performance, follow these steps:

- Turn virtual memory off. Virtual memory can be turned on and off from the Memory control panel.
- Turn file sharing off. File sharing can be turned on and off from the File Sharing control panel.
- Select the recommended color bit-depth setting. For example, turn your monitor's bit-depth from a display of millions of colors (24 bits) to 256 colors (8 bits). The monitor's color depth can be selected from the Monitors & Sound control panel. Although some CD-ROM software titles may require thousands of colors, the most common color depth setting is usually 256 colors.
- Turn AppleTalk off. AppleTalk settings are located in the AppleTalk control panel.

Print Settings

There are two types of printing configurations on a Mac: background and direct printing. These controls are located in the Chooser desk accessory. Printing performance becomes noticeable only if several documents are printed in a row, or if one long document is printed. Either way, the best printing performance will always be with direct printing. The downside of printing a large document to the printer directly is that you can't do anything else with the computer until that document finishes printing.

The benefit to printing in the background is that you can continue to work with another application or document while the printing. The downside of background printing is that overall system performance will slow down to some degree, and network performance will also be affected. Also, the document may take longer to print if the computer is tasked heavily while trying to process the print job.

Network Settings

To optimize network performance, avoid running background tasks such as background printing. Also, reduce the amount of disk and network activity for the computer. For example, turn off virtual memory and file sharing. Also, try not to download more than one item at a time from FTP or Web sites.

If you're using a modem to connect to another network or to the Internet, be sure the modem is configured to dial out at its maximum speed or at the maximum speed supported by the Internet service provider (or other network service). If you can, check local network activity to see whether performance slowdowns may be caused by the overall network. If only one computer on a network experiences performance problems, it may be the specific hardware attached to or configured with the computer, or it might be a misconfigured software setting.

7

Maximizing the Default OS Settings

Mac OS 8.5 installs three general categories of system software: 68040, Power Mac, and PowerBook system software. System software settings also vary depending on the Mac's memory configuration.

Finder Settings

In general, the default Finder settings provide optimal general performance for Mac OS 8.5. However, it's easy to change these settings, some of which will affect performance for specific tasks, for overall Mac performance. It isn't always easy to isolate whether a performance problem is related to Finder or some other features of system software. Performance slowdowns can also be caused by hard disk fragmentation.

Most system settings are located in the control panels installed with Mac OS 8.5. Almost all these control panels are performance oriented. However, a few play a larger part in affecting overall system performance than others.

Memory Control Panel

The Memory control panel in Mac OS 8.5 controls what the Mac does with available RAM (see Figure 7.2). This control panel can set aside portions of your Mac's RAM to be used for functions other than the normal RAM function. (Normally, RAM holds portions of software and data the CPU uses when it runs applications.)

The three settings—Disk Cache, Virtual Memory, and RAM Disk—can dramatically affect the performance of your Mac and also prevent or cause crashes. VM and RAM disk changes take effect only after the Mac is restarted. Also, Mac OS 8.5 allows only supported computers to run in 32-bit mode.

FIGURE 7.2.

The Memory control panel.

Previous versions of Memory control panel and system software allowed earlier Mac models to work in 24-bit mode for application compatibility and to support Macs with 8 MB or less of installed memory.

Previous Power Macs also have a choice between the Modern Memory Manager, which is native, and the older Memory Manager, which is based on 68K code. The Memory control panel in Mac OS 8.5 allows only Power Macs to use the Modern Memory Manager.

From the disk cache size to virtual memory to RAM disk size, almost all the options in this control panel have a direct affect on system software performance. The default settings for the Memory control panel set the disk cache at 96K or 128K and turn on virtual memory to either 20 MB total or 1 MB more than the amount of physical memory installed.

If the hard drive does not have enough free space to support virtual memory, the Memory control panel will turn VM "on," but it will actually be "off" because there isn't enough hard drive space to create the swapfile. The default setting for RAM Disk is "off."

Disk Cache

Disk cache is a section of RAM used to hold portions of applications and data files frequently used by the CPU. Applications are too big to fit entirely into RAM, so the disk cache acts as a kind of RAM overflow container to hold application information. Because accessing RAM is many times faster than accessing a hard disk, using the disk cache speeds up your Mac.

A bit of Mac trivia: Disk cache was incorrectly called "RAM cache" in System 6.

Unlike System 6, Mac OS 8.5's disk cache is always on (with a minimum setting of 96K). Increasing this amount will increase your Mac's performance, but the rate of increase becomes negligible at some point. In addition, the disk cache takes away the amount of RAM available to applications, so you don't want to set it too high; in extreme cases, too little available RAM will prevent some applications from launching. Luckily, in Mac OS 8.5, the Modern Memory Manager automatically sets the proper amount of cache. You have to physically shift from Default to Custom to change the cache. It's wise not to fool with cache (that is, unless you really know what you're doing).

To manually set your disk cache, click the Custom radio button in the Disk Cache section of the Memory control panel. The Mac gives you a dire warning that increasing the cache

7

will inversely affect the performance of your computer. If you're sure you want to set a custom number, click Custom. You then can type a new number or use the arrows to increase or decrease the number in the text box.

DISK CACHE SETTINGS

Disk cache settings in the Memory control panel can help a Mac ignore or work harmoniously with a Level 2 (L2) cache card and your Mac's RAM and hard drive. The default setting for the disk cache is 96K. If L2 cache is installed, the disk cache should be increased to match the size of the cache card. Depending on the type of work performed on your Mac, you may want to adjust the disk cache to a higher setting to see if you can notice any performance improvements.

Virtual Memory

Virtual memory is a feature of Mac OS 8.5 that uses an invisible file, known as the *swap-file*, as if it were RAM. This file extends the system's ability to support applications that require large amounts of memory to run. Virtual memory is slower than real memory for many reasons (one of which is that accessing a hard disk is slower than accessing RAM).

Older driver software for hard disk drives may be incompatible with Mac OS 8.5's virtual memory. In these cases, you can simply upgrade with a later driver. Use Drive Setup that comes with the Mac OS 8.5 CD-ROM or Disk Tools floppy or system installer disks to update the driver for your Apple hard drives. For other hard drives, you can use driver update software, such as FWB Software's Hard Disk Toolkit.

Even if you can run virtual memory, you may decide to keep it turned off if you have a 680x0-based Mac. The biggest problem with virtual memory in non–Power Mac models is speed, or more specifically, the lack thereof. Virtual memory can reduce your speedy Quadra to a crawling whimper. You should also avoid using virtual memory in PowerBook Macs on battery power. Virtual memory keeps the hard disk constantly spinning, which will quickly drain your battery.

Virtual Memory on Power Macs

The story is different for Power Macs, where virtual memory works better than it does in 68040 Macs. Your Power Mac requires less memory to run native software and will run faster if Virtual Memory is set to 1 MB more than the amount of physical memory installed in your Power Mac. If you double or triple the amount of virtual-to-physical memory, your Power Mac will still be slower than if the Virtual Memory setting was turned off, but it won't bring the machine down to a crawl.

> If you're not sure whether you should turn Virtual Memory on, try timing a task with VM off and then with VM on. If you notice one is faster than the other, pick the setting that creates the faster time. You may want to time several tasks before making a final decision about whether to leave VM on or off.

If you run many of the same applications frequently on a Mac, virtual memory can improve application launch times on both 68K and Power Macs over a period of time. Mac OS 8.5 virtual memory requires less system software overhead than in the first versions of System 7. This improves system performance with virtual memory on, and it also provides a performance-efficient workaround for not having enough memory to run software with Mac OS 8.5.

Default Virtual Memory Settings

When you first turn on the Virtual Memory setting on a 68K Mac, the default setting adds enough virtual memory to increase the amount of RAM up to 20 MB if there's less than 16 MB of memory installed. If there's more than 16 MB of memory, virtual memory will be set to 1 MB more than the amount of installed memory. On a Power Mac, Virtual Memory's default settings follow the same rules. It's best not to increase this amount. Instead, you should decrease it to the minimum amount you think you'll need.

> Another way to improve the performance of virtual memory is to set it up on a disk or partition that doesn't contain system software and applications. This way, the disk calls that are busy servicing virtual memory do not compete with the disk needs of application and system software.

Virtual Memory and CD-ROM Software

Another consideration when thinking about virtual memory is that many applications do not work well with it. CD-ROM software is probably the best example of software that suffers with virtual memory. Many CD-ROM titles will advise you to turn virtual memory off in order to be able to launch them. Video capture and playback is also not as efficient if Virtual Memory is on.

7

RAM Versus Virtual Memory

Virtual memory is also not a viable substitute for RAM in regards to performance. Large desktop publishing applications, such as Adobe Photoshop, work best if an adequate amount of RAM is installed prior to running the application.

File Sharing Control Panel

Both the Sharing Setup and File Sharing Monitor control panels have been consolidated into the File Sharing control panel (see Figure 7.3). File Sharing is turned off by default, and turning it on requires AppleTalk to be on. Turning File Sharing on increases the amount of memory system software uses to run and also affects the overall performance of the operating system.

FIGURE 7.3.

The File Sharing control panel.

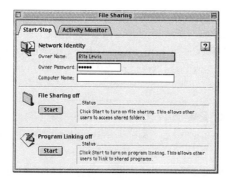

Additionally, slower performance occurs when another Mac logs into your Mac and copies files. The performance impact is greater when a slower network protocol such as LocalTalk is used (versus a higher-bandwidth protocol such as EtherTalk).

> If you don't need to share any files on your Mac, leave File Sharing off. Otherwise, you can use the Automated Tasks AppleScript to turn it off or on as needed, thus minimizing the impact of file sharing on your Mac's system performance.

AppleTalk Control Panel

When Mac OS 8.5 is installed, it restores the AppleTalk setting (for example, the Ethernet or printer port) from the previous version of system software installed. By default, the AppleTalk setting is off; however, Open Transport allows you to turn it back on without having to restart the computer. The AppleTalk control panel is provided so that you can easily toggle this setting on or off as needed for performance and communication with your printer or network (see Figure 7.4). If networking is not required for software applications used with Mac OS 8.5, AppleTalk can be disabled using the Extensions folder, or it can be turned off in the Chooser.

FIGURE 7.4.

The AppleTalk control panel.

If you're using a PowerBook and do not plan to be connected to a network, turning AppleTalk off also prolongs battery life.

PowerBook Performance Issues

PowerBook software is configured to take advantage of optimal performance when connected to a power outlet or, with different settings, when running off a battery. These settings can be configured in the PowerBook control panel. PowerBook performance is impacted the most by waiting for the internal hard drive to spin up after spinning down or sleeping. If a PowerBook is connected to a wall outlet, configure the PowerBook control panel not to spin down the drive so the performance remains as good as possible.

If you don't connect your PowerBook to a power outlet frequently, you probably rely heavily on having healthy battery performance for PowerBook use. Selecting applications that do not require hard drive access, turning Virtual Memory off, and using a RAM disk for system software can help extend the battery life of a PowerBook.

Battery performance can be easily maintained by using Battery Recondition on a regular basis, as well as by configuring your PowerBook control panel to trigger more energy-efficient settings to match your PowerBook use. Keep in mind that the life of a battery is somewhere between one and two years. Therefore, if it starts to have a real short recharge life, it might be time to replace the battery.

Tricks for Improving Performance

Finder and control panel preference settings for optimal performance are explained in this section. All settings do not need to be selected in order to improve system performance. However, following as many of the suggested settings as possible will increase the performance of Mac OS 8.5.

7

General Performance Improvements

Besides control panels, the Finder has several settings located in the View and Edit menus of Mac OS 8.5. Calculate Folder Sizes, shown in Figure 7.5, is one of the check boxes in the View Options window (change your view to "lists" before selecting View Options; otherwise, this check box will not be available). For faster performance, leave this feature off. Turning Calculate Folder Sizes on activates a background task in Finder that calculates the folder size in any selected window.

FIGURE 7.5.

Calculate Folder Sizes in Finder's View Options window.

Performance for opening and closing folders can be improved by keeping the number of files and folders stored in a single folder at a manageable level. The magic number of files and folders depends on what kinds of files and applications are on a Mac. Generally, however, it's a good goal to keep the total number below 100. This also applies to files and folders stored on the desktop.

Most control panel settings, such as those in General Controls, Mouse, and Keyboard, will not have a range of settings that impact performance. These control panels are introduced in Hours 1 through 5. Control panels that do impact performance are covered in the following section.

Improving Performance Using Connectix Products

Connectix has been extremely proactive about developing "fixes" for performance issues in Power Macs. Earlier in this hour it was mentioned that some commands are still "emulated" for PowerPCs, meaning that some older Mac 68K machine code has not yet been translated into PowerPC code and must be implemented in slower software (although each new version of the operating system requires less and less emulation). Connectix has developed two products that speed up software emulation on the Mac: Speed Doubler 8 and Ram Doubler 8. Speed Doubler is a more efficient emulator that replaces the emulator provided by Apple. This system extension is a must for users of older Macs, such as 6100s, 7100s, 7200s, and so forth, who want to run Mac OS 8.5. Ram Doubler provides a new caching scheme that provides better use of RAM for those Mac users who are using minimal (16 MB) RAM configurations.

In the future, these two Connectix products will not be necessary as the Mac world transitions to the more powerful 604e and G3 Macs, but in the meantime, it's good to know that this vendor is out there letting slower users take advantage of Apple's newest operating system.

Improving Performance of Extensions

You can increase the performance of your Mac by decreasing the number of extensions you have running at any one time. Each time you turn on a system extension, it adds a patch or change to the Mac OS. Every patch affects performance, because the Mac has to act on the patch before performing any other process. Use the Extensions Manager or a third-party extensions manager, such as Casady & Greene's Conflict Catcher 8, to toggle extensions on or off. (See Figure 7.6.)

FIGURE 7.6.

Use the Extensions Manager to turn startup extensions on or off.

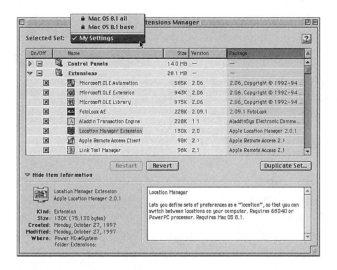

Items listed apply to the specific versions in Mac OS 8.5. It's possible newer versions of these control panels may, in fact, provide improved system software performance. However, do not forget that any control panels and extensions added to the System Folder can also slow down performance.

You can access the Extensions Manager or Conflict Catcher when starting up your Mac by holding down the spacebar. You must restart your Mac after making changes to either extension manager.

7

Tuning the Apple Menu Options Control Panel

Two sets of features can be found in the Apple Menu Options control panel: hierarchical menus and the Recent Items folder. Both sets of features in Apple Menu Options involve patching the system. This is the main reason performance is affected by turning on Apple Menu Options. Even if the hierarchical menus feature is off and the Recent Items folder is set to 0, Apple Menu Options will still have some patches running as the result of it loading at startup with the rest of the system. If all the features are turned off in this control panel, it's better to use Extensions Manager and move it to the Control Panels (Disabled) folder than to leave it in the Extensions folder.

Tuning the Menu Bar with Control Panels

Any software that needs to update the screen every second or so will also have an impact on system performance (albeit a small one). The Date & Time control panel has a clock option to flash the time separators. If this check box is selected, it means the system must process that information on your screen every second or so.

The performance hit is more obvious if the updated area involves a larger item that needs to be updated each second, such as a flashing Christmas light or hard drive access indicator in the menu bar. Optimizing performance means every little performance boost counts. Therefore, if you can live without this feature, leave it off.

Tuning the Control Strip

The wide range of module functionality in Control Strip attests to the likelihood of its patching the system in order to access settings or the status of settings such as File Sharing, AppleTalk, and Sound Volume. Also, Control Strip must always be the front-most item drawn on the screen. Again, these performance suggestions do not need to be followed to see performance improvements with Mac OS. However, if you do not use Control Strip on your desktop or PowerBook, disable it using Extensions Manager and see whether you can observe a performance increase in Mac OS 8.5.

Tuning the File Sharing Control Panel

File Sharing and Program Linking are two more background tasks that should be left off unless you absolutely need to use these features. To check these settings, go to the File Sharing control panel and make sure that both the File Sharing and Program Linking buttons read Start. This indicates that these features are turned off.

Tuning the Chooser

The Chooser contains two features that make a small performance improvement: turning AppleTalk off and deselecting Background Printing. To change the AppleTalk setting, go to Chooser in the Apple menu and select the Inactive radio button (see Figure 7.7). You can also change AppleTalk settings by going to the AppleTalk control panel and selecting the Options button.

> Background printing works differently with different Apple printer drivers in Mac OS 8.5.

FIGURE 7.7.

Chooser with AppleTalk and Background Printing off.

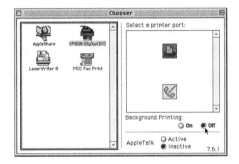

Improving Graphics and Video Performance

Video performance on your Mac can be improved by reducing the Color Depth setting in the Monitors & Sound control panel. Some Macs do not support the black-and-white setting. Even if you use color, selecting a smaller color depth can let your Mac update the items onscreen faster. See Hour 11, "Color," for a discussion of how to work with color and your monitor. Generally, the Monitors & Sound control panel is used to adjust your screen's resolution. Your OS version dictates where on the Monitors & Sound control panel this adjustment is located.

If Mac OS 8.5 is running a monitor that supports multiple screen sizes, performance will increase with the use of lower screen sizes. To select the resolution of a monitor, go the Monitors section of the Monitors & Sound control panel (see Figure 7.8). Lower resolutions appear at the top of the Resolution list; higher (or larger) desktop sizes, such as 1024×768, appear at the bottom of the list.

Selecting 640×480 will give you a smaller desktop, but it provides faster system performance for screen updates, especially on slower computers.

7

FIGURE 7.8.

Adjust your monitor size settings in the Monitors & Sound control panel to affect system performance.

Tools for Optimizing Hard Drives

Just when you thought you had reviewed all the software that might affect system performance, you find out there's more! Although you may have fast hardware when its first attached to your Mac, the software used with that hardware can become fragmented, run out of space to work with, or damaged over time. It's always a good idea to run regular maintenance checks on your hard drive and general computer components to check for both hardware and software integrity.

Updating Your Drivers for Better Performance

If you've already installed Mac OS 8.5 and are adding a new internal or external drive to your Mac, be sure it's updated with the latest version of driver software. If you're not sure what the hard drive was originally formatted with, you should reformat it before using it to store files. Most driver-formatting applications have an option to perform a low-level format. This option should be selected, as well as any settings that can optimize performance, such as a 1:1 access ratio.

Hard Drive Defragmentation

Several hard disk defragmenting products are available for Macs. Perhaps the most popular is included with Norton Utilities Speed Disk (see Figure 7.9). Speed Disk has a number of options besides just showing you how fragmented your hard drive is and then defragmenting it. It can color-code all the files on a drive and show you what percentage of the drive is used to comprise all the software on it. Defragmenting a disk can take a considerable amount of time.

FIGURE 7.9.

Speed Disk's main window.

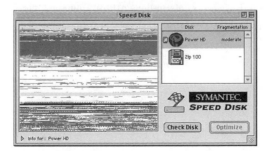

A good rule to follow is to leave somewhere between 5 and 100 MB of hard drive space free (or unused). Many software applications create temp files to store interim data while you're using them. If a hard drive doesn't have enough free space to support applications, this can cause slow performance or, possibly, software problems.

Also, some system software use hard drive space to perform basic tasks. For example, if an image is cut and pasted into Scrapbook, the file on the hard drive will grow in size.

Those of you who upgrade to HFS+ cannot use Speed Disk to optimize your hard drives. Speed Disk does not support the Extended File Format. There's currently (as of mid 1998) no defragmentation software available for optimizing HFS+ disks. Micromat's PlusOptimizer 1.1 will optimize disks formatted with HFS+. This $29 utility is fast and efficient and will defragment your startup disk while it's active.

Customizing Mac OS 8.5 for Performance

Customizing your system can sometimes be in opposition to optimizing performance with Mac OS 8.5. It's perfectly OK to use Mac OS 8.5 without having to add any software to change the way Mac OS looks or works. However, one of the best things about Mac OS is that you can easily customize it to reflect the latest cutting-edge features or the coolest (or the tackiest) software features. This section focuses less on customizing the System Folder by adding software, and more on reducing its size to help improve performance.

At some point, you may want to reduce the file clutter in the System Folder—either to improve performance or simply to free up hard drive space. If you're not sure which software pieces can be moved out of the System Folder without causing a software conflict (or inadvertently disabling some system software functionality), you've come to the right place! Files can be moved out of the System Folder for safe keeping, or they can be permanently removed using the Trash Can.

It's very easy to toss away the wrong system extension or control panel and end up with a dead Mac. Follow these two caveats when working with your System Folder:

- If you're unsure whether it's safe to move anything out of the System Folder, leave it there.
- Never trash any System Folder item. Move it to a holding folder. If, two or three weeks later, your Mac still works just fine after removing the item, copy it onto a floppy and then (and only then) trash it.

7

The Extensions folder is most likely the first place you'll start to find software that can be moved out of the System Folder and that will have the most affect on performance. Here are some items to look for:

- **Printer drivers.** The easiest files to choose are printer drivers that you don't have or won't use with your computer. Printer drivers are named appropriately after the printer families they support, so move any unneeded printer drivers out first. Don't forget: Some printer drivers work with other extensions. For example, the StyleWriter family of printer drivers use the Printer Share extension to share these printers across a network. If you don't have a StyleWriter type of printer connected to your Mac, you can toss the Printer Share extension as well as the StyleWriter family of printer drivers.

- **Subfolders.** The next place to look is in the subfolders, such as the Printer Description and Modem Scripts folders, in the Extensions folder. If you know what kind of printer you'll be printing to, you can remove any printer description files from the Printer Description folder. Similarly, if you know what kind of modem is attached to your computer, remove any other modem scripts from the Modem Scripts folder that do not apply to your computer configuration.

- **Apple Guide.** If you don't need support from Apple Guide, you can remove some of the Apple Guide files, such as Macintosh Guide, from the System Folder. Keep in mind, though, that once you trash these files, you also lose the helpful information contained in them. To get them back, you'll need to reinstall your System Folder. Therefore, if you're not sure whether you'll need these files, a better short-term solution is to make a backup of these files before removing them from the hard drive.

Summary

Making your Mac fast lets you experience Mac OS 8.5 at its finest. This hour covered how to configure Mac OS 8.5 for optimal performance as well as how to monitor it for performance.

Term Review

benchmark   A package of data designed to test the performance of a computer's hardware or software. The package can be run on more than one computer configuration to compare performance between competing models.

Conflict Catcher 8   A third-party extension manager that actively analyzes and fixes system extension conflicts.

Extension Manager An application that manages your system extensions, including their load order, on/off status, and conflicts with other system extensions.

fat applications These are applications that contain code for both PowerPC and 680x0 machines so that they can run equally well on either computer's hardware.

G3 processor The third-generation integrated circuits, actually called *PowerPC 750*, that operate the central processing units of new Macs.

Level 1 cache A piece of memory located on memory chips that's allocated for storing data and instructions for immediate processing. PowerMacs have 32- and 64-bit Level 1 cache addresses.

Level 2 cache Cache located on the processor chip (also called *backend cache*) used to store data and instructions for faster use by the CPU. Level 2 cache significantly increases the performance of Power Macs.

native code Operating system software written in PowerPC machine code rather than emulation code. Native code runs faster and more efficiently than emulated code.

software emulation Software written to act as an intermediary for interpreting machine code to enable incompatible applications to run on your computer. VirtualPC, SoftWindows, and the 680x0 code for Power Macs are emulators.

Q&A

Q How can I know that my Mac is performing at its optimum processor speed?

A Benchmark programs, such as MacBench (freeware from Ziff-Davis on http://www.zdnet.com) and MicroMat TechTools 2.0, are available that let you test the performance of your Mac under various processing conditions.

Q How do I know how much virtual memory I have running, if any?

A Select About This Computer from the Apple menu on the desktop. The resulting dialog box displays the amount of real and virtual memory you have currently running.

Q Why do my applications perform well for a while and then slow down during a session?

A If you open more than one application at a time, your Mac allocates memory partitions on a first-come, first-served basis. When you close an application, its memory remains allocated, thus fragmenting your memory. Eventually, depending on how much memory you have, your Mac runs out of memory to allocate and must swap out pages, thus slowing down your program. Try loading the programs with the

7

largest memory requirements first (such as Netscape Navigator or Internet Explorer) and then load your less piggy programs.

Q How can I speed up the performance of my input/output (I/O)?

A Several ways are currently available to provide faster I/O via the hardware/software combination of Ultra-Wide SCSI and FireWire. Faster I/O is being rapidly developed for the G3 and future G4 Power Macs.

Q What third-party software is available to manage fonts and control panels?

A Adobe Type Manager Deluxe 4.0 lets you manage your fonts outside of the Fonts folder, thereby increasing the performance of your Mac. ATM 4 allows you to load only those fonts you're currently using and store all others outside of your System Folder. Now Utilities also provides utilities for managing fonts and system extensions to increase performance, but they only work for Mac OS 8.0 or 8.1.

Symantec Suitecase lets you manage control panels and fonts outside of your System Folder, thus providing increased performance by limiting the number of control panels that are active at one time.

Workshop

The Workshop contains quiz questions to help you solidify your understanding of the material. You can find the answers to the quiz questions in Appendix B, "Quiz Answers."

Quiz

1. What hardware functions can affect the overall system performance of your Mac?
2. What software features can affect the performance of your Mac?
3. How can you minimize slowdowns while using networked volumes?
4. How can you maximize the performance of your CD-ROM player?
5. How can you ensure that a large and complex document can be printed successfully?
6. What's the best way to ensure that your disk cache is properly set?
7. When should you use virtual memory?
8. What are some general hints to enhance the performance of your Mac?
9. How can you increase the refresh performance of your monitor?
10. What software can you remove from your System Folder to improve performance without compromising the integrity of your system?

HOUR 8

Mobile Computing

In 1989, Apple introduced the first Macintosh Portable. It ran System 6.0.7 on a 68000 processor, had a 40 MB hard disk and black-and-white screen, and weighed a whopping 15.8 pounds. The best thing about the Macintosh Portable was that it was smaller than its desktop counterpart—the Mac Plus. Today's PowerBooks weigh from five to seven pounds and have up to 4GB of hard disk space, more efficient batteries, and larger color screens. Although the first PowerBook may not have seemed as revolutionary compared to PowerBooks of today, its software still carries forward into Mac OS 8.5. These control panels and extensions brought mobile computing into the '90s and introduced a whole new way of computing to the world. The concepts that define mobile computing center around key design elements only found in PowerBooks. Software and hardware must be optimized to use as little power as possible, yet they must provide the fastest possible performance from the processor, hard disk, any additional connected disks. Video and user interface performance must be fast, as well. This hour explains the origins and usage of mobile computing and Mac OS 8.5. Here are the topics covered:

- A short history of PowerBooks
- All about PowerBook hardware
- Identifying and using PowerBook software
- Optimizing the PowerBook operating system and application software
- A brief look at next generation technologies for mobile computing

Independence Day

The best thing about a PowerBook is that you can use Mac OS 8.5 anywhere you want to go. Both the hardware and software for PowerBooks are designed to take advantage of longer computing times when you're using your battery. They also take advantage of optimal computing equipment, such as a large color screen, and the placement of the CD-ROM and track pad. This all makes mobile computing a pleasant experience. This section covers all PowerBooks supported by Mac OS 8.5 and outlines the special mobile features for PowerBook products as they have evolved over the years.

The First PowerBooks

Mac OS only supports PowerBooks that have a 68LC040 processor or PowerPC processor. The PowerBook models that have 680LC040 processors include the PowerBook 190, 520 and 540 series, and PowerBook Duo 280 models. Earlier PowerBooks will work with Mac OS 7.6.1 and share most of the same software available with Mac OS 8.5. Some of the innovative features these PowerBooks introduced include the ability to turn the PowerBook into a hard disk to connect it to a desktop, the trackball or track pad, and small, but dazzling color screens (instead of the original black-and-white or grayscale screens). The PowerBook Duos introduced the concept of the Duo Dock to extend the hardware and software features of the comparatively light Duo. However, the Duo model ended with the PowerBook 2300, which upgraded this product with a PowerPC processor. The 190 and 520/540 series models have been superceded by the PowerBook 3400, which uses a PowerPC 603e processor.

When PowerBooks were first introduced, one of the larger issues to resolve was how to maximize battery life across the hardware system. Apple designed a power-management system to spin down the hard disk, and, with the 680LC040 Macs, slow down the processor speed when the PowerBook relies on batteries as its only source of power. When the PowerBook is connected to a power outlet, these features can be turned off to restore the maximum performance of the computer.

One feature that's common across all Macs is that they can use the Internet. PowerBooks can take advantage of this through a network or modem connection, similar to the way desktops connect to the Internet. The advantage PowerBooks have over desktops is that you can take any Internet information with you if you're travelling or if the nature of your job requires you to often be away from the office. Some PowerBook modems also support wireless or cellular phone connections, which let you take full advantage of the information on the Internet at any location.

PowerBooks Today

As with all technology, newer and faster products are always available if you wait long enough. The current PowerBooks models are the 2400, 3400 and G3 PowerBooks. Previous models, which share similar features to the current models, are the 5300 and 1400 series models. Some of today's PowerBook hardware features include relatively large 12- and 14-inch color screens, CD-ROM drives, and floppy, hard disk, and removable media drives. PC cards are the standard for adding a modem, network access, or file storage to PowerBooks. All PowerBooks now come standard with infrared receivers located at the back of the unit to provide wireless data transfer.

PowerBook software, shown in Figure 8.1, originally included several control panels for configuring power management and PowerBook settings, such as the SCSI ID of the machine. File Synchronization software allows the PowerBook to compare desktop files to those on the PowerBook drive, updating any that are newer on both computers. Control Strip was introduced with the first PowerBook to provide a shortcut to frequently used Mac OS settings, such as the battery level, monitor bit-depth, AppleTalk status, and sound settings. All these features continue to pervade the current and next generation PowerBooks using the latest G3 processors.

Mac OS 8.5 has actually brought some PowerBook software to the desktop world. Mac OS 8.5 brings the Control Strip feature to most desktop Power Macs. Earlier versions of Mac OS brought the Sleep feature to newer Power Macs. With Mac OS 8.5, Location Manager works with all desktop systems as well as with PowerBooks. Some of the hardware features from desktop software features that have moved to PowerBooks include CD-ROM drives, Ethernet, IDE hard disks, and internal PCI slots. Many consider today's PowerBook hardware and software to be equivalent to that available on desktops.

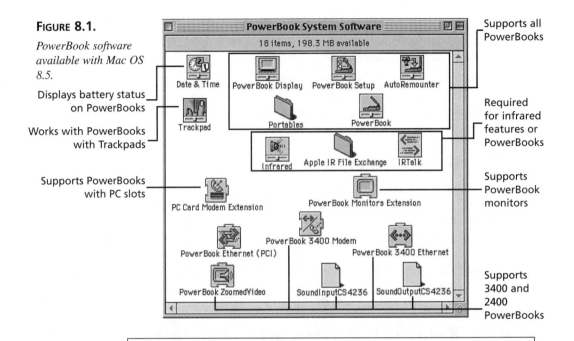

FIGURE **8.1.**

PowerBook software available with Mac OS 8.5.

Displays battery status on PowerBooks

Works with PowerBooks with Trackpads

Supports PowerBooks with PC slots

Supports all PowerBooks

Required for infrared features or PowerBooks

Supports PowerBook monitors

Supports 3400 and 2400 PowerBooks

Apple has announced that Rhapsody will work with the latest PowerBooks (that is, the 1400, 2400, 3400, and G3 models). This means that Macintosh hardware will be able to work with new Mac OS technology over the long term. Additional operating systems that support PowerBook hardware are Linux and Be OS.

Using PowerBook Hardware

PowerBook hardware is fairly straightforward and easy to use. There aren't any cables to work with (as there are with desktop systems) and when you don't have a power supply, the battery is right there in the case, ready to go. Some of the complicated technologies on the PowerBook are the swappable drives and the Plug-and-Play PC cards. In addition to these almost standard features for current PowerBooks, third-party peripherals (such as external monitors, keyboards, networks, and even digital cameras) and SCSI devices (such as external hard drives and scanners) are also supported via the ports located in the back of the PowerBook. This section will review PowerBook hardware features, such as working with battery power, swapping drives, and using PC cards with Mac OS 8.5. If you're already familiar with these technologies, you may skip ahead to the next section.

One of the advantages of a PowerBook is that you can easily move it from room to room or use it while traveling. However, as with desktop systems, you shouldn't use it in a location where moisture can build up on or near the computer. It's also a good idea to avoid locations that are extremely dusty or smoky.

8

Batteries

If any feature is required for a PowerBook, it's the battery. Without it, you wouldn't be able to do mobile computing. Having a battery introduces several additional considerations for PowerBooks owners: When do I recharge it? How do I maintain it? Which software do I use? Which type of battery do I buy? How many batteries do I buy? And when is my battery in danger? Most batteries will last for several years without needing to be replaced. However, the longevity of most current batteries will begin to deteriorate after about a year. The status of the battery is displayed in the Mac OS 8.5 menu bar, as shown in Figure 8.2. If the battery is being recharged, it will show a lightening bolt over the battery icon. The following is a list of general steps to follow to keep your battery maintained:

- If you use your battery, let it run out of charge before reconnecting to the wall outlet, which recharges the battery.
- Keep a spare battery handy, just in case you misplace or let your current battery run low on its charge.
- Recondition the battery regularly if you use it frequently.
- When not in use, the battery should be stored in a cool, dry place.

Apple provides battery recharging hardware for most PowerBooks. The recharger lets you recharge more than one battery at a time and will recharge the battery faster than if you're using the PowerBook to recharge it. Several third-party companies, such as VST, provide larger batteries for just about every PowerBook model. Larger batteries extend the amount of time you can use your PowerBook. However, they also usually add a good amount of heft to the PowerBook. Cigarette lighter adapters are also available for when you're travelling. Also, Keep It Simple Solutions makes a solar panel that can extend the battery life of PowerBooks while you're working in the sun.

FIGURE 8.2.

The battery indicator in the Mac OS 8.5 menu bar.

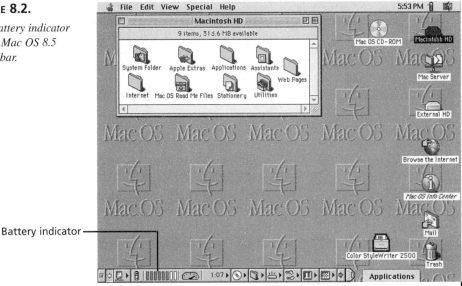

Battery indicator ────

When the battery runs low on a PowerBook, you may lose data. Mac OS 8.5 brings up a dialog box letting you know you're running low on battery power. However, in some situations (for example, when the PowerBook is asleep for a long period of time), you might not see this warning, and the PowerBook will shut itself down when it runs out of battery power.

Swappable Drives

Swappable drives are one of the more convenient features in PowerBooks. Most models include a floppy drive in addition to the CD-ROM drive. Third-party companies also provide hard disks, Zip drives, and AC/DC power adapters that you can swap while the PowerBook is asleep. The swappable drive port allows for the upgrading of these components with minimal software installation and virtually no learning curve. Any swappable device slides into the bay located at the right rear of the PowerBook. To remove the device, do the following:

- Unmount any volumes on the desktop
- Put the PowerBook to sleep using the Special menu in Finder
- Slide the button underneath the swappable drive
- Slide the mechanism out of the PowerBook

If you travel extensively and don't connect to your network long enough to backup your PowerBook, a good alternative is to use a Zip removable drive or a swappable hard disk to back up the data on your PowerBook. If you have a modem, you can also email an important file to yourself to create a short-term backup for any documents you might not want to back up into another folder on your hard disk.

PowerBook 1400s were the first PowerBooks to support internal CD-ROM drives. CD-ROM drives add a whole new dimension to mobile computing. Not only can they mount large read-only volumes onto the desktop, but they can playback audio CDs and support a bootable Mac OS 8.5 CD-ROM, just like Macintosh desktop systems. The CD Strip module installed on desktops and PowerBooks with Mac OS 8.5 allows you to control audio CD playback from the Control Strip, saving time and battery life by not having to leave the Apple CD Audio Player application open when you change audio CDs. The CD-ROM drive may also soon be upgraded with a DVD-ROM drive as Apple continues to add new technologies to its PowerBooks.

If you're running your PowerBook from its battery, you should be aware of the additional power consumption requirements of a CD-ROM or additional hard disk plugged in as a swappable device.

PC Cards

PC cards were first introduced with the first PowerPC PowerBook—the 5300 model. The first Apple product to use PC cards, which were formerly called PCMCIA cards, was the Newton. Actually, the Newton PC card works with the PowerBook PC card slot. However, it only lets you store 1 MB of data on it. A more practical application of PC card storage is as an adapter for other memory card formats. For example, I have an adapter card by Fuji that lets me take memory from my QuickTake 200 camera (which stores up to 40 images) and mount it on my PowerBook's desktop without having to install any additional software to have Mac OS recognize the card.

The most popular PC card products are Ethernet 10-Base T and modem cards. Current modem cards range in speed from 28.8, 33.6, and 33.6 × 2 (which supports up to 53Kbps). Most PC card modems work with cellular phones, thus boosting your mobility to almost anywhere your cell phone can dial. Although some PowerBooks, such as the 3400 and G3 series, have a modem and Ethernet port card installed inside, the PC card is a small, easy-to-upgrade form factor for adding networking and connectivity to your PowerBook.

Using PowerBook Software

PowerBooks have a more common set of system software than desktops that is largely associated with mobility. All PowerBooks use the same PowerBook control panels; however, PowerPC PowerBooks, including the PowerBook 190 series, have additional features, such as infrared networking, PC card support, and track pads. PowerBook Duos are unique because their Mac OS installation must support the docking option, which consists of Ethernet and additional external drives, including a CD-ROM drive.

Finder offers many alternative features for PowerBooks running Mac OS 8.5. You can put Finder to sleep, for example, instead of shutting down the system. Despite PowerBooks having a smaller screen space than desktop models, Mac OS 8.5 installs the Control Strip for fast access to controls such as AppleTalk and File Sharing. There's also a battery monitor in the menu bar, courtesy of the Date & Time control panel, as well as in the Control Strip. Location Manager also facilitates reconfiguring Mac OS settings if you travel to locations requiring unique software settings. These features are geared towards optimizing both ease of use and battery life for all supported PowerBooks.

Mac OS 8.5 PowerBook Features

For Mac OS 8.5, Apple created a program called Internet Setup Assistant. This program is included with Mac OS 8.5 in a folder labeled Internet. This assistant automates the process of configuring your Mac by walking you through 10 steps. Note that you need certain information provided by your Internet Service Provider or System Administrator in order to complete the dialog boxes in this assistant.

Control Panels

Out of all the system software Mac OS 8.5 puts into the System Folder, PowerBook software is probably the easiest to identify. Most of the files have the name PowerBook in them, and others have features, such as IR, that are not on most desktop computers. PowerBook control panels, such as TrackPad, PowerBook Display, Express Modem, and PowerBook Setup, are created specifically for hardware features found on PowerBooks. These control panels let you adjust settings for power management, external ports, devices, and software. This makes mobile computing easier to use from day to day.

Control Strip

It's not just for PowerBooks anymore! Control Strip is the narrow strip of software most commonly seen on PowerBooks. It provides easy access to many system software features, such as AppleTalk, File Sharing, CD-ROM playback, sound volume, and desktop printing, as well as various PowerBooks settings, such as battery level and hard disk sleep. Mac OS 8.5 installs Control Strip on all PowerBooks and Power Macs with PCI expansion slots (see Figure 8.3).

Each Control Strip module can be relocated within the Control Strip by dragging and dropping the module you want to move. The location of Control Strip can be changed by holding down the Option key and dragging Control Strip to either side of your screen. The font and font size can also be configured in the Control Strip control panel.

8

FIGURE 8.3.

The Control Strip control panel and modules.

Hides or shows control strip

Command key for hiding control strip

Sets font in control strip

The following are some Control Strip modules you're likely to see or use:

- **AppleTalk Switch.** Changes AppleTalk from active to inactive, or vice versa.
- **Battery Monitor.** Reflects the power source for your PowerBook, such as whether your battery is running out of juice or whether you're using a socket-based power source.
- **CD Strip.** A mini version of an Audio CD player with track selection, volume, pause, stop, and play controls.
- **File Sharing Strip.** Turns personal File Sharing on or off.
- **HD Spin Down.** Spins down a PowerBook's internal hard drive.
- **Location Manager.** This module gives you access to all the Location Manager modules installed in your System Folder. It lets you configure your PowerBook to adjust to changes in geographical location.
- **Monitor Bit-Depth.** Gives you access to change to any available bit-depth for the monitor(s) connected to your Mac.
- **Monitor Resolution.** Gives you access to all support monitor resolutions.
- **PC Setup Switch.** Lets you switch from your Mac to your PC, and back again.
- **Power Settings.** Contains power-related settings for PowerBooks.
- **Printer Selector.** Contains a list of desktop printers created by using Desktop Printing.
- **Sleep Now.** Puts PowerBooks and supported Macs to sleep.

- **Sound Volume.** Displays and lets you select the sound volume.
- **Video Mirroring.** Turns video mirroring on or off.

Most of the PowerBook-specific control panels listed here work across all PowerBooks running Mac OS 8.5. The following control panels are essential for configuring PowerBook-specific features (such as how the PowerBook runs on batteries versus how it runs when connected to a static power source):

- **AutoRemounter.** Keeps your network servers mounted on your desktop after you put your PowerBook to sleep and then wake it up. You can also reconnect any shared disks that were disconnected when you put your PowerBook to sleep. Automatic and password-required remounting are additional settings in this control panel.
- **Date & Time.** Displays how much life your battery has left.
- **Password Security.** Enables you to set password access to your 5300, 190, 1400, 2300,2400 or 3400 PowerBook at startup or when it's awakened from sleep. This control panel consists of On, Off, and Settings buttons. The Settings button brings up the Password dialog box as it will appear during startup or after the PowerBooks wakes from sleep.
- **PowerBook Display.** Lets you mirror your PowerBook display to an external monitor. This is a handy feature for presentations, such as working with a large-screen monitor.
- **PowerBook.** Sets several sleep-related settings for a PowerBook running on a battery or off a power source. This includes hard drive and system sleep, as well as screen dimming settings. Fewer or more settings are displayed in Easy or Custom mode, respectively.
- **PowerBook Setup.** Lets you set the SCSI ID of your PowerBook when it's in SCSI mode (using the darker gray SCSI cable). You can also change your modem settings to Normal or Compatible. The Automatic Wake-Up setting appears at the bottom of this control panel.
- **TrackPad.** Lets you set several options for PowerBooks with track pads. This control panel lets you set options for tracking speed, double-click speed, and usage of clicking, dragging, and drag lock.

Extensions

The following is a list of PowerBook-specific extensions in Mac OS 8.5. The PowerBook Monitors extension is the most general file and works across several PowerBook models:

- **PowerBook Monitors Extension.** Works with the Monitors & Sound control panel, as well as with the Monitors control panel, to support PowerBook displays.

- **PowerBook 3400 Ethernet.** Supports built-in Ethernet on this PowerBook model.

- **PowerBook 3400 Modem.** Supports the built-in modem on this PowerBook model.

- **SoundInputCS4236.** Supports sound input on PowerBooks newer than the 3400.

- **SoundOutputCS4236.** Supports sound output on PowerBooks newer than the 3400.

> Third-party software, such as Now Utilities Super Boomerang, provides easier navigation and file access for opening and saving files (available in the standard file dialog boxes).

Applications

PowerBook applications are located in the Portables folder and are installed in the Mac OS 8.5 Apple Extras folder (see Figure 8.4). These applications are supported on all PowerBooks, and they're almost a requirement if you want to make your PowerBook all it can be.

FIGURE 8.4.

PowerBook applications.

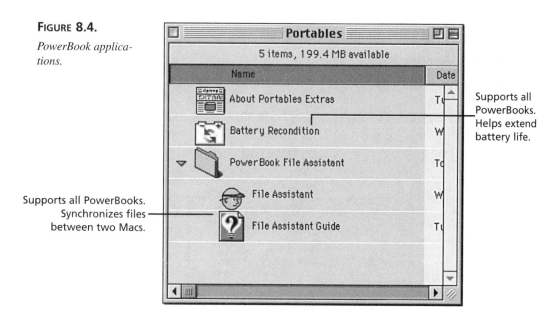

Supports all PowerBooks. Helps extend battery life.

Supports all PowerBooks. Synchronizes files between two Macs.

PowerBook File Assistant

PowerBook File Assistant 1.0 lets you synchronize your Mac's files and folders. Synchronization is helpful if you have two computers and want to keep the same set of data on both. File Assistant works with a PowerBook, with a desktop Mac or network server, or with a Duo and DuoDock. The File Assistant extension has been incorporated with the system file for Mac OS 8.5.

IR Software

One of the more advanced features in the latest Power Mac PowerBooks (all models except for the 2300 Duo) is their wireless networking capability. This technology is called *IRTalk*. PowerBooks can share data across their IRTalk ports in lieu of using a required cable for LocalTalk or Ethernet. The following list identifies each software piece for PowerBook IR and provides a brief explanation of the hardware supported and what each file does:

- **IRTalk.** This extension lets 5300, 190, 1400, and 3400 series PowerBooks network with each other by using their infrared modules. This extension works with Open Transport, LocalTalk, and Ethernet to enable Macs with IRTalk to send information to each other.

- **Infrared control panel.** Works with the IRTalk extension to let 5300, 190, 1400, and 3400 series PowerBooks share information across an infrared network.

- **Apple IR File Exchange.** The application that enables the IR technology to come to life with a PowerBook.

Battery Recondition

Battery reconditioning helps to restore small portions of the battery that can be lost during regular battery use. Reconditioning is not a requirement, but it gives your battery the best performance it can offer. The Battery Recondition application takes a battery and drains it completely. Once the application is finished, you'll need to let the battery recharge in the PowerBook before unplugging the PowerBook from a wall outlet power source. Figure 8.5 shows the main window of the Battery Recondition application.

FIGURE 8.5.

The Battery Recondition application.

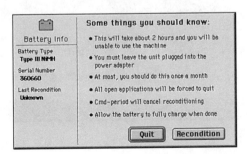

For best results, run Battery Recondition over night so the PowerBook can recharge the battery completely. The process of completely draining and then recharging allows the battery to perform optimally.

8

As Good as It Gets

Once you're familiar with all your PowerBook's hardware and software features, mobile computing is as good as it can be. Of course, a faster PowerBook always brings a more productive experience.

Using PowerBook Software

To synchronize files between two Macs, double-click the File Assistant icon, which should be located in the Portables folder in the Apple Extras folder on the hard disk. You can select the Guide for File Assistant to learn how to use it, or you can follow the general steps listed here:

- Select an item to synchronize
- Select the second computer, which contains the file with which you want to synchronize
- Select Synchronize Now from the Synchronize menu

To exchange a file over the IR port, open the Apple IR File Exchange application located in the Apple IR File Exchange folder in the Apple Extras folder on the hard disk. You can select the Guide for Apple IR File Exchange to learn how to use it, or you can follow the general steps listed here:

- Turn AppleTalk on
- Select IR Sender from the Windows menu
- Select Sending or Receiving Status to monitor the data being transferred over IR
- Quit the application when the file exchange is complete

If you have files named Assistant Tidbits 1 and Assistant Tidbits 2 in your System Folder, drag them to the Trash Can. These files are from previous versions of File Assistant.

Battery Recondition helps maintain and, in some cases, prolong the life of most PowerBook batteries. The latest PowerBooks, such as the 3400 and G3 series, which use Lithium Ion batteries, do not need to run Battery Recondition. To use Battery Recondition, double-click its icon, which should also be located in the Portables folder in the Apple Extras folder on the hard disk. This application might not work with some third-party batteries. If this is the case, Battery Recondition will return a message indicating this in its main window. Allow several hours for this application to recondition your battery. You'll not be able to use your PowerBook while this application is running.

Optimizing Software for Mobility

If you're happy with the overall performance of Mac OS 8.5 and your applications running on your PowerBook, you don't need to try to improve the performance of the software. Some applications are better suited for use with a PowerBook than others. For example, if an application always runs in memory, thus reducing the frequency it has to work the hard disk, this improves your battery life and gives you a faster software experience. Since PowerBooks have been introduced, many applications take mobile performance into account and try not to write to the disk more than necessary. Each time an application writes to the hard disk, you use up battery power, but you also must wait for the disk drive to spin up if it has not been in use. Figure 8.6 presents the optimum settings for the PowerBook control panel to provide the longest life for your battery.

FIGURE 8.6.

Recommended settings for the PowerBook control panel for a battery-conscious PowerBook.

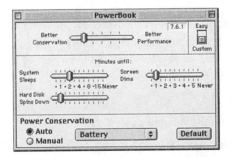

If you're not sure which application is best suited for your PowerBook, try using a demo version to see if you find its performance satisfactory prior to purchasing the full software product.

WANT TO LEARN MORE?

For the latest information about PowerBooks, go to Apple's URL for PowerBooks at
`http://www.powerbooks.apple.com`.

A Short Look at What's Coming Soon

Today's PowerBooks are some of the fastest computers in the world. However, this will change over the next few months, and along with this change, new technologies will arrive that will make mobile computing an even better experience. Some of the more visible technologies are DVD video and DVD-ROM drives. DVD technology is most visibly associated with Hollywood movie titles, which contain MPEG 2 video and Dolby 5.1 channel sound. DVD is likely to replace current CD-ROM technology found in today's PowerBooks.

USB is another new technology. It's an acronym for the Universal Serial Bus, which is a standard feature on PC desktops and portable computers. USB provides a higher bandwidth for data throughput than its current technology—the serial port. One of the more recent technology transitions has been the G3 processor. Apple has already announced it plans to take advantage of a new copper process that will be used with the next generation PowerPC processors for its next generation computers. The copper process will provide faster hardware performance than current processor technology. Lastly, hard disks are likely to provide more storage for a lower price. Look for PowerBooks with even more storage space and faster access times in addition to all the other great technologies on the horizon for PowerBooks.

Summary

In this hour, we reviewed mobile computing system software and applications installed with Mac OS 8.5. I explained hardware and software features common among PowerBooks and showed you how to identify and use them. You also learned how to select software to optimize your mobile computing experience. Finally, I briefly discussed the new technologies that are likely to be found in future PowerBooks.

Term Review

battery   Every PowerBook has one. The type of battery has changed from model to model, starting with lead acid in the original Mac Portable to Lithium Ion in the current PowerBooks. Different types of batteries can mean longer wireless computing time on your PowerBook. More than likely, new types of batteries that have longer lives between recharging will be available in the next-generation PowerBooks.

Battery Recondition   This application works with previous PowerBooks to maintain and help prolong the life of the battery.

File Synchronization   The PowerBook application that lets you synchronize files between your PowerBook and a desktop computer.

IR   The infrared connectivity features on PowerBooks. This technology works with Apple's IR File Exchange, enabling you to send files over a wireless network connection.

Location Manager   Apple's control panel for making it easier to change location settings as you move your PowerBook from location to location.

PC cards   Previously known as *PCMCIA cards*, PC cards are about the size of a credit card. The latest PowerBooks have two PC card slots. PC cards enable Ethernet, modem, and storage features on your PowerBook.

swappable drives   The latest PowerBooks let you plug and play CD-ROM drives, floppy drives, hard disks, Zip disks, and other devices.

USB   The Universal Serial Bus is a new standard that may eventually replace the serial port on PowerBooks.

Q&A

Q **Which PowerBook features can I use on my PowerBook?**

A If you have a PowerBook 520 or 540, you can use the PowerBook control panels and PC cards. The 5300, 190, and 2400 PowerBooks support IR, and the 1400, 3400 and G3 PowerBooks support all the previously mentioned features and they include a CD-ROM drive, as well. PowerBook Duos can be docked to support all the same hardware peripherals as desktops. When not docked, however, they only work with the standard PowerBook control panels, modem, and serial port.

Q **Which PowerBook software works with desktop computers?**

A Apple File Assistant.

Q **Which PowerBook should I buy?**

A As with all computers, always buy the fastest processor you can afford.

Q **What PowerBook software will I use most frequently?**

A Once the Mac OS 8.5 PowerBook control panels are configured, you probably won't be changing them very often. If you need to synchronize files across computers, you'll be using File Assistant frequently. Aside from this, you're likely to be watching the battery icon and using the Sleep menu item quite often.

Workshop

The Workshop contains quiz questions to help you solidify your understanding of the material covered. You can find the answers to the quiz questions in Appendix B, "Quiz Answers."

Quiz

1. What makes a PowerBook different than a desktop Power Mac?

2. Which PowerBooks support PC cards, IR, and swappable drives?

3. Which control panel lets you set the SCSI ID for the PowerBook?

4. How often should you recondition your battery?

5. Where does Mac OS 8.5 install PowerBook application software on the hard disk?

HOUR 9

Fonts

This hour covers the following font-related issues:

- Understanding fonts and type
- Knowing the difference between the varieties of type used on the Mac: bitmapped, PostScript, and TrueType
- Learning about OpenType and other future developments
- Installing and viewing fonts
- Adding the polish to your documents via well-behaved types

Let's begin by taking a brief look at how fonts have evolved on the computer as well as Apple's important role in that process.

History of Fonts

Looking at the world of microcomputers today, it's difficult to imagine the primitive font technology of 10 to 15 years ago. At that time, microcomputers (and printers) were text based and there was only the weakest of links between what was seen on screen and what appeared from the printer. The original microcomputers didn't even have the option of a graphics display— a single set of characters was all the display could handle.

The next generation of microcomputers enabled you to use *dual-mode* monitors to display graphics or text (the keyword here is *or*). You could work in text mode, where characters were retrieved from a character generator chip, or in a graphics mode, where graphics were drawn by selectively turning screen dots on or off. Text and graphics were kept completely separate. You had to switch between modes to edit text and to see the results of your work. Although still primitive, this is the method used by many microcomputer systems today. On these systems, the actual text editing is done with the system's built-in character set. You must use a special page preview to see even a rough approximation of the printed page.

Apple changed all of that with the introduction of a microcomputer based on the concept of *WYSIWYG*, which stands for "What You See Is What You Get" and is pronounced "wizzy wig." The effect of the Macintosh's new display technology was revolutionary. Most microcomputer developers today are scrambling to add WYSIWYG support to both their applications and to the operating environment.

The goal in a WYSIWYG environment is to have what appears on the screen be as close as possible to what appears on the printed page. Text and graphics can be intermixed intuitively, both on the screen and on the paper. Graphics are drawn onscreen directly, without you having to go into other modes of operation, and text is displayed as it will print. Although it's not an inherent requirement of a WYSIWYG environment, flexibility in the type and style of characters used for text has played an important role in the popularity of the WYSIWYG environment.

This flexibility in character styles, along with the ability to mix text and graphics, has revolutionized how personal computers are used. The Macintosh introduced the concept of publishing on the "desktop" to the business world. The horizons have expanded even further with the concepts of color desktop publishing, desktop animation, desktop sound studios, and desktop multimedia.

Along with the introduction of desktop publishing (DTP) came the introduction of a new vocabulary and a new set of standards. In reality, the creation and management of characters is much more complex than displaying and printing graphics. This hour begins with an introduction to the terms that are used to describe characters in the desktop publishing environment and the methods for displaying them on the screen and printing them on the page. Understanding these terms is crucial in order for you to get the most out of the WYSIWYG environment.

What Are Fonts and Type?

The most important term in this discussion is *font*. Unfortunately, the word *font* highlights one of the greatest problems in desktop publishing—people use it to refer to very different things. Working on the Macintosh, particularly in desktop publishing, requires an understanding of the technical jargon used to describe the font technology as well as the jargon of the typesetter. The desktop publishing terminology of the Macintosh is based on typography, but with some important differences.

To most Macintosh users, the term *font* refers to the name of the character style, such as Geneva, Palatino, or Times. To a graphics artist who is used to using the terms of typography, the term *font* refers to a single style of letters (for example, 12-point bold Palatino). To a Macintosh programmer, the term refers to the resource files used to store the information to create the image both on the screen and on paper. This section explains each of these meanings and why all of these views are important.

Basic Typography

Many of the original terms used to describe characters and character styles are still used today. Although in the electronic age, they no longer have physical equivalents. Originally, each character that appeared on the printed page was formed individually out of hot metal. Today, the letters are formed electronically with a collection of dots (or *pixels*).

Understanding Character Sets

Oned term that shares a common definition between the Macintosh DTP environment and typography is *character set*. A character set refers to the entire collection of symbols that can be printed in a particular character style. In the original microcomputer environment, this set was the ASCII character set and consisted of 128 characters of which approximately 70 are printable. ASCII stands for American Standard Code for Information Interchange and is pronounced "ask key."

All the characters sets currently used on microcomputers share these common characters, but most go far beyond the 128-character limit. Beyond the original standard characters, different character sets may contain different symbols. Most character sets on the Macintosh contain about 150 printable characters.

The characters in each character set consist of the characters typed from the keyboard with no modifier keys, those typed with the Shift key held down, those typed with the Option key held down, and those typed with both the Shift and Option keys held down. The characters produced without any modifier keys and those produced with the Shift key are shown on the actual keyboard keys (also called the *key caps*). The characters created with the Option and Shift-Option combinations are not represented on the keyboard. These characters include many useful symbols, such as the copyright, trademark, and registered trademark symbols as well as the degree symbol and other mathematical signs.

Unless you use these special characters regularly, it's difficult to remember the key combinations for them. Fortunately, Apple includes a desk accessory called Key Caps that enables you to identify the location of the symbol from a character set that you want to use.

A WORD ABOUT UNICODE

Unicode is the Wintel standard for depicting international character sets on the computer. Apple now supports Unicode in Mac OS 8.5. Unicode is a hidden update to Mac OS 8.5 that will enable you to transfer documents between Macs and PCs without requiring character substitutes for those pesky bullets, trademark symbols, circumflexes, and umlauts that you can create easily on the Mac but not so easily on the PC. With Unicode on the Mac, PCs can now display your fancy symbols, because they're now understood on the PC side. Unicode also brings the Mac into the worldwide standard for translating languages into computer code.

Key Caps is distributed as part of Mac OS 8.5 and is located on your Apple menu. When you select Key Caps, the screen blanks, except for the menu bar, and a representation of the keyboard is displayed. A new menu appears, called Key Caps, that lists all the available character sets by font name. Selecting a font name causes the symbols from that font to display on the keyboard in the plain style. Figure 9.1 shows a standard Key Caps window.

FIGURE 9.1.

This is the first level of Key Caps using the Palatino font.

Pressing a modifier key causes the characters that can be produced with that key to display. With no modifiers, the 8 key from the keyboard produces the number 8. With the Shift key held down, it produces an asterisk (*). In most fonts, holding down the Option key and pressing the 8 key results in a bullet symbol (ï). The Option and Shift key modifiers produce a degree symbol (_). Each key (including the letter keys) generally can create four symbols. Key Caps is simply a way to locate the special symbols; it's not needed to actually use these symbols. All the printable characters can be entered into any Macintosh program by first selecting the appropriate font name and then pressing the key combination. The symbols can be modified like any other member of the character set.

Understanding Font Families and Typefaces

The names listed on the standard Font menu in the Macintosh environment actually refer to *font families*. A font family is a collection of character sets that share a similar design. Each font family consists of a number of *typefaces*. A typeface is a particular style of character. There are two primary types of typefaces: those containing little hooks at the ends of their forms, called *serif* type (for example, Palatino, Times and New York), and those without these hooks, called *sans serif* type (for example, Helvetica and Geneva). The impact and readability of text is affected by whether serif or sans serif type is used.

The term *style* is used to refer to both the specific typeface being used and to the minor modifications made to that typeface. Some of the options on the Macintosh Style menu have nothing to do with the actual typeface. For example, Underline simply draws a line slightly below the characters, and Strikethrough draws a straight line over the original typeface. Other options modify the current typeface. Examples of this are Outline and Shadow. These commands work by creating a special effect based on the individual character. Outline simply draws a black line around the original character and then changes the character to white. Shadow adds a slightly thicker line along the bottom and to the left of all lines. Figure 9.2 shows the six most common effects from the Style menu.

FIGURE 9.2.

These are the type styles available for most fonts.

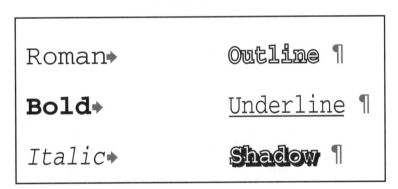

The difference between typefaces is most clearly shown with the italic style. The characters produced with the italic style are an entirely different typeface than those used for plain text. The text presented in Table 9.1 demonstrates this most clearly. The italic characters complement the plain text, but each character has its own design. Occasionally, the italic typeface is not available. In that case, it's represented by an *oblique style*. An oblique style simply takes the plain character and places it at an angle. When you select an italic PostScript font, it's displayed onscreen as an oblique style, but it prints as an actual italic typeface.

TABLE 9.1. PLAIN VERSUS ITALIC TYPEFACE.

A a	T t	Z z	2 8	& %	© _
A a	*T t*	*Z z*	*2 8*	*& %*	*© _*

Most of the typefaces in use today were designed for lead type and have been around for many years. As the industry has converted to electronic type, these typefaces have also been converted. Each company that produces an electronic version of a typeface may change the style slightly. Because of this, a document created in Palatino may look slightly different when produced on different printers or by different systems.

Understanding Fonts

In typography, the term *font* refers to a particular member of a font family (the *typeface*) in a particular size. In traditional typesetting, each variation of a letter was cut from a piece of metal. Not only did each typeface need to be cut independently, but each size of each typeface as well. Type is measured in terms of *points.* There are 72 points to the inch, and a single point is approximately .0138 inches. Using these terms, 12-point Palatino bold is an individual font, as is 10-point Palatino bold and 12-point Palatino plain. In Macintosh terminology, *Palatino* is the font (standing for font family), *12 point* is the size, and *bold* is the style. Therefore, each font in typography terms is represented by the font name, font size, and font style in Macintosh terms.

Fonts on the Macintosh do not act or look like the type on a typewriter. In typewriter type (and some computer type), each character has the same width and is therefore called a *monospaced* or *fixed-width* character. The advantage to fix-width fonts is that all the characters are positioned in a predictable location. Unfortunately, fixed-width fonts, such as Courier or Monaco, are not as legible as fonts whose character widths vary. The *proportional-spaced* fonts (where letters can have different widths) are easier to decipher and are therefore preferred for publishing. Figure 9.3 illustrates the difference between monospaced and proportional-spaced fonts.

FIGURE 9.3.

A comparison of monospaced and proportional-spaced fonts.

```
This is a monospaced font called Courier ¶
```
This is a proportional-spaced font called Palatino ¶

Spacing Between Letters

There are a number of special terms used to describe the position of characters. *Leading* is the space between baselines. When typesetters used to set type, they would place varying widths of leading in between the lines of type to separate them. Today, the distance between the baseline of one line of text and the next is called *leading* or *line spacing*. Leading is also measured in points.

The horizontal distance between letters is called the *letterspace*. Type is easier on the eyes if the space between letters is varied, based on the shape of the letter. For example, the letter combination "VAW" looks best if the three characters are moved closer together. The process of adjusting this distance for the best appearance is called *kerning*. Most sophisticated desktop publishing programs support the capability to vary the distance between letters.

It can be seen that the Macintosh revolutionized the display of text on the computer screen by providing an environment in which professional typesetting functions could be performed electronically. It takes very sophisticated software to control these functions. Not surprisingly, the computer side of desktop publishing developed its own special vocabulary.

The Computer Vocabulary

Each image produced using a computer must be available for three uses: display, storage, and printing. The various font technologies are actually different methods for dealing with requirements of each of these arenas. The needs of the display technology must always be balanced with the need to store data in a usable format.

Word processing files consist of the codes representing each of the letters (the ASCII codes and the Macintosh extensions). These codes are universal, regardless of the technology used to display them. In traditional systems, the codes were sent to the screen, which used a screen font to display the characters, and to the printer, which used a printer font to print the characters. As printers became more sophisticated and offered a wider variety of fonts, this system began to fail. A common solution used by other computer vendors was to display the text onscreen for editing using the built-in screen font and provide a graphics mode for previewing what it would look like on the printed page.

Apple's commitment to the WYSIWYG ideal required a different approach in the design of how data is presented than had been applied to personal computing in the past. In order to accomplish this realistic presentation, the Macintosh's designers found that the best way to display information was to operate in graphics mode at all times. The Macintosh replaced the cumbersome dual-mode method of displaying data onscreen with a bitmapped display method where every character, line, and complex graphic is created using a pattern of dots. This way, text is treated like a graphics object and drawn onscreen directly. There are no character-generator chips in a Macintosh.

The Macintosh screen drawing capability is controlled by a library of fast graphics routines collectively called *QuickDraw*. QuickDraw controls the drawing of any item on the Macintosh screen, including characters. Because everything is drawn onto the screen through these QuickDraw routines, the Macintosh can display a myriad of formats for information. QuickDraw enables the Macintosh system to display type in an almost-WYSIWYG fashion. Hence, different type styles can be displayed on the screen to look almost as good as they do in print.

> **A WORD ABOUT QUICKDRAW**
>
> QuickDraw was part of the original Macintosh system and was not intended for the complex output technologies currently available. The original QuickDraw routines have been supplemented by new code that's designed to be faster, more efficient, plus handle color. These new routines are variations of the original QuickDraw and are referred to as ColorQuickDraw, QuickerDraw, and a host of other names.

In the final analysis, both screens and printers create their images using small dots. In fact, the biggest difference between various output devices is the size of their dots. Whereas QuickDraw is always used to translate stored information into the dot pattern to be displayed on the screen, a variety of methods may be used to translate the stored information to the printed page.

Most font technologies get their names from the method they use to translate the stored information to the dot pattern used by the printer. The actual image for fonts may be from a stored bitmapped representation of the font or it may be created from an outline (using mathematical algorithms to represent each character). These two methods are the starting point for all the differences between font technologies. You should keep in mind that a single font technology might use bitmapped fonts for one purpose and outline fonts for another.

Bitmapped Fonts

The basic idea behind bitmapped fonts is that each dot in the final image is described individually. These dots may be screen dots, printer dots, or pixels. *Pixel* is probably one of the most misunderstood words in the computer industry. The following definitions are not universal (other authors may use the terms differently), but they are provided here in an effort to make the discussion of font technology a little clearer.

The term *pixel* comes from the phrase *picture element* and is used when discussing the storage of bitmapped images. Just as screen dots refer to the dots on the displayed image, and printer dots refer to the dots on the printed image, pixels refer to the "dots" used when storing the image in the computer's memory. However, unlike screen dots and printer dots, pixels cannot be measured in "dots per inch." Instead, images are discussed in terms of "bits per pixel." The number of bits used to store each pixel determines the number of colors (or shades of gray) recorded for the image. The relationship between pixels in memory and either printer dots or screen dots is called *bitmapping*.

HOW THE MAC STORES BITMAPPED IMAGES

The pixel information stored in memory corresponds directly to what's onscreen (and in some systems to those printed on the page). Each dot onscreen is *mapped* to a location in memory, and each entry in memory is recorded as a series of *binary digits* (or *bits*). On monochrome screens, each screen dot can either be black (a value of 1) or white (a value of 0). These are the only valid binary digits. To record color information for a screen dot requires using more than one bit for each screen dot. When you increase the number of bits in memory associated with each screen dot, you increase the variety of colors or shades of gray that can be stored for each screen dot. A 16-color (or 16-level grayscale) requires four bits for each screen dot. A 256-color (or 256-level grayscale) display requires eight bits for each screen dot.

Resolution is measured as the number of dots per inch an output device can produce. This may be either a monitor or a printer. The original Macintosh had a video resolution (on its built-in screen) of 71 dpi (dots per inch), and the original ImageWriter had a resolution of 72 dpi. Because the screens only produced black-and-white images, the pixels required only one bit. Therefore, an image could be stored in a single format using the same information used to create the screen dots and the printer dots. This is the simplest form of a bitmapped image, where a pixel, screen dot, and printer are all represented as being "on" or "off."

The video resolution of the Macintosh hasn't changed much since those days. Of course, screen sizes have changed, which means, given the same number of dots per inch, the absolute number of dots has increased. This is often measured in terms of the *pixel count* of the screen. What is actually being measured is the number of screen dots. The compact Macintoshes have 9-inch diagonal screens with a resolution of 74 dpi. The Apple color monitor has a pixel count of 480 vertically and 640 horizontally, and a resulting resolution of 80 dpi. Full-page and two-page displays retain the same pixel count ratios (80 dpi and 77 dpi, respectively). Because an image is stored with the same set of pixels, an image displayed on different-sized monitors will be a slightly different size on each one.

Outline Fonts

The description of an outline font is not based on pixels but rather on a mathematical equation describing the font's characters. Outline fonts are converted to screen or printer dots using a series of routines that convert mathematical descriptions into printable images. The most common page-description language used in printing is PostScript, which was developed by Adobe Systems. Apple and Microsoft have developed a second language called TrueType, which is discussed later this hour.

Outline fonts have a number of advantages over bitmapped fonts. Because outline fonts are not based on the static number of pixels in an area, each font instruction set can be used to create a character of any size or proportion by changing the equation proportionally to expand or contract the outline's shape and size. A related advantage is that outline fonts take up much less storage space, because a single file can manage all printing tasks. The most important difference is that outline fonts can be used at any resolution without distortion.

The process of converting an outline font to a series of pixels for use by an output device (whether the screen or printer) is referred to as *rasterizing*. When producing printed images, the rasterizing may be done by the computer or the printer. To produce an image for the screen, the outline must be rasterized by a portion of the operating system.

Some people think of outline fonts as being described in PostScript. PostScript is one of a variety of programming languages that can be used to describe the mathematical relationships of outline fonts. Its popularity comes from the fact that it was the first and, until recently, the only standard available for use with microcomputers. The Macintosh uses PostScript only as a printer language. PostScript fonts that are displayed onscreen are stored as bitmaps. As mentioned earlier, Microsoft and Apple joined forces to create the TrueType standard. The TrueType addition allows the use of outline fonts for screen display.

The process of rasterizing an image (converting it from outline form to a collection of dots that can be displayed or printed) consists of three steps:

1. The basic outline is scaled to the desired size.
2. The hinting program matches the scaled outline to a grid of pixels scaled to the resolution of the printer (or monitor). If there are places where a pixel is not clearly either on or off, a table of hinting information is consulted to determine the specific setting. This step improves the look of fonts at sizes that do not neatly match the resolution of the output device. At this point, the information describes each dot for a specific resolution.

3. The scanner converts the information from a collection of pixels to an actual bitmap. It's this bitmap that's passed to the printer or video memory.

Hinting is the most important phase of this conversion process. Hints are routines used to exactly fit the outline to the proper sized pixel grid and to adjust the character to fit that grid (known as *grid fitting*). Hints are most needed when there are few pixels to work with (such as with small size fonts or low resolution printers or monitors). Each character has a set of hints stored in its font file. Hints are rarely needed when printing or displaying above 600 dpi.

In spite of the work required to produce a usable image, outline fonts are more flexible to use, because they're not tied to a predetermined number of pixels. The amount of resolution information stored in an outline font is infinite. Only when the outline font is adjusted to a particular size and resolution is the information converted to pixels. Therefore, you can increase the resolution of the printer (for example, from a 600-dpi LaserWriter to a 2,540-dpi Linotronic) without distortion.

9

THE GRAPHICS ARENA

The distinction between bitmapped and outline images is also important in the production of graphic images. Traditional paint programs use a bitmapped approach. In fact, another way to understand the relationship between pixels and the actual dots used to create an image is to view a paint program's image at increased magnification. Many paint programs offer a view called *FatBits*, which enables the manipulation of individual pixels in a stored image. In FatBits, each of these pixels is represented by a square of screen dots (often eight by eight dots per pixel).

Draw programs, on the other hand, are based on describing the images in mathematical relationships. Most low-end draw programs use the mathematical equations associated with QuickDraw. This has a number of advantages for the display of information, but it presents some limitations for printing. Currently, higher-end graphics programs store the actual image in PostScript and use QuickDraw routines for screen display. With the integration of TrueType into the Macintosh system, it's possible that a new type of graphics application will emerge.

Working with Screen and Printer Fonts

It's important to remember that all output consists of a bitmap—bits are turned on and off in the Macintosh's video memory to represent the areas on the screen or black dots are applied to the page to create a permanent image. By definition, font technology involves both a method for displaying fonts onscreen and a method for creating a printed page.

Font technology may include a bitmapped image for both the printer and the screen, an outline image for the printer, and a bitmapped image for the screen or an outline image for both the printer and the screen. Although it would be possible to have a system using a bitmapped image for the printer and an outline image for the screen, it would not be practical, because the image required by the printer is always more complex than the one required by the screen.

Many font technologies use a bitmapped font for the screen display and another font for the printed output (either a higher resolution bitmap or an outline font. Bitmapped fonts that are used only for video displays are called *screen fonts*). Screen fonts are like typesetter's fonts in that a separate screen font must exist to represent each font size. Table 9.2 summarizes the most common font technologies currently used on the Macintosh.

TABLE 9.2. MACINTOSH FONT STANDARDS.

Font Technology	Screen Method	Screen Res.	Printer Method	Printer Res.
ImageWriter Fonts	Bitmap	71 dpi	Bitmap	72 dpi
QuickDraw	Bitmap	71 dpi	Bitmap	300 dpi
PostScript	Bitmap	71 dpi	Outline	Infinite
TrueType	Outline	Infinite	Outline	Infinite

The goal of these fonts is to provide as close a representation of what will be printed as possible. Adobe developed a system extension called Adobe Type Manager (ATM) to assist in producing a more WYSIWYG-like bitmapped font for screen display. Apple took a second approach and developed a mathematically derived description of each font, called TrueType, for use in displaying and printing WYSIWYG type. Both designs are compensating for the shortcoming of bitmapped fonts—each font is a fixed-size, and you must have a font file for each size you want to display. If you do not have a file, QuickDraw will approximate the size by using very simple mathematical ratios. The resulting screen display is not WYSIWYG.

Types of Type

Mac OS 8.5 uses three varieties of fonts:

- **Bitmapped.** You've already seen bitmapped fonts. These are the fonts displayed on your screen that are difficult to read for long periods of time. Not all bitmapped fonts are created equal. Since the advent of the Web and intensive screen reading requirements, developers are working feverishly on more legible screen fonts.

Fonts such as Mynion Web and Georgia are easier to read than the classic Times. In addition, ATM smoothes the rough edges (called anti-aliasing) of bitmapped fonts, making them slightly easier to read.

- **TrueType.** Apple and Microsoft got together to create a font that combines the screen image with the outline image into a single package. The result is TrueType, and it's rapidly replacing PostScript fonts for use on non-PostScript printers.

- **PostScript.** PostScript outline fonts remain the standard for desktop publishing, because they print at all resolutions beautifully. PostScript fonts are also called *Type 1 fonts* to differentiate Adobe's versions from third-party fonts (termed Type 3 fonts, because they emulate the PostScript language).

Much care has been taken to ensure that fonts print correctly, but not as much care has been taken to ensure that fonts display correctly or can be transported easily between computer systems. This portability issue is the new frontier of font development.

Because a problem occurs when you want to read a document created on one computer on another computer, software vendors such as Adobe, Microsoft, and Apple have been working diligently on ways to transport font information between computers and platforms. One of the developments that allows computers to display documents accurately and printers to print documents accurately (even if the proper fonts are not resident) is a new Type 1 font called *Multiple Master fonts*. All of these font formats are converging into a single open system called OpenType. Adobe and Microsoft developed OpenType to absorb TrueType and PostScript font technologies into a single package that holds information for both outline and bitmapped font images. Mac OS 8.5 supports OpenType.

Apple's Original Bitmapped Fonts

The original Apple bitmapped fonts were given the names of cities. These fonts were designed for legibility at 72 dpi resolution. City-named bitmapped fonts do not have accompanying outline fonts for page-description-based laser printing. If you try to print a city-named font on such a laser printer, it will re-create the 72 dpi bitmap for any size character you want to print. The result is a distorted character. The laser printer also tells you it's creating a bitmapped font for this font, because it doesn't have an equivalent outline font from which to work. Therefore, London, Sydney, Amsterdam, Boise, and San Francisco are all bitmapped fonts suitable for non-page-describing printing. Do not try to print them on a page-describing laser printer and expect high quality print.

Adobe PostScript Fonts

Adobe Systems developed PostScript, the page-description language used by graphics-based laser printers. Type 1 fonts are a subset of this language. The Type 1 font is a proprietary format, and until March, 1990, you had to get a license from Adobe to create Type 1 fonts. In March, 1990, Adobe released the specifications for this PostScript font format, enabling software companies to create new Type 1 fonts without paying Adobe a fee. Today, you can purchase font-creation tools such as Fontographer and FontStudio to create your own Type 1 fonts.

Type 1 fonts are outline fonts based on PostScript. As such, the font format always consists of two files—a printer file containing the outline font and a screen file containing the data about the font (such as kerning, character widths, line spacing, and the structure of the font's family). This data is used by the printer to create the specific bitmap for that character.

Sending an outline font to the printer is called *downloading*, and the font is sometimes called a *downloadable font*. Some PostScript printers have some fonts already hard-coded into their ROM. These fonts (usually a set or subset of 35 fonts: Avant Garde, Bookman, Helvetica, Helvetica Narrow, New Century Schoolbook, Palatino, Zapf Chancery, and Zapf Dingbats) do not have to be downloaded to print.

Type 3 PostScript Fonts

Type 3 fonts are fonts created by third-party vendors using the PostScript page-description language. Because they don't follow the proprietary standard set by Adobe for Type 1 fonts, they do not work with ATM. Furthermore, Type 3 fonts are not as clean and crisp as Type 1 fonts, and their files are also larger. The benefit of Type 3 fonts is that they can contain graphics, grayscale special effects, graduated fills, and variable stroke weights.

TrueType Fonts

The Apple and Microsoft TrueType font format consists of outline fonts that appear onscreen as legibly as they do in print, because each size character is generated from the outline algorithm and is not a fixed-size bitmap. Therefore, TrueType fonts print at the maximum resolution on PostScript, QuickDraw, and TrueImage printers. You don't need to add system overhead through the ATM INIT to use TrueType fonts. On Mac OS 8.5, TrueType is part of the operating system. TrueType fonts do not require a second file of screen fonts and are therefore easier to install than Type 1 fonts.

Multiple Master Fonts

A few years ago, at the dawning of the electronic publishing age, Adobe was bothered by the fact that you couldn't display text online properly if you didn't have the same fonts installed as those the document was originally created with. Therefore, Adobe came up with a solution based on its PostScript Type 1 font technology: Multiple Master fonts.

Multiple Master technology lets the computer draw or scale fonts that don't exist using the outlines of existing fonts. With Multiple Masters, computers can slant, skew, and horizontally scale fonts without changing the original type design. You can derive limitless numbers of font variations from a single typeface by editing the font in a program that supports Multiple Master technology, such as MacroMedia Fontographer.

The Multiple Master technology uses special fonts that offer style variations, called *design axes*. Every Multiple Master provides at least two axes: weight governing the lightness or boldness of the font, and width controlling the font's condensation or expansion. In addition, each design axis has two master designs—for example, the weight axis has a light weight and a bold weight axis. Every subsequent weight is interpolated between these masters.

There are two additional axes: an optical scaling axis to control very large and very small type sizes, and a style axis that controls sans serif, small serif, medium serif, or large serif fonts (or any other kind of sans serif or serif font). All of this wonderful magic is performed on your PostScript printer, which, in turn, eats memory. Adobe suggests that you have at least 3 MB of memory to process Multiple Master fonts.

OpenType and Open Font Architectures

Multiple Master fonts is a stop-gap solution to a raging problem: what to do if you don't have the fonts installed needed to print or display a document. Adobe and Microsoft realized that a new, open (meaning nonproprietary) system for rasterizing fonts was needed. Microsoft independently developed TrueType Open for use in embedding fonts into Web documents. Apple, meanwhile, implemented QuickDraw GX as a way of bringing the quality of PostScript printing to the computer screen. Also, Adobe developed an open standard for Type 1 fonts, called *OpenType*.

The benefit of OpenType is that you no longer have to reprogram applications to render TrueType or Type 1 fonts properly for the screen and then for the printer. OpenType uses plug-in rasterizers that tell applications what to do with Type 1 or TrueType. Future OpenType fonts can even contain the ligatures and kerning pairs introduced by QuickDraw GX. The final benefit of OpenType is that the plug-ins work on both PCs and Macs, making the exchange of documents transparent.

Needless to say, Microsoft and Adobe joined forces in 1995 and announced the OpenType standard, which would subsume Type 1 and TrueType fonts under one package. In 1998, with the advent of Mac OS 8.5, Apple abandoned QuickDraw GX and now supports OpenType.

Microsoft, Adobe, and Apple say that the goal of fonts is that they "just work." This means that all this rasterizing and formatting technology should be invisible. Therefore, you won't see any of this conversion when you use the fonts (except if you look closely at the names of the installed fonts, which might say TTF and OTF to indicate that they are TrueType or OpenType, but this won't matter to you as the end user).

Furthermore, until vendors start using the OpenType rasterizers, OpenType remains a technology without a home, but it is neat to know what's coming.

Fonts and the Printing Process

The Macintosh uses four tools to display text onscreen: your application program, QuickDraw, the Font Manager, and the Resource Manager. The Font Manager and Resource Manager are part of the system. When you want to format a font, you select a style from out of your application program using its procedures. QuickDraw receives this request from the application and requests the font, size, and style from the Font Manager.

Fonts are requested by their unique ID numbers (this is where Unicode character IDs come into play). The Font Manager uses the Resource Manager's routines to load the specified font into memory. If the appropriate font file is not available (that is, the bitmapped file for that size and style is not installed), the Font Manager derives the specific size by altering the description of an existing font. QuickDraw is responsible for deriving styles for fonts that lack actual files for different styles.

The Macintosh enables you to select the actual type style off the Font menu of the running application or select a style directing the Macintosh to identify the font file for that style. This two-pronged approach occurs because the Font Manager is not compatible with the formats all font vendors use to identify their font families. The Macintosh fixes this problem by displaying the font families' individual names and by allowing the Font Manager to find those fonts that do meet its specifications.

The system file also stores several other resources that provide information about font families: auto-leading information retained with each font tells QuickDraw how much space to leave vertically between baselines during an application's auto-line spacing operation, and the width table accompanies each font used by QuickDraw. In the future, OpenType fonts will provide this information to QuickDraw or Windows 95.

The Font Manager supports the stating of character widths in the width table in fractions rather than whole numbers. This is called *fractional character width* support. Fractional widths enhance the readability of text by varying its appearance. WYSIWYG using fractional character widths more closely approaches what the text would look like as output from the printer.

Installing Fonts

System 7.1 introduced an innovation to clean up the System Folder: a Fonts folder. If you don't have ATM installed, you must place both your bitmapped and outline fonts in this folder within the System Folder to operate properly. System 8 carries on this tradition but adds to its convenience. Screen fonts are kept in font suitcases that contain combinations of TrueType and bitmapped fonts (see Figure 9.4). You can open a suitcase by double-clicking it to reveal its contents. Outline printer fonts are stored willy-nilly all over the place, because you need an outline for each type style, not size.

9

Figure 9.4.

The Finder recognizes the difference between bitmapped screen fonts and outline printer fonts, although printer fonts may carry their own icon design.

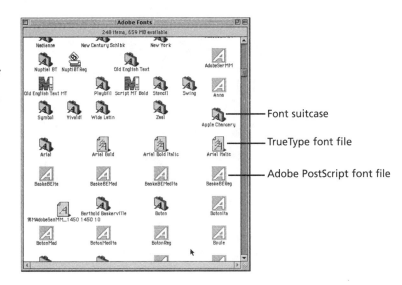

————— Font suitcase

————— TrueType font file

————— Adobe PostScript font file

To place fonts into the Fonts folder, drag the font onto the System Folder. Be sure to quit all programs before installing fonts, because open programs will not register the installation. Figure 9.5 illustrates the three types of fonts you have when you're done.

Figure 9.5.

ATM provides order out of chaos as well as identifies and deactivates damaged fonts, prevents font ID conflicts, and saves you RAM by only loading those fonts you actually use.

Here's another reason to get ATM. With Adobe Type Manager 4.0 installed, you can place your fonts anywhere on your Mac (or on a network). You activate fonts using ATM and organize them by folders.

Although you may have gazillions of fonts installed, you need to activate only those you use regularly. Add Adobe Type Reunion to further organize your fonts into sets for each project you undertake. (See Figure 9.6.)

Adobe Type Reunion also groups your fonts by family for easier viewing, and it displays the fonts in their actual forms on your menu bar. (See Figure 9.7.)

FIGURE 9.6.

Adobe Type Reunion lets you organize your fonts by project so that you display only those fonts you need.

FIGURE 9.7.

Adobe Type Reunion displays your fonts by family in their actual forms so you don't have to grope for the perfect font.

Viewing Fonts

You can see a sample of your font by double-clicking its icon. If the font is a TrueType font, it displays representative text in three sizes: 9, 12, and 18 points. (See Figure 9.8.)

FIGURE 9.8.

The dialog box displays text representing three sizes of Helvetica.

If the font is a bitmap or PostScript font, it only displays representative text for the font size you select. (See Figure 9.9.)

FIGURE 9.9.

The dialog box displays text representing 12-point Helvetica.

FONTS WITH MAC OS 8.5

You're probably wondering whether you get any fonts with Mac OS 8.5. The answer is yes. System 8.5 comes with 27 TrueType fonts as well as some bitmapped screen fonts. The following fonts are included: Geneva, Monaco, Times, New York, Helvetica, Charcoal, Sand, Techno, Gadget, Capitals (brand-new TrueType fonts), Chicago, and Zapf Dingbats.

Mac OS 8.5 and the Finder require certain of these fonts be installed in the Fonts folder in the System Folder so that menu bars, windows, dialog boxes, folders, files, and so forth can be correctly displayed onscreen. Always keep Geneva, Monaco, Charcoal, and Chicago in your Fonts folder. All other fonts can be removed safely.

Adding Professional Polish

The goal of layout is to increase the readability of a document. The spaces between words and lines, as well as the size and proportions of the type used in a document, are very important tools for this purpose.

TO SERIF OR NOT TO SERIF

The Macintosh's WYSIWYG display enables you to enhance your documents by adding different type faces, type styles, and sizes. Because you control almost totally what your document will look like, you must become a layout artist to use the Macintosh to its fullest potential. Over the years, commercial artists and layout specialists have developed "rules of thumb" to assist them in creating documents that are easy to read and yet strongly convey the information they were meant to convey.

Fonts were designed for aesthetics and usefulness. The first rule in using fonts wisely is *do not use a lot of different fonts on a page*. Use at most two fonts—a heading font and a text font. You can vary the heading levels by changing the typeface of the heading font, but use the same font for all headings.

Recall that all fonts fall into two categories: serif and sans serif fonts. (See Figure 9.10.)

Studies have shown that serif fonts are more readable in extended text than sans serif fonts. The thick/thin variations in serif fonts enables the eye to move naturally across a page without getting lost in the similarity of the shapes.

When using both a sans serif and a serifs font, use contrasting typefaces to increase the impact. For instance, if the serifs font is light and airy, use a strong bold sans serifs font for the headings.

FIGURE 9.10.

Serif and sans serif fonts serve different purposes in a document.

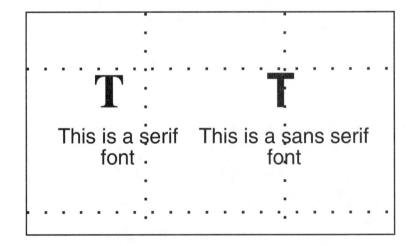

Kerning

Recall that kerning is a technical term for removing small spaces between letters to create visually consistent spacing. The key to correct application of kerning is your visual perception of words versus the whitespace between the words. Each character in proportional type creates its own perception of size and shape based on its roundness or squareness, as well as how the characters break down space into dark and light areas.

If you have software that supports kerning (that is, page layout software), the following list provides some rules for applying this technique:

- Place the most amount of space around two characters composed of mostly vertical lines, such as "H" and "L."
- Place less space between a vertical line letter and a curved letter, such as "H" and "O."
- When two curves are placed side by side, they require very little spacing.
- When two letters produce large amounts of white space, place them close together. For instance, a diagonal-line letter such as "A" can be placed very close to a vertical line letter such as "T."

You kern letters for the optical illusion that they appear evenly spaced more consistently on the page.

Leading

The spaces between lines in a paragraph should always be consistent. The space between lines should be 20 percent of the point size used in the paragraph. All auto-line spacing on the Macintosh is set at 120 percent or the point size plus 20 percent. When you increase the size of the font, the leading also increases automatically.

When you're typing in uppercase letters, the leading looks awkward because the letters lack descenders to break up the whitespace. Reset the leading to slightly less than the point size of the font to create the optical illusion that the spacing is 120 percent.

Use the Paragraph command in word processors or page layout programs to adjust the spacing before and after paragraphs so that a few extra points will be added to the leading before and after a carriage return. The rule of thumb is to add half a line space to the leading between paragraphs.

Typography

Because the Macintosh presents WYSIWYG displays, you can see on the screen what the printer will create on paper. This enables you to typeset your documents onscreen. Such powerful tools also presents you with a responsibility to follow some rules used by typesetters to make their documents easier to read:

- **Sentence spacing.** All spaces in typefaces on the Macintosh are proportional, meaning that each character varies in size. When using this sort of type, you don't have to use an extra space to designate where one sentence ends and another begins—the natural space created by a period and a space serves the same purpose as a monospaced period and a double space. Therefore, use one space after periods, colons, semicolons, question marks, quotation marks, exclamation marks, and any other punctuation.

- **Special characters.** The Macintosh provides many special marks that used to have to be applied by hand or awkwardly in type. The Macintosh provides three keyboard layouts: Option, Option-Shift, and regular. Utilities such as Apple's Key Caps or Norton Utilities KeyFinder assist you in identifying these hidden characters. Always use Option-R to produce the Æ mark, Option-2 to produce the ô mark, Option-G to produce the © mark, and any other special marks rather than creating these marks manually. Use the superscripts and subscripts provided by most Macintosh word processing and page layout programs when appropriate. The Macintosh also provides a fraction bar to make fractional numbers easier to read. To make fractions even more elegant, press the key combination Option-! to produce the fraction bar ($2^1/2$). Do not add a space between the whole number and the fraction. Highlight the numerator in the fraction and make it superscript. Make the denominator two-thirds the point size of the original text. Then, if you can, kern the numbers around the fraction bar. The following lists presents commonly used special characters and their keyboard positions.

ì	Option-[
î	Option-Shift-[
ë	Option-]
í	Option-Shift-]
–	Option-*hyphen* (en dash)
—	Option-Shift-*hyphen* (em dash)
…	Option-; (an ellipsis that cannot be separated at the end of a line)
ï	Option-8
©	Option-G
ô	Option-2
Æ	Option-R
_	Option-Shift-8
¢	Option-4
/	Option-Shift-1
£	Option-3

Layout Tips

The secret of good layout is to provide a seamless reading environment. Follow these layout rules of thumb when laying out a document:

- Replace all underlines with italics. The underline represents the emphasis for type-written documents that is now correctly expressed with italicized type. Also italicize the titles of books, periodicals, and so on, which were formerly underlined. The reason to avoid underlining is that it interferes with the legibility of your text.

- If you want to set a section of text off from the rest of the text, use a rule or line whose thickness and placement you choose. Most word processing programs and page layout programs provide you with a large assortment of rules. Rules are cleaner than underlining because they are drawn as a long line rather than a string of short lines.

- Avoid using all capital letters. Use different size fonts to create different level headings. Studies have shown that using all uppercase letters is hard to read, because letter groups are difficult to recognize without descenders or ascenders to break up the whitespace in words. Usually you read capitals letter by letter, not word by word. This slows down your reading speed and is therefore more tiring. Using all uppercase letters also takes up more room on the page. You can use larger type in the same amount of space when you vary the case of your words.

- Do not use the spacebar to arrange paragraphs or words in columns. Use the tab and indent keys instead. Tabs properly align text. For first-line indents, set the first-line indent tag on the word processor or page layout ruler.

- Avoid widows and orphans on a page. Single words (or seven characters) left dangling on the end of a paragraph are called *widows*. They leave the reader dangling as well. Sentences that cause paragraphs to end at the top of a new column are called *orphans*.

- Do not full-justify text. Always try to left-justify text, because the ragged-right margin makes text easier to read. Justified text also causes spacing problems within the paragraphs, because the word processor cannot compensate for the length of words versus the need to line up both ends of the margins, so it stretches some words and squeezes others to fit.

- When using more than one column of text on a page, align the first baselines of columns. Text lines should line up across the top of a page.

9

- Try to create as much whitespace (areas without text or graphics) as possible on a page. Whitespace makes the page easier to read. Use wide margins as well as empty space between important headings and their text. Also, place whitespace around text in boxes.

- Be consistent in your styles throughout a document. Use style sheets whenever possible to allow the computer to assist you in this endeavor.

Em, En, and Other Punctuation

The professional typography you can see on the WYSIWYG screen of the Macintosh should also be applied to punctuation. Typesetters have developed special symbols for quotation marks, quotes, long dashes, and short dashes to enhance the look of a document. Use these marks as follows:

Opening double quotation mark	"	Option-[
Closing double quotation mark	"	Shift-Option-[
Opening single quotation mark	'	Option-]
Closing single quotation mark	'	Shift-Option-]

Place commas and periods inside of the quotation marks and place colons and semicolons outside of the marks. Use the double-quotation mark to identify the beginning of each paragraph of a quotation that contains more than one paragraph, but place the closing double quotation mark only at the end of the last paragraph of the quote. Also, use the closing single quotation mark for apostrophes.

When a space/hyphen/space or a double hyphen is desired, replace it with the em dash (Shift-Option-*hyphen*). Use the shorter en dash (Option-*hyphen*) when indicating a duration, such as "from March–April." Do not place a space between the dash and the text. Use the hyphen only to break up words at the end of lines or to indicate compound words.

Summary

I guess you're slowly learning how wrapped up the Mac is in commercial art, typography, publishing, and all the arcane arts of printing. The Mac is the best platform for working with fonts for exactly this reason: The Mac OS supports the display and printing of type to the exacting standards of publishing and print houses. You can create great typographical masterpieces because the Mac makes typography almost transparent.

Term Review

bitmapped font   A method of drawing fonts whereby every dot on the screen is individually drawn by the printer. These fonts are also called "screen fonts" because they're used by QuickDraw to display fonts on your monitor.

character set   Refers to the entire collection of symbols that can be printed in a particular character style.

font   Refers to the name of the character style (such as Geneva, Palatino, or Times). To graphic artists as well as others who are used to the terms of typography, the term *font* refers to a single style of letters (for example, 12-point bold Palatino).

font families   A collection of character sets that share a similar design. Each font family consists of a number of typefaces.

kerning   Adjusting the space between letters to increase the legibility of type.

Key Caps   A Macintosh desk accessory used to view font families.

leading   The space between lines of type. The term comes from the old practice of placing lead between lines of type to separate the lines on a printing press.

monospaced fonts   Fonts such as Geneva, Monaco, and Courier, where each letter of type is given the same spacing on a line.

Multiple Master fonts   Special fonts (Serif MM and Sans Serif MM) developed by Adobe that give you the ability to create outline fonts on the fly. What's more, you can view a document as it actually will print without having to have the fonts it contains actually resident on your computer.

outline font   The description of a font based on a mathematical equation describing the font's characters. Outline fonts are converted to screen or printer dots using a series of routines that convert mathematical descriptions into printable images.

pixels   The dots per inch on your monitor screen used to define a bitmapped font.

points   A metric method of defining the size of fonts based on their pixel count.

PostScript   A page-description language developed by Adobe used to convert outline fonts into printable images.

proportional-spaced fonts   Fonts such as Palatino, Helvetica, and Times, in which each letter is given individual space (or weight) based on its shape.

QuickDraw   The page-description language used by the Mac to draw fonts on your screen.

9

Raster Image Processor (RIP)   The processor used by PostScript printers to convert a font from outline form to a collection of dots that can be displayed or printed.

style   Added qualities, such as bold, italic, outline, and shadow, drawn on fonts to increase their emphasis or graphic impact.

suitcase   A special folder that contains a font family.

TrueType   A method of describing fonts mathematically stored not on the printer (as in PostScript) but with the font itself. TrueType fonts can be accurately printed on any type of printer.

Type 1, 2, and 3 fonts   Different iterations of PostScript or outline fonts. Type 1 fonts are fonts developed by Adobe, whereas Type 2 and 3 fonts are copies of Adobe fonts or fonts with similar qualities to Adobe fonts developed by third-party vendors.

typeface   A particular style of character. Two primary types of typefaces exist—those composed with little hooks at the ends of their forms, called *serif* type (such as Palatino, Times, and New York) and those without these hooks, called *sans serif* type (such as Helvetica and Geneva).

typography   The science (or art form) of developing fonts.

WYSIWYG   An acronym for "what you see is what you get." Refers to the fact that the Mac is able to display onscreen practically what will be printed out on your printer.

Q&A

Q Which fonts are included with Mac OS 8.5?

A A total of 27 fonts are included with Mac OS 8.5. These fonts include Gadget, Sand, Techno, Capitals, New York, Geneva, Times, Courier, Monaco, Helvetica, Charcoal, and more.

Q How do I speed up the performance of my Mac with regards to fonts?

A Try to keep as few fonts as possible in your Fonts folder in the System Folder. Default fonts such as Charcoal, Geneva, Monaco, and Courier should be kept in the folder, but you can install other fonts outside of the System Folder and use a font management package, such as Symantec's Suitcase or Adobe's Adobe Type Manager Deluxe, to create sets of fonts for each of your tasks.

Q Which are better, Type 1 or TrueType fonts?

A That depends on your printer. Today, most fonts come in both outline and TrueType forms. If space on your hard drive is at a premium, store only the

TrueType versions of your fonts. If you have a PostScript printer, use the outline fonts because they're rendered more accurately than TrueType, and they print faster, too. However, with Mac OS 8.5's support of OpenType, this statement is fast becoming a moot point, because OpenType includes rasterizers for both TrueType and Type 1 fonts. PostScript will include support for OpenType fonts in the near future.

Q Do I need suitecases anymore?

A The short answer is no, because the Fonts folder does not require its fonts to reside in suitecases. The longer answer is that suitecases are a great way to organize font families. The problem is that Mac OS 8.5 does not support the creation of new suitecases. You need a third-party package such as Symantec's Suitecase or Adobe Type Manager Deluxe to create and manage suitecases of fonts. This use of a third-party font manager (another is FontReserve) is a good idea, because their use lets you unclog your Fonts folder, removing the hundreds of weird fonts you rarely use but acquire over time.

Q What's the best screen font to use in my browser or screen-readable document?

A A basic answer is anything but the browser default's 12-point Times. Times is a really bad screen font, although it provides a relatively good printed font. Spend $50 and purchase Web fonts from Adobe or Bitstream `http://www.bitstream.com`, such as Myriad Web, Minion Web, or Caflish Script Web, that have been optimized for screen viewing. Internet Explorer 4 from Microsoft, which comes as the default browser with Mac OS 8.5, includes several really good Web fonts, including Arial, Georgia, Comic Sans MS, Verdana, and Trebuchet. You can set these as the default in your browser or use as your default in documents that are going to be read online (such as help pages). Check out `http://www.microsoft.com/typography` and `http://www.adobe.com/prodindex/webtype/details.html` for listings of other Web fonts.

Q What can you do today to increase the legibility of online fonts?

A If you don't like those old Monaco, Geneva, and Courier fonts, check out Charcoal, Sand, Gadget, and Techno as alternative screen fonts. Change the default fonts used by your screen in the Appearance control panel's Fonts screen. Choose Gadget for your menu bar and dialog box font—it's more legible than Chicago. Stick with Geneva for your default screen font. Play around with other fonts and see which one hurts your eyes the least.

9

Workshop

The Workshop contains quiz questions to help you solidify your understanding of the material covered. You can find the answers to the quiz questions in Appendix B, "Quiz Answers."

Quiz

1. What is WYSIWYG?

2. What is a font?

3. What is typography?

4. What is a character set?

5. What is Unicode?

6. How do you change the font in Key Caps? How do you see the extra characters available for that font?

7. What is a font family?

8. What's the difference between a screen font and a printer font? What are alternative names for these font types?

9. Where, as a default, do fonts reside on a Mac?

10. What third-party products can you purchase that enhance the legibility and manageability of fonts on the Mac?

PART II
Afternoon Hours: Printing and Multimedia

Hour

10 Printing

11 Color

12 QuickTime

13 Sound and Audio

14 Video

15 Web Publishing

16 File Sharing

HOUR **10**

Printing

This hour covers the following print-related issues:

- Printing on the Mac
- Using PostScript
- Working with printer drivers
- Using the Page Setup and Print commands
- Printing with color

Let's begin by discussing the basic features of printing on a Macintosh.

Printing on the Mac

Before the advent of the Macintosh with its WYSIWYG environment and graphical user interface, displaying a document and printing it were two separate operations. Because the WYSIWYG screen display uses similar technologies to those used in printing a document, this is no longer true. QuickDraw guides both processes, ensuring that both text and graphics are drawn as specified.

Before the advent of desktop publishing and electronic typesetting, the term *letter quality* was used to define printing requirements. Letter quality meant output that looked type-written. Printers that produced this output were called *formed-letter printers*, and they used actual metal or plastic type brushed with ink, which was pressed onto the paper. Some of the type cartridges were removable, which allowed users to slightly vary the type characters, but they all looked typewritten versus typeset. Today, because users have seen examples of computer output that looks like it was typeset, *letter quality* has come to refer to high-quality dot-matrix printing. The Macintosh has changed the user perception of what is acceptable output. The Macintosh was originally sold with a dot-matrix printer called the *ImageWriter*. In 1986, Apple replaced the first ImageWriter with an updated one, called the ImageWriter II, that included a connection for sharing the printer over a network. As time progressed, users required a higher-quality, faster, quieter printing process for the Macintosh's graphics and text.

Vendors introduced laser printers, which increased the quality of the output. These lasers used either Adobe's PostScript page-description language to rasterize fonts, or, more recently, Macintosh's QuickDraw to rasterize images. Vendors have also developed bridges to enable Macintosh to print on non-PostScript laser printers, thermal printers, and inkjet printers. Color QuickDraw and PostScript Level 2 have been used to enable Macintoshes to print in color, as well. The Macintosh also supports high-end electronic typesetters, such as Linotronics, to produce extremely high-quality but expensive print-outs.

Today, printers are proliferating so fast and the technology for electronic typesetting is developing at such a rapid pace that truly paperless publishing is becoming more of a reality rather than a hyperbole. Table 10.1 provides an overview of the types of printers and their features available to Macintosh users.

TABLE 10.1. MACINTOSH PRINTER FEATURES.

Printer Type	Features	Possible Uses
Dot-matrix	144 dpi. Print wires and ribbon based	Printing mailing labels or any other print jobthat requires continuous-feed paper stock. Does not support individual paper sheets or envelopes.

Printer Type	Features	Possible Uses
Inkjet	360 to 720 dpi. Microscopic nozzles spray solid or liquid ink. Uses the Mac to control print job. Can support a software-based PostScript RIP	Home computing, draft printing, mailing labels, and low-quality printing jobs. Limited paper-stock control weights supported. Can support a software-based
QuickDraw laser printers	300 to 600 dpi. Photocopier technology that uses the Mac to control the printing process.	Good for printing text-heavy documents that do not rely on encapsulated PostScript for graphics and that lack emulators for other printers (therefore, they can only be used with Macs).
PostScript laser printers	300 to 1,200 dpi. Photocopier technology uses onboard computer to control printing process.	Desktop publishing and proofing output due to high resolution and accuracy of font and image reproduction.
Color PostScript laser printers	300 dpi on up to 1,200 dpi.	Color presentations using transparencies or film, business graphics, proofing color publications, scanned images, and illustrations (before submitting them to four-color printing processes).

Printing with Dot Matrix Printers

Dot-matrix printers produce images by hitting an inked ribbon with very small, moveable pins (called *print wires*). Each pin in the printer's print head produces a single dot. The pins are arranged in a matrix. The printer controls which pin strikes the ribbon and which ones remain stationary to direct the pattern on the paper. The resolution (clarity and crispness of the output) depends on the number of pins and their size.

Apple used to sell several dot-matrix printers under the name *ImageWriter*. Dot-matrix printers can print in three modes:

- **Draft mode.** The Macintosh sends the printer straight ASCII code and its spacing requirements only. The printer supplies the font in which it prints the document. Draft mode was designed to show you where each word would begin on the page if the actual bitmapped characters and graphics were used, making the spacing of the printer's internal font characters very disproportional.

- **Faster-print mode.** When the faster-print mode is used, the Macintosh does send the printer bitmapped images of fonts and graphics, but rather it sends a page image. Because the page image is too large to send in one piece, the Macintosh system's Print Manager generates the bitmap in stages in a process called *banding*. It flushes each section out of its memory after it sends them to the printer.

- **Best mode.** In best mode, the Macintosh also uses banding to transmit the bitmapped image to the printer. The quality is increased because the Macintosh generates a bitmap image that's twice the size of the page and then scales the image down to size before sending it to the printer. Because the larger image takes more memory, banding this image takes 47 passes to the printer.

  Best mode also increases the quality of the printout by causing the print head to make twice the number of passes over the paper. Before the second pass, the printer rolls the paper up one-half of a dot, causing the second pass to slightly overlap the first, thus filling in images and increasing the intensity of the print.

> The scaling process impacts how the Macintosh uses fonts to print on a dot-matrix printer in best mode. When you select best mode, the Macintosh selects a font twice the size of the one specified and then shrinks the bitmap by 50 percent. If you haven't installed a font twice the size of the specified font, the Macintosh uses one that's four times the required size, and if that font isn't available, the Font Manager scales to the next appropriate size. ImageWriter fonts typically provide fixed fonts for 9, 10, 12, 14, 18, 20, and 24 point sizes. Other sizes require the system to approximate the scaling using an available font size. This causes the output to look distorted.

TrueType fonts increase the number of high-quality fonts that can be printed on the dot-matrix printer, because QuickDraw scales the font to whatever size you specify using the outline font files as a template. Using TrueType, you can print any point size font. See Hour 9, "Fonts," for a discussion of fonts.

One way of making your images clearer when printing bitmapped graphics on a dot-matrix printer is to select the Tall Adjusted option in the Page Setup dialog box. This option adjusts the Macintosh output from 72 dpi to the 80 dpi vertical resolution of the printer, thus generating a proportional image.

To avoid the irregular word spacing that occurs in draft mode, change your document's font to a monospaced font, such as Monaco, for printing out a draft. The fixed-spaced font on the screen will then match the spacing of the printer's internal font, making the draft easier to read. Change your document to a more professional bitmapped font when you're ready to print your final copy.

To increase the quality of your printout in best mode, select fonts with uniform stroke widths, such as Geneva, Monaco, and Courier. These fonts scale more clearly than variable-stroke fonts, such as New York.

Always install fonts in groups of twos—9 point with 18 point, 10 point with 20 point, and so on—so that the Font Manager has the larger font available for scaling in best mode.

The clearest text font for use with the ImageWriter family is Boston II, which is a shareware font available from Apple Macintosh user groups. Use fonts with city names for best results, because these fonts were designed to be printed and displayed at 72 to 80 dpi.

The highest quality output in best mode is produced by using an older printer ribbon, because there is less smudging of characters from the double-pass process due to high levels of ink on the ribbon. Dot-matrix printers use inked ribbons that dry out over time, even without use. You should avoid stock-piling ribbons. Instead, buy them one at a time.

Printing with Inkjet Printers

Inkjet printers operate on the same principle as dot-matrix printers, only they use tiny squirts of ink on pins to print their dots on the page. Inkjet resolutions are better than dot matrix printers, but most are not as good as laser printer resolutions. Inkjet resolution averages 360 dpi in best mode, but Apple manufactures a color inkjet that averages 720 dpi in best mode for black-and-white text.

Most inkjet printers come bundled with Adobe Type Manager to rasterize Type 1 fonts on the Macintosh. They also come with their own set of outline fonts (Helvetica, Courier, Times, and Symbol) and can be upgraded to 35 or more resident fonts. Inkjets, like dot-matrix printers, receive rasterized images of TrueType fonts, which they use in conjunction with or in the place of their resident fonts. Therefore, Inkjet printers are not limited

in their ability to print Adobe and TrueType fonts, because all the hinting and scan conversion processes occur on the Macintosh.

Their only limitation is that they do not support PostScript-based graphic formats, such
as encapsulated PostScript, Adobe Illustrator, and MacroMedia FreeHand graphics. You
need a PostScript add-on card or interpreter to print PostScript graphics on an inkjet
printer. For example, InfoWave's StylePrint `http://www.infowave.net/printing_`
`solutions/html/ss_stylescript.html` provides a software-based PostScript 2
emulator that lets you print PostScript files on inkjet printers.

Inkjets use special inks that tend to bleed on regular printer paper, although the technology is better today than when inkjets were first introduced in the late '80s. Most vendors
recommend printing on special coated papers made for inkjet printers when printing
color images in best mode.

> AppleTalk doesn't get along with inkjet printers, because the inkjet must
> have a direct connection to the Mac, and AppleTalk manages the Mac's seri-
> al ports. In order to properly connect an inkjet, be sure to turn off AppleTalk
> by using the AppleTalk control panel or Chooser's AppleTalk Off radio but-
> ton as well as select Remote Only from the Connect Via pop-up menu in the
> AppleTalk control panel.

Printing with Laser Printers

Laser printers produce output that's better able to render the subtleties of electronic type
as well as the details of graphic drawings because they print at a resolution of 1,200,
800, 600, or 300 dpi versus the 144 dpi of high-quality dot-matrix printers and the 720-
by-360 dpi of inkjets. Laser printing is also faster than dot-matrix printing (and quieter).

Laser printers are more complex than dot-matrix printers because they use a laser to
shine a light to create the dots on the page. The laser printer consists of an engine (a type
of photocopier that manages paper feeding and printing the image) and a controller
(which accepts printing instructions from page-description languages and governs the
engine following those routines). The difference between PostScript printers and other
printers is that the controller is housed inside the printer case with PostScript laser printers (versus using QuickDraw to control the printing process).

The Laser Printer Engine

The printer engine consists of the following components:

- A light-sensitive rotating drum or belt.
- A laser assembly that's aimed at the drum through a series of mirrors and lenses.
- A toner reservoir. Toner is a fine plastic powder coated with a polymer that causes it to retain a negative electric charge. Some laser printers separate the toner from the developer (a second powder).
- Wires carrying high voltages (called *charging coronas*). Charging coronas electrically charge the drum as it rotates the paper through the engine, allowing the toner to be transferred to the paper.
- A fusing assembly to melt the toner particles so that they adhere to the paper.

Raster Image Processors (RIPs)

Laser printers that contain controllers use them to manage the rasterizing of images. Laser printers, like Macintosh video screens, are raster devices. A 300 dpi resolution laser inscribes over 3,300 scan lines per page on the photoconductive surface of the drum. Because the controller manages this process, it is sometimes called a *raster-image processor (RIP)*.

There are two types of RIPs, depending on the language they use to communicate an application program's page specifications—PostScript printers and QuickDraw printers.

Laser printers that do not have resident controllers to control the print engine are called *QuickDraw laser printers*. They do not use PostScript as their page-description language but rather use the power of QuickDraw to rasterize TrueType outline fonts or Type 1 fonts with Adobe Type Manager before printing the bitmap image.

The problem with some of the QuickDraw printers is that they cannot connect to Apple LocalTalk networks; therefore, they can't be shared among Macintoshes. They're also slower than PostScript printers and require more overhead storage on the Macs, because they perform their rasterizing, hinting, and scan converting on the computer. It's quite possible to run out of memory during a print job when using a non-PostScript printer.

The benefit of using a non-PostScript printer is that it's cheaper. It's also usually smaller and lighter, so it takes up less desk space.

Using PostScript to Print

PostScript is Adobe System's page-description language. PostScript printers use controllers that reside in the printer's case. The controller is a computer (usually based

10

on a RISC chip or Motorola CISC chips) that uses two or more megabytes of RAM as well as ROM chips that contain the printer fonts stored in outline form.

When you send a document to the printer by selecting the Print command in your application program, the Macintosh Printer Manager checks to see whether there's a communications link to the printer.

The Mac OS downloads the custom PostScript dictionary to the printer before the first use of the printer each time you turn it on. The PostScript dictionary contains translations for QuickDraw's shorthand commands, which speed up the printing process over AppleTalk networks. During the process of downloading, the desktop printer shows the message "Initializing Printer." Only those portions of the PostScript dictionary required to perform a specific print job are downloaded as needed. This also enables you to mix System 7 and System 8 versions of printer drivers on a network connected to the same printer.

SPOOLING AND PRINT QUEUES EXPLAINED

When you print a document using background printing, your document is "spooled" to a special file, called, naturally enough, the *spool file*, where it waits while the printer either finishes a previous job or is initialized. The waiting time is called *queuing*. If you don't have background printing turned on in the Chooser, your job goes directly to the printer and does not queue. Laser print jobs are not the only print jobs that can be printed in the background. You can have any print job spooled by selecting Background Printing in the Chooser. The benefit of spooling and queuing is that you can continue to work while your document prints. The downside of spooling is that it takes up processing power and memory, which can slow down the performance of your Mac or cause large documents to fail to print.

When initialization is complete, the Printer Manager sends the application's QuickDraw routines, translating the page layout specifications to the printer driver, which, in turn, translates QuickDraw into PostScript commands. The Print Monitor or desktop printer displays the alternating messages "Processing Job" and "Preparing Data" during this process.

During the transmission of the PostScript program, the printer's controller receives the code, which is read by the PostScript interpreter, and scan converts the image into a bitmapped page, which is stored in the controller's page buffer. The interpreter uses the font outlines stored in ROM to create the required fonts specified in the code. The controller then uses the bitmap to govern the engine's imaging mechanism and flushes the image and the PostScript code after the page is printed.

Benefits of PostScript Printing

PostScript printers provide extensive benefits in terms of performance, cost savings, and flexibility. Because PostScript scan converts the QuickDraw code, the application program doesn't have to know the resolution of the printer you're using. You can therefore print on many different PostScript printers using the same file and application program. The difference will be the quality of the output.

In addition, each bitmapped page takes up at least 1 MB of memory. Because the controller performs the scan, the page is stored in the printer's page buffer and not on the Macintosh, thus requiring less storage space on the Macintosh to be dedicated to printing. Multiple Macintoshes and PCs can share one printer, because the PostScript and page buffer reside in the printer.

Each PostScript printer contains print server software in its ROM that allows up to 32 machines to share the printer. The print server software acts as the interface between the Macintosh and the controller during the printing process. PostScript is a programming language that can be upgraded and improved to provide extended features, such as shading, gradients, special effects, and other modifications to fonts and graphics.

10

PostScript Level 2

In 1993, Adobe updated PostScript to PostScript Level 2 to add support for color printing and other new printer features, as well as to enhance existing features. PostScript Level 2 drivers (either LaserWriter 8.4 from Apple or PSPrinter 8.3.1 from Adobe) support the following features:

- **The addition of color extensions to the base language.** This gives PostScript the ability to describe and print colors as they are seen onscreen. Display PostScript (the screen-description language version of PostScript) is also included in the base language.

- **The compressing and decompressing of documents.** What's more, printers that support Level 2 can fax PostScript documents, cache patterns and forms between multiple printings of the same document, and generate accurate screen angles for smoother halftone printing.

- **Device-independent color support.** This feature provides a way to view documents on any monitor, print them on any printer, and have the colors appear the same from machine to machine. Apple's ColorSync technology manages color by providing support for the translation of RGB screen color schemes to CMYK data, which is used by printers to define colors. Full-color translation is not yet available except where applications provide the exact matches between color profiles used by the printer and the Macintosh. ColorSync and PostScript Level 2 are not 100 percent compatible in this regard, because they don't use the same device profiles to describe RGB colors.

Each version of ColorSync (now at version 2.5) and the printer driver (now at version 8.6) come closer to using the same profiles or substituting correct versions if profiles are not available.

- **Enhanced halftoning algorithm.** PostScript Level 2 describes more lines per inch and smaller angles onscreen, thus generating a higher-resolution image. Because more color and halftone information is available, color separations are smoother. You can also create a low-resolution version of a document for fast draft printing.

- **The inclusion of printer-specific features within printer drivers.** Each printer now provides a printer page-description (PPD) document, which is a portable ASCII file that tells the printer driver about the printer's specific features, such as what type of paper is in which tray and how long the printer stays awake before shutting down to save energy. Printer vendors can more easily upgrade their printers without worrying about creating a new driver by simply adding new features to the PPD for the driver to read. Any information located on the PPD is reflected in the Print and Page Setup windows in your applications.

- **Support for PostScript faxing.** PostScript Fax supports a base resolution for a fax of 200 dpi by 100 dpi (the CCITT Group III fax protocol) and includes the Error Correction Mechanism used by Group III faxes. If you purchase the PostScript fax card, you can turn your PostScript printer into a fax machine.

- **Increased speed and efficiency of printing.** PostScript Level 2 rewrote the way memory is allocated by the printer—all printer memory is now allocated to all printer tasks and is not partitioned to separate tasks in a linear fashion (as was the case in Level 1 PostScript). The addition of pattern and form caching—the ability to render and download forms and patterns that are used repeatedly (such as logos) to an area of printer memory—lets forms be used multiple times when multiple versions of the same document are printed.

- **Faster rasterizing**. Adobe incorporated a revamped Adobe Type Manager (ATM) rasterizer into Level 2. ATM is a set of PostScript subroutines that generates scalable font outlines on the fly for display onscreen, thus speeding up font rendering for non-PostScript output devices. Level 2 also supports TrueType font rendering.

PostScript 3

Adobe recently announced an upgrade to PostScript called *PostScript 3*. PostScript 3 is more than a printing description language but less than a programming language or printing environment. PostScript 3 provides many enhanced features for color prepress,

Webmasters, and heavy-duty printing. There are currently few printers that support PostScript 3, but new RIPs and printers will ship soon.

PostScript 3 promises smoother shading, the ability to remotely control printers via the Internet for direct Internet printing, and faster printing of both graphics and fonts, due to in-RIP processing such as chroma-key masking, 3D effects, and powerful trapping capabilities. In addition, PostScript 3 comes with an expanded set of 136 built-in fonts based on font-simulation technology from Ares Software.

Preparing Your Mac for Printing

When you install Mac OS 8.5, your computer is almost a blank slate when it comes to printing. The Mac knows that a printer is attached, but it doesn't know how to send the proper instructions to that specific printer. You have to inform it about your printer and its features. This instruction task contains three steps:

1. Set up your printer driver.
2. If you're printing with a PostScript printer, you must associate a page-description document (PPD) with the printer driver. If you're printing with a QuickDraw printer, you can set up who can share your printer using the Setup dialog box.
3. Select a default printer via its serial port.

Setting Up Your Printer Driver

A *printer driver* is an intermediary program that translates the QuickDraw commands used by an application to specify how a document should look into commands that can be used by a specific printer to print the document. These features, in turn, are displayed on the Page Setup and Print dialog boxes in all programs. Printer drivers are placed in the Extensions folder in the System Folder during the Mac OS installation process.

You can remove both printer drivers and PPDs for those printers you do not intend to use with your Mac. It's always a good idea to slim down the Extensions folder to speed the performance of your Mac and to release memory from the system. Open the Systems Folder's Extension folder and throw away all the drivers you don't need. Most PostScript laser printers, whether manufactured by Apple or another vendor, will use either the LaserWriter or LaserWriter 8 driver (depending whether the printer is an older one that still uses PostScript or a newer model that includes PostScript Level 2). If you're using an inkjet printer, throw away the LaserWriter drivers and stick with a StyleWriter driver.

Choosing Your Printer's Printer Driver

To select a printer driver, follow these steps:

1. Select the Chooser from the Apple menu.

2. In the Chooser, select your printer driver from the left list box (see Figure 10.1). Each driver is shown with its own printer icon. If you don't know which printer you're using, try to match the pictures. Apple only provides drivers for its own printers. You must go to your printer's manufacturer to obtain an up-to-date driver for your particular printer. Hewlett-Packard and Epson, being the only vendors still making printers for the Mac, maintain Web sites at `http://www.hp.com` and `http://www.epson.com/home.html`, respectively.

FIGURE 10.1.

Use the Chooser to select a printer driver that matches your printer.

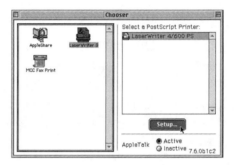

3. When you select your driver, the list box on the right displays one of several items. If you're connected to a network, the list box displays all the printers available for your use. If you're running the printer directly from your Mac, the list box displays a list of serial ports for you to choose to locate your printer.

4. Select either a printer (if you're networked) or a serial port (if you're printing directly) from the list box.

5. Close the Chooser.

Here's a rule of thumb to help you avoid getting confused by these two ports and their uses: Always run your printer from the printer port and your modem from the modem port. The downside of this rule is that you cannot use AppleTalk to communicate to other Macs if you're running a QuickDraw printer from the printer port. However, you can get a switch box to connect one cable for AppleTalk and another for your printer from the same printer port.

Be sure to turn off AppleTalk if you don't have a switch box installed.

Setting Up Page-Description Documents

PostScript is a special page-definition language that resides on your PostScript printer. Because PostScript is not resident on the Mac, the Mac needs some way to know about the specialized features of your PostScript printer. This information is provided by the PPD. You associate PPDs with your printer driver by selecting a printer driver from the Chooser and clicking Create.

Remember that this task is required only if you're using PostScript. QuickDraw printers use the Mac's processors and toolboxes to print and therefore do not require these files. If you're running a QuickDraw printer, just choose a serial port and you're done.

SOME MORE WORDS ON DRIVERS

Mac OS 8.5 comes with several QuickDraw printer drivers and one PostScript printer driver. The following drivers are QuickDraw drivers:

> Color StyleWriter Pro
>
> Color StyleWriter 2500
>
> Color StyleWriter 1500
>
> ImageWriter
>
> StyleWriter 1200
>
> LaserWriter 300/LS

The LaserWriter 8 (version 8.6.1) driver is required whenever you want to print on a PostScript printer.

Because Apple is getting out of the imaging business, it's no longer manufacturing printers. It's most likely that you'll be using another vendor's printer, namely an Epson or Hewlett-Packard inkjet. Each of these printers uses its own driver supplied by its vendor. PostScript laser printers by any vendor can be operated using the Apple LaserWriter 8 driver.

10

You can select the PPD that fits your printer using the resulting dialog boxes. (See Figure 10.2.)

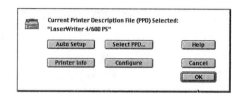

Creating a Desktop Printer

Mac OS 8.5 introduced the concept of *desktop printers*. The Mac chooses a default printer and places its icon on the desktop. This printer will be the first one used when you print a document. By creating a desktop printer, Mac OS 8.5 lets you skip the step of going to the Chooser and picking a driver, printer, or serial port each time you want to print. You can set up alternative printers in a special menu on the menu bar using the Printing menu's Default Printer command. The Printing menu appears when you select the desktop printer.

Mac OS 8.5 requires you to have a default or desktop printer. The last printer you select in the Chooser is this default.

After you create a desktop printer, its icon is placed on the desktop. You can then drag and drop documents from folders into the printer to invoke their associated programs and print them. You can also place multiple files into the printer, and they'll be queued and printed using the priority you set in the Printing menu. (See Figure 10.3.)

FIGURE 10.3.

Use the Printing menu to start, stop, and reconfigure print jobs.

Stopping and Changing Print Jobs

You can stop or delete print jobs using the same menu. To see which documents are in the queue and to check the status of your print jobs, double-click the desktop printer to open its Printing window. (See Figure 10.4.)

FIGURE 10.4.

The Printing window lets you view the status of your print jobs as well as start, stop, and prioritize jobs.

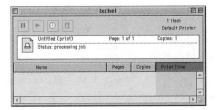

Printing a Document

A printer driver provides the Page Setup and Print dialog boxes used in the application program to initiate the printing process. Two commands are found in every application that let you print using these tools: Page Setup and Print. Both are typically located in the File menu.

Using Page Setup

Page Setup provides options to tell the printer driver how you want your document pages formatted. You can set the paper size (such as letter or legal size), the page orientation (either horizontal or vertical), how large you want the view of the page to be (a reduction or enlargement factor), as well as other options that affect how the document is arranged on the page. Each program also adds its own specific options to the Page Setup dialog box. In addition, the Page Setup dialog box provides a way to set up special effects, such as flipped views, inverted colors, and font-handling options.

Note that the Page Setup dialog box changes based on which printer driver is selected in the Chooser. Because most folks use either inkjet printers or PostScript laser printers, I'll focus the discussion on these two types of Page Setup screens. Figure 10.5 provides an illustration of the LaserWriter 8 Page Setup dialog box for Microsoft Word 6.

FIGURE 10.5.

The Page Setup dialog box lets you select a printer, the paper type, the size of the image on the paper, and the page orientation.

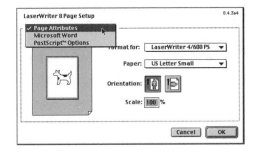

Selecting an item from the pop-up menu changes the dialog box from the default Page
Attributes screen to a second screen called *PostScript Options*.

Using PostScript Options

The PostScript Options screen gives you the opportunity to choose from a number of
special effects and printing-correction options. Figure 10.6 shows you the PostScript
Options screen.

FIGURE 10.6.

*The PostScript Options
screen lets you select
special effects to cor-
rect certain problems
with older printers.*

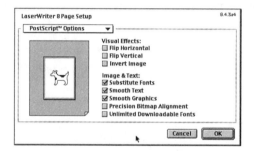

Select the appropriate boxes to create the following PostScript effects:

- **Flip Horizontal and Flip Vertical.** Selecting either box creates a mirror image of
  your document. Use the Flip Horizontal option to change the image direction from
  right to left. This is useful if you're creating film images on a Linotronic typesetting for transparencies or if the pages have to be emulsion side down. Don't use
  Flip Vertical; instead, just turn the paper around.

- **Invert Image.** Checking this option reverses the colored areas of your document so
  that all white areas become black, and vice versa. This option is useful if you're
  making negatives to use on a slide printer.

- **Substitute Fonts.** Checking this box replaces any fixed-size fonts (such as Geneva
  or New York) with their variable-size equivalents (even if these latter fonts are not
  available). The side effect of this process is that word and sentence spacing is lost,
  because these spaces do not change (even if you switch from fixed-size to variable-
  width fonts), thus making lines very jagged and hard to read. It's usually smart to
  leave this box unchecked.

- **Smooth Text.** Checking this box smoothes the jagged edges of fixed-size fonts for
  which there are no PostScript equivalents. The result is not always aesthetically
  pleasing. Leave this box unchecked. Always use variable-width fonts when
  printing.

- **Smooth Graphics**. Checking this box smoothes the jagged edges of bitmapped
  drawings, such as those produced by MacPaint, Painter, or any other bitmapped
  graphics program.

- **Precision Bitmap Alignment**. Checking this box corrects a problem that occurs when what you see onscreen is not necessarily what will be printed, especially when you're printing bitmapped graphics. This option reduces the entire printed image to enable the correct conversion of a 72 dpi screen image to a 300 or 600 dpi printed image (72 doesn't divide into 300 or 600 evenly). Reducing the image by 4 percent, effectively printing the image at 288 or 576 dpi (an even multiple of 72 dpi) aligns the bitmaps to produce a crisper output.

Setting Options with the StyleWriter

If you're using a StyleWriter, either the Color StyleWriter 1500 or 2500 or a StyleWriter II, selecting the appropriate printer driver in the Chooser presents a StyleWriter Page Setup dialog box, such as the one displayed in Figure 10.7.

FIGURE 10.7.

The StyleWriter dialog box provides fewer page setup options than those provided by the LaserWriter dialog box.

One special option provided by the StyleWriter Page Setup dialog box is the ability to print a watermark under your image and text. Click the Watermark button to display its options (see Figure 10.8). Use the pop-up menu to select the type of watermark you want; then use the slider bar to lighten or darken the mark and the pop-up menu to align the mark on the page.

FIGURE 10.8.

Use the Watermark button to add a water-mark to your document page.

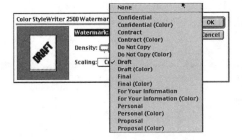

Using the Print Command

When you select the Print command from the File menu, depending on which printer driver you selected in the Chooser, a Print dialog box is displayed. Figure 10.9 illustrates the LaserWriter 8 Print dialog box.

FIGURE **10.9.**

*The LaserWriter Print
dialog box lets you
select which pages you
want to print, how
many copies you want,
and where the paper is
coming from.*

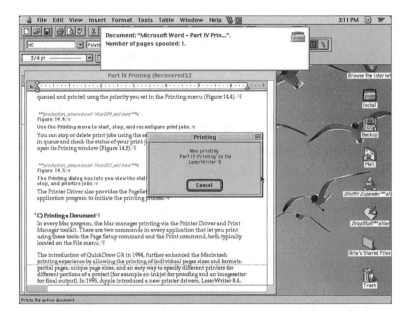

Use the pop-up menu to select options for color management, error reporting, general
printing (page numbers, copies, and so forth), and printing to a file. You can also choose
to print a cover page for your document.

What's more, you can save your print specifications so that the next time you want to
print, you can use one of your application's tools, such as a Print button or the
Command-P keyboard shortcut.

The StyleWriter's Print dialog box looks much the same as the LaserWriter's dialog box,
but with fewer options. My Epson Stylus 600 inkjet's Print dialog box provides similar
options. (See Figure 10.10.)

FIGURE **10.10.**

*The Epson Stylus Print
dialog box.*

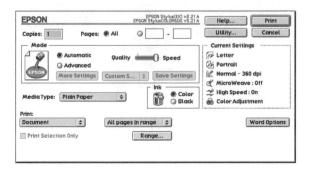

Printing to a PostScript File

If you're using a service bureau to print your document, it often will not have access to the program(s) you used to create your document. In this case, the easiest way to ensure that the document is printed correctly is to create an encapsulated PostScript (EPS) file of the document. You can embed the fonts into the file to ensure that they follow along with the document (although this makes the file extremely large). You create an EPS file by selecting the File option on the Destination pop-up menu on the General screen; then use the Print As File pop-up menu to select EPS options. (See Figure 10.11.)

FIGURE 10.11.

Use the Print As File menu to select the format options for your PostScript file.

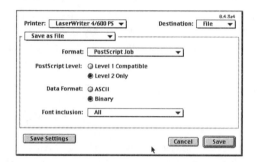

10

Use the pop-up menus to select the type of file to create (PostScript Job, EPS Mac Standard Preview, EPS Mac Enhanced Preview, or No Preview). You can also select to save the file as a Macintosh PostScript file (binary) or as a general PostScript file (ASCII) for use when you don't know what kind of computer the file will be printed from. Assume that any typesetter is a Level 2 PostScript device and select this radio button. Clicking Print causes the Save As dialog box to be displayed (see Figure 10.12). Give the PostScript file a name (notice the .PS suffix, identifying the file as an EPS file) and place it in the folder where you want it saved. Click Save to print the document to a file.

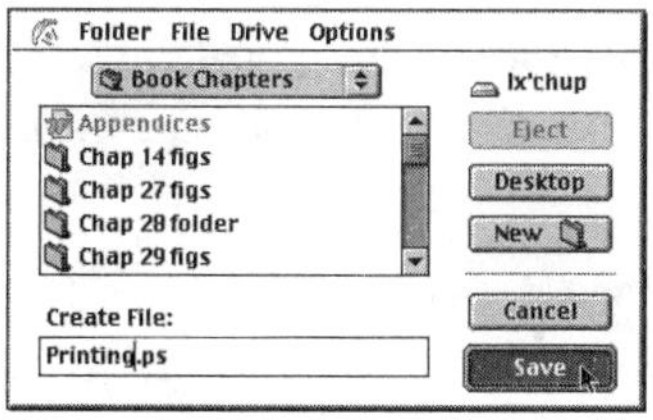

FIGURE 10.12.

Clicking Print saves the document to a PostScript file using the standard Finder Save As dialog box.

Folder File Drive Options

Book Chapters

- Appendices
- Chap 14 figs
- Chap 27 figs
- Chap 28 folder
- Chap 29 figs

Ix'chup

Eject
Desktop
New
Cancel
Save

Create File:

Printing.ps

Printing with Color

All color printers mix three pigments—cyan, yellow, and magenta—to produce all other colors. These colors are the primary colors and serve as the basis for all color printing. When all three colors are mixed equally, the result is a type of black. Many color printers add a real black for a richer mix. The resulting system is called *CMYK* or *process color*.

Color printers can take several forms: They can use liquid or solid ink sprayed on the page (inkjet and phase change inkjet), solid wax that's melted on a page (thermal wax), and pigments that are burned at different temperatures to produce the colors (dye sublimation). Some laser printers mix powdered toner in the four process colors. Printers are categorized by how they apply their pigments, so this section covers dye sublimation printers, thermal wax printers, color laser printers, and inkjet printers.

ColorSync 2.5 Calibrates Color During Printing

In Hour 11, "Color," the ColorSync color calibration system is discussed. Color printers use ColorSync to calibrate what you see on your monitor, displayed as combinations of red, green, and blue (RGB), to how printers create colors with CMYK colors. The Print command lets you use ColorSync 2.5 to ensure that your print colors match what you created on your screen. ColorSync 2.5 consists of three parts: a control panel where you set your RGB, CMYK, and Color Management default calibration files, the calibrator itself that you set up in the Monitors & Sound control panel, and an application program interface (API) used by vendors to enable ColorSync to coordinate their print drivers' various inputs to color printing.

Color Halftoning and Dithering

Halftoning and *dithering* are techniques used to generate color output. Color printers apply pigments by overlaying dots of primary colors. Therefore, a red dot is composed of a yellow dot overlaid by a magenta dot. Eight colors are relatively easily produced by overlaying two primary colors together for a resulting palette of cyan, yellow, magenta, black, red, green, blue, and white (the application of no pigment). Other colors can be created by a process called *dithering*.

Color dithering is the application of the primary color dots in complex patterns that create an optical illusion that one is seeing other colors. It's very difficult to hide the dot patterns, because all the dots are the same size, and different pattern arrangements cause different qualities of results. Only high-end printers can apply color to continuous areas of paper and avoid the dotting effect.

The other way color printers gain the effect of various color hues is through *color halftoning*. This is mostly used to print scanned images. First, the image is separated into its cyan, yellow, black, and magenta components (called color separations). Then, halftoning is used to create dots of different sizes to represent the different amounts of gray in a picture.

Color halftoning varies the amounts of cyan, yellow, magenta, and black in each separation to gain the illusion of various hues. Each separation screen is rotated to a different angle, causing their dots to overlap and form small circles called *rosettes*. Because the rosettes and dithering are noticeable to the naked eye at 300 dpi (the standard output quality of a color printer), this output is not usable to proof a color balance or the details of a color picture.

Inkjet Technology

Recall that inkjet printers are the cousins of dot-matrix printers. Rather than use wires tapping a ribbon, inkjet printers spray ink out of microscopic nozzles in the print head. Some inkjet printers send an electronic signal to a piezoelectric diaphragm within the print head that forces a drop of ink to be ejected from the nozzles. The colors of ink (cyan, magenta, yellow, and black) are all laid down on a single pass, causing fewer registration problems than printers that make four passes and lay each color down separately. Because the ink is a liquid, plain paper absorbs the ink, making clear images difficult to produce.

A second type of color inkjet printer uses a slightly different technology to lay down its colored dots. The phase change inkjet melts blocks of cyan, magenta, yellow, and black wax in ink reservoirs. The melted ink is sprayed onto the page through microscopic nozzles in the print head. Phase change inkjet printers also lay down the colored inks in a single pass. Because the inks are wax based, they solidify much more rapidly than liquid inks dry, thus allowing these printers to print more easily on plain papers. The downside is that less ink is absorbed by the paper, and the use of a high-pressure roller to flatten the solidified ink results the printing of images that are not as sharp as other technologies.

Color Laser Technology

Color lasers apply color by using a four-chamber toner developer unit containing cyan, magenta, yellow, and black toner powder. The image exposed by light onto the photosensitive drum takes on an electrical charge. Those charged areas attract toner as the drum rotates past the developing unit. The problem with this technology is registration errors. If the paper is not aligned perfectly onto the photosensitive drum, the colors will not be applied accurately, leaving fuzzy borders between colored areas.

Color laser printers can print color at higher resolutions than thermal wax or dye sublimation systems. The Apple Color LaserWriter series prints true 600 dpi resolution output. Many printers also use resolution-enhancement technologies, such as Color PhotoGrade from Apple or Hewlett-Packard's Resolution Enhancement Technology, to sharpen text or images by fine-tuning the dot sizes used to create the output.

Thermal Wax Technology

Thermal wax transfer printers use a system where wax-based pigments of each process color (cyan, yellow, magenta, and black) are positioned on a roll of transfer ribbon, one after another. The transfer ribbon is placed between the print head's thousands of heating elements and the paper. The heating elements in the print head are turned on and off, causing the different colors to melt onto the paper as dots. One color is applied for each of four passes of the paper over the print heads and transfer ribbon. The same problem of registration that occurs in the color laser process occurs here.

A newer technology used by Seiko's Professional ColorPoint PSF and Fargo's Primera Pro and Pictura 310 printers mix thermal wax transfer technology with dye sublimation technology. These hybrid thermal wax/dye sublimation machines remove the thermal wax ribbon and paper and replace them with the dye sublimation's plastic film. These printers produce more realistic colors, because the plastic film coated with process colors can produce continuous color, whereas the thermal wax system cannot. The system is cheaper than dye sublimation.

Dye Sublimation Technology

Dye sublimation and film recorders on the upper end of the color printing world do not have these drawbacks. Dye sublimation printing is performed by passing a plastic film coated with cyan, yellow, magenta, and black dye across a print head containing approximately 2,400 heating elements. Each heating element can produce 255 different temperatures, with more dye being transferred the hotter the element gets.

A special paper coated with polyester resin is passed over the heating elements four times for the four dyes; the dyes are sublimated into gases and diffused onto the coatings, thus producing dots of color. The variation in the density of the dyes that are transferred to the paper create continuous tones. Film recorders use red, green, and blue lights to produce images on 35mm slide film. A filter wheel controlled by the Mac produces the correct amounts of primary colors, which are then placed on the 4-by-5-inch Polaroid print or transparency film.

PostScript Options for Color Printers

Some printers, such as the color inkjets, use the Macintosh as the controller; others are more expensive because they contain a PostScript RIP. You can also add a software PostScript RIP to your Mac by installing a PostScript emulator such as ImageWave's StyleScript or TeleTypesetting Company's T-Script. These are software-based PostScript interpreters that run on your Mac.

Another option available for Apple's inkjets is a true Adobe PostScript Level 2 interpreter that runs on the Mac. Hewlett-Packard sells a PostScript RIP driver kit for the DeskWriter 560c. Each of these interpreters lets you print encapsulated PostScript illustrations, such as those from Adobe Illustrator or MacroMedia FreeHand, on your color printer, even if it doesn't contain a PostScript RIP.

Another option is to use software that turns your Mac into a print server, such as GDT Softworks StyleScript. High-end color printers rely on Adobe's Configurable PostScript Interpreter (CPSI) to process color PostScript print jobs and send them to printers.

10

Summary

Like most Macintosh technologies, printing has become quite sophisticated and complicated over time. Because many Mac users are graphic artists or in the publishing business, Macintosh printing has come to provide many high-tech typography features, such as ligatures, tighter control over color, and font management.

The most important thing to remember about printing on the Mac is that every program works the same way because the Mac, not the program, supplies the printer drivers that provide the engine for printing. Just remember to use the Chooser to pick a printer driver, the Page Setup command to determine page formatting, and the Print command to print.

Term Review

Chooser   The application used to select printer drivers and set up PPD files for your printer.

desktop printer   A feature of LaserWriter 8 that creates a drop box on your desktop that you can use to print documents by dragging and dropping.

dot-matrix printers   Printers that use small hammers to press dots of ink onto a page. These were the first computer printers.

dots per inch (dpi)   The measurement unit used to define the quality of printer output (how many dots a printer can place per inch onto a page). Printers range from high-end typesetters with 2,500 dpi levels to dot-matrix printers that print 72 dpi, but most modern business printers support resolutions of 1440, 600, and 300 dpi (or some combination thereof).

ImageWriter   Apple's version of the dot-matrix printer. ImageWriters are no longer supported by Apple.

inkjet printers   Printers that use small squirts of ink to make dots on a page. These printers use the Mac as a processor to rasterize data, but they can print at high resolutions.

laser printers   Printers that use lasers to melt toner onto a page. These printers contain their own microprocessors and memory where PostScript rasterizes data.

Page Setup command   The command that displays the dialog box used to set up how you want your page to appear, including special PostScript features, page size, image resolution, and so forth.

PostScript   Adobe's page-description language used to convert outline fonts to bitmapped images as well as to rasterize encapsulated PostScript (EPS) graphic images.

Print command   The command that displays the dialog box used to print a document.

printer driver   The intermediary software that lets an application communicate with the Mac's Printer Manager software. All printers have a printer driver that defines how they process information. You select the printer driver for your printer in the Chooser.

Printer Page Description (PPD) file   A document containing information about special features of a printer. Every printer has a PPD that resides in the Mac's Preferences folder in the Printer Description folder. You set up your printer by configuring its PPD via the Chooser's Setup button.

rasterizing   The process of converting EPS and outline font information into printable bitmapped images.

Q&A

Q How do I print a document that gives me a PostScript error?

A Often, PostScript errors have to do with one of two things: either you don't have all the fonts used in a document installed on your Mac, or you don't have enough memory on your Mac to perform background printing of your document. If you have a complicated document with lots of EPS graphics and varied fonts, use the Chooser to turn off background printing. This should free up enough memory to print the document. Also, try printing the document page by page.

Q How do I change my default printer?

A Use the Chooser to select a different printer. Note that only Apple printers can be made into default or *desktop printers* at this time. Mac OS 8.5 contains the software that enables third-party printers to be made into desktop printers, but vendors must update their printer drivers to take advantage of these new instructions.

Q How can I rename my printer?

A Run the Apple LaserWriter Utility to rename a default printer.

Workshop

The Workshop contains quiz questions to help you solidify your understanding of the material covered. You can find the answers to the quiz questions in Appendix B, "Quiz Answers."

10

Quiz

1. What's the difference between a dot-matrix printer, an inkjet printer, and a laser printer?

2. What are the two methods for printing on a Mac?

3. What is a RIP?

4. Name some benefits of PostScript printing.

5. What's a printer driver and how do you select the proper one for your printer?

6. When do you need a PPD and how do you create one?

7. What's the purpose of the Page Setup command?

8. How do you change the orientation of your paper?

9. How do you change the resolution of the image you want to print?

10. Where would you set up ColorSync calibration for your print job?

HOUR 11

Color

Color and graphics are like bread and butter to the Mac. One of the major uses of the Macintosh is for desktop and Web-top publishing. The results are often printed with a four-color process by a service bureau. Mac users often worry about the quality of color and graphics rendering—that is, the relationship between what you produce in your image-processing software and what's printed or published. Mac OS 8.5 delivers the tools in the form of ColorSync 2.5 and Color Picker to support the extraordinary precision demanded by prepress work. This hour focuses on using color tools, including the following subjects:

- A short lesson on color management systems (CMSs)
- A discussion of how QuickDraw and ColorSync work together to provide accurate color management
- Calibrating your monitor for prepress accuracy
- Working with specific color palettes for specific tasks, such as Pantone palettes for prepress color work and Netscape/Safe Color palettes for Web work via color palette plug-ins
- Using Color Picker to select the proper color palette for your requirements

What Is Color Management?

It's true that when you get something you want, you always want more. In 1984, Apple and Aldus (now Adobe) provided the tools to start a revolution. Desktop publishing was born when the Mac, running the Aldus PageMaker layout program coupled with Apple's laser printer supported by Adobe PostScript, toppled the preeminence of typesetters and prepress houses and moved manuscript design onto individual desktops. Because PostScript supported the printing of publication-level fonts and superior images, designers wanted more—more fonts, more images, and more photography support, and, in addition, the ability to print color.

Designers knew from years of experience that color commands attention. If you have a color manuscript, people are more likely to read what you have to say. Color advertisements are even more crucially important. The problem with color is that what you see on your screen is not what you necessarily get in your output. There was no way to control the quality of color to ensure its accuracy in print. This capability to match what is displayed onscreen with what is outputted is termed *color management*.

Why Don't Colors Match?

The study of color is a science—a part of physics. Scientists know a lot about how color works. The trick is to apply this knowledge to translating the medium of phosphorescence on your computer monitor or the electronics of a scanner bed to the chemistry of inks in your printer. There are two parts to this translation question: How do devices reproduce color, and how do desktop peripherals communicate in color?

Science has discovered that the human eye can see a wide range of colors. Light can be seen on a broad array of the electromagnetic spectrum between infrared and ultraviolet. Scientists display a model of what the eye can see, called the *color space*, on a chart called the *Chromaticity Chart*. The chart can display two dimensions of color: hue and saturation. A third dimension, called *lightness*, must also be taken into account, although charting its effects is difficult.

The Chromaticity Chart was devised by an international standards-setting organization called the Commision Internationale de l'Eclairage (CIE). In order to plot the color spaces of individual devices, CIE developed a measurement system called *LAB colors*. LAB colors are device neutral and thus provide a way to calculate and convert colors from one system to another without damaging the actual color values. The Chromaticity Chart is sometimes called the CIE Lab Color Chart.

What's frustrating to designers is that the color space your eye can see is a lot broader than the color space that can be depicted on a computer monitor, scanned into your computer, or printed. Scientists refer to the spectrum that a device can reproduce accurately as its *gamut*; thus, the popular saying *a whole gamut of colors*.

If you plot the gamut of a high-level display (such as your printer or scanner) onto the CIE chart, you can see that each device can handle only a small part of the total array. This subset of the larger area of color is called the *device's color space*. Different devices work in different color spaces, reproducing different gamuts of colors. The problem is how to translate one device's color space to another device's color space with as little loss of color as possible.

The development of LAB colors was a major breakthrough, because this measurement system provided a way to describe different coloring methods in a universal manner. LAB color is device independent, meaning that it isn't set to a particular printing or imaging technology. Color management is based on LAB colors.

Working with RGB and CMYK Colors

Let's take a closer look at color spaces. Monitors and scanners display colors using three basic hues: red, green, and blue (also called RGB). That's why displays are sometimes called *RGB devices*. Every color displayed on a monitor or scanned into your computer is derived from red, green, and blue phosphors. Printers and other output devices, on the other hand, create colors using a different color spectrum, sometimes called *process colors*, because the spectrum is based on the ink colors cyan, magenta, yellow, and black. Process colors are also called *CMYK*.

Converting RGB and CMYK to LAB colors enables color management software to correct and adjust colors in a unified way, allowing designers to use system-wide color management.

As stated earlier, each input and output device (printers, scanners, displays, and so on) use different colors to reproduce colors. The colors used to produce device-specific output and input colors are called *colorants*. CMYK color is extremely device dependent (because it's based on actual inks used in the printing process). RGB colorants are based on electronic signals and are therefore less device dependent. For this reason, it's a good idea to always avoid using CMYK colorants to input images. Stick to scanning using RGB or LAB colors so that your color management system can properly adjust these colors between devices. This means that you should always save your TIFF files in RGB rather than CMYK.

LAB color systems use profiles to describe the colors a device can convey. Profiles are dictionaries containing data on a specific device's color information. Every device comes from the factory with a color profile based on a scientific process called *device characterization*. Profile information has been standardized through the work of the International Color Consortium (ICC). ICC profiles can be used across multiple computer platforms.

Setting Up Color Profiles

Every device starts with a factory-set profile. However, each device varies from its factory norm. That's why devices must be calibrated regularly. The process of calibrating produces a corrective profile used by the color management system. I'll return to the subject of calibration later in this hour.

The same color profiles developed for device characterization and calibration are also used by color management systems (CMSs) to convert one color system into another. The process of conversion is called the *color matching method (CMM)*. There are many CMMs; you can think of them as universal translators that equate one color profile with another.

Because every device's color is slightly different, a CMS performs gamut-matching using the CMMs to select the next closest reproducible color. This is also known as *rendering styles*. Different images (such as photographs versus pie charts) require different rendering styles. CMSs take rendering styles into account when matching colors. For example, color matching must be highly accurate when you're printing a photograph, because it uses millions of colors to derive its image. On the other hand, you can get away with less accuracy when printing a chart, because it uses broad swaths of a single color to convey a message. Color management systems take these rendering style requirements into account to increase the efficiency of their performance.

Developing Color Management Systems

The problem with early color management systems was that each company that developed a system based that system on a proprietary architecture. You soon had a Tower of Babel, where every layout program used its own CMM to convert colors. This lead to a total lack of consistency in coloring as well as no compatibility between color profiles. You also couldn't exchange profile files between applications, because each application used a proprietary color management system. Therefore, no single system was widely adopted.

Apple decided to break down the walls between color management systems. In 1993, ColorSync 1.0 was introduced. ColorSync provides a common architecture for color management across all devices and applications. Therefore, all desktop publishing, image processing, and output devices could call on a single tool to perform color management.

ColorSync 1.0 was not perfect; its application programming interface (API) lacked enough information in each color profile to support high-end color processing needs. Therefore, ColorSync 1.0 was not widely adopted.

In 1995, Apple introduced ColorSync 2.0 (which has recently been updated to version 2.5) to handle a greater variety of CMMs and color profiles. ColorSync 2.5 is a system-wide color management system that provides device calibration, a default Apple CMM (although it supports third-party CMMs), and color management API support for programs such as Adobe Photoshop and QuarkXPress that also perform color management.

Figure 11.1 displays the architecture underlying ColorSync that lets it be the intermediary between disparate color devices. ColorSync uses LAB colors to convert and translate colors from input to output devices, based on the rendering styles, CMMs, and color profiles you select.

Figure 11.1.

ColorSync 2 sits between your image-processing applications, input devices, and output devices to convert and translate color information so that each device transmits accurate colors.

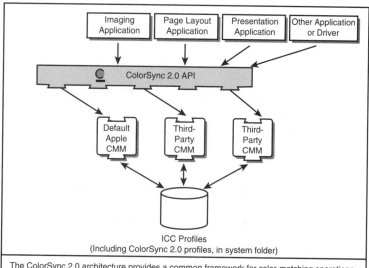

The ColorSync 2.0 architecture provides a common framework for color-matching operations. Because ColorSync is system-level software, input and output devices, as well as applications, all have a common solution for color matching.

Setting up your Mac for proper color work is a multistep process. The following sections describe each step.

Using QuickDraw

Before discussing how to calibrate your monitor, scanner, and printer to accurately work together to depict colors, I have to digress into a discussion of how the Mac works with images and color. QuickDraw is the Mac OS toolbox that supervises all the color management systems on the Mac, both hardware and software, to create the images you see on your computer display.

QuickDraw is able to communicate with your random access memory in 48-bit chunks, thus enabling the Mac to display 280 trillion colors (that is, if your eye could see and your monitor could display that many colors). Monitor video cards are designed with limited register sizes so that they can hold only so much color information for each pixel. The bit-depth of this address determines how many colors can be displayed. By the way, a pixel is the smallest possible area of screen that can be drawn. Color capabilities are generally given in "bits per pixel" measurements. Table 11.1 describes these pixel schemes.

TABLE 11.1. MONITOR PIXEL DEPTHS AND COLOR DISPLAY CAPABILITIES.

Pixel Depth	Displayed Colors	Bits Represented
1-bit	Black and white	0, 1
2-bit	Four colors	00, 01, 10, 11
8-bit	256 colors	--
16-bit	32 thousand colors	--
32-bit	16 million colors	--

A CLOSER LOOK AT QUICKDRAW

QuickDraw converts all color profiles to RGB values for display no matter what color model an application or device actually uses. The RGB model is quite ingenious. QuickDraw sets up a coordinate plane, called the *hyperdesktop*, that identifies every pixel that can be drawn. Each pixel is divided into four axes that are given color values— red, green, or blue (actually bit values from 0 to 65,535, providing a 16-bit number for each color). There's also a center point that represents the color being displayed. The center point is described by a value for each axis representing the amounts of red, green, and blue the color contains. This composite number has a possible size of 48 bits.

In the RGB model, any color can be created by mixing red, green, and blue in different amounts. The more of each color you add, the closer to white you get; the fewer colors you add, the closer to black you get. The most colors you can combine is called the *white point*. The white point is important for calibrating your monitor and peripherals.

Every color identified by QuickDraw's hyperdesktop model is listed as a 48-bit RGB description in a system extension called the Color Picker. QuickDraw uses the Color Picker to see which color profile you've requested and looks up the closest approximation from the hardware's Color Manager toolbox and the Graphics Device Manager toolbox's CLUT (color lookup table). The *CLUT* is a listing of every color your monitor or scanner can display, described in 8-, 16-, or 32-bit numbers (depending on what you've set in your Monitors & Sound control panel).

Here's where calibration comes in. When you have ColorSync 2.5 installed, you can calibrate your monitor to the Apple CMM (or any other CMM you have installed). ColorSync then exactly matches how your input and output devices display colors—converting scanner RGBs to display monitor RGBs to printer CMYK colors. ColorSync then attaches a color profile to each image for use by QuickDraw toolboxes to manage color on the Mac.

Color Calibrating Your Mac

As stated earlier, every Macintosh hardware device comes from the factory with a preset color profile. You can adjust this profile using ColorSync 2.5 to fit your document production needs. To change the color profile, you use the ColorSync Monitor Calibration Assistant in the Monitors & Sound control panel.

The assistant takes you through the steps required to set contrast, saturation, white point, brightness, and rendering style. When you're done, you give your new profile a name. You can use ColorSync to adjust the color profiles of your display, scanner, and any other input device (such as a tablet).

To calibrate your monitor, open the Monitors & Sound control panel and then click the Calibrate button. (See Figure 11.2.)

11

FIGURE 11.2.

Click the Calibrate button on the Monitors screen of the Monitor & Sound control panel to calibrate your monitor with ColorSync.

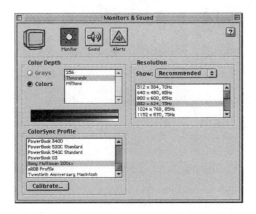

Monitor Calibration Assistant

The first task you need to do to calibrate your monitor is to adjust it physically so that it provides its best display. The first screen of the Monitor Calibration Assistant that appears after you click Calibrate enables you to set your brightness and contrast using an interactive panel on the assistant (see Figure 11.3). Push the appropriate buttons on your monitor to adjust the brightness and contrast. If you can adjust the white point, set that adjustment as well.

FIGURE 11.3.

Use the Monitor Calibration Assistant's first page to physically adjust the quality of your display.

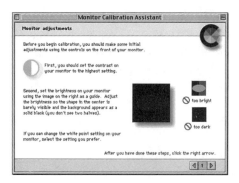

The next task you need to do is adjust the contrast between midtones (*called the gamma*) on your screen. You're really setting the density values of the red, green, and blue colors that generate all your screen colors. On the second page, shown in Figure 11.4, use the sliders to gently adjust the colors until the apple is barely noticeable on each of the three the interactive panels.

FIGURE 11.4.

Adjust the midtone contrasts of your screen by using the sliders on this page.

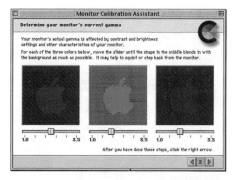

The third page has you set a target gamma for your monitor. Computer monitors and television screens display the same colors in wildly different ways. One of the ways to limit the change in color is to work from a monitor that mirrors what you think your final work should look like. One of the ways to adjust your display to represent different platforms is to change the screen's brightness setting.

The target gamma is a way to define different brightness settings for different platforms. Table 11.2 illustrates how different systems display the same picture. The lower the target gamma, the brighter the screen; the higher the target gamma, the darker the screen. Note that PC monitors display colors very darkly compared to Mac monitors.

TABLE 11.2. AVERAGE FACTORY SETTINGS FOR VARIOUS MONITORS.

Platform Type	Gamma Measurement
Macintosh monitors	1.8 gamma
Silicon Graphics monitors	1.7 gamma
Intel PC monitors	2.5 gamma
Television monitors	2.2 gamma

Select a radio button to change the gamma of your screen to represent a different platform (see Figure 11.5). The interactive panel changes to show you the result of your choice.

FIGURE 11.5.

Adjust the brightness of your screen by selecting a target gamma.

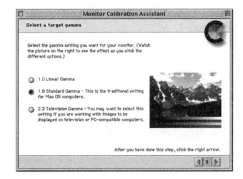

Remember those device color profiles? The fourth page, shown in Figure 11.6, has you select the color profile that best matches your monitor. You have to know the manufacturer and model of your monitor. If the model number is not there, pick the color profile that comes closest—in my case, it was a generic Sony profile.

FIGURE 11.6.

Choose the closest color profile from the list on this page.

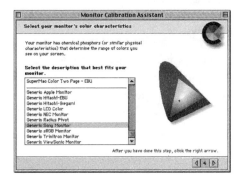

11

The last screen adjusts the background whiteness of your display. You can approximate the light quality of your resulting document by adjusting the white point of your monitor. Select the various radio buttons to see different white values. (See Figure 11.7.)

FIGURE 11.7.

Choose a screen whiteness value from this page.

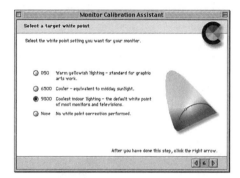

You've now calibrated your monitor to fit your design requirements. Click Save to create a *corrective profile*. Use this profile in the ColorSync 2 control panel. It comes up as your default profile for your system when you open the control panel. (See Figure 11.8.)

FIGURE 11.8.

The ColorSync 2 control panel's system profile setting reflects your calibration efforts.

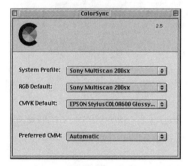

Calibrating Other Devices

You use the ColorSync 2 control panel to set the corrective profiles for your other input and output devices (refer to Figure 11.8). Note that I selected the Epson Stylus Color 600 glossy paper profile for CMYK, because this is the printer I generally use. Set the RGB profile to match your system or select a profile from the list. The RGB selection lets you calibrate scanners and other input devices.

Using Color Picker

You can pick the color matching method (CMM) used by your application in the Color Picker to match its gamut to the RGB profile used by QuickDraw. Color Picker is a system extension that controls the CMM used to convert colors from one device to another via ColorSync. All applications that use color call on Color Picker when you select a color or colors. Figure 11.9 shows you a type of Color Picker available in Adobe Photoshop 4.

FIGURE 11.9.

Many applications, such as Adobe Photoshop, use Color Picker to manage color selection.

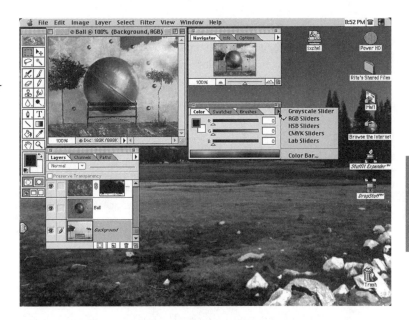

The quickest way to view Color Picker is to select Other from the colors list for highlighting on the Appearance control panel (Color Picker operates in the background in many image-processing and graphics applications). The color selection formats for the Color Picker dialog box include the following:

- **CMYK Color Picker.** Enables you to select a color based on cyan, magenta, yellow, and black colors (see Figure 11.10). Use this CMM to choose colors that reflect those produced by printers and other ink-based output devices. The color scale for each color ranges from zero to 100 percent. To create a color, move the sliders across the four colors to create the desired highlight color.

11

FIGURE 11.10.

The CMYK Color Picker dialog box.

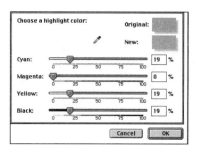

• **Crayon Color Picker.** Presents a selected color range, applicable in any color depth mode, using a crayon theme consisting of 60 colors (see Figure 11.11). To change the highlight color, select any crayon and click the OK button.

Some examples of colors you can select from are Apple, Banana, Fog, Ocean Green, Tangerine, Dirt, Cool Marble, Evening Blue, and Fern.

FIGURE 11.11.

The Crayon Color Picker dialog box.

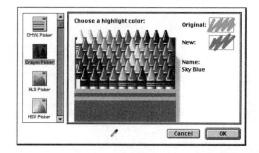

• **HLS Color Picker.** Presents the familiar color wheel from the original Color control panel (see Figure 11.12). The color wheel enables you to choose the highlight color. To select a color, click the color wheel and adjust the slider bar below it. The slider bar represents the Lightness value, indicated in the text box to the right of the bar.

You can also create or adjust a color by using the values in the Hue Angle, Saturation, and Lightness fields. Hue Angle is measured in degrees (0 to 360), Saturation is a percentage (gray to 100 percent of the selected color), and Lightness is a percentage (ranging from black to white).

• **HSV Color Picker.** Enables you to select a color from similar settings as HLS. The *V* in HSV stands for *Value*, however, which is reflected in both the slider bar and Value field of this Color Picker window. Hue Angle and Saturation are measured here the same as in the HLS dialog box. Value is a percentage ranging from black to 100 percent of the pure, selected color.

FIGURE 11.12.

The Hue, Lightness, and Saturation (HLS) Color Picker dialog box.

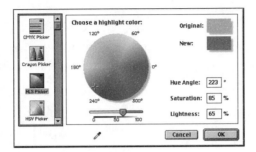

- **HTML Color Picker.** Consists of Red, Green, and Blue slider bars, with an HTML value in the lower-right corner of the window (see Figure 11.13). Use this CMM if you want to choose colors that represent those that a browser can use. This CMM is very useful when you're creating Web pages, because you can visualize the color represented by its hexadecimal code. The Red, Green, and Blue slider bars are followed by text fields that convert the color value into an HTML color value. Settings for each color range from 00, 33, 66, 99, CC, and FF. You can also input an HTML value into the HTML field, and the RGB sliders will reconfigure to show the input value's color.

FIGURE 11.13.

The HTML Color Picker dialog box.

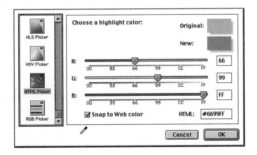

- **RGB Color Picker.** Enables you to select red, green, and blue to create the highlight color (see Figure 11.14). Each color is followed by a value field showing the percentage of each color used to create the highlight color. All slider bars share a scale starting at 0 and moving up 25 notches to 100 at the end of the sliding scale.

Other Uses of ColorSync

ColorSync 2.5 also xe "ColorSync" xe "ColorSync" includes a plug-in that you can drag into your image-processing or graphics application Plug-ins folder. This is the physical manifestation of the ColorSync API mentioned previously. When you install the

ColorSync plug-in, ColorSync takes over the task of matching filters, color separations, previews, and output colors in that application. Figure 11.15 shows an example of ColorSync in action, performing color separation (splitting out the layers of cyan, magenta, yellow, and black into separate documents for prepress use).

FIGURE 11.14.

The RGB Color Picker dialog box.

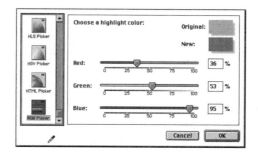

FIGURE 11.15.

Photoshop uses the ColorSync plug-in to manage color-separating tasks.

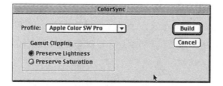

Read the documentation from your image-processing application for more information on how to use ColorSync with that software product.

Summary

During this hour, you've learned the rudiments of color management using ColorSync and Color Picker. You've learned how to calibrate your monitor, scanner, and printer to reflect your output requirements. You've also learned how QuickDraw manages color on your Mac and where ColorSync and Color Picker fit into the Mac toolbox.

ColorSync works in the background most of the time, translating colors to enable you to accurately reflect outputs on your screen. The hard part of using ColorSync comes when you apply its plug-in features in image-processing programs. Because you now know a lot more about how color works on your Mac, you should have no trouble learning how to apply its tools to specific applications.

Term Review

calibration   The process of adjusting a device to compensate for differences due to manufacturing, age, environmental conditions, and media inconsistencies.

color management system (CMS)   The process of controlling how colors are displayed and outputted on your computer. CMSs use color matching methods (CMMs) and color profiles to adjust color differences from one type of device to another to better match the intent of your work. ColorSync is a color management system.

color matching method (CMM)   The routine used by a color management system to apply transformations to color data. ColorSync uses the Apple CMM as a default but supports many third-party CMMs.

colorants   The colors used by a color device to produce colors. CMYK are colorants for printers.

Color Picker   The system extension in the Mac OS that manages which CMM is used to adjust colors in ColorSync to be displayed by QuickDraw.

ColorSync 2.5   The latest version of Apple's system-wide color management software suite. ColorSync calibrates input and output devices to ensure that their colors match what you created in your graphic or image-processing application.

11

device characterization   The process of creating a device profile. Manufacturers use spectrophotometers to accurately measure the color wavelengths emitted from devices to develop device color profiles.

gamma   A measurement of the contrast between the midtones in a gamut. *Gamma* is a way to describe the brightness of a device.

gamut   The range of colors that a device can reproduce.

gamut mapping   The process of altering a color so that it can be reproduced on a particular device.

International Color Consortium (ICC)   A committee formed in 1993 to establish standards for electronic color publishing.

process colors   The four primary colors used in printing: cyan, magenta, yellow, and black. Process colors are also called *CMYK colors*.

profile   A file containing the color reproduction capabilities of a given input, display, or output device. Color management systems use profiles to interpret color data between devices.

QuickDraw   The Mac OS software that manages how the Mac displays data on your monitor. All color management is controlled by QuickDraw.

rendering styles   The method in which color is reproduced, taking into consideration the intent of the color.

RGB colors   The three phosphors (red, green, and blue) used in computer displays and scanners to generate all colors.

Q&A

Q Which version of ColorSync comes with Mac OS 8.5?

A ColorSync 2.5. Mac OS 8.1 and 8.0 have ColorSync version 2.1.2 installed.

Q How do I get ColorSync 2.5?

A Download the program from `http://colorsync.apple.com/` or any of the many download sites, including Cnet's `http://download.com/`.

Q Where can I read more about ColorSync?

A Check out the whitepapers and tutorials at `http://colorsync.apple.com/info/`.

Q Which image-processing software supports ColorSync?

A Adobe Systems' PhotoShop 4.01, PageMaker 6.5, and Acrobat 3.0. Agfa Gevaert, NV ColorTune 3.0 (profile customizing and editing software), and ColorTune Pro. Color Solutions' ColorBlind Edit, Digital Zone PhotoImpress, Helios Software, GmbH ColorSync, QuarkXpress XT, and LinoColor VisuaLab.

Workshop

The Workshop contains quiz questions to help you solidify your understanding of the material covered. You can find the answers to the quiz questions in Appendix B, "Quiz Answers."

Quiz

1. Where do you find ColorSync on your Mac?
2. Which control panel is used to calibrate your monitor's colors?
3. Where are the device profiles for your printer and scanner stored on the Mac?
4. How do you change color-matching methods and choose another highlight color in the Finder?
5. What's the difference between CYMK and RGB color profiles in Color Picker?

6. How do you install the ColorSync plug-in on an image-processing application?

7. How do you change the target gamma of your monitor?

8. How do you assign ColorSync as the color manager in your color printer?

9. What bit-depth is used for producing images for the Web?

10. How do you change the color resolution and bit-depth of your monitor?

11

HOUR 12

QuickTime

QuickTime (now at version 3) is an Apple technology that works with software applications to synchronize image with sound. QuickTime is a highly successful multimedia architecture used on almost all multimedia CD-ROMs to produce the "wow" graphics. The following QuickTime-related issues are covered in this hour:

- Understanding what QuickTime is
- How to use QuickTime
- QuickTime components
- What's new in QuickTime
- Using QuickTime on the Internet

What Is QuickTime?

You've seen QuickTime in action if you have played Broderbund's Myst or Riven, used Microsoft Encarta, or played Id Software's Doom II. QuickTime enables your Mac to integrate text, still graphics, video, animation, 3D, virtual reality (VR), and sound into a cohesive whole. QuickTime has become the foundation in many video editing and multimedia creation programs for the production of video and audio documents. In addition, QuickTime provides the means to transmit and play real-time digital video over the Internet.

QuickTime is not a single program but a technology consisting of a host of small component programs that together provide digital video production and display. QuickTime resides on the Mac as a whole series of system extensions that enable the different pieces of the architecture (including QuickTime VR, QuickDraw 3D, QuickTime plug-in, QuickTime MPEG, and CODEC files) to function. The visible portion of the technology consists of two applications for viewing pieces of QuickTime: namely, Movie Player and PictureViewer. In addition, QuickTime 3.0 includes a plug-in for Netscape Navigator and Microsoft Internet Explorer to let you view streaming video in real-time on the Internet.

The latest version of QuickTime is QuickTime 3.0, which is included in Mac OS 8.5. Figure 12.1 shows you some of the system extensions installed to enable QuickTime.

QuickTime has two flavors: QuickTime 3.0 (a free set of tools to play QuickTime media) and QuickTime Pro (a software package that lets you create QuickTime applications). QuickTime Pro is a more robust version of QuickTime that lets you actually construct videos. You'll find when you first open QuickTime 3.0 that Apple places innumerable ads asking if you want to purchase the upgrade for $29.95.

FIGURE 12.1.

QuickTime adds many extensions and control panels to your System Folder to perform its powerful feats.

QuickTime 3.0 provides the following benefits:

- QuickTime 3.0 is one of the technology standards for delivery and playback of CD-ROM and Internet content on many platforms.

- Support for multiple data types (for example, multiple-language text tracks, video, sound, graphics, animation, text, music/MIDI, sprite, 3D, and virtual reality).

- If you upgrade to QuickTime Pro, you can create video productions on your Mac that can be played back on most platforms, including the creation of hybrid Windows/Mac CD-ROMs.

- Creation of videos is made easier because QuickTime provides advanced tools such as the automatic synchronization of sound, video, music, and other data tracks to a common time base.

Using QuickTime

Using QuickTime is almost a no-brainer because the applications do most of the work for you. In addition, Apple's got a great site for learning how to use QuickTime: `http://www.apple.com/quicktime/information/`. Applications that support QuickTime span a range of features, from authoring video, sound, and animation to playback of all these multimedia elements. Most of the authoring software packages, such as Adobe Premiere 5.0 and Macromedia Director and Authorware, are commercially available; however, they're more on the high end of the software spectrum for both cost and quality. In addition, Apple recently purchased Macromedia's fabled digital-video editing software called *Final Cut*, with hopes to release it soon as the ultimate QuickTime 3.0 authoring tool. As stated earlier, playback is supported by games, Web sites, and any other software that uses video, such as encyclopedias. In addition, QuickTime comes with MovieMaker 3.0, which lets you play QuickTime videos directly on your Mac.

12

Playing a Movie

QuickTime is invisible most of the time. When the Mac senses a digital video, it invokes QuickTime and plays the movie. (See Figure 12.2.)

FIGURE 12.2.

Movie Player automatically opens when you double-click a QuickTime movie icon.

You can also invoke the Movie Player application and then open a movie to play it.

Here's how to play a movie with Movie Player:

1. Double-click Movie Player (located in the QuickTime 3.0 folder installed with Mac OS 8.5).

2. Choose Open from the File menu.

3. In the resulting Finder dialog box, select a movie you want to play. (See Figure 12.3.)

FIGURE 12.3.

Open a digital video file like any other Mac file using a Finder dialog box.

4. Click Open.

5. The QuickTime screen is displayed and the movie plays.

Mac OS 8.5 installs the Movie Player application to the Applications folder on your hard drive. Movie Player prefers 2 MB of memory in order to support playback of QuickTime movies. Movie Player consists of many of QuickTime's standard interface features, such as the controller with its slider and button controls. It also has import, export, track editing, and window size controls for any image-based movie file.

Controlling the Video

Movie Player's controller interface lets you choose audio and video playback settings with a mouse click (see Figure 12.4). The sound volume button is located on the far left of the image playback window. Pressing the spacebar or pressing the Play button, located next to the sound volume button, begins playback of the movie.

FIGURE 12.4.

The Movie Player controller.

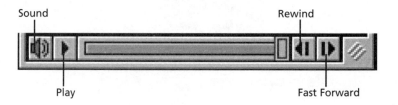

Sound   Rewind

Play   Fast Forward

During playback, you can press the arrow keys to step a frame forward or backward, or you can click anywhere on the slider bar to jump to a different location in the movie file. Pressing the "play backward" or "play forward" button, located at the lower-right corner of the image window, moves the slider bar and movie backward or forward.

Movie playback is set to the frame rate at which the movie was originally created. Playback performance is directly related to the hardware running Mac OS. If QuickTime cannot synchronize a large video window with audio, it will drop video frames during playback. Smaller window sizes provide more optimal performance than large window sizes, especially on slower computer hardware.

Movie Player can play back audio-only sound files as well as single or multitrack audio and video movie files. Opening a sound file with Movie Player will bring up both an open dialog box and a dialog box requesting where to save the QuickTime audio file. The controller for audio-only playback looks and works the same as with a movie file, except the audio-only file doesn't have an image window area. The controller allows you to play back part or all of the audio clip.

Movie and audio playback can be modified to loop all or part of the file at different window sizes and with single or multiple tracks of video and audio. Actually, there's only one video track and five sound tracks. Any track can be enabled, disabled, deleted, or extracted.

CALIBRATION AND CONFIGURATION ISSUES

Some configuration is involved to optimize QuickTime movie recording and playback. This includes setting the appropriate color depth and Mac OS settings (such as turning off virtual memory and file sharing). You should also refrain from initiating background tasks, such as printing.

Another issue to consider before playing a movie is how much memory is needed. Generally, the larger the recorded screen size, the more memory you'll need to allocate to the player application to play back the movie. It's not very easy to tell how much memory a movie needs before opening it, but sometimes the file size can indicate how much data is in the movie. If an application doesn't have enough memory to play a movie, it will issue an error message indicating this situation.

12

Playing Back a Movie in a QuickTime-Savvy Program

Any application that supports QuickTime (called *QuickTime-savvy*) can be used to play back a video. For example, SimpleText, the little text editor that comes with Mac OS 8.5, is QuickTime savvy. (See Figure 12.5.)

SimpleText's preferred memory is set to 512 KB. However, if you plan on using it for movie playback, you should increase the preferred memory size to 2 MB. If SimpleText doesn't have enough memory to open a movie file, it will display a message box saying so.

FIGURE 12.5.

SimpleText will also play QuickTime movies in a modal dialog box.

Opening a QuickTime movie with a savvy program such as SimpleText brings up the same window and controls as Movie Player, as well as a smaller set of menus. Running a movie within an application lets you play audio and video in QuickTime movies. The player lacks the loop and track menu features in Movie Player; however, it does support file import and export.

If you want to edit your movie, you need to downgrade from Movie Player 3.0 to Movie Player 2.5.1 or purchase QuickTime 3.0 Pro. Movie Player 3.0 provides only rudimentary playback controls and no authoring capabilities. Movie Player 2.5 can be acquired from shareware sites such as www.download.com, or you can select Movie Player from the custom screen of the Apple System 7.6 installation CD-ROM.

Saving a Video in the Scrapbook

Say you find a royalty-free movie on the Web you want to copy into a document. You can save the movie in the Scrapbook, where you can access it from any application on your Mac.

Audio-only or video and audio movies can be moved to the Scrapbook a couple of different ways. You can drag an entire movie out of Movie Player into the Scrapbook by dragging and dropping the open movie window into the Scrapbook window. The audio or image files can also be copied and pasted into the Scrapbook.

Once the image is in the Scrapbook, all the QuickTime controls for sound volume and playback are also available in the Scrapbook window. However, movie editing is not supported.

Scrapbook displays the duration and dimensions of the QuickTime movie as well as the file size in its main window. The window size of the movie is scaled to fit into the Scrapbook and is not a reflection of image quality if it were played back in Movie Player. Image resize information is also presented in the lower-right corner of the Scrapbook window containing the movie file.

Setting QuickTime Preferences

You use the QuickTime Settings control panel to select which features of QuickTime you want to run as well as how you want the technology to behave. The QuickTime Settings control panel contains five distinct sections: AutoPlay, Connection Speed, Media Keys, Music, QuickTime Exchange, and Registration. Through these settings panels you can control the transmission speed of incoming and outgoing video and audio signals, access secure media files, translate foreign media files into QuickTime-playable files on the fly, and manage how QuickTime replays video and audio.

Setting Up AutoPlay Preferences

AutoPlay lets you automatically play audio or CD-ROM titles when inserted into the computer (see Figure 12.6a). The Music section of the control panel lets you choose the setting or connection for music synthesis.

QuickTime allows you to enable or disable the AutoPlay feature for audio CDs. It provides control over when you want a CD to play. If you want to use the Apple Audio CD Player or a similar application to control audio CD playback, launch that application before inserting the CD. If the Apple Audio CD Player or a similar application is not running, the CD begins playing from Track 1 automatically when you insert the disc. Otherwise, you control when to start and stop the audio using your application software.

12

FIGURE 12.6A.

The AutoPlay section of the QuickTime Settings control panel.

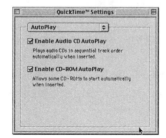

AUTOMATICALLY STARTING UP YOUR CDS WITH QUICKTIME

TheCD-ROM AutoStart feature also lets you create CD-ROMs that automatically launch an application when the disc is inserted. This is useful for entertainment and educational titles, because it's easier for users to begin playing the software. You can enable or disable AutoStart using the QuickTime Settings control panel.

To create an AutoStart-enabled CD-ROM, you specify a document or application file as the AutoStart file. If the file you specify is an application, you may set it to be invisible. Documents may not be invisible. If the AutoStart file is a document, QuickTime asks the Finder to launch the document. If an application is not available, the Finder will issue its normal warning, just as if the file had been double-clicked.

AutoStart works only with disks or other storage media that have been formatted as a Standard File Format (also called HFS). All information about AutoStart is contained in sector 0. The first two bytes in the sector must be either 0 or LK.

Setting Your Connection Speed

The speed of your modem has a great impact on the quality of the QuickTime movies you play back from the Internet. Use the control panel shown in Figure 12.6b to tell QuickTime the best performance your modem is capable of providing. QuickTime will adjust its streaming video to accommodate your requirements.

FIGURE 12.6B.

The Connection Speed section lets you tell QuickTime how fast your modem can transmit data.

Setting Up Music Preferences

Use the Music screen to select the default music synthesizer for QuickTime to use. Options available in the Music section of the control panel include QuickTime Music Synthesizer, General MIDI on Modem Port, General MIDI on Printer Port, and Plug-in Synthesizer and OMS. QuickTime Music Synthesizer is the default setting for the control panel unless MIDI hardware or some other music-related hardware is connected to the computer. Figure 12.6c presents the Music screen.

FIGURE 12.6c.

The Music screen lets you set up your MIDI Synthesizer preferences.

Applications and QuickTime movies can use QuickTime Music Architecture to play sounds through a general MIDI synthesizer, through the Macintosh's built-in speaker or external speakers, or through a hardware synthesizer. It also introduces atomic instruments. In previous versions of QuickTime Music Architecture, sounds were limited to the set of built-in sampled instruments. QuickTime 3.0 removes that limitation because you can create new atomic instruments and add them to a QuickTime Music Architecture instrument component.

The Movie Player and SimpleText applications let you open a standard MIDI file and convert it into a QuickTime music track. You can use either application to convert the MIDI file and save it as a QuickTime movie. After the file is saved, the music can be played back using the controller.

QuickTime Music Architecture is composed of four software components—note allocator, tune player, music component, and instrument component—and a set of music events. You can use the QuickTime Music Architecture components to play individual notes, play tunes, control MIDI devices, and include atomic instruments to increase the number of sounds available.

Setting Media Keys

The Media Keys control panel is rather obscure. Use this panel to set up password keys used to access proprietary or private servers. (See Figure 12.6d.)

FIGURE 12.6d.

Use the Media Keys screen to list the passwords used to access proprietary or secure servers that contain video files.

12

Setting Up QuickTime Exchange

Multimedia on computers is currently a Tower of Babel, with every digital video device
maker creating its own proprietary video format. Luckily, QuickTime can import foreign
formats and work with them. The control panel shown in Figure 12.6e lets you import
and export non-QuickTime video formats.

FIGURE **12.6E.**

*Use the QuickTime
Exchange panel to
enable QuickTime to
import, work with, and
export other video file
types.*

Editing Videos with Movie Player Pro

If you purchase QuickTime Pro, you get a beefed-up version of Movie Player. With this
high-octane version of Movie Player (called Movie Player Pro, naturally) you can manipulate your video and audio. Frames of an audio and video track can be cut and pasted to
the same file or to another movie file.

To select several frames, Shift-click and drag-select the frames you want to copy to
another part of a movie or to another file. Select Paste, or Command-P, to place the
frames into another part of a movie or to a separate movie file. The added frames will
appear with a black hue on the controller slide bar. Undo removes the added frames.
Creating a new movie in Movie Player creates an empty image window with the controller. Pasting frames into the window expands the window and displays the entire set of
frames added to the new movie file.

Editing Videos with Movie Player 2.5

As stated earlier, Apple did a sneaky thing with the upgrade of QuickTime. In upgrading
Movie Player to 3.0, all the editing and manipulation features available to version 2.5
users were removed. You're expected to pay $29.95 to upgrade to the Pro version of
Movie Player if you want to work with videos rather than just watch them.

Luckily, users have found a way around this glitch. When you install QuickTime 3.0, it
writes over only certain software, leaving such things as Movie Player 2.5 untouched.
Look and you'll find that you have both Movie Player 3.0 and Movie Player 2.5 resident

on your Mac. Moreover, when you launch Movie Player 2.5, you can take advantage of QuickTime 3.0's more advanced features. Here are some examples:

- You can play movies at half-normal and full-screen sizes.
- You can loop the movie and play it on a darkened background.
- You can cut, copy, and paste sequences.
- You can extract, delete, enable, and disable tracks.
- You can save changed videos or create new movies.
- You can export your movie in new formats, including BMP picture, Digital Video Stream, Wave sound files (.WAV), and mLaw sound files (.AU).
- You can give your videos special effects, such as blur, film noise, and sharpen. In addition, Movie Player 2.5 works with the freeware program MakeEffectMovie http://www.apple.com/quicktime/developers/tools.html to create effects such as Fire and Clouds and transitions such as Cross Fade, Iris, and Wipe.
- Movie Player 2.5 supports several industry-standard codecs (compression-decompression algorithms), including Sorenson Video codec and Qdesign Music and Qualcomm PureVoice codecs.

> To get the highest quality picture with these codecs, you must purchase the full-featured versions of these compressor/decompressor packages. The Qdesign and Sorenson products are available as a single package from Terran Interactive (http://www.terran.com) for $798.

12

However, there is one caveat: In order to obtain the full features of QuickTime 3.0, such as drag-and-drop editing, you do have to pay for the key that unlocks the Pro version.

For more information about working with Movie Player, check out Apple's QuickTime site at http://www.apple.com/quicktime/information/macmovieplayer/.

Drawing Vector Graphics in QuickTime

Another reason to upgrade to QuickTime Pro is to gain the ability to create vector graphic animations that are playable within QuickTime's Movie Player. The benefits of using object-based drawings rather than the standard bitmapped drawings is that vectors take up less space than bitmaps, resulting in smaller files. Although you cannot create the animations within QuickTime 3.0, you can purchase Lari Software's LighteningDraw/Web for $99 (http://www.larisoftware.com). LighteningDraw/Web lets you create vector animations for use on the Web via QuickTime. In addition, ObjectDancer by PaceWorks (http://www.paceworks.com) also supports vector animation.

Using Picture Viewer

QuickTime 3.0 introduced a new way to draw still images. Graphics importer components provide a standard method for applications to open and display still images contained within graphics documents. Graphics importer components allow you to work with any type of image data, regardless of the file format or compression used in the document. You specify the document that contains the image and the destination rectangle the image should be drawn into, and QuickTime handles the rest. The PictureViewer application, shown in Figure 12.7, in QuickTime Pro lets you manipulate these still images before placing them into a movie.

FIGURE 12.7.

Use PictureViewer to manipulate still images.

QuickTime and the Internet

There is a big difference between the QuickTime movies that work well over the Internet and the QuickTime movies you may be used to seeing on CD-ROMs. This section explains the reasons for the difference and some tips and tricks you can use to optimize your movies for playback over the Internet. You'll also learn how to embed QuickTime movies in a Web page.

Working with the QuickTime Plug-In

One of the most beneficial components of the QuickTime 3.0 package is the inclusion of a new QuickTime plug-in for Web browsers. QuickTime Plug-in 2.0 contains expanded browser support for Netscape Navigator 4.0 and Internet Explorer for Macintosh 4.0 (as well as for Windows 95/NT).

To use the QuickTime plug-in, you have to copy it into the Plug-ins folder for your browser. Then, whenever you start up your browser, it will initiate the QuickTime plug-in along with its other plug-ins to enable you to download streaming video.

One of the new features supported in the latest plug-in is support for QuickTime VR hotspots, which allow you to click on "hotspots" in a QuickTime VR movie to jump to a new page. The following is a list of new features included with QuickTime Plug-in 2.0:

- "Scaled movies" allows movies to play back at different sizes.

- "Cached movies" (Netscape 4.0 users only) caches movies you've recently viewed (just like other documents), so they don't need to reload when you return to them.

- Expanded Media Type Fast Start support (for the Macintosh only) lets you configure your browser to use the Apple QuickTime plug-in to play non-QuickTime files, such as AIFF audio files.

- MPEG playback support with the QuickTime MPEG extension.

- QTVR hotspots with embedded URL data. "Hotspots" in a QTVR movie can have URL data associated with them, enabling them to load new pages or media when they're clicked. (Requires QTVR Authoring Studit to create new URL hotspots with VR 2.1.)

- Expanded media type support for both Macintosh and Windows. You can configure your browser to use the QuickTime plug-in to play non-QuickTime files, such as WAV audio files. QuickTime 3.0 now supports playback of nearly 20 different media types.

- Full-feature parity across Windows 95, Windows NT, and Mac OS (with QuickTime 3.0 for Windows).

- A pop-up menu is always available for visible movies—even for sound only.

- You can disable playback of selected MIME types.

- You can save as original file type rather than movie (for example, AIFF).

- You can drag and drop a movie onto the desktop.

- Support for QuickTime VR 2.1.

- Support for QuickTime 3.0's URL-linking feature.

Saving Movies from the Web

Here's another annoyance issue with QuickTime 3.0: The new QuickTime plug-in (version 2.0) has removed the ability to save movies from the Web. In order to use a browser's contextual menu command Save Movie, you must purchase the Pro key and upgrade to QuickTime Pro. The professional version of QuickTime upgrades the plug-in, restoring the ability to save movies from the Web, which was standard in the older version 1.1 plug-in.

12

Creating QuickTime Movies for Fast Web Playback

When you have the QuickTime plug-in installed in your browser's Plug-ins folder, you can view movies as they are downloaded from the Web to your Mac. This ability is called *streaming video* and can be adjusted to fit the speed of your data transmission by clicking the arrow at the bottom of the QuickTime dialog box that appears automatically in your browser when it encounters a QuickTime movie. (See Figure 12.8.)

> The Movie Player that ships with QuickTime Pro prepares QuickTime movies so that the plug-in can present the first frame of an embedded movie almost immediately. It can begin playing even before the movie has been completely downloaded. Just click the Make Movie Self-Contained and Make Movie Playable on Other Computers items in the Save As dialog box.

FIGURE 12.8.

A QuickTime 3.0 streaming video coming at you in real-time from the Web.

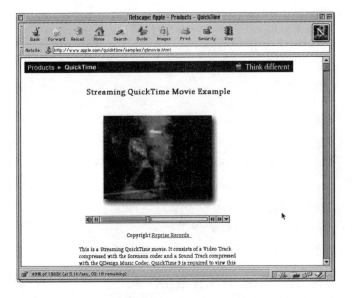

You can also use a utility called the *Internet Movie tool* to convert your movies to "fast-start." The Internet Movie tool is available on the QuickTime Software page located at (http://www.apple.com/quicktime/developers/tools.html). The Internet Movie Tool is convenient if you want to do a batch conversion of many movie files. To use the

Internet Movie tool, first make sure you have QuickTime 3.0 installed. Then you can simply drag and drop the movies you want to convert from the desktop or Finder window to the Internet Movie Tool icon and they will be converted.

When you convert a movie, the Internet Movie tool performs two tasks:

- A typical QuickTime movie file may have information located in an area (the resource fork) that machines other than the Macintosh would not be able to read correctly. The Internet Movie tool makes sure that all the data for the movie can be read on platforms other than Macintosh.

- A typical QuickTime movie file has certain important information (meta-data) at the end of the file. The QuickTime plug-in is constructed in such a fashion that it can start displaying the movie before all the movie file has been transferred from your Mac server—but only if this information is present at the beginning of the movie. Movies created with QuickTime 3.0 have this data at the beginning, but pre-2.5 movies do not. The Internet Movie tool moves this information to the front of the file so that the plug-in can fast-start the movie.

Embedding QuickTime in Your Web Page

This section briefly discusses the HTML code you need to use to embed a QuickTime movie into your Web site. A complete discussion of the code is beyond the scope of this book; see Hour 18, "Entering the Internet," for more information about using the Web.

The <EMBED> tag is used to embed different kinds of content (such as QuickTime movies) within an HTML page. When the document specified in the SRC parameter is a QuickTime movie, the QuickTime plug-in will be used to display it. Here's an example:

```
<EMBED SRC="SampleQT.mov" HEIGHT=176 WIDTH=136>
```

Replace the filename *SampleQT.mov* with the name of your movie, as well as the values for height and width of the movie with the dimensions of your movie (add 24 to the height of the movie for the default controller).

If you don't know these values, you can open your movie with the Movie Player and select Get Info from the Movie menu. Choose Size from the right pop-up menu. You'll need to add 24 pixels to the height reported by Movie Player for the height of the controller (unless you have specified CONTROLLER=FALSE). In addition to WIDTH and HEIGHT, there are a number of other parameters you can specify in the <EMBED> tag to control how your movie is presented.

12

Understanding QuickTime 3.0's Architecture

The more formal term for what QuickTime offers is an application programming interface (API) for multimedia tasks. The APIs are the QuickTime code that can be called by applications.

QuickTime provides APIs for compressing and decompressing audio and video data, as well as storing, retrieving, and manipulating time-based data. It provides services for applications to capture and play back a wide range of image and audio formats. The core API technologies within QuickTime are the Movie Toolbox, Image Compression Manager, Component Manager, and QuickTime Components. Many new features in QuickTime are added automatically to QuickTime-savvy applications.

What's more, no application changes are required to gain access to features in new versions of QuickTime, such as DVCam support in QuickTime 3.0. Other features added to APIs are accessible only by applications that are upgraded to support those new QuickTime APIs.

Introducing the QuickTime Media Abstraction Layer

QuickTime 3.0.0 brings new API support for digital video, as well as added API features for MPEG, video, audio, and new file formats (such as DVCam, OMF, AVI, and OpenDML).

The key to QuickTime's flexibility and performance is the QuickTime media abstraction layer. This foundation technology is an advanced, component-based software architecture that provides software and hardware developers full access to the built-in QuickTime services. It also specifies how to accelerate and extend QuickTime's capabilities through a powerful plug-in framework.

One of the most compelling features of the QuickTime media abstraction layer is the broad range of media types supported. QuickTime 3.0.0 includes built-in support for 10 media types (video, audio, text, timecode, music/MIDI, sprite/animation, tween, MPEG, VR, 3D). For each of the built-in media types, QuickTime provides a rich set of media-specific services appropriate for managing each particular media type.

QuickTime supports media types that are appropriate for all types of digital media publishing—whether the intended target is tape, CD-ROM, or the Internet.

The QuickTime media abstraction layer specifies a comprehensive set of services covering virtually all aspects of digital media creation, editing, and playback. Here's an abbreviated list of some of these services:

- Timing and synchronization
- Audio and image data compression and decompression
- Image splitting, format conversion, scaling, composition, and transcoding
- Audio mixing, sample rate conversion, and format conversion
- Audio and video effects and transitions
- Synchronized storage read and write
- Media capture
- Media import and export
- Standard user interface elements (such as movie controllers, media previewers, and media capture dialog boxes)

QuickTime 3.0. also extends the QuickTime media layer technologies by supporting new hardware associated with digital video, such as FireWire and digital video cameras.

Software written with QuickTime can take advantage of these new hardware technologies without having to rely on hardware services. The QuickTime media layer works with hardware services for the application.

In addition, QuickTime can be applied more easily to Web pages using the QuickTime plug-in for Web browsers. Web browsers require a QuickTime plug-in order support playback of QuickTime movies and other supported embedded data. Additional Internet software, such as Real Video, Real Audio, and Shockwave, can also work with QuickTime technology on the Internet.

12

Summary

QuickTime offers movie playback support for a wide range of file types for both traditional and Internet applications. Mac OS 8.5 includes QuickTime 3.0; however, QuickTime Pro is also available and can be installed with Mac OS 8.5 for a fee of $29.95. Applications such as Movie Player, SimpleText, and Scrapbook provide QuickTime file playback. Additional applications for authoring and manipulating other QuickTime features are available on the Net and as commercial products.

Term Review

DVCam   A method of storing video and sound images on CD-ROMs. QuickTime supports DVD-capable CDs and can create DVD movies.

Movie Player   The software included with QuickTime that lets you play QuickTime movies directly on your Mac. Movie Player Pro also lets you create and save movies in QuickTime.

MPEG   A method of compressing and decompressing sound for transmission. QuickTime MPEG 1.02 plays back MPEG-1 files.

QuickDraw 3D   This technology lets you create, manipulate, and incorporate 3D graphics into your documents and presentations. 3D applications that have been modified to support QuickDraw 3D and its associated user interface guidelines can produce standardized 3D images that can coexist with other leading applications. QuickDraw 3D images can also be incorporated into QuickTime movies.

QuickTime   A technology for creating and playing multimedia software, either locally on your Mac or via the Internet.

Q&A

Q Where can I see examples of QuickTime in action as well as gain more information on developing QuickTime multimedia?

A Surf to `www.apple.com/quicktime/information/`.

Q What's the difference between .AVI and .MOV files? Should I care?

A Microsoft Windows uses a video file format identified by the suffix .AVI. QuickTime can read and play these files as well as its own .MOV file format.

Q The play area is so small in Movie Player. How do I resize it to see the movie better?

A Select the Double Size command (Command-2) from the Movie menu.

Workshop

The Workshop contains quiz questions to help you solidify your understanding of the material covered. You can find the answers to the quiz questions in Appendix B, "Quiz Answers."

Quiz

1. What's QuickTime?

2. How do you start playing a movie?

3. How do you rewind a movie?

4. How do you stop a movie from playing?

5. How do you change the transmission speed to support T1 lines?

6. How do you automatically play an audio CD on your Mac?

7. How do you determine when you need QuickTime Pro versus QuickTime? How do you get this product?

8. How do you install the QuickTime plug-in?

9. How do you save Web-based QuickTime movies to your hard disk?

10. What's the QuickTime media abstraction layer?

12

HOUR 13

Sound and Audio

In this hour, I discuss in a very cursory way how to make your Mac make sounds. The basic components of the Monitors & Sound control panel combined with the Mac OS 8.5 Sound Manager and QuickTime let you use the Mac to record and play back music. With the proper additional MIDI equipment, you, too, can make music.

In a nutshell, this hour covers the following topics:

- A primer on sound
- A short discussion on MIDI and other music tools
- Using the Sounds and Alerts portions of the Monitors & Sounds control panel
- Recording and playing back sounds
- Configuring your sound input and output devices

History of Sound on the Macintosh

The hardware and software architecture of the Macintosh has always included sound as a basic part of the computer. However, its intended uses were mostly for system beeps, game sounds, and an elementary but effective form of speech synthesis called *MacInTalk*. Except for some entertainment software, speech synthesis had been ignored until the advent of the AV versions of Quadras and Power Macs. The reason for this is that acceptable speech requires massive amounts of computational power.

> High-end audio cards are available for Macintosh PDS, NuBus, and PCI slots for any Macintosh desktop computer. The most popular digital audio card is Digidesign's Audio Media product line. However, the PowerMac G3 and 8600, 8500, and 7600 series desktop computers come equipped with built-in video and can also capture digital audio in addition to video.
>
> The Quadra AV Macs (the 660AV and 840AV) included AT&T's 3210 DSP chip to drive the high-speed GeoPort connector used in telephony and telecommunications. The AT&T 3210 runs its own system software (Apple Real-Time Architecture, or *ARTA*) that independently performs signal processing, thus freeing up the CPU to perform other tasks.
>
> AV Quadras use the DSP chip on the motherboard to process sound. Power Macs do not require DSP chips to process audiovisual signals but use the Power PC processor for sound processing.

The synthesizer chip in the early Macs was monophonic, but Apple began using a stereo chip in the Mac II series. Performa-model Macs did not provide stereo output until the 5400/6400 models became available. All G3 Power Macs support stereo sound output. Although you can make music with the built-in synthesizer chip, you can't do much with it, except accentuate system beeps and game sounds. Conceptually, it contains an oscillator with selectable wave forms, plus a spectrum-shaping filter and an envelope generator (for attack and decay characteristics). With it, software developers can create distinctive sounds to alert you to various problems or simply to reinforce the fact that you have invoked a particular command or completed a task. This audio feedback remains one of the Mac's most powerful features.

> You can put MIDI instruments on the hard disk and use playback software and the MIDI features in QuickTime to play back music on the Mac (without the add-on MIDI hardware or external music keyboards).

Game developers, on the other hand, find the synthesizer chip limiting. Unique and attention-getting sounds can mean the difference between a successful game or a failure in the market. For this reason, computer games need striking sound effects. One solution is to use a library of sampled sounds. The concept is similar to the way wave table synthesizers use sampled sounds. Hit a key, and the sampled sound plays back for you (but without pitch changes or other alterations).

You can create your sampled sounds in any way: record natural sounds, develop new sounds on a large synthesizer, alter and manipulate sounds electronically in various ways, and even play sounds backwards. When you're finished, simply digitize them and store them as Mac sound files.

A Sound Primer

Mac OS and Macintosh computers are well known for their built-in and extendable sound and music technologies. Together, Sound Manager and QuickTime work with applications to bring a rich sound playback, editing, and integration environment to the computer. Applications that make use of sound and music range from games and interactive education software to professional music editing and video production authoring packages. Of course, the Mac has always been able to use interesting alert sounds, which can easily be expanded.

To understand music and sound on the Macintosh, it helps to know the basic principles of acoustics and human hearing. In physics, sound is mechanical vibration, carried through some medium (usually air). It has three basic properties: frequency, intensity, and spectrum. These properties correspond with the psychological sensations of pitch, loudness, and timbre (or tone color).

Human hearing is subjective: What we perceive is not always what we measure with test instruments. By using these two parallel sets of terms, we can distinguish between human perception and mechanical measurement, which provides a basis for a discussion of Mac sound.

13

Sound is also a series of tiny changes in air pressure. If the changes occur slowly, the frequency of the sound is low; rapid changes result high frequencies. If the amount of change in air pressure is small, the intensity is weak (soft). Larger changes in air pressure equate with greater intensity, or louder sounds. Ears and microphones are sensitive devices that can be used for measuring these microscopic variations in air pressure.

The two basic methods of working with sound and music on the Mac (or any computer, for that matter) are digital audio and MIDI (Musical Instrument Digital Interface). The difference between these two basic methods is substantial. Digital audio is a recording technique that's used to capture sounds and music as if the computer were a tape recorder. MIDI is more like a music device-controlling mechanism. MIDI does not record sound; it only records the data necessary to reproduce sound on a MIDI synthesizer. MIDI requires additional hardware to be added to the Macintosh to control additional hardware devices. Digital audio can be performed with a Mac, plus a built-in microphone or an audio CD (if the Mac has a CD-ROM drive built-in) as well as with high-end audio add-on cards and additional hard disks and other expensive equipment.

Digital Audio

Digital audio recorders work on the same principle as movie cameras. The digital audio recorder takes a series of snapshots (called *samples*) of the sound, just as a motion picture camera takes a series of snapshots (the individual frames on the film) of images. If the Mac samples the sound fast enough, the ear can perceive sounds individually. The human perceptual mechanism merges these "snapshots" into a sensation of sound or motion.

The sampling rate determines the highest frequency the machine can record. The sampling rate should be at least twice as high as the highest frequency you want to record. To record and reproduce the full range of human hearing (20Hz to 20,000Hz) on compact discs, the sampling rate must be 44.1KHz. Desktop and PowerBook Macs currently shipping (G3 models) all support recording 44KHz sound with stereo playback. Often, lower sampling rates will suffice, particularly when storage space is at a premium. For intelligible speech, sampling rates from 16KHz to 22KHz are adequate.

Quantizing

Quantizing is the process of measuring the intensity of the signal in each sample and assigning a digital number to that measured value. Each time the sampling circuit takes a snapshot, it must measure the intensity of the continuously varying analog signal (as a voltage) at that particular moment. Then the circuit must round off the value to the nearest digital number available, because inevitably the measured value will not correspond exactly to one of the digital values. These rounding errors cause noise and distortion.

To reduce this effect, you want to have as many digital numbers as possible to represent instantaneous voltage measurements. Note that 16-bit systems provide a much higher amount of numbers than earlier 8-bit systems. Remember, however, that lower quality recordings save storage space and are still acceptable for many uses.

Uses and Limitations of Digital Audio

After sound and music is digitized, you can manipulate the recorded data on your Macintosh. Instead of using the old cut-and-splice method of audio tape editing, you can edit down to the individual sample using software applications. Random-access editing software enables you to assemble a soundtrack for a multimedia production from a library of short excerpts simply by creating a list.

The amount of storage space required for all this audio data is the main limitation of digital audio. One minute of stereo at a 44.1KHz sampling rate with 16-bit quantization occupies about 1 MB; for this reason, you should have at least a 500 MB to 1 GB hard drive to do serious work with sound.

To permit random access editing, the drives must have an access time of less than 11ms and support high-speed (SCSI-2 or faster) transfer rates. In addition, make sure you have backup capabilities so that you can archive old projects and their source materials. Finally, you need a medium to store and transport the finished project; CD-R media, DAT tape, and Jaz cartridges are usually the best choices.

Musical Instrument Digital Interface (MIDI)

The Musical Instrument Digital Interface (MIDI) format began as a method of playing two synthesizers from one keyboard. MIDI captures all the data from every key that's pressed, including how long the key stayed down, how hard it was pressed, and so on, for every controllable parameter of the instrument. It also must capture the exact point in time that each event occurs.

The onboard microprocessor converts all this information into a digital data stream and sends it to the other synthesizer. In turn, that instrument's microprocessor sorts out the data and sends each signal to the proper device. Because it all takes place at a rapid rate, everything fits together, and the synthesizer plays music, automatically "pressing" the keys and holding them down exactly as they were pressed on the first synthesizer. Storing this data stream so that the information can later be played back is now easier than ever with the Mac.

Understanding MIDI Basics

MIDI is an 8-bit system, which means it can express 256 values for each parameter of the sound it's describing. The MIDI system transmits those numbers serially (one at a time) in rapid succession (at the rate of 31,250 bits per second). Each 8-bit byte describes the setting of a particular key, knob, button, or switch. Just to keep things straight, serial systems use start and stop bits to tell the microprocessor when each byte begins and ends. MIDI therefore adds one extra bit at each end of the byte, turning it into a 10-bit package. The actual data transmission rate in the MIDI cable is 3,125 bytes per second.

13

MIDI uses two types of bytes: status bytes and data bytes. Every MIDI message begins with the status byte and is followed by one or two data bytes (depending on what's needed). The *status byte* tells the receiving unit what control the following data will affect. It could be a Note On message, the setting of a foot pedal, or a change in a patch. To distinguish between the two types, MIDI assigns all data bytes a number from 0 to 127 and all status bytes a number from 128 to 255.

A typical stream of MIDI data contains status bytes, followed by one or two (sometimes none) data bytes. The status byte tells the synthesizer, "This data is for the Note On function." The first data byte tells it what pitch to turn on (that is, which key to strike). The second data byte tells it how hard to strike the key. Then the message ends. The next message may contain instructions about which instrumental sound (patch) to use, and so on.

Uses and Limitations of MIDI

Because MIDI involves only the data needed to control and play a synthesizer, it generates a fresh performance each time you play back the data. One advantage is that you can alter each performance in real-time. You can change the tempo, transpose the music to another key, add a crescendo, or play it with a different set of instrumental sounds.

You can edit the MIDI data in much the same way you edit a word processor file. The obvious disadvantage of MIDI is that it cannot record live sounds because it creates sounds by operating synthesizers. MIDI only consists of musical note and instrument data. MIDI does not contain any instrument or sound information, because this is stored on the computer or the keyboards it communicates with. Digital audio, in contrast, consists of both instrument and musical note content and occupies considerably more hard drive space than MIDI data.

Customizing Your Mac with Sounds

Modifying system sounds with your own sound library can be fun. The standard system sounds from Apple include the familiar System Beep, Sosumi, Quack, Droplet, and Wild Eep in the Monitors & Sound control panel. However, these sounds can become boring after awhile. You can attach new sounds to the system simply by dragging any sound file into the System Folder, as you do with fonts. Use either an external recorder or the built-in sound recording capabilities of Macs to capture the sounds and save them as System 7 sound files.

To add a system alert sound, open the Monitors & Sounds control panel and click the Alert button to bring up the Alert dialog box. Then click the Add button.

If you've selected CD as your input source in the Sound screen, you can slip an audio CD into your Mac and press Record to capture a smidgen of sound. Figure 13.1 shows you the recording dialog box you use to capture sounds. If you select External Input on the Sound screen, you can use your Mac's microphone to record a sound. When you're done recording, click Stop. Click Play to hear what you recorded. If you like it, click Save and give the sound a name. You can then select the name in the Alert list box.

FIGURE 13.1.

Use the Record dialog box to capture "alert" sounds.

Be very aware of copyright laws when copying music from audio CDs. Taking a smidgen of sound for use on your Mac is kosher; recording that sound and putting all over the Internet for others to use isn't.

An intriguing audio application is Kaboom! by Nova Development. This commercial version of the old shareware utility Soundmaster enables you to add sound effects to every Finder command as well as change system beeps. It comes with a large library of digitized sound effects, and it allows you to record your own. For example, Kaboom! can play the sound of trash cans rattling, flies buzzing, or a toilet flushing every time you empty the Trash Can. Kaboom! also saves sound files in nearly every format currently used. This capability allows you to add recorded sounds to multimedia presentations, QuickTime movies, and custom applications.

Audio File Formats

The following is a list of some common Mac sound file formats:

- AIFF is a standard sound format supported by cross-platform sound-editing applications.

- SND and SFIL are the type of resources saved to the system file for system beeps and alert sounds.

- MOOV is the QuickTime file format, but it also represents a QuickTime track that contains sound.

13

- MPEG Layer 2 is an audio file format that provides better audio quality than WAV. MPEG Layer 2 is a common audio file format used on the Internet.
- WAV is another standard sound file format supported by cross-platform sound-editing applications.

How to Use Sound

Part of what makes a Mac easy to use is that there's more than one way to change your settings on the computer. Sound is one of the settings that have several system software and application pieces. These pieces can change the sound volume, input, and output settings. This section focuses on the system software pieces that can adjust sound settings, such as the Monitors & Sound control panel, the Sound module of the Control Strip, Simple Sound, and the Sound control panel.

Playing Audio CDs on Your Mac

Did you realize that your Mac is the most expensive CD player you've ever owned? The Apple CD Audio Player application lets you play an audio CD in your Mac's CD-ROM drive. Figure 13.2 displays the features of the Apple CD Audio Player.

FIGURE 13.2.

The Apple CD Audio Player.

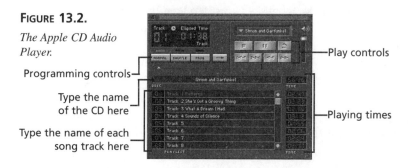

Programming controls

Type the name of the CD here

Type the name of each song track here

Play controls

Playing times

Remember to change the Sound input source to CD in your Monitors & Sound control panel before trying to play an audio CD. Make sure that the Sound Out and Sound Level sliders are not turned all the way down or muted; otherwise, you won't be able to hear your music.

You can personalize each audio CD you play by clicking the Audio CD text box and typing the name of the CD. The Mac saves the information you enter and brings it up each time you reinsert that CD. You can click each track's text box and enter the song's name next to its track number. You can type song names of up to 62 characters.

You can also program the play order of your songs by clicking the Program button. In the resulting Program dialog box, just drag the tracks from the list on the left to the order you want them to play on the right (see Figure 13.3). Imagine how powerful a tool this can be if you're burning your own audio CDs from your Mac.

FIGURE 13.3.

Program the play order in this dialog box.

Using the Monitors & Sound Control Panel

The Monitors portion of the Monitors & Sound control panel was discussed in Hour 11, "Color." This section focuses on how to use the Sound and Alert sections to change the input and output volumes, as well as how to set up and adjust the external speaker volume, internal or external CD volume, external or internal audio CD, and AV speaker volume controls.

There are actually two interwoven parts to the Sounds portion of this control panel: Sounds (which controls input and output sound quality and volume) and Alert (which controls the sounds used by the system for alert sounds). Figure 13.4 displays the Sounds portion of the control panel.

FIGURE 13.4.

The Sounds portion of the Monitors & Sound control panel.

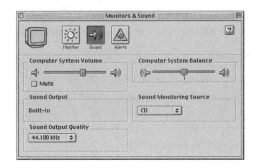

13

Setting Input and Output Levels

Most computers running Mac OS 8.5 have many sound input and output options. However, some, such as the PowerBook Duos, only have one option for sound input and output: microphone input and built-in output at 22.254KHz. In general, desktop computers have more sound input and output options available, compared to PowerBooks. PowerBook sound input and output options vary depending on the model.

Docking the Duo provides a way of extending sound capabilities with third-party audio cards and external speakers. You can also add a CD-ROM drive (external) to a Duo Dock if you want to capture sound from a CD and put it on the Duo.

The default for Sound Input depends on whether your computer has a built-in microphone or requires an external microphone. Either way, the microphone is the default sound input source in Monitors & Sound control panel. Desktop computers and newer PowerBooks can additionally choose from an internal or external CD or external audio input device. A pop-up menu appears in the Sound Input section of the Monitors & Sound control panel if more than one input option is available.

Sound output settings vary between desktop and PowerBook models. Some computers support only monophonic sound output, whereas most support stereo. The Sound Output Quality setting can also be selected from a general range of 11, 22, or 44KHz. The higher the KHz, the better the sound output is on the computer.

Both the internal computer speaker and external speaker have their own sound output (or volume level sliding bar) as well. Each sound output source can be muted or can share or have different sound volume settings. If external speakers or headphones are connected to the computer, the internal speaker volume is set to "mute" as the default.

Setting Alert Sounds

Click the Alert button to go to the Alert screen of the Monitors & Sounds control panel. Here you can select a built-in sound that alerts you to Mac trouble. You can also install your own set of sounds.

Using the Sound Control Strip Module

Sound volume can also be controlled from the Control Strip module that's installed with most Mac OS 8.5 computers. Some Performa models have sound volume control buttons located at the front of the case, below the monitor screen. The Control Strip module consists of a slider bar that represents volume levels from 0 through 7 (see Figure 13.5). Changing this setting also changes the sound volume settings in Monitors & Sound control panel.

FIGURE 13.5.

The Sound module of the Control Strip.

Some Performa models and AV monitors have sound volume control buttons located at the front of the case, below the monitor screen.

Using the Sound Control Panel

Mac OS 8.5 also installs the older Sound control panel for your use if you want more control over how sound is managed. The Sound control panel consists of four pop-up menus: Alert Sounds, Sound In, Sound Out, and Volumes. Each pop-up menu item changes the setting options available in the control panel window. Alert Sounds is almost identical to the Alert section of the Monitors & Sound control panel. Here you can also record sounds and create new system beeps.

Previous to Mac OS 8.5, the Sound control panel was installed on all computers and provided configuration settings that were a subset of the settings available in Monitors & Sound control panel. The Sound Control Panel folder is located in the Apple Extras folder.

The Sound Input window contains an icon view of the computer and an Options button. If no other sound input devices are available, the options button will be unavailable. The Options button brings up a dialog box with three icons: microphone, external audio, and CD-ROM (internal). If the internal CD-ROM drive is selected, also select the Playthrough check box to allow sound from the CD-ROM drive to play through the computer's internal speakers.

Sound output options are displayed in the Sound Out window. These settings are similar to those in the Monitors & Sound control panel. Most settings in this window cannot be altered, and they exist to reflect which sound output settings are supported by the hardware running the system software.

13

The volumes section of the control panel can display one or two sliders, representing internal and external speaker volume settings. This is the same as the volume slider bar and mute boxes in the Monitors & Sound control panel. You can use both the Monitors & Sound and the Sound control panels to configure your sound input and output settings with Mac OS 8.5.

Recording Sound with Mac OS 8.5

The Simple Sound and SimpleText applications, the Sound control panel, and the Monitors & Sound control panel all use the same window for recording sound resources that can be used for system beeps. Before recording sound, keep in mind that sound recording relies on memory and hard drive availability—that is, having enough memory and disk space free to record sound.

The easiest way to adjust the loudness or quietness of a sound recording is to position the audio source farther away or closer to the microphone. The goal of sound recording is to record as little distortion as possible at the highest supported sound recording quality.

Internal and External Microphones

Many kinds of microphones, including the built-in microphone, can create a sound clip for the Mac OS. Apple began including a microphone with their computers beginning with the LC, Iisi, and IIfx. PowerBooks and AV Mac monitors (by Apple) have built-in microphones. Before that, an external serial device, MacRecorder, was used to record monophonic or stereo sound. The latest Macs ship with a newer microphone than those first computers. It's also referred to as the PlainTalk microphone and has a slightly longer mini plug than the earlier microphone. Some Macs require the newer microphone in order to support sound recording.

When recording sound into the computer, avoid holding the microphone too close or too far away from you. Try some test recordings to see how loud or soft your initial sound recording is. Before doing the final recording, try to reduce background noise, and once you start recording, try to keep the dead space at the beginning and end of the recording to a minimum. Once the sound is recorded, you can leave it in the system file and select it for the system beep in the Alert section of the Monitors & Sound control panel.

CD-ROM Sources

You can also record sounds from the internal Apple CD-ROM drive and use them as system beeps. To record from the CD-ROM drive, configure Monitors & Sound to use the Internal CD-ROM drive as the Sound Input device. Put an audio CD into the computer and play it using the Apple CD Audio Player application.

Before recording, adjust the sound volume using the Apple CD Audio Player application. Then record a few seconds of sound and play it back by selecting it in the Alert section of the control panel. If the sound is not loud enough, try increasing the Sound Out or Apple CD Audio Player levels. Once you're content with the quality of sound recorded, it can be used as a system beep in the Monitors & Sound control panel.

Configuring Speakers for Playback

The placement and number of speakers connected to the Mac can affect how you hear sound playback of existing or newly recorded sounds. You can use headphones to help objectify sound playback quality, or you can connect a couple speakers to tweak sound playback.

A basic goal is to place external speakers equal distances apart from the computer. If you have more than one pair of speakers connected to the computer, try to place the second pair behind you, or at a higher level than the first pair of speakers. Some computer speaker systems include a subwoofer, which should always be placed somewhere on the floor at a location more central to where you sit in front of the computer.

MIDI Hardware

MIDI synthesizers offer many possibilities for creating music and sound effects with the Mac. Unlike hard disk–based digital audio recording, MIDI synthesizers use control signals from your Mac to play music automatically. Each performance is new, rather than a reproduction of an earlier one. Before you can do this, however, you need a sequencer application running on your Mac to record, store, and send out the MIDI control signals. In addition, you need a MIDI interface to connect your Mac's serial port to a chain of MIDI instruments.

MIDI works in much the same way as LocalTalk and SCSI, in that it can send data to several devices connected together as well as route specific data to specific devices. MIDI also lets you capture data from synthesizers and store it as a Mac data file. In other words, when you play music on a synthesizer, your sequencer records the data needed to reproduce that performance exactly as you played it.

Using your sequencer application, you can edit the data and alter the performance, add more tracks (corresponding to vocal and instrumental parts), and create a finished composition and performance. At any point, you can play it back to hear how it sounds.

MIDI-to-Mac Interface

Every Macintosh needs a MIDI adapter to connect it to a synthesizer. This device connects to one of the serial ports (printer or modem) and provides the electrical interface

13

between the computer and the MIDI system. It has three connectors labeled In, Out, and Thru. A MIDI interface box serves the same function as a LocalTalk adapter but operates at a different voltage. A simple, basic MIDI adapter usually costs under $100; you can get one from Apple and many other vendors. A slightly more elaborate version, a MIDI Thru Box, has several Thru ports, each of which sends out an identical copy of the signal. Thru boxes typically sell for about $500 to $600.

If you have a large and complex MIDI system, consider an "intelligent" or "smart" MIDI interface. Unlike the basic interface, it contains its own microprocessor. A smart MIDI interface can generate its own clock signals and keep the entire system synchronized more effectively than a basic MIDI adapter. In addition, microprocessor-equipped MIDI interfaces usually offer Society of Motion Picture and Television Engineers (SMPTE) time code, the industry-standard format for synchronizing multiple audio, video, and film devices. Apple does not make an intelligent MIDI interface, but they are available from Opcode, Mark of the Unicorn, and other companies. Prices vary, but most are $1000 or more, depending on features.

MIDI Connections

Connecting your Mac to a single MIDI instrument is simple. Plug the MIDI interface into the modem or printer port. Take a MIDI cable, plug one end into the Out connector on the interface and the other end into the In connector on your instrument. This connection permits MIDI data to travel from the Mac to the instrument. So far, so good.

If you need to send data back to the Mac, you need to connect the Out port on the synthesizer to the In port on the interface. Some MIDI instruments don't have an Out port, however. Sending MIDI data back to the Mac is important because that's how the sequencer records whatever you play on a MIDI instrument. Playing the notes on a MIDI instrument usually is a much easier way to enter musical data than selecting notes from a palette and dragging them onto the staff.

If you have more than two MIDI devices (the Mac with its adapter counts as one), you have more choices to make. In most cases, you'll want a daisy-chain connection, using the Thru ports instead of the Out ports. Because the MIDI Out port only sends output data from that unit's microprocessor, you won't be able to control the other synthesizers in the chain from the first one (the Mac).

The Thru port copies the control signals the unit receives from the Mac, adds the output data from that instrument, and passes them on so the next unit can use them. You can daisy-chain as many instruments as you want (subject to some practical limitations).

Some instruments route the signal through the microprocessor before copying it and passing it to the Thru port. This routing process delays the signal slightly. The more times this happens, the longer the delay, which is commonly known as *MIDI lag*. After passing through about four or five such Thru ports, the signal is so late arriving at the next synthesizer that you can hear the delay. It sounds like everyone's playing off beat, and it's quite irritating. Some instruments have a nondelaying Thru port, enabling you to build long daisy chains. Check the owner's manual to see which kind of Thru port your MIDI interface has.

Still another configuration is the star network, which requires either a smart interface or Thru box. The Thru box sends the same signal to all its Thru ports. The smart interface uses its own onboard microprocessor to receive the control signals from the Mac and send identical copies, all synchronized in time, to each of its Thru ports.

This process ensures that all instruments play at exactly the same time, thus preventing MIDI lag. A Thru box and a smart interface solve the basic MIDI timing problem. A smart interface extends the synchronization capabilities by generating its own timing signals so that you can control external equipment such as video and audio recorders via SMPTE time code.

A smart interface can translate MIDI time code (MTC) and SMPTE time code to synchronize the synthesizers with audio and video recorders (useful for synching music and sound effects with actions onscreen in a video production).

Sound and Music Software

Two major classes of audio software are available. The first enables you to record and edit digital audio. This software works with and manages actual sound samples. High-end software of this type turns your Mac into a multitrack recording studio. Low-end digital audio software behaves more like an ordinary stereo tape recorder, but with some digital editing capabilities thrown in.

Another class of software allows you to work with MIDI data but not actual sound. These MIDI sequencer applications operate MIDI synthesizers to produce sound. Most sequencer software programs use the onscreen metaphor of a multitrack tape deck, but they only record and play back MIDI data rather than sound itself.

This distinction is becoming blurred because many sequencers now allow you to add digital audio tracks to MIDI tracks. For example, you can record a vocal on top of a complex MIDI arrangement so that the synthesizers accompany the voice in perfect synchronization.

13

Software Options

Some other types of musical software don't quite fit into these categories. One valuable addition to any Mac-based musical system is a patch editor/librarian. With one of these, you can create and edit the patches (instrument definitions) on your synthesizer. Advantages to this kind of software include the capability to work on a larger, more legible screen, and a dedicated database manager to store and retrieve the patches from a library.

Automatic composition and accompaniment programs appeal to many users. Some, such as Band-in-a-Box and Jam, play chords and bass lines with the stereotypical accompaniment figures of a waltz, march, blues, and so on. Finally, some applications can teach you to play an instrument and tutor you on music theory.

Applications for Editing and Creating Sound Files

If you feel comfortable using the sound-recording features in the Monitors & Sound control panel and want to explore more sound playback and recording options, there are many shareware and commercial sound applications available for the Mac OS.

The following is a brief list of sound applications. Many of the sound-editing applications support MIDI, multitrack and track sequencing, and mixing:

- **Sound Edit 16.** One of the first packages available for sound editing and creation on the Mac OS. It's a commercial product available from Macromedia.
- **Deck II.** Another sound-editing application available from Macromedia. It's a higher-end sound-editing package that supports up to 64 simultaneous, real-time 16-bit tracks as well as provides multiprocessor support.

Macromedia, Incorporated

600 Townsend Street

San Francisco, CA 94103 415 252-2000

http://www.macromedia.com

- **Sound Maker.** An affordable recording and editing application by MicroMat Computer Systems.

MicroMat Computer Systems

8934 Lakewood Drive, #273

Windsor, VA 95492

707 837-8012

Email: techsupport@micromat.com

http://MicroMat.com/mmcs/

- Professional applications at music retailers provide more high-end editing and authoring capabilities for audio. Developers of these software products include Digidesign, Opcode, and Mark of the Unicorn, among others.

Summary

This chapter reviewed how to use sound and audio with your Mac OS 8.5 computer. Several configurations and ways to adjust sound input and output were discussed, including the system software control panels and applications that work with sound input and output.

Term Review

digital audio   A recording technique used to capture sounds and music as if the computer were a tape recorder.

MIDI (Musical Instruments Digital Interface)   A software interface used to control devices that make and play music. Music is created by translating digital signals from the Mac and synthesizing them into sound on the MIDI player.

quantizing   The process of measuring the intensity of a sound signal in volts in each sound sample and assigning a digital number to that measured value. Today, the Mac uses a 16-bit measuring system to lessen the amount of distortion produced.

sampling   A series of "snapshots" of sound taken by the Mac. The sampling rate is the highest frequency of sound a machine can record. Audio CDs record sounds at 44.1KHz; human speech is sampled successfully at 16 to 22KHz.

Sound Manager   The Mac OS 8.5 toolbox that manages sound production.

Q&A

13

Q Why would I choose to use the Simple Sound control panel rather than the Monitors & Sound control panel?

A There are no real differences. Both provide almost exactly the same features. Some features are just labeled differently (for example, sound quality items in the Simple Sound menu versus the KHz settings in the Monitors & Sound control panel).

Q How can I increase the sound quality that outputs from my Mac?

A You can attach external speakers to your Mac or to the external CD-ROM drive of your Mac. You cannot control the volume of your speakers from the Apple CD player nor can you record CD sounds from your external drive without connecting your external drive's output jacks to your computer's sound input port with a stereo patch cord. Remember that the jacks have to fit both the CD player's output port as well as the Mac's sound input port, but luckily the standard RCA-style headphone jack you use for your Walkman will fit.

You can also increase the quality of sound output from your Mac by attaching any line-level audio source, such as a VCR, cassette player, or audio CD player to your Mac if it supports line-level sound. (Luckily, all PowerPCs, Quadra 605, 630, 660AV, and 840Avs, as well as LC 475, 575, and 630 support these devices, as do PowerBook 500s.)

Workshop

The Workshop contains quiz questions to help you solidify your understanding of the material covered. You can find the answers to the quiz questions in Appendix B, "Quiz Answers."

Quiz

1. How do you adjust the sound volume?
2. How do you change the alert sounds?
3. Can you add sounds to your Mac? How?
4. How can you record alert sounds?
5. Can you record sounds directly to the Mac? How?
6. What's the difference between MIDI and digital audio technologies?
7. Are there any prerecorded sounds available commercially?

HOUR 14

Video

You know the special effects you see in movies such as Independence Day and Mission Impossible? Those digital images were produced with Macintosh computers. The Mac was used to create preproduction, or prototype, 3D animations to work through scenes prior to dedicating the more expensive custom software and hardware to generate the final high-resolution 70mm big-screen image containing the special effects. Mac OS 8.5 provides the tools so that you, too, can record and playback video on your Mac.

Apple Video Player coupled with QuickTime and the proper video hardware, such as a G3 Desktop or Performa, lets you produce great movies and stills. This hour describes how to use Apple Video Player to record and play back video, as well as the cabling requirements for the external devices you need to accomplish this task. It also discusses what software you can add to enhance the editing process once you've captured your images. If you're even curious about digital video on the Mac, read this chapter to find out how it's done.

In this hour, the following topics are covered:

- Setting up and using the Apple Video Player
- Some performance tips and techniques for recording video
- Video hardware and cabling requirements
- Third-party software available for video editing and manipulation

You, Too, Can Be in Pictures

If your Mac has video inputs or a TV tuner card, you can use Apple Video Player to record or capture video or still frame images on the computer's hard drive from your television, VCR, camcorder, or other video production device. The Movie Player application, which is part of QuickTime 3.0, can play back any movies captured by Apple Video Player. The Apple Video Player works with the following Macs:

- Those Macs with built-in video ports, such as the PowerMac 7300, 7500, 7600, 8500, and 8600.
- Those Macs that have the Apple Video System card or Apple TV/Video System card installed. Performa 630 and Power Mac or Performa 5200, 5300, 5400, 5500, 6300, 6400, and 6500 come with these add-on PCI cards.
- Those Macs with audiovisual (AV) cards containing AV connectors, such as the PowerMac 6100AV, 7100AV, and 8100AV.

You can add video recording and playback capabilities to your Mac by installing a video card made by Apple, ATI Technologies (www.atitech.ca), IMS (formerly IXMicro; (www.ixmicro.com), or Radius, Inc. (www.radius.com). Third-party vendor video cards often require their own video player software. For example, the ATI card uses the Xclaim video player.

You need more sophisticated applications, such as those from Adobe (Premiere) or Avid (Cinema), to actually produce production-quality video with music, cutaways, sophisticated edits, and so on. However, as mentioned earlier, you can do the basic capturing and viewing with Apple Video Player, which comes installed with Mac OS 8.5. (See Figure 14.1.)

FIGURE 14.1.

*The Apple Video
Player interface.*

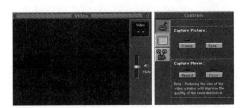

Apple Video Player consists of a few files, as shown in Figure 14.2: the Video Startup extension, the Apple Video Player application, and the Apple Video Player Guide. The version of the Video Startup extension must match the version of the Apple Video Player application used with Mac OS.

Apple Video Player can view MPEG files and record or capture video or still frame images to the computer's hard drive. You can also pause while recording to skip any video you don't want to use. Apple Video Player 1.7.1 is fully scriptable and can work with the AV ports or tuner cards installed on a computer. It requires a color depth set at "thousands of colors." Video capture performance can also be improved by turning off Virtual Memory, AppleTalk, and File Sharing.

FIGURE 14.2.

The Apple Video Player software.

What Is Apple Video Player?

As mentioned previously, Apple Video Player lets you use Apple's AV hardware—the built-in AV ports in PCI Power Macs and the tuner and AV cards in Power Macs with NuBus slots. Apple Video Player works differently with different Apple AV hardware. For example, the tuner card can support TV and video input sources, but the AV ports on PCI Macs only support video and S-video inputs. You can view television broadcasts on both systems; however, the tuner card takes a direct feed, whereas the AV port works indirectly with VCR, LaserDisc, or digital camera input.

APPLE VIDEO PLAYER OR MOVIE PLAYER?

Actually, except for playing back MPEG1 files, these two applications perform two very different tasks. Apple Video Player records video with Apple's AV hardware. Apple's Movie Player application plays it back and even lets you edit or add additional content to your QuickTime movie.

Apple Video Player's user interface contains two main windows and a few menus that let you set input sources and application preferences. The video window only displays an image if Monitors & Sound is set to thousands or millions of colors. The Controls window consists of three main sections: Capture, Video Source, and MPEG File Playback (for files on a CD or hard disk).

14

But there are also other ways to find help while using UnInstaller. UnInstaller's online Help feature can help you out in any jam. But there are also other ways to find help while using UnInstaller.

APPLE VIDEO PLAYER HARDWARE REQUIREMENTS

Memory requirements for Apple Video Player are a minimum of 550K, with a preferred size of 2 MB. Don't forget to check your amount of free disk space before capturing video. Apple Video Player works with any color monitor using a 640×480 desktop and larger. It will only launch if the same version of the Video Startup extension is in the System Folder and if the application can find any AV hardware on the computer.

Using Apple Video Player

Apple Video Player can be used for many kinds of video-related tasks—watching television is probably the easiest of any of its features. Using either the cable feed or a connected camera, you can also record video or capture a single frame of video on your hard drive. Apple Video Player uses keyboard controls to begin single-frame or longer-term video recording.

Before recording, check the screen's color adjustments to ensure that the color scheme of what you want to capture matches the expected output. Also, focus any external devices, such as a camera or an external image source. Adjust the image for sharpness and focus as well.

Capturing Video Pictures

While you watch video on your computer screen, you can capture a single frame of video in the Clipboard or on your hard disk for future use. You can also capture continuous video to create QuickTime movies with Apple Video Player.

You capture a single frame in the Clipboard by selecting Copy Video Display from the Edit menu. You capture QuickTime movie files or SimpleText pictures by using the Capture window. Click the video camera icon in the Controls window to display the Capture window. You can also use Apple Video Player's Apple Guide for additional instructions on how to use these features.

The Capture window consists of two parts: Capture Picture and Capture Movie (see Figure 14.3):

- To record a picture, freeze the video by clicking the Freeze button. If the frozen image is worth saving, select the Save button. Note that the video source will continue to display video unseen unless you pause or stop it at its source (that is, the VCR or camcorder controls).
- To capture a movie, select the Record button. Once recording begins, the Record light will turn red and the button's caption changes to Stop. Clicking the Pause button stops recording momentarily, but it continues recording to the same movie file if Resume is selected.

FIGURE 14.3.

The Video Capture options in Apple Video Player.

Helpful Hints for Quality Pictures

The Mac uses QuickTime to compress your movie so that it takes up less hard disk space. The Mac also ensures that you capture just enough video for good quality without compromising computer performance by optimizing the number of frames it records per second while only previewing selected frames. The key to creating quality video is to let the Mac process as many frames per second as possible (the more frames, the smoother the picture). To ensure that the Mac has sufficient processing power, turn off any extraneous functions such as background processing, Virtual Memory, File Sharing, Internet access, and RAM Doubler. You can also save processing by inserting floppies and CDs into their drives so that the Mac doesn't have to periodically check to see if one has been inserted.

The file size and frame rate (the number of frames the Mac can capture per second) for your movie is affected by three other considerations:

- **Use a small video window.** Your video window size affects not only the frame rate but also the quality of the video picture and the file size of the captured movie. For the best quality picture and the smallest file size, try to set up your window no larger than 160×120 pixels (select Smallest Size from the Video Player's Window screen). The Normal option sets your window at 320×240 pixels.
- **Compress those videos.** Video compression does degrade the quality of your picture. Selecting Normal in the Preferences dialog box (on the Setup menu) lets you

14

reduce file size by 12 to 50 percent. The Apple Video compression method works best when you've set the number of colors in the Monitors & Sound control panel to thousands of colors.

- **Reserve your disk space.** Capturing a normal frame size (320×240 pixels) requires 2 to 4 MB of disk space for each second of video, depending on your frame rate. You must have at least 4 MB initially available so that Video Player can save the first captures in an uncompressed temporary file. Compression occurs only after you've finished recording your movie.

Playing Back Your Video

To play back an MPEG1 video, you need to have an MPEG 1 video file available on your hard disk or CD-ROM. Then, follow these steps:

1. Select the video source from the left side of the Controls window by clicking the appropriate button: either Television, S-Video, or Standard Camcorder Video. (See Figure 14.4.)

2. Adjust the picture quality from the right side of the Controls window. You can adjust picture brightness, sharpness, contrast, and color by using convenient sliders.

3. If a tuner source is found, the Player will display a Preferences window for that input. From there, Apple Video Player will search for any valid channels and save them—only valid channels will appear when you surf with the keyboard controls.

4. Audio volume can be controlled using the up and down arrow keys.

The main video window of Apple Video Player can be adjusted to any desired size. The Windows menu supports three standard settings, the largest of which grows the video window to fill the screen, thus hiding the application's menu bar. Clicking the screen will bring the menu bar back. You can also use one or two keyboard commands to resize the video window to a smaller size.

FIGURE 14.4.

The Video Source options in Apple Video Player.

Video Playback and CDs or Servers

Apple Video Player supports playback of MPEG 1 files located on a CD or hard drive (see Figure 14.5). If you're not sure which files are MPEG files, Apple Video Player can search your server or local disk via the Preferences menu item. If no MPEG files are found, the Playback section of the Controls window remains blank.

FIGURE 14.5.

MPEG playback in Apple Video Player.

Hardware Considerations

Apple's TV tuner card works with a cable TV connection or F cable connection to bring a television signal into Quadra 630, Power Mac 52*xx*, 62*xx*, 53*xx*, 63*xx*, 54*xx*, 55*xx*, 64*xx*, 65*xx*, and Twentieth Anniversary Power Mac computers. If a cable feed is not available, the tuner card requires an antenna connection using an F connector. Apple Video Player supports NTSC and PAL input, although NTSC is the only video format used in the U.S. Most countries in Europe use the PAL video standard for television broadcast instead of NTSC.

The best feature about the tuner card is that you can view television using keyboard controls at a real-time frame rate of 30 frames per second. Of course, the quality of the broadcast is only as good as the source. However, the tuner card supports closed caption and AppleScript, so if you want, you can create a transcript of a closed caption program and save it for reading at a later date. Performa models that ship with the tuner card also include a remote control that works with Apple Video Player to let you change channels and sound volume with a click of a button.

AV Macs

Apple Video Player supports similar video playback features with AV hardware as well as the tuner card. However, with AV hardware, you cannot change or configure channels as you can with the tuner card. AV hardware supports an RCA connection to an external video device, such as a VCR or camera, for movie or still frame capture. Brightness, sharpness, contrast, and color can also be adjusted in the application.

Video images that are prerecorded on videotapes are typically copyrighted and cannot be copied for secondary use. Be careful when you use prerecorded materials from tape or the Internet. Make sure they are "royalty free" or can be copied for personal use. Do some research before copying. This way, you'll be safe and honest.

14

One feature Apple Video Player supports on both the tuner and AV hardware is video recording.

Cabling Considerations

Before you can record video with an AV Macintosh, such as the 8600, 8500, 7600, 7500, and 7300 models or the 8100AV, 7100AV, or 6100AV Power Macs, you have to connect your video source to your Mac. Like setting up a VCR, the cabling of your video Mac can be confusing, because you have to worry about audio and video connections for both input and output. You also need two-headed jacks to capture stereo sound.

Depending on the Mac, you'll connect a cable TV connection to the TV tuner card, or you'll connect a cable from your video input jack on your VCR or camcorder to the video input port on your Mac. Then, you have to connect a cable from the audio output jack(s) of the camcorder or VCR to your Mac's audio input port or microphone port.

The type of video cable you use depends upon the type of output jack used by your VCR or other video equipment. You either need an S-video jack (a nine-pin connector similar to that used by your serial devices) or a composite jack (which resembles the RCA-type jack you see on stereo components). Most camcorders, VCRs, and televisions use composite output jacks. High-end video equipment typically uses S-video jacks.

You can also connect a composite output jack to an S-video port using a composite cable adapter that should have come with your Mac.

Make sure you have the correct connectors (RCA type, composite, or stereo minijacks) on both ends of your cables; otherwise, you cannot make proper connections.

Video Applications

Apple Video Player provides recording and frame capture features for only three kinds of video input. For a more complete video authoring system, third-party commercial applications, often combined with hardware, provide the video solution. Because video performance and editing require more memory and hardware assistance to support higher-end features, video editing on a computer can become an expensive investment. Most video-authoring products use image compression and decompression to efficiently use hard disk space and maximize playback frame rates. Here's a selected list of video-editing software and hardware products.

- **Adobe Premiere.** Supports movie and video editing. Its feature set can be extended using plug-in software. Adobe After Effects is another useful tool for editing and adding effects to digital video.

- **Macromedia Director.** Used to combine video with still image, sound, animation, and Director's scripting language. Director is more of a postproduction tool than a video-authoring product.
- **Media 100.** A hardware and software video system for Macintosh computers.
- **ATI XClaim VR.** Provides a fairly low-cost video capture and playback solution for PCI Power Macs. It also support 3D acceleration and video output features.

Summary

Apple Video Player, installed with Mac OS 8.5, is one piece of the arsenal of multimedia tools provided on the Mac. Apple Video Player lets you record and play back video on your Mac. You can connect a video source, such as a camcorder, VCR, or other digital video camera, to the Mac and use the Player to record from it. You can install third-party software to edit your masterpiece, and you can produce broadcast-level quality video as well. Apple Video Player also supports Apple AV and tuner card hardware to bring video to your computer.

Term Review

Apple Video Player   The software application that comes with Mac OS 8.5. On properly configured Macs (those with video cards or AV chips) you can capture and replay video on your computer.

audiovisual (AV) Macs   Macs, such as the Quadra 660AV and 840AV, that have digital signal processor (DSP) chips installed, enabling the recording and playing of digital video.

composite jack   A cable with an RCA-type metal jack typically used to connect VCRs to other video or audio components.

frame rate   The number of images captured by the video source per second. The more frames per second, the smoother the picture quality.

S-video connector   A nine-pin connector (similar to a printer cable or other serial port cable) used to connect high-end video components to your Mac.

video card   The integrated circuit board containing audiovisual signal conversion chips that you add to your Mac to make it ready to record and play video.

14

Q&A

Q **What third-party tools are available for creating digital video productions?**

A There are several authoring software packages available, including the following:

- **Apple HyperCard.** HyperCard is a programming language that lets you create simple animations and establish links between hotspots on your screen and other cards in the HyperCard deck.

- **Allegiant's SuperCard.** SuperCard is a cousin of HyperCard; it provides enhanced color and animation support. In addition, SuperCard's database and calculation capabilities are superb.

- **Voyager Company's Expanded Book Toolkit.** This toolkit is used for electronic book publishing and is therefore useful for creating interactive multimedia presentations. It provides such features as automated word searching and annotation.

- **Apple Media Tool.** This is a desktop publishing vehicle for the production of multimedia. You can import art, movies, text, and sounds that you then manipulate within AMT. You can also create hotspots for links, buttons, and actions and then compile the parts to create standalone applications that run on many platforms.

- **Macromedia Director and Authorware.** You can create interactive animated multimedia presentations by importing and manipulating multimedia components. Add interactions using the Lingo language and run the resulting program on the Director player.

Q **What hardware is available for video production?**

A The Apple Video System ($199) is a circuit board that installs in an expansion slot to provide digitizing features similar to those provided on the AV Macs. Using this card, you can connect a videocassette recorder, camcorder, or other video source to the Mac.

Workshop

The Workshop contains quiz questions to help you solidify your understanding of the material covered. You can find the answers to the quiz questions in Appendix B, "Quiz Answers."

Quiz

1. What hardware do you need to begin recording video on your Mac?

2. How do you cable your video source to your Mac?

3. Where do you find your copy of Apple Video Player?

4. How do you change the video screen size?

5. How do you adjust the picture quality while watching a video?

6. What do you do if you get a low memory alert while trying to capture a video?

7. What formats can you use to save your video?

8. How do you increase the frames per second used to record video?

9. How do you turn off the compression feature to increase the quality of your pictures?

10. What do you need to edit your video once you have it captured?

14

HOUR 15

Web Publishing

A few years ago, desktop publishing was the "in" thing to do on a Mac. It still is, but the so-called "paperless office" is starting to catch up. So, how do you convert those skills you have in desktop publishing to electronic publishing? Easy, just learn a new markup language (HTML), learn some new file formats for graphics (GIF and JPEG), learn some new skills to produce animation and videos to add to your publications, and become computer-savvy about how client/server systems work, and you're on your way. Wow!

Luckily, Mac OS 8.5 is a great platform to rapidly learn new tricks. Vendors are quickly developing desktop-publishing-type programs for electronic publishing to take the pain out of using HTML and make it behave (for example, to let you place objects anywhere on a page with great precision). This hour reviews how to use the Mac to publish your work electronically, including the following topics:

- Electronic publishing on the Web
- Constructing your site so it's aesthetically pleasing
- HTML basics
- How to gain access to the Web

Planning for Electronic Publishing on the Web

The Internet is in its infancy. There are organizations dedicated to setting standards for the tools used to manage the World Wide Web (such as HTML), security issues, and so forth, but browser developers, commercial artists, and businesses are rushing in to use the Web way ahead of the planners. Creating a Web publication is always a work in progress, because you don't know how well your readers are able to access your work. For example, some users have browsers that support every whiz-bang extension to HTML, whereas other users have modems that will not support large file sizes at adequate speeds. Designing for the Web is more than just storyboards and layout—it requires an understanding of human interface design and computing as well.

The design of a Web site includes two parts:

- **Content Design.** What are you going to publish? What is the purpose of your site? Who is its audience? How will you structure the site to enable that audience to move efficiently through its pages? You can call this the *strategic* step.

- **Appearance Design.** When you've determined the contents of the site, you need to design the themes, look, and methodology of the site. You must take into account copyright laws, the logistics of downloading your graphics (and how it affects the readability of your site), and other issues dealing with the tactics of site building. You can call this the *implementation* step.

Content Design: Determining What to Say

The goal of a Web site is to communicate. How you communicate is based on what it is you want to say as well as who you're speaking to. Therefore, when you plan your Web site, first figure out answers to the following three questions:

- **What is the intended purpose of your site?** For example, will you be using the site to train new personnel in your company across the U.S. or to let people know what's being done about animal cruelty issues in New Hampshire?

- **Who is the site's audience?** For example, if you were the Webmaster of Apple Computer, you would know your typical audience consists of well-educated, computer-savvy, urban professionals seeking information about computer updates and computer-related news.

- **How will you construct your site?** Given the site's purpose and its audience, how can you design it to meet your goals? For example, should your site be one long page or should you break your content into several pages? Will it be in database form or will it be very graphical without containing much information?

Intended Purpose of Your Site

A good design rule is that *form follows function*. The first thing you have to do is figure out what you're doing. Why are you building this site? What do you want to say? People surf the Web looking for many things. Sometimes they're doing research for a book they're writing. Other times they're looking for a specific piece of information about a subject, such as discipline issues in child rearing, or they want to buy something, such as a piece of software. Mostly though, they're just looking around to have fun.

Each of these purposes use different methods of navigating:

- If you're researching, you probably use a search engine, such as Yahoo or Alta Vista, to locate a Web site by URL that covers the topic you're seeking.

- If you're looking for people who have answers to specific questions you're asking (such as "Should you use 'time outs' for disciplining a two year old?"), you start with a search engine and then use hypertext links within sites that describe other sites to jump to destinations that meet your needs.

- If you're shopping, you look for a catalog or store site that uses forms and databases to present products you can order online. The purpose of the site drives how its navigation features are designed (in other words, how people move around the site).

Therefore, the first task of Web site planning is to figure out what you want it to be. For example, do you want your site to be a catalog, a store, a public relations vehicle introducing a product, a library that points to other sites, a newspaper, an artist's studio? Each type of site has different types of content and ways of presenting information.

One way of figuring out what you want is to surf the Web and look at other people's sites. By researching what's out there, you can determine how jazzy you want to make your site, where do you want to take the reader, how often the site will need updating (in order to keep the information current), and so forth.

What the site is about dictates how it looks. For example, a site dedicated to listing a compendium of other sites is different than a site that shows off a company's products. The first site will have a lot of text and linked headings with very few graphics, and the latter will probably be more artsy with lots of images linked to descriptions of products and services.

Use a search engine, such as Yahoo or Alta Vista, to identify sites from your industry. The search engine lets you search by keywords and categories, and it displays a listing of hypertext that fits your search criteria. Go to each identified site and bookmark those that appeal to what you want to say.

Note how the home pages of other sites in your industry work: Are the sites attractive and well organized? Do they contain up-to-date content?

It's okay to take the ideas behind such sites. You can even copy the source HTML to see how a site is constructed. Save the source document and open it in PageMill to display its WYSIWYG image and underlying HTML.

When you dissect the site, replace its text and pictures with your own. Do not take any content, such as pictures or text, without permission.

A good rule of thumb is that every image you find on the Web or take from a clip art collection is copyrighted material. Get permission to use anything you do not create yourself. Even photographs in the public domain are copied from something that may have a copyright. Speak to a lawyer if you have questions about using an item. Check out the InfoLawAlert newsletter at http://www.infolawalert.com for information about electronic copyright and patent law issues.

Now that you've figured out what you want your Web site to be, you have to determine who your audience is.

The Audience

Who your audience is might be the most important consideration when creating your Web page. After all, you're publishing information for the public. Understanding characteristics of your audience helps you make smart decisions when designing your page. Here are some examples:

- The Mac-savvy, educated consumer will be looking for snazzy, up-to-the-minute plug-ins, such as fading text, animation, frames, and so forth.
- The "newbie" (someone who's just starting out) doesn't know what to look for and needs more navigation aids and less "noise."
- Researchers want quick, no-frills connections to what they're searching for and often turn off the graphics to speed up their searches (they might be under monetary constraints, and online time costs plenty, depending on the service provider).

If you're designing the site for people who know your industry (say, as an example, you're selling environmentally friendly kitchen items), you should give them good visual cues to quickly move them to where they want to go. Humor and up-to-date information are good ways to keep these people coming back to your site. Your goal is to be "bookmarked" so that your readers can easily return again.

Therefore, the audience dictates both the content and the appearance of your site. If you determine, for example, you want to attract buyers of environmentally friendly products, you then have to decide whether you want existing customers to come to your site or you want to attract new customers who've never thought of the subject. Existing customers will not require as much advertising via special effects as new customers will. New customers will remember your site through its visual impact.

Other important issues include deciding what browser capabilities and what type of Internet connection (modem, ISDN, T1, and so on) your audience will have. This helps you decide what information you serve, how you serve it, and the size and number of graphics you place on your page.

There are as many different Web site design philosophies as there are Web publishers, so create your Web site in a form that feels right for your anticipated audience's browsers.

For More Information

Check out Microsoft's Site Builder Network site (`http://www.microsoft.com/ sitebuilder/site06.htm`) for a wealth of whitepapers, tools, how-to guides, standards, and software you can use to plan the conceptualization and tactical phases of your site design project. A great article you can find there is "So You Want to Build a Web Site? Everything You Need to Consider from Initial Planning Through Launch," by Dominick J. Dellino.

Appearance Design: Organizing Your Information

Now that you've figured out the purpose of your site and who the site is for, it's time to actually design the physical layout of the Web site. The act of designing the physical body of the site is called *prototyping*. The prototype should answer three questions:

- **What information are you going to include in the site?** Collect a list of all the information you want to include, such as mission statements, product descriptions, product pictures, URLs you want to link the site to, company history, various graphics, and so forth.

- **How is the site supposed to work?** Create a thumbnail sketch of all the pages in your site. Place arrows where you want your readers to be able to move. These storyboards create a visual picture of the site on paper that you can use to ensure you don't forget anything. This way, you can make sure everything is properly positioned so that the links will work.

- **Where you are going to place links and what they will link to?** Your storyboard will help you make sure you've given your reader ways to return to the home page, as well as move up and down long documents, move horizontally between pages, and jump out and back into the site easily.

Physically Prototyping the Site

The purpose and appearance of your site dictates how the site is constructed. Here are four steps to building a site:

- **Collect your materials.** Create a resource file (both paper and electronic) containing all the text and graphic images you'll use on the pages. Make sure you have permissions to use any copyrighted materials (including photographs, clip art, documents, and other previously published works).

- **Build the site.** Construct nonworking prototypes of your pages that include all the technologies you'll use: hypertext links, frames, form parts, tables, inline graphics, splash sheets (title bars), imagemaps, buttons, and so forth. This builds the HTML you need and gives you a list of CGIs you have to check out with your Webmaster. You can also determine where you might need actual HTML programming to accomplish your goals (for example, special Java or ActiveX parts or nonsupported HTML, such as style sheets).

- **Test the site.** Check out what the site looks like under a number of different browsers, such as Netscape Navigator 2 and 3, and 4, Microsoft Internet Explorer 3, and 4, and Mosaic. Check out the site with beta versions of these browsers, as well. Look at the sizing of text and graphics on different computer platforms, such as Macs and PCs, as well as on different resolution monitors. Also, check the speed of graphic image downloads on different modem models and speeds.

- **Upload the site.** Load your site on your ISP's server. Find out how to upload the HTML documents to the Web server. Different providers have different methods and requirements for uploading. Some providers use FTP protocols; others let you have direct access to the server.

Collecting Your Materials

Now you're down to the nitty-gritty of creating visuals, buttons, splash banners, and so forth. Because HTML does not specify any specific fonts, you must create any special use of fonts, shows, drop caps, and so forth. Your best tools are an image processor, such as Adobe Photoshop, an illustration package, such as MetaCreations Painter, Adobe Illustrator, or Macromedia Freehand, and a word processor, such as Microsoft Word or Corel WordPerfect.

In preparing your files for inclusion on the Web page, you must be aware of how each image will appear (its width on the computer screen as well as how long the image will take to download). Remember, almost everything you place on a page will be a graphic, whether it's a background image (such as a tiled pattern), an inline image and layered text, or future images for imagemaps and buttons. Because each image is a file and each file must download separately, the most important issue to consider when designing your files is color management (that is, in order to lessen the time it takes to download a page).

Most readers will be using computers that lack power and modems that lack baud rate. Most users are running 14.4K or 28.8K baud modems. With these modems, a 60K file takes about a minute to download (one second per kilobyte). A good target size for your files is half of that, or 30K, which will download in 30 seconds with a 14.4K baud modem. Get those file sizes as small as possible.

Selecting the Right File Format

Two image formats are supported on the Web: JPEG and GIF. Both have pluses and minuses in terms of file size versus image quality:

- JPEG (Joint Photographic Expert Group) compresses color bitmapped images (scanned images such as photographs are bitmapped). JPEG enables variable rates of compression (called *lossy* compression). With this compression scheme, images tend to lose some of their quality when compressed and decompressed by browsers. Use JPEG formats for soft photographic images continuous in tone (avoid gradients and three-dimensional pictures). Don't use the JPEG format for line drawings or images with wide areas of flat colors. These line drawings and broad color-based drawings will appear distorted after decompression.

  Set your image compression to Maximum in Photoshop to get the lowest compression factor so that little data is lost during compression. JPEG produces smaller files with 24-bit images (16.7 million colors) than the GIF format can produce with its 8-bit image (256 color) limit.

  When selecting compression factors for JPEG images, remember that most of your readers only have 8-bit (256 color) monitors available for viewing your pictures. In addition, each browser interprets higher color bit rates differently. Try to limit your colors to under 256 by removing colors from your images in Photoshop. In fact, even if your file is smaller using JPEG than GIF, because the browser performs the decompressing of JPEG images, they take longer to download than larger GIF images.

- CompuServe's GIF (Graphics Interchange Format) is the industry standard for Web pages. GIF supports moving just about any type of graphic between computer platforms without a loss of quality. It does this by supporting only 256 colors (8-bit images). Use the Indexed Color setting in Photoshop to save a graphic with 256 colors. GIF uses LZW compression (also called *lossless* compression) and therefore doesn't loose any quality when compressed and then decompressed.

The compression is performed by looking for repeating patterns of color along each horizontal line and then compressing those pixels (deleting them but keeping track of the location of the deletions so that the colors can be replaced during decompression). Those images with the most repeating patterns horizontally create the smallest files. Therefore, flat-colored images are small in GIF format without loosing quality. One way to limit the amount of vertical pixels is to turn off *dithering* (a way of increasing the detail in an image by adding intermediate colors) in Photoshop before converting your images to 8-bit color. You need to tune your graphics (add and subtract colors) and visually determine where degradation begins to occur. Stick right on the edge to keep your files small (under 40K).

> Use Lynda Weinman's browser-safe palette (available on the Web at http://www.lynda.com/hex.html) in Photoshop to ensure your images are optimized at 216 colors so that they look good on both Macs and PCs. This palette works best on images with flat colors or that use a lot of one single color.

GIFs have a benefit over JPEG formats in that you can create transparent images. Transparency enables you to lay a graphic on top of a background and let the background shine through the image. This is also called *masking*. Avoid using transparency if you see a halo effect when laying the graphic on top of a color (this is the colored edge around a picture, also called *anti-aliasing*).

> Web technology does not provide a way to avoid anti-aliasing. If you're using a solid background without a pattern, make sure you create an image with the same color background. This creates the illusion of an *aliased* edge on the graphic (no halo).

Converting Graphics For The Web

Generating graphics that work on the Web isn't a straightforward endeavor. Right now, you must use several image-processing programs to perform a conversion. Here's a sample step-by-step guide on how conversions are done:

1. Create your graphic in a graphic package such as Adobe Illustrator, MetaCreations Painter 5, or Macromedia Freehand.

2. Save the graphic as a PICT file.

    You can also scan a permissible image into Photoshop or Create IT and edit the
    scanned graphic until you've created what you want.

    You can also get an image from a clip art collection such as IMSI's Art Explosion
    Gold.

3. Open the PICT file in a program that can perform conversions, such as Lempke's
   GraphicConverter (a wonderful shareware program).

4. Select Save As from the File menu.

5. In the resulting standard Finder window, shown in Figure 15.1, click the Format
   pop-up menu and select GIF or JPEG as the file format.

FIGURE 15.1.

*GraphicConverter pro-
vides image editing
and conversion tools to
simplify getting your
graphics ready for
the Web.*

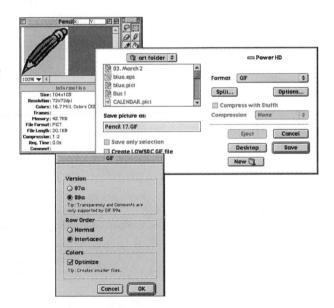

6. Click the Options button.

7. If you're saving the file as a GIF, select GIF 87a and Interlaced.

8. Make sure the name of the file changes to include a suffix representing the new file
   format (either .GIF or .JPG).

The beauty of GraphicConverter is that you can change many graphics to GIF or JPEG
formats simultaneously via a conversion batch processor (see Figure 15.2). Select
Convert More from the File menu. In the resulting Conversion dialog box, find the
images you want to convert in the left list box and select a storage location from the right

list box. Click the button for the process you want to perform (convert, rename, move, and so on). You can also change file formats using the Format button, create new folders, and set image options.

FIGURE 15.2.

Use GraphicConverter's batch processor to convert multiple files at the same time.

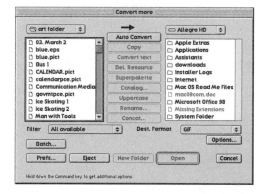

One piece of good news is that the multistep task of converting images will soon be a thing of the past. Adobe has introduced an all-in-one package for image editing and conversion called ImageReady (http://www.adobe.com/prodindex/imageready/). The program is supposed to let you swap images among Photoshop, Illustrator, and ImageReady to create animations, convert files, and optimize images more efficiently.

GraphicConverter is a shareware program. Please honor the pact with these brave programmers and pay for your copy. Figure 15.3 provides the information you need to acquire and register your copy.

FIGURE 15.3.

GraphicConverter is shareware, which means you'll pay $35 for the privilege of using this program.

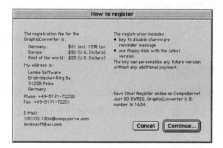

Constructing Your Site

Now that you've created all these beautiful graphics, amazing movies, animated GIF files, sound effects, and so forth, you need to put them together on your Web site. (A series of linked Web pages makes up a Web site.)

The first page your reader sees when going to your site is always named INDEX.HTML (if you're working on a Mac) or INDEX.HTM (if you're working on a PC that only supports three-letter suffixes). This page becomes the default document and can be your actual home page or an entrance vestibule enabling your reader to choose between a text-only version or advanced browser version of your site (if you decide to create these options).

The following sections introduce the components of the home page and its supporting pages.

The Home Page

Web sites are broken into pages and sections. Sections are parts of a page, often divided by headings (type larger than the rest of the content), rules (horizontal lines), or graphics.

A home page can introduce the reader to your site, give some information about what is offered at the site, or tell who created the site and why. Of course, all this information depends on the type of site you're creating.

Home pages can have a clickable imagemap using pictures, icons, or images as a navigation guide for the Web site (see Figure 15.4). An imagemap is a graphic containing *hot spots* (places that link you to other URLs or anchors when you click them). A simpler way is to offer a table of contents that links viewers to specific places on the Web site.

FIGURE 15.4.

This home page provides buttons that link to external and internal pages in the site.

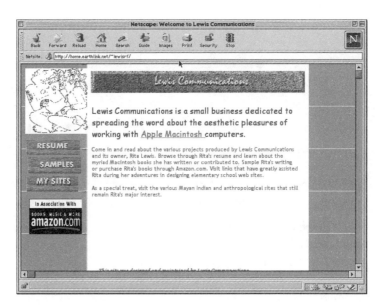

Support Pages

Support pages can include a common graphic as a header to give the site some consistency as well as an identity. However, the information within delves deeper into the Web site's topics. The home page of the site uses a series of graphics to indicate various Web site groups the reader can travel to. Each button leads to a supporting page that lists these sites. You then use hypertext links on the supporting pages to jump to these sites. (See Figure 15.5.)

FIGURE 15.5.

Sams is a support page in the Macmillan Computer Books (MCP.com) site.

Clickable imagemap

Hypertext links

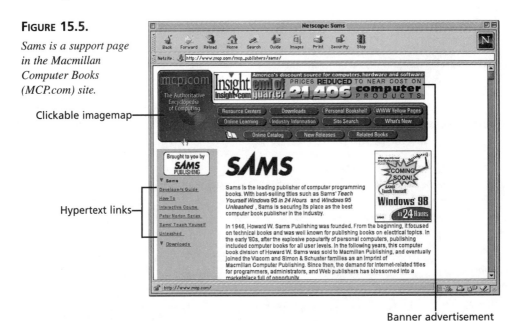

Banner advertisement

Designing Your Graphics for Navigation

Graphic images are not just pretty pictures—they can provide a way to navigate around a Web site. Some graphics advertise important subjects in a site. These images can be *imagemapped* (that is, hypertext links can be added to designated portions of a graphic that, when selected, jump you to a supporting page describing the subject of the image).

Some graphics are used as standalone icons (representations of ideas). These graphics can be placed in a toolbar and linked to direct readers from any page to other areas (such as back to the home page, to a feedback page, and so on). The more redundant your application of toolbars and icons, the better, because your goal is to let your readers know exactly where they are in your site and where they can go at all times.

Setting Up Your Resources

One of the most important tasks you must do while constructing your site is to set up the folders holding the images and text. The best time to do this is when you're collecting materials and producing your Photoshop images.

Most servers run under some flavor of UNIX, including Macintosh network servers. Set up your folders under Windows 95 or the Mac OS by grouping files according to type (GIFs with GIFs, and HTML with HTML). Then, place these format-based folders into folders by location, such as News page, Gallery page, and so forth. The folder system you devise on your Mac or PC will be converted to a system under UNIX that uses directories and subdirectories equivalent to your top folder (the root directory) and all nested folders (the subdirectories) in the hierarchy.

Because UNIX is unforgiving (meaning, move a file, lose a link), you should organize your Web resources carefully. Try to limit the number of items in a folder (or directory) to 15 to 25 files or pages. Try to limit the number of subdirectories (or subfolders in your folder hierarchy) to a depth of two, because numerous directories create complex URLs as well as file management problems.

If you're not going to manage your Web page yourself on a personal server located on your computer, you need to tell your HTML editor and the Web server how to find your top folder (the root directory). This is done by giving the folder (directory) a name that includes all the directories the server must pass through to reach it. This is called the folder's *pathname*. You must type the complete pathname for the root directory of the remote server. Ask your Webmaster or the system administrator for this name if you don't already know it.

Tips for Speeding Up Download Times

Here are some more tricks for speeding up download times:

- Reuse your images on a page. The first time an image is used, it's stored on the user's computer. That stored version is displayed any subsequent time the image is called for.

- Use textured or gradated background images so that you can make your GIF files transparent and avoid anti-aliasing effects.

- When using tiled patterns, make the tiles small so that they load quickly.

- Use specific color schemes on your pages. The fewer colors you use, the better the compression and faster the download time.

- Try to use 6- or 4-bit color in your images to create smaller files.

Check out the Microsoft Site Builder Network site at http://www.microsoft.com/sitebuilder/site06.htm for more articles and tips on Web construction. Read the article titled, "Decreasing Download Time Through Effective Color Management," by Kate S. Knight.

Testing Your Site

When you've placed all your artwork, text files, hypertext links, advanced plug-ins, and so forth into your pages, you need to make sure they all appear and work consistently with most browsers. To do this, open your Web pages using different versions of Netscape Navigator, especially the oldest (version 1) and the newest (version 4). If you can, get a hold of a beta version of Netscape Navigator to ensure that the page remains compatible. Also, do the same testing for Microsoft Internet Explorer (versions 1, 2, and 3, and 4). Make sure you click all links to see if you go where you're supposed to. Also, check the appearance and download times of your images. You need to test your browsers on both the Mac and PC platforms to see if your site operates across platforms.

Here's a nice checklist for testing:

- Is the layout easy to comprehend?
- Are all the images loading?
- Is any raw HTML showing?
- Do all links and anchors work?
- Do the counters or scripts work?
- Is the performance on a slow computer reasonable compared to the performance on a fast computer?
- Is there too much information on one page?
- Does the information fit appropriately on the screen?
- Has the page been proofread?
- Is the overall look pleasant and not cluttered? Is the overall look consistent with the message you want to convey with the readers?

You need to correct all bugs in hypertext links and imagemaps. Go back to Photoshop and tweak those images that load slowly or appear compromised on either the Mac or PC platforms.

A Quick Primer on HTML

All Web pages consist of HTML tags, and it's the creative use of graphics and tags that make a great page. For example, Figure 15.6 displays the Macmillan Computer Publishing home page (www.mcp.com). As you can see, the Web page is a huge imagemap with hot spots that light up when you pass your mouse over them. The hot spots are links to supporting pages. The lights indicate that the Web page is full of JavaScripts or Java applets.

FIGURE 15.6.

An advanced Web page that uses color and symbols to convey multiple messages about its subject matter.

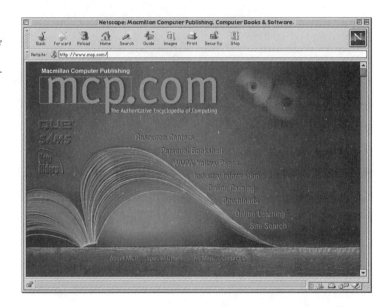

Figure 15.7 shows what must be coded in HTML to create the tables, Java applets, hypertext links, and active images and inline images presented on the page.

Notice that most of the text is actually imported into the Web page as graphics files (those instances of `<IMG SRC="...">`). If you want fancy text or colorful logos, you have to create them in separate software packages, such as Adobe Illustrator, Adobe Photoshop, Macromedia Xres, and Macromedia Freehand (available on both Mac and Windows platforms), and place them on the page. HTML does not provide any capability to perform advanced desktop publishing, such as rotating text, adding three dimensions, or even creating gradients of color.

HTML does no formatting. It simply tells the viewer's browser how to present the information contained within the bracketed tags. That's why it's called a *markup* language.

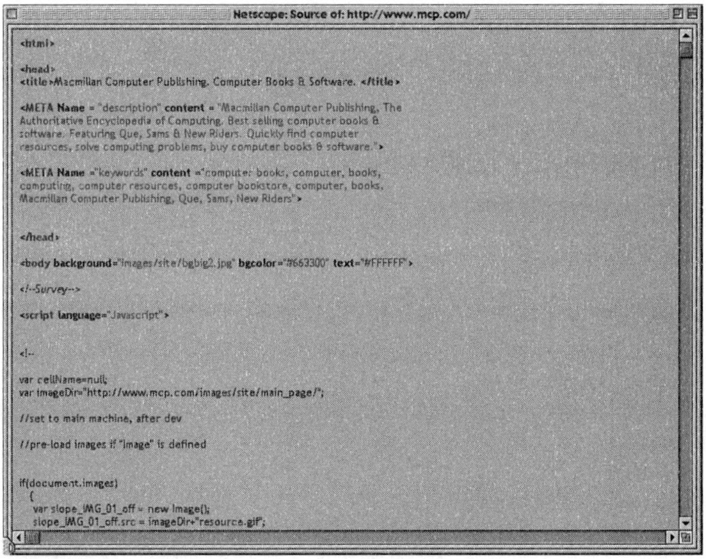

FIGURE 15.7.

The HTML and JavaScript that actually generate the Web page.

How HTML Works

All HTML documents consist of a shell—a basic set of tags that defines the parameters of your page. PageMill bases its total philosophy on this basic template, because you can build any page by adding bells and whistles to this basic format:

```
<HTML>
<HEAD>
<TITLE> This is the Title</TITLE>
</HEAD>
<BODY>
   <H1> Major document heading here</H1>
      text and markup
   <A HREF="URL"> anchor title</A>
<ADDRESS>Author and version information</ADDRESS>
</BODY>
</HTML>
```

HTML is not sensitive to case. You can type in all caps, initial caps, or lower-case letters—it's all the same to the markup language. However, it's wise to differentiate your tags from the text or image it's containing. Type items that don't change, such as tags, in all caps; type items that do change, such as attribute values (you'll learn about these later), in lowercase letters. This makes it easier to read the HTML source code, should you have to edit it.

Table 15.1 presents commonly agreed upon HTML 3.0 tags as well as the agreed upon Netscape 1.1 extensions that modify these tags.

TABLE 15.1. COMMON HTML 3.0 TAGS.

Tag	Description
<A> </A>	Defines a location that can be linked to or defines links to other resources.
<Address> </Address>	Identifies the author of the document.
<B> </B>	Makes what it surrounds bold.
<Base>	A Head section element that identifies the URL of the current document.
<Basefont>	Defines the default text size for the document. You can give this tag a value from 1 to 7. The standard setting is 3. This is a Netscape-only supported extension.
<Blink> </Blink>	Makes its contents blink.
<Blockquote> </Blockquote>	Identifies its contents as a quote from another source.
<Body> </Body>	Defines the body of your document. You can modify how the page looks with the following attributes: Background Image, Background Color, Text Color, Link Color, Visited Link Color, Active Link Color.
 	Inserts a soft return (also called a *line break*). A Netscape 1.0 extension adds the attribute Clear, which defines where the content can begin the next line of the document. You can give Clear the value Left, Right, or All.
<Center> </Center>	Centers the enclosed object or text on the page. This isn't really supported by HTML standards, but all browsers understand that it means. Another way to indicate Center is as an attribute of a heading: <H1 Align=Center> </H1>.
<Form> </Form>	Defines its contents as a from containing input fields (INPUT), selection lists (SELECT), or input boxes (TEXT AREA). You can modify forms using the following attributes: Action (defines the CGI used to process the form), and Method (defines the procedure used for passing information to the CGI and can be Post or Get).
<H1> </H1> to <H6> </H6>	Six hierarchical levels of headings. Each one must have a beginning and an ending tag.

continues

TABLE 15.1.   CONTINUED

Tag	Description
<Head> </Head>	Defines the header section of the document, which provides information about the originating program, the level of HTML used, the title of the page, and other information needed to identify the page.
<Hr>	Inserts a horizontal rule. Netscape 1.0 extensions add the following attributes: Width, Size, Noshade, Align Left, Align Right, and Align Center.
<Html> </Html>	Defines the document as an HTML document.
<I> </I>	Makes everything within its boundaries italic.
<Img>	Inserts an image file. The Img tag uses the following attributes: Src (source of the associated image file), Alt (provides an alternate text string for browsers that do not support graphics), Ismap (Imagemap), Align Top, Align Middle, Align Bottom, Align Left, Align Right, Align Texttop, Align Absmiddle (absolute middle), Align Baseline, Align Absbottom (absolute bottom), Hspace (defines the space along the horizontal edges of an inline graphic), Vspace (defines the vertical space), Width, Height, Border, and Lowsrc (low resolution version of the graphic).
<Isindex>	This is a Head element tag that lets you set up keywords for simple searches. The tag is used with the Prompt attribute, which lets you place a customized message in the search dialog box or window. You need a search engine (CGI) on your server to use this tag.
<Li>	Defines a new item in a list. You can modify the listed item using the following attributes: Type (defines what type of dingbat is used as a bullet or number) and Value (lets you set where to begin numbering the items in the list).
<Link>	This is a Head element tag that defines relationships between the current document (identified by the Base tag) and another document.
<Meta>	This is a Head element tag that lets you present information about the document that's not displayed by the browser.
<Ol> </Ol>	This tag set identifies an ordered list of items with sequential numbers.
<P>	Inserts a hard return (also called a *paragraph break*).

Tag	Description
`<Table> </Table>`	This tag defines its contents as a table that contains rows (`Tr`), cells (`Td`), headers (`Th`), and captions (`Caption`). You can modify tables by using the following attributes: `Border`, `Cell-Spacing`, `Cell-Padding`, `Width`.
`<Title> </Title>`	This is a `Head` element tag. It defines the title of the document (the name that the browser places in the title bar).
`<Ul> </Ul>`	This tag set defines an unordered list of items.

Applying Tag Pairs to Format Items

As stated previously, all HTML consists of pairs of tags—one in the front of the item it modifies and one that follows the item. Tags are sometimes called *containers*, because they come in pairs and hold the text or images you want to include on the page. Here's an example,:

```
<h1>Welcome to Joe Webhead's Home Page!</h1>
```

This tells the browser to display the text "Welcome to Joe Webhead's Home Page!" as a first-level heading (according to that browser). All you know is that first-level headers have the largest font size and boldness, and each subsequent heading levels (`<H2>` down to `<H6>`) are less prominent. You can set up different text and paragraph formats to tell the browser how to display the text.

Using Attributes and Values to Modify Tags

Tags are the primary way of telling the browser how to display what the tags contain. Tags, such as `<H1> </H1>`, are modified by *attributes*, which are secondary tags that offer layout options, such as center, left align, and so on. You can add details to how the browser is supposed to display the contained text by adding an attribute/value pair (written *attribute=value*).

Attributes describe optional specifications, such as height and width of an image, that modify a tag. Values are the different options from which you can select (center, right, left, and so on). Whenever you see a phrase that includes an equals sign (for example, `ALIGN=LEFT`), you're looking at an attribute/value pair.

Creating Hypertext Links

HTML has an extremely powerful tool for jumping your browser from computer site to computer site—the concept of hypertext links (also called *hotlinks*). The HTML tags for these links use two structures: an anchor and a hypertext reference. Here's an example:

```
<a href="the URL you are linking to"</a>
```

If, for example, you want to point to the Macmillan Computer Publishing home page, you type the URL for Macmillan in place of "the URL you are linking to":

```
<a href="http://www.mcp.com"</a>
```

Placing Objects in a Page

You cannot simply paste graphics into a Web page; you must point the browser at where the image is stored and let the browser load the appropriate image. You use an image tag (`<IMG>`) to indicate you want to import a graphic. On many pages, the buttons for jumping to other pages are graphics with Java applets applied. The code would look something like

```
<IMG SRC="graphics/dot.gif">
```

where "graphics" is the directory and "dot.gif" is the name of the image file being placed.

The most important thing to remember when placing images (or any other type of self-contained object) is to name your files using appropriate extensions (the two to four-letter addition applied to the end of a filename after a period). It's very important to name your files correctly. Table 15.2 presents a list of common file extensions and their meanings.

TABLE 15.2. FILE EXTENSIONS AND THEIR MEANINGS.

Extension	Description
.GIF	A graphic image file
.MOV, .MOOV, .QT	A QuickTime movie
.CLASS	A Java applet
.AIF, .AIFF, .AU	A Macintosh sound file
.WAV	A Microsoft sound file
.DOC	A text file
.HTML, .HTM	A Web page
.AVI	A Microsoft Video for Windows file
.MID	A MIDI music file
.MP2, .MPEG, .MPG	A video/sound file
.JPG, .JPEG	A photographic image file
.STY	A style sheet file

Working With Paragraph and Line Spacing

The only other thing you need to know is how dumb HTML really is. You need to designate all paragraph endings, line endings, and line spaces. When you press the Return/Enter key in PageMill, a <P> tag is inserted for hard paragraph return. If you press Shift with the Return/Enter key, a <BR> tag is inserted, indicating a line feed or soft return. Anytime you see a <P> tag in HTML, it indicates a new paragraph. That's why <P> is used to indicate a blank line as well as an actual paragraph.

The Logic Behind HTML

Now, here's where HTML gets a little more complicated. When I said earlier that all HTML tags come in pairs, I was lying. Actually. *most* HTML tags come in pairs. These tags are called *containers* and toggle on and off a function (such as a paragraph style). A specialized type of tag operates as a single tag. These noncontainer tags perform specific tasks, such as creating a horizontal rule.

An HTML document consists of two parts:

- **The head.** The Head area uses *document structure tags* to identify information about the document, such as its name, its originating application, what type of HTML is being used, and so on. These tags consist of the <HTML>, <HEAD>, and <TITLE> tags.

- **The body.** The Body area uses *content tags* (also called *body elements*). Content tags are every other tag offered in HTML, including <BODY>, <H1>, <IMG>, and so on. Body elements come in two flavors: block-level elements, which cause paragraph breaks (such as <P> and <ADDRESS>) and the text-level elements, such as <STRONG> and <B> (for bold text). Block-level elements can act as containers for text-level elements and other block-level elements. Text-level elements may only contain other text-level elements.

The following sections discuss these parts in more detail.

The Head Area

The following HTML code is the Head area, which contains mostly the stuff that tells the browser what to do with the rest of the HTML source code:

```
<HTML>
<HEAD>
<TITLE> This is the Title</TITLE>
</HEAD>
```

The Head section of the document provides information for browsers and other applications that access HTML files. The Head section can include the title of the document, the relationship between it and the HTML document, and where its associated files are stored (that is, its file directories). It sometimes provides keywords that can be used in indexes to identify the document.

> You use the <TITLE> </TITLE> tag portion of the Head area to provide a name for your page. This is the information that appears on the browser's title bar. You're not limited as to how long to make the title, but remember that most browser title bars are not large and they also contain the name of the browser. Therefore, try to limit the title to 64 characters so it will not be truncated by the browser.

The Body Area

This following HTML code shows the Body area (the stuff that appears on the graphical browser's screen):

```
<BODY>
    <H1> Major document heading here</H1>
        text and markup
    <A HREF="URL"> anchor title</A>
<ADDRESS>Author and version information</ADDRESS>
</BODY>
</HTML>
```

The body of an HTML document contains all the data you want to show the reader's browser. The body of the document is set off by the <Body> </Body> tags. This is where the bulk of the HTML appears.

Adding Special Characters

Because HTML is an international markup language, it accepts the standard ASCII code set of special characters (called *Latin-1*). The problem in PageMill is that you cannot add the special characters by simply using the keystroke equivalents you're used to, because HTML must see an ampersand before the symbol and a semicolon after the symbol to recognize it as an ASCII character. The Latin-1 extended character set uses both literal codes (those that spell out what they do, such as adding an accent agrave to a letter— typed as à) and numerical equivalents (those that use numbers to specify what they do; an accent agrave can also be typed as Ç). You can use either literal or numerical notations in HTML to get the extended character to appear.

Table 15.3 presents the Latin-1 ASCII character set and what you must literally type into the HTML source window to get them to appear.

TABLE 15.3. THE LATIN-1 EXTENDED CHARACTER LIST.

Character	Literal	Numerical	Description
~		&#136;	Circumflex accent
–		&#150;	En dash
–	&emdash;	&#151;	Em dash
™		&#153;	Trademark symbol
			Nonbreaking space
¢		&#162;	Cent sign
©	&copy;	&#169;	Copyright symbol
-	&shy;	&#173;	Soft hyphen
™	&reg;	&#174;	Registered trademark symbol
2		&#179;	Superscript 2
1/4		&#188;	Fraction one-fourth
1/2		&#189;	Fraction one-half
3/4		&#190;	Fraction three-fourths
<	&lt;	&#60;	Less than sign
>	&gt;	&#62;	Greater than sign
&	&amp;	&#38;	Ampersand
o		&#178;	Degree sign

Using Cascading Style Sheets

A newly developing standard that's currently supported by Netscape Navigator 4.0 and Microsoft Internet Explorer 4.0 is Cascading Style Sheets. (See the W3 committee Web site at `http://www.w3.org/put/WWW/TR/WD-css1.html` for information about this developing standard.) This indicates you want standard values applied to attributes every place they're encountered. Files containing style sheets use the .STY extension.

Style sheets are a set of new tags that present a series of statements or rules describing a document. You set up a style by typing

```
selector {property = value}
```

where *selector* is the tag element being lent a style, such as a header or paragraph, a list, and so on, *property* is something about the selector that varies, such as its alignment, text color, spacing, and so on (you can think of the property as the attribute of the selector), and *value* is the variable you select for the property, such as `Left`, `Right`, `Center`, and so on.

Therefore, you can set up a style sheet that states that each Level 1 header will be red, Helvetica or Arial, 12-point type with 2-point leading, and bold faced:

```
H1 {
   text color=red
   font-family=helvetica
   alt-font=arial
   font-size=12pt
   font-leading=2pt
   font-weight=bold
   }
```

In addition, you can use the <CLASS> attribute to add power to your style sheets by defining special styles to classes of tags. For example, let's say you want to define some lists as being in the classification "key." By adding the <LI CLASS=key> attribute to your HTML, every time this attribute is encountered, the LI.key style is applied to the list. This is a great way to set up paragraph styles for specialized formatting.

Right now, anything goes with how styles are applied to HTML, because each browser developer works on her or his own system of applying styles. You can also use a new tag called <STYLE> </STYLE> to define the style of a paragraph as you go along. For example, the previous list with the "key" classification would be manually formatted with a text color of lime green by adding the HTML <STYLE>LI {text-color=#00ff00"}</STYLE> to the document.

Using Java Applets and JavaScript Macros

Java is a portable programming language developed by Sun Microsystems. The usefulness of this language is that it can run on any computer with access to the Web. Suddenly, you can write programs and store them on the Web for use by anyone who has access to your site. True "groupware" is born.

Java programs are fully compiled applications that contain only a little code, thus the name *applets*. Java applets perform a certain task, such as displaying an analog clock that tells time in an animated fashion. Netscape developed a scripting language (such as you use in Excel spreadsheets to write a macro that runs as a tiny program to do automatically what you regularly do manually) based on Java called *JavaScript*. You can write JavaScript macros directly in your HTML that cause the browser to perform some task as ordered by your HTML, such as increasing an incremental counter one unit.

Web Publishing Software

The one conclusion you should come to while reading this hour is that for basic Web publishing, you really don't need to go through a bunch of coding and testing. It's still helpful to understand the basics of HTML code so that you can tweak the code after it has been written by the software; therefore, the time spent learning HTML in this hour is still a good idea.

Several vendors have developed WYSIWYG HTML editors that let you do layout in a more standard desktop publishing manner, leaving the program to interpret what you've done and then write the proper HTML tags. The following companies have good Web publishing software available. All these packages are cross platform, thus enabling many users to work on a Web site design and share their results online:

- **Adobe PageMill 2.0.** This is the granddaddy of Web publishers and is still the one that contains the most support for HTML 3.2 standards. PageMill lets you work on a word-processing-based window to create tables, frames, and other advanced HTML features by clicking and dragging. PageMill requires SiteMill to maintain pages across a site.

- **Microsoft FrontPage.** FrontPage is a port from Windows and is not as powerful or intuitive as PageMill. FrontPage also provides a bird's-eye view of your Web site so you can manage changes while not disturbing links between pages.

- **GoLive CyberStudio.Personal and Professional.** These packages provide the most up-to-date collection of Web authoring tools in a WYSIWYG interface. You can drag and drop objects onto a grid for extremely precise layout work, or you can code directly in the source HTML. A very powerful site maintenance section is also provided. (This is my favorite authoring tool.)

- **NetObjects Fusion.** This is an expensive (approximately $500) site management and layout program that lets you leave the linear HTML-based layout for true precision placement of items on your page. In addition, you can create master style sheets that carry items across a site to create headers, footers, buttons, and so forth to ease navigation.

Gaining Access to the Web

The World Wide Web is only one method of accessing the information on the Internet. The Internet communicates through special networking rules via TCP/IP (Transmission Control Protocol/Internet Protocol). TCP/IP is the network standard used on most UNIX computers and has become the *de facto* standard for large networks running different types of computers.

The "IP" portion of TCP/IP lets multiple processes communicate with each other over a network using packet-switching technology. The goal of TCP/IP is reliability, regardless of how congested the transmission traffic gets. IP enables multiple networks to connect to form "internetworks" by routing data via *datagrams* (packets of information routed over a common network) between networks.

The "TCP" portion of the network standard manages how dissimilar computers speak to one another. Together, TCP/IP provides communications between networks and operates on a variety of computer platforms, from Apple Macintosh computers, DOS-based personal computers using Windows 3.1, Windows 95 and Windows NT systems, to IBM mainframes and RISC-based UNIX workstations.

TCP/IP uses two types of network protocols to connect to the physical LAN media: the X.25 packet protocol for wide area networks, and the IEEE 802 specifications (such as Ethernet and Token-Ring) for local area networks.

Most computers using TCP/IP are permanently connected to some sort of high-speed network (such as Ethernet, ISDN, or T1 lines). You also can dial into a TCP/IP network using a modem. If the modem is used to connect with the network, one of two types of protocols assists the connection: SLIP (Serial Line Internet Protocol) or PPP (Point-To-Point Protocol). Either way, you call into a central computer whose software controls the flow of talk between computers and provides the files and directories that can be accessed via the Net. This software is known as *server* software. The term *server* describes both the hardware on which the software runs, such as an Intel Pentium personal computer or an Apple Power Macintosh, as well as the software managing the process, such as Microsoft Windows NT 4.0, Netscape Enterprise Server, or Netscape Fastrack Server 2.0 for Windows operating systems, HTTPd or Apache for Unix operating systems, or StarNine's WebStar server for the Macintosh operating system.

If your computer is connected to a high-speed network, you have direct access to the server. Today, however, most people who use the Web use an intermediary service accessed via a modem. In this case, the Internet Service Provider's hardware and software connects you with the Web server.

Uploading Your Page

After you've determined the remote server (typically your ISP's server) where you want to publish your Web site, you need to upload it. This is a two-step process: setting up a folder or directory to store your Web site files and then actually uploading the files.

This discussion assumes that you'll be communicating with a UNIX server, because this is a ubiquitous server system (with Windows NT servers coming in a close second). Setting up the UNIX server for your Web site entails working with Telnet (or some similar terminal emulation software) to communicate with the UNIX operating system and work with the FTP server to send folders and documents to the correct directories. Assuming you're installing your Web site on an ISP's UNIX-based system, can use Fetch (http://www.dartmouth.edu/pages/softdev/fetch.html) or a similar FTP utility to manage the task.

You must speak to the Internet Service Provider (or the system administrator of your organization) to set up an account with a user ID and password prior to uploading. You should find out how to gain an account and what the rules for working with your server are before you start.

> Note that many ISPs do not allow you to upload files but rather make you use their proprietary HTML editors to build home pages. Find out if you can upload home pages prior to beginning the uploading process. You might find you can bypass the Telnet session because your provider has preselected a remote directory for your use.

When you've completed uploading your page files, you can check to see whether your site is really live by opening your browser and selecting the URL for your new site. The URL should be formatted as follows:

```
http://your ISP's site name/~your shell account log-in name/
```

If you don't purchase a name for your site, you must use your ISP's server as your home base. This home base computer is known as a *domain*. A domain name lets other servers and browsers know where your site is located. You can register your own domain name—remember those virtual servers on many Web servers? Ask your system administrator or ISP for instructions and fees for registration. The domain names must be registered with InterNIC (`http://www.internic.net`), because all domain names must be unique. InterNIC researches the availability of names and sells them on a first-come, first-served basis. Be sure to think of several domain names, because someone may have already registered your first choice.

Summary

This hour has provided a quick-and-dirty overview of Web publishing. To get the best results publishing on the Web, you need to purchase a Web publishing program and get space on a server. Then you can let the Mac OS 8.5 Internet access software (Fetch 3.0 and Netscape Communicator/Navigator or Microsoft Internet Explorer) support your endeavors.

Term Review

absolute pathname   A detailed and explicit way of locating a file or device on a network by starting with the name of the computer on which the object or file resides and then listing any intermediate folders or directories, thus ending with the name of the file or object. For example, `<http://upubs-71.uchicago.edu/wwwbook/appendixes/glossary.html>`.

animated GIF   A method of providing moving images on a Web page. Animated GIFs are based on the GIF89 file format, which enables you to include multiple pictures in a single file. You can place animated GIF files (designated by the .GIF extension) in your PageMill document by using the Place Object command.

applet   A program written in an independent language (for example, Java) that executes within an HTML document displayed by a Web browser without requiring the application or language that created it.

attribute   A qualifying property of an HTML tag.

browser   A program designed to read HTML files and retrieve and display information on the Web. Also called a *client*. Graphical browsers have the capacity to display images, colors, and other graphic elements. Nongraphical browsers display textual information but not graphics. (See *Netscape Navigator*.)

browser   The application used to interpret HTML, as well as download and display Web pages on your computer screen. Includes Netscape and Microsoft Explorer.

CGI   Common Gateway Interface. A standard interface between a Web server and an external (or *gateway*) program such as a Web browser. A program that handles a request for information and returns information or performs a search or other routine. CGI can be written in a number of programs.

cgi-bin   The secure directory containing all bundled CGI programs on UNIX Web servers.

cyberspace   A term originally used in the novel *Neuromancer* by William Gibson to describe a computer network of the future that can be connected directly to peoples' minds. *Cyberspace* now represents the Internet or the Web.

domain name   A textual alias for an IP address based on the domain name system. Components of a domain name are separated by periods. For example, an IP address for a computer might be `197.99.87.99`; it might then have several aliases, such as `www.mycomputer.com`.

GIF   Graphics Interchange Format. A file format commonly used with graphics or photos displayed on Web documents. It's the most supported and popular graphics format on the Web. Originally popularized by CompuServe.

GIF animation   Combining several GIFs into one image through scripting. When viewed through a Web browser, the image flips through the various frames, thus creating animation.

GIF89a   An extension of the GIF standards that enables transparency of selected colors.

home page   The welcome page of a Web site; the place where visitors are supposed to start when finding out about a particular site.

hypertext link   Also called an *anchor*. A hypertext link in an HTML document is usually distinguished by underlined or highlighted text that, when selected, takes the user to another file or Web page. The hypertext link is added to the document by using the HTML tag <A HREF> </A>.

Hypertext Markup Language (HTML)   The markup language that instructs browsers how to lay out your document on a computer screen.

imagemap   The CGI program provided by HTTPd-based servers that processes active image hotspots during server-side imaging. Also, the name of the file that contains the mouse click coordinates and associated URLs for an active image. Imagemap files usually use the .MAP extension. *Imagemap* is also an older term for an active image, which is going out of use with the advent of client-side imaging.

Interlaced graphics are best used for large static images that take a long time to load. This way, the user can see the image building while waiting for the entire image file to download. It's better that just staring a blank spot.

interlacing   A process that loads a GIF file in sections when viewed through a browser. Because different lines of an image are loaded rather than from the first line to the last, the image becomes recognizable more quickly. The browser displays a low-resolution version first, then a better version, and finally the full-blown version.

Internet   An international network of networks, originally started for military purposes, that connects about 40 million higher education, government, military, and commercial users.

Internet Explorer   Microsoft's fast, easy-to-use Web browser. Internet Explorer runs on Windows and Macintosh systems and is a direct competitor to Netscape Navigator.

Java   A computer language developed by Sun Microsystems that enables the creation of "applets" or "live objects," which execute in response to mouse clicks and produce sound, video, or other effects within Netscape 2.0 or other Web browsers.

JPEG   Joint Photographic Experts Group. A graphic image compression format.

Netscape Navigator   A fast, easy-to-use graphical information browser for the World Wide Web that was developed by some of the same people who created Mosaic. Created by Netscape Communications Corporation.

newbie   A newcomer. Someone just getting started on the Internet.

Photoshop   Common parlance for Adobe Photoshop. Image editing software that allows a number of sophisticated graphics functions, such as retouching and editing of images, on personal computers.

style sheet   A text file that defines the stylistic elements of a series of HTML files. Style sheets are not supported by PageMill, except as objects that can be placed in HTML placeholders. Style sheet files, designated by the .STY extension, are a part of HTML version 3.2 and provide the benefit of allowing organizations to impose a "house style" on Web pages that can be changed on all pages by editing a single .STY file.

tag   An HTML notation that identifies formatting for text.

transparent GIF   A GIF image that appears to float directly atop a Web page without its own background or border. A specific number in the GIF color palette (#89) is assigned to be the same color as the background of the page, giving the image a transparent appearance.

URL   Uniform Resource Locator. A standard address for a file or location on the Internet. URLs always begin with an Internet protocol (FTP, Gopher, HTTP), followed by an Internet host name, folders, and the destination file or object.

Web publisher   A person who creates Web pages.

Web site   A collection of Web pages residing on a Web server. Web sites are usually synonymous with a URL. One server can host several Web sites by providing URLs that define a path to the Web site. Some types of computers can support multiple unique URLs on a single server.

Webmaster   Someone who both creates Web pages and manages a Web server.

Q&A

Q Why did you include this hour's information in a Mac OS 8.5 book?

A Sixty-seven percent of all Web sites are designed on Macs. The Mac OS provides a nearly perfect platform to design multimedia for the Web, providing accurate color representation, excellent graphics performance, and font-handling capabilities. You'll soon want to write HTML from your Mac, so this hour is provided to begin to teach you how.

Q What are those HTML editors that I've been reading about?

A HTML editors, such as GoLive Cyberstudio, NetObject's Fusion, Adobe PageMill, Claris HomePage, and Macromedia DreamWeaver, provide you with an environment that generates the HTML code from items that you lay out using various desktop publishing metaphors. With these applications, you almost don't have to know HTML to publish documents on the Web.

Q Where can I find out more about Web publishing?

A Several fabulous books are available that teach about the aesthetics and physical techniques of Web site design:

- David Siegel, *Creating Killer Web Sites* (Hayden Books, 1996, 1998)
- Lynda Weinman, *<designing web graphics>* (New Riders, 1996, 1998)
- Mary Jo Fahey, *Web Publisher's Design Guide for Macintosh* (Coriolis Group Books, 1995)
- Darcy DiNucci, Maria Giudice, and Lynne Stiles, *Elements of Web Design* (PeachPit Press, 1997).

Q What's the future of Web publishing look like?

A Professional Web site designers want more control over what their pages look like. To centralize control, propositions have been presented to the World Wide Web Consortium to create a new form of HTML called *Extended Markup Language (XML)*, which would let designers define tag definitions directly in each set of HTML. Another trend directly on the horizon is the inclusion of Cascading Style Sheets in HTML, again to provide more control over how pages appear on all browsers. HTML 4.0 is almost approved. It will bring more support for Java applets and dynamic HTML (another way to automate the production of tags so that designers retain control of a page's appearance).

Workshop

The Workshop contains quiz questions to help you solidify your understanding of the material covered. You can find the answers to the quiz questions in Appendix B, "Quiz Answers."

Quiz

1. What are the two parts to designing a Web site?
2. What's the goal of a Web site?
3. What three questions must you answer to determine a Web site's content?
4. How are site navigation techniques related to the intended purpose of a site?
5. What is a search engine?
6. Your prototype should give you information on the following issues:
7. What graphics and publishing tools are available to create the components you want to use on your Web page?
8. What are the two file formats for graphics accepted by the Internet? How do they differ?
9. What's the standard name given to a home page when saving it to the server?
10. What's HTML and how does it work?

HOUR 16

File Sharing

The goal of this hour is to cover File Sharing in all its glory. Here are the topics covered:

- What is File Sharing?
- Setting up File Sharing
- Understanding the concept of permissions
- Setting up Print Sharing
- Connectivity options

What Is File Sharing?

As early as 1984, Macintosh computers enabled their users to communicate with other Macs and Apple printers to share data and programs without having to pass through an intermediary centralized file server. This ability is sometimes called *point-to-point* or *peer-to-peer networking*.

Apple Macs provide a perfect environment for this type of networking, because networking protocols, software, and hardware (such as AppleTalk

Filing Protocol, AppleShare software, and LocalTalk hardware) are built into every Mac's design. The AppleTalk protocols underlying this structure enable transparent communications between computers without the installation of additional devices or software. This is called *distributed file sharing*.

Distributed file sharing has benefits and drawbacks that should be accounted for when determining network needs. The advantages of a distributed system are as follows:

- A distributed network is inexpensive to install on Macintoshes. Because Mac OS 8.5 comes complete with File Sharing, you have no additional expense for software. The only expense for small networks is the cable and connectors. Farallon's PhoneNET system uses shielded twisted-pair cabling or telephone wire to complete the LocalTalk network.

- A distributed network is flexible, because network users can make part or all of their hard disks accessible to other participants on the network. Each owner determines which files to make available, based on the requirements of the workgroup. These files can be changed at any time, based on need, by simply selecting a different folder in the Sharing command dialog box and then selecting the Mac using the Chooser.

- A Macintosh distributed network is easy to learn and use, because it's based on the pervasive Macintosh interface. Mac OS 8.5's File Sharing system can be learned in a couple of hours.

On the other hand, the nature of distributed systems can be described as "controlled anarchy." Any user can become a file server at any time, any other user can access any Mac on the network. Also, messaging between Macs is nonexistent. Therefore, one Mac can crash or simply shutdown, disabling the rest of the users accessing its data. There are no rules in distributed networking.

The bottom line is that distributed networks are excellent options for small workgroups in a single area—workers who can talk to each other while they're sharing data between their Macs. When users become more spread out, centralized servers become a requirement to maintain order and security.

What's Under the Networking Hood in Mac OS 8.5?

The Mac's file sharing capabilities build upon this built-in foundation. Right out of the box, Macs provide five print and file services for peer-to-peer network support (Figure 16.1 displays the system extensions supporting these services):

- **Chooser.** The Chooser is an application used to select network services that support AppleTalk Filing Protocol (AFP).

- **LaserWriter Chooser extension.** This extension allows users to connect to most AppleTalk-compliant laser printers via the Chooser.

- **Shared printing extensions.** LaserWriter 8.4 created an innovative way to print using a desktop printer with expanded print spooling capabilities. To support this innovation, you'll find four extensions where once you had one: the PrintMonitor, Desktop PrintMonitor, Desktop PrintSpooling, and PrintShare extensions provide spooling support for multiple print jobs along with drag-and-drop printing from the desktop.

- **AppleShare Chooser extension.** This extension provides the capability to connect to any AFP-compatible server volume through the Chooser.

- **File Sharing.** This extension provides the capability to turn parts of your hard disk into sharable volumes available to other users on the network.

FIGURE 16.1.

The Mac provides a strong platform for distributed networking via its array of networking system extensions.

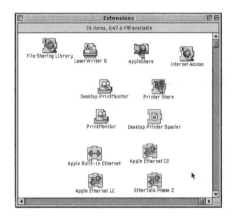

All Macs provide access to network services via the Chooser utility, located under the Apple menu. All AFP-compliant networks support the use of the Chooser, thus providing a consistent network interface that can be easily learned by Mac users new to networks.

Because of AppleShare, all such shared volumes appear as new hard disk icons on your desktop that can be accessed in the same manner as accessing a local hard disk (for instance, double-clicking to open the disk where a window would appear containing folders and files). File Sharing is a special augmentation of the networking support provided by older Mac operating systems. With the File Sharing extension, your Mac provides limited distributed file sharing for networked Macs.

As stated earlier, File Sharing is a distributed network, meaning that each Macintosh controls its connection to the network. You can use the File Sharing software in Mac OS 8.5's multitasking environment as if it and its files were another application and its documents were located on your Mac (although they may actually be located elsewhere on the network).

The software is relatively small, taking up only 200K of storage space. This economy of scale allows you to share a file on another Macintosh while someone is using your local shared file. Up to ten users can be given permission to share a file, although only one person may access any one file at any one time.

With application programs that allow more than one person to simultaneously share documents, File Sharing enables multiple accesses to the same document at the same time. The File Sharing software also works as a file server, replacing AppleShare, so that your Macintosh can control a centralized network. File Sharing is also compatible with AppleShare so that it can run on larger and faster networks.

File Sharing provides a complete suite of networking tools, although internal support is somewhat limited for features commonly associated with larger networks, such as accounting, electronic mail, and data integrity.

PERFORMANCE ISSUES WITH FILE SHARING

You can minimize the tendency of shared Macs to have degraded performance by following a few tips:

- Assign an alias to a shared volume that you've accessed from another Mac. Then, the next time you want to use it, simply double-click the alias to bring its volume onto your system.
- Limit the number of folders you allow to be shared by placing all the files you're sharing into a single folder; then designate that folder as the shared item. Note that if you have different access privileges for each file, this strategy doesn't work, because a folder's entire contents are assigned a single access privilege.
- Limit the number of people who access your Mac. Make it a rule that work is performed on the local Mac, not on remote nodes.
- Share as few files as possible. This is a good security procedure, because the fewer files available, the less possible damage can be performed.
- Limit the security levels. Keep it simple so that managing and untangling a confusion of passwords and access permissions doesn't take up all of your time.
- Use the same registered names on all Macs on the network to avoid confusion.
- Avoid launching an application on a volume you're sharing. The performance of both Macs will become too slow to do anything else on these computers. For best performance, you should copy a file to your local disk, edit it, and then copy it back to the other file-shared disk.

Setting Up File Sharing

Setting up your Mac to share files is a multistep process. Once you've set up your permissions, users, and groups, actually turning on File Sharing is very easy.

The first step in setting up File Sharing is creating the network. You do this by identifying your network's users and then associating these users with groups. *Groups* are those users who are permitted to share folders and files with each other. Set up the network using the Users & Groups control panel. (See Figure 16.2.)

16

FIGURE 16.2.

The Users & Groups control panel is the first stop in creating your distributed network.

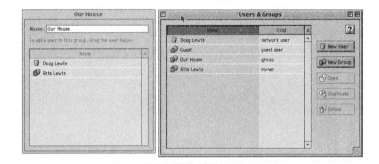

You'll notice that you already exist. Double-click the User icon with your name to see your password and computer's name (see Figure 16.3). The Mac OS Setup Assistant has placed this information here. If the information is missing, you can type it in.

FIGURE 16.3.

Use this dialog box to identify yourself to the network.

Use the pop-up menu to shift to the Sharing screen (see Figure 16.4). Use this screen to assign permissions as to who can share your computer.

FIGURE 16.4.

Use the Sharing screens of the dialog box to identify which parts of your computer you're willing to share.

The second step of the process is to identify your Mac to the network. You do this through the File Sharing control panel (see Figure 16.5). One of the tasks undertaken by the Mac OS Setup Assistant is setting up File Sharing for you. When you open the File Sharing control panel, your name, your computer's name, and your password should already be entered. If a glitch occurs and these items are missing, go ahead and type them in.

FIGURE 16.5.

The File Sharing control panel turns File Sharing on and off.

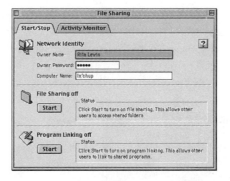

Click Start to turn on File Sharing. You can also select the AppleScript "Start File Sharing" under Automated Tasks.

AppleTalk needs to be "on" before you can turn File Sharing on. You can also use the Control Strip module to turn File Sharing on and off. The following fields need to be filled in.

- **Owner's Name.** If your first name is unique on your network, you only have to enter your first name. If someone else has the same name, enter your last name as well.

- **Owner Password.** The password is a number and letter combination up to eight characters in length. It should be easy for you to remember, but unique enough that it cannot be guessed by others.
- **Macintosh Name.** The name entered in this box is how other users find your Macintosh on the network. The name you give your Macintosh should be descriptive enough so that people associate it with the files they use on your system.
- **File Sharing.** You cannot turn on File Sharing if you haven't completed the boxes listing your name, password, and Macintosh.

16

After turning on File Sharing from the File Sharing control panel, you can select the folders and/or hard disks you want shared on the network. Only you can designate how your files will be accessed and by whom. The Sharing command on the Desktop File menu is the tool used to designate access privileges for your files and folders.

The Sharing command activates a window with the same name as the file you want to share (see Figure 16.6). The top of the window describes the location of the sharable folder. Place files you want to share with other users into a folder. Only folders and disks can be shared across a network. In this way, files you do not want to share can be kept separate from sharable files.

FIGURE 16.6.

Select a file or folder and choose Sharing from the File menu to permit sharing.

If you haven't turned Sharing on by using the File Sharing control panel, the Sharing command will appear dimmed in the menu. It will also appear dimmed if you have not preselected a folder before highlighting the command.

Creating an alias of the documents you want to share protects the original file from being accidentally destroyed by someone using your disk. The person using your disk can make changes to the alias that are reflected by the original, but he or she can only remove the alias.

Place your shared folder at the root or highest level of your folder hierarchy—the desktop. A disk cannot be shared if it contains an already-shared folder. By making the disk or root folder the sharing level of your shared files, you avoid having the system give you a message that the folder you want to access to is not accessible because there's a shared folder inside it.

Sharing a Volume

File Sharing is transparent once you've set up the network. Access to the network is performed via the Chooser utility program. Volumes selected in the Chooser are displayed on your Mac as hard disks and can be opened and used in the same way that you use your own local disks. After opening the Chooser from the Apple menu, clicking items in its dialog box provides you with access to networked volumes, folders, and files. (See Figure 16.7.)

FIGURE 16.7.

The Chooser is a multipurpose utility for selecting network and printer drivers, as well as zones and nodes.

To access these items, use the following steps:

1. Select the AppleShare driver icon from the "printer driver" box and highlight the file server you want to access from the list of file servers. If necessary, select the network node where the file resides. When you're done, click the OK button.

2. The system brings up a dialog box requesting your AppleShare user status (see Figure 16.8). Click the radio button for Registered User if you've been given a password and registered name by the owner of the Macintosh you want to access.

FIGURE 16.8.

File Sharing has built-in security that requests your user ID and password before it lets you access another person's folders.

Click the radio button for Guest if you're not a registered user and the owner has given guest privileges (if there are no guest privileges for the file, the button will be dimmed). If you're a registered user, enter your registered username and password in the spaces provided. When you're done, click the OK button.

3. The system displays a list of sharable files you can access (see Figure 16.9). Any files that are not currently available or are already accessed by you appear dimmed. Select the file or files you want to access and click the OK button.

FIGURE 16.9.

Folders you've been given permission to share are listed in the dialog box. Select a folder to mount it on your Mac.

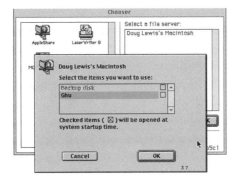

4. An icon depicting the shared folder, called a *volume*, appears on your Macintosh on the right side of the screen and acts like a hard disk. (See Figure 16.10.)

AppleTalk must be active for you to link to another Macintosh on the network. Click the radio button labeled Active if it's not already on.

Before you can access another person's shared items as a registered user, you must know your registered name and password on the other person's system. If the network is large, you may also have to know the zone where the other Macintosh is located.

FIGURE 16.10.

The shared volume is displayed on your desktop. Its networked icon indicates it's a shared disk.

Opening a Shared Volume at Startup

Mac OS 8.5's Startup folder allows you to go directly to remote files that you regularly access, letting the system run through the File Sharing access routines to automatically bring up the specified files onto your desktop.

The Chooser's dialog box along with the related File Sharing dialog boxes load the selected volumes into the Startup folder, enabling you to automatically open networked volumes whenever you turn on your Mac. Follow these steps:

1. After you select a volume in the Chooser, the system displays a list of sharable files you can access. Any files not currently available or already accessed by you appear dimmed. Select the file or files you want to access and click OK. Check the boxes next to the files to pick the files you want to access at startup.

2. The system adds two more lines to the dialog box. Click the appropriate box to select the way you want to access the files at startup: completely automatic, where the system enters your name and password, or partially automatic, where the system supplies your name and you supply your password when the system requests it.

3. An icon depicting the shared file appears on your Macintosh on the right side of the screen and acts like a hard disk. When you next start up your Macintosh, the files you selected for startup documents will appear automatically or semiautomatically, depending on your choice.

4. Should the Mac that contains the file you want to share be down when you start up your Mac, you'll get a message saying that the volume you want is not available.

> You must be a registered user of the files to automatically access them upon startup.

Ending a File Sharing Session

Mac OS 8.5 treats shared volumes in the same manner as local volumes, providing a simple method to end a File Sharing session by ejecting the shared files from your Macintosh. To end a File Sharing session, simply throw the shared file or volume into your Trash Can.

> Dragging the shared folder or disk into the Trash Can also ejects it from your system. You can also shut down your Macintosh and the share items will be flushed from your system. Note that if you did not turn off File Sharing before shutting down, the Macintosh will automatically bring you back to the files you were using when you next turn on your machine.
>
> When you throw away a shared file, the owner Macintosh receives a folder on its desktop labeled Network Trash Folder. As long as the Trash Can isn't emptied, the item can be restored by dragging it out of the Trash folder and renaming it.
>
> Each user on the network who trashes one your files sends you a Trash folder with a consecutive number. You can also prevent the trashing of shared folders by changing the access privileges for your shared files.

Understanding Network Permissions

Networking on a Macintosh works in exactly the opposite fashion from most other networking software. File Sharing and AppleShare enable you as the owner of your Macintosh to designate what files can be used by other users on the network. Until you allow people to see your files, they are not permitted to access them. Once you've allocated files to the File Sharing system, they are open to every user on the network until you set up who has permission to use them.

You must restrict access to control shared file use. Mac OS 8.5 is designed to enable you to easily set up permissions to restrict the access to your files. The system is based on several concepts: the owner of the files, a registered user of the files, and a guest user of the files. In addition, registered users can be arranged into groups of users with specified privileges granted to members of that group.

The Owner

The owner of a Macintosh is represented by a special bold-outlined icon in the Users & Groups control panel. It's created automatically when you identify yourself and your Macintosh in the File Sharing control panel. The owner's name on the owner icon is the same as that entered in the Owner's Name box in the File Sharing control panel. As the owner of your Macintosh, you have special rights and privileges:

- You have the right to access your Macintosh remotely over the network.
- You have the right to work with all your files, whether they have been designated as sharable or not.
- You can remotely change your password.

Three other types of privileges are associated with ownership of a volume:

- **Allow user to connect.** This allows the owner to connect to a Macintosh from a remote Macintosh.
- **Allow user to change password.** This allows the owner to change a password from a remote Macintosh.
- **Allow User to see entire volume.** This allows the owner to use all files on the system, even if they're not designated as shared files.

Guests

A *guest* is any other Macintosh user connected to the network but not registered as a user. Without any access restrictions, any guest can use any designated sharable file on your Macintosh. Use the icon labeled Guest to change the permitted behavior of guests. You can also disallow all guest access, permitting only registered users to access your files.

Registered Users

A *registered user* is authorized to use shared files on a Macintosh. Each registered user is given a registered name and password that must be used to gain access to the shared files. Typically, these names are derived from the registered users' own File Sharing dialog boxes so that consistency is maintained across the network. If you use a different name, notify the person so that he or she can record the proper name to use. Each time registered users log on to your Macintosh, they must type their registered names.

You can also set up an additional security level by assigning passwords to each of your registered users that must be used to gain access to your shared files. Again, tell the users the assigned passwords so that they can record them. Registered users are granted privileges with shared files, as follows:

- You can allow or disallow them to connect to your Macintosh.
- You can allow them to change their passwords.

Each type of user can be granted various types of permissions: for example, See Folders, See Files, and Make Changes. These permissions are discussed in more detail in the section, "Access Privileges."

Groups of Users

Mac OS 8.5 enables you to set up groups of users who can share common items needed to perform their work. Such groups can be organized around projects, departments, organizations, or work-groups. A group is considered by the system to be a special type of registered user and has the same privileges for individuals in the group as are granted to individual registered users.

An alternative way to add members to a group is to open the group icon by double-clicking it and then dragging the members' icons into the group window.

Hold down the Shift key while selecting users (or create a marquee with the cursor around the users you want to transfer) to select more than one user at a time.

Also, always check with the people you're assigning as registered users to get the accurate names they've assigned themselves as owners. Use these names as your registered names for them to avoid confusion on the network. You can use single names if they're unique on the network.

Keep in mind that although a registered user may have been transferred into a group, his or her registered user icon will remain in the window, because a single user may have access privileges beyond those granted to the group. A user can also be a member of multiple groups.

Finally, note that you don't need to include your owner's icon in any group on your Macintosh.

Access Privileges

Each user of your shared files can perform the following three actions:

- **See Folders.** If you grant the privilege of seeing folders, it allows users to show or hide folders enclosed in a shared folder or disk. Without this privilege, users cannot open folders within the shared folder.

- **See Files.** If you grant the privilege of seeing files, it allows users to show or hide files enclosed within folders within the shared folder or disk. Without this privilege, users cannot open or copy to their disk files within shared folders.

- **Make Changes.** If you grant the privilege of making changes, it allows users to make changes to any shared item, including copying, deleting, and saving the item.

Table 16.1 presents some combinations of these privileges and their resulting permissions.

TABLE 16.1. PRIVILEGES AND THEIR RESULTING PERMISSIONS.

See Folders	See Files	Make Changes	Resulting Permission
Yes	Yes	No	Allows users to open files and folders and copy files to their own disks, but they cannot add new files to the shared folder or change an existing item.
No	Yes	Yes	Allows users to open and see files within the shared folder or disk and make changes or add new files. Any folders inside the shared item are invisible. (Good for keeping private folders within a shared folder.)
Yes	No	Yes	Allows users to see and open folders but not files within them. They can save new items to the shared folder but cannot change files within the folder.
No	Yes	No	Allows users to only view or copy files within a shared folder without making changes to the shared item.
No	No	Yes	Allows users to save items to the shared folder without being able to view files or folders within the shared folder. (This is the "drop box" option.)

The access privileges are set at the shared folder or disk level. Each folder is granted different privileges for the owner and/or users and groups. The following list displays the privilege icon for each level of access:

- **Plain folder.** A plain folder means that you can open the folder. It does not tell you anything about other privileges you may have.
- **Tabbed folder.** A folder with a darkened tab indicates that you have File Sharing turned on and that the folder is available for sharing.
- **Belted folder.** A folder with a belt around it is off-limits to you. You cannot open it and do not have any privileges for it. It will appear gray in the list of sharable files.
- **Belted folder with an arrow.** A folder with an arrow above its belt means that you cannot open the folder but you can save items into it. This also called a "drop box." This is created by checking the Make Changes privilege.

Shared Folders versus Shared Volumes

Mac OS 8.5 adds an additional layer to your security on the network. If you set up a shared folder during the Mac OS 8.5 setup session, your fellow users will not be able to read or write to any file or folder (or even see them) except for items you place in your shared folder.

You can click the shared folder and set up sharing criteria, which makes access to this folder and its contents even more stringent (for example, read only or drop box). When the Shared Folder feature is enabled, only the shared folder is accessible from the Chooser.

So, what do you do with your shared folder? Make aliases of those folders you want to share and place the aliases in the shared folder. Then, users can access those aliases to gain access to specific folders on your hard drive. For example, if you're working on a proposal, you can place an alias of the proposal folder in your shared folder and make it read only. Make a drop box for submissions to the proposal. Then, only you can open the drop box alias, but everyone can read the proposal to give their reviews.

If someone tries to access another part of your computer, he or she receives the alert shown in Figure 16.11.

To turn off the Shared Folder, make sure File Sharing is turned off and simply throw the Shared folder in the trash.

Any software, artwork, or sounds that you want to place on the network must be licensed with the right to share them over a network. Do not place any unlicensed items on the network.

FIGURE 16.11.

Mac OS 8.5 will not let users open any other volume on a computer that has a shared folder.

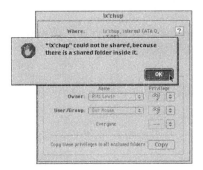

Using Networked Programs from Your Mac

If your organization has applications such as databases, spreadsheets, or desktop publishing programs that are licensed for group use, File Sharing enables you to access this software from your Mac using the Program Linking tool. The File Sharing control panel provides a Program Linking button that turns on this function, allowing you to select networked programs from the Chooser.

MORE ON PROGRAM SHARING

Apple has taken the capability to perform live cutting and pasting (publishing and subscribing) and has expanded it to allow programs to work together as a unified whole. Apple calls this capability *interapplication communications (IAC)*. Mac OS 8.5 has incorporated IAC into its design through the capability to pass messages between programs. The language used to pass these messages is called *AppleEvents*.

The Finder uses AppleEvents to open, print, and close programs and documents. In addition to these four messages, Apple has provided a list of another 24 messages that programs need to understand in order to participate in data sharing. Most Macintosh programs already incorporate these messages, such as close, save, undo, cut, copy, paste, and clear.

In addition, related programs (such as different word processors) can already understand text manipulation messages, and different drawing programs can understand graphic manipulation messages. AppleEvents enables the Publish and Subscribe features of Mac OS 8.5 to work, as well as enables you to use other dynamic communications features across applications and networks.

You select the application programs that you'll allow to be shared on the network using the Sharing command, located under the File menu. When the Sharing dialog box appears, click the Allow Remote Program Linking box to turn on linking.

> You don't have to use the Sharing command to link to other programs on your own Macintosh; you do so only if you want to link with a remote program.
>
> If you haven't turned Sharing on by using the File Sharing control panel, the Sharing command will appear dimmed in the menu. It will also appear dimmed if you have not preselected a program before highlighting the command or if the program does not support program linking.
>
> The Sharing command activates a window with the same name as the program you want to share. The top of the window describes the location of the sharable folder.

16

Connectivity Options

Connecting computers together on a network requires transmission rules, called *protocols* (such as AppleTalk), a transmission medium (such as cabling and connectors), and software (such as drivers).

AppleTalk provides the rules by which Macintoshes talk to other computers in the form of network protocols. As a protocol, AppleTalk supports a whole suite of connectivity options, based on the network driver you select. The most common drivers are LocalTalk, EtherTalk, and TokenTalk, although newer drivers are being developed to support fiber optics and infrared network methodologies. The following section describes the cabling designs and drivers used to interconnect Macintoshes in networks.

Cabling Mediums

The original connectivity medium for AppleTalk was also called *AppleTalk*—a cause of much confusion. In approximately 1986, Apple renamed the AppleTalk transmission mechanism *LocalTalk* to clear up this confusion. LocalTalk and the original AppleTalk both consist of the same shielded or unshielded (telephone wire) twisted-pair cabling and connectors.

Third-party vendors manufacture alternatives, such as Farallon's PhoneNET, but all such cabling options transmit data at 230,400 bits per second (baud) and are limited to relatively short distances. (Token Ring networks also use shielded twisted-pair cable but transmit data at different rates using a different methodology.)

The AppleTalk protocol also supports coaxial cabling media, such as the half-inch thick coaxial cable (called *thicknet*) used as the backbone along with transceiver cables in large, long-distance Ethernet networks or the three-sixteenths-inch coaxial cable (called *thinnet*) used in shorter Ethernet networks.

Cabling Topologies

Topology refers to the physical arrangement of devices and cabling on a network. The design of the network also includes the rules used by devices to access the network and communicate with other nodes on the system. The network media and type depends on the topology selected. A topology can take three basic forms: bus, star, and ring.

If thicknet is selected for the cabling media of your Ethernet, you must use a bus architecture, because the thicknet is not flexible enough to be strung from device to device without intervening smaller transceiver cables.

Ethernet, using twisted-pair cabling, can be arranged in the smaller star architecture, whereas Token Ring networks typically use ring topologies to take the best advantage of the token-passing rules associated with that networking system. Internetworks, or *interconnected networks*, provide the means of using the best topology for each group of devices that want to communicate, because each internetwork can consist of many different physical shapes.

Bus Designs

The *bus* is the cable through which signals travel between computer nodes. AppleTalk supports both daisy-chain and backbone bus topologies.

The Daisy-Chain Topology

The simplest network topology is the daisy-chain cabling system. This network consists of pieces of cable that are strung between computers and linked via special connectors so as to form a chain (see Figure 16.12). The first and last computer on the chain are terminated with special terminating resistors. The length of all the cable used among the network computers also has a limit. As an exaggerated example, you can't simply drag a super long cable from a computer on the first floor to a second computer on the fiftieth floor (to network them together) and expect the network to work as efficiently as two computers networked with 10 feet of cable between them. LocalTalk networks have a limit of 32 devices on a daisy-chain. Additional devices will degrade network performance and efficiency.

Daisy-chain networks are inexpensive, because the only cost is the cabling and connectors. As mentioned earlier, twisted-pair cables, such as telephone wire, make excellent daisy-chain vehicles. Farallon manufactures connectors, called PhoneNET, that are cheaper than those sold by Apple but just as durable and efficient. Daisy-chain networks are the lowest common denominator of Apple network topologies and can be mixed with other topologies to create effective internetworks. Most small LocalTalk networks (such as a group of Macs sharing a printer) use daisy-chains.

FIGURE **16.12.**

The daisy-chain topology is used for small LocalTalk networks.

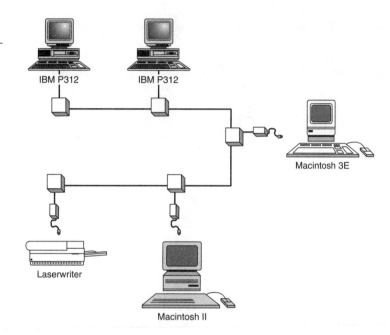

16

Because this topology consists of pieces of cable strung from machine to machine, the loosening of one cable connection on the chain brings the total system down. This fragility can be combated by limiting the number of computers on a single chain. In addition, because each connector requires two interfaces to function, daisy-chain networks must be short. The addition of too many cables weakens the signal.

The Backbone Bus Topology

The most common type of network topology is the backbone bus. This cabling scheme uses a cable laid linearly along a path with terminating resistors at both ends. Computers are connected to the bus via drop cables, which, in turn, are connected to the backbone using taps or transceivers. (See Figure 16.13.)

LocalTalk networks that use shielded twisted-pair cables are typically implemented as bus topologies. In addition, Ethernet thicknet and thinnet cabling schemes also typically use buses. TokenTalk is unique in its use of a ring topology.

The bus is the cabling medium used to transmit signals. Bus networks use another system to manage these data transmissions. On buses, each computer contends with each other to gain access to the cabling medium. This is called *distributed system control.*

FIGURE 16.13.

The bus topology is used for medium to large networks.

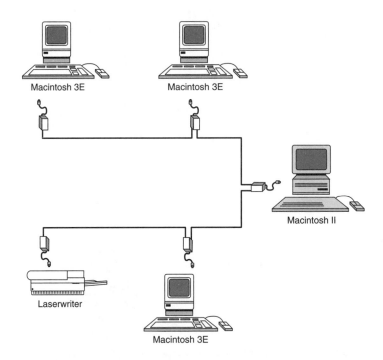

The most typical distributed system for AppleTalk networks is called *carrier sensing*. In this methodology, each device listens to the network before transmitting, and if it senses a signal on the medium (meaning that another node is transmitting), it backs off and tries to send its message later.

In this system, data transmissions are broadcast to all devices connected to the cabling medium. Devices receive transmissions by recognizing their own addresses. On LocalTalk networks, collisions of data signals are avoided by the addition of another protocol, *collision avoidance*. This protocol says that each node must wait until the network has been idle for a specified minimum amount of time, plus an additional random interval, before attempting to transmit. If transmissions collide despite this protocol, the data is sent again. Ethernet networks use another protocol, called *collision detection*, that specifies how to sense a data accident and retransmit the signal.

Backbone bus networks are more fault tolerant than their daisy-chain cousins because there are fewer cables to weaken the signals, as well as fewer cables that may become loose, causing a breakdown of the network. In addition, backbones are more flexible, because taps can be placed anywhere on the bus. You can even place unused cables for future expansion without causing a degradation of the performance of the network.

Backbones support more devices for longer distances because there's only one cable involved in transmitting the signal along the total length of the network. In addition, backbone buses can grow through the addition of repeaters to boost the signal.

Star Topologies

The star topology is based on a design whereby each computer is connected to a hub (such as a telephone punch-down block or wiring box or an intelligent controller) via its own cable and connector. Most LocalTalk networks that use unshielded twisted-pair cables (telephone wiring) are laid out as stars to take advantage of existing telephone wiring.

Ethernet networks that are based on unshielded twisted-pair cables also use stars. Stars can be mixed with buses by dropping the backbone from the hub. Such a cabling design is called a *branch*.

Cabling in a Nutshell

Table 16.2, assembled from information provided by Apple Computer, compares the three network architecture's in terms of cabling, performance, and ease of use.

TABLE 16.2. A COMPARISON OF NETWORK TYPES.

Network Architecture	Medium	Trans- mission Rate	Top- ology	Max. No. of Devices	Max. Length	Ease of Instal- lation
LocalTalk	Shielded TP	230.4 Kbps	Bus	32	1,000'	Easy
	Unshielded TP (phone wire)	230.4 Kbps	Bus Passive star Active star	20 to 40 varies 254	2,000' 4,000' 3,000'/branch	Easy Requires installer Requires installer
	Infrared light	230.4Kbps	N/A	128/ trans- ceiver	Transceivers must be within 70' diameter	Easy
Ethernet	Thicknet	10Mbps	Bus	100/seg. 1,024/ network	8,250;	Requires installer
	Thinnet	10Mbps	Bus	40/seg 1,024/ network	3,300'	Easy with Apple Ethernet product
	TP	10Mbps	Star	1,024	330' from hub to device	Requires installer
	Fiber-optic	10Mbps	Bus	1,024	14,256'	Requires installer

continues

TABLE 16.2. CONTINUED

Network Architecture	Medium	Trans- mission Rate	Top- ology	Max. No. of Devices	Max. Length	Ease of Instal- lation
Token Ring	Shielded TP	4/16Mbps	Star-wired ring	260/ring	990' from MAU to device	Usually requires installer
	Unshielded TP	4/16Mbps	Star-wired ring	72/ring	330' from MAU to device	Usually requires installer

Summary

The Mac supports workgroup computing through its system-deep networking capabilities. Mac OS 8.5 File Sharing gives workgroup members the ability to share files, folders, and programs, using them as if they were working with their own files and folders. AppleTalk is a relatively slow networking scheme that has been augmented in Mac OS 8.5 with TCP/IP.

Term Review

access privileges   The settings used to set up what a permitted user can do to files on your Mac: See Folders, See Files, or Make Changes.

AppleShare   The client and server software used to manage an AppleTalk network.

AppleTalk   The network protocol used by Macs.

client/server networking   A networking scheme in which a Mac or other computer acts as the centralized location where all information and programs are stored and managed. This computer is called a *server* because it serves data to its network. Other computers on the network are called *clients* and can receive information from the server and pass information to the server for processing.

EtherTalk   The driver used to operate a Mac on an Ethernet network.

File Sharing   The name the Mac gives to its peer-to-peer network. This is a decentralized network that the provides the ability to share files, folders, and volumes among computers.

LocalTalk   The physical hardware required to create the network (for example, cables and drivers).

peer-to-peer networking In a peer-to-peer network, each Mac acts as its own server, passing information to other computers on the network. In this setup, there is no centralized server.

permissions The settings used to exclude or include computer users in sharing files on your Mac.

program sharing The ability for another computer user to use an application on your Mac over the network.

TokenTalk The driver used to operate a Mac on a Token Ring network.

16

Q&A

Q What's the difference between File Sharing and AppleShare IP?

A File Sharing is a distributed networking option for a limited number of Macs (and PCs). When you determine that you need a centralized server to handle network traffic, AppleShare IP 6.0 provides the file server software needed to manage the server. AppleShare IP supports TCP/IP protocol running on top of AppleTalk. TCP/IP is the networking protocol used by internetworks.

Q What's the difference between AppleTalk, EtherTalk, and TokenTalk? What hardware and software do I need to set up an Ethernet system versus a LocalTalk system.

A AppleTalk, EtherTalk, and TokenTalk are the software protocols automatically supported by Mac OS 8.5's Open Transport software. You need an Ethernet PCI card and an external 10-Base T transducer in order to connect your Mac to an Ethernet-based network. Luckily, most G3-based Macs come with the Ethernet card preinstalled. Token Ring is IBM's networking protocol and requires its own PCI card. AppleTalk runs on the Mac's built-in LocalTalk hardware.

Q When do I need to install routers and gateways on my network?

A Routers are used to connect two networks together. Gateways are used to bridge the two networks. You use routers to build internetworks from your networks. Routers let you create logical groups of computers, called *zones,* linking disparate computers together to share resources such as printers and file servers. Gateways let you link incompatible network protocols, such as AppleTalk and TCP/IP networks, together on a single network.

Q What are some good basic books to read that explain about networking Macs?

A Here are a few resources to check out:

- Apple Computer, Inc. *Understanding Computer Networks.* Addison-Wesley, 1989.

- Apple Computer, Inc. *A Guide to Apple Networking and Communications Products.* Apple Computer, 1990.
- Apple Computer, Inc. *Planning and Managing AppleTalk Networks.* Addison-Wesley, 1991.
- Kosiur, Dave and Joel Snyder. *MacWorld Networking Bible, 2nd Edition,* IDG Books, 1994.

Workshop

The Workshop contains quiz questions to help you solidify your understanding of the material covered. You can find the answers to the quiz questions in Appendix B, "Quiz Answers."

Quiz

1. What's the difference between distributed and centralized file serving?
2. What is peer-to-peer networking?
3. What is AppleShare? What is the difference between AppleShare IP server software and AppleShare client software?
4. What does Open Transport do?
5. What control panel is used to turn on File Sharing?
6. What is the Sharing command used for?
7. How do I end a file sharing session?
8. How do I access a shared volume?
9. What are the possible causes of performance degradation during a file sharing session?
10. How do I make my file or hard disk sharable?

PART III

Evening Hours: Networks and Internet

Hour

17 Personal Web Serving

18 Entering the Internet

19 Using the Internet

20 Talking to the Other Guys

HOUR 17

Personal Web Serving

Apple believes you should walk before you run. During this hour, I am assuming you've connected your Mac to an organization's intranet or to the Internet. Intranets are like private Internets within a company/organization that only the group has access to. Now, suppose you need some content and a way to publish it on your intranet, but you don't feel ready for a full-blown dedicated server.

Apple provides the Personal Web Sharing feature in Mac OS 8.5. Personal Web Sharing lets your Mac become a server to electronically publish materials—including bulletin boards, chat rooms, forms, and Web pages that you would ordinarily need a dedicated server to manage. Because it's assumed that you'll be serving a limited number of people who have access to your domain address, your Mac can handle the load. When you find that you're getting too many "hits," Apple provides the Internet Server Solution for the World Wide Web package to create that dedicated server you now need.

This hour describes how to set up Personal Web Sharing and run it on your Mac. The hour includes the following lessons:

- Turning on and configuring Personal Web Sharing
- Setting up a personal FTP site
- Graduating to a dedicated Web server

Personal Web Sharing

Personal Web Sharing makes the serving process relatively painless. Think of Web Sharing as Mac OS File Sharing over the Internet. Web Sharing is a distributed server that lets others on your intranet access and send documents.

The way Web Sharing works is that any file placed in your Web Pages folder can be served using the Personal Web Sharing server.

You can place HTML documents, CGIs, Java applets, and so forth in your Web Pages folder, and your server will process these files and serve the results to those users that access your address. This means anyone with a browser—be it a PC or a Mac running Netscape Navigator, Communicator, or Microsoft Internet Explorer—can read what has been published and respond interactively (if the proper software resides in the Web Pages folder).

SOME IMPORTANT DEFINITIONS: CGIs AND APPLETS

A *CGI* or *Common Gateway Interface* is not a programming language but a set of conventions or rules for setting up two-way communications between the server's computer and the browser's computer. CGIs provide the roadmap for the way Web clients and servers handle requests for executing and sending out the results of programs processed on the server. CGI scripts have been written for every computer platform (including Macintosh, Windows, and UNIX) and can be written in almost any programming language. Web servers can pass information to CGIs as well as receive information from CGIs. CGIs can be launched by the Web server and can interact with applications other than the Web server.

Applets are small programs—mostly written in an open programming language called *Java*—that perform single functions, typically graphic in nature. Those revolving pictures you see on Web sites are usually performed using Java applets. HTML calls on the applets that reside on the server to perform these functions.

Personal Web Sharing makes training easy, because you can publish information with jazzy Java animations or activities and let people access the documents and learn at their own pace. You can use Web Sharing to collect information from your workgroup, for example.

The Personal Web Sharing server also can be secured so that only certain people can access its contents. Web Sharing works with the Sharing command to set up access privileges in the same fashion as File Sharing. (For more information, see Hour 16, "File Sharing.")

Setting Up Web Sharing

This section assumes that you already have access to the corporate intranet or the Internet established. For more information on Web setup, see Hour 15, "Web Publishing."

After you've logged on to the Internet or corporate intranet, you can set up Personal Web Sharing, as follows:

1. Open the Personal Web Sharing control panel from the Control Panels hierarchical menu on the Apple menu.

2. In the resulting Personal Web Sharing control panel, click the Select button next to Web Folder to indicate where on your hard disk you're storing the folders and files you want to share over the Internet (see Figure 17.1). Select a folder from the Finder list box.

3. Click the Select button next to Home Page to indicate which file is your default or starting page (it's typically named INDEX.HTML). Select a file from the resulting Finder list box.

   The default page will be the page that users see every time they log on to your site. This is your "portal" (in much the same way that Yahoo, Excite, Earthlink, and Netscape offer their home pages as portals for delving deeper into the Internet).

FIGURE 17.1.

*Click the appropriate
Select button to assign
a sharing folder and
default start page.*

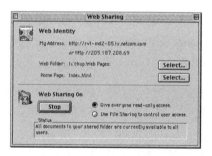

Remember that links stay linked only if you do not move documents out of their subfolders. Use Adobe SiteMill to ensure that all your links work before you turn on the Web server.

Turning On Web Sharing

To turn on Web Sharing, select the Web Sharing control panel from the Control Panels pop-up menu on the Apple menu. In the resulting Web Sharing dialog box, click Start.

17

Notice that the server checks to see whether an IP address has been assigned, and if not, it calls the intranet or Internet service provider (ISP). Web Sharing uses Open Transport/PPP to dial into an Internet Service Provider's server and get an IP address. Remember this address and hand it out to anyone who you want to give access to your server. The IP address is always listed in the Web Identity area of the dialog box. If you forget the address, open the control panel and it will be displayed whenever the server is active.

Notice that the Web Address space contains two addresses. The first address is the domain name for your server, and the second is the actual IP address of your server. You can surf for your default Web page using either the domain name or IP address and give either out when announcing your site. You can also pay $100 to NIC to purchase an actual domain name such as http://www.yourcompany.com, which you can then lease for $50 per year. Either way, remember either of these two addresses.

> You can also copy the IP address to your Clipboard for pasting into documents or emails by selecting Copy Address from the File menu when the Web Sharing control panel is open.

Accessing the Server

Anyone with a browser can type your server's IP address and gain access to either your default home page or the Personal NetFinder (see Figure 17.2). Notice that the IP address on the Web Sharing control panel matches that on the browser.

FIGURE 17.2.

You can access the Web site using a relative URL or the actual server IP address of the Mac.

I've placed my own Web site in the Web Pages folder that resides on my Mac. When the Web Sharing server is on, this site is what people will be able to view and use. Use an HTML editor such as PageMill 2 or Claris HomePage to create your own pages. Figure 17.3 illustrates that what resides in the Web Pages folder becomes the contents of the server. Drag and drop files into the folder to change the contents of the server.

FIGURE 17.3.

Any file placed in your Web Sharing folder is available for browsing over the Internet.

Your Web server can be a document repository instead of an electronic publishing house when you set the home page identifier to None and use the Personal NetFinder (see Figure 17.4). Personal NetFinder causes a list view of the contents of the Web Pages folder to appear on a surfer's browser. The user can then choose which document to view by clicking it (the same as selecting a document in list view in the Finder).

Such a listing is useful if you're using the Web Sharing server to upload and download files (as an FTP server).

You can add a message banner as a header and a special footer to the folder listing by placing two text files called FOLDER_HEADER.HTML and FOLDER_FOOTER.HTML into the Web Pages folder. Whatever you place in these special HTML documents will appear on any SimpleText document that you serve. You can add graphics, imagemaps, and so forth to these files. The only restriction is that you should not add the standard <HTML>...</HTML> tag pair to these files.

You can control how many people can access your server (and hence its performance) by limiting or increasing the amount of memory allocated to the server. Select the Web Sharing extension in the Extensions folder of your System folder and use the Get Info dialog box (Command-I) to increase the preferred memory size. Make sure your server is turned off before increasing or decreasing its memory. When you turn the server back on, you'll have changed its performance parameters.

FIGURE 17.4.

Your Mac can become a personal FTP server with Personal NetFinder.

Working with CGIs in Personal Web Serving

CGI scripts extend the interactivity of your Web site by enabling you to add intelligence to your HTML via preprocessing so that each browser is given a personalized version of your Web page. For example, CGI can personalize your email, provide fill-in form processing, perform database searching, do image hotspot processing (although most of this is pushed over to the client-side and handled by the browser), provide point-of-sale processing (setting up online stores that accept and process credit card accounts), and supply access counters or give the time of day or date. The excitement of Web pages is provided via CGI scripts. For example, a CGI script can personalize a response to a reader's completion of an order form with "Thanks, Joe for placing an order with WizzyWig. Your order is scheduled to ship next Wednesday." CGI scripts can create HTML text and pull in images on the fly, which are then returned and displayed on your reader's computer screen via a browser. CGI is a standard within HTML version 2.0, which means you can pull in CGI scripts from any type of server supporting HTML version 2.0 (such as UNIX, Windows NT, and Mac).

There are three parts to CGI:

- A special URL the reader enters into a browser either directly or via a hidden hot link you placed on your page. (Remember the Inspector's Form mode screen from Hour 8, "Mobile Computing"?)
- CGI-compatible Web server software, which in this case is Personal Web Sharing.

- The CGI application. CGIs can be purchased that perform specific tasks, such as form processing, or you can write your own programs using practically any programming language—most are written in a UNIX scripting language (such as Sh or Perl) or some Mac or Windows equivalent (such as AppleScript or MacPerl on the Mac or Visual Basic on the Windows side). Scripts written in full-blown programming languages, such as C or C++, must be compiled to create executable code before they are usable. Most scripts, on the other hand, are interpreted (in other words, they're run line-by-line by the server).

CGIs are provided by third-party vendors to perform a variety of actions. Yahoo's CGI section is a good place to start if you want to find CGIs. The address is `http://www.yahoo.com/Computers_and_Internet/Internet/World_Wide_Web/CGI_Common_Gateway_Interface/`.

Apple does not provide any CGIs with Personal Web Sharing. Consult the documentation or descriptive information provided for the CGI to determine how to use it with your Web server.

You have to do three things to get a CGI script to run on a server. The trick is that you have to configure the CGI script to recognize where the files relating to your Web site are located on the Web server (if they have been moved). Here are some key points:

- Every CGI script must be configured to run on your local server. A .SETUP file comes with many public domain CGI scripts that centralizes server-specific variables and options so that you can update them in one place. If no .SETUP file exists, you'll find the options and server-specific variables you have to set in the first lines of the main script.

- You must always check the instructions that come with CGI scripts to see how they need to be configured (how to set up variables) to run properly. Each script has different instructions.

- You also have to ensure you have an interpreter on your server that can read the script—either AppleScript or MacPerl, for example. You then have to make sure the interpreter is referenced correctly on the first line of the script.

- You need to ensure that the permissions are set correctly for each file in the script so that the Web server will run any applications, read any data, or setup fields and write to any supporting files that the script requires.

You also have to let Personal Web Sharing know that you're using a CGI by including it in the Actions section of the Preferences dialog box.

17

To add an action (CGI) to your Web server, follow these steps:

1. Check the documentation for the CGI you want to add to see what type it is and how to use it.

2. Open the Web Sharing control panel and choose Preferences from the Edit menu.

3. Click the Actions tab (if necessary).

4. Click New.

5. In the Action dialog box, select the type of action from the pop-up menu.

6. Click Select and then pick your CGI from the resulting Finder Open dialog box.

7. Click OK to add the new action to the list.

8. Click Save.

Personal Web Sharing can handle a maximum of 32 CGIs.

Running a Dedicated Server

After researching the different avenues open to you for publishing your Web site, you decide to run your own Web server. Three issues are involved in this decision: How powerful a computer do you need? What kind of software do you need to manage your site? And, how big of a "pipe"—the physical transmission line—do you want to purchase?

Making Hardware Decisions

There are three basic types of processors and many manufacturers of hardware suitable for Web serving. You must get enough hardware to handle a large number of simultaneous connections to your server. This entails judging four issues:

- **Which operating system do you want to use?** Three different operating systems provide support for Web servers. The traditional operating system that still runs most Internet servers is UNIX. UNIX is able to perform more than one task at a time (called *preemptive multitasking*), provide secure areas to run multiple applications without memory problems (called *protected memory*), communicate easily with Ethernet LANs using the TCP/IP protocol, and support many users simultaneously. Therefore, it's a natural server platform. All other operating systems are judged against UNIX when determining their applicability to Web serving.

  Today, Microsoft Windows NT 4.0 and Apple Macintosh System 8.5 also support Internet servers. Both Windows NT and the Macintosh offer a more user-friendly, intuitive computing environment than UNIX. In addition, Windows NT offers the multithreading, preemptive multitasking, and protected memory features of UNIX on a cheaper-to-manage platform. The Macintosh is harder to break into than either UNIX or Windows, but it carries a higher performance overhead because of its heavily graphics-based user interface. Only UNIX is robust enough to handle very large networks—neither Macs nor computers running Windows NT offer the input/output (I/O) speeds provided by UNIX machines.

- **Which computer processor offers the best price/performance for your needs?** The processor technology is speeding up through the implementation of multiple parallel processors, Reduced Instruction Set Computers (RISC), and new Intel Pentium chip technologies. The speed of the computer chip is not the only influence on the performance of a server, because the I/O throughput speeds and other networking concerns play a larger part in the performance of a hardware system. The best platforms are still the larger computing systems (called *workstations* or *minicomputers*) based on RISC chips and fast I/O, including systems manufactured by Silicon Graphics, Inc. (SGI), Digital Electronics Corporation (DEC), Sun Microsystems, Hewlett-Packard, and IBM. Although it's far cheaper to purchase, the Apple Macintosh is much slower than those more expensive UNIX-based workstations. Hardware based on the Intel Pentium chip that runs Windows NT falls in between the Macintosh and the workstations in terms of price and performance. Prices for the computer processor range from Macintosh Internet Server Solutions (approximately $7,000) to Sun Microsystems' Netra i600 system (approximately $16,000).

- **What local area network connections do you want to use?** Bandwidth is the bottleneck for Web performance. The faster the network and the broader the frequency spectrum provided, the better the performance. The standard base connection for Web networking is Ethernet (both AUI thicknet and 10-Base T thinnet). Today, more and more networks are running wide area networks using ISDN and T1 leased lines. Some workstations come with internal ISDN terminal adapters, such as the SGI Indy WebForce and Sun Netra i600. Most other hardware systems require the purchase of a third-party ISDN adapter at an additional cost. If modems are an option, the faster the better. Today, 28.8Kbps, 34Kbps, and 56Kbps modems are standard (although many people dialing up the Web still use slower 14.4Kbps modems).

- **How many simultaneous connections are you willing to support?** The number of users able to log on to your server at any one time depends on the amount of random access memory (RAM) you have installed and the amount of memory allocated per connection. Large Web servers may have 100,000 TCP/IP sockets open at any one time. Multimedia files are big and require these sockets to be open longer than the simple text transfers of the past. On the Macintosh, each WebStar

17

connection requires about 100K. On UNIX, each Netscape connection requires 200K when idling and 300K to 500K when running. Users may use four or five simultaneous connections while a page with several GIF images is downloading. The browser determines the number of simultaneous client connections allowed.

A recent Web server hardware and software benchmark study by *NewMedia Magazine* published by Hyperstand at
`http://www.hyperstand.com/NewMedia/96/08/td/Web_Servers_Need_Power.html`)
was reported in an article titled "Web Servers Need Power, Speed, and Multimedia Savvy," by Sam Murphy and Bob Doyle. This article reports that the RISC-processor-based workstations won the throughput war. Doyle and Murphy tested the following representative systems:

- Apple Internet Server Solution running Macintosh System 7.5.3 on a 132MHz PowerPC 604 RISC chip system configured with 32 MB RAM and a 2GB hard drive. The computer had an internal Ethernet thicknet and thinnet terminal and optional ISDN connection, three PCI slots, CD-ROM and floppy disk drives, and three drive bays. It's street price was $6,879.

- DEC Internet AlphaServer 1000 4/266 running either OSF1 UNIX or Windows NT 3.51 on a 266MHz Alpha RISC chip system configured with 64 MB RAM and a 2GB hard drive. The computer had an internal Ethernet (both thicknet and thinnet) and an optional ISDN terminal connection. It came with a CD-ROM and floppy disk drive, seven EISA slots, three PCI slots, and ten drive bays. It's street price was $15,990 for the Windows NT version and $18,990 for the UNIX version.

- Hewlett-Packard HP 9000 running HP UNIX 10.0 on a 100MHz PA-RISC chip system configured with 32 MB RAM and 1GB hard drive. The computer had a thinnet Ethernet internal terminal and optional ISDN connection. It came with CD-ROM and Digital Audio Tape (DAT) drives, seven EISA slots, and seven drive bays.

- IBM RS/6000 Internet POWERsolution running AIX UNIX 4.1 on a 133MHz PowerPC 601 RISC chip-based system configured with 32 MB RAM and 1GB hard drive. The computer had an internal Ethernet (both thick and thinnet) and an optional ISDN terminal connection. It came with a CD-ROM and floppy disk drive, three MicroChannel slots, and two drive bays.

- Intergraph Computer Systems Intergraph InterServe Web-300 running Windows NT Server 3.51 on a 150MHz Pentium Pro chip system configured with 64 MB RAM and a 2GB hard drive. The computer had an internal Ethernet (both thicknet and thinnet) and an optional ISDN terminal connection. It came with a CD-ROM and floppy disk drive, two EISA slots, three PCI slots, and three drive bays.

- Silicon Graphics SGI Indy WebForce running IRIX UNIX 5.3 on a 132MHz MIPS R40 RISC chip set configured with 32 MB RAM and a 1GB hard drive. The computer had an internal Ethernet (both thicknet and thinnet) and an optional ISDN terminal connection. It came with a CD-ROM and floppy disk drive.

The problem with personal computers is not their computing power but their throughput capabilities. You can use a standalone IP router connected to the Mac via Ethernet to handle automatic data compression and other TCP/IP communications tasks. You also need high-speed serial ports, such as FireWire (available on PCI cards as an upgrade), to handle many simultaneous I/O requests.

Web Server Software

The following sections provide an overview of the various server software options available for the Intel, UNIX, and Macintosh platforms. This is not an exhaustive review, by any means, because the picture changes daily.

Based on an article in the January, 1997 edition of *ZD Internet Magazine*, "Does Your Web Server Measure Up?" by Lisa L. Sweet, over 100 Web servers are available either as shareware or commercial products.

In October, 1996, Netcraft, an independent service, performed a survey of Web server software (available at `http://www.netcraft.co.uk/survey/`). This survey was used by Ziff-Davis Labs, along with an update of newer servers, to illuminate which software packages had the largest install bases. Ziff-Davis and Netcraft found nine packages (ranked by Ziff-Davis Labs Benchmark Performance from fastest to slowest) that were the most popular for corporate Web serving:

- Microsoft Internet Information Server 2.0 for Windows NT
- Netscape Enterprise Server 2.0 for Windows NT
- Internet Factory Commerce Builder Professional 2.0 for Windows NT
- Process Software Purveyor Encrypt 1.2b for Windows NT
- Netscape Enterprise Server for UNIX
- Stronghold for UNIX
- O'Reilly Website Professional for Windows NT
- NCSA Apache for UNIX
- Quarterdeck StarNine WebStar for Macintosh

Web serving began on UNIX machines. Because most corporate computer organizations are Windows NT based, Microsoft Windows NT has become the operating system of choice for Web serving in corporations. Macintosh is the server of choice for small-scale Web services, such as single sites and low-volume services.

Netscape holds approximately 14 percent of the market and offers several flavors, depending on the needs of the server (for example, commerce versus intranets versus Internet Service Provider). Microsoft comes in second with 10 percent of the server market. O'Reilly comes in last with 4 percent of the market for Windows NT servers. Macintosh software (predominantly Webstar) serves over 60 percent of the current Web sites.

All the previous servers provide certain universal capabilities:

- The capability to perform back-end processing via CGIs, configurable MIME (Multipurpose Internet Mail Extensions) settings, and URL suffix mapping (to be able to use relative URLs). MIME settings and URL mapping lets you configure your server to support new innovations in data (such as PDF files), new types of sound files, and so on, by telling the server it should recognize a new suffix (such as .PDF for PDF files).

- The use of access security features (such as realm control and allow/deny control). These two functions provide both active and passive security. *Realms* are groups of folders and documents. You gain active security because with realm control, you allow or deny permission to access realms via passwords. Allow/Deny provides passive security because the server enables only certain IP addresses to access certain domains names.

- The capability to maintain more than one site on a Web server (called *multihoming*) and to run more than one copy of the server software on the server at a time (called *multiserving*). This way, you can maintain a public and private server over different serial ports.

Server software is purchased based on price/performance. In other words, what you are willing to pay for performance? Most of the expense is in hardware, because you want the fastest machine with the most memory and storage capacity available to support your server software.

You should consider leasing space and data transmission bandwidth from an ISP and then moving your site to your own server when the cost of maintaining a leased site equals the cost of setting and managing your own. The benefits of running your own site includes not having any other domains (Web sites) competing for space and bandwidth, easily gaining access to the site for maintenance, and updating the site without having to ask permission.

CGI Script Examples

The following paragraphs provide a short overview of the types of CGI scripts available for three platforms: UNIX, Windows, and Mac. This list is by no means exhaustive.

Forms and Guest Books

As mentioned throughout this chapter, most CGIs process information via Web page forms, because forms offer a flexible way to getting information from your reader and return it back to the reader. *Guest books* are specialized forms that collect information about your site's visitors. You can use this information to tailor the site to the interests of the readers you're getting. Other forms take information and return data to your readers. Still other forms offer ways to email or fax information.

Scripts in Perl

Here's a list of available Perl scripts for guest books:

- Selena Sol's Guestbook 3.0 (Perl)
- Guestbook.cgi (Perl) by Matt Wright
- Poll it 1.0 (Perl) by Jason Berry

Scripts in C

Forms.acgi by Steve Johnson (`http://www.biola.edu/cgi-bin/forms/`) takes the data input from a form and puts it into an email message and sends it to the recipient. Most of the configuration for Forms.acgi is done with hidden fields in your form, including names and addresses for both the sender and receiver, and the subject line. Therefore, if you want a message to go to different people, you need to create separate fill-in forms for each.

NetForms, by John O'Fallon, Maxxum Development (`http://www.maxum.com/NetForms`), runs native on Power Macs. In addition to taking the data from a form and dumping it into a text file (the text is tab delimited, so you can easily import it into a database), you can also have it formatted as HTML. This way, you can have user-input information posted at your Web site and create bulletin board–style discussion areas on your Web site. You can also embed hotlinks into the text file that point to other related forms or hidden fields that, in turn, point to other CGIs that can further process the data. This forms-processing CGI is useful for collecting information that records user feedback, registers products online, reports problems, tracks information collection, and takes online orders. In fact, any information placed in a text file and analyzed offline can be collected via NetForms.

17

Scripts Written in AppleScript/Frontier

Email.acgi, by Eric Lease Morgan (http://www.lib.ncsu.edu/staff/morgan/email-cgi.html), is an AppleScript-based program that does the same thing as Forms.acgi: It takes information from a form and drops it into an email. Email.acgi, like ROFM.cgi, needs a few commercial AppleScript scripting additions (such as Parse CGI and TCP scripting additions) to work.

> In addition to a Web server, you also need to be running a Simple Mail Transfer Protocol (SMTP) server to use these CGIs. The CGI creates a mail message and sends it through your Internet email server. If you're running Delphic's NetAlly, you probably won't need another application, because SMTP is part of the package. If you're running any other server, check out the Apple Internet Mail Server (AIMS), available from Apple's Web site at http://www.apple.com.

If you have information in Claris's FileMaker Pro database program, you can use ROFM, by Russell Owens (http:// rowen.astro.washington.edu/), to serve as the intermediary between the data and your server.

Interaction/IP, written by Terje Norderlaug and available from the Media Design inProgress site (http://www.ifi.uio.no/~terjen/interaction), performs the same text dump functions and bulletin board support functions as NetForms. The benefit of Interaction/IP is that it supports numerous plug-ins and tool scripts (such as a tool that creates a collaborative calculator for jointly solving math problems over the Web).

Counters

Not long ago, having a counter on your Web site's home page became incredibly popular. There's really no point to this other than to let people know how popular your site is and to show off your Web "know how" (counters require CGIs).

Muhammad Muquit wrote an elegant counter called Count in Perl (available at http://warm.semcor.com/~muquit/) that keeps a raw count of hits on your site and displays the number in a digital clock format.

You can also hire a company called Internet Audit (http://www.internet-audit.com) to link to your site and record all the information about your visitors for you. An inline GIF file linked to their home page uses a unique personal code that activates recording software. You can get the results by clicking another GIF connected to a statistics script.

Analog, by Stephen Turner, is written in Perl and can be downloaded from ftp://ftp.statslab.cam.ac.uk/put/users/sret1/analog. Analog records usage statistics for a Web site.

Logger.cgi, by Rod Clark and available through the CGI Collection, is a program written in Perl that keeps a log of every person who "hits" your page.

You can also purchase a commercial counter program for $695 from Interse called Market Focus (`http://www.interse.com`). The program analyzes the use of Web sites or pages and downloads the results to a Word 6.0 document.

ServerStat (for the Macintosh) processes your log and creates an HTML page, giving you the vital statistics of your Web site. ServerStat charts connections by the day and hour and tells you how many connections were made from various domains (such as education, commercial, and government). ServerStat is available at `http://165.247.199.177/ss.html`.

Count WWWebula is a C-based shareware package from Kagi Software (available at `http://198.207.242.3/`). The counter displayed on your Web page is a GIF image (when you are using a CGI) rather than just a number. A few GIFs come with the package, plus you can have your own GIFs displayed as the numbers. The coolest GIF is the odometer graphic.

NetCloak, from Maxum Development, is listed here as a counter CGI, but providing a quick way to display a counter is only a small part of what NetCloak can do. In reality, NetCloak provides about 30 new HTML commands, giving you control over what information is displayed on your Web site.

Besides displaying a counter, NetCloak can have items randomly displayed. It can change the look of your page depending on any number of qualities of the browser software (for example, you can display information to clients viewing from educational sites differently than those viewing from commercial sites). NetCloak can even change the information on your page depending on the date or time of day.

NetCloak is made by Maxum Development, the same people who make NetForms. You can download a sample copy of NetCloak from `http://www.maxum.com`.

Active Images

Active images are graphics with "hotspots" that can be clicked to access their underlying hypertext link. Two types of active images exist, depending on where the information used to create the link resides—server-side and client-side active images. For server-side active images to work, however, you need to have a CGI on the server that can process in-coming information.

The most common CGI script available for the Macintosh is ImageMap.acgi, from Lutz Wiemann. Wiemann's CGI is fast, somewhat easy to use, and free. You can download ImageMap.acgi at `http://weyl.zib-berlin.de/imagemap/Mac-ImageMap.html`.

What ImageMap.acgi does is provide the server with the intelligence needed to read the map file you created in HTML. It also tells the server what URLs to serve when a particular coordinate is clicked. This is a prime example of CGIs extending the functionality of the Web server. The server only wants to serve files, not figure out what a set of coordinates means, so it passes that information to the CGI and lets the CGI figure everything out.

MapServe is another CGI for the Mac that works similarly to ImageMap.acgi. The basic concept is the same. The Web server software provides the CGI with the coordinates returned when a viewer clicks a hotspot on an imagemap. The CGI converts these coordinates to a URL based on information it has in a map file and then sends the URL to the server. MapServe can be downloaded from
http://www.spub.ksu.edu/other/machttp_tools/mapserve.

NetAlly is the Macintosh server software from Delphic Software. Delphic has a vision of a single software package that can handle just about any Internet server requirement you may have. Part of this is built-in support for active images.

If you're using NetAlly, you won't need another application to turn the coordinates into a URL (the server will have this capability built in). You still need to produce the map file and create a link to it in the Inspector, but you won't need to install another application.

Animation

You can create moving pictures on your Web page without having to use video or movie files. Animated GIFs can be created just like cartoons used to be—by drawing a sequence of pictures, each one slightly different, and displaying them rapidly one after another.

Three types of animation are available to receive moving pictures on your Web page: client-pull animation, server-push animation, and animated GIFs.

Client-Pull Animation

Client-pull refers to the fact that the browser requests an object from the server (meaning that the animation is initiated by the browser). The browser requests the next page automatically through a command embedded in the HTML. You can embed scripts that create random backgrounds or replace images randomly using client-pull techniques. The secret to client-pull is the <META> tag in the HEAD area of the page (see Hour 15 for a discussion of the parts of an HTML document). You provide an attribute/value pair, called HTTP-EQUIV="Refresh", that causes the server to automatically replace the page with another page within a specified time period. The limitation of client-pull animation is that the entire page is replaced each pass. A more sophisticated way to animate an image is via *server-push animation*.

> The <META> tag is supported only by Netscape Navigator browsers.

Server-Push Animation

The benefit of server-push animation is that it's triggered on the server side by a CGI and is therefore able to affect individual elements on your page. The CGI sends a series of individual GIF images to the browser during a set time frame. An example of a server-push animation CGI is RandPic 1.0, by Robert Niles (available via the CGI Collection). This random image generator uses server-side includes (SSIs) that you must configure (*SSIs* are additional variables and data you must enter into your HTML). Robert Niles also wrote RandImg in Perl, which does the same thing without SSIs.

Animated GIFs

Netscape Navigator uses a feature called *GIF animation*, which incorporates all the animation frames into one file. This is a more efficient use of the server and saves storage space as well. GIF animation uses a special format for images called *GIF89a*. GifBuilder, which is shareware for the Mac, assists you in creating GIF animations by collecting the frames and providing you with options for the number of repetitions, image transparency, and so on.

For More Information

For more information about working with client-pull animation, server-push animation, and animated GIFs via CGIs, surf Meng Weng Wong's Perl page at
`http://www.seas.upenn.edu/!mengwong/perlhtml.html`.

Online Stores

If you're creating your Web site to sell items, you can use a standalone CGI program that serves as a product catalog. Then another CGI is used to process the orders. Therefore, you can generate dynamic catalog pages and take electronic orders. Catalog and order processors can create dynamic HTML documents that personalize the use of your catalog for each browser. One such program suite is iCat's Electronic Commerce Suite 2.0, available at iCat's site (`http://www.icat.com`). The two parts of the suite are iCat Commerce Publisher (for building and maintaining online catalogs) and iCat Commerce Exchange (for processing electronic orders, including processing credit card transactions). The Publisher lets you build a database of products on either a Mac or Windows platform. It then creates dynamic HTML documents based on a reader's queries. The Publisher comes with many predefined templates through which you can add product information and objects (including images, movies, video, audio, PDFs, and animated GIFs). The

17

Exchange portion of the suite uses the Secure Sockets Layer standard to provide encryption for credit card transactions.

Database Processing

When you collect information, you need to put it in a database. Database CGIs take the information from a browser's form and places it in a semipermanent repository. It's then able to retrieve parts of the information, based on options selected by the user, and redisplay them on a page. Typically, several pieces of script and HTML are required to handle database management:

- The data repository (typically a commercial relational database of some sort)
- A CGI script that writes to the database
- A CGI script that takes information from the database
- A page to display the retrieved information

The CGI script that retrieves the data does most of the work. CGI scripts can also connect to SQL-based database management systems via embedded SQL queries. Microsoft markets a SQL server, called Microsoft SQL Server, that runs on Windows NT and can be linked to the Web via a CGI script. UNIX can use the shareware mSQL server (available for $129 from `http://hughes.com.au/product/w3-msql/`).

Other database CGI scripts and SQL server software are available—for example, Tango, by EverWare software (`http://www.everyware.com`), for the Mac. The Macintosh does not come bundled with a relational database such as Access. Only one serious SQL-based relational database is available for the Mac: namely, EveryWare Development's Butler SQL 2.02. Butler SQL is a database server that supports both AppleTalk and TCP/IP network protocols (it's a great cross-platform Internet database server). Butler also supports queries from any ODBC-capable client, thus providing your Mac with connections to Windows- and UNIX-based database servers. You cannot, however, query the database from your Web page unless you also have EveryWare's Tango 1.5.

Tango takes data capturing to the next level. It's a complete CGI, enabling you to tie Butler to your Web site. By using Tango, you can make queries to any ODBC-compatible SQL database, including but not exclusive of Butler and those running on Windows and UNIX platforms. Tango includes a query definition editor so you can define HTML snippets—thus letting Tango capture both the query request and the results in a single file. Tango then uses these snippets to build HTML pages on the fly. Suddenly, you can publish an entire site from within the database. You can also edit individual forms and update your database through your Web page. You do need to know HTML to make use of Tango and Butler because the CGI is not particularly user-friendly (unlike PageMill).

Just like the FileMaker CGI, you need to have a Butler database before you can use Tango.

EveryWare Development, the maker of Tango and Butler, has several examples of what can be done with these tools on its Web site. One example includes a slick online store that uses a shopping cart metaphor to enable users to click through several pages and pick up products as they go.

ACI US manufactures one of the major relational database environments for the Macintosh: Fourth Dimension (or 4D). The 4D environment is a complete programming language used to develop applications.

Some developers, however, have created externals for 4D. These externals are little pieces of software that enable 4D programmers to create complex applications without having to rewrite code.

ForeSight Technologies has created a 4D external that enables a 4D database to interact with a Macintosh Web server. The software, called NetLink 4D, gives you all the capabilities of having a database integrated into your Web site (enabling users to input data, perform searches, and assemble dynamic pages to be published on your site), plus the serious data-crunching power of a 4D database.

Apple has a powerful document search engine working over local networks called AppleSearch. Robin Martheus, a programmer at Apple, has released a CGI that enables you to search through AppleSearch archives over the Web.

Using the CGI requires you to have the AppleSearch application either on the same Macintosh as the Web server or on a Macintosh accessible over your network. AppleSearch.acgi has the same problem with custom configuration that Forms.acgi has—you have to poke around in the resource with ResEdit.

This CGI is free, but AppleSearch is not. However, AppleSearch does come bundled with the Apple Internet Server Solution. Download the latest version of AppleSearch.acgi from http://kamaaina.apple.com.

TR-WWW (found at http://www.monash.edu.au/informatics/tr-www.html)is another solution for providing searching capabilities on your Web site. TR-WWW is a standalone application that searches all documents you've placed in a particular folder. The advantages of TR-WWW over AppleSearch.acgi are that you don't need another application running in addition to the CGI and you don't need to prepare the documents to be searched the way that you do with AppleSearch.

The downside is that TR-WWW needs some configuration that's not very intuitive. It has a dreaded configuration file—a long text file with strange codes that tell TR-WWW how to behave. You also need to create your own form (not so with AppleSearch).

For More Information

For information about ActiveX, search `http://www.activex.org`. To find out more about ActiveX controls, go to `http://www.microsoft.com/activex/controls/`.

To learn more about CGI scripting, check out `http://hoohoo.ncsa.uiuc.edu/cgi/intro.html` or `http://www.yahoo.com/Computers_and_Internet/Internet/World_Wide_Web/CGI_Common_Gateway_Interface/`.

For more information about Perl CGI scripts, surf Selena Sol's Pubic Domain CGI Script Archive and Resource Library at `http://www.eff.org/~erict/Scripts`.

Another source for Perl and C scripts is Matt's Script Archive at `http://www.world-widemart.com/Scripts/`.

More CGI scripts for UNIX servers are available at The CGI Collection at `http://www.selah.net/cgo.html`.

Check out Jon Weiderspan's CGI Applications Directory at `http://www.comvista.com/net/www/cgi.html` for more CGI scripts as well as a good tutorial on writing CGI scripts for the Mac.

For more information about Java and JavaScript, check out these sites:

- `http://java.sun.com`
- `http://www.javaworld.com/javaworld/jw-06-1996/jw-06-vm.html`
- `http://www.gamelan.com`
- `http://java.sun.com/sfaq/`
- `http://www.netscape.com/comprod/producats/navigator/version_3.0/building_blocks/jscript/index.html`
- `http://home.netscape.com/eng/mozilla/3,0/handbook/javascript/index.html`
- `http://www.freografx.com/411/tutorial.html`.

For more information about VBScript, set your browser to `http://www.microsoft.com/vbscript/`.

Summary

In this hour, you have learned how to use the Personal Web Sharing software included with Mac OS 8. This little application turns your Mac into a Web server for light browsing use. Setting up personal Web serving is as easy as dragging all of the files and folders you want to share into a single folder and identifying that folder to the Personal Web Sharing program. The application dials your ISP, gets an IP address for your personal server, and manages traffic. You can also configure your personal server to act as an FTP server to upload and download files over the Internet.

When you have outgrown a personal server (which happens very rapidly given that you have to have your Mac on 24 hours to serve files), you can graduate to dedicated Web serving software. I provided a brief overview of how Web servers operate.

Term Review

File Transfer Protocol (FTP)   A server that manages the uploading and downloading of files. FTP servers resemble the list view of the Finder.

IP address   The Internet Protocol address that identifies the location of your Web server.

Personal Web Sharing   The desk accessory provided with Mac OS 8.5 that lets you create a small Web server on your Mac.

Web server   The software that manages the sharing of files between users via the Internet.

Q&A

Q How do I know that the Personal Web Sharing server is actually serving files?

A The Personal Web Sharing control panel provides rudimentary information on who is accessing your server. Install traffic measurement software, such as ServerStat, to gain better information.

Q How can I make locating my home page easier for users?

A Ask your users to bookmark your start page. That way, they don't have to type in your IP address each time.

Q How much does a dedicated server cost to set up?

A Lots and lots of money. Figure $10,000 for the computer, $2,500 for the server software, and a salary for a Webmaster to run the server.

Q What do I have to do to keep my personal Web server open 24 hours a day?

A Keep your Mac and modem on 24 hours a day. Personal Web Servers are best used in office settings where you can announce that you have turned the server on or off.

Workshop

The Workshop contains quiz questions to help you solidify your understanding of the material covered. You can find the answers to the quiz questions in Appendix B, "Quiz Answers."

Quiz

1. Where is Personal Web Sharing stored?
2. Where should you place your Web Sharing folder?
3. How do you assign a folder for Web sharing?
4. How do you assign a default start page?
5. What happens if you do not select a start page?
6. How do you start Personal Web Sharing?
7. How do you set up permissions in Personal Web Sharing?

Hour 18

Entering The Internet

So, what's all this jive about webs, surfers, highways, and such got to do with the Macintosh? In a word—everything. The Internet provides interactive communications in the form of electronic mail, telephony, published documents, and avenues to gain direct access to software and information. This is the Information Superhighway.

This hour discusses how to use the various Mac products to access the Web. The following topics are included:

- Setting up your Mac using Internet Setup Assistant
- Using the Internet control panel to set up your browser preferences
- A look at the individual control panels: Modem, Remote Access, and TCP/IP
- A brief overview of Open Transport and Apple Remote Access (formerly called PPP and Open Transport/PPP)

The Mac's Role on the Web

Mac OS 8.5 is constructed to support the four underpinnings of the Internet/Web (component software, open standards, multimedia, and networking):

- *Component software* lets you build applications specifically tailored to your exact needs by adding together small building blocks (such as a spell checker, spreadsheet, and calculator). Mac OS 8.5 supports two technologies that allow you to construct programs on-the-fly: Open Doc and its successor, RunTime Java.

- *Open standards* refers to the fact that you can run a piece of software on your Mac that was written in an alien programming language for an alien chipset, and vice versa. This is the power of the Java programming language as well as its offshoots. Materials viewed on the Internet reside in a space that can be manipulated by anyone with a computer, a connection, and the proper software. The trend is to bring this transparent usability to each computer so that you can run someone else's application locally without accessing a network or share a program over a network to collaborate across a distance. RunTime Java, again, provides the vehicle to accomplish this mission.

- The Macintosh is the computer of choice for multimedia developers because its architecture deeply supports the integration of sound, graphics, text, and animation. QuickTime is truly a cross-platform tool for developing and playing video productions in real-time, regardless of their format. QuickTime technologies (QuickTime, QuickTime Virtual Reality, QuickTime MPEG, and QuickTime Musical Instruments) are also leading helper programs (called *plug-ins*) that let you view and manipulate moving images on your Mac downloaded from the Internet. In fact, QuickTime is also the accepted standard on the PC side of the computer universe, making it a *de facto* standard for viewing online images—and you had it first on your Mac!

  The integration of sound, image, and text tools with the Mac operating system also makes the Mac the most popular platform for creating Web pages. The ability to accurately display text and graphics means that what you program in Hypertext Markup Language (HTML) is really what you get (unlike on the PC side).

- The Macintosh has always included built-in networking capabilities. Mac OS 8.5 continues this trend but ups the ante with Open Transport. Open Transport 2.0 provides support for TCP/IP, AppleTalk, EtherTalk, and TokenTalk. Apple Remote Access (ARA) provides a convenient way to dial into your Internet Service Provider. You don't need any additional hardware except a modem to connect to the Internet.

The Underlying Architecture

This section gets into the nitty-gritty of what actually happens when you connect to the Internet. This information isn't really required in order to access the Web, but it helps to understand the basics when you have to troubleshoot. If you only want the basics to getting online and already know how you'll be connecting, you can skip to the section titled "Using Internet Setup Assistant."

Because the Internet is composed of millions of disparate computers and networks, your connection is not necessarily anywhere near your home server. Here's a short tutorial on connecting to the Web on the Internet.

If you have a local telephone number and network ID, you can use your modem to call a *point of presence (POP)* provider. You use ARA to manage the calling and connecting via the POP provider onto your ISP's server. You typically don't see ARA's Open Transport components in operation, but you can sense its progress when you use Apple Remote Access.

The POP3 server dials another computer and connects you to the Internet backbone via MCI, Sprint, or AT&T telephone lines. The network backbone cables and satellites route you to your server (as identified in your network ID). The server takes over and identifies you as having permission to access its computer and hence the Internet by checking your password and ID. If everything matches up, you're logged on.

ARA passes control of your computer to your browser. You can see this happen when the Internet Dialer closes and your browser's splash screen appears. The browser then connects to your default home page on the Internet. A default home page doesn't have to be your ISP's stated home page—it can be any URL you've designated.

All of this takes about one or two minutes (depending on how busy the POP3, backbone, and server are at the time you dial). The speed at which data can be transmitted over the backbone via your server is also dependent on how much bandwidth is available to each caller—that is, how busy the system is when you call. This is why you can have a fast new 56Kbps modem and still only be able to transfer information at 21Kbps or less. For this reason, you should find out what your ISP's busiest times are and try calling during the off-peak hours. Netcom, for example, is busiest early in the morning and about 10 p.m. EST; other ISPs may have different bottleneck periods.

How TCP/IP Works

The Internet operates using special networking rules known as *TCP/IP (Transmission Control Protocol/Internet Protocol)*. TCP/IP is the network standard used on most UNIX computers and has become the *de facto* standard for large networks running different

18

types of computers. The IP portion of TCP/IP lets multiple processes communicate with each other over a network using packet-switching technology.

The goal of TCP/IP is reliability, regardless of how congested the transmission traffic gets. IP enables multiple networks to connect to form internetworks by routing data via datagrams (packets of information routed over a common network). TCP, on the other hand, manages how dissimilar computers speak to one another. Together, TCP/IP provides communication between networks and operates on a variety of computer platforms—Apple Macintosh, DOS-based PC using Windows 3.1, Windows 95 or Windows NT systems, IBM mainframes, and RISC processor–based UNIX workstations.

You can gain access to a TCP/IP server in a few ways:

- **You can use an Internet Service Provider (ISP).** For a monthly fee, you can use the ISP's server as the intermediary between you and the Web. Many ISPs offer personal home page space (about 1 to 2 MB) for free or they offer Web site space leases for an additional fee.

- **You can join a commercial online service.** Commercial online services provide *gateways* (or doors) to the Web. America Online is the main commercial online services with access to the Web. You can publish your Web pages using your online service's servers for free or for an additional fee.

- **You can use a corporate server.** If your company lets you have access to its server, and its server has access to the Internet via leased T1 lines, and if you have permission of the system administrator, you can publish your Web page on your corporate server. You can also use remote access software, such as Apple Remote Access, to dial into a network or the Internet.

Internet Service Providers

Internet Service Providers (ISPs) offer relatively cheap access to the Internet. Typically, an ISP provides you with a server address you can dial into using a local telephone number—called a *point of presence (POP)* connection. This is your conduit to the Internet. You can use the software typically provided by the ISP. Note that most ISPs do not serve the Mac community well when it comes to software, because they're oriented toward the larger PC world. Mac OS 8.5 contains all the software you need to surf: ARA, Internet control panel, and a browser of your choice. Once you get the server address, domain name, and local phone number, you're ready to surf.

EarthLink (called *Total Access*) and Netcom (called *NetComplete*) do provide fairly strong Mac-centered Internet access packages with software that configures the connection just as the Apple Internet Setup Assistant provides with Mac OS 8.5. Just note that most ISP software packages are based on the older shareware versions of PPP and TCP (called *MacPPP* or *FreePPP* and *MacTCP*) that will not run concurrently with Open Transport's versions of these protocols. You do not have to run FreePPP to connect with your ISP; just select PPP in the TCP/IP control panel and remove the FreePPP system extension from your Extensions folder.

ISPs are proliferating and consolidating. You can separate ISPs into local home-grown ISPs (such as zianet), national services (such as Netcom or Earthlink), and communications companies (such as AT&T, Sprint, and MCI). In addition, cable companies such as TCI are looking to break into the business. Also, local telephone companies, long-distance carriers, entertainment conglomerates (such as Time-Warner), and former video rental operators (such as Erols) are all getting into the ISP business. National companies such as EarthLink, Netcom, and GNN offer an extensive array of Internet connection services at escalating prices based on the speed and size of the their POP connection.

ISPs typically charge a flat monthly fee. However, due to the unprecedented growth of the Internet, these flat "one size fits all" monthly fees are giving way to escalating fee structures based on the quantity and quality of access required.

Small businesses may receive several email addresses, storage space on an FTP server, home page space, and unlimited access for one fee, whereas large companies may receive actual site management support, Web page management, and all the small business features for a larger fee. Lowly home users may be billed by the minute of access time. What do you get for your monthly access fee as a single user? Most ISPs offer an email address, connection to the Internet via an Internet address, 1 to 2 MB of space (sometimes more) for personal home pages, and possibly space for uploading files for FTP serving.

Make sure your ISP offers a local point of presence (POP) so that you don't have to pay long-distance telephone rates on top of the monthly Internet access rate. If you live near a metropolitan area, a local telephone number should be available.

18

Corporate Servers

Many large companies and most universities offer access to the Internet over very fast leased telephone lines (called *T1 lines*). Users in these environments can connect to the Internet from their desktops using their organization's local area network and server. The downside of this free access is that users must go through their computer operations or MIS department to gain access and permission to maintain a Web site. Often, users are limited in the access to the server due to security measures such as firewalls (strong separations of the network from the Internet) and proxy servers (virtual servers that act as the real server in order to filter access to ensure security).

Open Transport Technologies

Hold on to your hat, because it's going to be a bumpy ride for awhile. Therefore, if you don't want to know the skinny on Open Transport and how it speaks TCP/IP, you can skip this section and go directly to the next.

Apple recently realized that it has outgrown proprietary systems, so it embraced the industry by introducing a communications technology that supports many protocols. Apple calls its new communications subsystem *Open Transport*. Figure 18.1 displays the OSI model for Open Transport.

Open Transport is the mother of all network activity on the Mac. It must be installed to use Ethernet, LocalTalk, AppleTalk, IP, OT PPP, and IR (on PowerBooks). Open Transport completely replaces the older Communications toolbox, providing the Mac OS with a robust communications architecture that supports the following networking standards:

- X/Open Transport Interface (XTI) to support POSIX-compliant applications
- Datalink Provider Interface (DLPI) to support network interface controller (NIC) drivers
- UNIX System V release 4.2–compatible STREAMS environment for network protocol development

Figure 18.1.

The OSI model and Open Transport proto-cols.

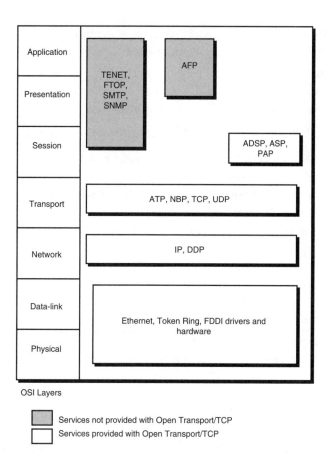

What's in Open Transport 2.0

When you install Open Transport 2.0 with the Mac OS 8.5 system, the following files are installed in the Control Panels folder:

- **AppleTalk.** A new control panel that replaces the classic Network panel.
- **TCP/IP.** A new control panel that replaces the classic MacTCP and AdminTCP panels.
- **Remote Access.** A new control panel used to dial and manage calls to the Internet. It replaces the retired PPP control panel.

- **Modem.** The control panel that manages the configuration of your modem and allows OT to communicate successfully.
- **Dial Assist.** The control panel that lets you store and automatically use telephone suffixes and prefixes. It also contains specialized dialing information needed to complete telephone calls from your Mac.

Also, the following files are installed in the System Extensions folder:

- **Shared Library Manager and Shared Library Manager PPC.** These are the extensions that implement the Apple Shared Library Manager for 680x0 and PowerPC Macintoshes, respectively. Both libraries are required for Open Transport to operate properly on Power Macs.
- **Open TransportLib and Open Transport Library.** These are the shared libraries that implement core Open Transport services on PowerPCs. Open TransportLib contains the modules and APIs for PowerPC-native applications; Open Transport Library contains modules to support 680x0 applications running in emulation on PowerPCs. You need to install both libraries on Power Macs to allow Open Transport to function properly.
- **OpenTptAppleTalkLib and Open Tpt AppleTalk Library.** These are the shared libraries that implement Open Transport AppleTalk protocols and services on PowerPCs. The first library, OpenTptAppleTalkLib, contains PowerPC-native models and APIs; Open Tpt AppleTalk Library contains emulator modules and APIs. Both files should be installed for proper operation of Open Transport and AppleTalk on Power Macs.
- **OpenTptInternetLib and Open Tpt Internet Library.** These are the shared libraries that implement Open Transport TCP/IP protocols and services on PowerPCs. Again, both files should be installed for proper operation of Open Transport and TCP/IP on Power Macs.
- **OpenTpt Modem, OpenTpt Remote Access, and OpenTpt Serial Access.** These are the shared libraries that implement ARA protocols and services on PowerPCs. You need to install all three components for the proper operation of ARA.

Configuring Open Transport

For Mac OS 8.5, Apple created a program called *Internet Setup Assistant*, included in the Internet folder. This assistant, shown in Figure 18.2, automates the process of configuring your Mac by walking you through ten steps. You do need certain information provided by your ISP or system administrator in order to complete the dialog boxes in the assistant.

FIGURE 18.2.

The Internet Setup Assistant leads you step-by-step through the TCP/IP configuration process.

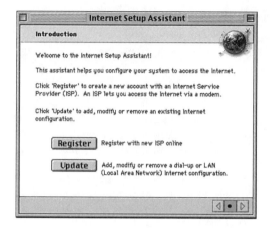

You should ask your ISP for the following information:

- **The telephone number of your local connection.** This is sometimes called a *POP* or *dial-in* number.

- **Your username (also called your *user ID* or *login name*) and password.** Without these two pieces of information, you cannot access your ISP's server or the Internet. These are the first pieces of information your ISP will send you when you open an account. Don't loose them.

- **The name of the ISP's domain.** The domain name should be a compound word separated by periods, such as ix.netcom.com. All the subdomains, such as email and newsgroups, will use this name in their identifiers.

- **The numeric name of your ISP's server(s).** This is called the *DNS (domain name server)* or *router address* and is very important to ensure that you connect to the right server. The number typically consists of four parts separated by periods. For example, Netcom's address is 199.182.120.203. These numbers represent the unique actual address on the Internet for your server.

- **The name of the incoming mail server or POP server.** This is your email server. The name consists of the server's domain and POP identification. Netcom's is popd.ix.netcom.com.

- **The name of the outgoing mail server or SMTP server.** This is the server that handles the delivery of emails and attachments. The name consists of the server's domain name and an SMTP identification. Netcom's is smtp.ix.netcom.com.

- **Your email address.** This is typically your user ID joined to the ISP's domain name by an "at" sign (@). For example, your email address would be *yourname*@highflying.net.

- If you're interested in joining any Usenet newsgroups, you need to know the newsgroup's domain name. This is typically the newsgroup server (or NNTP) and your ISP's domain name. For example, to use Netcom, again, the newsgroup's name is nntp.ix.netcom.com.

> If you're using Open Transport, you'll connect to the ISP using ARA under Mac OS 8.5. If you look on the TCP/IP control panel, you'll see where you're asked how to connect. Always select PPP. MacIP, MacPPP, and other connection methods are used if you're running shareware connection kits, such as FreePPP. The Internet Setup Assistant assumes you're using ARA and automatically selects this connection method in the TCP/IP control panel. If you're not using ARA for some reason, you'll have to know the name of the software you're using to connect to your ISP so you can update the TCP/IP control panel manually.

Using Internet Setup Assistant

Now you're ready to run the Internet Setup Assistant. The Internet Setup Assistant is very conversational and thorough. You progress through its pages by clicking the appropriate radio buttons to either add, update, or remove an existing ISP configuration. The following paragraphs review this process.

If you're updating an existing configuration, the first important page in the application is the sixth screen (see Figure 18.3). Here, you must type the telephone number for the local connection to your ISP. Be sure to add any area codes. Note that the new Mac OS 8.5 DialAssist control panel handles any prefixes and suffixes that your PBX might require (such as dialing 9 for an outside line prior to placing a call or disabling call waiting by dialing 077).

FIGURE 18.3.

Entering a local telephone number for an ISP.

Internet Setup Assistant
Configuration information
What is the phone number for this configuration? Your computer calls this number to connect to the Internet.
301 555-8690
What name do you use with this service? (also known as your login name or user ID)
#janepropeller
What is your password?
•••••
You can leave this blank, but you will have to enter your password each time you use the Internet service.
To continue, click the right arrow.
◁ 6 ▷

Figure 18.3 also shows where you enter your user ID and password. Note that the password is shown onscreen as black dots so that no one else can see it. ARA automatically enters your ID and password during the dial-up process if you've designated that ARA should remember your password.

The next relevant page that requests information from you is the tenth screen (see Figure 18.4). Here's where we get into configuring TCP/IP. Carefully type the router address for your ISP. (This is the four-part numbers mentioned earlier.) Double-check that you have the number correct, because this is the real way the network locates your specific server.

FIGURE 18.4.

Type the domain name server number in the box.

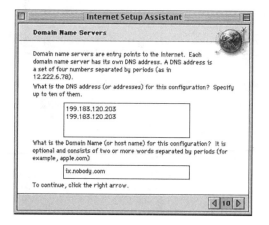

If you get the number wrong, the Internet Setup Assistant will tell you; it then asks you to reenter the number. The assistant checks for the correct number of digits, proper period placements, and so forth to ensure that you get the information right.

You now have two more items to complete: you need to set up your email account and point your browser to your newsgroup address. Figure 18.5 presents the screen used to set up your email account. Remember the terminology on this screen, because you'll see different iterations of it on many Internet configuration dialog boxes. Later in this section, I'll show you a trick you can use to make setting up other configurations easier.

You're basically done. If you want to ensure that the information you entered is correct, click the Overview button to display a review of your configuration when you get to the fourteenth screen (see Figure 18.6). You can go back and change anything that's wrong or incomplete. (Actually, the assistant is so smart that it will prompt you to correct overtly wrong information.)

FIGURE 18.5.

*Fill in the text boxes
with your email
domain names and
email ID.*

FIGURE 18.6.

*Use this screen to
review your Internet
configuration informa-
tion.*

Now click Go Ahead to have the assistant automatically complete the Modem, TCP/IP,
Remote Access, and Internet control panels (see Figures 18.7 to 18.10). When you're
done, you can open each panel to ensure that the data has been entered correctly. You can
also change these panels individually (but be careful, because one wrong number bungles
all three panels).

FIGURE 18.7.

The Modem control panel tells the Mac the capabilities of your modem.

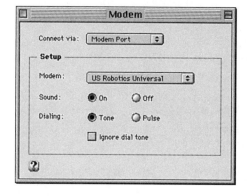

FIGURE 18.8.

The TCP/IP control panel tells the Mac information about the Internet.

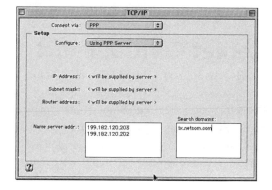

18

FIGURE 18.9.

The Remote Access control panel tells the Mac information about your connection to the Internet.

FIGURE 18.10.

The Internet control panel replaces Internet Config as the repository of your Internet preferences.

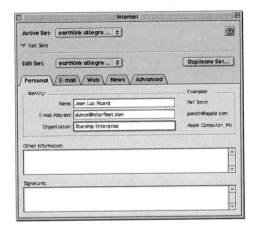

Using the Internet Control Panel

Apple has provided a new control panel called Internet, which is really a version of the venerable Internet Config control panel, to make your life easier (see Figure 18.11). Use the Internet control panel to select preferences for different parts of your Web browsing experience: home page, email, newsgroups, and general settings. You can then group your settings under a name (called a *set*). Using sets lets you switch configurations to fit your browser and browsing requirements. You simply select a new set from the Active Set pop-up menu.

FIGURE 18.11.

The Internet control panel lets you set up configurations for Internet browsing.

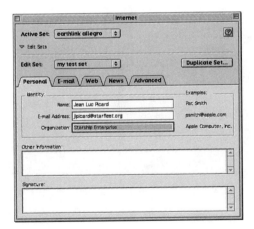

Working with Configuration Sets

With the Internet control panel open, you can activate, edit, rename, and remove sets of configurations. Here are some key points:

- You can activate another configuration set by selecting a name from the Active Set pop-up menu.

- You can create a new set of configurations by selecting Untitled from the Edit Sets pop-up menu. Enter the information requested on each tab and make your preference selections. When you're done, select Rename from the File menu. In the resulting dialog box, type a new name in the text box and click Rename. You can use this command to rename existing sets as well.

- You can duplicate an existing set to make slightly different configuration settings by selecting an existing set from the Edit Sets pop-up menu and clicking the Duplicate button. Make sure the copy is selected in the Edit Sets menu when you make your changes.

- You can delete a set by making sure the unwanted set is not active or in edit mode and then selecting Delete from the File menu. In the resulting Delete dialog box, select the set you want to delete and click Delete.

- You can save a set by closing the control panel. Your changes are always saved prior to quitting the Internet control panel.

Working with the Personal Tab

When you use the Internet Setup Assistant to set up your Internet system on Mac OS 8.5, your user ID, password, company name, username, and email information is automatically entered into the Internet control panel. The Personal tab contains your username, ID, password, and company name information (refer back to Figure 18.11). In addition, you can add a signature to your name by typing a message in the Signature text box. Using signatures is a fun way to tell a little about yourself, and they're included in your emails when you select Internet Config as your configuration manager in your browser.

> For some reason, Netscape Communicator does not support Internet Config's (and hence Internet control panel's) Signature text box. In order to use signatures in Netscape Communicator, you must place your signature data in a SimpleText file and identify the file to Communicator in its Messenger preferences screen.

Working with the Email Tab

As is the case with the Personal tab, information is automatically entered for you in the Email tab when you set up your Internet connection (see Figure 18.12). In addition, you can select how you want to be alerted when you receive mail by selecting the appropriate check box for either a flashing icon, an alert box, or a sound.

Use this tab to set your default email program. Apple has made an agreement with Microsoft to make OutLook Express the default email program, but you don't have to stick with it. If you want to change programs, choose Select from the Default Email pop-up menu. In the resulting Finder Open dialog box, select another email program such as Netscape Communicator, Qualcomm's Eudora Pro or Eudora Lite, or whatever your organization uses. The new program will now automatically appear in the Default Email pop-up menu.

FIGURE 18.12.

The Email screen lets you select a default email program. It also lists your email user information as well as preferences.

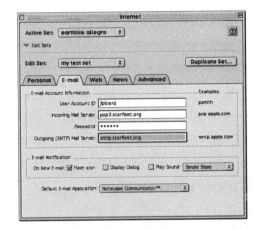

Working with the Web Tab

The Web tab, shown in Figure 18.13, lets you pick a home page and search page that will automatically open whenever you invoke your browser. This tab is also used to select a default browser and to set up color options for types of links (active, selected, used, and default). Whichever browser you've selected has its own default home page that appears in the Home Page text box. If you don't like this page, copy a URL from a portal you do like and paste the data into this text box. For example, I don't like to use Netscape's Netcenter home page as my portal to the Internet because it does not offer enough news. I've changed my home page to http://my.excite.com. This is all up to your personal preference. Home page/portal sites are the latest war zone for the hearts and minds of users. You should change yours often so you can sample many types of sites.

SETTING A DEFAULT BROWSER

Note that Mac OS 8.5 dutifully assigns Microsoft Internet Explorer 4.01 as your default browser. Choose Select from the Default Web Browser pull-down menu to locate your copy of Netscape Navigator 4.0 or Communicator (if you want to use that browser instead). Once you've specified an alternate browser, it's easy to use the pull-down menu to switch browsers.

FIGURE 18.13.

*The Web screen lets
you select a home page
and search page as
well as a default
browser.*

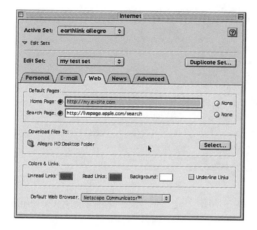

Using Other Internet Configuration Tabs

Two additional tabs appear on the Internet control panel: News and Advanced (note that you cannot use the Advanced tab without first changing user modes by selecting User Modes from the Edit menu and then selecting Advanced). The News tab controls information about newsgroups. See Hour 19, "Using the Internet," for a discussion of how to work with these older Internet areas.

The Advanced tab lets you adjust FTP, helper file, font, and server settings—subjects that are beyond the scope of this book. Use your browser manual to learn how to change these settings.

Getting Ready for the Web

Now you're ready to get on the Web. How do you dial your modem? How do you know you've connected correctly? How do you tell your Mac which browser to use once you are connected? Ah, more problems to solve!

Dialing the Internet

You have a few ways available to you for dialing into the Internet. For example, there's the hard way, a not-so-confusing way, and a relatively easy way.

First, the hard way. Open the Remote Access control panel, shown in Figure 18.14, and click Connect.

18

FIGURE 18.14.

Use Remote Access to dial up your ISP.

Next, the easier but less informative way is to click the ARA icon on your Control Strip and select Connect from the resulting pop-up menu. This way provides very little information concerning the status of the call, but it does confirm a proper connection once you've reached your server (a little network symbol appears under the icon). When you quit your browser, click Disconnect to hang up the modem.

Directly related to the Control Strip are two other ways to dial: You can use the Remote Access Status application on the Apple menu or you can double-click the Browse the Internet AppleScript on the desktop (this script can also be selected from the Internet Access pop-up menu on the Apple menu). The Remote Access Status desk accessory, shown in Figure 18.15, is very similar to the old Internet Dialer included with the Apple Internet Connection Kit. You can use the window to connect and disconnect from the Internet as well as keep track of how long you've been connected.

FIGURE 18.15.

Use the Remote Access Status desk accessory to connect and disconnect from the Internet.

The Browse the Internet icon on your desktop and Apple menu opens your browser and then dials the Internet via an AppleScript.

Finally, let's say you want to get quickly in and out of the Internet and you know exactly where you're going. In this case, you can use the Connect To command on the Internet Access pop-up menu on the Apple menu. (See Figure 18.16.)

FIGURE 18.16.

Use the Connect To command on the Apple menu item to dial the Internet from any application.

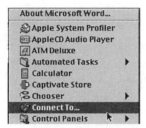

For example, let's say you're reading an article in Adobe Acrobat and want to get more information about a certain topic in the article. You can copy the URL from the screen, paste it in the Connect To dialog box, click Connect, and away you go. You can then copy information from the Web and read it at your leisure offline. When you are done, just quit the browser to return to your previous document.

Now That You're In

If you've successfully dialed up your ISP, your browser will display your default URL or startup page (it's called the *startup page* because this is the first Web page your browser downloads whenever you connect to the Internet).

> Note that all these various ways of connecting assume you've set up the Remote Access control panel to automatically open your browser after you dial or to dial whenever you open your browser. To set up Remote Access, open the control panel and click Options. Then click the Protocols tab and select the check box Connect Automatically Whenever Starting TCP/IP Applications. With this option selected, any time you open your browser, PPP will automatically dial into the Internet. In fact, PPP will dial from any application that requires an Internet connection, such as games, Fetch, Eudora, Outlook Express, and so on.

Now you can move around the World Wide Web. But how? One way is to use the arcane addressing system known as the *Universal Resource Locator* (or *URL*). You can also go to a page you've previously identified as a Favorite (MSIE) or Bookmark (Navigator) by selecting that page from your Favorites/Bookmarks menu or toolbar button.

Welcome to the Browser Wars

Today, 90 percent of all Internet users use commercial browsers rather than home-grown varieties. Commercial browsers are increasing in capabilities as to what they can interpret and display. Microsoft and Netscape are competing to create the ultimate browsing machine. Microsoft offers Internet Explorer, whereas Netscape provides Netscape Navigator.

Microsoft Internet Explorer 4.01 for the Macintosh, shown in Figure 18.17, is included on the Mac OS 8.5 CD-ROM. This browser is entering its fourth iteration as a suite of tools that can be used to browse Web pages and online multimedia, as well as to email, chat, publish, and conference. It also incorporates new concepts such as the ability to select the information you want to view and have it download on a scheduled basis to your computer (this is known as *push technology*).

FIGURE 18.17.

Internet Explorer is a popular browser from Microsoft.

Microsoft has made an agreement with Apple that Mac OS 8.5 should include Microsoft Internet Explorer as the default browser. This means that unless you consciously change browsers, you'll be using Internet Explorer. Also note that you can download a free copy of the newest version of Microsoft's browser from http://www.microsoft.com/ie/download/. You can also get the update by ordering a CD-ROM from that site.

Netscape Navigator 4.0 (which does not include Netscape Messenger email or the other members of the Netscape suite) is also included on the Mac OS 8.5 CD-ROM (see Figure 18.18). You can download a free copy of Netscape Communicator 4.04 (which includes the entire suite) from http://www.netscape.com/download/index.html.

WATCH THAT MEMORY AND DISK SPACE!

As more bells and whistles are added to these browsers (for example, the ability to send and receive HTML in email, play real-time audio and video files, and so on), they get bigger and therefore require more real estate on your Mac. Netscape Navigator wants 12 MB of memory and takes up almost 7 MB of hard disk. Communicator is even larger. Microsoft Internet Explorer is less of a memory hog, but it still takes up about 10 MB or more of your precious disk space (Internet Explorer 4.0 with all its components takes up about 40 MB of hard disk space).

FIGURE **18.18.**

*Netscape
Communicator is a
fourth generation
browser package.*

Summary

In this hour, we reviewed those portions of Mac OS 8.5 that let you surf the Web almost
as an extension of your operating system. I covered how the Internet works and presented information on how to get connected. I also reviewed how to use the Internet Setup
Assistant to make your TCP/IP settings virtually failsafe. In addition, I showed you the
many ways to access the Internet from your Mac as well as how to navigate the Web
once you're there. Finally, I described some third-party software that will enhance your
Internet experience and discussed some of the technologies on the horizon.

Term Review

browser   The software that resides on your Mac to translate codes downloaded from
the Internet and use them to display Web pages. The browser serves as the intermediary
between your computer and the Internet.

DNS (Domain Name Server)   One of the components of a Web server that translates
IP addresses into understandable Web site names.

domain   A single Web server.

Internet   The international network of networks of computers.

ISP (Internet Service Provider)   A company that leases connections to the Internet by providing you with a server address you can dial into from your Mac.

Microsoft Internet Explorer   Microsoft's fourth generation browser, which comes as the default browser with Mac OS 8.5.

Netscape Communicator   Netscape's fourth generation browser that's actually a suite of several integrated applications.

Netscape Navigator   The browser portion of Netscape Communicator. Navigator is now offered independently of Communicator for those users who want a slim browser and do not require email, collaboration, construction, and push services.

Open Transport   The Mac OS architecture developed to manage AppleTalk and TCP/IP protocols.

POP   The point of presence connection (the local telephone number you use to dial up your ISP's server).

PPP (Point-to-Point Protocol)   A connection protocol for use with modems.

TCP/IP (Transmission Control Protocol/Internet Protocol)   The IP portion of TCP/IP lets multiple processes communicate with each other over a network using packet-switching technology. This part enables multiple networks to connect to form internet-works by routing data via datagrams (packets of information routed over a common network). The TCP portion of the network standard manages how dissimilar computers speak to one another.

URL (Uniform Resource Locator)   An address used to identify Web pages based on translations performed by the domain name server.

World Wide Web   A way of viewing the Internet that allows the display of graphics, sounds, movies, and color on your computer.

Q&A

Q How do I find out the best deal for Internet access?

A The answer really depends on the purpose for which you're going to use the Internet. If you need email, want a community of forums and chat rooms, and will only be briefly browsing, a commercial provider (such as America Online) is probably your best bet. If you find yourself spending a lot of time browsing and have a

18

hankering for designing your own Web site or starting a business, the different rate plans offered by ISPs is for you.

Q How do I find an ISP?

A The Internet Setup Assistant will dial a central database at Apple and assist you in selecting and setting up a new ISP. Both Netscape Navigator and Microsoft Internet Explorer (using the Internet Connection Wizard included with IE4, which is automatically installed with Mac OS 8.5) provide startup tools to assist you in selecting an ISP. Be aware that the ISPs who list with these three companies have paid for the privilege, so they might not provide you with the best price.

Most computer magazines, software, and even newspapers these days come stuffed with CD-ROMs from national ISPs, such as EarthLink and AT&T. Most ISPs offer you a limited access to check them out before they bill you. Also, the business sections of newspapers are full of ads for local ISPs, such as Erols in the Washington, D.C. area. Try your local Yellow Pages as well.

Q What's going on with the so-called Browser wars?

A Life is getting interesting. Microsoft Internet Explorer has gained about 56 percent of the browsing market (and is sure to grow with the introduction of Windows 98 and its integrated browser). Netscape has taken a new tactic: It has integrated its browser with active information on a new portal Web site called *Netcenter* (`http://home.netcenter.com`). Netcenter can be personalized to your browsing preferences. Netscape Communicator 5 (available as this book is being published) will include software that lets you perform customized searches and collect favorite sites interactively.

Workshop

The Workshop contains quiz questions to help you solidify your understanding of the material covered. You can find the answers to the quiz questions in Appendix B, "Quiz Answers."

Quiz

1. How do you switch browsers from the default browser?
2. How do you access the Internet Setup Assistant?
3. How do you find the proper local telephone number to use to call your ISP's server?
4. What happens if you forget your password or user ID?

5. What's the easiest way to hang up after an Internet session?

6. How do you maintain more than one Internet configuration on your Mac?

7. What's a home page?

8. How do you make the Internet Connection icon stop flashing?

9. How do you make the Email icon flash?

10. How do you select a folder to use to receive downloads?

18

Hour **19**

Using the Internet

The Mac operating system has always supported easy-to-use networking. Mac OS 8.5's Open Transport technology provides almost seamless connections to the Internet by melding Apple's proprietary AppleTalk networking architecture with the open architecture of the Internet (known as *TCP/IP*). This hour continues the discussion of Internet services from the last hour and covers the following topics:

- A deeper look at what exactly the Internet is
- An introduction to Internet services and the software required to support them—electronic mail, conferencing, newsgroups, and chatting
- An introduction to Apple's new Data Detector technology using Internet Address Detectors

What Is the Internet?

The *Internet* is a conglomeration of computers linked by myriad networks into a baffling, decentralized global network. An *intranet* is a corporation's version of the Internet—an internal "Internet" for that organization.

The Internet and intranets provide several types of services to their members, all based on the capability to pass information along wires and other telecommunications equipment between disparate computers and have the contents of these information packets understood and usable on the other side. Internet services are functional, meaning they provide ways to use the Internet technology. You can use the Internet to perform the following types of tasks:

- **Electronic mail.** The reason most people connect to the Internet is to pass messages between computers. The ability to send and receive data almost instantaneously between two points no matter where they are in the world makes email one of the most compelling uses of the Internet.

- **Research.** The second reason most people connect to the Internet is to perform research. The use of hypertext and interactive images makes retrieval of information almost instantaneous, opening the Internet to be used as a medium for broadcasting news and entertainment, corporate information, research data and images, advertising, consumer goods, and on and on.

- **Discussion.** One of the oldest uses of the Internet involves a form of email that's broadcast to many people at once—newsgroups. Just think of an interest and you'll probably find a group of people who are receiving and responding to lists of messages about this subject via a listserver. Once you subscribe to a newsgroup, you receive all the messages submitted by members of the group within a certain time period, which is determined by the group's system operator (or *sysop*). You can read threads of queries and responses using a news browser. This is usually included in your browser software as an adjunct to your email browser.

- **Chatting.** This is the capability to send and receive messages in real-time. Remember, email allows you to send and receive messages as packets of information that you must open, reply to, and send back to an address. Chatting lets a group of people get together anywhere in the world and type messages to each other over the Internet. There are chat rooms for just about every interest. You need special software to use the Internet to chat, however. One of the most common Mac chatting tools is called *Global Chat*, a piece of shareware typically provided by your Internet Service Provider (ISP).

- **Interactive games.** One of the fastest growing features of the Internet is the ability to play computer games in real-time. Online gaming is an adjunct to chat rooms and newsgroups, melding the WWW with a dose of virtual reality thrown in for good measure. Games such as Doom and Bungie's Marathon are played using client software (games that reside on your Mac) and a modem connection to the Internet. Responses to your moves are reflected in your game as they happen.

LIFE ON THE NET

Like an isolated tribe, the Internet has developed its own language and culture. The collective knowledge of how to behave on the Internet is termed *netiquette*. Basic netiquette rules follow:

- Be a lurker and just read along for a few days before jumping into a mailing list or Usenet group. Learn what topics are appropriate to query and how not to repeat stale topics.

- Read the FAQs before responding. FAQs are a series of basic questions and answers that give you background information about a group. Knowledge of FAQs lets you be "in the know" and not repeat universal knowledge or ask silly questions.

- DON'T TYPE IN CAPITAL LETTERS. Typing in capitals is considered shouting and is very impolite. If you mean to emphasis a word, type it all in caps or place asterisks around it.

- If you want to quote someone else's message within your message, don't copy the entire quote but rather the snippets you want to comment on. Keep your posts short.

- Don't broadcast if you mean to send a message to a single individual. Respond to Sender and not to the entire list.

If you follow these rules, you can avoid two pernicious responses from obnoxious mailing list members: flaming and spamming. *Flaming* is the stuffing of your mailbox with very hostile and personally nasty posts. *Spamming* is the sending of junk mail over the Internet (offers of business opportunities, unwanted press releases, and worse).

Enter the World Wide Web

19

The World Wide Web is a front-end system to data, not a place or network. It provides a way to intuitively navigate through tons of data via pictures and hypertext. The invention of the Web (the `http:` you see in URLs when you surf the Web indicates that you're using this method to communicate on the Internet) provided a way to move around the Internet by exchanging documents via hyperlinks (internal and external computer addresses included with the documents). It was revolutionary.

By 1992, one million host computers were connected to the Internet. The public's interest in using these networks to communicate was astounding. Today (mid 1998), there are more than 10 million Web users.

Browsers and the Web

The Web is simply a way of looking at the Internet. This vast network consists of computers that manage data and the communications links via software and hardware called *servers.* Web servers receive requests for information, go out and find the data in their databases, and return the proper "pages" of data to the requesting computer.

The operating systems that run the server computers can vary. The challenge of early efforts to share information was cutting through this operating system Tower of Babel to share information between dissimilar computer environments. HTTP was developed as a way to find information and retrieve it over telephone lines in a coherent fashion.

The revolutionary portion of HTTP is the separation of collecting data from displaying the data. On your computer, a *Web browser* translates what is sent over the wires into the pictures and words you see onscreen as a Web page. Figure 19.1 shows Apple's home page as an example of such a display.

FIGURE 19.1.

The browser controls how a page appears on your computer screen.

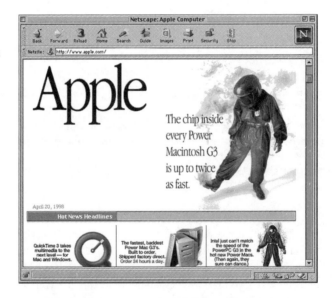

How did browsers come to be? Early users of the Internet, prior to the advent of HTTP, had to be UNIX gurus to understand UNIX communications protocols, because in order to communicate with another computer using the Internet, you still had to deal with the server software to query and receive information. Data coming across the Internet was in textual form, because nothing stood between you and the server except UNIX.

What's more, the question of how to increase the amount of data that crossed a limited amount of bandwidth could not go unanswered. Computer science students began to write programs that could understand the HTTP protocol. These browsers served as intermediaries between the server and the user.

Print shops already were accepting print jobs on tape from their clients about this time. The digital version of a print job used tags to tell the printers how to output data (as a paragraph, a list, or a citation, for example). This tagging method was called *Standard Generalized Markup Language (SGML)*. Computer scientists looked at SGML and simplified it considerably. This simplified version of the markup tags was to travel with the data and be interpreted by the retrieving software—the browser. This was the first HTML language.

Hypertext (such as Apple's HyperCard) supplied ways to connect disparate pieces of data that resided on separate computers using more tags. Together, the hypertext and display tags tell the computer how to interpret Internet documents. This came to be known as *Hypertext Markup Language (HTML)* and is the standard way to tag pages of information traveling over the Internet via the Web.

Hypertext was revolutionary, because it freed up bandwidth by enabling a piece of software, called a *browser*, that resides on each client computer to interpret tags and properly display data a page at a time. Two main browsers have become ubiquitous: Netscape Navigator and Microsoft Internet Explorer. As these browsers matured, they became more powerful interpreters, able to translate and display movies, animation, sounds, and pictures as well as hypertext links. In addition, as with all software today, more and more programs are now packed into the browser packages: conferencing, email, Web page design, server push support (channels), as well as Java Virtual Machines. With Windows 98 and Mac OS 8.5, browsers are becoming more and more integrated into the basic operating systems that run the computers.

Using Commercial Online Services

19

Commercial online services, such as America Online (AOL) and its subsidiary CompuServe, offer gateways to the Internet. To access the Internet as well as the rest of the service, you need to set up an account. AOL and CompuServe supply free access software through attachments to computer magazines, by mail, or in stores. Part of the access software is a browser for connecting to the Web. Both online services also enable you to publish your own Web page. Apple makes it very easy to use AOL by including its software (version 3.0) on the Mac OS 8.1 CD-ROM. Note that Mac OS 8.5 does not include AOL software, but every magazine about Macs usually includes an AOL CD-ROM.

Using AOL

I'm going to talk predominantly about AOL because it's the most Mac-friendly service. CompuServe offers Internet access but is less user-friendly and Mac friendly than AOL. You can count Prodigy out of the equation entirely, because it doesn't really provide Mac-friendly software.

AOL is a very popular way to surf the Net. For this reason, you might find it difficult to gain access to AOL or the Internet at certain times of the day.

AOL can be accessed in two ways: via its own TCP/IP software, called *AOLLink*, that it installs in your Extensions folder, or via Open Transport and Remote Access if you've already set up an ISP account. Note that if you do have Mac OS 8.5's Remote Access/Open Transport upgrade and an ISP account, AOLLink will not work. You can install AOL with Open Transport by not using AOLLink and connecting to AOL via your Remote Access software as described in the previous hour.

In either case, be sure to click the Setup button on AOL's Welcome dialog box and select TCP as your linking method in the resulting Setup dialog box. (See Figure 19.2.)

FIGURE 19.2.

Use the Setup dialog box to use ARA and your ISP account to link to AOL.

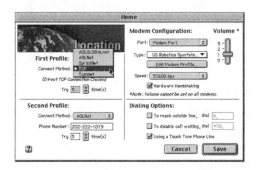

AOL uses a modified version of Microsoft Internet Explorer that lacks a mail tool and some of the commercial browser's other bells and whistles, such as built-in search engines, a robust bookmark system, and so on (see Figure 19.3). Note that you can still use Netscape or IE in addition to the AOL connection. Also, AOL has its own mail software built into it.

FIGURE 19.3.

AOL's browser is a rudimentary version of Microsoft Internet Explorer.

AOL uses the metaphor of a television channel to identify its various interest areas. Each channel offers both proprietary and public (Web-based) areas. When you click a red swirl symbol (designating an AOL link), AOL automatically invokes its browser and takes you to the designated Web site. You can also reach sites that you specify by selecting the World Wide Web area on the Internet channel. Type a URL in the text box and press the Go to the Web button, and AOL takes you to your specified site.

AOL offers an extensive array of search engines via the Web page displayed in Figure 19.3 (http://www.aol.com). AOL also provides descriptions of its user's favorite sites to guide you in your perusing endeavors.

Email and AOL

AOL provides a very good email system, which includes attachment capabilities. AOL email accepts inline images and the posting of Web pages or URLs within its messages. Click the red flag in the right corner of the window to attach a page to the Clipboard for future use. To attach files to AOL email, you can also drag and drop them into the attachment window/tab area of the email.

You can send mail to recipients using other services by knowing their email addresses. If you use AOL as your mailbox, your address is *YourAOLName*@aol.com. One neat thing about Mac OS 8.5 is that the Mail icon on the desktop lets you automatically download mail from AOL at scheduled times without having to actually enter AOL. In addition, you can send email to other AOL users by only using their account name (for example JLPicard instead of JLPicard@aol.com).

19

Web Page Publishing Using AOL

AOL provides two options for publishing Web pages: *My Home Page* for beginners and *My Place* for Webmasters. My Home Page is a template where you fill in the blanks to create a single page. You cannot add anything to the format provided by AOL. You're allowed up to five free screen names of up to 2 MB each per account.

You can upload graphics to your page using AOL's proprietary file transfer program. Modifying the page can be costly because you can only make changes to the page while online.

For more serious Web page builders, AOL offers the more advanced area called My Place. You can create your Web site using Adobe PageMill (or any other HTML editor) and upload it to the area. You use an online utility to manage your files, and you need to know UNIX to work with subdirectories to the directories created by AOL's program. My Place is an anonymous FTP site where any files or directories you create become accessible to anyone who knows your screen names (although you do have a private directory).

> **WEB SURFING AND PUBLISHING VIA COMPUSERVE**
>
> CompuServe uses a less-integrated system to access the Web. You must set up a separate PPP connection and launch individual Internet applications (a Web browser, Telnet software for communicating with the server, Usenet newsgroup software, file transfer protocol (FTP) software, and so forth). CompuServe provides Web site space in an area called *Our World*. You can build very creative Web sites offline and upload your files to CompuServe's server. You're allocated 1 MB of hard disk space at no extra charge, but no additional space is available. Also, you cannot import HTML pages from outside the program.

Growing Beyond AOL

AOL works great if you're interested in small snippets of information about a topic or have only a few emails to send or receive daily. AOL provides connections to software companies, entertainment companies, shopping, travel, and chat rooms. Each channel provides newsgroup forums as well as links to selected Web sites related to that channel. AOL also provides message boards for discussion as well as access to Internet news-groups. Also, many special interest groups, services, and magazines are available (in other words, e-commerce is alive and well on AOL).

AOL limits the amount of information you can find on a topic to those vendors who have signed up to be participants. For example, *MacWorld* retains a presence on AOL, whereas

MacWeek does not. Therefore, if you're looking for articles on Mac topics, you won't have access to Ziff-Davis publications on AOL; instead, you must link to the Web using the Internet Channel's WWW area where you can type `http://www.zdnet.com/macweek`. Unfortunately, AOL's method of gaining access to alternative sources of information outside its proprietary world is clumsy and slow.

When you find yourself linking to the Web more than you're using AOL's channels, you've probably are outgrowing AOL and are ready to move up to the grownup world of ISPs. Refer to Hour 18, "Entering The Internet," for a discussion of how to get an Internet Service Provider (ISP).

Other Internet Services

As you've probably noticed by now, the whole world is turning to the Internet for functions that used to be handled by individual proprietary software packages. The most important shift in functionality has occurred in how electronic mail is handled within offices and outside organizations.

Very recently, companies began abandoning proprietary closed email systems such as cc:Mail from Lotus (IBM), Microsoft Mail, or other similar software and turning to the Internet (and intranets) to handle email. The most popular use for the Internet is email, and Netscape and Microsoft is very aware of this fact. Browsers from these two companies are beefing up the quality of their electronic mail packages to support old and new features, such as filters to avoid spamming, automatic address book updates, mail scheduling features, and embedded HTML. Meanwhile, other software companies are selling individual Internet email systems that provide even more enhanced features.

The other categories of Internet communications that are popular are Usenet newsgroups and chat rooms. Browsers are beefing up the feature set to support filters, sorting, and embedded HTML in newsgroups, as well as three-dimensional (virtual reality) chat rooms with avatars (the characters that represent you and the other users in these rooms). Let's look at some of these developments in email, Usenets, mailing lists, and chat rooms.

Electronic Mail

Two ways are currently available to transmit messages between computers using the Internet: general-purpose electronic mail packages operating via ISPs (such as Qualcomm's Eudora Lite or Pro or Microsoft Outlook Express) and proprietary email systems built into commercial online services (such as CompuServe or America Online).

19

Browsers also provide email functions that are a subset of the general-purpose email managers. However, there are good and bad points to both these systems. The other email system alternative is a closed loop with gateways to the Internet, such as First Class or CE Software's QuickMail. Although it's more difficult to send mail and file attachments through the gateways accurately, proprietary closed systems are more manageable for system administrators than open systems based on the Internet, because anyone can send anything to anybody at any time on the Internet.

General-Purpose Email Managers

The upside of general-purpose software is that each package has been designed specifically for its function. Therefore, although you have to switch back and forth between a Web browser, Telnet remote connection program, mail manager/reader, and news reader, each program is more friendly and has a larger feature set than can be packed into browser suites.

One benefit provided by general-purpose programs is that retrieval of email can be automated. Your email manager can be programmed to go online at specified times and automatically download your mail, sort it, and present it in an organized way offline that makes it easier for you to manage. Another benefit of standalone systems is that some will respond to specified mail with automatic replies or will automatically trash junk mail based on preset criteria (a great solution for *spamming*, the sending of gobs of unrequested emails).

Mac OS 8.1 comes bundled with Claris Emailer version 4. Mac OS 8.5 uses Microsoft Outlook Express as its default email program. A real boon is a new feature of Mac OS 8.5 that lets you open your default email program from your desktop by clicking the Mail icon. You set your default email by selecting a program from the Email screen of the Internet control panel. Clicking Mail opens the default email program (in this case Outlook Express), and if you're not online, it dials your ISP via Remote Access. The email program (if set up to do so) can then send and receive mail very rapidly without having to actually load an Internet browser or commercial service.

Free Email

A very new offering from large search engines is free email. Bigfoot (www.bigfoot.com), Excite (www.excite.com), and Yahoo (www.yahoo.com) offer mailboxes on their systems and the ability to forward your mail from an assortment of email addresses to your free mailbox. Today, just about any portal site offers their own mailboxes, including e-greetings (www.outpost.com), hotmail (www.microsoft.com), ivillage (www.parentsoup.com), Disney (www.disney.com), and so forth. Watch out for these Web-based emails because they're not secure. Information may be sent directly across the Internet without encryption, unless the email service states that it uses secure sockets (SSL). Don't send anything you wouldn't want someone else to read.

Commercial Mail Services

America Online and CompuServe maintain internal email systems. Whenever you see an Internet address of *somebody*@aol.com or *1234.234*@compuserve.com, you know you're going through a gateway to these proprietary services. Mail managers such as those within Netscape Navigator and Microsoft Internet Explorer are able to send and receive email from commercial online services. As stated previously, Claris Emailer can even poll commercial services on a set schedule to retrieve email.

Usenet Newsgroups

Newsgroups are the place where you must tread lightly, because around every bend is a weird or eclectic group of people talking to each other via words and emoticons. Usenet newsgroups provided some of the earliest uses of the Internet for communication.

Every newsgroup is part of a hierarchy of groups. The top-most level of the hierarchy are Usenet sites with names beginning in .sci, .talk, and .soc. Within these categories you'll find sites covering almost any topic imaginable, organized into three basic areas: alternative newsgroups (identified by the prefix .alt), standard newsgroups (identified by the prefixes .comp, .misc, .news, and .rec), and local newsgroups (set up for the benefit of a local community, organization, or university). Local newsgroups can have any name.

Sometimes these groups are made accessible to the general public (in fact all of the "junky" names you see in your newsreader are probably local newsgroups). Table 19.1 presents a general definition of the contents of some of the Usenet prefixed groups.

19

TABLE 19.1. USENET PREFIX DEFINITIONS.

Prefix	Contents
.alt	Alternative newsgroups that can be founded and managed by any Internet user
.biz	Another alternative newsgroup type dedicated to discussing business news, marketing, and advertising
.comp	A standard newsgroup maintained by a Usenet site
.misc	A standard newsgroup in which anything can be discussed that doesn't fit into other categories
.news	A Usenet site
.rec	A standard newsgroup where discussions center on hobbies and sports

continues

TABLE 19.1. CONTINUED

Prefix	Contents
.sci	A standard newsgroup dealing with science topics
.soc	A standard newsgroup dealing with social issues and socializing
.talk	A standard newsgroup dealing with social issues

Usenet can handle only basic text. You can send graphics, sounds, and animation as *binaries* that must be decoded by your newsgroup reader software.

The two main browsers provide newsgroup readers. Internet Explorer's reader is called News and can be accessed in Outlook Express. Netscape Communicator's newsgroup reader is called Collabra. Figure 19.4 shows you a screenshot of the message center within Collabra. Note that it closely resembles Netscape Messenger. Both newsreaders list Usenets by their hierarchical names. Search for a group by its top-level prefix and then burrow down within a newsgroup by its subname listings (typically depicted as a name separated by a period, such as alt.tv.highlander. Subscribe to groups that interest you. Subscribing merely copies the newsgroup's name to your message center for easier access.

FIGURE 19.4.

Netscape Collabra is one of many newsgroup reader applications that lets you manage the thousands of Usenet posts available for reading.

Chat Rooms

Newsgroups present interactive communication on a delayed basis, whereas chat rooms provide interactive communication almost in real-time. (I say *almost* because you type furiously to send your message to a group of people who then furiously type a message back for you to be read line by line). WebChat is a Macintosh-based system run by the Internet Roundtable Society that experiments with the sending of images along with text during chats. Check out `www.irsociety.com/webchat/talkform.html`. Excite (`www.excite.com`) runs many "chat rooms" where people with similar interests can gather to exchange information.

There are two types of chats. The first type I call *static* chats, because they resemble newsgroups in that you send a query out to the group and wait for someone to submit a response. Figure 19.5 shows you this type of chatting.

FIGURE 19.5.

Chatting can resemble Usenet newsgroups, only Web-based.

The second type, the *classic* chat room, is fully interactive. Netscape Navigator and Internet Explorer both offer Java-based chat engines that let you type messages in real-time.

19

Although it's mostly safe, the Internet does have some demons lurking on it (just as there are everywhere in society). They seem to show up most often in chat rooms and Usenet newsgroups. In chat rooms, everyone is anonymous and no one is who they seem to be. Therefore, you can get caught in situations you would never get caught in if you were chatting face to face with a group of people. Vile language, innuendo, smut, and stupidity run rampant. In addition, most of what you read is rumor and cannot be believed. Be cautious and politic when using chat rooms and Usenets. Here are some key points to keep in mind:

- Don't give out your address and telephone number
- Don't indicate where you live
- Don't give out your email address
- Avoid providing your true identity
- Stay away from chat rooms or Usenets whose subjects you feel uncomfortable about
- Leave if you don't like what you're reading
- Use a filter such as SurfWatch, which comes with Internet Explorer, to screen out Usenets and chat rooms you feel are inappropriate for children.

Using Apple Data Detectors

Mac OS 8.5 can be augmented with a new software tool called the *Apple Data Detector*. *Data detectors* are small programs that use the Apple Data Detector 1.0.2 software to locate currency rates, information about cities or states, or open Internet addresses.

These clever pieces of software can scan selected text in a document and perform actions with the results it finds. Data detectors are AppleScripts (of which you'll read more about in Hour 22, "Automating Your Mac with AppleScript") that automate the finding and processing of information.

So far, Apple has developed three data detector applications: Internet Address Detector, Currency Detector, and U.S. Geographic Detector. Because Internet Address Detector (IAD) relates the most to the subject of this hour, we'll take a closer look at this neat product.

You can get a copy of IAD from
`http://applescript.apple.com/data_detectors/detectors.00.html`. IAD includes
the required Apple Data Detector 1.0.2 software. IAD recognizes URLs, email addresses,
Internet host names, FTP sites, and newsgroups. The software will open a URL and save
the URL or its contents to a file on your hard drive, create a new email message and send
it to the identified email address, open a Telnet connection to an Internet host for conferencing, retrieve a file from an FTP site, or read an identified newsgroup's entries.

Figure 19.6 shows you how IAD works. Highlight paragraphs in a document where you
know URLs, email addresses, and so forth are listed. IAD is a contextual menu. Pressing
Control while clicking activates IAD, presenting you with a contextual menu of options.
Select an option, such as Mark as a Bookmark in Netscape Navigator, and IAD performs
this task.

FIGURE 19.6.

IAD acts on Internet sites while still in a document.

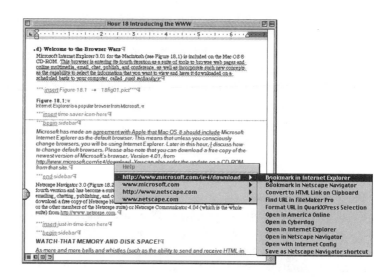

You can specifically target IAD to identify and act on certain Internet URLs, email
addresses, and so forth by selecting them in the Apple Data Detectors control panel (see
Figure 19.7). This control panel lets you adjust the Apple Data Detector software to recognize any new detector you install. Apple is encouraging third-party vendors to write
detectors to cover any research item you may need. For example, the current stock price
of Apple can be captured from the Internet and placed in your document given the proper
detector. This is ground-breaking stuff.

FIGURE 19.7.

Use the Apple Data Detectors control panel to identify the data you want captured and the actions you want taken.

Uploading and Downloading Documents

One of the joys of the Internet is access to software and information almost immediately. The vehicle for getting these items is another portion of the Internet known as a *File Transfer Protocol (FTP) site*. Here's where the speed of your modem and the popularity of the software may conspire to make your experience exasperatingly slow. Today's software is very large (even in compressed form), and FTP sites are crowded during evening hours. This makes getting software, such as Apple's updates, from online sites such as `http://info.apple.com/` or `http://www.cnet.com/download.com/` take a long time. For example, a 10MB program such as Netscape Navigator may take two hours to download. Just be warned. However, you can find lots of stuff worth reading offline via downloading.

The Mac OS 8.5 makes it relatively easy to download short items because even though most documents or software programs have been compressed for quicker transfer, Aladdin's StuffIt Expander is included in the Apple Internet Connection Kit. This software not only decompresses almost every compression format known to computers, but it translates BinHex files (encoded files) into a readable format that can then be decompressed. All of this is done automatically and quickly. Just tell your browser where to put the download so you don't loose the file on your computer. I make a folder called Downloads and place it on my desktop or with my browser software and direct all materials to that folder.

Uploading files to a server is a whole other matter. You may want to send material to an FTP site or upload a Web site to your ISP's server. For this, you need special software.

After you've determined where you want to publish your Web site, you need to upload the files to the Web server. This is a two-step process: setting up a folder or directory to store your Web site files and actually uploading the files. The uploading of files is beyond the scope of this book.

Using Fetch to Upload Files

The following paragraphs assume that you'll be communicating with a UNIX server, because this is the most popular server system (with Windows NT servers coming in a close second). Setting up the UNIX server for your Web site entails working with Telnet (or similar terminal emulation software) to communicate with the UNIX operating system and work with the FTP server to send folders and documents to the correct directories. Assuming you're installing your Web site on an ISP's UNIX-based system, use Fetch (http://www.dartmouth.edu/pages/softdev/fetch.html) or a similar FTP utility to manage the task.

You must speak to the ISP (or the system administrator of your organization) to set up an account with a user ID and password prior to uploading. Find out how to gain an account and what the rules for working with your server are before you start.

Note that many ISPs do not allow you to upload files but rather make you use their proprietary HTML editors to build home pages. Find out if you can upload home pages prior to beginning the uploading process. You might find you can bypass the Telnet session because your provider has preselected a remote directory for your use.

Summary

This hour covered the rest of the Internet and its relationship with Mac OS 8.5. As you can see, you can reach out and touch people in many ways directly from your desktop. Email lets you collect mail and send mail from your desktop's default mail program or browser. Usenets let you converse with people having similar interests. Lists let you receive these conversations via email either as separate missives or as digests. Chat rooms let you converse in real-time with your peers. Tying all these communication methods together is the new Apple Data Detector applications, which automate the collection of information from within documents.

19

Term Review

America Online (AOL)   AOL is a commercial online service that provides exclusive e-commerce services, special interest groups, chat forums, message boards, as well as a gateway to newsgroups, Web pages and email on the internet, all for a monthly fee (similar to an ISP).

AOLLink   AOL's point of presence (POP) gateway on to the Internet for use with commercial browsers such as Netscape Navigator or Microsoft Internet Explorer.

Apple Data Detector   A new component of Mac OS 8.5 providing the ability to scan a document and act on the results of the scan. Apple Data Detector works with AppleScript to provide services such as opening a URL cited in a document in your browser, getting information about identified topics from the Internet, and creating bookmarks. Three data detectors are currently available: Internet Addresses, U.S. Geography, and Currency.

CE Software QuickMail   An electronic mail package for the Macintosh that uses dedicated LANs to transmit messages. QuickMail provides a gateway to the Internet for transmission of electronic mail.

chat room   An environment where subscribed users can type messages back and forth in real-time on identified topics.

Claris Emailer   The proprietary electronic mail package that comes bundled with Mac OS 8.5.

electronic mail   Provides the ability to transmit messages and files over telephone lines and dedicated wires via the Internet.

emoticons   Icons used in electronic mail and newsgroup messages that provide a quick way to express an emotion.

First Class   A commercial proprietary electronic mail system with a gateway to the Internet.

flaming   The act of sending angry and hostile messages to a person.

free mail   A new service offered on the Web (mostly by search engines such as Excite, Yahoo, and Outpost) that provides a universal mailbox where you can receive all your consolidated electronic mail messages.

gateway   A software doorway from a proprietary local area network service on to the Internet.

Internet Address Detector   An Apple Data Detector component that provides a way to open identified Web pages directly in documents.

listserv   An Internet server dedicated to managing mailing list transmissions. You subscribe or unsubscribe to listservs to receive or stop receiving mailing list messages.

Lotus cc:Mail   A proprietary electronic mail system with a gateway to the Internet.

mailing lists   A collection of users who uses a listserv server to communicate back and forth via electronic mail.

Microsoft Outlook Express   Microsoft Internet Explorer's electronic mail program.

Netscape Collabra   Netscape's newsreader. Collabra is a component of Netscape Communicator.

Netscape Messenger   Netscape's electronic mail program. Messenger is a component of Netscape Communicator.

newsgroup   A collection of users who use a Usenet server to transmit messages on a specified topic.

Qualcomm Eudora   A proprietary electronic mail system with a gateway to the Internet.

spamming   The act of sending unsolicited junk mail to many electronic mail addresses.

Usenet   A type of server that manages communications on newsgroup topics.

Q&A

Q How do I find a newsgroup?

A Your ISP typically provides a newsgroup server that gives you access to the Usenet. You need to enter the server name of the news server into your browser or the Internet Config control panel to gain access. Then, use the news reader in your browser to search for newsgroups. Subscribe to those groups that interest you and your newsreader will automatically update messages for that group whenever you open its folder.

Q How do I find chat rooms?

A Check the People and Chat channel of most search engines, such as Excite (www.excite.com) and Yahoo! (www.yahoo.com). Netscape maintains a chat area for businesspeople at its Netcenter site (www.netscape.com/netcenter/). Also, http://www.talkcity.com is a very popular chat site on the Internet.

Q How do I get an electronic mail user ID and password?

A Your ISP will provide you with the POP3 and SNMP domain names (such as earthlink.net and mail.earthlink.net) as well as a personal ID and password you use to gain access to your mailbox.

Q What do I have to know to download a file from an FTP site?

A You need to know the URL of the FTP site. Typically, FTP sites require a user ID and password for access. Anonymous FTP access is available at some sites where you use your Internet ID as a password to gain access to information.

Q What do I need to know about the security of messages I transmit over the Internet?

19

A There's very little innate security on the Internet. Any message you publish on a newsgroup is available to other subscribers to that group. Messages sent via electronic mail can be encrypted and digitally signed to ensure that they come from you and that no one else has read the message. Verisign provides digital IDs to sign Web pages and electronic mail for a price at their site: www.verisign.com. Electronic commerce sites, such as Amazon Books (www.amazon.com), Etoys (www.etoys.com), and so forth secure the transmission of credit card information via a TCP/IP technology called *secure sockets layer (SSL)*. This is an actual protocol within TCP/IP that encrypts and ensures that eavesdroppers cannot read an SSL-based transmission. The downside is that your ISP must support SSL for it to operate. Newer and even more secure encryption methods are on the way that do not require special server-based software for their use.

Workshop

The Workshop contains quiz questions to help you solidify your understanding of the material covered. You can find the answers to the quiz questions in Appendix B, "Quiz Answers."

Quiz

1. Who invented the World Wide Web?
2. What's the difference between the WWW and the Internet?
3. What's a newsgroup and how do you gain access to one?
4. What's a private chat room?
5. What are emoticons?
6. How do you prevent minors from accessing pornographic materials on the Internet?
7. What do you need to run an Apple Data Detector?
8. Where can you change the data that a data detector scans for?
9. How do you specify the processes performed on scanned data by the data detector?
10. What do you need to know to download a file using an FTP program?

Hour 20

Talking to the Other Guys

So, you've created the ultimate report containing beautifully typeset text, sophisticated illustrations, and a brilliant analysis on spreadsheets. Now you want to share it electronically with the world (or your workgroup). Immediately, three information-sharing concerns hit you in the face:

- How can you provide other users who don't have Macs with the capability to open and view your document on their computers?

- If your coworkers can't open the document, how can you share the information contained within it?

- If the document can be opened and viewed on other users' computers, how do you ensure that all your formatting, including typography, is visible?

Don't fret. Mac OS 8.5 provides a series of tools that make it relatively easy to share documents—or their contents—with those other users, whether or not they use a Mac.

Sharing Data versus Sharing Documents

One of the ways that the Macintosh is different than the Intel world is in the imposition of standards on software that runs on the operating system. On the Mac, traditionally, you could take data from one program and use it in another because all the software programs recognized basic features of Mac files. You may not realize that on a PC, individual software hasn't a clue about which file goes with which program. Windows 95 has gotten smarter about this, but underneath the surface, even Windows 95 is still DOS.

Understanding File Types

The Mac is different. From its inception in 1984, the Mac operating system, through the Finder, has linked programs with their documents. This is done by applying invisible four-letter codes to programs and documents called *file types* or *creators*.

> You don't have to know any information about these file types or creators to work with documents on a Mac. In fact, the only way you would ever know anything about this is if you've had to share information with a PC, which depends upon suffixes to identify its documents. Then, it's good to know that somewhere on the Mac the computer is keeping this information safe.

First, the Finder gives each file a type code. This identifier, such as TEXT for any ASCII text document (regardless of its originating program), PICT for many graphics documents, and APPL for any application program, tells the Finder what type of file it's dealing with. This used to be enough to share data between programs via the Open Command, the Clipboard, or drag and drop (because so many programs recognize TEXT or PICT as appropriate file types).

> Today, many programs use proprietary type codes that cannot be shared (such as many Adobe programs—for example, PageMaker, PhotoShop, and Illustrator). The file type is assigned to a document when you use the Save As command and select a format from the standard pop-up menu. You can select a more universal type, such as PICT, EPSF, or TEXT, instead of the proprietary default type if you know you want to open the document in another program.

The Finder also assigns another four-letter code to all files during the Save process—this is the creator code. The creator code identifies for the Finder which application program goes with which document file. The creator identification lets the Finder launch the correct application when you double-click an associated document, present documents with the icon identifying their owning software on the desktop, or create aliases of documents that launch the proper programs. Every program has a unique creator code. For example, Microsoft Word documents are given a creator code of MSWD, whereas Adobe PageMill's documents are given a creator code of StMI.

Table 20.1 provides a list of common file types and creators. You don't really need to know these, but just in case you're curious, here they are.

TABLE 20.1. COMMON FILE TYPES AND CREATORS.

Type of File	File Type	Creator
Any application	APPL	Varies
Any text file	TEXT	Varies
ClarisDraw document	dDoc	dPro
MacPaint document	PNTG	MPNT
MacWrite document	WORD	MACA
Microsoft Excel 4 document	XLS4	XCEL
Microsoft Word document	WDBN	MSWD
TIFF images	TIFF	Varies
PICT graphics	PICT	Varies
PageMaker 4 document	ALB4	ALD4
QuarXPress document	XDOC	XPRS
System file	zsys	MACS
Finder	FNDR	MACS
Desktop file	FNDR	ERIK
System extension	INIT	Varies
Control panel	CDEV	Varies
Chooser extension	RDEV	Varies
FKEYs	FKEY	Varies
SimpleText document	TEXT or ttro	ttxt

20

What Are File Formats?

The goal in computing is to produce information that can be used and shared. This sounds simple enough, except for one small problem: Software that does this work on computers handles the task of telling the screen and printer how to display and manipulate text and graphics in many different ways.

The codes used to display and print information in a document compose the file format. The file format tells the program how information (both text and graphics as well as formatting) is stored. The trouble is that one program's file format may not be legible to another program. Therefore, you might not be able to view the information in a document if you don't have the program installed on your computer that produced the document. If the program you're importing the document into doesn't contain the same feature set as the document's originator, you'll lose the formatting based on the missing features. Sometimes trying to open a foreign file may crash the importing program. You must be aware of file formats when importing and exporting files.

Many file formats exist. The ones that will concern you the most are those used to share information between software packages, called *file interchange formats*. The granddaddy of all interchange formats is ASCII, an acronym for the American Standard Code for Information Interchange (pronounced "as-key"). The Macintosh understands an extended version of ASCII that contains 256 characters (those Option key characters such as ô, Æ, [c], and foreign language markings are added to the standard 128 characters).

ASCII assigns a unique number to every letter, number, and symbol. These numbers are understood by most software programs. The program takes the ASCII codes and matches them to corresponding characters. ASCII is the underlying character code that most programs build on to handle text, although ASCII itself is "raw" text without formatting. You can always move ASCII (called *Text* on the Mac) between software programs, but you'll lose any bolding, italics, tab stops, hanging indentations, and so forth in the conversion process.

Several file interchange formats are available that capture more formatting than simple ASCII. The problem is that with more formatting comes additional danger that the importing program will not support the format feature, and you lose your data. Not all formats are supported by all programs. You should try out each flavor to find the one that transfers the most information to the new program. Here's a list of some of the most common types of formats:

- **Document Content Architecture (DCA).** This is a PC-based file format that can be translated by MacLink Plus/PC and MacLink/Translators. When using this format, you lose fonts, styles, and size information.

- **Rich Text Format (RTF).** This is the strongest interchange format, retaining a lot of information about font, styles, and sizes across programs. Not all Mac word processors support RTF, but it's a good bet if you're moving PageMaker or QuarkXPress files across platforms between Windows and Mac.

- **Data Interchange Format (DIF).** This is another PC-based file format that assists in the transfer of spreadsheet and database information. Cell formatting and width information is lost in the translation. MacLink Plus/PC and MacLink/Translators supports DIF.

- **Symbolic Link (SYLK).** This file format translates spreadsheet and database information while retaining some formatting, including commas, column width, and cell alignments. Font, style, and size information is lost in the transfer.

- **Encapsulated PostScript (EPS).** This file format converts PostScript-based graphics and special effects from native formats to one that most PC programs can accept. Only PostScript devices (such as PostScript level 2 laser printers) can understand and print EPS graphics.

- **Tagged-Image File Format (TIFF).** A file format that transfers bitmapped graphics between computer platforms. TIFF is supported by many PC and Mac scanners and is independent of specific computer or graphic resolutions. The files are very large and cumbersome to store and load.

- **PICT Format.** This is the basic Mac graphics file format encoded into the Mac's screen description language, QuickDraw. You can combine bitmapped with object-oriented graphic images into a single PICT file. Minimal PC program support is available for PICT, although MacLink Plus/PC and MacLink/Translators do provide translators for PICT to Windows metafile format.

Many popular software applications provide file format translators that go beyond ASCII to translate the special codes used to indicate formatting from one file format to another. For example, WordPerfect, Microsoft Word, and Nisus NisusWriter will translate documents from their respective native formats to another program's format. However, not all programs are as accommodating.

You set the file format in the Save As dialog box (opened by selecting Save As on the File menu of almost every Macintosh program). Use the File Format pop-up menu, shown in Figure 20.1, to select a file interchange format for your document. The formats listed are those supported by the program you're using. Each program supports a different range of formats, from Word's extensive list to Freehands' very short list (Freehand, PICT, and EPS).

20

Figure 20.1.

Use the Save As dialog box to select a file interchange format for your document.

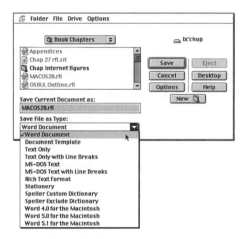

Sharing Data Between Files

The Mac has two tried and true methods for copying information between files. One is very, very old and the other is relatively new. You can copy and paste information via the Clipboard (very old technology) or drag and drop the information between files (introduced in System 7.1 and upgraded to support the Finder in System 7.5).

Dragging and dropping is neat. Simply select the item you want to copy while holding down the mouse and then move the cursor to where you want to copy the information to. When you release the mouse, the selected material is copied to the new location.

Use drag and drop to copy items between files or to copy graphics from files to the desktop for use as backgrounds on Web pages or as wallpaper in the desktop screen of the Appearance control panel. This latter method creates a *picture clippings file*, as shown in Figure 20.2. (Be sure to save the new clippings file in the Desktop Pictures folder in the Appearance folder in the System folder).

You can also select text and drag it to the desktop. You can then use the text repeatedly by dragging its clippings file from the desktop to an open document in any program that supports drag and drop. This is handy for inserting your address, telephone number, URL, email address, and other information into multiple places.

Not all software programs support drag and drop. Check with each program's user manual to see whether this technology is supported. Applications that do support drag and drop include SimpleText, Scrapbook, Stickies, Note Pad, ClarisWorks, Claris Emailer, and Corel WordPerfect.

FIGURE 20.2.

Click and drag an item from the Scrapbook or another file to the desktop to create a picture clippings file.

Publish and Subscribe

Another technology that has been around for a couple years is Publish and Subscribe. This technology builds on the old copy and paste method to provide live updates to material that you copy from one document to another. Publish and Subscribe copies material from one document to another bypassing the Clipboard.

The benefit of live updates is that the copied material is still linked to its original document so that when you change anything in the original, it's automatically updated in the copy. In addition, because you copy information from an intermediary file that can be located anywhere on a network, you don't have to have the originating programs to access the information, and you can be located anywhere on the network and still access the edition file.

Many programs support Publish and Subscribe, making it very useful for workgroups who create joint documents and want to synchronize their work. Each person subscribes to an edition that is published on a network.

20

The key to maintaining the link between the originating document and any destination documents is through the edition file. You must save the edition file, because if it gets deleted or corrupted, the link between documents is broken.

To create an edition file, select the text, graphic, table, or spreadsheet that you want to copy. Select Create Publisher from either the File or Edit menu. The standard Save As dialog box appears, as shown in Figure 20.3.

FIGURE 20.3.

Publish an edition file to copy updateable information between files.

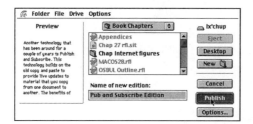

Give the edition file a name and click Publish. When you want to use an edition file, open the document you want to use as the destination and select the Subscribe To command from the File or Edit menu. The standard Open dialog box, shown in Figure 20.4, is used to locate the edition file.

FIGURE 20.4.

Subscribe to an edition file to place update-able information into your document.

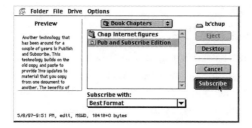

When you click Subscribe, the contents of the edition file appear at your insertion point. You can specify how often and when you want the edition file updated by selecting options from the Publisher Options dialog box (found on either the Edit menu or on a Publisher submenu on the File menu). Figure 20.5 shows this dialog box.

FIGURE 20.5.

Set the update schedule for your edition file.

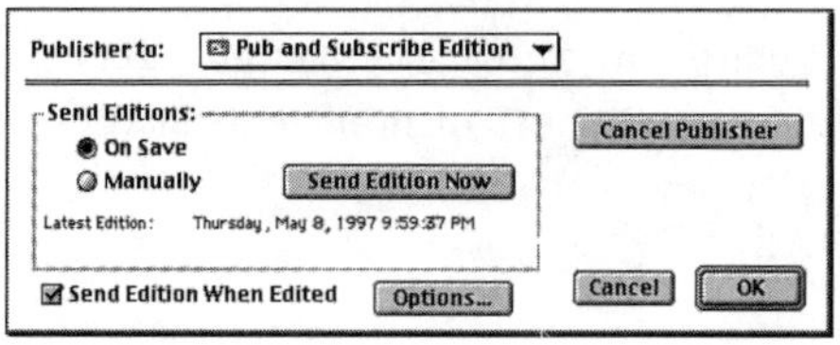

Object Linking and Embedding (OLE)

Microsoft, of course, took another tactic for data sharing called *object linking and embedding (OLE)*. With OLE, you can copy material (or whole documents) from one program (called an *object*) into another document without the need for an intermediary file. The object and its originating document are linked so that any changes you make in the original are automatically represented in its objects.

The downside of Microsoft's method is that you have to have both the originating software and the destination software open on your desktop at the same time (which means that you have enough memory installed to support two Microsoft programs running simultaneously—no small matter).

Note that you cannot copy objects from programs you do not have resident on your machine, and it's not particularly network or workgroup oriented (for example, you have to have the document you want to embed as well as its originating program accessible for OLE to work). For this reason, although OLE is the underpinning of many technologies on Windows 95 computers, it has not really caught on in the Mac universe. OLE embeds the object into your document, meaning that you can open the originating program by double-clicking the object, thereby updating its information on-the-fly.

To embed an object in an OLE-supported document, select Insert Object from the Insert menu (say, in Word or Excel). In the resulting dialog box, shown in Figure 20.6, select the program whose document you want to take the object from. If the file exists, click the From File button to open a standard Open dialog box.

FIGURE 20.6.

Select a program from the OLE-savvy applications in the list to embed an object.

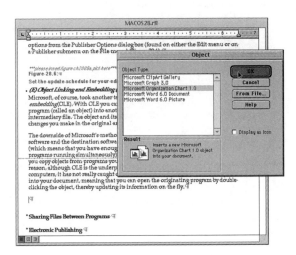

20

If you want to create a new object, click the OK button to open the desired program (for example, another Word document). Now, whatever you type in the originating document will be updated in its embedded version when you close the "document in a document" file. Use this method to add addresses, URLs, and other information maintained in a Word file so that all objects can be updated whenever the information changes in the original file.

Sharing Files Between Programs

It's one thing to share files between Macintosh programs, and another related but more challenging thing to share Macintosh files with Windows programs, and vice versa. File sharing on a Mac is relatively straightforward because of the advent of Easy Open.

Using File Exchange for Translation

The File Exchange control panel's File Translation screen, shown in Figure 20.7, maps orphan files with compatible applications so that they can be opened and read. Double-clicking any file, whether it has a creator identified or not, will launch an application that can read the file. If File Exchange cannot identify the creator of a file, it displays a dialog box asking you to select the most likely candidate.

FIGURE 20.7.

File Translation lets you manually or automatically map orphan files to compatible applications.

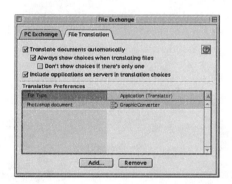

File Exchange's File Translation tool gets a strong helping hand from a third-party application called MacLink Plus/Translators (from DataViz), which was bundled with Mac OS 8.1 but is not included with Mac OS 8.5. You can still purchase MacLink Plus/Translators, current version 10, from DataViz (www.dataviz.com) MacLink Plus contains a vast array of formatting filters that convert file formats from one format to another, including Internet formats such as HTML, GIF, and JPEG. MacLink Plus works with Easy Open to convert orphaned files to legible files by linking appropriate converters to applications.

See, we go around and around and end up right back at the issue of file formats again.

Macs and PCs are not the same species. These two computer systems cannot readily communicate because information is stored and processed (disk and file formats) in much different ways. Reading PC files on a Mac used to be impossible. However, Apple has developed two tools (included with Mac OS 8.5) that make exchanging files with PCs much easier: PC Exchange and Easy Open. Mac OS 8.5 further simplifies file conversion by combining these two tools into one single control panel called File Exchange. I've already discussed the File Translation screen portion of File Exchange, but you can also use File Exchange's PC Exchange screen to automatically translate PC file formats to Mac file formats on-the-fly.

Now, let's discuss PC Exchange.

THE MAC SPEAKS WITH A FORKED TONGUE

Remember I said that Macs and PCs are different species. One of the most clever ways that the Mac differentiates itself from the Intel world is how it saves information about programs and files. All Mac programs and some Mac documents consist of two pieces of information, called *forks*. The *resource fork* saves information about the structure of a program, such as how it formats its data for storage. The *data fork* contains all the information used to run a program, such as macros, formulas, the actual data, and so forth. The creator and type codes mentioned earlier are stored on the resource fork. The trouble with communicating with PCs happens because PCs don't know about forks.

Using the PC Exchange Screen

In this day and age of mixed platform offices, it's sad but true that you'll run into people who do not use Macs. Sometimes these PC users may have information they want to share with you. How can you get a PC file (or even a floppy disk) recognized by your Mac so that the appropriate program can read the file? In 1988, Apple introduced the SuperDrive on the Macintosh II. These new disk drives could read the then common 1.4 MB floppy disks used by Macs and PCs. But reading and understanding are two different things.

20

Macs still couldn't read the PC directories and therefore couldn't display the contents of PC disks on the desktop or in the Finder's Open and Save As dialog boxes. Third-party vendors offered several programs that provided the software required to read PC directories and properly display PC files on Macs.

Programs such as AccessPC from Insignia and Software Architects' DOS Mounter 95 are the most recent iterations of these hoary programs. With the advent of System 7.5, Apple introduced its version of this software, called *PC Exchange*. Mac OS 8.5 rewrote PC Exchange and bundled it into File Translation to become *File Exchange* (see Figure 20.8). The PC Exchange portion of File Exchange performs several hidden jobs. For example, it allows the formatting of disks for PCs. PC Exchange also allows the reading of PC disks on Macs, lets you copy files from your Mac to a PC-formatted disk, and allows you to open PC files in their corresponding Mac programs.

FIGURE 20.8.

The PC Exchange screen lets you mount and read PC files on your Mac.

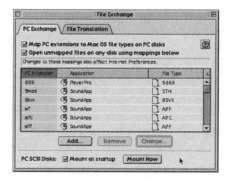

PC Exchange works invisibly to display PC files on your Mac. However, PC Exchange goes further than simply allowing you to see files on the screen. PC Exchange is a control panel that lets you map file extensions between PCs and Macs. Extension mapping lets you create a relationship between the Mac's types and creators with a PC file's extensions (the three-letter suffix) in most PC filenames. You can then open PC files by double-clicking them as you would a Mac file.

In older versions of PC Exchange, you had to know which PC extensions went with which Mac type and creator. In the most recent version of PC Exchange that comes with Mac OS 8.5, the control panel provides the ability to pick a program to associate with an extension and to further link the creator and type by looking at all the options on a hierarchical menu. This is very handy, because a PC extension such as .TIF can be read by many Mac programs, such as ClarisWorks, MacDraw Pro, Color It, Macromedia Freehand, Adobe PageMaker, and so forth. You can also set up proper MIME types for transmission of files over the Internet between Macs and PCs.

WATCH THE FILENAME LENGTHS!

With the advent of Windows 95 came a glitch with PC Exchange you should be aware of. Windows 95 lets you create filenames of up to 256 characters, but Macs can only handle 31 characters. Worse still, PC Exchange works with the older Windows 3.1 rules of an eight-character limit on filenames. Therefore, when files are copied to and from PC disks, filenames are truncated to eight characters and a three-character suffix.

For example, a perfectly good Microsoft Word Mac file name such as "My Word File" gets copied over to the PC disk by PC Exchange as My!Word!.fil. Notice that the three-character suffix in this case ended up being added as a continuation of the file's name and not a true extension, which causes the PC file to lose its identify and be unreadable (the three-character suffix is not really part of the name on PCs but is added by Windows to link the document with its associated application).

One solution is to give your files eight-character names if they're going to be read by Macs and PCs. You could also get a more robust conversion program, such as Software Architect's DOS Mounter 95, that supports Windows 95 filenaming conventions (note that you should still limit your filenames to 31 characters so that the Mac can recognize it). Always try to add the suffix to Mac files that are bound for PCs—even though these suffixes have no meaning on the Mac side, they are crucial for safe computing on the PC side.

PC Exchange adds another function to Macs—the ability to mount PC-formatted removable disks such as Iomega Zip or Jaz drives, SyQuest EZ135s, or Bernoulli cartridges on the Mac desktop. With this option selected, you can slip PC-formatted removable media in your appropriate drives and they will properly appear on your desktop.

Sharing Files over a Network and the Internet

When you want to exchange files over a network to PCs or between your Mac and an online service, you want to retain the information stored in the data and resource forks. The most secure way of making sure that you can reconstruct your Mac files or applications once they're downloaded is to convert your Mac files to MacBinary format prior to sending them.

MacBinary is a special file format for telecommunications that strips the information off the data and resource forks and creates a special header containing this data along with the file's Finder attributes that it installs at the beginning of the file. Most telecommunications programs and FTP programs let you specify that you want to transmit the Mac files in MacBinary. Note that programs such as Fetch rename your files with

20

a .BIN suffix to indicate that they are MacBinary files. You can also manually translate your files to MacBinary format using Aladdin Software's StuffIt Deluxe.

When you download files to your Mac, software such as Aladdin Software's StuffIt Expander, which comes with Mac OS 8.5's Internet Access package, converts the file back to a standard Mac file format. You'll know that a file is in MacBinary format because it is labeled with a .BIN suffix.

You may also see .HQX or .UU as suffixes. These are two other communications file formats used to transmit Mac or PC files. The BinHex format (.HQX) is used to convert Mac files to reside safely on UNIX servers (such as those used on the Internet). The UUcode format (.UU) is used to convert files for use on PCs. You can set up StuffIt Expander to automatically decode these formats as well (see Figure 20.9). Double-click the StuffIt Expander icon on your desktop and select Preferences from the File menu. Select the options you want to automatically invoke when you drop items onto the icon (or download files using the Netscape Navigator browser).

FIGURE 20.9.

Set up StuffIt Expander to automatically decode communication file formats such as BinHex, UUcode, and MacBinary.

Note that the DropStuff application, which also comes with the Internet Access software in Mac OS 8.5, will convert files to BinHex format during the stuffing process if this is set in its Preferences dialog box (located on the File menu). Then, whenever you drag and drop a folder or file onto the DropStuff alias icon residing on your desktop, its contents will be encoded and stuffed automatically.

The Mac is smart, but PCs are dumb. If you download a Mac file to a PC, it doesn't have the software to convert and decompress MacBinary files. Use sneaker net to carry the file from the PC back to a Mac and decode and decompress the file using StuffIt Expander. You can also retransmit the file from the PC to your Mac and have it automatically decoded as it downloads.

Sharing Documents Online

One of the most frustrating things about exchanging documents is how messed up fonts, typographical formatting, and layout can get if the person you're exchanging a file with doesn't have the same program or fonts installed as you. Before documents could be published on CD-ROMs, intranets, or other online document distribution systems, this problem had to be resolved.

We are not at the "paperless office" yet, but we're getting close. Many vendors have searched for a method to embed fonts and formatting in a document and still keep the size of the document manageable for transmitting. Several solutions to this problem have been proposed, and the winner at this time seems to be Adobe Systems Acrobat.

Portable Document Format (PDF)

All electronic publishing tools operate by "printing" a document to a special file. Some programs require you to select a driver in the Chooser prior to printing. Acrobat's Distiller operates through a command on the File menu of Acrobat-savvy programs (such as Adobe PageMill) to create a Portable Document Format (PDF) file.

Adobe created this PDF format based on PostScript, thus preserving the format and layout of text and graphics as if they've been printed on a PostScript laser printer. The PDF does not contain embedded fonts but rather the PostScript-based descriptions of how to build the fonts (their height, width, weight, names, and styles, and so forth). Acrobat uses several substitution fonts and a technology called Multiple Masters to build missing fonts on-the-fly. Because the actual fonts are not resident in the files and because the files are compressed, Acrobat files are very small and easy to transmit online.

You need to have Adobe Distiller installed to create a PDF. Distiller is part of a suite of five programs that together constitute Adobe Acrobat Pro 3.0. You view Acrobat files using the Acrobat Reader that's freely distributed by Adobe all over the Internet (check out http://www.adobe.com) and is included the Internet Access component of Mac OS 8.5. Acrobat also includes collaboration software (Acrobat for Workgroups), Acrobat Search (a powerful indexing tool for creating searchable documents), Acrobat Catalog, and Acrobat Capture (an optical character recognition package that lets you scan items and automatically convert them to PDFs for distribution). With the Acrobat Reader and Adobe Type Manager (ATM) installed, you can read PDFs containing text, animated graphics, movies, and sounds. (See Figure 20.10.)

20

FIGURE 20.10.

Adobe Acrobat PDF files are easily downloaded and read using the Acrobat Reader with ATM.

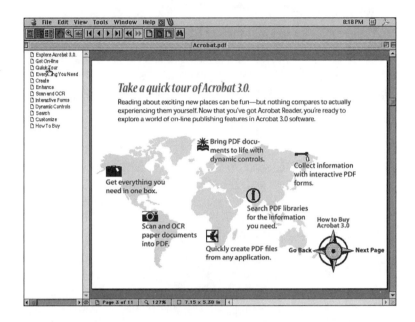

Acrobat Distiller provides the ability to convert documents to PDFs in the background. Just set up a Watcher folder and place any documents you want to convert in the folder, and Distiller converts them while you're working on something else.

Adobe Acrobat Pro is expensive ($450) as well as a memory and storage hog. Other companies have created less popular but more efficient, portable document converters. These are discussed in the next section.

Common Ground, Envoy, and Replica

Adobe is not the only vendor to create electronic publishing tools. Common Ground Software (formerly No Hands Software) provides Common Ground for considerably less than Adobe's Acrobat. Common Ground costs $100 and can create "digital paper" versions of documents that can be viewed using the Common Ground viewer. Like PDFs, DPs can be annotated, searched, and indexed. You can add hypertext links and PostScript graphics to digital paper files. The benefit of Common Ground is that you can embed its very efficient MiniViewer in your digital paper file so that the recipient doesn't need to have access to a viewer to be able to read your document.

Corel has inherited Envoy from Novell when it bought WordPerfect. Envoy is another electronic document tool that lets you create portable documents from WordPerfect files.

Farallon offers Replica, another electronic publishing tool. Common Ground, Envoy, and Replica have not had the success of Acrobat. The more Acrobat becomes ubiquitous on the Net, the more of a *de facto* standard it becomes, thus driving these other products out of the market.

Summary

File formats are a dicey subject because their components are invisible to the user. You have to know about types and creators if you want to share Mac files with other computer platforms, because these other platforms rely on different tools to identify what type of application created a file and how it should be displayed and read. Mac OS 8.5 provides several tools to make file conversion relatively painless. This hour described Easy Open, PC Exchange, StuffIt Expander, Adobe Acrobat, and MacLink Plus/Translators. All these software tools make the Mac truly a cross-platform communicator.

Term Review

ASCII   American Standard Code for Information Interchange is the oldest file interchange format. No formatting information is contained in ASCII, but the Mac understands a modified version of ASCII that contains 256 characters, including special symbols and accent markings.

BinHex   A method of converting Mac files for safe transmission on UNIX servers. BinHex files are indicated by a .HQX suffix.

clippings file   A selection of data dragged on to your desktop.

creator   A four-letter code assigned by the Finder during the Save process that identifies which application program runs the specified document.

data fork and resource fork   All Mac programs and some Mac documents contain two pieces of information, called *forks*. The resource fork saves information about the structure of a program, such as how it formats its data for storage; the data fork contains all the information required to properly run the program, such as macros, formulas, and the actual data. Creator and file types are resource fork data.

DCA   Document Content Architecture. A PC-based file format that contains only text without font or style information.

DIF   Data Interchange Format. A PC-based file format used to transfer spreadsheet and database information between applications. Cell width and height information is lost during translation.

20

drag and drop   A method of moving and copying data between places by selecting the information with your cursor and dragging the data (or Option-dragging for copying) to another place. You can drag and drop information between documents in the same application as well as between documents in different applications (assuming those applications support drag and drop).

Easy Open   A desk accessory that maps orphan files with compatible applications so that these documents can be opened and read. Easy Open works in conjunction with MacLink Plus/Translators.

EPS   Encapsulated PostScript. A file interchange format for converting PostScript-based graphics and special effects from native formats to a printable format. Only PostScript devices can understand and print EPS graphics.

file format   The codes used to display and print information in a document. The file format tells the program how information (both text and graphics as well as formatting) is stored.

file interchange formats   File formats that permit the sharing of information between application software packages.

file type   An identifying code applied to files by the Finder that tells the Finder what type of application created the file and how it should be displayed and read.

MacBinary   A file interchange format used for transmitting Mac files securely over networks. MacBinary files are indicated by a .BIN suffix.

MacLink Plus/Translators   A vast array of file conversion tools provided by DataViz in the Mac OS 8.5 package. MacLink Plus automatically identifies and translates PC file formats into Mac-readable formats.

object linking and embedding (OLE)   A way to copy information between applications and documents in OLE-savvy applications (mostly created by Microsoft, who invented OLE). Using OLE lets you update copied information automatically in the target file should you change it in the original file. Data is actually embedded in your document with a link to its originating application.

PC Exchange   A desk accessory that enables your Mac to read PC-formatted floppies, Iomega disks, and CD-ROMs.

PDF   Portable Document Format. Used to display documents on computers that might not have the document's original application or fonts resident. Adobe offers a free reader, called Acrobat, and a suite of software for sale that you can use to create PDF files.

PICT   The basic Mac graphics format encoded into QuickDraw.

RTF   Rich Text Format. A popular file interchange format that retains a great deal of formatting and font information when files are exchanged by applications.

SYLK   Symbolic Link. A spreadsheet and database file interchange format that retains some cell formatting while losing font and style formats during translation.

TIFF   Tagged-Image File Format. Used to transfer bitmapped images between computer platforms. TIFF is useful because it's independent of specific computer or graphic resolutions.

UUcode   A method of converting files on PCs for safe transmission.

Q&A

Q   What software do I need to send, receive, and translate files from the Internet?

A   Mac OS 8.5 comes bundled with two products from Aladdin: StuffIt Expander and DropStuff EE. These programs contain the tools to archive .HQX, .BIN, .SIT, .ZIP, and .UUC files.

Q   How can I know what the creator and file type of a document is so that I can properly convert it to readable format?

A   File types and creator information is sometimes listed in the Get Info box when you select a document on the desktop. You can also use any number of shareware programs to change file types and creators manually. PC Exchange lists PC equivalents to Mac file types for use in file conversion.

Q   How do I make sure that a PC program can recognize my Mac file?

A   Always label your Mac documents with the appropriate PC application suffix (file type) if your files are going to be transferred between platforms. Try to limit your file names to eight characters and a three-character suffix.

Q   How do I attach multiple files to an email successfully?

A   Place all the files you want to transmit into a single folder and stuff the folder using DropStuff or StuffIt Deluxe into a single file with a .SIT or .SEA suffix. Note that .SEA files are special self-archiving StuffIt files that can be opened without having StuffIt resident on your system.

Q   What's the best format to save Adobe PhotoShop and Illustrator or Macromedia Freehand files to ensure their readability by other programs?

A   These proprietary formatted applications let you convert your files to EPS or PICT format. Note that PICT formatted files lose vector information in the translation,

20

and EPS files are only readable by programs that can recognize them. Another solution is to use a file conversion program such as $30 shareware called GIF Converter to translate files in batches for use on Web pages or by other programs.

Workshop

The Workshop contains quiz questions to help you solidify your understanding of the material covered. You can find the answers to the quiz questions in Appendix B, "Quiz Answers."

Quiz

1. How do you change the format of a file?
2. How do you open a foreign file?
3. What format is best for transmitting files over the Internet?
4. What's a creator?
5. What's a resource fork?
6. How do PC and Mac files differ in format and structure?
7. What do you need in order to read PDF files?
8. How do you know that a file is readable by a specific Mac program?
9. How do you make sure that PC programs can read your Mac filenames?
10. What program does the Mac use to perform file conversions on-the-fly?

PART IV

Night Hours: Advanced Mac OS 8.5

Hour

21 Working with Java

22 Automating Your Mac with AppleScript

23 The File System Extended

24 Troubleshooting Your System

HOUR 21

Working with Java

Java. A slang for coffee? A country in Indonesia? A rage in computing circles? The next wave of computing? The Mac's future? Yes, yes, yes, yes, and yes.

The press has literally been gushing coffee bean metaphors all because Sun Microsystems developed the first programming language and environment for running software that's truly portable across platforms.

Apple is one of the first companies to incorporate a Java Virtual Machine into an operating system. Mac OS 8.5 comes with Macintosh Runtime Java (MRJ) version 1.0.2, which lets you run actual Java programs, such as those found on Web sites, directly on your Mac without really being aware that what you're doing is special—meaning the Java engine is all but invisible.

This hour looks at how this is done and what it all means to you. Included in this lesson are the following topics:

- What is Java?
- Macintosh Runtime Java
- Running Java applets
- Component software and Java
- Native Java applications

What Is Java?

Java is both a programming language and an environment used to run programs. Confused yet? What makes Java special is that programmers do not have to recompile their programs to carry them from one computer platform to another. All you need is a Java virtual machine running on your computer to run Java-based or Java-savvy programs.

Each programmer who has written a Java-based application in the past has also had to write a runtime engine to operate the program. That's a big and expensive step. No standard exists for the quality of these engines or how much of the Java code they support. That's why until recently you've mainly seen Java as the animation and cursor controllers on Web sites via either Netscape Navigator and Internet Explorer. These browsers are some of the only commercial programs containing Java runtime engines. The Java code that they run are small, self-contained programs, called *applets*, that have been embedded into a Web page.

Java Capabilities

Macintosh Runtime Java (MRJ) installs a tiny world, called the *Java Virtual Machine (VM)*, that can play on top of the Mac OS. Java has become a standard for distributing software over the Internet, for writing standalone software with Java functions, such as NisusWriter and Corel WordPerfect, and for writing component software (called *beans*) that can run within containers, such as the Apple Applet Runner that comes with Mac OS 8.5.

Right now, Java is in its infancy, meaning that very little actual Java-based software exists. However, software developers are excited about Java because it provides very advanced features that make its programs more secure (automatic memory management and protection), faster (built-in threading), and compatible (innate cross-platform compatibility).

In fact, Apple is so excited about Java that it recently decided to chuck OpenDoc and replace its component functionality with that of Java Beans in future releases of both Mac OS and Rhapsody.

With MRJ, you can open components, such as the small drawing program displayed in Figure 21.1, within another program (that is, if it's MRJ or Java savvy).

Programs such as Adobe PageMill and Claris HomePage let you drag and drop such components into Web pages to be viewed online or locally using a browser. Figure 21.2 displays an applet I loaded onto a Web page using PageMill. I can use this applet locally with my browser or I can upload it to a server and link to it via its URL. Either way, I now can actually draw on a Web page.

FIGURE 21.1.

The DrawTest applet lets you draw simple shapes with different colored lines. It's an example of an interactive applet.

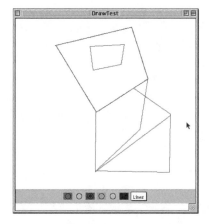

FIGURE 21.2.

You can use the DrawTest applet in an HTML document and view the results in any browser when you have MRJ installed.

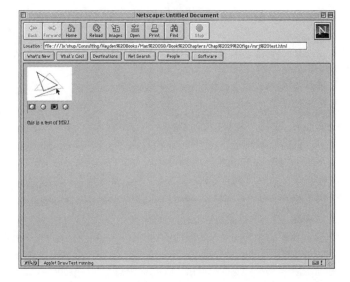

Can you see how transparent the Internet is becoming? You don't know whether you're using a program locally or over the Net, and you don't care.

Understanding the Java VM

What makes Java a cross-platform environment is that it actually operates in its own little world that calls on the resources of its temporary home, in this case the Mac OS 8.5 toolboxes, in order to operate. The environment where Java runs is called the *Java Virtual Machine*. Macintosh Runtime Java is just one of several Java VMs available for the Mac. The two other Java VMs are part of the two major commercial browsers: Netscape Navigator and Microsoft Internet Explorer.

21

WHAT DO ALL THESE ACRONYMS AND TERMS MEAN?

As is the case with all new technologies, Java has erupted with a whole new vocabulary. Here are some translations:

- **Abstract Windowing Toolkit (AWT).** The tools used by MRJ to define the look and feel of Java applications running on Mac OS 8.5.

- **Applet.** A standalone program written in Java that's distributed over the Internet or can be invoked within HTML using the <APPLET> tag.

- **Bongo.** Marimba's transmitter development program for Windows 95 and Windows NT. *The Macintosh version is announced but not published.*

- **Castanet.** A new technology from Marimba Software that lets you download Java files from the Internet and run the resulting application and data directly on your Mac rather than within a browser. Support for Castanet is included in version 1.5 of the MRJ.

- **Channels.** Combinations of Java code and associated data that your computer can "subscribe to" via a special "tuner" (you double-click an icon on a special Web page). You can download the channel's contents and run the resulting Java applet on your Mac. Channels can be automatically updated by the tuner that's linked to the subscription Web pages.

- **Java Beans.** Component applications, such as buttons, dialog boxes, and check boxes, that can be inserted into Java-savvy containers, such as the Apple Applet Viewer Live Object. Java Beans is the replacement technology for creating component software now that OpenDoc has been retired.

- **Java Foundation Class (JFC).** A new set of tools that combines the best of JavaSoft's AWT and Netscape's IFCs to provide a unified framework for how Java applications are displayed and how they function on all computer platforms. JFC is an outgrowth of a collaboration between Sun Microsystems, Netscape, Apple, and IBM.

- **Java VM (Java Virtual Machine).** The emulator that runs on computers to let them process programs written in Java.

- **Java.** The programming language and software environment for running standalone Java code.

- **JavaScript.** Netscape's implementation of Java for use directly in HTML documents.

- **JavaSoft.** The company founded by Sun Microsystems to develop Java code.

- **JBScript.** Microsoft's implementation of Java for use in HTML documents.

- **Just In Time compiler (JIT).** A special Java compiler that converts Java code to byte-codes on the fly. JIT negates the need to recompile a Java instruction each time it's encountered—JIT can store compiled code and recall it when necessary if the instruction needs to be performed again. JIT is already included with Microsoft Internet Explorer's Java VM and will be included with MRJ with version 1.5.

- **MRJ (Macintosh Runtime Java).** The Java VM for Macs.

- **Transmitter.** A Web site containing channels suitable for downloading and management by Castanet.

- **Windowing Internet Foundation Classes (IFC).** Netscape's implementation of JavaSoft's AWT in Netscape Navigator and Communicator browsers.

Java and the Internet

As stated earlier in the hour, the only current place you can actively use Java today is on the Internet via HTML documents. To read HTML documents, you need a browser. The most current versions of Netscape Navigator and Microsoft Internet Explorer include Java VMs that let you run Java applets within HTML pages.

The two most important issues to consider when selecting a browser or applet viewing method are performance and stability. Because each Java VM is slightly different (especially in their implementation of the Abstract Windowing Toolkit), each machine has various pluses and minuses. The inclusion of the Just In Time compiler considerably speeds up the processing of Java bytecodes, because code that's already been compiled doesn't have to be recompiled if it's required more than once. Only Microsoft Internet Explorer includes a JIT compiler at this time. The other Java emulators will include JIT compilers in future versions currently in beta or alpha testing.

The Microsoft Internet Explorer 4 Java VM comes in two flavors: with and without JIT. Both machines are not very stable and crash often. Microsoft also gives you the option of using the Apple MRJ in the place of either Microsoft Java VM. Although MRJ 1.5 is slightly slower (because it lacks the JIT), it's much more stable than the Microsoft implementations. Note that the version of Apple Macintosh Runtime Java (version 2.0) that comes with Mac OS 8.5 does include a JIT compiler from Symantec.

Netscape Navigator 4 does not come with a JIT compiler as of yet. The Navigator 3 Java VM is more stable than the one provided by Microsoft Internet Explorer, but it cannot implement all the features of the Abstract Windowing Toolkit (such as threading of graphics). Netscape Communicator, like MRJ 2.0, includes Symantec's PowerMac JIT 1.5. The new Java VM is more stable and can execute all the functions of the Abstract Windowing Toolkit.

MRJ includes a small program called Applet Runner that works like a browser to let you run Java applets over the Internet by linking to the URLs where the applets reside. Although you cannot view the rest of the HTML document within Applet Runner, you can operate or download the applet to your desktop.

Using Macintosh Runtime Java (MRJ)

On the Mac, the Java VM, called *Macintosh Runtime Java (MRJ)*, installs as a shared library, available to any software that can call upon its code. Apple designed MRJ to install in this fashion to allow Java components to run in any application, not just in a browser. Four shared library components are installed in the Extensions folder:

21

- **Jmanager.** An application programming interface (API) that allows existing applications to embed or host Java applets and applications.

- **Jshell.** An API that lets you write standalone "clickable" Java programs on your Mac.

- **Jbindery.** A tool to convert .ZIP, .JAR, .CLASS packages that arrive over the Internet into Jshell-based applications that can be opened using the standard Mac icon method.

- **JRI.** The standard Sun Java API used to call Java code from C/C++ code.

Figure 21.3 illustrates how these four MRJ components work with the Apple Applet Runner or any other Java-savvy program to run Java-based code using the Mac OS 8.5 toolkit.

FIGURE 21.3.

The MRJ includes two technologies and a utility that let you run Java applications and components on your Mac.

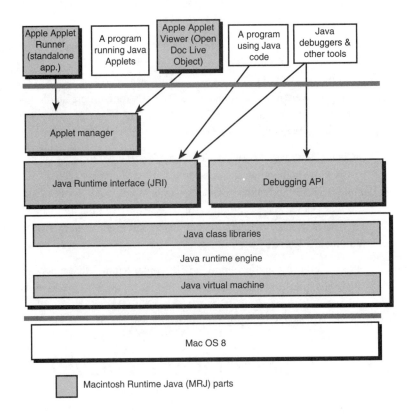

When you run the MRJ installer, it places several folders on your Mac in several places:

- **Mac OS Runtime for Java folder.** The MRJ folder is placed in the Apple Extras folder on your root folder on your startup disk (the window that opens when you double-click the startup disk icon on your desktop). This folder contains the Apple Applet Runner and assorted sample applets from JavaSoft.

- **MRJ Libraries folder.** This is placed in the Extensions folder and contains the four shared APIs mentioned previously. In addition, the MRJ Libraries folder contains two additional folders required by Java: the MRJLib folder and MRJClasses folder.

- **Text encoding converter.** This is placed in the Extensions folder and helps translate Java applet classes and code to a format that's readable by Macs.

- **Text Encodings folder.** This is placed in the System folder and contains the resulting conversion documents created by the Jbindery API.

After running the Apple Applet Runner for the first time, you'll also find a new file in the Preferences folder called Apple Applet Runner Preferences.

More About Applets

Most applets come from the Web where they're called upon on Web pages via the HTML tag pair <APPLET>...</APPLET>. The applet itself is a file that's stored with the Web page, along with supporting files such as sounds, images, and text, or even plug-ins that further enhance the performance of the applet.

Two types of applets are available for your use: distributed applets and server-bound applets. *Distributed applets* can be run remotely by referencing the applet (calling its URL) in the Apple Applet Runner or by using the CODEBASE parameter to identify its URL in an HTML file. Figure 21.4 displays a distributed applet (one being run from the Web) operating on the MRJ engine. Although you can't see it in action, the applet in Figure 21.4 is fully interactive—I can take my cursor and turn the object 360 degrees in the window.

FIGURE 21.4.

MRJ doesn't care whether the applet resides on your computer or on the Internet. (This one is running on the Internet.)

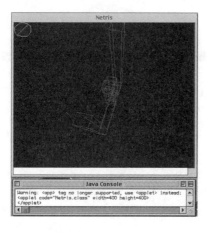

21

Applets that reside on your computer are called *server-bound applets*. There's no difference in how they are displayed and operated under MRJ.

Because Java applets have stringent security devices built into their code, a difference exists between the way the Java VM engine handles distributed applets versus server-bound applets. You can't see this difference, but it has to do with check points and firewalls between the engine, the Internet, and your Mac.

Basically, an applet may access only files that reside on the same computer as the applet itself. What makes distributed applets so safe is MRJ. The Runtime Java engine is a traffic cop, stopping applets from accessing any files that do not belong to them. Therefore, if you want to modify an applet or add images or sounds, you cannot use a distributed applet—you must download the applet and its attendant files to your computer.

You can choose how the applet is displayed and behaves because the Java VM controls how the applet is displayed and operates. You just cannot reference any files that do not reside on the same server as the applet.

As an example of how an applet can be modified, I changed the Blink applet that comes with the Mac OS 8.5 CD-ROM. Figure 21.5 illustrates in static form what Blink originally looked like. Notice the Java Console displays the HTML that calls the applet and defines in parameters how the applet behaves.

FIGURE 21.5.

Here's Blink running on the Apple Applet Runner.

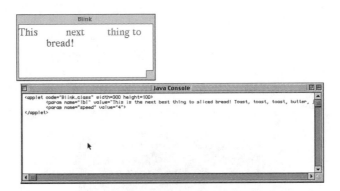

I then copied the HTML from the Java Console into PageMill, my HTML editor (or you can actually open the file EXAMPLE1.HTML). In the editor, I made the following changes to the applet's HTML tags:

```
<APPLET CODE="Blink.class"
WIDTH=300 HEIGHT=100>
    <PARAM NAME="lbl" VALUE="Now is the time for all good people
to come to the aid of their country.">
    <PARAM NAME="speed" value="3">
```

```
       <PARAM NAME="font" VALUE="MS Comic Sans">
       <PARAM NAME="fontsize" VALUE="18>
</applet>
```

I then saved the edited HTML page as EXAMPLE2.HTML and open it in Apple Applet Runner. Figure 21.6 illustrates in static form how the parameters changed. You can do this with any applet as long as the HTML file is stored with the Java applet (identified by the .CLASS suffix). Notice that the words that blink have changed as have their font and size.

FIGURE 21.6.

Here, the parameters that tell Blink how to behave have been changed.

Notice that I didn't touch the actual Java applet, only the surrounding HTML tags that identify how the applet should be used. The ability to use applets for many purposes is part of their power. Notice also that Apple Applet Runner does not display any of the rest of the HTML, but only the resulting applet as modified by its parameters. You have to view the HTML file in a browser to see the rest of the HTML.

In order for the Java VM to process an applet, it must find the <APPLET> tag along with three settings, called *attributes*, that tell the engine how large a window to use to display the Java applet's output and which applet to use. These parameters are CODE (the name of the applet file identified by the .CLASS suffix), HEIGHT (how tall to make the window displaying the applet in pixels), and WIDTH (how wide to make the window displaying the applet in pixels). The rest of the attributes set how the applet performs and is displayed.

Running an Applet

You can run Java applets in several places on your Mac. To view applets all by them-selves (or to search the Web for applets), open the Apple Applet Runner. Select an applet from the Applet menu and it will open in a window on your desktop.

You can control the applet's operation by using the Applet menu's commands to suspend restart, reload, and display the HTML tags in the Java Console (see Figure 21.7). You display the Applet menu by making the Applet window the active window (click the win-dow to bring it to the front).

21

FIGURE 21.7.

*Click the applet win-
dow and use the Applet
menu to control the
operations of the
applet.*

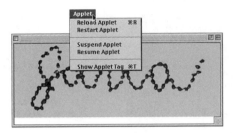

The Apple Applet Runner is more than simply a tool to demonstrate applets that have
been packaged with the Mac OS 8.5 CD-ROM. You can run distributed applets by using
Open Transport/PPP to dial up the Internet and grab an applet from a specified URL. Just
select the Open URL command from the File menu and Apple Applet Runner displays a
list of URLs it remembers (this program remembers URLs where applets have been
found). Select an applet and its URL is displayed in the dialog box (see Figure 21.8).
Click Open to get and run the applet.

FIGURE 21.8.

*Use the Open URL
dialog box to run
distributed applets
directly on your Mac.*

You can also call up other URLs by using the Add button. Clicking Add displays a new
dialog box that lets you give the URL a name (typically the name of the applet and the
Web site where its found) as well as type in the URL. Clicking OK adds the new applet
to the URL list. Selecting the new URL name and clicking Open grabs that URL. Apple
Applet Runner will even invoke Remote Access to dial the Web if you're not already
connected.

Are you seeing the possibilities inherent in being able to run Web-based applets on your
Mac? Suddenly, you're not limited to the software residing on your local Mac—you can
share programs over an intranet, play interactive games over the Internet, use remote
applets to perform quick calculations (on specialized spreadsheet macros or charts), or
get stock quotes that automatically update themselves. The list is endless. What's more,
your Mac becomes an almost seamless adjunct to the Internet (or intranet).

Unfortunately, there's a downside. Right now, MRJ is slow. Luckily, Apple added a Just In Time compiler from Symantec to the MRJ (version 1.5) and updated the compiler for version 2, which is included with Mac OS 8.5. The JIT tool should speed up MRJ so that it's really useful. Update your Java VM by accessing the Apple Web page (www.apple.com/).

Using Component Software

The newest trend in programming, called *component-based programming*, is extending its reaches to the World Wide Web. Currently, a battle is raging for the right to be the ultimate standard for how components work on the Web. *Components* are small programs that can be fit together to form a modular, customized application in real-time. The beauty of components is that they can be written in cross-platform languages and rapidly compiled to work on many platforms. For example, if you want a spell checker for your spreadsheet, just use a component and you don't have to purchase a large program such as Microsoft Excel to gain that function.

Component-based programming has come to the Web in the form of a fight for acceptance as standards among Sun's Java programming language, Apple/IBM's OpenDoc technology, and Microsoft's technology (formerly called OLE). Basically, Netscape Navigator has chosen to use Java applets and its own JavaScript to provide extensions to basic browser functions. Microsoft has built Internet Explorer from ActiveX technologies but plans to support Netscape Navigator's JavaScript and Sun's Java via ActiveX controls. This is confusing, isn't it? Wait, it gets better.

Basically, the battle is over two models of how Web browsers will grow, and hence, how Web pages will be enhanced using component software. Microsoft depends on the Distributed Component Object Model (DCOM), whereas Netscape, Apple, IBM, and Sun have agreed upon the Object Management Group's Common Object Request Broker Architecture (COBRA). These competing models make you decide which browser to use, but you must publish your Web pages for both Internet Explorer and Netscape Navigator (as well as other browsers of lesser capability, such as UNIX's Lynx and NCSA's Mosaic).

Luckily, the technologies do the same thing—that is, they enable you to view objects placed into HTML, such as GIF animation, virtual reality, and Shockwave objects (FreeHand illustrations and Director animation, for example). The difference is in how they do it.

One of the compelling features of the Java programming language is the ability to write small, self-contained programs that can be placed in a container, such as an HTML file

21

or Java-savvy document, to build a customized application that does only what you want it to do.

The software from JavaSoft that lets you create these components is called *Java Beans*. Java Beans is an extension to the Java platform that creates applets that are usable in other Java programs. Each component is called a *bean*. Java Beans is designed to optimize the creation of small, single-purpose applications, such as buttons, radio boxes, and so forth, with which you can build your own applications that are independent of any specific computer platform.

THE END OF OPENDOC AND BEGINNING OF JAVA BEANS

Now for the bad (or good) news. As of April, 1997, Apple abandoned OpenDoc and fully embraced Java Beans as a more compatible option for creating component software that meets "industry standards"—meaning that it will run on any platform and be available via the Internet. Therefore, although Cyberdog and OpenDoc objects are included in Mac OS 8.1 and some independent vendors are still working with this technology, you'll see no more development of OpenDoc or Cyberdog by Apple or inclusion of this technology in Mac OS 8.5.

FOR MORE INFORMATION

For more information about component-based software, surf the following Web sites:

- **ActiveX.** Go to `http://www.microsoft.com/activex/` or `http://www.activex.org/`.
- **OpenDoc.** Go to `http://opendoc.apple.com/dev/dev.html` or `http://applenet.apple.com/`.

You can learn more about JavaScript at the following sites:

- **Netscape's Official JavaScript Reference Guide.** Go to `http//home.netscape.com/eng/mozilla/2.0/handbook/javascript/index.html`.
- **Tecfa's JavaScript Manual.** A JavaScript tutorial. Go to `http://tecfa.unige.ch/guides/java/tecfaman/java-1.html`.
- **JavaScript 411.** A JavaScript FAQ, tutorial, and more. Go to `http://www.freqgrafx.com/411`.
- **JavaScript 411's Snippet Page.** Provides advanced JavaScript code. Go to `http://freqgrafx.com/411/library.html`.
- **Example Site.** Provides examples of JavaScript macros, including a temperature converter, a metric converter, a calendar greeting program, and a loan interest calculator. Go to `http://www.cis.syr.edu/~bhu/javascript.d/`.

Running Java Applications

Recall that, currently, the only way to run Java applets has been to embed them in HTML documents. Delivering software as embedded objects has several drawbacks. First, if you want to run an applet, you have to be connected to the Internet and the applet has to be run in a browser window.

A few good people from Sun Microsystems Java team got together to form a new company called *Marimba*. Marimba manufactures a technology called *Castanet*, which breaks the browser/Internet hurdle for delivering Java applets to your computer. With Castanet, Java programs and their data are delivered to your computer as applets. They can be executed as if they were applications on your desktop with their own icons.

Castanet contains three parts: the tuner, the transmitter, and the channel. You can download the tuner from the Marimba Web site (`www.marimba.com`) or load it from your Mac OS 8.5 CD-ROM. The tuner is the Java applet that manages the downloading and updating of Java programs.

The tuner is written completely in Java. It has its own icon that you can either use directly or create aliases for and place anywhere you want. Double-click the Castanet icon to invoke the tuner. You'll wait a long, long, time because the tuner has to open MRJ and dial up the Internet before it's fully operational. (A good idea is to keep the tuner open on your desktop at all times, because it also updates the Java software you've subscribed to on-the-fly.)

The idea behind Castanet is that software vendors will create special sites on the Web that contain various Java applets, called *channels*. These special sites are called *transmitters*. Figure 21.9 shows the current transmitters available via Castanet. As Castanet becomes more available, these transmitters will grow. Developers write transmitters using the Marimba software called *Bongo*. Bongo currently only runs on Windows 95 or Windows NT machines and can upload transmitters to Windows NT or UNIX servers. Mac versions are forthcoming.

You subscribe to channels. Castanet downloads the applet and its data to your hard disk and creates an icon that you use to invoke the software when needed.

The result is a fully functional piece of Java software that can run on your Mac under MRJ. InfoBook is an example of such an applet. InfoBook is a contact manager that works directly with your browser to store contacts and their Web connections.

21

Castanet is part of the future. Netscape recently announced that Castanet will be included in its new push technology, called *NetCaster*. Castanet "pushes" programs of your choice to your computer and keeps them automatically updated via the Internet.

FIGURE 21.9.

Castanet provides access to Java applets residing on special Web sites called "transmitters."

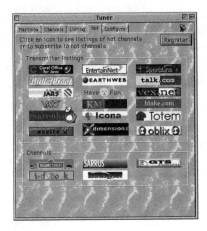

Summary

I spoke about some heady stuff—the Java programming language, Java Virtual Machines, Macintosh Runtime Java, component software, beans, Castanet, and so on. What these technologies have in common is that they're computer platform independent. These technologies are new, and some of them are not yet available. However, it seems that Java and the Macintosh will be linked for the foreseeable future.

Term Review

Apple Applet Runner   An MRJ-based program provided with Mac OS 8.5 used to run Java applets on your Macintosh.

applets   Small programs written in Java and distributed on the Internet via HTML. Applets can run using either the browser's runtime engine or the Mac's MRJ.

component software   Modular chunks of software that perform small specific actions. You can build software applications by putting together components that perform very specific functions.

Java   Both an open, nonproprietary programming language and an environment for running software that's portable to most computer platforms without needing to be recompiled.

Java Beans   Component software written with Java.

JavaScript   Special Java instructions written directly in HTML to be interpreted line by line by your browser.

Macintosh Runtime Java (MRJ) A Java Virtual Machine written for the Macintosh operating system. MRJ 1.5 comes bundled with Mac OS 8.5.

Runtime Engine A software emulator written to accompany a Java program to provide a little virtual machine where Java runs. Originally, each Java program had to have a run-time engine for each computer platform—a very expensive proposition. When Java run-time engines moved to operating system software, Java became a viable open system language.

virtual machine A software-based environment that emulates another operating system. Java uses a virtual machine to function on many different computer platforms. The software emulator is written for each computer, but the Java programs run on any virtual machine. The Mac's virtual machine is called Macintosh Runtime for Java.

Q&A

Q What's the status of Castanet and other push technologies based on Java?

A Push is currently a technology in flux. Java as a programming language has been extensively introduced throughout the Web, but programs that you can download via engines such as Castanet do not seem to be developing as rapidly. This is still a technology waiting for a reason to exist.

Q What books can I read to find out more about Java?

A The following books are very enlightening:

- *Java for Dummies* by Aaron E. Walsh (1996, IDG Books Worldwide).
- The Sunsoft Press Java Series by Peter van der Linden, including *Not Just Java* and *Just Java* (1997, Prentice-Hall and Sun Microsystems).
- *Teach Yourself Java for Macintosh in 21 Days* by Laura Lemay and Charles L. Perkins, with Timothy Webster (1996, Hayden Books).

Q What's the difference between MRJ 1.5 and MRJ 2.0?

A Mostly speed and support for the newest version of SunSoft's Java System Development Kit (SDK), currently at version 1.2.

Q Which runtime engine should I install as the default on my Mac: Netscape Navigator's, Microsoft Internet Explorer's JIT, MRJ, or all of them?

A The answer depends on the amount of RAM you have installed on your Mac. Supposedly, at the time of this writing, Netscape's Java is slightly faster than Internet Explorer's Java engine without JIT, and both are faster than the Mac version. You'll need a lot of RAM to operate Microsoft's Java with JIT, but if you want power, that's the one to use.

21

Workshop

The Workshop contains quiz questions to help you solidify your understanding of the material covered. You can find the answers to the quiz questions in Appendix B, "Quiz Answers."

Quiz

1. How do you run an applet on your Mac?
2. How do you control the operation of your applet?
3. What else does Applet Runner do?
4. How do you run an applet on the Internet from your Mac?
5. What's the Add button on Applet Runner used for?
6. What's the status of OpenDoc?
7. What do you need in Netscape Navigator to run Java applets? In Internet Explorer?
8. What's the difference between Applet Runner and the Apple Applet Viewer?
9. Where's MRJ installed on your Mac?
10. What good is all this Java stuff today?

HOUR 22

Automating Your Mac with AppleScript

One of the nice things about computers, especially Macs, is that they can take care of drudge work for you. For example, instead of driving up the stock prices of white out companies, you can just use the mouse and the Delete key to banish typos. You'll find that you can save a lot of time and be more efficient by investing a little effort in learning and using AppleScript. This hour covers the following topics:

- How AppleScript works
- Working with the Apple Script Editor
- Recording scripts
- AppleScript's scripting language
- Some advanced tools and where to find more information about scripting and AppleScript

What Is AppleScript?

AppleScript is a scripting language that's designed to allow you to automate actions performed by the Finder and by a wide spectrum of Mac applications. The actual script looks a lot like standard English, with verbs, nouns, adverbs, and adjectives. Even if you haven't had any programming experience, you should be able to quickly master AppleScript.

Although your Mac is an incredibly sophisticated and easy to use machine, it's brainless. Everything it does is based on instructions someone has given it. The Mac can understand a whole bunch of different languages, but most of them are complex and would require you to invest years learning them. AppleScript is an English-like language that's designed to make it easy for you to tell your Mac what to do. The language lets you work with the arcane four-letter codes, called *Apple Events*, without having to actually manipulate these beasts. AppleScript does the interpreting of your commands to boss around Apple Events and get the job done.

> AppleScript comes in two flavors, depending on which Mac OS 8 version you're running. The newest version of AppleScript, version 3.0, works *only* with Mac OS 8.5. *Do not* install AppleScript 3.0 on an older version of Mac OS 8. If you're working with Mac OS 8.0 or 8.1, use AppleScript 1.1.3.

Things You Can Do with AppleScript

AppleScript can help you in the following three ways:

- It can save you time by automating tasks you currently do manually, such as clearing out your browser's cache file.
- It can save you effort by converting something that takes a bunch of mouse clicks or a lot of repetition into a single mouse click.
- It can let you do things you couldn't easily do manually—for example, fixing emailed files that have lost their icons. In many cases, a script will help you in more than one way.

To give a better idea of what scripts can do, here are some examples:

- A script can let you delete all the files in your Netscape Navigator cache so that Navigator runs better.
- A script can record video.

- If you're using Qualcomm's Eudora and FileMaker, Inc.'s FileMaker Pro, you can create an AppleScript to dump all email into a database and then re-send email out of the database to Eudora. (A script that fixes files that can't be opened.)

- A script can find all the copies of SimpleText on your hard disk and deletes all but a single copy of the most recent version.

- A script can read your Netscape Navigator bookmark file and find all the URLs in the file and create entries in a FileMaker Pro database for each URL, including the page name, the URL, and any comments you've entered for each bookmark. This way, you can search for sites using keywords.

- A script can take the database built by the aforementioned script and automatically build a Web page with those links sorted by category to enable visitors to your site to jump to those pages.

- A script can log onto the Internet, download news from your favorite sites, find articles that interest you, put them into a FileMaker Pro database, and construct a personal newspaper with those articles in QuarkXpress or PageMaker.

The good news is that with just what you'll learn in these few pages, you'll be able to write most of these scripts. The last three examples will take a bit of work, but you'll have all the tools you need to get started.

The Downside of Using AppleScript 3.0

A catch is also involved with anything that sounds too wonderful to be true. The same holds true for AppleScript 3.0. The downside of using the newest version of AppleScript is that older scripts that ran under System 7 might not work with this version, because the Finder has changed how it relates to AppleScript under Mac OS 8.5. You need to update your older scripts to support new Finder features, such as independent view properties for each window, and then recompile them before they will run.

AppleScript 3.0 is very smart and knows which Finder terminology is defunct. When AppleScript comes upon an out-of-date term, it adds the word *OBSOLETE* next to the term. Clean out these terms from your script, and the script will run with Mac OS 8. On the other hand, if you update the script for Finder 8.0, it will no longer run successfully with older Finders. Catch-22.

What's Under the Hood?

AppleScript works directly with the Mac's operating system to perform work. Because the language is so intimate with your Mac's innards, the program inserts several components into your System Folder. To make things more fun, AppleScript's other components, namely Scripting Additions files and the Script Editor, are located in two other places on your hard disk: the Scripting Additions folder in your System Folder, and the AppleScript folder in your Apple Extras folder. In addition, Mac OS 8.5 creates a Scripts folder in your System Folder to hold active scripts that have been dragged onto the System icon. I'll talk more about those folders and how they function later in this hour.

What's in the Extensions Folder?

Here's a list of what you'll find in your Extensions folder:

- **The AppleScript extension.** This extension contains the actual AppleScript code.
- **AppleScript Lib extensions.** These extensions are shared libraries used by scriptable Mac OS components. As indicated by their inclusion in your Extensions folder, many more Finder components are now scriptable, including the Appearance and Apple Menu Items control panels, the Application Switcher and ColorSync System extensions, the File Exchange control panel, the Find application, the Apple Help Viewer application, and the System Profiler application. In addition, two special tools have been provided in the AppleScript folder in Apple Extras to support Open Transport via the Open Transport Configuration database: the Desktop Printer Manager and the Network Setup Scripting application.

- **SOMobjects for Mac OS extensions.** These extensions are shared libraries used by PowerPC-native applications that incorporate AppleScript. Shared libraries contain code used by multiple programs or application components. You'll notice that Microsoft Office 98 products use many shared libraries.

- **Folder Actions extension.** This extension controls the actions of folders and is a new scriptable Finder component. Mac OS 8.5's Finder supports attachable folders for five actions: opening a folder, closing a folder window, adding items to an open folder, removing items from an open folder, and resizing or moving a folder window. If you include any of these actions in your AppleScript, it triggers adjunct scripts assigned or "attached" to the targeted folders. Mac OS 8.5's CD-ROM includes ten Folder Action scripts.

What Other Script Folders are Hiding in the System Folder?

Two other folders are used by AppleScript that reside in your System Folder—the Scripting Additions and Scripts folders:

- **Scripting Additions (also called OSAX).** These are add-on modules that provide special resources or commands to the AppleScript programming environment. AppleScript version 1.3, which ships with Mac OS 8.5, has consolidated the previously unbound Scripting Additions files into a single scripting addition called *Standard Additions*. Other scripting additions included in the folder are FileSharing Commands, Keyboard Addition, MonitorDepth, Network Setup Scripting, Remote

Access Commands, Set Volume, and Desktop Printer Manager.

Another folder resides within the Scripting Additions folder: the Dialects folder. If you want to write scripts for languages other than American English, you can because localization support for English, French, and Japanese via dialect files stored in this folder.

- **Scripts.** Mac OS 8.5 is very tidy. Rather than throw active scripts all over the System Folder, scripts are collected and stored in one place: the Scripts folder. Place any script you want to activate within this folder (or drag it onto the System Folder's icon). Another very important function of the Scripts folder is to contain those script sets that can work with the new Scripting Additions menu (also called the *OSA Menu Script menu*).

A PRESENT FROM APPLE

Apple includes a very useful tool called OSA Menu Lite, written by Leonard Rosenthol (freeware), in the AppleScript folder on the Mac OS 8.5 CD-ROM. The OSA menu extension installs a new menu bar item: the OSA menu. Compiled scripts placed in the Scripts menu in your System Folder will be displayed on this menu for your easy access. Apple also includes three sets of scripts for use with the OSA menu: Finder scripts, Universal scripts, and Script Editor scripts. Additional script sets as well as the full version of OSA Menu are available on the AppleScript site at http://www.applescript.apple.com /script_menu/script_menu.01.html.

 Note that those scripts that you want to appear on the Apple menu should have aliases placed in the Automated Tasks folder located in the Apple Extras folder.

What's Stored in the AppleScript Folder?

The AppleScript folder that's included in the Apple Extras folder (although you don't have to keep it there) contains three folders: Automated Tasks, More Automated Tasks, and the Script Editor. The automated tasks folders contain third-party scripts provided by Apple for your use.

Scripting Fundamentals

You can make your Mac work for you by presenting it with a list of things you want it to do. This list is called a *script*. A script is a series of instructions that contain words that work like nouns, adjectives, adverbs, and verbs. You use these instructions to tell the Mac what to do.

The Mac OS supports several different scripting languages (the way you write your lists):

- **UserTalk.** UserLand's Frontier scripting language (http://www.scripting.com).
- **MacTcl/Tk (Tool Command Language/Toolkit).** Sun Microsystems' scripting language (http://sunscript.sun.com).
- **AppleScript.** Apple Computer's scripting language (included free with Mac OS 8.5).

Because the Mac comes with a very powerful scripting language (and for free), why use anything else?

The AppleScript language is very simple. It consists of groups of actions and their attendant targets. There are really only five objects that AppleScript uses to work with an application's capabilities: Get, Set, Count, Copy, and Run.

AppleScript works by sending commands, called *events*, between applications. *Apple Events* are the glue that holds the Mac OS together. AppleScript learns which Apple Events the targeted program (that is, the one you want to affect) can understand by reading that program's dictionary. This dictionary is very important and underlies everything that AppleScript can do.

The dictionary tells AppleScript which objects the application is able to work with. For example, the Finder can work with files, folders, and disks. The dictionary also provides AppleScript with translations for the four-letter event codes so that you can write a command in English in the script and have AppleScript send the correct code to the application to trigger the event. Figure 22.1 shows the Finder's dictionary.

FIGURE 22.1.

Every scriptable application contains a data dictionary.

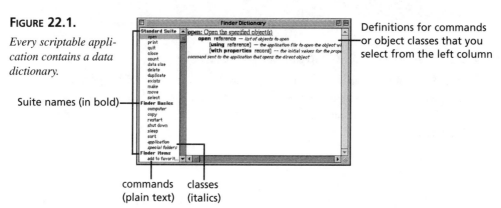

Suite names (in bold)

commands
(plain text)

classes
(italics)

Definitions for commands
or object classes that you
select from the left column

You can view the dictionary of a scriptable application when you're in the Script Editor by selecting Open Dictionary from the File menu. Select the application (for example, the Finder) from the Open dialog box and then click Open. The Script Editor displays a new window with the application's dictionary entries. Select a command, class, or type of command (called a suite) from the left column to display its list of object classes and commands in the right column.

Using Apple's Script Editor

As mentioned previously, the program you use to write, edit, and record scripts is called the *Script Editor*. You find the Script Editor in the AppleScript folder in the Apple Extras folder that Mac OS 8.5 places on your Mac during installation. In this hour, you'll use the Script Editor that comes with AppleScript. Double-click the Script Editor to launch the application. Figure 22.2 shows you the Script Editor's window. The script window can contain one script.

FIGURE 22.2.

The Apple Script Editor window.

The script description area is where you type in an explanation of what your script does. The Record and Stop buttons are used to control the recording of a script. The Run button lets you tell your Mac to follow the instructions you've written. The Check Syntax button lets you ask the Mac whether it understands what you've typed. You'll type the scripts you want the Mac to run into the area below these buttons.

Four basic processes are involved in creating a script (although there are several methods of performing these steps). The flowchart displayed in Figure 22.3 illustrates what the process looks like.

FIGURE 22.3.

*The script writing
process.*

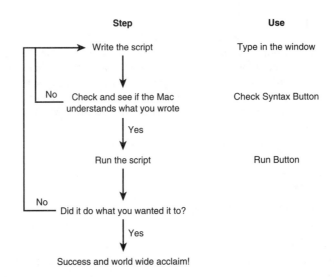

Scripts require the following steps:

1. **Generating a script.** There are two ways to write a script: have the Mac do it for you, called *recording*, and doing it yourself, called *scripting*.

2. **Editing your script.** You can move lines around in your script just as you would in a word processing document. You can also format your script for easier reading and better comprehensibility.

3. **Checking the syntax of your script.** This step is also called *debugging*. Syntax is the grammar of the script. If this is correct, the script will actually work.

4. **Compiling the script.** This step changes the script into machine code that can be understood by the Mac.

Generating a Script

The Script Editor is an application just like any other you've encountered on the Mac. Double-click it's icon to open the Editor. You can open any script with the Apple Script Editor except those saved as run-only scripts. To open an existing script, choose Open from the File menu (or press the keyboard combination Command-O).

You can only record actions in a recordable application (one that recognizes the recorder), such as the Finder. Not all actions are recordable. Only actions that result in changes to a document can be recorded. Therefore, random mouse movements cannot be recorded.

Recording Scripts

AppleScript allows you to make an application or set of applications write scripts for you. The basic technique is that you work in an application, such as PageMaker or Netscape Navigator, selecting menu items and clicking buttons, while AppleScript and the application watch what you do, converting your actions into a script.

To see how powerful recording can be, let's record a script that empties out the Netscape Navigator cache folder—that's where Navigator stores all the pages you've visited. Cleaning out the cache can help Navigator run faster and possibly crash less often; therefore, emptying it periodically is not a bad idea. Follow these steps:

1. Open a new script window in Script Editor by selecting New from the File menu.

2. Click the desktop to return to the Finder and open the Cache folder—the Netscape folder in the Preferences folder inside your System Folder.

3. Now go back to Script Editor and click the Record button in the script window. It will turn green (shown in gray in Figure 22.4). A small flashing icon also replaces the apple in the menu bar at the top of the screen.

FIGURE 22.4.

Be quiet, you're recording!

4. Now go back to the Finder, select the Cache window, and choose Select All from the Edit menu. Then drag the files to the Trash Can.

5. Empty the Trash Can using the Empty Trash command in the Special menu.

6. Now go back to the Script Editor and click the Stop button in the Script window.

7. AppleScript displays the resulting script in the script editing area.

Why Recording Isn't the Best Option

Recording is not the best means of creating a script because it does not provide the flexibility needed to fully exploit the power of scripting. Recording faces the following problems:

- Not that many scriptable applications are also "recordable." However, some really useful ones, such as the Finder and Word, are recordable.
- Recorded scripts can't include `if` and `repeat` statements. This means that recorded scripts are simple linear scripts that can't make decisions or repeat the same task (that is, unless you manually repeat the task while recording the script).

Even with these limitations, you can still record useful scripts. More important, you can see how to use the commands in an application's dictionary.

Recording actions to create scripts lets you create linear scripts that do one action after another. If you want to create more complicated or elegant scripts that make decisions, you need to write them yourself, as covered in the next section.

Writing Your Own Scripts

If you're a logical thinker, you can use AppleScript's full-blown programming language to write your own scripts. If you learn its verbs, adjectives, nouns, and adverbs, as described in the "AppleScript Language Basics" section (later in this hour), you can create some powerful tools. The following exercise provides a small feel for how script writing works.

EXERCISE #1: HELLO WORLD

All right, it's now time for you to write your first script:

1. Click the mouse in the script editing area and type **display dialog Hello World**.

2. Click the Check Syntax button to see whether the Mac understands what you typed.

3. Surprise! I tricked you. These instructions do not work. AppleScript displays an alert box to that effect.

Although the error message—called a *syntax error*, because something's wrong with the structure of your script—may seem incomprehensible, the part of the script that has a problem is shown in a little box. So what could be wrong with the Hello World script? Well, the answer is that `Hello World` should be in quotes. Follow these steps to fix the problem:

1. Dismiss the error by clicking the Cancel button. Then, add quotes around `Hello World`. Next, click the Check Syntax button again.

2. The scripting window should now look like the one shown in Figure 22.5.

FIGURE 22.5.

A script the Mac can understand!

22

Scripts can get long and cumbersome to read and comprehend. Luckily, they are actually composed of parts—operators, keywords, comments, and so forth. The Script Editor keeps track of these parts. There are two actions you can take on your script: adding text, tabs, and line breaks and adding formatting.

To add text, tabs, or lines to a script, just type them in the script window. You can use this method to add more commands and actions to your script than can be performed using the recording method.

You can indicate where these different parts occur in your script by using the Formatting command to change the formatting of the different parts from their default colors, styles, and type. Table 22.1 presents the different parts of an AppleScript script that can be delineated using the Formatting dialog box.

TABLE 22.1. FORMATTABLE SCRIPT PARTS.

Script Part	Default Format	What It Does
New text	Courier 10pt	Any portion of a script typed before saving, running, or syntax checking.
Operators	Geneva 10pt	"Verbs" that perform an action or operate on values: plus and minus are operators.
Language keywords	Geneva 10pt bold	AppleScript code available to all scripting applications.
Application keywords	Geneva 10pt	Scripting code specific to a particular application (found in that program's data dictionary).
Comments	Geneva 9pt italic	Explanations and documentation you typed into your script. Comments are ignored by AppleScript.
Values	Geneva 10pt	Information entered into a script that's used by the AppleScript code to perform an action.
Variables	Geneva 10pt	Containers (definitions) for values.
References	Geneva 10pt	Identification of specific objects (such as a specific word on a line of a document) that can be acted upon by the script.

To change the formatting of your script, choose AppleScript Formatting from the Edit menu. In the resulting dialog box, select a type of scripting device, such as Comments, and use the Fonts and Style menus to change its formatting. Click OK to return to your script and see the result. Click Default to return to AppleScript's original settings.

Saving Your Script

Congratulations, you've now mastered the basic mechanics of writing a script. There's one last thing to learn: how to save a script you've written. As with any other Mac application, the Script Editor has a Save As command in the File menu. After selecting Save As, use the Kind pop-up menu to save your script as one of three types of applications: a text file, a compiled script, or a standalone application.

The only unique issue about saving a script is that you must decide the format in which to save it. The three available format options are listed in Table 22.2.

TABLE 22.2. APPLESCRIPT FILE FORMATS.

File Type	Description
Text	A standard text file that can't be executed.
Compiled script	A file that can be executed. Double-clicking the icon launches the Script Editor, where you can use the Run button.
Application	A standard Mac "double-clickable" application that will run your script.

When you save a script as an application, you get two additional options. The first, Stay Open, is your way to tell the Mac to leave the script running once you've started it. This is a useful option when you're creating agents.

The second option, Never Show Startup Screen, lets you prevent the display of the normal startup message. What startup message, you may ask? Well, if you add some information to the description area of the Script window, save your Hello World script as an application, and then double-click it, you'll see the message displayed in Figure 22.6.

FIGURE 22.6.

Your first script's start-up message describes what your script does.

Note that I added the phrase *A script to greet the world!* to the script description area. The phrase will be displayed in the startup screen. If you check the Never Show Startup Screen option in the Save dialog box, the user will not see this dialog box.

Congratulations! You now know 98 percent of all you'll ever need to know about the mechanics of writing a script. You can find out more about Script Editor by reading the `Using AppleScript Part 2` file in the AppleScript folder. Your next challenge is to learn the AppleScript language so you can write your own scripts.

Debugging and Compiling

There are two final steps in creating a script: debugging (checking your script for errors and correcting them) and compiling (or running) the script.

Syntax checking is the most frustrating and time-consuming process involved in script development. You use the Check Syntax button on the Script Editor to see whether the Mac understands the instructions you've given it. If the Mac doesn't understand what you wrote, you need to go back and modify your script so that it's comprehensible to the Mac. To do so, follow these steps:

1. Once you get the green light from the Mac, you can run the script using the Run Button.

2. Make sure the script did what you wanted it to do. Just because the Mac understood what you typed doesn't mean it did what you wanted it to. Therefore, if your script is designed to delete all the items in the Netscape Navigator Cache folder, you should check that folder and confirm that it's empty after you've run the script. (You should also check to see whether or not it's empty before you run the script.)

You can tell that the Mac feels comfortable with what you've typed because no error messages appear. Now you're ready to take the great leap from being an everyday Mac expert to being a scripting superhero.

Extending the AppleScript Language

Although AppleScript is very powerful by itself, its real strength comes from its extensibility. You can extend AppleScript in two ways: by using Scripting Additions or scriptable applications:

- Scripting Additions (also called OSAXs) add functionality to AppleScript via additional routines and resources. AppleScript 1.3, which comes with Mac OS 8.5, provides several new OSAXs, including scripting the Clipboard, a delay command for pausing scripts, displaying lists of text items, mounting AppleTalk and AppleShare IP volumes, speaking text, summarizing text, and the ability to have dialog boxes

automatically close after an indicated period of time. In addition, a new Internet
suite is included for creating Common Gateway Interfaces (CGIs) for use in
automating browser and server behavior.

- Scriptable applications are programs that support scripting. Not all programs are
  scriptable (that is, respond to AppleScript commands). What's more, applications
  that are scriptable are "AppleScript savvy" to differing levels. Table 22.3 presents
  an annotated list of scriptable applications. See
  `http://www.applescript.apple.com/applescript_overview/scriptable_soft`
  `ware/enabled.00.html` for a full listing.

TABLE 22.3. SCRIPTABLE APPLICATIONS.

Scripting Level	Applications	Description
Scriptable/Recordable/ Attachable	Century Software's ClockWork	A day planner
	Multi-Ad Creator's Creator2	Page layout application for advertising
	Late Night Software's Script DeBugger	Script editing application
Scriptable/Recordable	Apple Media Tool	Application for creating cross platform multimedia presentations
	Canto Software's Canto Cumulus	Networkable image database
	Dartmouth College's Fetch	FTP communications software
	Quark, Inc.'s QuarkXpress	Desktop publishing application (Requires Street Logic's ScriptMaster Xtension for recording)
	Tex-Edit Plus	Text editor
	Farrallon's Timbuktu Pro	Remote control/connection software for data transfer
Scriptable	Adobe FrameMaker	Long document desktop publishing application
	Adrenaline Software's Adrenaline Numbers & Charts	Chart and graph creation software
	BareBones Software's BBEdit	HTML editor

Scripting Level	Applications	Description
	Butler SQL	Client/server database management system
	MetroWorks' CodeWarrior	Programming environment
	FileMaker Pro by FileMaker, Inc. (formerly Claris Software)	Database application
	ImSpace's Kudos Image Browser	Image management database application
	Apple HyperCard	Mac OS interactive application development environment
	Dantz Retrospect	Backup software
	Aladdin StuffIt Deluxe	Compression/decompression application

22

AppleScript Language Basics

What follows is a crash course in AppleScript's programming language. If you've already programmed in some other language, such as HyperCard's HyperTalk, you should be able to digest this and do some simple things. If you've never programmed before, you'll probably have to pick up an AppleScript book in order to fully learn how to script.

Let's discuss AppleScript grammar for a moment. Like all languages, AppleScript uses nouns (called *data types*), adjectives (called *variables*), and verbs (called *operators* or *commands*) to function coherently. The next paragraphs describe AppleScript's data types, variables, and operators.

Data Types

Like a noun, a data type describes a thing (in this case, your information). Data types are the different formats that AppleScript uses to express types of information, such as numbers, dates, logic, and so forth. AppleScript contains a number of different data types, but the main ones are listed in Table 22.4.

TABLE 22.4. APPLESCRIPT DATA TYPES.

Data Type	Description	Example
Integer	A whole number	1, 2, 378, 19944
Real	A number with a fractional part	1.23, 0.14, 3.1415, 199876.45
String	Regular text	"Hello World", "Yes"
Boolean	A logical value	True, False (no other values allowed)
List	A group of values	{7, "b", 3.2}, {"a", "test", "c", "work"}
Date	A point in time	"Friday, May 16, 1997 12:00:00"
Reference	An indirect description of something	Word two of paragraph three of document "Business Plan"
Record	A group of values where each value has a name.	{text returned:"Alien Monster", button returned:"Zap It!"}

Variables

An adjective modifies a noun, thereby giving you more information about the quality of the noun. Variables provide more information about a script in the same manner. A variable is a place to store a data type so you can reuse it later. To store something in a variable, you write a script line like one of the following:

```
set x to "this is a string"
set y to 2
```

Each of the lines of script shown here tells the Mac to set the value of the variable—*x or y* in these examples—to the value listed after **to**. You probably remember with great joy the variables you used in algebra, right? Actually, you'll find the variables in AppleScript to be pretty simple.

BOLD KEYWORDS

When a script compiles, certain words will be shown in bold. These are called *keywords* (not all keywords turn bold, however). Script Editor writes these keywords in bold to help you see the structure of your program.

Unlike some other programming languages, you don't have to "declare" a variable (in other words, you don't have to tell the Mac what type of data the variable will hold) prior to using it. You can store any type of data in any variable. You can even store one

22

type of data—say, a string—in a variable in one part of your script and another type—how about an integer—in the same variable elsewhere in the same script.

POINTS TO REMEMBER WHEN NAMING VARIABLES

Follow these basic guidelines when naming the variables you use in your scripts:

- Variable names can contain any letters (either uppercase or lowercase).
- Variable names can contain numbers but not decimal points.
- Variable names can contain the underscore character (_).
- Case doesn't matter; therefore, average_score and Average_Score are treated the same.
- Select variable names that indicate what the variables store rather than using cryptic names you won't remember later (such as color versus co).
- Don't use keywords for variable names (you'll get an error message if you try).

Operators

Verbs describe what your noun is doing—some action or process it is performing. There are two types of verbs in scripting: operators and commands.

Most scripts involve performing tasks and manipulating information. Operators are tools that allow you to transform information in ways ranging from the straightforward (for example, 2 + 2 uses the addition operator to add two numbers) to the elegant (for example, the use of the ampersand symbol lets you append strings). Table 22.5 shows the most useful math operators and what they do.

TABLE 22.5. THE APPLESCRIPT MATH OPERATORS.

Operator	Description	Example	Final Value of x
+	Addition	set x to (2 + 2)	4
-	Subtraction	set x to (7.4 - 1.2)	6.2
*	Multiplication	set x to 3*5	15
/	Division	set x to 3/4	0.75
^	Exponentiation	set x to 5^2	25.0
mod	Remainder	set x to 26 mod 5	1
div	Integer division	set x to 7 div 3	2

Operators tell AppleScript to evaluate the variables in a line of code based on what the operator does and to write the result on the next line. Typically, operators give you an actual answer that's placed in a result window.

Another type of operator gives you a "true" or "false" response based on the operator. These are called *logical* or *comparison* operators. AppleScript also has a whole bunch of logical and comparison operators, such as AND, OR, and > (greater than), which you learn more about in the section on making decisions. There are two logical operators, shown in Table 22.6, that you'll find yourself using often as you write scripts.

TABLE 22.6. LOGICAL OPERATORS.

Operator	Description	Example	Final Value of x
as	Coercion	set x to 7.23 as string	7.23
&	Append	set x to "this " & "that"	this that
		set x to "this " & 7	this 7

The as operator lets you convert one type of data value to another. Not all data types can be coerced into every other data type, so you should consult one of the sources list at the end of this hour or do some experiments to see what you can and cannot coerce.

The & operator lets you append strings. It will automatically coerce nonstring arguments to strings.

Commands

Commands are specialized instructions that tell AppleScript to perform certain actions. Table 22.7 shows the most useful commands.

TABLE 22.7. USEFUL APPLESCRIPT COMMANDS.

Command	Description	Example	Final Value of x
activate	Launches an application or brings it to the front	activate application "Netscape Navigator"	Nothing returned but Navigator is in front and running
copy	Makes a copy of a value and puts it into a new variable	copy 37 to x	37

Command	Description	Example	Final Value of x
count	Gets the number of some type of item in a container	set x to count {1,2,3}	3
		set x to number of integers in {1,2.3,"a",7}	2
current date	Returns the current time and date	set x to current date	date "Saturday, May 17, 1997 14:06:53"
info for	Returns info about files and folders in a record	set x to info for file "MetroWorks:Read Me"	{name:"Read Me", creation date:date "Monday, April 3, 1995 09:58:01", modification date:date "Thursday, May 4, 1995 16:31:37", icon position:{128, 104}, visible:true, size:4425, folder:false, alias:false, locked:false, file creator:"ttxt", file type:"ttro", short version:"", long version:"", default application:alias "Ted:SimpleText"}
list disks	Returns a list of the currently mounted disks	set x to list disks	{"Ted", "System", "Kate", "Scripting", "Mary", "Therese"}

continues

TABLE 22.7. CONTINUED

Command	Description	Example	Final Value of x
list folder	Returns a list of file and folder names in a folder	`set x to list folder "Ted:Apple Extras:AppleScript ..."`	{"Automated Tasks", "More Automated Tasks", "Script Editor", "Using AppleScript part 1", "Using AppleScript part 2"}
offset	Finds the location of one string inside another	`set x to offset of "y" in "maybe"` `set x to offset of "y" in "no"`	3 0
path to	Returns the location of standard Mac folders such as the System folder	`set x to path to System Folder`	alias "Ted:System Folder:"
random number	Returns a random number between 0 and 1	`set x to random number`	0.149589591869
round	Rounds a real number to an integer	`set x to round 3.2`	3

Note that many of these commands have more complex options than those shown here. For example, the `random number` command lets you specify the upper and lower limits for the random numbers.

Advanced Tools and Scripting Resources

AppleScript is so powerful that a cottage industry has developed around it. I can't cover all the useful shareware and freeware that exists, but here are some short overviews of tools that will help you automate your drudgery work. You can find a complete list of useful stuff at the ScriptWeb site (`http://www.scriptweb.com/`).

- **Scripter 2.0 (Main Event Software).** This shareware is a nice AppleScript development tool that has a debugger for tracking down mistakes in your script and a bunch of utilities to make writing scripts easier. Although Script Editor is free, if you spend any significant amount of time scripting, you'll appreciate Scripter 2.0's more powerful development environment. (`http://www2.mainevent.com/bis/mainevent/mainevent/products/scripter/home_frame.html.`)

- **Script Debugger (Late Night Software LTD).** This shareware is another powerful AppleScript development environment with a debugger. It also comes with a ton of useful scripting additions. (`http://www.latenightsw.com/.`)

- **TCP/IP Scripting Addition (Mango Tree Software).** This shareware lets you write scripts that work directly with the Internet. (`http://www.mangotree.com/.`)

- **FaceSpan 2.1 (Digital Technology International).** This shareware is a nice tool designed to let you build full applications with menus and all the other standard Mac interface elements. Instead of programming, though, you just write AppleScripts to define what the program will do. An excellent way to get more user interface tools than the standard display dialog box. (`http://www.dtint.com/facespan.html.`)

- **Marionet 1.1(Allegiant).** This shareware is a set of scripting additions that allows you to provide Internet access from your scripts. Marionet supports getting Web pages, email, and FTP. This is a really nice way to add Internet capabilities to your tools. (`http://www.allegiant.com/marionet/.`)

- **OSA Menu.** This is a nice freeware utility that you can find at most online sites. It puts a menu of scripts in the upper-right side of the menu bar. You can run the script by selecting its menu item. Hats off to Leonard Rosenthal for this nice tool.

- **Frontier 4.2.3 (UserLand Software).** Frontier is the first scripting language to have been developed for the Mac. It's free (it used to cost over $400) and it's fast. Unlike AppleScript, Frontier is a full-fledged development environment with a debugger, database, and lots of nifty tools. It's also very good for managing Web sites. The one drawback is that Frontier's language is not as "English like" as AppleScript. However, it's nowhere near as complex as C++ or Java. (`http://www.scripting.com/frontier/.`)

- **Macro Tools.** These are tools that let you fake typing keys, clicking the mouse, and selecting items from inside a script. In general, these tools are designed to automate tasks without scripting; they're useful for controlling applications with minimal or no scripting support. Although Tempo II, QuickKeys, and OneClick are all useful, in general, PreFab Player (`http://www.tiac.net/prefab/`) is designed to work with scripts and nothing else.

Summary

AppleScript provides a powerful way to augment the features of Mac OS 8.5. Using AppleScript, you can automate repetitive or boring tasks, such as downloads, backups, and file cleanups. Many programs are "AppleScript savvy," meaning that their dictionaries are accessible to AppleScript for use in preparing appropriate Apple Events.

This hour provided a quick review of the syntax (grammar) inherent in AppleScript's instructions as well as provided tables of objects, variables, operators, and commands for your use in future scripting efforts.

Term Review

agent   A script that runs in the background all the time.

Apple Events   The system software used by AppleScript to interact with applications. Applications send event messages between themselves. When an application receives an Apple Event, it takes an action based on the content of the event.

AppleScript   The scripting language that comes bundled with Mac OS 8.5.

control structure   A special type of AppleScript command that teaches AppleScript how to perform other commands.

data types   The different formats that AppleScript uses to express types of information, such as numbers, dates, logic, and so forth.

dictionary   The listing of commands, object classes, and suites used by an application along with their definitions and relationships. Data dictionaries reside in the System Folder and are accessible by Script Editor.

object classes   A series of linked data types and commands that together perform a function.

operators   Tools that allow you to transform numerical and alphabetical information.

programming   The act of writing instructions using a language that's translatable by the computer into code that it can process.

recording   Enabling AppleScript to follow your actions on the Mac in order to build a script.

Script Editor   The application that comes with AppleScript used to write, run, and edit scripts.

scripting   The act of writing your own instructions in AppleScript from scratch.

Scripting Additions   Files you place in the Scripting Additions folder inside your System Folder. Scripting Additions can provide just about any type of functionality, ranging from advanced text manipulation features to control over the PPP control panel.

22

syntax   The structure of an instruction. In other words, how to use data types, operators, variables, and commands to construct a script that can be understood by the computer.

variables   A place to store a data type so you can reuse it later. Variables can hold various values.

Q&A

Q   Where can I go on the Mac for more help with AppleScript?

A The AppleScript Help files feature a full tutorial on all aspects of script production. On the desktop, choose Help Center from the Help menu. In the Help Browser, click AppleScript Help link.

Q   Does AppleScript support Unicode (the international standard for type display)?

A Yes, version 1.3 that comes with Mac OS 8.5 supports Unicode text.

Q   How does AppleScript support enterprise workflow through database scripting?

A AppleScript fully supports the linking of databases, image processing applications, and desktop publishing applications via third-party OSAXs, Adobe PhotoShop plug-ins, and QuarkXpress Xtensions. You can use AppleScript to automatically convert electronic publications to Web pages that link to databases. Check out `http://www.applescript.apple.com/applescript_overview/dbase_lessons/` `DBASE_LESSON.00.HTML` for more information.

Q   What is the optimum hardware configuration requirements for running AppleScript applications?

A If you want to run publishing automations involving multiple applications and data transfers, you need a powerful Mac with extensive amounts of RAM. A G3-based PowerMac with at least 24 MB of free RAM (after the 12 MB used by the Mac OS) is the minimum configuration.

Workshop

The Workshop contains quiz questions to help you solidify your understanding of the material covered. You can find the answers to the quiz questions in Appendix B, "Quiz Answers."

Quiz

1. What is AppleScript?
2. What are some problems with using the newest version of AppleScript (version 3.0)?
3. Where would you look to find your Scripting Additions files?
4. Where would you look to find your active scripts?
5. What new application lets you use a menu to access scripts and additions?
6. How do you record a script in Script Editor?
7. What is Syntax Check?
8. Where would you look to find a specific application term?
9. How can you set up the Script Editor so that a script is more comprehensible?
10. What are the four processes used when you create a script?

HOUR 23

The File System Extended

This hour delves into the inner workings of one of the newest features available in Mac OS 8.1 and higher—the Mac OS Extended File System (or HFS+). During this hour, you'll learn about the following topics:

- How your hard drive and the Mac OS File Manager work together to record and manage files
- What logical formatting entails and how HFS differs from HFS+
- What happens when you save a file
- The benefits and pitfalls of upgrading to HFS+
- How to reformat your hard drive

What Is a Hard Drive?

Your hard drive is the same thing as your hard disk—the terms are synonymous. Hard disks are composed of iron-oxide-coated aluminum platters (or some other flexible metal) encased in a hard shell.

Two types of hard disks are used in Macs: SCSI and IDE. Each type of hard disk requires a unique initialization/format. IDE only works as an internal hard disk on Macs. SCSI disks can be internal or external, as long as the Mac has the correct internal cabling to connect the SCSI disk internally to the hardware bus.

Hard disks consist of a rigid, usually nonremovable series of round, flat platters placed one on top of each other. Figure 23.1 displays a schematic of a generic hard disk drive. The read-write heads and their arms are lined up above and below each disk where they float a hair's breath above and below the platter. Unlike the floppy disk, which spins only when a read or write operation is requested, hard disks platters are continuously spinning. IDE drives tend to have a lower rpm rate than SCSI drives. Current SCSI drives (at the high end of the product line) run at 7,200 and 10,000 rpm. A minimum of 10ms access time is required for video capture or audio recording, so 7,200-rpm drives are a minimal configuration for doing multimedia on Macs.

FIGURE 23.1.

A schematic of a hard drive.

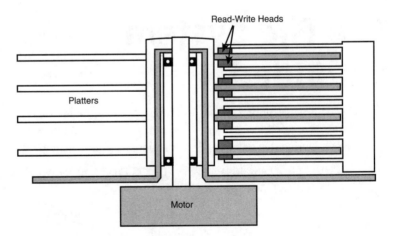

Hard disks also can hold more data in the same amount of space than a floppy because data is packed more tightly on the platter (due to the difference in the substrate—plastic in the floppy and aluminum or some other flexible metal in the hard disk; also, the magnetic particles that coat this substrate are smaller). For this reason, the read-write arms do not have to travel as far along the platters to retrieve or replace the data; this also makes the hard disk perform more efficiently than a floppy disk.

Disks and drives are the tools by which the Macintosh gains information. Those tools are useless if they are not instructed in how to perform work in the Macintosh environment. The Macintosh teaches the disks how to behave during a process known as *initialization*.

Initializing Disks

In order for the Macintosh's disk drives to read a disk, the disk must be organized into some sort of pattern. Initializing a disk places the Macintosh disk layout requirements on to the media, making it usable to the Macintosh. These patterns lay out how the data will be stored and tracked on the disk. The correct layout of the patterns is the key to repairing damaged disks and finding lost files so that they can be recovered. All disk information analysis is based on these markings.

23

Interleaving

Initialization patterns affect how the Macintosh stores its data on the disk, as well as how it designs its databases to track the location of files on the disks. The Macintosh models differ in how the tracks and sectors are identified on the disk based upon how fast their disks can be accessed. This identification patterning is produced when the disk is initialized (or *formatted*). The system by which the IDs are assigned is called the *interleave factor*.

When you buy a hard disk, it usually comes already initialized (or formatted) from the factory. If it has not been formatted, each hardware vendor usually provides formatting software to use with their disk drive. FWB also provides hard drive management software to OEM vendors. You can purchase the FWB Hard Disk Toolkit to initialize and manage most hard disks. Apple provides the Drive Setup program with Mac OS 8.5.

Each of the various Macintosh model families operate at different computer speeds. Remember that the hard disk contains platters that are continually spinning at 3,600 to 10,000 rpm (revolutions per minute). Read-write heads float on horizontally moving arms over the platters. The read-write arms move at a set speed, as do the platters. Therefore, the Macintosh computer must be able to read sectors into memory at the same speed that the mechanical parts of the disk drive are moving. The time it takes to read a sector is important, because you want the computer to be able to read all the sectors on the disk so they can all be usable.

The Macintosh can store vast amounts of data, but this data would not be available if the Macintosh did not have a means to organize the tracking of its location on the various peripheral hard disks attached to the CPU. The Macintosh manages this task by using a protocol or set of rules by which it recognizes communications from these peripherals. This set of rules is called the *SCSI protocol*.

Tracks and Sectors

One type of pattern installed is the magnetic divisions used to organize the stored information. These magnetic divisions are called *tracks* and *sectors*. Each computer platform, such as a Sun, Silicon Graphics (SGI), Wintel, or Mac computer, has its own unique track and sector configuration recognizable only to that system. Figure 23.2 displays an illustration of a generic disk platter's tracks and sectors.

FIGURE 23.2.

How a generic disk is formatted into tracks and sectors.

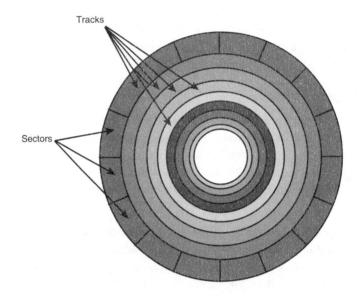

Tracks are laid down in concentric circles around the platter's circumference.

Hard Formatting

When the disks are initialized as Macintosh disks, each sector's address (physical location) is electronically coded into the sector itself. This is called *address stamping*. Along with this sector preamble data, special synchronization bytes are written to tell the disk controller that it's about to read a sector address. The formatting process also lays down *gap bytes* (meaningless filler bytes of data between sectors) to create a timing tolerance so that the spinning platters are synchronized with the swinging of the read-write head and arm.

More data is written into the sector directly after the address stamp—the *cyclical redundancy check (CRC)* bytes. These bytes of data are the result of a checksum calculation based on the value of all the bytes written to that sector. Whenever the sector is later read from the disk, its CRC bytes are also read and the checksum recalculated. The two values are compared; if they do not match, a read error has occurred.

The laying down of the sector addresses, sync bytes, gap bytes, and CRC bytes is performed by the hardware with minimal instructions from the Macintosh software. This formatting process is called *low-level formatting* or *hard formatting*. The next task before a disk can be used is to format it logically.

Logical Formatting

In order for the Macintosh operating system to find data out of all the myriad megabytes of information on a disk, it's necessary to impose some order by dividing the disks up into areas reserved for specialized identification information as well as for the storage of data. The operating system builds a series of indexes and directories defining what is where and which sectors and tracks are free (as opposed to which are already assigned). It also identifies any damaged sectors that are unusable on the disk. The process of setting up this organization is called *logical formatting*. Since 1986, the Macintosh operating system has organized disks into five main areas: the boot blocks, the volume info blocks, the catalog tree, the extents tree, and the data area. When any hard disk is formatted, some of the raw disk space is allocated to replace bad blocks and to store file system data. Partitioning will reserve additional raw hard disk space for the OS and file system to track this additional configuration information for the hard disk.

The result of logical formatting is the creation of a *volume* (or a *logical disk*). Each physical hard disk can hold more than one logical disk, or volume, by partitioning. Partitioning is splitting the disk up logically into separate sections. The software used to perform the partitioning writes special bookkeeping information at the front of the hard disk to tell the Macintosh how many volumes are on the disk, the location of each, as well as their sizes. Floppy disks, removable disks, and most hard disks that cannot or are not partitioned do not have this information.

The volume contains the bookkeeping data in rigidly specified locations on the disk. If the information is missing, is presented in a nonspecified manner, or is in the wrong location, the Macintosh cannot read the disk.

Understanding Mac OS Extended Format (HFS+)

The Hierarchical File System (HFS) used by the Mac to manage disks has not been updated in 12 years. Mac OS 8.1 finally provides a modern filing system for the Macintosh called Mac OS Extended or HFS+.

The old HFS is very rigid (meaning that the number of blocks on a disk does not change regardless of the size of the disk). It divides your hard drive into 65,536 equal-sized blocks. Each block stores a chunk of data; whether the data requires 4K or 64K doesn't matter, the block is taken. This allocation formula was fine when all the Mac was working with was 20 MB hard drives. On a 20 MB drive, each allocation block is tiny. But because hard disks have grown huge (1, 2, 4, even 9 GB), this system no longer proves efficient. Let's see why.

Mapping 65,536 blocks into 20 MB provides nice 8K blocks so that the Mac can allocate data to storage in 8K chunks. When you map 65,536 blocks on to a 4 GB disk, suddenly each block takes up 64K. Because the smallest file size a Mac understands is one block, files are allocated in blocks, one to one. When you put a 4K block into a 64K space (because the Mac cannot allocate anything smaller), you waste 97 percent of the storage capacity within a block. Therefore, a 70K file actually swallows 128K of space because the file requires two 64K blocks for its storage.

In addition to the vastness of the wasted space, HFS limited the number of blocks of data you could save on your hard drive to 65,536, which can get filled mighty fast.

Enter HFS+. With the new Mac OS Extended Format, the maximum number of blocks that can be mapped on a hard disk has been expanded to 4.29 billion. That's *billion*. Now, large hard disks can be mapped in smaller block chunks, thus wasting much less space.

Mac OS 8.1 and later offer you two file format modes: the Mac OS Standard (that old HFS method) and Mac OS Extended (the new HFS+ method). Now, you must decide which method you want to use on your hard drive or partitions.

Drawbacks of HFS+

It sounds great to be able to maximize the storage space on your hard disk. There are some caveats, however.

You probably won't get much disk space savings on disks smaller than 1GB, or if you're saving very large files. You can see why immediately. The block sizes remain adequate on smaller disks, and large files take up all the larger block sizes anyway. On the other hand, if you're using very large hard drives (1 GB or larger) or saving lots of small files, your savings will be enormous. For example, reformatting a 1 GB hard drive gains over 100 MB. (In fact, I got back 200 MB when I reformatted my 2.5 GB hard drive.)

You cannot initialize volumes smaller than 32MB as Mac OS Extended (HFS+). If you attempt to do so, the Drive Setup application will state "Initialization Failed." You also cannot initialize floppy disks in HFS+.

A second caveat is that you cannot use a hard disk initialized with HFS+ as the startup disk of a 68040-based Mac. This newfangled thing is for Power Macs only.

Here's a third warning: Once you do it, it's done. You can only access disks formatted with HFS+ from Macs running Mac OS 8.1 or higher. If you try to mount your Extended File–formatted disk on a Mac running an earlier system, you get an ugly surprise. All you will see is a single ReadMe file called `Where_have_all_my_files_gone?`. This helpful document explains how to upgrade to Mac OS 8.1 so you can see your files again.

23

One last caveat: Make sure you upgrade all your system utilities, such as Norton Utilities, TechTool, CD-ROM Toolkit, HardDrive Toolkit, and so forth, to a version that supports HFS+. Currently, the following versions support HFS+:

- MicroMat TechTool Pro 2.0
- FWB Hard Disk Toolkit 2.5.2
- FWB CD-ROM Toolkit 3.0.1
- Apple Disk First Aid 8.1

Note that Norton Utilities does not support disks formatted with HFS+.

Initializing HFS+ Disks

The good news is that you gain many megabytes when you update your hard disk to HFS+. The bad news is you have to reinitialize your hard drive to do it. What does this mean? You lose all your data when you reformat your drive because initialization erases all the data on the hard drive.

> Always back up your hard disk before attempting to reformat your drive. In fact, back it up twice, once for security and once for use in restoring your files after you've moved to HFS+. Use the Get Info window for the hard disk to see if the disk is formatted for HFS (standard) or HFS+ (Extended).

You have two ways in which to reformat your hard drive. If you're formatting an external hard drive that's not your startup disk, use the Erase command on the Special menu. If you want to reformat your startup disk, you need to boot from the Mac OS 8.5 CD-ROM and run the Drive Setup application.

When you're finished initializing your disk, you must restore the original files from your backup disk(s). You'll probably lose all your alias connections in the restoration process.

Using Erase to Format a Disk

Here is the simplest way to format a disk. You get two choices: Erase or Cancel. Follow these steps:

1. Select the volume you want to format.
2. Choose Erase Disk from the Special menu.
3. In the resulting dialog box, select a formatting option from the pop-up menu (see Figure 23.3). Select Extended Format to use HFS+.

FIGURE 23.3.

The Erase/Format dialog box provides two different formatting methods: Standard and Extended.

4. Type a name for your disk in the text box.
5. Click Erase.
6. The Mac proceeds to erase the contents of your drive. It then reformats the drive.

If you purchase PlusMaximizer from Alsoft (www.alsoftinc.com), which is $10 with the purchase of PlusMaker, you can maximize the size of your hard disk savings by minimizing the size of blocks down to 0.5K. PlusMaximizer is a system extension.

Using Drive Setup to Format a Disk

Drive Setup provides more options for initializing your disks, such as setting up partitions. Make sure you're using the Mac OS 8.1 version of Drive Setup (version 1.4). Note that with HFS+, you don't really need to partition the hard disk because the file system will minimize the file size on the larger, single partition disk anyway.

You can use Drive Setup on your startup disk to initialize an external hard disk. If you want to reformat your startup disk, you need to reboot from the Mac OS 8.1 CD-ROM and use its copy of Drive Setup. Either way, open Drive Setup, select the drive you want to format, and click Initialize. In the resulting dialog box, click Custom Setup and then choose Mac OS Extended (HFS+) from the Type pop-up menu.

Using Alsoft PlusMaker

Now that I've covered the down-and-dirty way to initialize a disk, let me introduce you to the best way. Use Alsoft's PlusMaker (available for $29.95; go to www.alsoftinc.com). PlusMaker provides a way to format your hard disk without you having to remove its contents. PlusMaker converts the directory file to HFS+ without touching the actual data on your disk.

To run PlusMaker and convert your existing disk to HFS+ format, follow these steps:

1. Reboot your system using the Mac OS 8.1 CD-ROM (or any other CD-ROM that contains Mac OS 8.1 or later).

2. Place a floppy disk with PlusMaker into your Mac. Open PlusMaker from the floppy.

3. In the resulting dialog box, select the volume you want to convert (see Figure 23.4). PlusMaker will tell you if you can proceed and how much disk space you'll gain in the process.

FIGURE 23.4.

The PlusMaker dialog box provides information about your drive and the results of the proposed conversion.

4. Click Graph to view how much space you'll gain (see Figure 23.5). Note that when I converted my 100 MB Zip drive, I only recovered a little space. When I converted my startup disk, I recovered 65 percent of my hard drive that had been in use.

FIGURE 23.5.

The graph presents a picture of your proposed space savings with HFS+.

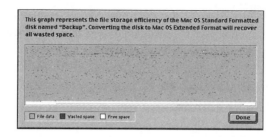

5. If you decide to go ahead and convert, close the graph and click Convert on the original dialog box.

6. You're presented a warning about what you're going to do. There's no turning back once you click Proceed.

7. Note that eight steps are involved to verify your drive's directories and to perform the conversion. Do not stop the process until it is complete.

Summary

During this hour, you learned how the Mac OS controls your storage system. You learned how the hierarchical file system works and what happens when you save a file. You also learned the benefits and drawbacks of upgrading your hard drives to Mac OS Extended Format (also called *HFS+*). Finally, you learned two ways to perform the conversion: the hard way (initializing your hard drive and restoring its data) and the easy way (running PlusMaker and converting your hard drive in-place). Always, always back up your drives before proceeding.

Think twice about converting to HFS+, because once you do it, you cannot use the hard drive on any other system but Mac OS 8.1 or higher. If you do decide it's worth pursuing, you'll see a benefit in storage space savings.

Term Review

address stamping   When the disks are initialized as Macintosh disks, each sector's address (physical location) is electronically coded into the sector itself.

Apple Drive Setup   The utility that's bundled with Mac OS 8.5 that provides enhanced initialization support beyond what's provided by the Erase command.

boot blocks   The first two sectors of every disk volume is reserved for the boot blocks. Boot blocks store information needed by the Macintosh to learn how to read its internal ROM and thereby perform its startup routines.

Catalog B-tree The Catalog B-tree contains an entry for every file describing its folder location (the hierarchical structure), as well as the size and location (starting point and ending point) of the three pieces that make up a file: the header, resource fork, and data fork.

cyclical redundancy check (CRC) bytes These bytes of data are the result of a checksum calculation based on the value of all the bytes written to that sector. Whenever the sector is later read from the disk, its CRC bytes are also read and the checksum recalculated. The two values are compared; if they do not match, a read error has occurred.

desktop file An invisible file created during the initialization of a disk. The desktop file maintains a catalog of icons, ensuring that the desktop displays the correct icon for each type of document and application.

Extents B-tree When files become *fragmented* (scattered in bits and pieces across the disk's tracks and sectors), an Extents file is opened. It contains information about the location of each file fragment (the rest of the pieces or extents of the forks).

File Manager The Mac OS toolbox that works with the Finder and manages storage and files on your Mac.

gap bytes Meaningless filler bytes of data between sectors that create a timing tolerance so that spinning platters are synchronized with the swinging of the read-write head and arm.

hard drive The series of hard platters, read/write heads, and mechanisms that provide permanent storage for your data. Hard drive and hard disk are synonymous.

Hierarchical File System (HFS) The original or standard file system used by the Mac. HFS allocates 65,356 blocks on your hard disk where data can be stored in one-block increments.

HSF+ The Mac OS Extended file system provided with Mac OS 8.1 and later, which increases the number of blocks allocated to drives to 4.26 billion, thus making each individual block considerably smaller and more efficient in storing chunks of data.

initialization Initializing a disk places the Macintosh disk layout requirements onto the media, thus making it usable to the Macintosh. These patterns lay out how the data will be stored and tracked on the disk.

interleave factor The system by which identification patterning is assigned on a disk. The Macintosh models differ in how the tracks and sectors are identified on the disk based on how fast their disks can be accessed. This identification patterning is produced when the disk is initialized or formatted.

logical formatting   The process of setting up an organization system used by the Macintosh operating system to find data out of all the myriad megabytes of information on a disk. Logical formatting divides the disks up into areas reserved for specialized identification information as well as for the storage of data.

low-level formatting   The process of laying down sector addresses, sync bytes, gap bytes, and CRC bytes performed by the hardware with minimal instructions from the Macintosh software. This process is also called *hard formatting*.

PlusMaker   An Alsoft product that converts existing hard drives containing data to HFS+ without requiring the initializing of the drive.

volume   A logical disk whose information matches the physical composition of the disk. Each partition or separate area you create on your physical hard drive is a separate volume to the operating system.

volume bitmap   This file keeps track of the usage patterns of tracks and sectors on the disk, identifying which areas are free and which are filled.

volume directory   The Macintosh stores data on a volume in the sectors in each track. Information does not remain consecutive but is read and written into any free sectors that are available. Therefore, the Macintosh needs some way to track where the bits and pieces of a document are stored on the volume. This invisible file really consists of two parts   a Catalog B-tree file and an Extents B-tree file.

volume information block   Located in this reserved area are the locations of other critical bookkeeping information areas, such as the Catalog and Extents trees. Other information such as the name and size of the volume, how much space is available, the location of the system folder (if this is a startup volume), and so forth is also stored in this area. The volume info block also maintains the identification numbers used to label each new folder, assigning the next available ID to the next new folder you create.

Q&A

Q Is there any "gotchas" involved in updating a Mac clone to HFS+?

A Yes. If your clone's system does not use the Apple CD-ROM driver, you cannot boot your Mac using the Mac OS 8.1 CD-ROM as required, because your Mac will not be able to read the CD-ROM. This is a catch-22. I've found that the CD-ROM will boot if you have the FWB CD-ROM Toolkit, because it includes the correct driver. A second solution is to boot from a second, external disk containing Mac OS 8.1 or use Alsoft's PlusMaker. You can also make an 8.1-bootable Zip disk or Jaz cartridge as a workaround for clones (so they can startup from 8.1 in emergencies).

Q How can I defragment a disk formatted with HFS+?

A You currently can't. Rumors of an upgrade to Symantec Norton SpeedDisk to support HFS+ are in the air, as is an additional component to TechTool Pro that would optimize disks. At the moment, however, no tool exists.

Q Why is it a good idea to also install PlusMaximizer?

A The default allocation block size with HFS+ is 4K, up to eight times the block size the format actually supports. PlusMaximizer brings the default block size down to 0.5K, the minimum block size supported by HFS+, thus saving you more disk space.

Q How do I know which format is used on my hard drive?

A Select the volume and choose Get Info (Command+I) from the File menu. The Format line on the dialog box tells you whether the disk is formatted as a Mac OS Extended or Standard disk.

Workshop

The Workshop contains quiz questions to help you solidify your understanding of the material covered. You can find the answers to the quiz questions in Appendix B, "Quiz Answers."

Quiz

1. What's the difference between a hard disk, a removable disk, and a floppy disk?
2. What's initialization and why is it important?
3. When should you use the Apple Drive Setup application to initialize a disk?
4. Explain logical formatting and how it differs from hard formatting.
5. What's the Mac OS Standard format?
6. What are the benefits of upgrading to HFS+?
7. What are the pitfalls of upgrading to HFS+?
8. What's the most important thing to do before you upgrade to HFS+?
9. What's the easiest way to convert your volumes to HFS+ in-place?

HOUR 24

Troubleshooting Your System

You'll learn in this hour about some of the things that can go wrong with your Mac and how to deal with them. Troubleshooting is a multifaceted issue that covers hardware, software, peripherals, networks, and the Internet and how they affect your Macintosh experience. Not all circumstances of failure can be covered in this type of introductory book, but when we're done, you'll know where to look for the answers. Topics discussed this hour include the following:

- How Apple Disk First Aid 8.5 automatically troubleshoots and affects repairs before startup any time you improperly shutdown your Mac
- General problems you may experience
- Building a software toolkit
- What to do if you are the problem
- Software problems and how to solve them

What to Do If There's a Problem

When you feel sick and can't put your finger on why, you call a doctor who examines your symptoms and comes up with a diagnosis. Often the diagnosis has a cure, but sometimes it doesn't. We've learned in this day and age of managed medicine to make informed decisions about our health. Troubleshooting a Mac works the same way. Here are the basic steps involved:

1. **A problem occurs.** Something happens that crashes your computer.
2. **Identify the problem.** You run a diagnostic software suite or check out the possible causes yourself.
3. **Come up with a solution.** You or the assisting software come up with a definition of the problem and a possible solution.
4. **Perform the solution.** You try to implement the cure, let a specialist (a Mac technician) fix the machine, or buy a new Mac.

The head banging comes during two stages of this process: finding out what's wrong and coming up with a solution.

What exactly is meant by "crash"? Several things, actually:

- Your Mac's cursor freezes and moving the mouse produces nothing.
- The Finder displays an alert with a bomb and a very cryptic error message. It might not let you restart, depending on the severity of the problem.
- A blank alert box appears and the Mac freezes.
- You get a low memory alert and a few seconds later your program dies; you're returned to the desktop and then the Finder bombs.

What all these various messages mean is that you can no longer produce work on your Mac.

The good news is that Macs seldom crash without something you've added being the cause—for example, a system extension that conflicts with others, a noncompliant application (one that doesn't follow Apple's Human Interface Guidelines), or a peripheral device that's not installed correctly. These are all problems that can be researched and solved.

The bad news is that when the Mac crashes, it crashes. Therefore, preventive measures (backups, frequent defragmentation, and regular checkups) should be performed so that crashes don't happen (and if they do, you won't loose much of your work).

Let's examine what can go wrong with your Mac and how to resolve these problems.

Problems You May Encounter

Here are several general categories of problems you may encounter:

- **User error**. Hey, we all make mistakes. Sometimes, we cause our own troubles by not properly using the tools we have (for example, installing hardware using the same SCSI ID for two separate devices) or by not following instructions (for example, installing new software without turning off the virus protection or, if required, nonessential system extensions). User errors are among the most common type of error. Fortunately, these problems are also among the easiest to solve.

- **Software problems**. One of the most common problems on a Mac is a system extension conflict. Another very common (and preventable) problem is application software that doesn't follow Apple guidelines and treads where it isn't supposed to go. A third possible software issue is viruses.

- **Hardware problems**. Sometimes hardware fails. Hardware failures can be caused by something you do, such as installing an upgrade. Failures can also happen when a piece of hardware wears out. Hardware failures can be very expensive. Fortunately, though, most hardware is very reliable, and you aren't likely to have trouble in this area.

24

Strangely enough, hardware failures are the most likely when your computer is brand new. This is called *burn-in*, the result of minor quality defects or design problems that lead to premature failures of hardware components. Fortunately, almost all hardware is warranted past the burn-in period; therefore, these failures—while annoying—are not likely to cost you money.

Collecting a Software Toolkit

Once you've identified a problem, you can solve it in two general ways. The first is to manually work through the solution by moving files, changing settings, rebuilding the desktop, and so on. This way can work for many problems; however, others require a more sophisticated approach via a software tool. Although the "manual" approach works, it's often very time consuming and is limited by your knowledge. The upside is that you often learn a great deal while trying to solve problems—just you and your Mac, *mano a mano*.

Here's some more good news, Wintel PCs crash a lot. That means software vendors have seen a business opportunity and have developed software to do battle with errors. Mac users have benefited from the experience and expertise of these vendors (such as

Symantec, Qualcomm, MicroMat, and FWB, as well as other utility players such as Alsoft and MacAfee). Several good diagnostic tools are available on the market to assist you in your identification task. It's a good idea—even if you're a "newbie" and are possibly apprehensive about getting into the guts of your Mac—to purchase diagnostic software to have on hand if and when something bad happens. To get you started, here's a list of some tools I strongly recommend:

- **Backup software.** You currently have three ways to maintain a backup copy of the contents of your hard drive: manually, locally (via a backup program), and remotely (via an Internet-based backup system). Don't manually perform a backup unless you have a very small hard drive or few important files. Usually, the volume of files is too great. Use a backup system such as Dantz Retrospect locally or Netscape's Atreiva remotely.

- **Diagnostic and repair software.** Next, you need an automated helper to delve into the internals of your hard drive, system files, and ROM to scurry out errors. Two powerhouse programs are available on the market that perform this work: Symantec's Norton Utilities version 5.0 and MicroMat's TechTools 2.0. Norton Utilities provides a plethora of tools that you can use to do disk maintenance (such as optimization and defragmentation) as well as to recover from a variety of software and hardware problems. It also provides tools that enable you to recover your files in the event of an accidental deletion. Norton Utilities also helps you protect your system when one of your applications crashes and enables you to rate your Mac's performance so that you can see whether problems are degrading it. Norton Utilities is an essential part of your toolkit for both preventive and "emergency" tasks. The problem with Norton Utilities is that it doesn't support extended file systems (HFS+). If you've upgraded your drives to HFS+, upgrade to TechTools 2.0. TechTools provides two levels of diagnostics: basic and advanced. Although it lacks the range of tools provided by Norton Utilities, TechTools checks your Mac and its peripherals much more deeply and thoroughly than what's performed by Norton. I like TechTools and use it regularly.

- **System extension management software.** Another very important piece of preventive measures is the management of your startup files and system extensions. Apple provides the Extension Manager in Mac OS 8.5, but this program is unwieldy and does not allow you to actively rearrange INITs, rename them on-the-fly, delete them, synchronize them from old to new system files, or customize them to fit your working style. Therefore, you should purchase Casady & Greene's Conflict Catcher 8. This essential utility provides industrial strength tools for troubleshooting software conflicts. Conflict Catcher helps you determine which parts of your system are fighting with others. Conflict Catcher also provides extensive information on the extensions, control panels, plug-ins, and other software add-ons and helps you know when these items need to be upgraded. It even helps you contact the companies that produce the problem software. You can also use Conflict Catcher to prepare a detailed report on your hardware and software configuration—information that's essential for troubleshooting your system. Conflict Catcher can also be used to optimize your Mac's performance for whatever task you're working on.

- **Antivirus software.** There are bogeymen in those woods—people who get their jollies by writing software that undermines and destroys the computers of strangers. Because you often need to share software, you need to protect yourself from infection from viruses. There are several products available that provide protection: Symantec's Norton Anti-Virus for Macintosh 4.0, Dr. Solomon's Virex 5.9, and the shareware program Disinfectant. All these programs provide background scans of any disk or volume that comes in contact with your Mac, whether locally via a disk drive or remotely via a network or the Internet.

- **A Mac OS startup disk.** Keep a startup disk handy that's composed of a limited Mac OS 8.5 system (Finder, System, minimal extensions, and control panels) along with Disk First Aid and HD Setup, either on a Zip disk or a CD-ROM. The easiest way to start up your Mac is from a CD-ROM; keeping your original Mac OS 8.5 CD-ROM is the best bet. To boot from a CD-ROM, press C during startup.

I suggest you get all these tools as soon as you can. When the time comes, you don't want to obtain—and learn to use—new software at the same time you're trying to solve your problems.

Identifying the Problem

Mac OS 8.5 introduces a diagnosis and repair solution that smoothes out what used to be a frustrating experience: system crashes. With Mac OS 8.5, the first thing you do when your Mac crashes is simply restart it. Mac OS 8.5 takes over the diagnosis and repair of common hard disk problems by running Disk First Aid before system startup.

To restart a crashed Mac, do one of two things: Press the keyboard combination Command-Control-Power key or press the restart button on the side or front of your computer.

Disk First Aid is initialized any time you use the above radical restart methods to shutdown and restart your Mac. Disk First Aid simply verifies the status of your Mac and repairs any hard disk errors it encounters. You receive no information about what was performed or discovered—your Mac just checks itself. In fact, this diagnostics system is

24

automated so that you don't even press the Done button at the end of the process; the Disk First Aid program times out and begins the startup process for your Mac.

If you are smart—which you are—you'll be concerned that something's going on with your Mac that's causing problems. Therefore, whenever Disk First Aid runs, you should collect your software toolkit and begin to identify the possible causes.

Continuing Your Research

When you run into a problem that's not clearly a hardware or software problem (see the following sections for symptoms of these problems), one of the first things you should think about is what you're doing (or not doing, as the case may be).

Many sources of information are available on the possible trouble spots on a Mac. Sometimes it feels like there's too much information. However, you're becoming knowledgeable about your Mac and will be able to ferret out the false from the sane, given the facts. Here are some places to look for facts:

- **ReadMe files.** Most software comes with ReadMe files. These files are provided to give you information that could not be included in the printed documentation that comes with the software. If you have trouble with a particular application, you should read through these files. They will often provide essential information.

- **The manual and online help.** Most applications come with a paper manual, online help (Apple Guide or Balloon Help), or both. You should peruse this information to help you understand what you're doing and to prevent problems.

- **The Internet.** Just about every software vendor in the world now has a Web site containing technical information, customer support FAQ (Frequently Asked Questions) areas, user group forums, and upgrade areas for your use. In addition, these sites often contain the newest information about your software—stuff the manuals couldn't contain because it wasn't known when they were written. The Internet is the richest place for information collection.

- **Apple's various Web sites.** Especially Apple Product Information (www.info.apple.com). Apple's technical information memos, whitepapers, literature, and even its marketing materials provide a wealth of information not only about Apple products, but about third-party software as well.

Before asking for any kind of troubleshooting help, you need to understand the configuration of your hardware and software. You can use Apple System Profiler to do this. (See Figure 24.1.)

FIGURE 24.1.

The Apple System Profiler will tell you everything you need to know about your system.

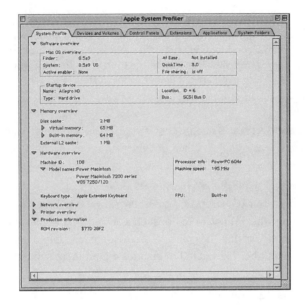

- **E-zines, Web sites, and magazines.** There are also a lot of e-zines and paper magazines that contain information that will help you prevent yourself from causing problems. For example, MacFixIt (http://www.macfixit.com), Adam Engst's TidBits site (http://www.tidbits.com), MacInTouch (http://www.macintouch.com), MacWorld, MacTech, and MacHome (http://www.macweek.zdnet.com).

Working with Problems

So you've run your analysis and have identified where the problem with your Mac lies. This section describes some of the possibilities for software and hardware problems you may encounter during your identification phase.

Software Problem Symptoms

A lot of individual symptoms can indicate a software problem, but they usually fall into one of the following kinds of behaviors:

- **Quits and Type "Whatever" Errors**. Sometimes the application you're using will suddenly quit. You might get an error message saying something like, "The application has unexpectedly quit because of a meaningless number error." When this happens, you lose all the changes you made to the open document since the last time you saved it. This is not a good thing.

> If the application you work with doesn't have an autosave feature, you should consider adding a utility that will issue a save command at predetermined intervals. This way, in the even of a quit, you won't lose much work. If all else fails, just remember to save often.

- **Hangs and freezes**. Sometimes software errors will cause your application—or Mac—to freeze or hang. When this happens, your machine will seem to lock up and you won't even be able to make the pointer move on the screen. This is also very bad if you haven't saved your work recently.

- **Not doing what it's supposed to**. Many times, errors will occur that prevent you from doing what you want to do, such as using a particular function of the software, printing, saving files, and so on. Also, menus might become grayed out when they shouldn't be. These kind of errors are a bit more subtle than the others, but they can still be a big problem for you.

- **Error messages during startup**. Software conflicts can cause various error messages and other problems to occur during startup.

- **Generic icons**. One of the great things about the Mac is that it keeps track of which applications can be used to edit specific documents, so you don't have to worry about it yourself. You open a document by simply double-clicking it. Each icon has a distinctive look, based on the type of file it is (for example, Word documents have the Word document icon). Sometimes, however, the Mac will seem to lose its mind and all the icons will suddenly become generic (just a plain looking rectangle).

- **Lost preferences**. You make your Mac your own by setting various preferences that tell it how you want it to work and look. Occasionally, you'll find all your preferences gone.

Hardware Problem Symptoms

Hardware problems are different from software problems. Although software problems can be very tough to troubleshoot, hardware problems often aren't—hardware failures usually make themselves abundantly obvious. Whereas software problems usually can be solved by you with a minimal cost, major hardware problems often require a service technician and a fair amount of money. Fortunately, hardware problems are fairly rare, especially when compared to software problems.

The major symptoms of a hardware failure are usually pretty obvious. Your system won't work. It's usually that simple. It may be that your Mac won't boot up, you might hear the dreaded chimes of death, or you might not be able to mount a drive. In all these cases, it will be very clear that you have a problem, and you'll also know what the nature of that problem is.

Your Mac always—*almost* always anyway—keeps track of the time and date. This is important for many reasons, the most important of which is stamping the files you create and modify with the proper dates. Once in a while, your Mac may seem to lose its watch and won't know what time it is. This is usually a sign of a more subtle hardware problem.

 If you've never heard the chimes of death, be glad. You know that pleasant sound your Mac makes when you restart it? The chimes of death are just about the worst sound you can hear. Although they're tough to describe, you'll know them if you ever hear them. They are usually accompanied by a sad Mac. Both clues mean the same thing: trouble for you.

24

Finding Solutions

You've identified the problem, narrowed down the culprits, and collected your repair tools; now it's time to get down to the business of the actual repair. This section discusses how to use your various tools and new knowledge to fix hardware and software problems.

Software Problem Resolutions

Unfortunately, software problems are unpredictable. Once they happen, there usually isn't much you can do to recover from them. You simply save and restore as much of your data as you can, reboot your machine, and begin the task of figuring out how to *prevent* future occurrences of the problem. The bulk of your troubleshooting efforts for software problems are therefore prevention of future problems rather than treatment of problems that have occurred.

If your application is "acting up," save your work and begin preventive troubleshooting as soon as you can. Once you've recovered from the immediate problem, you need to figure out what to do to prevent future occurrences of that problem.

Quits

When an application quits unexpectedly, you can't do much about it. It's simply gone. Sometimes, you can recover your data, sometimes you can't. Usually you'll need an additional piece of software that captures your keystrokes to be able to recover your work.

For example, Casady & Greene's excellent Spell Catcher will capture and save all your keystrokes in its GhostWriter function. You can go back to the GhostWriter file for the application that quit and restore the keystrokes you made since the last save. This process also records all keystrokes, even command keys. This is helpful for recovering some of the work, but all formatting and graphics are lost. Still, it can help you recover a substantial portion of your data.

Hangs

When an application hangs, you can attempt to shut it down by pressing Command-Option-Esc. This is a force quit, and it will sometimes shut down the hanging application. When you attempt this, you'll see a dialog box asking you if you want to force the application to quit. You'll also see Force Quit and Cancel buttons. If you click Force Quit, the Mac will attempt to shut down the problem application. If it works, you'll be returned to the desktop. You need to immediately save all the work in other open applications and then restart your Mac. A force quit is only a last resort measure and might cause problems for the system.

If the force quit doesn't work, you need to reboot your Mac by pressing the keyboard combination Command-Control-Power key. You should use this method only when left with no alternative.

If Mac OS 8.5 were a fully multitasking and memory protected operating system, one application crashing would not affect the other applications running at the time. Unfortunately, you see such an OS for awhile. Mac OS 8.5 offers more memory protection than previous versions, but it does not offer full memory protection.

If you use a PowerPC Mac and have Norton Utilities, you can use Norton's CrashGuard feature. TechTool Pro also has a feature called TechTool Protection that works similarly to Norton FileSaver in that it snaps a picture of your computer on a specified schedule giving you a restore file to use when you want to restore lost volumes. CrashGuard enables you to quit the problem application or try to fix it so you can save your data. CrashGuard also maintains a record of crashes and other problems. If CrashGuard is able to help you save your data, you still need to reboot your Mac immediately so that other parts of the system are affected.

Until the Mac has a fully protected memory structure, using CrashGuard or TechTool Protection is the best you can do.

Battling Software Conflicts

The more extensions, control panels, and applications that you use, the more likely it is that some of this software will conflict. What happens when software programs battle it out? In short, you lose. You can experience startup errors when conflicting software tries to load into the system, or you may experience quits, hangs, and performance problems. The most likely source of conflicts are extensions and control panels, but applications can occasionally conflict with each other as well.

 Known conflicts will often be listed in ReadMe files and on Web sites for the software you install. You should check these sources for known conflicts before purchasing or installing new software.

24

Isolating Extension Conflicts

The basic technique to root out extension and control panel conflicts is to systematically remove items until the problem goes away. Then, return the removed items until the problem occurs again. The last item added back to the system is the likely source of the conflict.

The primary tool you can use for this is Apple's own Extensions Manager. Extensions Manager enables you to turn various extensions, control panels, and other items off and on. You can also save sets of these items so that reconfiguring your system is simply a matter of selecting the appropriate Extensions Manager set.

Follow these steps when using Extensions Manager to try to find the software that's causing conflicts:

1. Choose Extensions Manager from the Control Panels folder from the Apple menu. Extensions Manager will open. (See Figure 24.2.)

2. Choose New Set from the File menu, enter a name for your set (try something like Set1), and click OK.

3. Scroll through the lists of control panels, extensions, and other items, clicking the on/off check boxes for those that might be related to your problem.

 Try and focus on items that are related to the application or function you were using at the time of the problem. For example, if you were trying to connect with your modem, choose the items that are related to that activity.

FIGURE **24.2.**

*Extensions Manager
in action.*

4. Continue this process until you've turned off about half the items.

5. Restart the computer.

6. Once the machine is up, try to duplicate the problem. If it doesn't happen again, you know that the problem item is one that you've turned off.

7. Go back to Extensions Manager and turn on about half of those that you turned off the first time. Save this group of settings.

8. Restart the computer to see whether the problem happens again. If it doesn't happen, you know the problem isn't caused by one of the items you turned back on and the culprit is still off.

9. Repeat steps 7 and 8 until the problem happens again.

10. Once the problem happens, you know that the conflicting software is in the group you just turned on. You need to continue turning items off and on and narrowing the groups down until you're left with a single item that proves to be the culprit.

This process can be difficult and time consuming. For example, it can be hard to keep track of all the items you've turned on or off. You have to be very disciplined about keeping things straight, and this takes some time.

Eventually you'll identify the software causing the problem. To correct it, you can do one of the following:

- **Live without it**. If you can do without the problem software, you can solve the problem by leaving the item turned off.

- **Get an upgrade**. You can try to get an upgrade for item to see if the conflict has been solved.

- **Change the loading order**. You can rename items to change the order in which they load into the system. (Try adding Z's or spaces to the item's name.) Sometimes conflicts can be eliminated by changing the loading order.

Using Conflict Catcher

Earlier, I said that Conflict Catcher is an essential part of your software toolkit. Once you see how it can help you troubleshoot conflicts, you'll understand why I said that.

Conflict Catcher provides a complete management tool for your system extensions, control panels, plug-ins, and other items. In addition to the extremely powerful troubleshooting that Conflict Catcher can do for you, it also offers the following features:

- **Displays information on your startup files**. After you install a few dozen extensions, control panels, and other startup files on your computer, it's not hard to forget what they all do. With Conflict Catcher, you can easily get very detailed information on almost all the startup files on your system.

- **Provides contact information for important vendors**. In addition to the detailed technical information Conflict Catcher provides, it also gives you contact information for the vendors of the startup files in your system. This is a great help when you need to contact the vendor for support or to obtain an upgrade.

- **Enables you to create custom groups**. With Conflict Catcher, you can make custom sets of startup files to maximize the performance of your computer for specific tasks.

- **Provides a complete report on your system's configuration**. This is similar to the Norton Utilities System Info function.

> Conflict Catcher also identifies startup files by grouping them in functional groups (for example, the Apple CD-ROM group, which contains all the startup files needed to use a CD-ROM drive). This makes it easy to identify all the startup files associated with a particular technology.

Once Conflict Catcher is installed, it can be launched in a variety of ways. The simplest is to choose Open Conflict Catcher from the custom Conflict Catcher menu installed next to the Application menu. The control panel will open. The right pane of the Conflict Catcher window lists all the startup files in your system.

These files can be sorted in various ways using the pop-up menus at the top of the pane. In the lower right corner, the Group Links area can be used to quickly turn all the startup files associated with a particular technology on or off. The left pane of the window is the area where Conflict Catcher displays detailed information about individual files. The Set pop-up menu at the top of the left pane enables you to quickly select a particular set with which to work. At the bottom are buttons that enable you to start the conflict-testing process and to generate a report on your system configuration.

> If you already have a version of Conflict Catcher installed, you must upgrade it to version 4.1.1 to be compatible with Mac OS 8.0 or 8.1. If you've installed Mac OS 8.5, only Conflict Catcher version 8 works accurately.
>
> You can get an upgrade from Conflict Catcher 4 to 4.1.1 from www.download.com or from Casady & Greene's Web site (www.c&g.com). Although you'll need to purchase the upgrade to version 8, Casady & Greene might be offering discounts to users of previous versions.

Detecting Buggy, Poorly Designed, and Conflicting Applications

Some applications are just plain buggy. You may encounter trouble despite having plenty of RAM and no conflicts or any other system-level problems—the software just doesn't work very well. Symptoms of this can include quits, hangs, and odd performance.

In the case of a buggy application, the only real solution is to get a bug fix release of the application (assuming that the publisher will issue one, of course). You may just have to live with the problem or live without the application. If it conflicts with another application you also need, one of them may have to go.

The bottom line is that some things you won't be able to fix. If an application is basically flawed, there probably isn't much you can do about it. The best bet in this case is to either get a bug fix or get an alternative application.

Detecting Viruses

Viruses can also cause software problems for you. Again, problems caused by a virus can be quits, hangs, and poor performance. Suspect a virus if something particularly strange is happening; for example, weird messages, strange dialog boxes appearing on your screen, or persistent crashes.

If viruses do infest your machine, you'll need to use an antivirus tool such as Symantec Norton Anti-Virus for Macintosh or Dr. Solomon's Virex 5.8. These applications have features that can identify and eliminate viruses from your machine. (See Figure 24.3.)

FIGURE 24.3.

Fighting viruses with Virex.

Hardware Problem Resolutions

Although many hardware failures require a trip to a service technician, there are several hardware problems that you can troubleshoot and fix on your own.

Start Simple

When you have a hardware problem, start simple. Check all the cables that connect various components to your system. Turn the power off and check each cable to make sure that it's properly plugged in. Sometimes a loose cable will prevent the system from operating properly. Always try a simple reboot before taking any more drastic measures.

Another good idea is to strip the system down to its basic components. Disconnect everything except what you need to start the machine. If the machine boots in the stripped condition, you know that the problem lies in one of the peripherals. If the machine still doesn't boot, you know that the machine is the problem.

Never plug or unplug SCSI (disk drives, tape drives, scanners, and so on) or ADB (mice, keyboards, joysticks, and so on) cables while your system is on. If you do so, you run the risk of destroying your motherboard, which means you'll need to make major repairs. It's okay to do so with serial cables (modem and printer), however.

Zapping the PRAM

Parameter RAM (PRAM) is an area of your Mac that stores the information that needs to be retained when the power to the computer is turned off. These settings include time and date, system preferences, and so on. Occasionally, your Mac will start acting oddly and will seem to lose its mind every time you restart it. If you have problems with your date and system preferences, try zapping the PRAM.

Note that if you zap the PRAM, you'll lose all your system settings and will have to reconfigure everything you've changed from the defaults.

To zap the PRAM using the keyboard, hold down Command-Option-P-R while you restart your Mac. When it starts back up, the PRAM will have been cleared. You'll then have to reset the date and time as well as all your other custom settings.

Changing the Battery

All RAM requires power to store data, and PRAM is not an exception to this. So how does PRAM maintain data when the machine is powered down? Simple. Your Mac has a battery in it that provides power to the PRAM so that certain settings will be maintained even when the power to the machine is turned off.

Sometimes, these batteries fail. When this happens, your Mac will forget the time and date and most of the preferences you've changed (this happens every time you turn the power off and then on again). When this occurs, try zapping the PRAM. If that doesn't help, you'll need to replace the battery in your machine. See the manual that came with your Mac to learn how to do so.

> Losing the battery can also affect your monitor. If you restart your Mac but the monitor won't come back on, it may be due to a failed battery. Weird things can happen when good PRAM goes bad.

TechTool Pro 2.0 is especially useful in checking those parts of your Mac that Norton Utilities cannot touch, such as chips, floppy drives, CD-ROMs, RAM, and other problems that aren't related to the hard disk. Because TechTool 2.0 is fully compatible with HFS+ disks and Norton is not, I urge you to purchase TechTool Pro 2.0 from MicroMat (www.micromat.com).

Corrupted Disk Structure

As you use your disk drives, the constant writing and reading of data to the drive can lead to the data structure of the disk becoming corrupted. When this happens, the disk may not mount, or if it does, you may get disk errors when you try to write data to it. You can use a variety of tools to check and repair a disk's data structure. These include Apple Disk Tools, which comes with Mac OS 8.5, as well as third-party tools such as Norton Utilities or MicroMat TechTools 2.0.

Here's how you can use Norton to repair a disk:

1. Launch Norton Utilities and then click the Norton Disk Doctor button. You'll see the Disk Doctor window.

2. In the window, select a disk to check and repair.

3. Click the Examine button. You'll see a progress window as the good doctor checks your drive. The application will perform a series of six checks on this drive.

> If you want to skip a particular test, click the Skip Test button. If you want to stop the check, click Stop.

4. As problems are found, you'll see various dialog boxes that tell you what the problems are and ask if you want to fix them. You should fix all the errors the disk doctor finds.

   Don't be shocked if you see numerous problem dialog boxes, you'll often encounter several during this process.

5. Continue to have the doctor fix errors as they are found.

   Eventually, you'll reach the end of the tests and will see the doctor's clipboard showing the results of your checkup.

6. Click Show Report to see the details of the problems found and the repairs made to your disk. If you don't want to see the details, just click Done.

> Note that you'll need to boot from the Norton CD-ROM that has the active system software on it in order to fix problems on the disk. In other words, keep a version of Norton on the original disk or CD-ROM so that you can repair straight from it if need be.

After Norton finishes repairing your drive, you should notice fewer problems. Sometimes these repairs can have very dramatic results and will make a nonmountable disk mountable again. Other times, you might not notice much difference. It just depends on how bad the errors on your disk are.

Inadequate Hardware

Sometimes your system won't operate properly because you're trying do something that the hardware is simply not capable of doing. You might not have enough RAM, the processor may be underpowered, or your video system might not be capable of supporting the number of colors or resolution needed. You can avoid this by paying attention to hardware requirements that are listed on all the software and hardware that you buy.

24

If the hardware requirements are greater than your system, you can expect to have troubles if you try to use the device or software. Also, the minimum requirements are usually optimistic. If your system just barely meets these requirements, you may have trouble.

SCSI Devices

Each SCSI device on your system must have a unique ID number in order to be recognized by the system. If you attach two devices with the same ID number, your system won't boot. Usually this is pretty obvious. When you connect an additional device and the system won't start (but it does start when you remove the device), you have a SCSI ID conflict. You'll have to change the ID number on one of the conflicting devices in order to get your system to boot.

> Remember that all SCSI devices have an ID number, even the internal devices such as hard drives and CD-ROM drives. Usually the internal drives have low SCSI ID numbers (0 or 1) or high numbers (6). Various utilities are available that will let you see the SCSI ID numbers of the devices on your system. For example, you can use the System Info function in Norton Utilities to view this information.

Upgrade Problems

When you install new hardware in your system—such as RAM or VRAM chips, a new drive, or a PCI card—you always run the risk of not installing the item correctly or moving something that's already installed. If these devices are not seated properly, you'll hear the chimes of death and your system will not start. If this happens, open the case again and make sure that everything is installed properly. If you find no problems, the new device may be bad. Remove it and see whether the system will start without the new hardware. If it does, either the new device was bad or you installed it improperly. Try again in that case.

> If you still can't make it work, you might consider reading the instructions! I know, I know, drastic situations require drastic measures.

Failed Hardware

Sometimes hardware fails due to it wearing out—even during the initial period of operation (this is usually due to quality problems). In this case, you usually have to replace the item or have it repaired.

You can often tell when hard drives and other rotating devices are on their way to failure. Usually you'll hear louder than normal noises from these devices before they fail. If you start hearing unusual or loud noises from your equipment, make sure your data is backed up. Hearing an unusual noise is never good news.

Summary

During this hour, I discussed solutions to various problems you might encounter. I began by reviewing the different types of failures can run into and then briefly discussed some software you really need to have in your toolkit to be adequately prepared to deal with these problems.

Term Review

Apple System Profiler A desk accessory that analyzes your system and produces a report on all components, both software and hardware, you've installed. Use the System Profile when reporting problems to help desks.

AppleGuide The Mac OS 8.5 automated help system. AppleGuide interactively shows you how to perform operations when it's invoked in any application that supports guides.

AutoSave A former piece of Norton Utilities that automatically saves files at a pre-arranged interval. Microsoft Word and other applications also provide their own autosave functions to ensure that you don't lose data from failure to save files.

Balloon Help The descriptive help system provided by Mac OS 8.5 and supported by assorted applications. If a program supports this feature, when you select Show Balloons from the Help menu and point to an item, a balloon appears that describes what that item does. Select Hide Balloons to turn this feature off.

burn-in The period right after you purchase a new computer when any factory-based errors in hardware or software will likely appear.

Conflict Catcher 8 Casady & Greene's superb utility for managing system extensions, analyzing system conflicts, and assisting in their repair. Note that only version 4.1.1 is compatible with Mac OS 8.1 only. You must upgrade to version 8 to run this program with Mac OS 8.5.

corrupted disks Storage disks that contain errors—whether misplaced bits of data or something more serious—that are causing the disk to malfunction.

24

force quit   A last-ditch operation for closing an application without rebooting your Mac. Any unsaved information you may have in a document will be lost. Press the keyboard combination Command-Option-Esc.

Hanging   When your system freezes and you can do nothing in an application.

Norton CrashGuard   A component of Norton Utilities that attempts to fix application or system hangs (or at least lets you perform a proper shutdown of your Mac before repairing an error).

Norton FileSaver   A utility (part of Norton Utilities) that runs in the background, periodically taking a snapshot of your system for use in data recovery.

Norton Utilities 3.5   A suite of programs that provides disk analysis, repair, and recovery support for your Mac.

PRAM   Parameter RAM is a nonvolatile RAM chip that holds special system parameter data that's separate from your hardware and software. For example, the data on PRAM teaches the Mac to use a mouse, to know which hard disk is your startup disk, and other mission-critical information needed to startup and maintain your Mac.

ReadMe files   SimpleText documents that accompany most software that provide late-breaking news about the programs, such as known bugs, compatibility issues, installation issues, and so forth, that may not have made it into the written documentation.

Rebuild Desktop   A procedure that forces the Finder to construct fresh, invisible desktop directory files, replacing files that may have become unstable or corrupted. Press the Command-Option keys while your Mac is starting up to rebuild the desktop.

restart   The process of turning off and on your Mac while allowing the system to properly put away documents and applications. Select Restart from the Special menu or press the Power key and click Restart on the resulting alert box.

Retrospect   Dantz Software's very good file backup program.

Symantec Anti-Virus for Macintosh (SAM) 4.0   Symantec's virus-protection and repair program for your Mac. Version 4.0 is compatible with Mac OS 8.1 and later.

TechTool Pro 2.0   MicroMat's application that provides disk, RAM, chip, and peripheral analysis, repair, and recovery services. TechTool Pro 2.0 is HFS+ savvy.

TechTool Protection   MicroMat's utility (part of TechTool Pro 2.0) used to take periodic snapshots for data recovery purposes.

Virex 5.8   DataWatch's virus-protection and repair program.

Q&A

Q What Web sites support Macintosh troubleshooting?

A Many Web sites provide extensive support for Mac troubleshooting. Here are just a few:

- **Macintosh software and hardware conflicts site.** Lists troubleshooting resources and known system conflicts (http://www.quillserv.com/www/c3/c3.html).

- **Ric Ford's MacInTouch site.** Lists known bugs and fixes for Macintosh problems. This was one of the first bug-reporting and repair sites. It's also really up-to-date (http://www.macintouch.com/).

- **MacDirectory's help desk.** Called "Ask the Baroness" (http://www.macdirectory.com/pages/Baroness.html).

- **Apple's customer support site.** Provides Apple Tech Info files online (http://www.apple.com/support/).

- **Ted Landau's MacFixIt.** Lists potential problems and solutions as well as update links for Macs. This is a fantastic site (http://www.macfixit.com/).

- **Phoenix Macintosh Repair.** Provides information and advice on how to repair older Macs. Phoenix provides a printed manual for a nominal fee as well as excellent Web site pages (http://www.mainelink.net/~deceiver/phoenixmacrepair.html).

Q Where do I go to get a Power Computing computer fixed? How about other clones?

A There are two places: Decision One (http://www.decisionone.com/powercomputing.html) will fix your computer if you mail it to them. Apple also has a hotline for Power Computing questions that you can contact via SOS-Apple. Local Apple-approved repair centers, such as CompUSA, will also fix Apple Mac clones, but be sure to ask first.

Q How do I find out about late-breaking Mac OS 8.x issues?

A MacFixIt's site (www.macfixit.com/reports/macos8.1.shtml) contains an extensive array of information and links to special reports on issues related to Mac OS 8.1 and later. Apple's Tech Info document "About Mac OS 8.1" contains many known issues.

Q What about the Apple warranty? How many free calls do I get and how can I extend the warranty?

A Apple has a one-year warranty that allows 90 days of free calls from your first call. After that time, Apple charges $35 per call, unless you buy an extended warranty.

Q What basic steps can I follow when troubleshooting a problem with my computer?

A Follow these steps:

1. Try listing the exact steps that produce the problem and specifically identify the exact problem you're experiencing.

2. Select the Mac OS 8.5 base set of extensions and restart the computer. Then try to reproduce the problem. If the problem goes away, you probably have an extension conflict.

3. If the problem continues to occur, start your computer from the Mac OS 8.5 CD-ROM or Disk Tools floppy and run Apple's Disk First Aid on all hard disk volumes. Check to see whether it finds any errors on the hard disks and then try to repair them. Then restart and see if the problem persists.

4. Check for viruses or damage to the software files. You might need to reinstall your software application, rebuild the desktop, or create new preferences files if these files were damaged by a virus or by a software crash.

5. If all else fails, visit the publisher's Web site or give the technical support group a phone call to see whether there's an update available for the software problem.

Workshop

The Workshop contains quiz questions to help you solidify your understanding of the material covered. You can find the answers to the quiz questions in Appendix B, "Quiz Answers."

Quiz

1. What are the first three things you should try when experiencing problems with your Mac?

2. What software tools from third parties should you purchase to assist your troubleshooting and repair efforts?

3. Where can you find information about known bugs or software/hardware problems?

4. What are the symptoms of software problems?

5. How can you fix intermittent software problems?

6. What can you do if your application does not have enough RAM?

7. How do you solve system extension conflicts with Conflict Catcher?

8. How can you avoid bringing viruses on to your Mac?

9. How do you quit a malfunctioning program without rebooting your Mac?

10. How can you restart your Mac with no extensions running, and what does this help you troubleshoot?

24

APPENDIX **A**

Internet Sources for Mac OS 8.5

Table A.1 provides a list of Apple, Developer, and catalog vendors of Mac products. Support for these products is also provided.

TABLE A.1.

Adobe Acrobat	Adobe Home Page	http://www.adobe.com/ prodindex/acrobat/ main.html
Apple Computer	Home Page	www.apple.com
Apple Computer	Support and Information Page	www.info.apple.com
Apple Computer	Developers Page	www.apple.com/developer
Background images	MIT Site	the-tech.mit.edu/KPT/bgs.html
Browser-safe palettes	Lynda Wynman's Home Page	www.lynda.com/hex.html
Browsers	Browser Watch	www.browsers.com

continues

TABLE A.1. CONTINUED

HTML editors	BBEdit Home Page	www.barebones.com
HTML editors	PageMill Home Page	www.adobe.com
HTML editors	FrontPage Home Page	www.microsoft.com/frontpage/
HTML specs	WWW Consortium Home Page	www.w3.org
Java Applet Foundry	Gamelan Home Page	www.gamelan.com
Microsoft	Microsoft Home Page	www.microsoft.com
Netscape	Netscape Home Page	www.netscape.com
Shockwave	Macromedia Home Page	www.macromedia.com/shockwave/
TrueType Fonts	Web Fonts for Free	www.microsoft.com/truetype/free.htm
Web Page Design Firms	Various home pages	
	Atomic Vision	www.atomic.vision.com
	Avalanche	www.aval.com
	c|net	www.cnet.com
	Construct	www.construct.net
	Hot Wired	www.hotwired.com
	Organic Online	www.organic.com
	Studio Architype	www.studioarchitype.com
	Vivid Studios	www.vivid.com
Web Site Registration Services	Various sites	
	Submit-It	www.submit.com
	Barnsides	www.barnsides.com/links.htm

APPENDIX B

Quiz Answers

Hour 1

1. In addition to several new features, such as spring-loaded folders and pop-up windows, Finder now sports multiple Copy dialog boxes, context-sensitive menus, sticky menus, window view preferences (located in the Views menu), Finder preferences, tighter or wider grid spacing for icon views, and a simpler Finder setting.

2. Control panels that are no longer supported include Color, Views, Sharing Setup, File Sharing Monitor, Desktop Patterns, Labels, Monitor, Sound, and Window Shade. The features of these control panels are now found in renamed control panels or they're part of Finder 8.

3. The Macintosh Extended file system (also called *Hierarchical Filing System Plus* or *HFS+*) provides a cure for the storage bloat caused by the growth of hard disk capacity versus the capability of the Mac Standard file system to allocate appropriate block sizes. The Standard (or *HFS*)file system allocated 65,536 blocks regardless of the size of

the hard drive, whereas the new Extended (or *HFS+*) file system allocates up to 4.26 billion blocks, thus enabling each individual block where data is stored to be smaller, which means less wasted space.

4. QuickTime 3.0 is an extensive update to the Apple multimedia support system that lets you view all the newest audio and video formats on your Mac. In addition, you can update to QuickTime Pro to gain creation and editing tools for making your own audio and video documents.

5. ColorSync 2.5 provides color calibration support used by many image processing and desktop publishing applications. ColorSync also lets you calibrate your monitor and peripherals to support these imaging products.

6. Open Transport is the Mac's suite of networking components. Open Transport lets the Mac communicate using many network platforms, including AppleTalk, Ethernet, Token Ring, and TCP/IP.

7. Internet Config 1.3. Note that this software is no longer bundled with Mac OS 8.5, because the Internet control panel performs the same function.

8. The Finder lets you pop open folders by clicking a click-and-a-half; it generates contextual pop-up menus of commands you can access within applications or on the desktop; it lets you create "file drawers" on your desktop that contain active information you can open and shut by passing your cursor over the folder's title tab; and it provides a new Finder dialog box (used by the Open and Save As commands) that replicates the new behavior of the list view in dialog boxes.

9. Web Sharing is a control panel and system extension that turns any folder on your Mac into a small Internet server. Consider Web Sharing to be File Sharing for workgroups.

10. The Appearance control panel provides a handy place to customize the colors, fonts, sounds, and windows used on your desktop. You can even create combinations of features into themes to personalize your Mac.

Hour 2

1. To ensure a smooth transition of the new technologies provided by your new system, follow these steps:

    1. Check to see how much memory and hard disk space you have available for the installation.

    2. Ensure that your hard disk is error and virus free.

    3. Update your hard disk driver.

    4. Back up your hard disk's contents.

    5. Turn off all nonessential system extensions.

    6. Run the Mac OS Install application.

    7. Restore third-party control panels, preferences, and extensions from the old system to your new System Folder.

2. A normal system software installation modifies and updates the existing System Folder. A clean install disables the existing System Folder, leaving all files in place, and forces the installer to create a new System Folder.

B

A clean system install brings the system software back to the standard configuration. This is necessary when system software has been damaged or modified, thus preventing a normal installation. It's also useful for troubleshooting.

The main drawback of performing a clean installation is the work it entails. When you're finished, your work has really just begun, because you must restore all the third-party control panels, extensions, preference files, and folders you were running on your old system.

3. You'll need 154 MB of storage and at least 12 MB of RAM to perform an entire installation.

4. Open a folder on your hard drive. Look on the top of the window. The installer also calculates how much disk space you need and how much is available when you select a hard disk as your startup disk.

5. Disinfectant, Symantec Anti-Virus for Macintosh (SAM), and Dr. Solomon's Virex.

6. Let the installer update the drive during the installation via the Options dialog box. You can also use the Disk Setup program that comes with Mac OS 8.5. Select Update Driver from the Drive Setup's Functions menu.

7. Use FWB Hard Disk Toolkit 2.5.2 and select Update Driver from the Devices menu.

8. Restart your Mac and hold down the C key while it starts up.

9. Choose Custom Installation from the accompanying pop-up menu for that application. In the resulting dialog box, select the components you want to install from the list.

10. Open the old System Folder and new System Folder and slowly compare the contents of every subfolder. Pay strict attention to the contents of the Extensions, Preferences, Apple Items Menu, Fonts, and Control Panels folders. Drag any third-party icons into the appropriate new folder and copy any application folder from the old to the new System Folder.

Hour 3

1. Double-click the Trash Can icon and drag the contents of the folder back onto your desktop.

2. Dialog boxes use the following types of Finder tools:

   - **Check box.** Provides a way to select more than one option.
   - **Radio button.** Provides a way to select only one option from a list.
   - **Text box.** Provides a way to type information into a dialog box.
   - **Pop-up menu.** A hierarchical menu of options from which you can select one item.
   - **Button.** A tool used to initiate or stop a process (such as OK or Cancel). Also a method of switching between volumes (for example, the Desktop button or the New Folder button).
   - **Finder list box.** A list of documents and folders used to locate a file (or files).

3. Collapse the folder using the Collapse button. You can also collapse a folder to its title bar by double-clicking the title bar.

4. A local disk is available only to your Mac, because it resides at your computer. Local disks can be removable or fixed. Volumes are shared disks that you access via a network. Volumes are indicated by the small AppleTalk symbol on their icon and can be thrown away when you no longer need them available. (Do not throw away a fixed startup disk.)

5. Press the Option key while dragging a control strip icon to move it to another location on the Control Strip. Drag and drop Control Strip applications onto the Control Strip to add the item.

6. Create a new folder and give it a name starting with an Option-8 bullet. Then drag the new folder onto the Launcher title bar or into the Launcher Items folder in the System Folder.

7. Drag the item onto the Launcher window or onto a Launcher folder.

8. Choose Preferences from the Edit menu. In the resulting Preferences dialog box, specify a new folder speed using the slider bar.

9. Control-click an item on the desktop or in applications that are context menu savvy.

10. Click a different title to sort the folder by that subject—for example, Name, Date Created, Version Number, Size, and so on.

Hour 4

1. The lowest-level folder on your desktop is the one representing the contents of a disk or volume. You get to the root by double-clicking the hard disk icon on the desktop.

2. Select the alias you want to identify. Choose General Information from the Get Info pop-up menu on the File menu. In the resulting General Information dialog box, click Select New Original.

3. Select the item and perform one of the following tasks:

   - Choose Make Alias from the File menu (Command-M).

   - Control-click to bring up a contextual menu. Then select Make Alias.

   - Drag the item onto the Launcher or its title bar.

4. Select Hide <*filename*> from the Application menu. You can also collapse a window so that only its title bar is showing by clicking the collapse button on its window or double-clicking its title bar.

5. The startup disk cannot be dragged into the Trash Can, nor can the Trash Can icon.

6. Drag the item into the Launcher window or onto a button on the Launcher's title bar. You can also open the Launcher Items folder in the Systems Folder and manually insert the items.

7. Choose New Folder from the File menu (Command-N). Give the folder a name starting with a bullet (Option-8) and then drag the new folder onto the Launcher window.

8. Use the Find application's Search Context tab. Click Index. Select the local volume you want to index and then click Index. You create an index to speed up content searches.

9. Select the folder and choose View Preferences from the View menu. In the resulting dialog box, set up how you want icons to be viewed for that folder. Close the dialog box to apply the changes.

10. Mac OS 8.5 provides a way to "burrow" through folders (opening one hierarchical folder after another until you reach the document you're seeking). This burrowing feature is indicated by a magnifying glass cursor and is invoked by single-clicking and then half-clicking the mouse.

B

Hour 5

1. The Appearance control panel's Desktop tab lets you assign desktop patterns and pictures.

2. The Appearance control panel's Appearance tab lets you assign desktop themes.

3. The Appearance control panel's Sound tab lets you assign sounds to system functions.

4. The Appearance control panel's Color tab lets you assign primary and system highlight colors. Double-click Other Color to display the Color Picker. Use the Color Picker's various color system options to select an alternative color scheme.

5. The Appearance control panel's Font tab lets you assign fonts to large displays (such as menu bars) as well as basic system fonts.

6. Select a new monitor resolution from the Resolution list in the Monitors tab of the Monitors & Sound control panel.

7. Open the Desktop tab of the Appearance control panel and click Remove Picture and then Set Desktop.

8. Use the Alert tab of the Monitors & Sound control panel. Select another sound from the list.

9. Use the Keyboard control panel. Select a keyboard template from the list. You must set up a keyboard layout during installation to have these layouts available in the control panel.

10. Use the Extensions Manager to turn on and off system extensions and control panels. Press the spacebar during startup to display the Extensions Manager.

Hour 6

1. Applications are independent programs that run on the Mac, whereas control panels (called CDEVs) and system extensions (called INITs) are pieces of software that work with the Mac OS to perform a function. You can tell the difference because applications use their own windows, menu bars, and dialog boxes, whereas CDEVs and INITs rely on the Finder's menu bar and dialog boxes to perform their functions.

2. Here are four ways:

   In the Finder, select the application you want to open and choose Open from the File menu (or press the keyboard combination Command-O). Double-click the application's icon on the desktop. Select the applications' button in the Launcher.

Select the application's name from the Recent Applications Apple menu item's pop-up menu.

3. Here are four ways:

   Drag the document's icon over its application icon on the desktop. Double-click an application's icon. Select the document's button from the Launcher. While in an active application, choose Open from the File menu (or press the keyboard combination Command-O).

4. In an application's active window, choose Save As from the File menu. Use the Finder list box to drill through folders until you locate the folder where you want to save your document. Use the Desktop button to change from a local to a remote volume, if necessary. Use the title bar to navigate through a folder's hierarchy, if necessary. If available, click New Folder to create a new folder at the location where you want to save the file. Then, follow the standard process to save a document.

5. In the older Finder Open dialog box, click the Desktop button to move to a different volume. The Desktop button takes you to the desktop (naturally), where you can choose another volume from the Finder list box.

   In the new Navigation Services Open dialog box, click the "pointing finger" button to access the Finder pop-up menu. Select a volume from those listed or click Internet or Network to open another volume not currently loaded on your Mac.

6. Choose Hide *<application name>* from the Application menu's pop-up menu.

7. Here are the two ways:

   Choose another open application from the Application menu or click another window to bring it to the front and activate its application.

8. Here are the two ways:

   Click the close box on the top-left corner of a window or choose Close from the File menu (you can also press the keyboard combination Command-W).

9. Save the document using the PC naming convention of an eight-character name followed by a three-character suffix, which indicates the originating application that produced the document. It's also smart to use the Format pop-up menu to save the document in a format readable by most PC programs (for example, Word for Windows instead of Word 98).

10. Run the installer for the program (if it uses an Apple installer) and hold down the Option key while clicking the Install button. In the resulting Customize dialog box, select Remove from the Easy Install pop-up menu.

B

Hour 7

1. Performance is affected by the speeds of your input/output bus, hard drive, floppy drive, and removable media, as well as the number of times your Mac has to access peripherals. Also, which video components are installed is a factor as well.

2. Loading too many system extensions, such as Now Utilities various startup extensions, Norton Utilities startup extensions, and so forth, can bog down your Mac's performance. Installing an extensive amount of fonts in your Font folder also tends to slow your Mac's performance.

3. Turn off all extraneous processes, such as background printing and copying. Copy applications to your local volume before using them. Try not to open documents on the server, but rather copy documents to your hard disk and open them locally.

4. CD-ROM media ranges from audio CD to interactive multimedia to 3D animation-packed software applications. To maximize CD-ROM playback performance, do the following:

   - Turn the Virtual Memory setting off. Virtual Memory can be turned on and off from the Memory control panel.
   - Turn the File Sharing setting off. File sharing can be turned on and off from the File Sharing control panel.
   - Select the recommended bit-depth setting. The monitor's color depth can be selected from the Monitors & Sound control panel.
   - Turn AppleTalk off. AppleTalk settings are located in the Chooser or the AppleTalk control panel.

5. Turn off background printing. Also, make sure you don't include too many fonts or graphic images in your document. A rule of thumb is to include only two font families per page and one or two images. Also, you can increase the memory in your printer.

6. Do not change the default setting in Mac OS 8.5's disk cache in the Memory control panel. The new Memory control panel manages disk cache for you, providing the proper amount automatically.

7. You should set Virtual Memory in the Memory control panel to 1 MB greater than your available hard disk space if you're using a Power Mac. The default for Mac OS 8.1 and 8.5 is to have this setting already turned on.

8. A general rule of thumb for increasing performance is to turn off any bells and whistles. For example, the Finder has several settings located in the View and Edit

menus of Mac OS 8.5. Calculate Folder Sizes is one of the check boxes in the View Preferences window (change your view to "lists" before selecting View Options or this check box will not be available). For faster performance, leave this feature off. Turning Calculate Folder Sizes on activates a background task in Finder that calculates the folder size in any selected window.

Performance for opening and closing folders can be improved by keeping the number of files and folders stored in one folder at a manageable number. The magic number of files and folders depends on what kinds of files and applications are on your Mac. Generally, however, it's a good goal to keep the total number below 100. This also applies to files and folders stored on the desktop.

B

9. Video performance on your Mac can be improved by reducing the Color Depth setting in the Monitors & Sound control panel. Some Macs do not support the black-and-white setting. Even if you use color, selecting a smaller color depth can let your Mac update the items onscreen faster. See Hour 11 for a discussion of how to work with color and your monitor. Generally, the Monitors & Sound control panel is used to adjust your screen's resolution. Your OS version determines where on the Monitors & Sound control panel this adjustment is located.

10. You can safely remove any system extension or control panel that doesn't work with your Mac. For example, if you're not using a PowerBook, you can safely remove PowerBook-only control panels. Delete printer drivers for those printers you don't use. Remove extraneous printer description files from the Printer Description folder in the Preferences folder. If you're not using Ethernet, you can turn off the built-in Ethernet system extension, the TokenTalk extension, and the EtherTalk extension.

Hour 8

1. Battery, power consumption, hard disk spin-up, smaller screen size, and portability.

2. The 3400 and G3 series PowerBooks as well as the next-generation PowerBooks.

3. The PowerBook Setup control panel.

4. Once a month, unless your PowerBook (that is, the 3400) doesn't need to have it reconditioned.

5. In the PowerBook folder located in the Apple Extras folder.

Hour 9

1. "What you see is what you get." The goal in a WYSIWYG environment is to have what appears onscreen be as close as possible to what appears on the printed page.

2. To most Macintosh users, the term *font* refers to the name of the character style such as Geneva, Palatino, or Times. To a graphics artist, the term refers to a single style of letters (for example, 12-point bold Palatino). To a Macintosh programmer, the term refers to the resource files used to store the information to create the image both on the screen and on paper.

3. *Typography* is the physical creation of fonts, formerly out of hot metal, and today on the computer. All font terminology stems from the printer's trade.

4. A *character set* refers to the entire collection of symbols that can be printed in a particular character style. All the character sets currently used on microcomputers share these common characters, but most go far beyond the 128-character limit. Beyond the original standard characters, different character sets may contain different symbols. Most character sets on the Macintosh contain about 150 printable characters.

5. *Unicode* is an international standard for the listing of font character IDs used by the Font Manager on the Mac to render fonts for printing and display. Up until Mac OS 8.5, the Mac used WorldScript as its international character standard. With Mac OS 8.5, the Mac supports the more popular Unicode standard.

6. Use the Font menu to select another font. Press the Option key or the keyboard combination of Shift-Option to view the additional characters in the set.

7. A *font family* is a collection of character sets that share a similar design. Each font family consists of a number of typefaces. A *typeface* is a particular style of character.

8. A screen font, or *bitmapped* font, is a font composed of pixels, one shape for every font size. Many files are required to produce a font family. Bitmapped fonts are created at screen resolutions (72 dpi) and therefore display cleanly and can be drawn onscreen quickly. Printer fonts, also called *PostScript* or *outline* fonts, are based on mathematical algorithms that can recalculate the shape of a font for any size, based on a single outline (this is known as *resolution independence*). PostScript fonts are paired with bitmapped fonts so that every font requires two types—a single printer file and many screen files—for proper rendering. TrueType fonts are special printer fonts that consist of outline fonts that can be properly rendered as bitmaps onscreen. TrueType fonts do not require a second font type for their use and are therefore more space efficient than PostScript fonts.

9. When fonts are installed on your Mac, they are placed in the Fonts folder in your System Folder.

10. Adobe Type Manager Deluxe 4.0 lets you manage your font families so that only those fonts you require for each project need to be activated at any one time. ATM also smoothes the jagged edges of bitmapped fonts (known as *anti-aliasing*), corrects any corruption that may creep into your font files, and controls the character ID chart. Adobe Type Reunion lets you see the actual families as they appear onscreen in the Font menu of most applications (even Word 98). Symantec Suitecase also manages your font families.

   With the advent of OpenType fonts, ATM and Suitecase should no longer be needed, because fonts are automatically anti-aliased, and font families are more controlled.

B

Hour 10

1. A dot-matrix printer and an inkjet printer use small, movable pins, called *print wires*, to create dots, which in turn are used to create images. Dot-matrix printers use inked ribbons to create the dots, whereas inkjet printers squirt ink onto the pins to create the dots. Laser printers use a totally different technology to create images. Lasers shine a light to create the dots used to create images. Lasers are controlled by onboard computers, whereas dot-matrix printers and inkjets are mechanical devices controlled by your Mac.

2. Printers come in two types: those that contain a computer and a page-description language interpreter in their cases (such as PostScript printers), and those that use the power of QuickDraw on the Mac to describe how pages are drawn.

3. Laser printers that contain controllers use them to manage the rasterizing of images. Laser printers, like Macintosh video screens, are raster devices. Because the controller manages this process, it's sometimes called a *raster-image processor (RIP)*. There are two types of RIPs, depending on the language used to communicate an application's page specifications: PostScript printers and QuickDraw printers.

4. PostScript printers provide extensive benefits in terms of performance, cost savings, and flexibility. Because PostScript scan converts the QuickDraw code, the application program does not have to know the resolution of the printer you're using. You can therefore print on many different PostScript printers using the same file and application program. The difference will be the quality of the output.

5. A printer driver is software that acts as an intermediary between the Mac and the printer. Also, a printer driver is the intermediary program that translates the QuickDraw commands used by the application to specify how a document should look into commands that can be used by a specific printer to print the document. These features, in turn, are displayed on the Page Setup and Print dialog boxes in all programs.

   To select a printer driver, open the Chooser and select a printer driver from the Driver list on the left side of the dialog box.

6. A PPD is a page-description document used by PostScript laser printers to describe the specific features of the printer. You create a PPD by selecting a printer driver and printer in the Chooser and then clicking Create.

7. The Page Setup command describes for the printer how you want to print the image. Whenever you change printer drivers in the Chooser, make sure to open Page Setup in your document to inform the program that you've changed printers.

8. Select the Page Setup command from the File menu and click the landscape or portrait diagrams in the Orientation section.

9. Select the Page Setup command from the File menu and type a new percentage in either the Enlarge or Reduce text box.

10. Select the Print command from the File menu and then select ColorSync as your Color Manager in the Color section.

Hour 11

1. ColorSync is a control panel.

2. The Monitor & Sound control panel.

3. In the Extensions folder in your System Folder.

4. Select Other from the Colors list in the Appearance control panel. Color Picker's dialog box is displayed. Pick a new CMM and select a color using the new method.

5. CYMK uses process colors (cyan, magenta, yellow, and black) to create colors, whereas RGB uses electronic colors (red, green, and blue) to create colors.

6. Drag the ColorSync plug-in to your application's Plug-ins folder.

7. Go to the Monitors & Sound control panel's Color screen and click the Calibrate button. Follow the instructions on the resulting screens to calibrate your monitor. Save the results as a corrective profile.

8. Choose Print from the File menu. In the resulting Print dialog box, find the Color section. In the Epson Stylus 600 dialog box, you click the ColorSync color management button. Other printers have their own dialog boxes with similar instructions.

9. Set your monitor to 256 colors or 8-bit depth. In image-processing applications, this setting is known as the Netscape or Safe Color profile.

10. Open the Monitors & Sound control panel and specify the appropriate measurements in the list boxes.

Hour 12

1. QuickTime is a set of technologies that let you create and play multimedia presentations.

2. Click the left-facing arrow on the Movie Player control pad.

3. Click the right-facing double arrow set on the Movie Player control pad.

4. Click the square stop button on the Movie Player control pad.

5. Use the Connection Speed dialog box in the QuickTime Settings control panel to select a data transmission speed.

6. Use the AutoPlay screen of the QuickTime Settings control panel to check the AutoPlay setting before inserting an audio CD into your CD-ROM drive. Use the Apple CD Audio Player to control the play options.

7. If you want to create QuickTime movies, you need to purchase QuickTime Pro (available for around $29.95). Apple makes it very easy to purchase the product online by providing a QuickTime video and links to the Apple Store on the Registration dialog box in QuickTime Settings. There's also an annoying advertisement that pops up when you first use the QuickTime plug-in.

8. Drag the plug-in into the Plug-ins folder in your browser's folder. The Netscape Navigator and Microsoft Internet Explorer folders are located in the Internet Applications folder, which in turn is located in the Internet folder.

9. Upgrade your QuickTime package to QuickTime Pro to update the QuickTime plug-in. When you want to save a video from the Web, hold down the mouse to display the browser's contextual menu. Select Save Movie from the menu. Follow the resulting instructions for saving a file to your Mac's hard drive.

10. This foundation technology is an advanced, component-based software architecture that provides software and hardware developers full access to the built-in QuickTime services. It also specifies how to accelerate and extend QuickTime's capabilities through a powerful plug-in framework.

One of the most compelling features of the QuickTime media abstraction layer is the broad range of media types supported. QuickTime 3.0.0 includes built-in support for 10 media types (video, audio, text, timecode, music/MIDI, sprite/animation, tween, MPEG, VR, 3D). For each of the built-in media types, QuickTime provides a rich set of media-specific services appropriate for managing each particular media type.

Hour 13

1. Use the Sound tool on the Control Strip to adjust the volume, or you can open the Monitors & Sound control panel and adjust the volume on the Sound screen.

2. Open the Monitors & Sound control panel and click a new sound from the Alert list on the Alert screen.

3. Yes, drag an SND file onto your System Folder to install it in your system file. Choose the new sound from the Alert list on the Alert screen of the Monitors & Sound control panel.

4. Click the Add button on the Alert screen of the Monitors & Sound control panel. Click the Record button to start recording sounds from a microphone attached to your Mac or an audio CD playing on your CD-ROM drive. Press Stop to stop and Play to play back your sound sample. Save the sound and then select it from the Alert list box.

5. No, you need some sort of software to record sounds. The Mac has the technology to interpret input and output sounds to support MIDI and digital audio devices and software.

6. MIDI synthesizes sounds created on your computer and plays them back on external MIDI devices. Digital audio is a method of recording external sound and manipulating it on your Mac.

7. Yes, scads of sounds are available on the Internet and AOL. Also, Kaboom! prepackages copyright-cleared sounds for your use.

Hour 14

1. You need a video source, such as a television, camcorder, VCR, or digital camera. You need a video capture card in your Mac, and you need enough memory and

space to capture and replay your video. PowerMac 7500, 7600, 8500, and 8600 as well as some configurations of the G3 are "video ready" out of the box.

2. Each video source has its own connector and cable requirements. Most VCRs and camcorders use composite jacks (similar to RCA-type stereo jacks) for connecting outputs and inputs. You need at least four connections: video and audio input and output. High-end systems use S-video connectors. Read the manual for your video source for details on which cables to connect to which ports. You also have to consult the instructions for your third-party video card to properly connect it to your source.

3. In the Applications folder installed by Mac OS 8.5 on your hard disk.

4. Choose Normal Size, Smallest Size, or Largest Size from the Window menu.

5. Use the picture controls in the Controls window to adjust sharpness, contrast, color, and brightness.

6. Quit the Video Player. Select its icon on the desktop. Then choose Get Info (Command-I) from the Edit menu and increase the memory allocated to the application's partition.

7. You can save video in QuickTime movie format (MOV) or as a PICT file for still images.

8. Turn off all background processes including File Sharing, Virtual Memory, and menu bar items such as the clock and RAM Doubler.

9. Choose Preferences from the Setup menu. Set Movie Compression to None.

10. You need third-party software such as Adobe Premiere or Macromedia Director. Here are some of the input sources supported:

- Antenna
- Cable feed
- Digital camera
- VCR
- LaserDisc
- S-video devices

Apple Video Player is also fully compliant with AppleScript and supports playback of MPEG 1 movie files from CD or hard disk.

Hour 15

1. Content design (determining what you want to say) and appearance design (determining how your Web site will look).

2. The goal of a Web site is communication.

3. Here are three questions you must answer to determine a site's content:
   - What is the intended purpose of the site?
   - Who is the site's target audience?
   - How will you construct the site?

4. A good rule of thumb to use when designing site navigation is *form follows function*. For example, if you're designing a site used for academic research, it will probably be accessed using a search engine such as WebCrawler or Alta Vista. If you're providing general information in more of a newsletter presentation, your audience probably will access your home page using a site index such as Excite, Yahoo, or NetCenter and then jump to links they are interested in using your hypertext links. If you're building a commercial site, your audience will use a database or form approach to finding information about your site's contents.

5. There are two types of search engines: a so-called Web bot that goes crawling through the entire Internet compiling URLs by keywords. These are the earliest type of search engine such as Alta Vista or WebCrawler. There are companies, such as Snap, Yahoo, or Excite that have people who review sites that are registered with them and only list those sites that pass their approval. A third newer concept is the "portal" a home page sponsored by a search engine company that lists indexed sites and contains a Web-bot for general searching. Netscape's NetCenter (www.home.netcenter.com), Excite's My Excite (my.excite.com), and Yahoo's My Yahoo (my.yahoo.com) are three such portals. The portals can be personalized to meet your specific work habits.

6. Your prototype should give you information on the following issues:
   - What information will actually be included in the site?
   - How is the site supposed to work? What interconnections will actually be built between components?
   - Where will your links be made and what outside URLs will be included?

7. Your best tools are an image processor, such as Adobe Photoshop, an illustration package, such as MetaCreations Painter, Adobe Illustrator, or Macromedia Freehand, and a word processor, such as Microsoft Word or Corel WordPerfect.

8. There are two standard image file formats suitable for publishing on the Internet:

   - JPEG (Joint Photographic Expert Group) compresses color bitmapped images (scanned images such as photographs are bitmapped). JPEG enables variable rates of compression (called *lossy* compression). JPEG is the best compression method for images such as photographs, which contain many colors in varying amounts.

   - CompuServe's GIF (Graphics Interchange Format) is the industry standard for Web pages. GIF supports moving just about any type of graphic between computer platforms without a loss of quality. GIF is the best compression format to use when your images contain solid areas of relatively few colors, such as raster or vector drawings.

9. The standard name for a home page is INDEX.HTML.

10. HTML stands for Hypertext Markup Language. HTML consists of tags that tell the browser how to display the data contained within the tags. All HTML documents consist of a shell, a basic set of tags that defines the parameters of your page. PageMill bases its total philosophy on this basic template, because you can build any page by adding bells and whistles to this basic format:

```
<HTML>
<HEAD>
<TITLE> This is the Title</TITLE>
</HEAD>
<BODY>
    <H1> Major document heading here</H1>
        text and markup
    <A HREF="URL"> anchor title</A>
<ADDRESS>Author and version information</ADDRESS>
</BODY>
</HTML>
```

Hour 16

1. Distributed file serving, the type of networking provided by Apple File Sharing, operates without a central file server to manage the transport and sharing of files. Each computer shares the job of file serving. Centralized file serving uses a dedicated computer to contain and serve all the data and files used by computers connected by the network. Centralized serving is also called *client/server networking*, because it uses two types of software: file serving software on the dedicated computer and client software to manage serving files on each connected computer.

B

2. *Peer-to-peer networking* is a type of physical cabling that links computer to computer. This can be used instead of a backbone cable with drops to each computer (including the file server). Peer-to-peer networks are typically used with distributed file servers.

3. AppleShare is two things: AppleShare 3.5.7 is the current version of the client networking software that resides on every Mac to run networks using the AppleTalk protocol, and AppleShare is the general name for Macintosh networks. AppleShare IP 6.0 is the file server software that works with AppleShare client to manage a Macintosh client/server network.

4. Open Transport is a technology composed of various pieces of software that together drive networking via both AppleTalk and TCP/IP on the Mac.

5. The File Sharing control panel.

6. To set up access privileges for your Mac.

7. Turn off File Sharing using the File Sharing control panel. Throw away the shared volume into the Trash Can.

8. Select AppleShare in the Chooser. Select a zone from the AppleShare list and a volume from the resulting list of shared volumes. If more than one volume is available for sharing at a location, select the volume you want to mount from the resulting dialog box after entering your password.

9. You can minimize the tendency of shared Macs to have degraded performance by following these tips:

   - Assign an alias to a shared volume you've accessed from another Mac. Next time you want to use it, simply double-click the alias to bring its volume onto your system.

   - Limit the number of folders you allow to be shared by placing all the files you're sharing into a single folder and designate that folder as the shared item. Note that if you have different access privileges for each file, this strategy does not work, because all the folder's contents are assigned a single access privilege.

   - Limit the number of people who access your Mac. Make it a rule that work is performed on the local Mac and not on remote nodes.

   - Share as few files as possible. This is a good security procedure, because the fewer files available, the less possible damage can be performed.

   - Limit the security levels. Keep it simple so that managing and untangling a confusion of passwords and access permissions doesn't take up all your time.

   - Use the same registered names on all Macs on the network to avoid confusion.

- Avoid launching an application on a volume you're sharing. The performance of both Macs will become too slow to do anything else on these computers. For best performance, you should copy a file to your local disk, edit it, and then copy it back to the other file-shared disk.

10. Select a disk or file you want to share. Choose Sharing from the Get Info pop-up menu on the File menu. Make sure File Sharing and AppleTalk are on by opening their control panels first. In the Sharing dialog box, click the check box for Share This Folder. Close the Sharing dialog box.

Hour 17

1. Personal Web Sharing is a control panel that can be accessed from your Apple menu.

2. At the highest level of your Mac (preferably your desktop).

3. Click Select next to the Web Folder text in the Web Sharing control panel.

4. Click Select next to the Start Page text on the Web Sharing control panel's dialog box.

5. The Personal NetFind scheme is automatically set up. Basically, your browsers see a list of folders and files similar to your Finder that they can download.

6. Click Start on the Web Sharing control panel's dialog box.

7. Select the File Sharing radio button to have your File Sharing permissions apply to Personal Web Sharing. See Hour 16, "File Sharing," for a discussion of file sharing.

Hour 18

1. Use the Internet control panel's Web tab. Select another browser from the Default Web Browser pop-up menu.

2. If you're first installing Mac OS 8.5, the Internet Setup Assistant will automatically open after the Mac OS Setup Assistant is finished. If you want to make changes to your setup, the Internet Setup Assistant has an alias in the Internet folder.

3. Contact your ISP. Many ISPs offer software programs, such as EarthLink's TotalAccess, that retrieve this information for you.

4. You're in trouble. Luckily, Remote Access will remember your password and ID if you check the Remember Password box on the Remote Access control panel. You can also call or email your ISP's technical support hotline if you lose your account information and don't mind a delay.

5. Select Disconnect from the Remote Access Control Strip tool or click Disconnect from the Remote Access Status desk accessory found on the Apple Menu.

6. Open the Internet control panel and click Duplicate. Make your changes in the copy of the configuration. Use the Rename command on the File menu to give your second configuration a name. Select the configuration you want to use from the Active Set pop-up menu.

7. A *home page* is the first Web page that opens when you invoke your browser. Web search companies are fighting fiercely to be your home page, because companies pay to have their URLs referenced on this page. You can switch home pages regularly by typing the page's URL in the Home Page text box of the Web tab on the Internet control panel.

8. Open the Remote Access control panel and select Options. Turn off the check box for Flashing Icon in the Connection screen.

9. Select the Email Flash check box on the Email screen of the Internet control panel.

10. Open the Web tab on the Internet control panel. In the Download Files To section, click Select. Choose a folder or create a new folder and click Select. Your designated folder appears in the section.

Hour 19

1. Tim Berners-Lee invented the concept of Web pages and the hypertext markup language that supports their transmission. Marc Andreeson invented the browser that translates HTML into readable documents.

2. The *WWW* is a method for viewing information graphically from the Internet. The Internet is the overall network of networked computers containing the information.

3. A *newsgroup* is a collection of messages about an identified topic. Use a newsreader such as Netscape Collabra or Microsoft News to search Usenet servers for pertinent newsgroup topics.

4. A private chat room is an area of the Internet you can create using security that allows you to communicate with subscribers without being overheard by the rest of the Internet. Private rooms limit the publication range of a message to specific recipients.

5. *Emoticons* are small symbols that indicate an emotion—for example, :) or ;).

6. Install special screening software, such as Surf Nanny or SurfWatch, that blocks access to sites having specified alert tags.

7. To run an Apple Data Detector, you need to install the Apple Data Detector 1.0.2 software that comes with the Internet Address Detector. You also need to have AppleScript and Open Transport 1.3 installed and running on your Mac.

8. Use the Apple Data Detector control panel to specify which data to use in data detection scans.

9. Use the subheadings under each data detector in the Apple Data Detector control panel to control the actions taken on scanned information.

10. You need to know the URL of the FTP site you want to access, any subdirectory names, and your user ID and password.

Hour 20

1. To change the format of a file, select a different file format from the Save File as Type pop-up menu in the Save As dialog box.

2. To open a foreign file, double-click the file or drag it onto a Mac application. File Exchange will automatically translate the file into a readable format. Note that Word uses its own conversion tools and bypasses File Exchange.

3. Use Aladdin StuffIt Deluxe or Drop Stuff EE to convert files into SIT archives before transmission.

4. *Creator* is a four-letter code assigned by the Finder during the Save process that identifies which application program runs the specified document.

5. The *resource fork* saves information about the structure of a program, such as how it formats its data for storage. File type and creator information is saved in the resource fork.

6. The Mac hides its file type information in a resource fork, whereas PC-based documents need each file to be manually named with a file type so that an application can be associated with that file based on the suffix.

7. To read PDF files, you need the Adobe Acrobat plug-in. Acrobat is available at www.adobe.com or on just about every site that uses PDF files.

8. The document displays an icon representing its creator application. Orphan files lose their icon bundle bits.

9. Make sure you use the eight-character naming convention and three-character file type suffix in the filename.

10. MacLink Plus/Translators version 10 on the Mac and MacLink Translators/PC on Windows.

Hour 21

1. To view applets all by themselves (or to search the Web for applets), open the Apple Applet Runner. Select an applet from the Applet menu, and it opens in a window on your desktop.

2. You can control the applet's operation by using the Applet menu's commands to suspend restart, reload, and display the HTML tags in the Java console. You display the Applet menu by making the Applet window the active window (click the window to bring it in front).

3. The Apple Applet Runner is more than simply a tool to demonstrate applets that have been packaged with the Mac OS 8.5 CD-ROM. You can run distributed applets by using Open Transport/PPP to dial into the Internet and grab an applet from a specified URL.

4. Just select the Open URL command from the File menu, and Apple Applet Runner displays a list of URLs that it remembers (this program remembers URLs where applets have been found). Select an applet, and its URL is displayed in the dialog box. Click Open to run the applet.

5. Clicking Add displays a new dialog box that lets you give the URL a name (typically the name of the applet and the Web site where it's found) as well as type in the URL. Clicking OK adds the new applet to the URL list. Selecting the new URL name and clicking Open grabs that URL. Apple Applet Runner will even invoke OT/PPP to dial the Web if you're not already connected.

    OpenDoc is currently no longer supported by Apple. Mac OS 8 and 8.1 include OpenDoc and CyberDog in their installations for the developer population developing Live Objects. As far as Apple is concerned (as illustrated by the exclusion of OpenDoc from Mac OS 8.2), OpenDoc has been superseded by Java.

7. Nothing. Java runtime engines are included with both browsers.

8. *Apple Applet Runner* is the application that lets you run applets on your Mac's MRJ engine. *Apple Viewer* is a Live Object used by CyberDog to run Java applets and, as such, is no longer supported.

9. The Mac OS Runtime for Java folder in your Apple Extras folder.

10. There are currently fights between the different vendors marketing their own versions of Java. These versions are incompatible with each other and need their own engines to run. Until Microsoft, Sun, Hewlett-Packard, and Netscape agree on a Java standard, Java will be an interesting future tool within Mac OS 8.5.

Hour 22

1. *AppleScript* is a scripting language that's designed to allow you to automate actions performed by the Finder and by a wide spectrum of Mac applications.

2. Version 3.0 can only be used with Mac OS 8.5. Related to this issue is the fact that older scripts may not run under AppleScript 3.0 and Finder 8.0 due to changes in the Finder.

3. The OSAX files are stored in the Scripting Additions folder that resides in the System Folder.

4. Active scripts are stored in the new Scripts folder in the System Folder.

5. The OSA menu (found in the AppleScript folder on the Mac OS 8.5 CD-ROM) lets you access your active scripts from the menu bar.

6. The record and stop buttons are used to control the recording of a script.

7. Syntax Check is a button used in the Script Editor to automatically check the logic used in your scripts. The Syntax Editor flags errors for your correction.

8. Every scriptable component of an application contains a terminology dictionary you can use to input codes. You can view the dictionary of a scriptable application when you're in the Script Editor by selecting Open Dictionary from the File menu. Select the application (for example, the Finder) from the Open dialog box and then click Open. The Script Editor displays a new window with the application's dictionary entries. Select a command, class, or type of command (called a *suite*) from the left column to display its list of object classes and commands in the right column.

9. Change the formatting options of the different script parts by selecting AppleScript Formatting from the Edit menu.

10. Four basic processes are involved in creating a script, although several methods are required for performing these steps. Scripts require the following steps:

    1. **Generate a script.** There are two ways to write a script: have the Mac do it for you (known as *recording*) or doing it yourself (known as *scripting*).

    2. **Edit your script.** You can move lines around in your script just as you would in a word processing document. You can also format your script for easier reading and comprehensibility.

    3. **Check the syntax of your script.** This step is also called *debugging*. Syntax is the grammar of the script. If this is correct, the script will actually work.

    4. **Compile your script.** This step changes the script into machine code that can be understood by the Mac.

B

Hour 23

1. Hard disks consist of a rigid, usually nonremovable series of round, flat platters placed one on top of each other. Unlike the floppy or removable disk that spins only when a read or write operation is requested, hard disk platters are continuously spinning. Hard disk drive platters spin at an approximate rate of 3,600 to 5,400 revolutions per minute.

2. In order for the Macintosh's disk drives to read, the magnetic iron-oxide dust on the disk must be organized into some sort of pattern. New disks consist of randomly scattered coatings on their substrates. Until they're initialized, they cannot be read or written to by the Macintosh (because it cannot recognize any identifying markings). Initializing a disk places the Macintosh disk layout requirements onto the media, making it usable to the Macintosh. These patterns lay out how the data will be stored and tracked on the disk.

3. When you want to partition your hard disk into individual logical volumes with different qualities (HFS versus HFS+, and so on) per volume.

4. *Hard formatting* physically arranges the substrate on a disk in a pattern understood by the Mac, whereas *logical formatting* creates the directories and invisible files that tell the Mac what information is stored on which track or sector of the disk.

5. The original formatting scheme for Macintosh disks based on the hierarchical file system. HFS creates 65,536 blocks on the hard disk of equal size where chunks of data can be stored.

6. Now, large hard disks can be mapped in smaller block chunks, thus wasting much less space.

7. You probably won't get much disk space savings on disks smaller than 1 GB or if you're saving very large files.

8. You cannot use a hard disk initialized with HFS+ as the startup disk of a 68040-based Mac. Once you do it, it is done. You can access disks formatted with HFS+ only from Macs running Mac OS 8.1 or higher.

9. The most important thing to do before you upgrade to HFS+ is to back up your hard disk.

10. The easiest way to convert your volumes to HFS+ is to use Alsoft PlusMaker.

Hour 24

1. Reboot by pressing Command-Ctrl-Power key. Rebuild the desktop by pressing Command-Option while restarting. Restart without extensions by holding down the Shift key while restarting.

2. Norton Utilities or TechTool Pro. The following tools are also helpful:

   • Dantz Retrospect 4.0.

   • Symantec Norton Utilities 4.

   • Casady & Greene Conflict Catcher 8.

   • Symantec Norton Antivirus for Macintosh 5.0.

3. There many sources of this information, including the following:

   • ReadMe files.

   • The manual and online help.

   • Various software vendor sites on the Internet as well as Apple's product information site (`http://www.info.apple.com`).

   • Books and magazines.

4. They usually fall into one of the following categories:

   • Quits

   • Hangs and freezes

   • Won't do what it's supposed to

   • Error messages during startup

5. Save and restore as much of your data as you can, reboot your machine, and begin the task of figuring out how to *prevent* future occurrences of the problem. The bulk of your troubleshooting efforts for software problems is the prevention of future problems rather than the treatment of problems that have already occurred.

6. Use the Memory dialog box accessed using the Get Info pop-up menu on the File menu (File|Get Info, or Command-I) and increase the program's preferred memory size. Add more RAM to your Mac if you're running out of memory in general.

7. Use Conflict Catcher and run an analysis of your system. Conflict Catcher automatically corrects any conflicts it finds.

8. Install a virus-scanning program such as SAM or Virex. Do not download any alien file without first scanning it with your virus protection program. Isolate your network from the Internet by using a firewall or proxy system.

9. Use the Force Quit procedure by pressing the keyboard combination Command-Option-Esc. Note that when you do this, your Mac exits the program without saving; therefore, you may loose a lot of work if you haven't saved recently. You should restart your Mac after performing a Force Quit because it causes your Mac to become unstable.

B

10. To restart your Mac with no extensions, press the Shift key while restarting. Note that Mac OS 8.5 requires certain extensions, such as CD-ROM, hard drive, and its invisible Startup extensions to function. Your best bet to isolate conflicts is to press the spacebar while restarting (to bring up your conflict management software) and turn off everything except the Mac OS 8.5 basic extensions.

INDEX

Symbols

4D database environment, 369
4D relational database, 19

A

A tag, 309
About This Computer window, 119-120
Abstract Windowing Toolkit (AWT), 444
access privileges (network permissions), 338
    privilege icons, 339
accessing America Online, 404
Acrobat Reader 3.0, 17
active images, 365-366
active windows, 44
    switching between, 118

ActiveX Web site, 452
ADB cables, 509
address stamping (initializing disks), 484
Address tag, 309
Adobe Distiller, 433
Adobe PageMill 2.0, 317
Adobe Type Manager (ATM), 180
    fonts, installing, 185-186
Adobe Type Reunion, organizing fonts into sets, 186
Adobe Web site, 433, 519
alert sounds
    changing, 96-97
    setting, 272
Alert window (Monitors & Sound control panel), 97
aliases, 52-53, 62-64
    creating, 63
    manipulating, 63-64
Allegiant Web site, 477
Allegro, 1
Alsoft PlusMaker, initializing disks, 489-490

Alsoft Web site, 488
America Online (AOL), 404-406
    accessing, 404
    email, 405
    limitations, 406-407
    Web page publishing, 406
American Standard Code for Information Interchange (ASCII), 422
Analog counter, 364
animation, 366
    animated GIFs, 367
    client-pull, 366
    server-push, 367
anti-aliasing, 181, 300
antivirus software, 26, 499
AOL (America Online), 404-406
    accessing, 404
    email, 405
    limitations, 406-407
    Web page publishing, 406
AOLLink (TCP/IP software), 404

**API (application program-
ming interface),
QuickTime, 258**
**Appearance control
panel, 86**
  Appearance tab, 87
  Desktop tab, 88-90
  Fonts tab, 88
  Options tab, 91
  Sound tab, 90-91
  Themes tab, 87
**appearance design (Web
sites), 297**
Appearance Manager, 8
APPL file type, 420
**Apple Applet Runner, run-
ning applets, 449-451**
**Apple CD Audio Player,
270-271**
**Apple Data Detector,
412-414**
**Apple Data Detectors con-
trol panel, 413**
Apple Events, 458, 462
Apple Guide, 148
**Apple Macintosh CD-ROM,
clean installations, 30-31**
Apple menu
  navigating files, 68-69
  organizing, 79
**Apple Menu Options con-
trol panel, tuning, 144**
**Apple Product Information
Web site, 500**
**Apple Real-Time
Architecture (ARTA), 264**
**Apple Remote Access
(ARA), 17**
Apple System Profiler, 500
Apple Video Player, 282-289
  capturing video pictures,
  284-285

hardware considerations,
287
  AV hardware, 287-288
  cabling considerations,
  288
hardware requirements,
284
hints for quality pictures,
285-286
playing back videos, 286
  CD drives, 287
  hard drives, 287
software, 283
user interface, 283
  Capture window,
  284-285
video applications,
288-289
Video Source options, 286
video window, resizing,
286
see also QuickTime
**Apple Web site, 12, 364,
414, 451, 519**
  Developers page, 519
  Support and Information
  page, 519
AppleEvents, 340
AppleScript, 458-462
  Apple Events, 458, 462
  data dictionaries, 462-463
  extending, 469-471
    scriptable applications,
    470-471
    Scripting Additions,
    470
  Extensions folder, 460
  OSA menu, 461
  programming language
  basics, 471
    commands, 474-476
    data types, 472
    operators, 473-474
    variables, 472-473

Script Editor, 463-471
  compiling scripts, 469
  debugging scripts, 469
  editing scripts, 467-468
  generating scripts, 464
  recording scripts,
  465-466
  saving scripts, 468-469
  script window, 463
  script writing process,
  464
  writing scripts,
  466-467
Scripting Additions folder,
460
scripts, 458-459
  old script compatibility,
  459
Scripts folder, 461
tools/resources, 477-478
Web site, 461
AppleScript folder, 461
**AppleScript Lib extensions,
460**
**AppleSearch search engine,
369**
**AppleShare Chooser exten-
sion, 327**
Applet Runner, 445
APPLET tag, 449
AppleTalk
  control panel, 140-141
  inkjet printers, 204
  protocol, 341
    bus topologies,
    342-345
    cabling mediums, 341
    cabling topologies, 342
**applets (Java), 316, 352,
442-444, 447**
  channels, 453
  distributed applets,
  447-448

DrawTest, 443
editing, 448-449
InfoBook, 453
running, 449-451
server-bound applets, 448
AppleWorks 5.0, 19
application heap, 119
Application menu, 106
Hide command, 64
multitasking, 117-118
Application Switcher,
118
switching between
applications, 118
**application programming
interface (API),
QuickTime, 258**
**Application Switcher,
64, 118**
applications, 106
accessing with
Launcher, 65
closing, 111
compatibility, 106
fat applications, 134
General Information win-
dow, 80-81
grouping, 75-76
installing, 108-109
Kaboom!, 269
Macintosh built-in tool-
boxes, 108
Macintosh Human
Interface Guidelines, 106
mapping files to, 428
memory
error messages, 122
fragmentation, 123
managing, 121-123
moving between, 64

opening, 75-76, 110-111
Navigation Services,
111
Open dialog box,
110-111
PowerBook, 161-163
Battery Recondition,
162-164
File Assistant, 162
IR software, 162
protection, 109
removing, 109
scriptable applications,
470-471
data dictionaries,
462-463
SimpleText, 107
types, 107
see also software
**ARA (Apple Remote
Access), 17**
**architectures (networks),
comparing, 345-346**
**ARTA (Apple Real-Time
Architecture), 264**
**ASCII (American Standard
Code for Information
Interchange), 422**
assistants, 10
**ATI Technologies Web site,
282**
**ATM (Adobe Type
Manager), 180**
fonts, installing, 185-186
Atomic Vision Web site, 520
**attributes (HTML tags),
311, 449**
CLASS attribute, 316
audio, 265
alert sound, changing,
96-97
audio CDs, playing,
270-271

audio file formats, 269
audio files, playing, 247
Control Strip module, setting volume, 272-273
desktop sounds, setting,
90-91
digital audio, 266-267
Macintosh history,
264-265
MIDI, 267-268
connections, 276-277
data bytes, 268
hardware, 275-277
MIDI lag, 277
MIDI-to-Mac interface,
275-276
status bytes, 268
uses/limitations, 268
Monitors & Sound control
panel, 271-272
physics of, 265
recording, 274-275
CD-ROM sources, 274
microphones, 274
speaker configuration,
275
software, 277-279
editing/creating sound
files, 278-279
Sound control panel,
273-274
synthesizer chip, 264-265
system sounds
customizing, 268-269
Kaboom! application,
269
audio cards, 264
**audio CDs (QuickTime
AutoPlay feature), 249**
**AutoPlay preference
(QuickTime), 249**

autosave features (software), 502

AutoStart preference (QuickTime), 250

AV hardware, 283
    Apple Video Player, 287-288

Avalanche Web site, 520

AWT (Abstract Windowing Toolkit), 444

B

B tag, 309

backbone bus topology, 343-345

backgrounds (desktop)
    customizing, 88-90
        pictures, choosing, 89
        removing desktop pictures, 90
    positioning, 90

backing up the System Folder, 29

backup software, 498

Balloon Help system, 120

banding, 202

Barnsides Web site, 520

Base tag, 309

Basefont tag, 309

batteries
    Macintosh, 510
    PowerBook, 155-156

Battery Recondition application (PowerBook), 162-164

BBEdit 4.0, 19

BBEdit Web site, 520

beans (Java), 442, 452

benchmarks, 128

best mode (dot-matrix printers), 202

Bigfoot Web site, 408

binary digits, 177

BinHex file format, 432

bitmapped fonts, 176-177, 180-181
    Apple's original bitmapped fonts, 181
    screen fonts, 180

bitmapped images, 177

bitmapping, 177

bits, 177

Blink tag, 309

Blockquote tag, 309

Body area (HTML documents), 314

Body tag, 309, 314

bold keywords (AppleScript), 472

Bongo, 444, 453

Br tag, 309

branches, 345

Browse the Internet icon, 390

Browser Watch Web site, 519

browser-safe palettes, 300

browsers, 392
    Internet Explorer, 392
    Java Internet browsers, 445
    memory requirements, 393
    Netscape Navigator, 393
    opening automatically, 391
    Web browsers, 401-403

bug fix releases (software), 508

built-in memory, 119

built-in toolboxes, 108

burn-in, 497

burrowing cursors (click-and-a-half), 11

bus, 342

bus topologies (connectivity), 342-343, 345
    backbone bus topology, 343-345
    daisy-chain topology, 342-343

Butler SQL 2.02, 368

button view, 67

bytes (MIDI), 268

C

cabling considerations (Apple Video Player), 288

cabling mediums (connectivity), 341

cabling topologies (connectivity), 342

calibrating
    devices, 234
    monitors, 231
        Monitor Calibration Assistant, 231-234

Canvas 5.0, 19

Capture window (Apple Video Player), 284-285

carrier sensing, 344

Casady & Greene Web site, 508

Cascading Style Sheets (HTML), 315-316

Castanet, 444, 453

ccMail, 19

CD Audio Player, 270-271

CD-ROMs
    Apple Macintosh CD-ROM, clean installations, 30-31

drives, 76-77
  playing MPEG1 video
    files, 287
  PowerBook, 157
  ejecting, 55
  files, viewing, 70
  Mac OS 8.5 CD-ROM,
    clean installations, 31
  performance settings,
    134-135
  QuickTime AutoStart fea-
    ture, 250
  recording sound, 274
  virtual memory, 139
CDs, playing audio CDs,
  270-271
Center tag, 309
CGIs (Common Gateway
  Interfaces), 356
  active images, 365-366
  adding to servers, 358
  animation, 366
    animated GIFs, 367
    client-pull, 366
    server push, 367
  components of, 356-357
  counters, 364-365
  database processing,
    368-370
  finding, 357
  forms, 363-364
  guest books, 363-364
  online stores, 367-368
  running scripts, 357
  see also scripts
channels, 444, 453
character sets, 171-172
  font families, 173
  Key Caps, 171-172
  Unicode, 172
chat rooms, 400, 411-412
  classic chats, 411
  static chats, 411

Chooser
  network access, shared
    volumes, 332-333
  network services, 326
  printer drivers, selecting,
    210
  tuning, 144-145
Chromaticity Charts,
  226-227
CIE Lab Color Chart,
  226-227
Claris Home Page 3.0, 19
CLASS attribute (HTML),
  316
classic chats, 411
clean system installations,
  30-31
  with Apple Macintosh
    CD-ROM, 30-31
  with Disk Tools disk, 30
  with Mac OS 8.5
    CD-ROM, 31
click-and-a-half (mouse), 67
click-and-a-half cursor, 11
client-pull animation, 366
clone drivers, updating, 28
Close command, 112
closing applications, 111
CLUT (color lookup table),
  230
CMM (color matching
  method), 228
  Color Picker, 234
  rendering styles, 228
CMYK, 218
CMYK Color Picker dialog
  box, 235
CMYK colors, 227-228
Cnet Download Web site, 49
Cnet Web site, 414, 520
Collabra (Netscape
  Communicator), 410
collapse button, 65
collapsible windows, 46

collision avoidance, 344
collision detection, 344
color calibration, 231
  Monitor Calibration
    Assistant, 231-234
color depth (monitors),
  95-96
color dithering, 218
color halftoning, 219
color lookup table (CLUT),
  230
color management systems,
  226-229
  CMYK colors, 227-228
  color profiles, setting up,
    228
  ColorSync, 228-229
  developing, 228-229
  QuickDraw, 229-231
    Color Picker, 230
    hyperdesktop, 230
  rendering styles, 228
  RGB colors, 227-228
color matching method
  (CMM), 228
  Color Picker, 234
  rendering styles, 228
Color Picker, 230, 234-237
Color Picker dialog box,
  235-237
Color PostScript laser
  printers, 201
color printers, 218-221
  ColorSync color calibra-
    tion system, 218
  dithering, 218
  dye sublimation, 220
  halftoning, 219
  inkjet printers, 219
  laser printers, 219
  PostScript options, 221
  thermal wax transfer print-
    ers, 220

color profiles, setting, 228, 233

color spaces, 226-227

colorants, 227

colors
Chromaticity Charts, 226-227
CMYK colors, 227-228
customizing desktop, 87
device characterization, 228
gamut, 227
LAB colors, 226-227
lightness, 226
printing, 218-221
ColorSync color calibration system, 218
dithering, 218
dye sublimation, 220
halftoning, 219
inkjet printers, 219
laser printers, 219
PostScript options, 221
process color, 218
thermal wax transfer printers, 220
RGB colors, 227-228
white point, 230

ColorSync, 228-229, 238
color calibration, 231-234

ColorSync 2.5, 13

commands
AppleScript, 474, 476
Close, 112
Erase, formatting HFS+ disks, 488
Internet Access menu, Connect To, 390
Page Setup, 213-215
PostScript Options, 214-215
StyleWriter Options, 215
Print, 215-217
PostScript files, 217
Quit, 111
Sharing, 331, 340-341

comments, viewing file comments, 70

commercial mail services, 409

commercial online services, 403-407
America Online (AOL), 404-406
accessing, 404
email, 405
limitations, 406-407
Web page publishing, 406
CompuServe, 406

Common Gateway Interfaces, *see* **CGIs**

Common Ground Software, 434

Communicator (Netscape), Collabra, 410

comparison operators (AppleScript), 474

compatibility, applications, 106

compiling scripts, 469

component memory and space requirements, 25-26

component software, 451-452
Internet, 374
Java Beans, 452

component-based programming, 451

compression
lossy compression, 299
LZW compression, 299
StuffIt compression utility, 108
video compression, 285

CompuServe, 406

configuring
Apple System Profiler, 500
QuickTime, 247
speakers, 275

Conflict Catcher, 8, 29, 36-37, 498, 507-508
features, 507
upgrading, 508

conflicting software, 505-508
Conflict Catcher, 507-508
features, 507
Extensions Manager, 505-506
isolating extension conflicts, 505-507

Connect To command (Internet Access menu), 390

Connection Speed preference (QuickTime), 250

connections
Internet
dialing, 389-391
ISPs, 376-377
open transport technologies, 378
T1 lines, 378
underlying architecture, 375
MIDI, 276-277
MIDI lag, 277

connectivity options (networks), 341
bus topologies, 342-345
backbone bus topology, 343-345
daisy-chain topology, 342-343
cabling mediums, 341

cabling topologies, 342

network types, comparing, 345-346

star topologies, 345

Connectix products, 142

Construct Web site, 520

containers (HTML), 311-313

content design (Web sites), 294-297

audience considerations, 296-297

intended purpose of site, 295-296

Microsoft Site Builder Network Web site, 297

context-switching multitasking, 114

contextual menus, 11, 46-47

data detectors, 11

control panel conflicts, 37

control panels

Internet, 386

Advanced tab, 389

configuration sets, 386-387

Email tab, 387-388

News tab, 389

Personal tab, 387

Web tab, 388

PowerBook software, 158-160

Remote Access, connecting to Internet, 389

Control Strips, 47-49

PowerBook software, 158-160

types, 48-49

Control Strip module, setting volume, 272-273

converting graphics, 300-302

cooperative multitasking, 114-115

Copy feature, 56

copying

data between files, 424

IP addresses, 354

copyright laws (music), 269

corrective profiles, 234

corrupted disk structure, 510-511

Count counter, 364

Count WWWebula counter, 365

counters, 364-365

crashes, 496

restarting Macintosh, 499

CrashGuard (Norton Utilities), 504

Crayon Color Picker dialog box, 236

CRC (cyclical redundancy check) bytes, 484

creators, 420-421

cursors, 67

click-and-a-half, 11

magnifying glass cursor, 67-68

Custom Install dialog box, 32

customizing

desktop format, 85-86

Appearance control panel, 86

appearance, setting, 87

backgrounds, setting, 88-90

fonts, setting, 88

scroll options, 91

sounds, setting, 90-91

themes, setting, 87

Extension Manager sets, 93-94

Extensions Manager, 91

Finder 8.0, 81-82

custom icons, changing, 81-82

files, changing, 82

folders, changing, 82

Keyboard control panel, 98-99

Key Repeat settings, 98

Mac OS 8.5 installation, 32-34

determining what to install, 34

suggested options, 33

Mac OS 8.5 for performance, 147-148

Monitors & Sound control panel, 94-97

alert sound, changing, 96-97

Alert window, 97

color depth, 95-96

multiple displays, changing, 97

resolution, 95-96

Numbers control panel, 99

system sounds, 268-269

Kaboom! application, 269

Text control panel, 99-100

cyclical redundancy check (CRC) bytes, 484

D

daisy-chain connections (MIDI), 276

daisy-chain topology (bus topologies), 342-343

DAs (desk accessories), 114

data, sharing
between files, 424
creators, 420-421
file formats, 422-423
file types, 420-421
OLE, 427-428
Publish and Subscribe,
425-426
data bytes (MIDI), 268
data detectors, 11, 412-414
data dictionaries, 462-463
**Data Interchange Format
(DIF), 423**
**data types (AppleScript),
472**
**database processing Web
sites, 368-370**
**databases, desktop data-
base, 69-70**
datagrams, 317
DataViz Web site, 428
**DCA (Document Content
Architecture), 422**
debugging scripts, 469
Deck II, 278
default OS settings, 136-141
AppleTalk control panel,
140-141
File Sharing control panel,
140
Finder settings, 136
Memory control panel,
136-140
disk cache, 137-138
virtual memory,
138-140
PowerBook performance,
141
**defragmenting hard drives,
146-147**
deleting
applications, 109
items from desktop, 55
print jobs, 212

**design axes (Multiple
Master fonts), 183**
designing Web sites
appearance design, 297
content design, 294-297
audience considera-
tions, 296-297
intended purpose of
site, 295-296
Microsoft Site Builder
Network Web site,
297
folder system setup, 305
navigation graphics, 304
prototyping, 298-302
collecting materials,
298-299
graphic conversions,
300-302
selecting file formats,
299-300
speeding up downloads,
305-306
desk accessories (DAs), 114
desktop, 41-44
Browse the Internet icon,
390
changing format, 85-86
Appearance control
panel, 86
appearance, setting, 87
backgrounds, setting,
88-90
fonts, setting, 88
scroll options,
setting, 91
sounds, setting, 90-91
themes, setting, 87
hard drive icon, 43
Mac OS 8.5, 10-11
menu bar, 43
navigating files, 68-69

organizing, 62-66
aliases, 62-64
Application Switcher,
64
collapse button, 65
Hide command, 64
Launcher, 65
removing items, 55
throwing away items, 55
Trash Can icon, 44
desktop database, 69-70
**desktop printers, creating,
212**
detecting viruses, 508-509
device characterization, 228
devices
calibrating, 234
SCSI devices, 512
diagnostic software, 497-499
**dialing into the Internet,
389-391**
dialog boxes
CMYK Color Picker, 235
Color Picker, 235-237
Crayon Color Picker, 236
Custom Install, 32
Epson Stylus Print, 216
Erase/Format, 488
Finder, 76
HLS Color Picker, 236
HTML Color Picker, 237
LaserWriter Print, 215
Open, 110-111
Open URL, 450
Page Setup, 213
PostScript Options,
214-215
StyleWriter Options,
215
PlusMaker, 489
Preferences, 45
Program (Apple CD Audio
Player), 271

Record, 269
RGB Color Picker, 238
Save As, 112-113
Setup (AOL), 404
Sharing, 340
StyleWriter Page Setup, 215
DIF (Data Interchange Format), 423
digital audio, 266-267
quantizing, 266
samples, 266
software, 277-279
uses/limitations, 266
Digital Technology International Web site, 477
digital video files, *see* **movies**
directories, 27
Web site directory setup, 305
disk cache, settings, 137-138
Disk Doctor (Norton Utilities), 510-511
disk drives, corrupted disk structure, 510-511
Disk First Aid, 26
running, 499-500
Disk Tools disk, clean installations, 30
disks
ejecting, 55
hard disks, 481-482
initializing, 483
address stamping, 484
cyclical redundancy check bytes, 484
gap bytes, 484
hard formatting, 484
interleaving, 483
logical formatting, 485

sectors, 483-484
tracks, 483-484
logical disks, 485
Mac OS Extended Format (HFS+), 485-486
drawbacks, 486-487
initializing HFS+ disks, 487-488
partitioning, 485
Disney Web site, 408
Distiller, 433
distributed applets, 447-448
distributed file sharing, 326
distributed networks, 326
creating (File Sharing setup), 329-332
networking system extensions, 326-328
distributed system control, 343
dithering, 218, 300
Document Content Architecture (DCA), 422
documents
HTML documents, 313
Body area, 314
Head area, 313-314
opening, 42
page-description documents, setting up, 211-212
saving, 112-113
selecting all items, 56
sharing
Common Ground Software, 434
Envoy software, 434
PDF files, 433-434
preserving formatting, 433
Replica software, 435
text layout, 187-188
kerning, 188-189
leading, 189

punctuation marks, 192
tips, 191-192
typography rules, 189-190
watermarks, adding, 215
see also files
domain names (Personal Web Sharing), 354
domains, 319
dot-matrix printers, 200-203
banding, 202
best mode, 202
draft mode, 202
faster-print mode, 202
fonts, 202
hints for better printing, 203
ImageWriter, 202
print wires, 201
double-clicking (mouse), opening files, 75
downloading
Internet files, 414
Mac OS 8.5 updates, 31
outline fonts, 182
speeding up download times, 305-306
draft mode (dot-matrix printers), 202
drag-and-drop, 56, 424
dragging (mouse), opening files, 75
draw programs, 179
DrawTest applet, 443
drive capacity
adding hard drive space, 25
checking before Mac OS 8.5 installation, 24-26
Drive Setup, formatting HFS+ disks, 488
Drive Setup application, 27-28

drivers

hard disk drivers

Extended Format, 132

updating, 27-28

Mac clone drivers, updating, 28

printer drivers, 148

LaserWriter 8, 211

Page Setup command, 213-215

Print command, 215-217

QuickDraw drivers, 211

selecting, 210

setting up, 209-210

drives

CD-ROM drives, 76-77

PowerBook, 157

corrupted disk structure, 510-511

hard drives, *see* hard disks

indexing, 72

swappable drives (PowerBook), 156-157

DropStuff application, 432

DropStuff Expander, 17

dual-mode monitors, 170

dye sublimation printing, 220

E

e-greetings Web site, 408

editing

Java applets, 448-449

QuickTime movies, 248

with Movie Player 2.5, 252-253

with Movie Player Pro, 252

scripts, 467-468

formattable script parts, 467-468

sound files, software, 278-279

edition files, creating, 426

ejecting disks, 55

em dash, 192

email, 400

alert options, 387

America Online, 405

default program, setting, 388

flaming, 401

Internet email, 407-409

commercial mail services, 409

free email, 408

general-purpose email managers, 408

spamming, 401

Email.acgi script, 364

EMBED tag, 257

embedding

objects, 427

QuickTime movies in Web sites, 257

Empty Trash command, 55, 77-78

emulators (software emulators), 134

en dash, 192

Encapsulated PostScript (EPS), 423

files, creating, 217

Envoy software, 434

EPS (Encapsulated PostScript), 423

Epson Stylus Print dialog box, 216

Epson Web site, 210

Erase command, formatting HFS+ disks, 488

Erase/Format dialog box, 488

error messages

application memory, 122

Mac OS 8.5 installation, 34

software, 501-502

syntax errors (scripts), 466

errors, hard disk errors, 26-27

Ethernet networks, 341-345

Eudora Pro 4, 19

events (AppleScript), 462

Exchange preferences (QuickTime), 252

Excite Web site, 408

exporting non-QuickTime video formats, 252

extended characters, 314-315

Extended Format (hard disk drivers), 132

Extended Format file system, 18

extending AppleScript, 469-471

scriptable applications, 470-471

Scripting Additions, 470

extension conflicts

isolating, 505-507

troubleshooting, 37

extensions

AppleScript Lib extensions, 460

file extensions, 312

Folder Actions extension, 460

improving performance, 143-145

Apple Menu Options control panel, tuning, 144

Chooser, tuning,
144-145
File Sharing control
panel, tuning, 144
menu bar, tuning, 144
networking system exten-
sions, 326-328
PowerBook software,
160-161
SOMobjects for Mac OS
extensions, 460
Extensions folder, 148, 460
Extensions Manager,
29, 91-94, 498
improving extension per-
formance, 143
isolating extension con-
flicts, 505-506
launching, 92
sets, creating, 93-94
viewing modes, 93
external microphones, 274

F

FaceSpan 2.1, 477
failed hardware, 512
faster-print mode (dot-
matrix printers), 202
fat applications, 134
FatBits, 179
Favorites folder, 68
Favorites menu, 69
Fetch utility (uploading
files), 415
Fetch Web site, 318
File Assistant (Powerbook),
162
file comments, viewing, 70
File Exchange, 428-429
File Translation tool, 428
PC Exchange, 429-431

file format modes
Hierarchical File System
(HFS), 485-486
Mac OS Extended Format
(HFS+), 485-486
drawbacks, 486-487
initializing HFS+
disks, 487-488
file formats, 422
ASCII, 422
BinHex, 432
DCA, 422
DIF, 423
EPS, 423
GIF, 299-300
JPEG, 299
MacBinary, 431
PDF, 433-434
creating files, 433
viewing files, 433
PICT, 423
RTF, 423
saving scripts, 468
setting (Save As dilaog
box), 423
SYLK, 423
TIFF, 423
translators, 423
UUcode, 432
File Sharing, 325
connectivity options, 341
bus topologies,
342-345
cabling mediums, 341
cabling topologies, 342
network types, compar-
ing, 345-346
distributed file sharing,
326
networking system
extensions, 326-328
ending File Sharing ses-
sions, 335
network permissions, 335

access privileges, 338
group user privileges,
337
guest privileges, 336
networked programs,
using, 340-341
owner privileges, 336
registered user privi-
leges, 336-337
shared folders versus
shared volumes, 339
performance issues, 328
setting up, 329-332
shared volumes
accessing, 332-333
opening at startup,
334-335
File Sharing control panel,
140
tuning, 144
file system, 27
File Transfer Protocol
(FTP) sites, 414
File Translation tool, 428
file types, 420-421
FileMaker Pro 4.0, 19
filenames, 82
files, 50
aliases, creating, 52-53
audio file formats, 269
creating, 51-52
customizing (Finder), 82
digital video files, *see*
movies
edition, creating, 426
encapsulated PostScript
files, creating, 217
exchanging over IR ports
(PowerBook), 163
Extended Format file sys-
tem, 18
file extensions, 312
grouping, 74-76

Internet files
  downloading, 414
  uploading, 414-415
Location Manager, 12
mapping to applications,
  428
moving, 53
MPEG1 video files, play-
  ing, 286-287
naming conventions, 113
navigating, 68-70
  Apple menu, 68-69
  desktop, 68-69
  desktop database,
    69-70
  with mouse, 67-68
nesting, 50
opening, 74-76
  double-clicking tech-
    nique, 75
  dragging technique, 75
PostScript files, printing
  to, 217
protecting, 53
ReadMe files, 500
saving, 112-113
searches, 71-74
  Find a File search,
    71-72
  indexing drives, 72
  Search by Content
    search, 72-73
  Search the Internet
    search, 73-74
sharing, 428
  data, 424
  File Exchange,
    428-429
  File Translation tool,
    428
  MacLink
    Plus/Translators, 428
  name lengths, 431

  networks, 431-432
  PC Exchange, 429-431
spool files, 206
swapfiles, 138
synchronizing between
  Macs, 163
viewing, 66-67
  CD-ROMs, 70
  hard drives, 70
  removable media, 70
  see also documents
Final Cut, 245
Find application, see
  Sherlock
Find command, 71-74
  Find a File search, 71-72
  Search by Content search,
    72-73
  Search the Internet search,
    73-74
Finder
  dialog boxes, 109-110
    Open, 110-111
    Save As, 112-113
  multitasking, 115
  Open dialog box, 110
Finder 8, 10-11, 62
  Application menu, Hide
    command, 64
  Application Switcher, 64
  applications
    grouping, 75-76
    opening, 75-76
  CD-ROM drives, 76-77
  click-and-a-half cursor, 11
  contextual menus, 11
  customizing, 81-82
    custom icons, chang-
      ing, 81-82
    files, changing, 82
    folders, changing, 82
  desktop, organizing, 62-66

files
  desktop database,
    69-70
  grouping, 74-76
  navigating, 67-70
  opening, 74-76
  viewing, 66-67, 70
  General Information win-
    dow, 80-81
  GUI, 10-11
  Launcher, accessing appli-
    cations/folders, 65
  menu bar, 78-79
    Apple menu, organiz-
      ing, 79
  settings, 136
  Trash Can, 77-78
    emptying, 77-78
    Move to Trash com-
      mand, 78
  windows, collapse
    button, 65
  see also Sherlock
Finder dialog box, 76
fixed-width fonts, 174
flaming, 401
floppy disks, ejecting, 55
Folder Actions extension,
  460
folder systems, 305
folder window, 51
folders, 50
  accessing with
    Launcher, 65
  aliases, creating, 52-53
  AppleScript
    Extensions folder, 460
    Scripting Additions
      folder, 460
    Scripts folder, 461
  AppleScript folder, 461
  creating, 51-52
  customizing (Finder), 82

Extensions folder, 148
Favorites folder, 68
Fonts folder, 185
  placing fonts into, 185
Macintosh Runtime Java,
  446
moving, 53
nesting, 50
Preferences, 53
protecting, 53
shared folders, comparing
  to shared volumes, 339
Shut Down Items
  folder, 55
Startup folder, opening
  shared volumes at startup, 334-335
Startup Items folder, 55
subject folders, 50
System Folder, 53
  combining extensions
    and control panels,
    100
  memory, 121
  reducing size to
    improve performance,
    147-148
  volumes, *see* volumes
font families, 173
Font Manager, displaying
text onscreen, 184
fonts, 170, 174, 180-184
  bitmapped fonts,
    176-177, 180
    Apple's original
      bitmapped fonts, 181
  customizing desktop, 88
  document layout, 187-188
    kerning, 188-189
    leading, 189
    punctuation marks, 192
    tips, 191-192
    typography rules,
      189-190

dot-matrix printing, 202
fixed-width, 174
font technologies, 175-176
history, 169-170
inkjet printers, 203
installing, 185-186
Mac OS 8.5, 187
Macintosh font standards,
  180
monospaced, 174
OpenType, 183-184
outline fonts, 178-179
  downloading, 182
  hinting, 179
  rasterizing, 178-179
Palatino, 174
PostScript fonts, 181
  Type 3, 182
printer fonts, 179-180
printing process, 184
proportional-spaced, 174
sans serif, 188
screen fonts, 179-180
serif, 188
TrueType fonts, 181-182
  dot-matrix printing,
    202
Type 1 fonts, 181
  Multiple Master fonts,
    181-183
  OpenType, 183-184
Type 3 fonts, 182
type styles, 173
viewing, 187
Fonts folder, 185
force quits, 504
Form tag, 309
formatting
  disks, 483
    address stamping, 484
    cyclical redundancy
      check bytes, 484

    gap bytes, 484
    hard formatting, 484
    HFS+ disks, 487-490
    interleaving, 483
    logical formatting, 485
    sectors, 483-484
    tracks, 483-484
  scripts, 467-468
formed-letter printers, 200
forms (CGIs), 363-364
Forms.acgi script, 363
Fourth Dimension database
environment, 369
fractional character widths,
184
fragmentation (application
memory), 123
free email, 408
Frontier 4.2.3, 477
FrontPage, 317
FrontPage Web site, 520
FTP (File Transfer
Protocol) sites, 414
FTP servers, creating, 355

G

Gamelan Web site, 520
gammas, setting target
gamma, 233
gamut, 227
gap bytes (initializing
disks), 484
General Controls control
panel, 64, 75
  Documents section, 76
  Protect an Application set-
    ting, 109
General Information win-
dow, 80-81, 121

general-purpose email managers, 408
Get Info window, 52
GIF file format, 299-300
Global Chat, 400
GoLive CyberStudio, 317
GraphicConverter, 301-302
graphics
    active images, 365-366
    converting for the Web, 300-302
    improving performance, 145-146
    navigation graphics, 304
Graphics Interchange Format (GIF), 299-300
grid fitting, 179
group user privileges (network permissions), 337
grouping
    applications, 75-76
    files, 74-76
groups, 329
guest books (CGIs), 363-364
guest privileges (network permissions), 336

H

H tag, 309
halftoning, 219
hard disk drivers
    Extended Format, 132
    updating, 27-28
hard disks, 481-482
    adding space, 25
    checking available space, 24
    checking for software/hardware errors, 26-27
    defragmenting, 146-147
    files, viewing, 70

IDE, 131, 482
indexing, 72
initializing, 483
    hard formatting, 484
    interleaving, 483
    logical formatting, 485
    sectors, 483-484
    tracks, 483-484
Mac OS Extended Format (HFS+), 485-486
    drawbacks, 486-487
    initializing HFS+ disks, 487-488
optimizing, 146-147
    defragmentation, 146-147
    drivers, updating, 146
partitioning, 70, 485
performance issues, 131-132
playing MPEG1 video files, 287
schematic, 482
SCSI, 131, 482
hard drive icon, 43
hard formatting, 484
hardware
    Apple Video Player hardware considerations, 287
    AV hardware, 287-288
    cabling considerations, 288
    AV hardware, 283
    MIDI hardware, 275-277
    connections, 276-277
    MIDI-to-Mac interface, 275-276
    performance limitations, 129
    PowerBook, 154-155, 157
    batteries, 155-156
    PC cards, 157
    swappable drives, 156-157

problems, 497
    batteries, changing, 510
    corrupted disk structure, 510-511
    failed hardware, 512
    inadequate hardware, 511
    Paramter RAM (PRAM), zapping, 509-510
    resolutions, 509-513
    SCSI devices, 512
    symptoms, 502-503
    upgrade problems, 512
servers, 358
    example systems, 360-361
    LAN connections, 359
    memory, 359
    operating systems, 358-359
    processors, 359
Head area (HTML documents), 313-314
Head tag, 310
Help systems (Balloon Help system), 120
Hewlett-Packard Web site, 210
HFS (Hierarchical File System), 485-486
    Standard File Format, 132
HFS+ (Hierarchical Filing System Plus), 18
    hard disk drivers, 132
    Mac OS Extended Format, 485-486
        drawbacks, 486-487
        initializing HFS+ disks, 487-490
Hi-Tech theme (desktop), 86
hinting, 179

HLS Color Picker dialog
  box, 236
home pages, 303, 391
  selecting, 388
hot spots, 303
Hot Wired Web site, 520
hotlinks, creating, 311
hotmail Web site, 408
Hr tag, 310
HTML (HyperText Markup
  Language), 307-308, 403
  Cascading Style Sheets,
    315-316
  case sensitivity, 308
  CLASS attribute, 316
  containers, 311-313
  documents, 313
    Body area, 314
    Head area, 313-314
  hypertext links, creating,
    311
  images, placing in pages,
    312
  Java applets, 316
  JavaScript macros, 316
  Latin-1 extended charac-
    ters, 314-315
  line spacing, 313
  paragraph spacing, 313
  placing objects in pages,
    312
  tags, 309-311
    APPLET, 449
    applying pairs to for-
      mat items, 311
    EMBED tag, 257
    modifying with attrib-
      utes/values, 311
  Web publishing software,
    316-317
HTML Color Picker dialog
  box, 237

Hue, Lightness, and
  Saturation Color Picker
  dialog box, 236
hyperdesktop (QuickDraw),
  230
hypertext links, creating,
  311
HyperText Markup
  Language, see HTML

I

I tag, 310
I/O (input/output), performance issues, 131
IAC (interapplication communications), 340
IAD (Internet Address
  Detector), 412-413
iCat Web site, 367
ICC (International Color
  Consortium), 228
icon view, 67
icons
  custom icons, changing,
    81-82
  hard drive icon, 43
  privilege icons (access
    privileges), 339
  Trash Can, 44, 55, 77-78
    ejecting disks/
      volumes, 55
    emptying, 77-78
    Move to Trash com-
      mand, 78
    throwing away
      items, 55
ID numbers (SCSI devices),
  512
IDE drives, 131

IDE hard disks, 482
IFC (Internet Foundation
  Classes), 444
ImageMap.acgi, 365
imagemapping, 304
imagemaps, 303
ImageReady Web site, 302
images
  active, 365-366
  bitmapped images, 177
  browser-safe palettes, 300
  file extensions, 312
  GIF file format, 299-300
  JPEG file format, 299
  placing in pages (HTML),
    312
  rasterizing, 178-179
ImageWriter, 202
Img tag, 310
importing non-QuickTime
  video formats, 252
IMS Web site, 282
indexing drives, 72
InfoBook, 453
InfoLawAlert Web site, 296
InfoWave Web site, 204
initializing disks, 483
  address stamping, 484
  cyclical redundancy check
    bytes, 484
  gap bytes, 484
  hard formatting, 484
  HFS+ disks, 487-488
    Alsoft PlusMaker,
      489-490
    Drive Setup, 488
    Erase command, 488
  interleaving, 483
  logical formatting, 485
  sectors, 483-484
  tracks, 483-484

inkjet printers, 201-204
AppleTalk, 204
colors, 219
fonts, 203
PostScript graphics, 204
input
performance issues, 131
sound input options, 272
Install Mac OS, 9
installers, 108-109
installing
applications, 108-109
fonts, 185-186
Mac OS 8.5, 23, 29-32
clean install, 30-31
components,
adding/reinstalling/re-
moving, 35
custom installations,
32-34
downloaded up-
dates, 31
drive capacity, check-
ing, 24-26
error messages, 34
hard disks, checking
for errors, 26-27
memory, checking,
24-26
restoring System
Folder, 36
security/virus protec-
tion, turning off, 29
System Folder, backing
up, 29
troubleshooting exten-
sion conflicts, 37
updating hard disk dri-
vers, 27-28
virus-proctection, 26
Interaction/IP script, 364
**interapplication communi-
cations (IAC), 340**

**interleave factor (initializing
disks), 483**
internal microphones, 274
**International Color
Consortium (ICC), 228**
Internet, 399-403, 407
browsers, 392
Internet Explorer, 392
Java, 445
memory requirements,
393
Netscape Navigator,
393
chat rooms, 400, 411-412
classic chats, 411
static chats, 411
component software, 374
connections
dialing, 389-391
ISPs, 376-377
open transport tech-
nologies, 378
T1 lines, 378
underlying architec-
ture, 375
data detectors, 412-414
document sharing
Common Ground
Software, 434
Envoy software, 434
PDF files, 433-434
preserving formatting,
433
Replica software, 435
downloading files, 414
email, 400, 407-409
commercial mail ser-
vices, 409
flaming, 401
free email, 408
general-purpose email
managers, 408
spamming, 401

file sharing, 431-432
BinHex format, 432
DropStuff application,
432
MacBinary format,
431-432
UUcode format, 432
File Transfer Protocol
(FTP) sites, 414
interactive games, 400
multimedia, 374
navigating, 391
netiquette rules, 401
networking, 374
newsgroups, 400, 409-410
prefix defintions, 409
open standards, 374
QuickTime movies,
254-257
creating for fast play-
back, 256-257
embedding in Web
sites, 257
QuickTime plug-in,
254-255
saving, 255
searching, 73-74
services, 400
streaming video, 256
TCP/IP, 317-318, 375-376
servers, accessing, 376
uploading files, 414
Fetch utility, 415
World Wide Web, 401-403
see also Personal Web
Sharing
**Internet Access menu com-
mands, Connect To, 390**
**Internet Address Detector
(IAD), 412-413**
Internet Audit Web site, 364

Internet control panel,
16-17, 386
Advanced tab, 389
configuration sets,
386-387
Email tab, 387-388
News tab, 389
Personal tab, 387
Web tab, 388
Internet Editor utility, 10
Internet Explorer
(Microsoft), 17, 392
Just In Time compilers,
445
News (newsgroup reader),
410
Internet Foundation Classes
(IFC), 444
Internet management com-
ponents, 8
Internet Movie tool, 256-257
Internet Protocols (IP),
Open Transport, 13
Internet Service Providers
(ISPs), 376-377
Internet Setup Assistant, 10,
17, 382-384
information needed,
381-382
PowerBook, 158
Internet software, 16-17
Internetworks, 342
InterNIC Web site, 319
intranets, 399
see also Personal Web
Sharing
IP (Internet Protocols),
Open Transport, 13
IP addresses, 354
IR ports, exchanging files
(PowerBook), 163
IR software (PowerBook),
162

Isindex tag, 310
ISPs (Internet Service
Providers), 376-377
italic typeface, 173
ivillage Web site, 408

J

Java, 442
Abstract Windowing
Toolkit, 444
applets, 316, 352,
442-444, 447
channels, 453
distributed applets,
447-448
DrawTest, 443
editing, 448-449
InfoBook, 453
running, 449-451
server-bound applets,
448
beans, 442
Bongo, 453
Castanet, 453
channels, 444
Internet browsers, 445
Just In Time compiler
(JIT), 444-445
Mac OS Runtime for Java
(MRJ), 13
Macintosh Runtime Java
(MRJ), 442-451
distributed applets,
447-448
editing applets,
448-449
folders, 446
library components,
446

running applets,
449-451
server-bound applets,
448
terminology, 444
transmitters, 453
Java Beans, 444, 452
Java Foundation Class
(JFC), 444
Java Virtual Machine (VM),
443-444
JavaScript, 444
JavaScript 411 Web site,
452
JavaScript macros, 316
Web site, 452
JavaSoft, 444
Jbindery, 446
JBScript, 444
JFC (Java Foundation
Class), 444
JIT (Just In Time compiler),
444-445
Jmanager, 446
JPEG file format, 299
JRI, 446
Jshell, 446
Just In Time compiler (JIT),
444-445

K

Kaboom! application, 269
kernels (multitasking),
116-117
kerning, 175, 188-189
Key Caps, 171-172
Key Repeat settings, 98
Keyboard control panel,
98-99
Key Repeat settings, 98

keyboard layout, changing, 98

keyboard shortcuts, 56

keywords (AppleScript), 472

L

LAB colors, 226-227

Label menu item, 79

LAN connections (Web servers), 359

Lari Software Web site, 253

laser printers, 200, 204-205
   Color PostScript, 201
   colors, 219
   PostScript, 201
   printer engine, 205
   QuickDraw, 201
   QuickDraw laser printers, 205
   raster-image processors (RIP), 205

LaserWriter 8 printer driver, 211

LaserWriter Chooser extension, 327

LaserWriter Print dialog box, 215

Late Night Software LTD Web site, 477

Latin-1 extended characters, 314-315

Launcher, accessing applications/folders, 65

Launcher control panel, 49

layout (document text), 187-188
   kerning, 188-189
   leading, 189
   punctuation marks, 192

tips, 191-192

typography rules, 189-190

leading, 175, 189

letter quality, 200

letterspace, 175

Li tag, 310

library components (Macintosh Runtime Java), 446

lightness (colors), 226

line breaks, 309

line spacing, 175
   HTML, 313

Link tag, 310

list view, 67
   Extensions Manager, 92

LocalTalk, 341

Location Manager, 12

Logger.cgi counter, 365

logical disks, 485

logical formatting, 485

logical operators (AppleScript), 474

lossless compression, 299

Lotus Notes, 19

low-level formatting, 485

Lynda Wynman's Web site, 519

LZW compression, 299

M

Mac OS 8.5
   CD-ROM, clean installations, 31
   component memory and space requirements, 25-26
   memory, managing, 120-121

Mac OS 8.5
   components
      assistants, 10
      Finder 8, 10-11
      Install Mac OS, 9
   customizing for performance, 147-148
   desktop, 10-11
   Extended Format file system, 18
   fonts, 187
   installing, 23, 29-32
      clean install, 30-31
      components, adding/reinstalling/removing, 35
      custom installations, 32-34
      downloaded updates, 31
      drive capacity, checking, 24-26
      error messages, 34
      hard disks, checking for errors, 26-27
      memory, checking, 24-26
      restoring System Folder, 36
      security/virus protection, turning off, 29
      System Folder, backing up, 29
      troubleshooting extension conflicts, 37
      updating hard disk drivers, 27-28
      virus-protection, 26
   Internet control panel, 16-17
   Internet software, 16-17

multimedia tools, 14
  QuickDraw 3D, 16
  QuickTime 3.0, 14-15
  QuickTime VR, 15
new features, 8-9
software, 12
  ColorSync 2.5, 13
  Location Manager, 12
  Mac OS Runtime for
    Java (MRJ), 13
  Open Transport, 13
third-party software, 19
Web Sharing control
  panel, 17-18
**Mac OS Extended Format
(HFS+), 485-486**
drawbacks, 486-487
initializing HFS+ disks,
  487-488
  Alsoft PlusMaker,
    489-490
  Drive Setup, 488
  Erase command, 488
**Mac OS Runtime for Java
(MRJ), 13**
**Mac OS Runtime for Java
folder, 446**
Mac OS Setup Assistant, 10
MacAddict Web site, 49
MacBinary file format, 431
MacFixIt Web site, 501
MacInTalk, 264
Macintosh
hardware problems
  batteries, changing,
    510
  corrupted disk struc-
    ture, 510-511
  failed hardware, 512
  inadequate hardware,
    511

Parameter RAM
  (PRAM), zapping,
    509-510
resolutions, 509-513
SCSI devices, 512
symptoms, 502-503
upgrade problems, 512
preparing for printing,
  209-213
  desktop printers, creat-
    ing, 212
  page-description docu-
    ment setup, 211-212
  print jobs,
    stopping/deleting,
    212
  printer driver setup,
    209-210
restarting, 499
software problems
  conflicts, 505-508
  hangs, 504
  quits, 503
  resolutions, 503-504
  symptoms, 501-502
  viruses, detecting,
    508-509
troubleshooting, 496-497
  basic steps, 496
  crashes, 496
  Disk First Aid, run-
    ning, 499-500
  hardware problems,
    497
  information sources,
    500-501
  software problems, 497
  user error, 497
  with diagnostic soft-
    ware, 497-499
**Macintosh built-in
toolboxes, 108**

**Macintosh Human Interface
Guidelines, 106**
**Macintosh Runtime Java
(MRJ), 13, 442-451**
applets, 447
  distributed applets,
    447-448
  editing, 448-449
  running, 449-451
  server-bound applets,
    448
folders, 446
library components, 446
MacInTouch Web site, 501
**MacLink Plus/Translators,
428**
**Macmillan Computer
Publishing Web site,
304, 307**
Macro Tools, 478
**Macromedia Web site,
278, 520**
**macros, JavaScript macros,
316**
MacTcl/Tk Web site, 462
**MacWeek Web site,
407, 501**
**magnifying glass cursor,
67-68**
mail, *see* **email**
**Main Event Software Web
site, 477**
Make Alias command, 63
**MakeEffectMovie Web site,
253**
**Mango Tree Software Web
site, 477**
MapServer, 366
Marimba, 453
Marionet 1.1, 477
Market Focus counter, 365
markup languages, 307

masking, 300
math operators
    (AppleScript), 473
media abstraction layer
    (QuickTime), 258-259
Media Keys preferences
    (QuickTime), 251
memory, 119
    About This Computer
        window, 119-120
    application heap, 119
    application memory
        error messages, 122
        fragmentation, 123
        managing, 121-123
    built-in memory, 119
    checking before Mac OS
        8.5 installation, 24-26
    determining amount,
        119-120
    fragmentation, 123
    General Information win-
        dow, 80-81
    largest unused block, 120
    managing, 119-123
    playing QuickTime
        movies, 247
    System Folder, 121
    system heap, 119
    virtual memory, 119
    Web servers, 359
Memory control panel,
    136-140
    disk cache, 137-138
    virtual memory, 138-140
        CD-ROM software,
            139
        comparing to RAM,
            140
        default settings, 139
        on Power Macs,
            138-139

memory management, 119
menu bar, 43, 78-79
    tuning with control panels,
        144
menus
    Apple menu
        navigating files, 68-69
        organizing, 79
    Application menu, 106
        Hide command, 64
        multitasking, 117-118
    contextual menus,
        11, 46-47
        data detectors, 11
    Favorites menu, 69
    OSA menu, 461
    Printing menu, 212
Meta tag, 310
MicroMat Computer
    Systems Web site, 278, 510
microphones, 274
Microsoft FrontPage, 317
Microsoft Internet
    Explorer, 17
    Just In Time compilers,
        445
    News (newsgroup reader),
        410
Microsoft Office 98, 19
Microsoft Site Builder
    Network Web site,
    297, 306
Microsoft Web site, 520
MIDI (Musical Instrument
    Digital Interface), 267-268
    data bytes, 268
    hardware, 275-277
        connections, 276-277
        MIDI-to-Mac interface,
            275-276
    MIDI lag, 277
    software, 277-279
    status bytes, 268
    uses/limitations, 268

MIDI synthesizer,
    QuickTime Music prefer-
    ences, 250-251
MindVision installer, 108
MIT Web site, 519
Mixed Mode Manager, 134
modems, QuickTime
    Connection Speed prefer-
    ences, 250
monitors
    color calibration, 231
        Monitor Calibration
            Assistant, 231-234
    color depth, 95-96
    color display capabilities,
        230
    dual-mode, 170
    gamma factory settings,
        232
    multiple displays, 97
    pixel depths, 230
    resolution, 95-96, 177
    selecting, 145
Monitors & Sound control
    panel, 94-97, 271-272
    alert sound, changing,
        96-97
    Alert window, 97
    Color Depth setting, 145
    monitors
        color depth, 95-96
        multiple displays,
            changing, 97
        resolution, 95-96
    Monitors screen, 231
    screen resolution, adjust-
        ing, 145-146
    Sounds portion, 271
        alert sounds, setting,
            272
        input/output levels, set-
            ting, 272

monospaced fonts, 174
mouse
    click-and-a-half, 67
    double-clicking technique, opening files, 75
    dragging technique, opening files, 75
    navigating files, 67-68
Move to Trash command, 78
Movie Player (QuickTime)
    controller interface, 246-247
    editing movies, 252-253
    movies
        editing, 248
        playback settings, 246-247
        playing, 245-248
Movie Player Pro, editing movies, 252
movies (QuickTime)
    Apple Video Player, 282-285
        Capture window, 284-285
        capturing video pictures, 284-285
        hardware considerations, 287-288
        hardware requirements, 284
        hints for quality pictures, 285-286
        playing back movies, 286-287
        software, 283
        user interface, 283
        video applications, 288-289
        Video Source options, 286

        video window, resizing, 286
    editing, 248
        with Movie Player 2.5, 252-253
        with Movie Player Pro, 252
    Internet movies, 254-257
        creating for fast playback, 256-257
        embedding in Web sites, 257
        QuickTime plug-in, 254-255
        saving, 255
    playing, 245-246
        in QuickTime-savvy programs, 247-248
        playback settings, 246-247
    saving in the Scrapbook, 248-249
    streaming video, 256
moving
    between applications, 64
    files, 53
    folders, 53
MPEG1 video files, playing, 286-287
MRJ (Macintosh Runtime Java), 13, 442-451
    applets, 447
        distributed applets, 447-448
        editing, 448-449
        running, 449-451
        server-bound applets, 448
    folders, 446
    library components, 446
MRJ Libraries folder, 447

mSQL server shareware, 368
multimedia (Internet), 374
multimedia tools, 14
    QuickDraw 3D, 16
    QuickTime 3.0, 14-15
    QuickTime VR, 15
multiple displays (monitors), 97
Multiple Master fonts, 181-183
    design axes, 183
multitasking, 8, 114-118
    Application menu, 117-118
        Application Switcher, 118
        switching between applications, 118
    context-switching multitasking, 114
    cooperative multitasking, 114-115
    desk accessories, 114
    Finder, 115
    kernels, 116-117
    preemptive multitasking, 115
music, 265
    audio CDs, playing, 270-271
    audio file formats, 269
    Control Strip module, setting volume, 272-273
    copyright laws, 269
    digital audio, 266-267
    MIDI, 267-268
        connections, 276-277
        data bytes, 268
        hardware, 275-277
        MIDI lag, 277
        MIDI-to-Mac interface, 275-276

status bytes, 268
uses/limitations, 268
Monitors & Sound control
panel, 271-272
alert sounds, setting,
272
input/output levels, set-
ting, 272
physics of, 265
recording, 274-275
CD-ROM sources, 274
microphones, 274
speaker configuration,
275
software, 277-279
editing/creating sound
files, 278-279
Sound control panel,
273-274
**Music preferences
(QuickTime), 250-251**
**Musical Instrument Digital
Interface (MIDI), 267-268**
data bytes, 268
hardware, 275-277
connections, 276-277
MIDI-to-Mac interface,
275-276
MIDI lag, 277
software, 277-279
status bytes, 268
uses/limitations, 268

N

**naming conventions (file
sharing), 113**
**naming variables
(AppleScript), 473**
native software, 134

navigating files, 68-70
Apple menu, 68-69
desktop, 68-69
desktop database, 69-70
with mouse, 67-68
navigation graphics, 304
Navigation Services, 110
opening applications, 111
**Navigation Services toolbox,
75, 109**
Navigator (Netscape), 17
Just In Time compilers,
445
nesting files/folders, 50
NetAlly software, 366
NetCaster, 453
NetCloak counter, 365
NetForms, 363
netiquette rules, 401
NetObjects Fusion, 317
**Netscape Communicator,
Collabra, 410**
Netscape Navigator, 17, 393
Just In Time compilers,
445
Netscape Web site, 520
**Netscape's Official
JavaScript Reference
Guide Web site, 452**
network permissions, 335
access privileges, 338
privilege icons, 339
group user privileges, 337
guest privileges, 336
networked programs,
using, 340-341
owner privileges, 336
registered user privileges,
336-337
shared folders versus
shared volumes, 339
**networked programs,
340-341**

networking (Internet), 374
**networking system exten-
sions, 326-328**
networks
archtitectures, comparing,
345-346
connectivity options, 341
bus topologies,
342-345
cabling mediums, 341
cabling topologies, 342
network types, compar-
ing, 345-346
creating, File Sharing
setup, 329-332
distributed networks, 326
networking system
extensions, 326-328
document sharing
Common Ground
Software, 434
Envoy software, 434
PDF files, 433-434
preserving formatting,
433
Replica software, 435
Ethernet networks,
341-345
file sharing, 431-432
BinHex format, 432
DropStuff application,
432
MacBinary format,
431-432
UUcode format, 432
Internetworks, 342
performance issues, 133
performance settings, 135
Token Ring networks, 342
**News (Internet Explorer
newsgroup reader), 410**
newsgroup readers, 410

newsgroups, 400, 409-410
  prefix definitions, 409
Norton Anti-Virus 5.0, 26
Norton Utilities, 498
  CrashGuard feature, 504
  repairing disks, 510-511
Norton Utilities 3.5, 26
Norton Utilities Speed Disk, 146-147
Numbers control panel, 99

O

object linking and embedding (OLE), 427-428
objects
  embedding, 427
  placing in pages (HTML), 312
oblique style, 173
Ol tag, 310
OLE (object linking and embedding), 427-428
online gaming, 400
online services, 403-407
  America Online (AOL), 404-406
    accessing, 404
    email, 405
    limitations, 406-407
    Web page publishing, 406
  CompuServe, 406
online stores, 367-368
Open dialog box, 110-111
open standards (Internet), 374
Open Transport 2.0, 13, 379-380
  configuring, 380-384
    information needed, 381-382

open transport technologies, 378
Open URL dialog box, 450
OpenDoc, 452
opening
  applications, 75-76, 110-111
    Navigation Services, 111
    Open dialog box, 110-111
  documents, 42
  files, 74-76
    double-clicking technique, 75
    dragging technique, 75
OpenType, 183-184
operating systems
  kernels, 117
  Web servers, 358-359
operators (AppleScript), 473-474
  logical operators, 474
  math operators, 473
optimizing
  hard drives, 146-147
    defragmentation, 146-147
    drivers, updating, 146
    PowerBook software, 164
Organic Online Web site, 520
organizing the desktop, 62-66
  aliases, 62-64
    creating, 63
    manipulating, 63-64
  Application Switcher, 64
  Hide command, 64
  Launcher, accessing applications/folders, 65
  windows, collapse button, 65
original items, 62

orphans, 191
OSA menu, 461, 477
OSAX folder, 460
OSAXs (AppleScript Scripting Additions), 470
outline fonts, 178-179
  downloading, 182
  hinting, 179
  rasterizing, 178-179
output
  performance issues, 131
  sound output options, 272
owner privileges (network permissions), 336

P

P tag, 310, 313
PaceWorks Web site, 253
Page Setup command, 213-215
  PostScript Options, 214-215
  StyleWriter Options, 215
Page Setup dialog box, 213
  PostScript Options, 214-215
  StyleWriter Options, 215
page-description documents, setting up, 211-212
PageMill 2.0, 317
PageMill 2.1, 19
PageMill Web site, 520
pages
  home pages, 303
  images, placing with HTML, 312
  objects, placing with HTML, 312
  publishing
    America Online, 406
    software, 316-317

support pages, 304
uploading, 318-319
paint programs, FatBits, 179
Palatino font, 174
paragraph breaks, 310
paragraph spacing (HTML), 313
Parameter RAM (PRAM), zapping, 509-510
partitioning, 485
partitions (hard disk drives), 70
password keys (QuickTime Media Keys preferences), 251
Paste feature, 56
pasting IP addresses, 354
pathnames, 305
patterns (desktop)
    customizing, 88-90
        choosing pictures, 89
    positioning, 90
    removing, 90
PC cards (PowerBook), 157
PC Exchange, 429-431
PDF files (portable document format), 433-434
    creating, 433
    viewing, 433
peer-to-peer networking, 325
performance, 128-135
    benchmarks, 128
    customizing Mac OS 8.5, 147-148
    default OS settings, 136-141
        AppleTalk control panel, 140-141
        File Sharing control panel, 140
        Finder settings, 136

Memory control panel, 136-140
    PowerBook perfor-mance, 141
    determinants, 128
    File Sharing, 328
    hard drive performance issues, 131-132
    hardware performance limitations, 129
    I/O performance issues, 131
    improving, 141
        Apple Menu Options control panel, tuning, 144
        Calculate Folder Sizes option, 142
        Chooser, tuning, 144-145
        Connectix products, 142
        extensions, 143-145
        File Sharing control panel, tuning, 144
        graphics, 145-146
        hard drives, optimizing, 146-147
        menu bar, tuning, 144
        video, 145-146
    network performance issues, 133
    PowerMac G3 processor, 129-130
    system software, 133
        CD-ROM settings, 134-135
        native software, 134
        network settings, 135
        print settings, 135
    video performance issues, 132

Personal Web Sharing, 352
    access memory allocation, 355
    accessing server, 354-355
    as FTP server, 355
    CGIs, 356
        adding to servers, 358
        components of, 356-357
        finding, 357
        running scripts, 357
    domain names, 354
    IP address, 354
    setting up, 353
    turning on, 353-354
PICT file format, 423
PICT file type, 420
Picture Viewer (QuickTime Pro), 254
pictures (desktop)
    customizing, 88-90
        choosing pictures, 89
    positioning, 90
    removing, 90
pixels, 177, 230
    pixel count, 177
placing images (HTML), 312
placing objects (HTML), 312
platinum appearance, 44
plug-ins
    Sherlock, 74
    QuickTime, 254-255
PlusMaker, initializing disks, 489-490
PlusMaximizer, 488
point of presence (POP) connections, 376-377
point-to-point networking, 325
Point-To-Point Protocol (PPP), 318

points, 174
POP (point of presence) connections, 376-377
pop-up windows, 46
portable document format files (PDF files), 433-434
  creating, 433
  viewing, 433
positioning desktop pictures, 90
PostScript
  color printer options, 221
  printing, 205-207
    benefits, 207
PostScript 3, printing, 208
PostScript files, printing to, 217
PostScript fonts, 181
  Type 3, 182
PostScript graphics, inkjet printers, 204
PostScript laser printers, 201
PostScript Level 2, printing, 207-208
Power Macs, virtual memory, 138-139
PowerBook, 152
  applications, 161-163
    Battery Recondition, 162-164
    File Assistant, 162
    IR software, 162
  Control Strips, 47-49
  current features, 153-154
  hardware, 154-157
    batteries, 155-156
    CD-ROM drives, 157
    PC cards, 157
    swappable drives, 156-157
  Location Manager, 12
  new technology, 165
  old features, 152-153

performance issues, 141
software, 153, 158-161
  control panels, 158-160
  Control Strip, 158-160
  exchanging files over IR ports, 163
  extensions, 160-161
  Internet Setup Assistant, 158
  optimizing, 164
  synchronizing files between Macs, 163
sound input/output levels, 272
Web site, 165
PowerMac G3 processor, 129-130
PPP (Point-To-Point Protocol), 318
PRAM (Parameter RAM), zapping, 509-510
preemptive multitasking, 115
PreFab Player Web site, 478
preferences (QuickTime), 249-252
  AutoPlay preference, 249
  AutoStart preference, 250
  Connection Speed preference, 250
  Media Keys preferences, 251
  Music preferences, 250-251
  QuickTime Exchange, 252
Preferences dialog box, 45
Preferences folder, 53
prefix definitions (newsgroups), 409
Print command, 215-217
  PostScript files, 217
print jobs, 212

print performance settings, 135
printer drivers, 148
  LaserWriter 8, 211
  Page Setup command, 213-215
    PostScript Options, 214-215
    StyleWriter Options, 215
  Print command, 215-217
    PostScript files, 217
  QuickDraw drivers, 211
  selecting, 210
  setting up, 209-210
printer fonts, 179-180
printers, 200
  Color PostScript laser printers, 201
  color printers, 218-221
    ColorSync color calibration system, 218
    dithering, 218
    dye sublimation, 220
    halftoning, 219
    inkjet printers, 219
    laser printers, 219
    PostScript options, 221
    thermal wax transfer printers, 220
  desktop printers, creating, 212
  dot-matrix, 200-203
    banding, 202
    best mode, 202
    draft mode, 202
    faster-print mode, 202
    fonts, 202
    hints for better printing, 203
    ImageWriter, 202
    print wires, 201

dye sublimation, 220
features, 200-201
formed-letter printers, 200
inkjet, 201-204
  AppleTalk, 204
  colors, 219
  fonts, 203
  PostScript graphics,
   204
laser, 200, 204-205
  colors, 219
  printer engine, 205
  QuickDraw laser print-
   ers, 205
  raster-image processors
   (RIP), 205
PostScript laser printers,
  201
QuickDraw laser printers,
  201
resolution, 177
thermal wax transfer printers, 220
printing, 199-205
color, 218-221
  ColorSync color cali-
   bration system, 218
  dithering, 218
  dye sublimation, 220
  halftoning, 219
  inkjet printers, 219
  laser printers, 219
  PostScript options, 221
  process color, 218
  thermal wax transfer
   printers, 220
dot-matrix printers, 201
  banding, 202
  best mode, 202
  draft mode, 202
  faster-print mode, 202
  fonts, 202

hints for better print-
  ing, 203
  ImageWriter, 202
  print wires, 201
inkjet printers, 203-204
  AppleTalk, 204
  fonts, 203
  PostScript graphics,
   204
laser printers, 204-205
  printer engine, 205
  QuickDraw laser print-
   ers, 205
  raster-image processors
   (RIP), 205
letter quality, 200
Mac preparations, 209-213
  desktop printers, creating, 212
  page-description docu-
   ment setup, 211-212
  print jobs,
   stopping/deleting,
   212
  printer driver setup,
   209-210
Page Setup command,
  213-215
  PostScript Options,
   214-215
  StyleWriter Options,
   215
PostScript, 205-207
  benefits, 207
PostScript 3, 208
PostScript Level 2,
  207-208
Print command, 215-217
  PostScript files, 217
queues, 206
spool files, 206
Printing menu, 212
**privilege icons (access privi-
leges), 339**

process color, 218
processors
  PowerMac G3 processor,
   129-130
  Web servers, 359
**Program dialog box (Apple
CD Audio Player), 271**
Program Linking tool, 340
**programs, networked pro-
grams, 340-341**
**proportional-spaced fonts,
174**
protecting
  applications, 109
  files, 53
  folders, 53
protocols, 341
  AppleTalk, 341
   bus topologies,
    342-345
   cabling mediums, 341
   cabling topologies, 342
  SCSI protocol, 483
  TCP/IP, 375-376
   servers, accessing, 376
**prototyping Web sites,
298-302**
  collecting materials,
   298-299
  graphic conversions,
   300-302
  selecting file formats,
   299-300
**Publish and Subscribe,
425-426**
  edition files, creating, 426
publishing Web sites, 294
  America Online, 406
  appearance design, 297
  content design, 294-297
   audience considera-
    tions, 296-297
   intended purpose of
    site, 295-296

Microsoft Site Builder Network Web site, 297
prototyping, 298-302
    collecting materials, 298-299
    graphic conversions, 300-302
    selecting file formats, 299-300
    software, 316-317
punctuation marks, 192

Q

Quadra AV Macs, 264
quantizing (digital audio), 266
queuing, 206
QuickDraw, 176, 229-231
    Color Picker, 230
    displaying text onscreen, 184
    hyperdesktop, 230
QuickDraw 3D, 16
QuickDraw laser printers, 201, 205
QuickDraw printer drivers, 211
Quicken 98, 19
QuickMail, 19
QuickTime, 243-249
    API (application programming interface), 258
    benefits, 244
    configuration issues, 247
    Internet movies, 254-257
        creating for fast playback, 256-257
        embedding in Web sites, 257

QuickTime plug-in, 254-255
    saving, 255
media abstraction layer, 258-259
Movie Player
    controller interface, 246-247
    movies, editing, 248, 252-253
    movies, playing, 245-248
Music Architecture components, 251
preferences
    AutoPlay, 249
    AutoStart, 250
    Connection Speed, 250
    Media Keys, 251
    Music, 250-251
    QuickTime Exchange, 252
    setting, 249-252
Scrapbook, saving movies in, 248-249
Web site, 245
QuickTime 3.0, 14-15
QuickTime Pro, 14
    Movie Player Pro, 252
    Picture Viewer, 254
    vector graphics, 253
QuickTime Software Web site, 256
QuickTime VR, 15
QuickTime Web site, 253
Quit command, 111
quiz answers, 521
    Hour 1, 521
    Hour 2, 522
    Hour 3, 524
    Hour 4, 525
    Hour 5, 526
    Hour 6, 526

Hour 7, 528
Hour 8, 529
Hour 9, 530
Hour 10, 531
Hour 11, 532
Hour 12, 533
Hour 13, 534
Hour 14, 534
Hour 15, 536
Hour 16, 537
Hour 17, 539
Hour 18, 539
Hour 19, 540
Hour 20, 541
Hour 21, 542
Hour 22, 543
Hour 23, 544
Hour 24, 544

R

Radius, Inc. Web site, 282
RAM (random access memory), 119
    comparing to virtual memory, 140
raster-image processors (RIP), 205
rasterizing, 178
    images, 178-179
ReadMe files, 500
rebuilding desktop database, 69-70
Record dialog box, 269
recording scripts (Script Editor), 465-466
    limitations, 466
recording sound, 274-275
    CD-ROM sources, 274
    microphones, 274
    speaker configuration, 275

registered user privileges (network permissions), 336-337

Remote Access control panel, connecting to Internet, 389

removable media, viewing files, 70

removing items from desktop, 55

rendering styles, 228

Replica software, 435

resolution (monitors), 95-96, 177
  selecting, 145

Resource Manager, displaying text onscreen, 184

restarting
  Mac OS, 53
  Macintosh, 499

RGB Color Picker dialog box, 238

RGB colors, 227-228

RGB devices, 227

RIP (raster-image processors), 205

ROFM script, 364

rosettes, 219

RTF (Rich Text Format), 423

running Java applets, 449-451

S

samples (digital audio), 266

sans serif fonts, 188

sans serif type, 173

Save As dialog box, 112-113

Save Search Criteria command, 74

saving
  files, 112-113
    Save As dialog box, 112-113
  QuickTime movies
    from the Internet, 255
    in the Scrapbook, 248-249
  scripts, 468-469
    file formats, 468

Scrapbook, saving QuickTime movies, 248-249

screen capture options, 56

screen fonts, 179-180

screen whiteness value, setting, 234

Script Debugger, 477

Script Editor, 463-471
  compiling scripts, 469
  debugging scripts, 469
  editing scripts, 467-468
    formattable script parts, 467-468
  generating scripts, 464
  recording scripts, 465-466
    limitations, 466
  saving scripts, 468-469
    file formats, 468
  script window, 463
  script writing process, 464
  writing scripts, 466-467

scriptable applications
  AppleScript, 470-471
  data dictionaries, 462-463

Scripter 2.0, 477

Scripting Additions (AppleScript), 470

Scripting Additions folder (AppleScript), 460

scripting languages, 462
  AppleScript, 458-462, 471
    Apple Events, 458, 462
    commands, 474, 476
    data dictionaries, 462-463
    data types, 472
    extending, 469-471
    Extensions folder, 460
    old script compatibility, 459
    operators, 473-474
    OSA menu, 461
    Script Editor, see Script Editor, 463
    scriptable applications, 470-471
    Scripting Additions, 470
    Scripting Additions folder, 460
    scripts, 458-459
    Scripts folder, 461
    tools/resources, 477-478
    variables, 472-473
    Web site, 461

scripts, 458-461
  compiling, 469
  debugging, 469
  editing, 467-468
    formattable script parts, 467-468
  generating, 464
  recording, 465-466
  saving, 468-469
    file formats, 468
  writing, 466-467
  script writing process (Script Editor), 464
  see also CGIs

Scripts folder (AppleScript), 461

ScriptWeb Web site, 477
scroll options (desktop), setting, 91
SCSI (small computer serial interface)
cables, 509
devices, 512
drives, 131
hard disks, 482
SCSI protocol, 483
searching for files, 71-74
Find a File search, 71-72
indexing drives, 72
Search by Content search, 72-73
Search the Internet search, 73-74
sectors (disks), 483-484
security protection
applications, 109
turning off for installation, 29
selecting all items in documents/windows, 56
serial cables, 509
Serial Line Internet Protocol (SLIP), 318
serif fonts, 188
serif type, 173
server software, 318
server-bound applets, 448
server-push animation, 367
servers
FTP, creating, 355
hardware, 358
example systems, 360-361
LAN connections, 359
memory, 359
operating systems, 358-359
processors, 359

Personal Web Sharing, 352
accessing, 354-355
CGIs, 356-358
domain names, 354
IP address, 354
memory allocation, 355
setting up, 353
turning on, 353-354
software, 361-362
capabilities, 362
Netcraft survey, 361
UNIX, 415
uploading files, 414-415
Fetch utility, 415
Web servers, 401
ServerStat counter, 365
sets (Extensions Manager), creating, 93-94
Setup dialog box (AOL), 404
SGML (Standard Generalized Markup Language), 403
shared folders, comparing to shared volumes, 339
Shared printing extensions, 327
shared volumes
accessing, 332-333
comparing to shared folders, 339
ending File Sharing sessions, 335
opening at startup, 334-335
sharing
data
between files, 424
creators, 420-421
file formats, 422-423

file types, 420-421
OLE, 427-428
Publish and Subscribe, 425-426
documents
Common Ground Software, 434
Envoy software, 434
PDF files, 433-434
preserving formatting, 433
Replica software, 435
files, 428
File Exchange, 428-429
File Translation tool, 428
MacLink Plus/Translators, 428
name lengths, 431
networks, 431-432
PC Exchange, 429-431
Sharing command, 331, 340-341
Sharing dialog box, 340
sharing files, 325
connectivity options, 341
bus topologies, 342-345
cabling mediums, 341
cabling topologies, 342
network types, comparing, 345-346
distributed file sharing, 326
networking system extensions, 326-328
network permissions, 335
access privileges, 338
group user privileges, 337
guest privileges, 336
networked programs, using, 340-341

owner privileges, 336
registered user privileges, 336-337
shared folders versus shared volumes, 339
performance issues, 328
setting up File Sharing, 329-332
shared volumes
accessing, 332-333
ending File Sharing sessions, 335
opening at startup, 334-335
Sherlock, 71
Find a File search, 71
indexing drives, 72
plug-ins, 74
Search by Content search, 72
Search the Internet search, 73-74
see also Finder 8
shortcuts (keyboard shortcuts)
Copy feature, 56
Paste feature, 56
Show Original command, 63
Shut Down Items folder, 55
shutdown process, 53-54
SimpleText, playing QuickTime movies, 247-248
SimpleText application, 107
SLIP (Serial Line Internet Protocol), 318
small computer serial interface (SCSI) drives, 131
software
antivirus software, 499
autosave features, 502
backup software, 498

bug fix releases, 508
component software, 451-452
Java Beans, 452
diagnostic software, 497-499
emulators, 134
error messages, 501-502
PowerBook, 153, 158-161
control panels, 158-160
Control Strip, 158-160
exchanging files over IR ports, 163
extensions, 160-161
Internet Setup Assistant, 158
optimizing, 164
synchronizing files between Macs, 163
problems, 497
conflicts, 505-508
hangs, 504
quits, 503
resolutions, 503-504
symptoms, 501-502
viruses, detecting, 508-509
server software, 318
servers, 361-362
capabilities, 362
Netcraft survey, 361
sound/music software, 277-279
editing/creating sound files, 278-279
standards, 420
system software performance, 133
CD-ROM settings, 134-135
native software, 134
network settings, 135
print settings, 135

Web publishing software, 316-317
see also applications
SOMobjects for Mac OS extensions, 460
sound, 265
audio cards, 264
audio CDs, playing, 270-271
audio file formats, 269
Control Strip module, setting volume, 272-273
digital audio, 266-267
quantizing, 266
samples, 266
uses/limitations, 266
Macintosh history, 264-265
MIDI, 267-268
connections, 276-277
data bytes, 268
hardware, 275-277
MIDI lag, 277
MIDI-to-Mac interface, 275-276
status bytes, 268
uses/limitations, 268
Monitors & Sound control panel, 271-272
alert sounds, setting, 272
input/output levels, setting, 272
physics of, 265
recording, 274-275
CD-ROM sources, 274
microphones, 274
speaker configuration, 275
software, 277-279
editing/creating sound files, 278-279

Sound control panel, 273-274
synthesizer chip, 264-265
system sounds
customizing, 268-269
Kaboom! application, 269
Sound control panel, 273-274
Sound Edit 16, 278
Sound Maker, 278
sounds
alert sound, changing, 96-97
desktop sounds, setting, 90-91
spamming, 401
speakers, configuring, 275
special characters, 314-315
speech synthesis, 264
Speed Disk, 146-147
Spell Catcher, 504
spool files, 206
spring-loaded windows, 44-45
Standard File Format (HFS), 132
Standard Generalized Markup Language (SGML), 403
star network (MIDI), 277
star topologies (connectivity), 345
startup (Extensions Manager), 92-93
startup disks, 499
Startup folder, opening shared volumes at startup, 334-335
Startup Items folder, 55
startup pages, 391
selecting, 388

startup process, 53-54
static chats, 411
status bytes (MIDI), 268
streaming video, 256
Studio Architype Web site, 520
stuffing files, DropStuff application, 432
StuffIt compression utility, 108
StuffIt Expander, 17
style sheets (HTML), 315-316
STYLE tag, 316
styles, 173
StyleWriter Page Setup dialog box, 215
subject folders, 50
Submit-It Web site, 520
support pages, 304
swapfiles, 138
swappable drives (PowerBook), 156-157
SYLK (Symbolic Link) format, 423
synchronizing files between Macs, 163
syntax errors (scripts), 466
synthesizer chip, 264-265
system components, 9
system configuration (Apple System Profiler), 500
system extension conflicts, 37
System Folder, 53
backing up, 29
combining extensions and control panels, 100
memory, 121
reducing size to improve performance, 147-148
restoring after installation, 36

system heap, 119
system performance, 128-135
benchmarks, 128
customizing Mac OS 8.5, 147-148
default OS settings, 136-141
AppleTalk control panel, 140-141
File Sharing control panel, 140
Finder settings, 136
Memory control panel, 136-140
PowerBook performance, 141
determinants, 128
hard drive performance issues, 131-132
hardware performance limitations, 129
I/O performance issues, 131
improving, 141
Apple Menu Options control panel, tuning, 144
Calculate Folder Sizes option, 142
Chooser, tuning, 144-145
Connectix products, 142
extensions, 143-145
File Sharing control panel, tuning, 144
graphics, 145-146
hard drives, optimizing, 146-147
menu bar, tuning, 144
tricks, extensions, 143
video, 145-146

network performance issues, 133
PowerMac G3 processor, 129-130
software, 133
    CD-ROM settings, 134-135
    native software, 134
    network settings, 135
    print settings, 135
video performance issues, 132

system sounds, customizing, 268-269
Kaboom! application, 269

T

T1 lines, 378
Table tag, 311
Tagged-Image File Format (TIFF), 423
tags (HTML), 309-311
A tag, 309
Address tag, 309
APPLET, 449
applying pairs to format items, 311
B tag, 309
Base tag, 309
Basefont tag, 309
Blink tag, 309
Blockquote tag, 309
Body tag, 309, 314
Br tag, 309
Center tag, 309
EMBED tag, 257
Form tag, 309
H tag, 309
Head tag, 310

Hr tag, 310
Html tag, 310
I tag, 310
Img tag, 310
Isindex tag, 310
Li tag, 310
Link tag, 310
Meta tag, 310
modifying with attributes/values, 311
Ol tag, 310
P tag, 310, 313
STYLE tag, 316
Table tag, 311
Title tag, 311, 314
Ul tag, 311
Tango software, 368
target gamma, setting, 233
TCP/IP, 317-318
(Transmission Control Protocol/Internet Protocol), 375-376
servers, accessing, 376
TCP/IP Scripting Addition, 477
Tecfa's JavaScript Manual Web site, 452
TechTool Pro, 510
TechTool Protection feature, 504
TechTool pro 2.0, 26-27
Terran Interactive Web site, 253
testing Web sites, 306
text
character sets, 171-172
    Key Caps, 171-172
    Unicode, 172
document layout, 187-188
    kerning, 188-189
    leading, 189
    punctuation marks, 192

tips, 191-192
typography rules, 189-190
font families, 173
fonts, 170, 174, 180-184
Apple's original bitmapped fonts, 181
bitmapped, 180
bitmapped fonts, 176-177
downloading outline fonts, 182
fixed-width, 174
font technologies, 175-176
history, 169-170
installing, 185-186
Mac OS 8.5, 187
Macintosh font standards, 180
monospaced, 174
Multiple Master fonts, 181-183
OpenType, 183-184
outline fonts, 178-179
Palatino, 174
PostScript fonts, 181
printer fonts, 179-180
printing process, 184
proportional-spaced, 174
sans serif, 188
screen fonts, 179-180
serif, 188
TrueType fonts, 181-182
Type 1 fonts, 181
Type 3 fonts, 182
Type 3 PostScript fonts, 182
viewing, 187
kerning, 175

leading, 175
letterspace, 175
orphans, 191
punctuation marks, 192
typefaces, 173-174
    italic typeface, 174
    styles, 173
widows, 191
Text control panel, 99-100
Text encoding converter folder, 447
Text Encodings folder, 447
TEXT file type, 420
themes (desktop)
Hi-Tech, 86
settting, 87
thermal wax transfer printers, 220
thicknet, 341
thinnet, 341
third-party software, 19
TidBits Web site, 501
TIFF (Tagged-Image File Format), 423
tiling, 89
Timbuktu Pro, 19
time sharing, 114
Title tag, 311, 314
Token Ring networks, 342
toolboxes
built-in toolboxes, 108
Navigation Services, 109-110
    opening applications, 111
TR-WWW search application, 369
tracks (disks), 483-484
Transmission Control Protocol/Internet Protocol, see TCP/IP, 375
transmitters, 444, 453

Trash Can icon, 44, 55, 77-78
ejecting disks/volumes, 55
emptying, 77-78
Move to Trash command, 78
throwing away items, 55
troubleshooting, 496-497
basic steps, 496
crashes, 496
    restarting Macintosh, 499
Disk First Aid
    running, 499-500
extension conflicts, 37
hardware problems, 497
    batteries, changing, 510
    burn-in, 497
    corrupted disk structure, 510-511
    failed hardware, 512
    inadequate hardware, 511
    Parameter RAM (PRAM), zapping, 509-510
    resolutions, 509-513
    SCSI devices, 512
    symptoms, 502-503
    upgrade problems, 512
information sources, 500-501
software problems, 497
    conflicts, 505-508
    hangs, 504
    quits, 503
    resolutions, 503-504
    symptoms, 501-502
    viruses, detecting, 508-509

user error, 497
    with diagnostic software, 497-499
TrueType fonts, 181-182
dot-matrix printing, 202
tuner cards, 287
turning off the Mac, 53-54
turning on the Mac, 53-54
TV tuner card, 287
type, points, 174
Type 1 fonts, 181
Multiple Master fonts, 181-183
    design axes, 183
OpenType, 183-184
Type 3 fonts, 182
type styles, 173
typefaces, 173-174
italic typeface, 174
sans serif type, 173
serif type, 173
styles, 173
    oblique style, 173
typography
character sets, 171-172
    Key Caps, 171-172
    Unicode, 172
document layout, 189-190
font families, 173
leading, 175
letterspace, 175
typefaces, 173-174
    italic typeface, 174
    styles, 173

U

Ul tag, 311
Unicode, 172
Uniform Resource Locators (URLs), 392

Universal Serial Bus (USB), 165

UNIX servers, uploading files, 415

updating, hard disk drivers, 27-28

updating shared data, 425-426
edition files, creating, 426

upgrade problems, 512

upgrading Conflict Catcher, 508

uploading
Internet files, 414
Fetch utility, 415

uploading Web pages, 318-319

URLs (Uniform Resource Locators), 392

USB (Universal Serial Bus), 165

Usenet newsgroups, 409-410
prefix definitions, 409

user error, 497

UserLand Software Web site, 477

UserTalk Web site, 462

utilities
StuffIt compression utility, 108

UUcode file format, 432

V

values
HTML tags, 311

variables (AppleScript), 472-473
naming, 473

vector graphics (QuickTime Pro), 253

video
improving performance, 145-146
performance issues, 132

video cards, 282

video compression, 285

video files, see movies, 254

Video Player, 282-289
capturing video pictures, 284-285
hardware considerations, 287
AV hardware, 287-288
cabling considerations, 288
hardware requirements, 284
hints for quality pictures, 285-286
playing back videos, 286
CD drives, 287
hard drives, 287
software, 283
user interface, 283
Capture window, 284-285
video applications, 288-289
Video Source options, 286
video window, resizing, 286

video-editing software/hardware, 288-289

viewing
file comments, 70
files, 66-67
CD-ROMs, 70
hard drives, 70
removable media, 70
fonts, 187

viewing modes, Extensions Manager items, 93

Virex 5.8, 26

virtual memory, 119
comparing to RAM, 140
settings, 138-140
CD-ROM software, 139
default settings, 139
on Power Macs, 138-139

virus protection
Mac OS 8.5 installation, 26
turning off for installation, 29

viruses, detecting, 508-509

Vivid Studios Web site, 520

volume settings
Control Strip module, 272-273

volumes, 485
shared volumes
accessing, 332-333
comparing to shared folders, 339
ending File Sharing sessions, 335
opening at startup, 334-335

W

W3 committee Web site, 315

watermarks
adding to documents, 215

Web browsers, 401-403

Web browsers, see browsers

Web pages
  images
    placing with HTML,
      312
  placing objects with
    HTML, 312
Web publishing software,
316-317
Web servers, *see* **servers**
Web Sharing control panel,
17-18
Web Sharing, *see* **Personal**
  Web Sharing
Web sites
  active images, 365-366
  ActiveX, 452
  Adobe, 433, 519
  Allegiant, 477
  Alsoft, 488
  Analog counter, 364
  animation, 366
    animated GIFs, 367
    client-pull, 366
    server-push, 367
  Apple, 12, 364, 414,
    451, 519
    Developers page, 519
    Support and
      Information page,
      519
  Apple Product
    Information, 500
  AppleScript, 461
  ATI Technologies, 282
  Atomic Vision, 520
  Avalanche, 520
  Barnsides, 520
  BBEdit, 520
  Bigfoot, 408
  Browser Watch, 519
  Casady & Greene, 508
  Cnet, 414, 520

Cnet Download, 49
Construct, 520
Count counter, 364
Count WWWebula, 365
counters, 364-365
database processing,
  368-370
DataViz, 428
designing
  folder system setup,
    305
  navigation graphics,
    304
  speeding up down-
    loads, 305-306
Digital Technology
  International, 477
Disney, 408
e-greetings, 408
Email.acgi script, 364
embedding QuickTime
  movies, 257
Epson, 210
EveryWare software
  (Tango), 368
Excite, 408
Fetch, 318, 415
forms, 363-364
Forms.acgi script, 363
FrontPage, 520
Gamelan, 520
guest books, 363-364
Hewlett-Packard, 210
home pages, 303
  selecting, 388
Hot Wired, 520
hotmail, 408
iCat, 367
ImageMap.acgi, 365
ImageReady, 302
IMS, 282
InfoLawAlert, 296

InfoWave, 204
Interaction/IP script, 364
Internet Audit, 364
InterNIC, 319
Interse (Market Focus
  counter), 365
ivillage, 408
JavaScript 411, 452
JavaScript macro, 452
Lari Software, 253
Late Night Software LTD,
  477
Lynda Wynman's Web
  site, 519
MacAddict Web site, 49
MacFixIt, 501
MacInTouch, 501
Macmillan Computer
  Publishing, 304, 307
Macromedia, 278, 520
MacTcl/Tk, 462
MacWeek, 407, 501
Main Event Software, 477
MakeEffectMovie, 253
Mango Tree Software, 477
MapServer, 366
Marimba, 453
Maxum (NetCloak
  counter), 365
MicroMat Computer
  Systems, 278, 510
Microsoft, 520
Microsoft Site Builder
  Network, 297, 306
MIT, 519
mSQL server shareware,
  368
NetForms, 363
Netscape, 520
Netscape's Official
  JavaScript Reference
  Guide, 452

online stores, 367-368
OpenDoc, 452
Organic Online, 520
PaceWorks, 253
PageMill, 520
PowerBooks, 165
PreFab Player, 478
publishing, 294
    America Online, 406
    appearance design, 297
    content design,
      294-297
    prototyping, 298-302
QuickTime, 245, 253
QuickTime Software, 256
Radius, Inc., 282
ROFM script, 364
ScriptWeb, 477
Sherlock plug-ins, 74
ServerStat, 365
Studio Architype, 520
Submit-It, 520
support pages, 304
Tecfa's JavaScript Manual,
  452
Terran Interactive, 253
testing, 306
TidBits, 501
uploading, 318-319
UserLand Software, 477
UserTalk, 462
Vivid Studios, 520
W3 committee, 315
WebChat, 411
WWW Consortium, 520
Yahoo, 408
WebChat Web site, 411
whiteness value, setting, 234
widows, 191

**Windowing Internet
  Foundation Classes (IFC),
  444**
windows, 44-46
  About This Computer
    window, 119-120
  active windows, 44
    switching between, 118
  Alert window (Monitors &
    Sound control panel), 97
  collapse button, 65
  collapsible windows, 46
  folder window, 51
  General Information win-
    dow, 80-81, 121
  Get Info window, 52
  Launcher window, 49
  pop-up windows, 46
  selecting all items, 56
  spring-loaded windows,
    44-45
**World Wide Web (WWW),
  401-403**
  accessing with TCP/IP,
    317-318
  browsers, 401-403
  publishing sites, 294
    appearance design, 297
    content design,
      294-297
    prototyping, 298-302
  see also Internet
writing scripts, 466-467
**WWW Consortium Web
  site, 520**
**WYSIWYG environments,
  170**

X-Y-Z

Yahoo Web site, 408

**zapping Parameter RAM
  (PRAM), 509-510**